ENCYCLOPEDIA OF
CIVIL WAR SHIPWRECKS

ENCYCLOPEDIA OF
CIVIL WAR
SHIPWRECKS

W. CRAIG GAINES

LOUISIANA STATE UNIVERSITY PRESS  BATON ROUGE

Published by Louisiana State University Press
Copyright © 2008 by Louisiana State University Press
All rights reserved
Manufactured in the United States of America
FIRST PRINTING

DESIGNER: Barbara Neely Bourgoyne
TYPEFACE: Goudy, display; Minion Pro, text
PRINTER AND BINDER: Maple-Vail

Library of Congress Cataloging-in-Publication Data

Gaines, W. Craig, 1953–
  Encyclopedia of Civil War shipwrecks / W. Craig Gaines.
     p. cm.
  Includes bibliographical references and index.
  ISBN 978-0-8071-3274-6 (cloth : alk. paper) 1. United States—History—Civil War,
1861–1865—Naval operations—Encyclopedias. 2. United States—History—Civil War,
1861–1865—Antiquities—Encyclopedias. 3. Shipwrecks—United States—History—
19th century—Encyclopedias. I. Title.
  E591.G35 2008
  973.7′5—dc22

                                                                        2007019754

This book is dedicated to my wonderful wife, Arla,
who accompanied me to numerous libraries, Civil War battle sites,
and museums during the writing of this work.

I also dedicate this book to the memory of
the soldiers, sailors, and civilians whose legacies live on within these pages.

Contents

Illustrations follow page 76

Preface

I wanted to write this book on Civil War shipwrecks from the time I was in the sixth grade. When I began, I thought there would just be a few hundred shipwrecks, but I was wrong. This book covers more than two thousand American or American Civil War period–related shipwrecks between the years 1861 and 1865. It is likely that I failed to find information on a few shipwrecks, but I feel confident that the vast majority of wrecks related to the Civil War are included. For some shipwrecks I found very limited information, while in the case of others there is much published and unpublished material.

In this book *shipwreck* means a vessel sunk, scuttled, burned, grounded, lost, capsized, missing, blown up, one that collided with another vessel or object and sank, or one that was generally made unusable without salvage and substantial repairs. Vessels temporarily grounded or beached have generally been excluded. For several vessels it was difficult to decide whether or not they were shipwrecks. Some blockade-runners listed as sunk in Union or Confederate records were actually grounded and quickly refloated. Examples of vessels that experienced temporary groundings are the blockade-runners *Annie* and *Ranger* off Cape Fear, North Carolina, and the *Havelock* and *Flamingo* off Charleston, South Carolina. Rowboats, small boats, most ferries, and canoes are excluded because of their small size. Several very small sloops and schooners are included, as they were listed in the Union or Confederate official records.

The entries are formatted to get as much information in as little space as possible. Each entry provides an overview of a shipwreck. There is a wealth of information on Civil War shipwrecks, with more becoming available all the time because of continuing cultural resources exploration. Environmental and cultural resources laws have resulted in a number of investigations that have discovered many shipwrecks from the Civil War period in recent years.

I did my best to determine the site of each shipwreck from various sources, but some locations are vague or unknown. The vessels I have listed in the "Shipwrecks of Unknown Location" section near the end of the book have no location given where they were lost in the information I reviewed.

Otherwise, I divided the shipwrecks in this book into geographic location by state, country, or body of water, as seemed most logical to me. Because rivers meander over the years and are often dividing lines for states, I often list shipwrecks in river sections, since it is sometimes unclear in which state a shipwreck occurred. I list vessels without names, with unknown names, and with names I could not locate under "Vessels without Names"—by vessel type—at the end of each geographic section.

In general location names at the time of the shipwreck are used in the book. Many place names have changed since the Civil War. Some towns have disappeared. Rivers have moved or meandered, often leaving shipwrecks below dry land. The metropolis of New York is listed as New York City, and well-known cities are often referenced without their state (e.g., Boston without Mass.).

Vessels often had several names over their careers. Each vessel's name when it was sunk or its most common name is listed first, and its previous names or nicknames are listed in parentheses. Some vessel names are pre–Civil War, and a few names were post–Civil War names, in cases in which the vessel was raised and refitted. Some vessels served in both the Union and Confederate navies or as commercial vessels on both sides. Blockade-runner names were frequently changed to deceive Union spies, so there is frequently some confusion regarding their names. A number of vessels had the same name. It is likely that several vessels are listed twice if they had different data associated with different names. I have noted where I think there may be multiple listings of the same vessel.

At the start of each entry I have noted whether the vessel was in Union or Confederate service or, if neither, what its nationality was (unless it is unknown). Vessels listed as "USS" served in the Union navy or United States Navy, while those listed as "CSS" were part of the Confederate navy. Vessels noted as "Union" were American vessels under Union control, while the label "Confederate" means the vessels were under Confederate control. Vessels noted as "U.S." were ships privately owned by Americans in 1861 prior to the start of the war or in 1865 after the war's end. Many foreign vessels traded with the Union and the Confederacy, so some vessels are designated as "British," "Spanish," "French," and so on. If the allegiance or nationality is unclear from the sources, which is often the case with blockade-runners, I have indicated that the nationality is unknown.

Information in this encyclopedia came from a wide variety of sources. Not surprisingly, data are often conflicting on dimensions and tonnage. Vessels were frequently modified or rebuilt to include technical innovations, to increase cargo capacities, or to be repaired. Many underwent dimension changes during conversion from commercial vessels to warships or from warships to commercial vessels. The most reliable information, in the author's opinion, is given first, with alternative information following in parentheses.

Hull dimensions generally are linear center-line distances from the stem to the main stern transom. The beam is the widest part of the hull. On stern-wheelers the vessel length could be extended considerably by the paddle wheel diameter at the stern. For side-wheelers the beam or width of the vessel could be extended because of the supporting structures for the side-wheels. Depth is usually defined as the vertical distance from the bottom of the main deck floor to the bottom of the vessel amidships.

Tonnage is given in the sources as displacement tons, British gross tons, registered tons, gross tons, net tons, burden tons, bulk tons, or simply tons. The measurement of tons was very loose and differed significantly, depending on the weight system or carrying capacity used and its tax consequences. Where the term *tons* was used, it generally meant about 100 cubic feet of vessel space to the ton. Tons could also be the number of tons of water a vessel would displace, such as the total vessel weight plus its cargo. Gross or registered tons were often based on internal cargo volume without non-cargo areas, such as the crew's quarters, engine room, and so forth.

Some vessel tonnages were estimates and others were precise measurements. A new measurement system was

started in 1864. Until about 1865 tonnage also used fractions of 95th tons. After 1865 tons were rounded up or down to the whole ton.

Vessel modification also changed the tonnages assigned to some vessels as the length and beam increased or decreased. Many vessels had several published tonnages over the course of their lives. Merchant vessels converted to military vessels and then converted back to merchant vessels could have several different sets of tonnages based on the tonnage system used and type of vessel modification.

Vessel armament also varied through time. The first armament listing is my best guess for the vessel at the time of sinking, with armaments from other sources listed in parentheses. Crew size or complement was another variable, depending on the vessel's mission and modifications for combat or cargo.

Salvage and excavation information is provided where possible. Salvage boats and divers were widely available during the Civil War but were used only when military security could be provided. Some shipwrecks were salvaged and returned to commerce at the close of the war. Many shipwrecks were removed after the war by the U.S. Army Corps of Engineers as hazards to navigation when waterborne commerce returned to the southern states.

With the wide underwater access SCUBA has brought, many shipwrecks have been discovered and explored by divers, historians, treasure hunters, and archaeologists since the 1960s. Magnetometers, remote sensing devices, and remote operated robot submarines have helped discover many shipwrecks. There are many points of view relating to the exploration and recovery of material from shipwrecks. I have used information from sources with a wide range of views on these issues.

Salvage of the *Bertrand* (Missouri River, Neb.), USS *Cairo* (Yazoo River, Miss.), CSS *Muscogee* (Chattahoochee River, Ala./Ga.), USS *Monitor* (Cape Hatteras, N.C.), CSS *Alabama* (European waters, France), *Brother Jonathan* (Pacific Coast, Calif.), CSS *H. L. Hunley* (Charleston, S.C.), and *Republic* (Atlantic Ocean, off Ga.) has greatly increased public awareness of Civil War era shipwrecks and their place in American history. More shipwreck investigations and salvage remain to be completed on many shipwrecks.

Efforts to raise or excavate several of these old vessels are continuing, usually by the combined efforts of individuals, interested groups, universities, and state and federal agencies.

It is my hope that this book will provide interesting and useful information to students, historians, archaeologists, Civil War buffs, divers, and others. It should be noted that the U.S. Navy has laid claim to all Union and Confederate military warships and enforces its claims where the federal government has control. Also, many commercial vessels had insurance, and their cargo may still be subject to claims from the insurers. The Shipwreck Act set up a method by which all those interested in the discovery and recovery of these vessels' history may participate within United States waters.

A shipwreck is more than just an object for historical commentary. It can also be a habitat for water-dwelling species and a place of recreation and wonder for SCUBA divers as well as a kind of time capsule of discovery for archaeologists and historians. Treasure hunters look at the recovery of gold, silver, and valuables from shipwrecks as part of the capitalist process. Shipwrecks are a site where the present can touch the past. As time passes, we will continue to learn more about these time capsules of the nation's past.

I wish to thank the National Park Service, the U.S. Army Corps of Engineers, the Tulsa City-County Library, the Sacramento Public Library, the California State Library system, the University of Tulsa, and many other libraries for help, guidance, and the use of their archives, books, and facilities in the preparation of this book.

Abbreviations

CWC	U.S. Department of the Navy, *Civil War Chronology, 1861–1865* (Washington, D.C.: Government Printing Office, 1971).
DANFS	U.S. Department of the Navy, *Dictionary of American Naval Fighting Ships,* 8 vols. (Washington, D.C.: Government Printing Office, 1959–81).
EAS	Bruce D. Berman, *Encyclopedia of American Shipwrecks* (Boston: Mariners Press, 1972).
LLC	Stephen R. Wise, *Lifeline of the Confederacy: Blockade Running in the Civil War* (Columbia: University of South Carolina Press, 1988).
MSV	William M. Lytle and Forrest R. Holdcamper, *Merchant Steam Vessels of the United States: 1790–1868, "The Lytle Holdcamper List,"* ed. C. Bradford Mitchell (Staten Island, N.Y.: Steamship Historical Society of America, 1975).
NUMA	National Underwater and Marine Association, founded by Clive Cussler, www.numa.net.
OR	*The War of the Rebellion: A Compilation of the Official Records of the Union and Confederate Armies,* 128 vols. (Washington, D.C.: Government Printing Office, 1880–1901), ser. 1 unless noted otherwise.
ORA	Thomas Yoseloff, ed., *The Official Atlas of the Civil War* (New York: Harper and Row, 1967).
ORN	*Official Records of the Union and Confederate Navies in the War of the Rebellion,* 30 vols. (Washington, D.C.: Government Printing Office, 1894–1922).
SCH	Robert Wilden Nesser, *Statistical and Chronological History of the U.S. Navy, 1775–1907* (New York: Burt Franklin, 1970).
WCWN	Paul H. Silverstone, *Warships of the Civil War Navies* (Annapolis, Md.: Naval Institute Press, 1989).
WPD	Frederick Way Jr., *Way's Packet Directory, 1848–1983* (Athens: Ohio University Press, 1983).
WSTD	Frederick Way Jr. and Joseph W. Rutter, *Way's Steam Towboat Directory* (Athens: Ohio University Press, 1990).

ENCYCLOPEDIA OF
CIVIL WAR
SHIPWRECKS

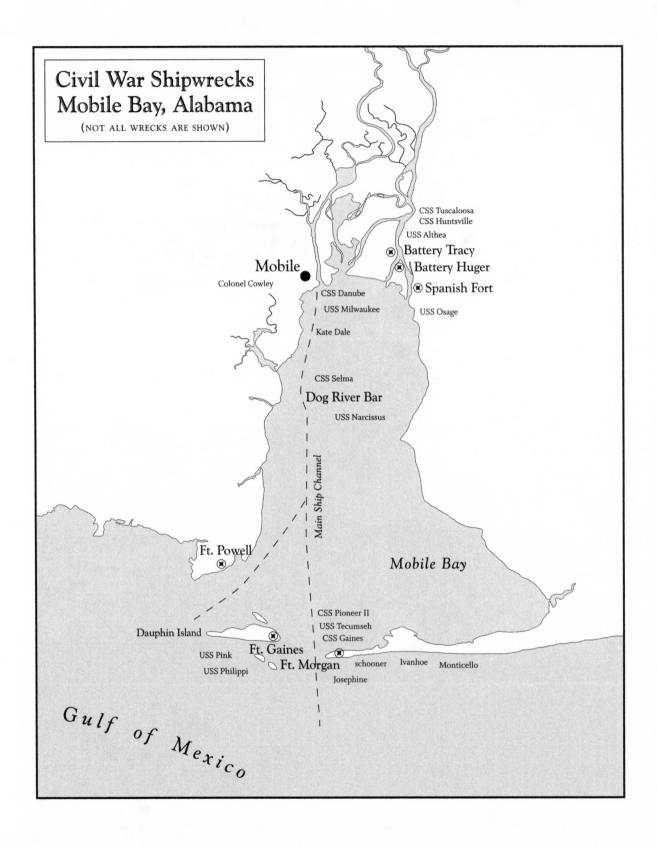

Civil War Shipwrecks
Mobile Bay, Alabama
(NOT ALL WRECKS ARE SHOWN)

CSS Tuscaloosa
CSS Huntsville
USS Althea
⊗ Battery Tracy
⊗ Battery Huger
⊗ Spanish Fort

Mobile

Colonel Cowley

CSS Danube
USS Milwaukee
USS Osage

Kate Dale

CSS Selma
Dog River Bar
USS Narcissus

Main Ship Channel

Ft. Powell
⊗

Mobile Bay

CSS Pioneer II
USS Tecumseh
CSS Gaines

Dauphin Island

USS Pink
Ft. Gaines ⊗
USS Philippi
Ft. Morgan ⊗   schooner   Ivanhoe   Monticello
Josephine

Gulf of Mexico

Alabama

Civil War shipwrecks in Alabama were concentrated mostly in and around Mobile Bay. The port of Mobile and Mobile Bay were blockaded by Union naval forces early in the Civil War. Mobile Bay was not permanently closed to blockade-runners until Adm. David G. Farragut's fleet ran past Fort Morgan into Mobile Bay on August 5, 1864, and defeated the Confederate Mobile fleet. Farragut's force lost the monitor USS *Tecumseh* and small gunboat USS *Philippi*, while the Confederates lost the gunboat CSS *Gaines*, which was sunk, as well as the ironclad CSS *Tennessee* and gunboat CSS *Selma*, which were captured.

The siege of Mobile continued until the end of the Civil War, with the Confederate defenses along the Blakely River being attacked by land and sea. The entrances to Mobile, the Blakely River, and the Spanish River were blocked by several rows of scuttled vessels and the extensive use of torpedoes. Union naval losses due to torpedoes in the Blakely River and Mobile Bay were the greatest in the war. Torpedoed Union vessels included the USS *Althea*, USS *Ida*, USS *Itasca*, USS *Milwaukee*, USS *Narcissus*, USS *Osage*, *R. B. Hamilton*, and USS *Rose*, as well as a launch from the USS *Cincinnati*. The Confederates scuttled the Mobile fleet, which included the CSS *Danube*, CSS *Huntsville*, CSS *Phoenix*, and CSS *Tuscaloosa*.

During Gen. James Harrison Wilson's Union cavalry raid through Alabama at the end of the war, five steamboats were burned at Montgomery; the ironclad CSS *Muscogee* was scuttled on the Alabama side of the Chattahoochee River near the Columbus, Ga., Navy Yard; and the ironclad CSS *Chattahoochee* was scuttled on the Georgia side of the Chattahoochee River.

USS *Althea* (*Alfred A. Wotkyns*). Union. Steam tug, 72 bulk tons. Length 70 feet, beam 16 feet 4 inches, depth 7 feet. Maximum speed 9 knots. Complement of fifteen, with a 12-pounder. Built in 1863 at New Brunswick, N.J. On March 12, 1865, as it was removing a Confederate torpedo in the Blakely River, its chain ran afoul of an old wreck abreast of Battery Huger, and it ran into the torpedo. Was sunk in 10–12 feet of water, with two killed and three wounded. Was raised on November 7, 1865. Sold on December 8, 1866. (*ORN*, 22:96, 132–33; ser. 2, 1:33; *WCWN*, 113; *MSV*, 6.)

Atlantic No. 2. U.S. Stern-wheel steamer, 53 tons. Length 101 feet 6 inches, beam 22 feet 3 inches, depth 3 feet. Built in 1863 at New Albany, Ind. Snagged on October 9, 1865, at Demopolis on the Tombigbee River or Black Warrior River. (*MSV*, 15, 243; *WPD*, 32–33.)

Augusta. Confederate. Steamer. Cargo of cotton and bacon. Was captured with the *Henry J. King* and *Milliner* in the Coosa River on April 14, 1865, by the Union 4th Ky. Cavalry Regiment during Wilson's Raid and taken to Montgomery, where all three boats were burned. (*OR*, 49:1:352, 497–98.)

California. Confederate. Schooner, 77 tons. Only 1 mast. Length 84 feet, beam 29 feet, depth 4 feet 10 inches. Built in 1855 at Mobile, Ala. Was scuttled to act as an obstruction at the Dog River Bar in Mobile Bay in 1862 or 1863. (Irion, *Mobile Bay Ship Channel, Mobile Harbor*, 35, 62.)

Carondelet. Confederate. Side-wheel steamer, 87 tons. Length 160 feet. Built in 1849 at St. Louis. Was sunk to act as an obstruction while filled with bricks at the Dog River Bar in Mobile Bay in 1862. Part of the vessel was discovered by archaeologists in 1985. (Irion, *Mobile Bay Ship Channel, Mobile Harbor*, 35–37, 58; *MSV*, 30.)

Clipper. U.S. Side-wheel steamer, 242 tons. Built in 1865 at Cincinnati. Was burned on October 5, 1865, 70 miles above Mobile, Ala., with eight members of the crew killed. (*MSV*, 40, 251.)

Colonel Clay. Confederate. Two-masted side-wheel steamer, 257 tons. Length 145 feet, beam 35 feet 8 inches, depth 7 feet. May have been built in 1847 at Louisville or in 1851 at New Orleans. Was scuttled with a load of bricks to act as an obstruction by Confederates at the Dog River Bar in Mobile Bay in 1862 or 1863. Was probably removed in 1871 by the Mobile Harbor Board. (Irion, *Mobile Bay Ship Channel, Mobile Harbor*, 36–37, 58; *MSV*, 40.)

Colonel Cowles. U.S. Ship. Was destroyed at Mobile, Ala., with the *Kate Dale* when a captured Confederate supply depot, Marshall's Warehouse, exploded on May 25, 1865, with 20 tons of gunpowder and numerous shells at the corner of Lipscomb and Commercial streets. (*OR*, 49:1:556–67; 49:22:913.)

Cremona. Confederate. Stern-wheel steamer, 268 or 243 tons. Length 182 feet, beam 30 feet, depth 6 feet 6 inches. Built in 1852 at New Albany, Ind. Was scuttled with a load of bricks by Confederates to act as an obstruction at the Dog River Bar in 1862. Investigated and mapped by archaeologists in 1984 and 1985. (Irion, *Mobile Bay Ship Channel, Mobile Harbor,* 46, 58; Irion, "Confederate Brick Fleet of Mobile," 45–47; *MSV*, 47.)

C.S.M. Confederate. Steamer. Was sunk at a Mobile Bay wharf by a collision with the guard boat steamer *Mary* in mid-October 1864. (*OR*, 39:3:841, 851.)

Cuba. Confederate. Side-wheel blockade-runner steamer, 604 bulk tons. Length 250 feet, beam 32 feet 7 inches, draft 9 feet. Cargo worth $1,250,000. Built in 1854 at Greenpoint, N.Y. Was chased on May 19, 1863, by the USS *Huntsville* for 90 miles, and then the USS *De Soto* joined the chase. To prevent capture by the Union ships, the crew set it afire, at latitude 28° 47' north, longitude 87° 58' west, off the Alabama coast. The crew was captured. (*ORN*, 17:442, 444; *MSV*, 48; *LLC*, 295.)

CSS Danube. Confederate. Floating battery, 980 tons. Length 170 feet 4 inches, beam 30 feet 11 inches, draft 16 feet 11 inches. Battery of four 42-pounders. Built in 1854 at Bath, Maine. Confiscated by Confederates in Mobile Bay in May 1861. Was sunk to act as an obstruction in December 1864, in the upper line of obstructions in the Spanish River Gap at the Apalachee Battery in Conways Bayou. (*OR*, 39:3:887; *CWC*, 6-218; *ORA*, pl. 71, no. 13.)

Duke W. Goodman. U.S. Stern-wheel steamer, 196 tons. Built in 1858. Was burned in November 1865 at Rainwater. (*MSV*, 57, 256.)

CSS Dunbar. Confederate. Side-wheel steamer, 213 tons. Probably built in 1859 at Brownsville, Pa. Was sunk up to the guards off the Tennessee River in Cypress Creek, about two miles below Florence in February 1862, to prevent capture by advancing Union vessels. Was burned on April 21, 1862, by the USS *Tyler*. Was raised by the Union army and later sold in 1865. (*ORN*, 22:782, 822; 23:77; *MSV*, 67; *CWC*, 6-223; *WCWN*, 246.)

Eclipse. Confederate. Stern-wheel steamer, 156 tons. Length 150 feet, beam 27 feet, depth 4 feet. Built in 1864 at California, Pa. Was sunk to act as an obstruction with a load of bricks at the Dog River Bar in 1862. Probably removed in 1871 by the Mobile Harbor Board. (Irion, *Mobile Bay Ship Channel, Mobile Harbor,* 35, 36, 59; *MSV*, 59.)

Emma Boyd. Confederate. Stern-wheel steamer, 172 tons. Built in 1863 at Wheeling, Va. (now W. Va.). Snagged on August 26, 1864, at Selma, Ala. (*MSV*, 64, 258.)

CSS Gaines. Confederate. Wooden side-wheel gunboat, 863 tons. Length 202 feet, beam 38 feet, depth 13 feet, draft 6 or 7 feet 3 inches, speed 10 knots, armor 2-inch iron. Complement of 130–74, with one 8-inch rifle and five 32-pounder smoothbores. Built in 1861–62 at Mobile, Ala., from unseasoned wood. Shot to pieces on August 5, 1864, by Adm. David G. Farragut's Union fleet in a heated engagement in Mobile Bay. The vessel left the battle in a sinking condition after being hit by 17 shells with water in the magazines, aft hold, and shell room. Its wheel ropes were cut. Grounded within 500 yards of Fort Morgan in two fathoms of water. The vessel's ammunition, small arms, and cannon were salvaged by the crew. The crew scuttled and burned the vessel to prevent capture. Two crewmen were killed, and 3 or 4 were wounded in the engagement. Six boats with 129 crewmen rowed across Mobile Bay to the safety of Confederate-held Mobile in spite of the bay being controlled by Admiral Farragut's victorious Union fleet. May have been located by Clive Cussler's survey in 1989. (*OR*, 35:2:224; 39:1:443, 449–53; *ORN*, ser. 2, 1:253; *CWC*, 6-230; NUMA Web site, "Survey of Civil War Ships.")

USS Glasgow (Eugenie) (General Buckner). Union. Side-wheel steamer, 252 bulk tons, 428 or 168 registered tons. Length 150 feet or 119 feet 2 inches, beam 23 feet or 22 feet 1 inch, depth 11 feet 9 inches, speed 13 knots. Complement of thirty, with one 20-pounder rifle and one 12-pounder smoothbore. Built in 1862 at Keypost, N.J. Formerly the blockade-runner *General Buckner*. Was captured as the blockade-runner *Eugenie* by the USS *R. R. Cuyler* off Mobile on May 6, 1863. Converted to a Union navy dispatch and supply ship. Hit a submerged obstruction as a Union gunboat off Mobile and sunk on May 8, 1865. Was raised on June 19, 1865. (*ORN*, 22:188, 202, 212; *WCWN*, 108; *LLC*, 301.)

Henry J. King. Confederate. Side-wheel steamer, 409 tons. Cargo of cotton and bacon. Was captured on April 14, 1865, along with the steamboats *Augusta* and *Milliner* by the Union 4th Ky. Cavalry Regiment during Wilson's Raid. Was taken to Montgomery and burned with four other steamboats. (*OR*, 49:1:352, 497–98; *MSV*, 94.)

CSS Huntsville. Confederate. Screw ironclad floating battery. Length 150 or 152 feet, beam 32 feet, draft 7 feet, speed 4 knots, armor 4-inch iron. Complement of forty, with three or four 32-pounders and one 6.4-inch rifled gun. Launched in 1863 at Selma, Ala. Completed at Mobile. Had defective engines and lacked a full battery. Escaped up the Spanish River after the fall of Mobile. Was scuttled by Confederates on April 12, 1865, about 12 miles from Mobile. In 1985 divers found small sections of the stern and deck of what was believed to be this vessel. Divers hoped to raise the vessel. (*ORN*, 22:95, 139; ser. 2, 1:256; *CWC*, 6-251; Irion, *Mobile Bay Ship Channel, Mobile Harbor*, 13; *WCWN*, 207; Hand, "Gunboats of the South to Rise Again," *Skin Diver*, 140–41.)

USS Ida. Union. Side-wheel steam tug, 104 bulk tons, 77 tons. Armed with one gun. Built in 1860 at Gretna, La. Was blown up in the Main Ship Channel near Choctaw Pass, Mobile Bay, on April 13, 1865, with three killed and three wounded when a torpedo hit the starboard side, bursting the boiler. Was sunk with water up to the upper deck. The gun and engine were later removed from the wreck. The wreck was raised then sold on September 11, 1865. (*ORN*, 22:96, 128–33, 256; ser. 2, 1:106; *EAS*, 173; *WCWN*, 123; Perry, *Infernal Machines*, 187–88.)

Isabel. Nationality unknown. Blockade-runner steamer. Cargo of 200 bales of cotton. Grounded within 200 yards of Fort Morgan. Was captured by boats from the USS *R. R. Cuyler* on May 18, 1863, along with the vessel's master and six men. As the CSS *Gaines* approached the *Isabel*, Union Acting Master's Mate N. Mayo Dyer and nine of his sailors set fire to the *Isabel* to prevent recapture. (*ORN*, 20:198–99; Shomette, *Shipwrecks of the Civil War*, 435.)

Isabel. Confederate. Two-masted schooner. Length 48 feet 8 inches, beam 15 feet 2 inches, depth 4 feet 11 inches. Built in 1861 at Charleston, S.C. Was scuttled to act as an obstruction by Confederates at the Dog River Bar in Mobile Bay. (Irion, *Mobile Bay Ship Channel, Mobile Harbor*, 62.)

Ivanhoe. British. Iron side-wheel steamer, 308 bulk tons, 266 gross tons, 173 registered tons. Length 201 feet 5 inches, beam 20 feet 2 inches, depth 9 feet 6 inches. Built in 1864 in Scotland. Ran hard aground by the USS *Glasgow*, about 2 miles east of Fort Morgan on the night of June 30, 1864, while trying to enter Mobile Bay. Between seven hundred and eight hundred shells were fired at the vessel by the USS *Hartford*, USS *Metacomet*, USS *Kennebec*, and other Union vessels. In spite of the Union attacks, the Confederates saved most of the vessel's cargo. Was destroyed on the night of July 5–6, 1864, by three boats from Adm. David G. Farragut's fleet. One Union sailor was killed in a skirmish with Confederates on the beach. The *Ivanhoe*'s crew brought the feared yellow fever to Mobile. The Confederates salvaged the vessel's machinery. The wreck was thought to have been located under dry land by Florida State University archaeologists using a magnetometer and ground penetrating sonar in 1991 and 1992, about a meter below the water table. (*OR*, 39:2:687, 693; *ORN*, 21:353–57, 904–5, 907, 936; Florida State University, "Remote Sensing Investigation of the Civil War Blockade Runner *Ivanhoe*," Web site; *LLC*, 178–79, 306.)

Josephine. Confederate. Sloop. Forced ashore by the USS *Aroostook* and burned near Fort Morgan on March 5, 1863. (*ORN*, 19:649.)

CSS Julius (Julius H. Smith). Confederate. Side-wheel steamer, 224 tons. Cargo from evacuated from Fort Henry. Built in 1859 at Paducah, Ky. Was burned by Confederates upon the approach of the USS *Tyler*, USS *Conestoga*, and *Sam Orr* on February 8, 1862, in the Tennessee River at Florence, at the foot of Muscle Shoals. (*OR*, 7:154; *ORN*, 22:782, 821; *CWC*, 6-257; *MSV*, 118, 273; *WCWN*, 247.)

Kate Dale. U.S. Wooden side-wheel steamer, 428 bulk tons. Length 193 feet 9 inches, beam 37 feet, depth 8 feet 4 inches. Built in 1855 at New Albany, Ind. Was captured while outbound from Mobile Bay on July 14, 1863, by the USS *R. R. Cuyler* near Dry Tortugas and put into Union service. Set afire at Mobile when a captured Confederate supply depot, Marshall's Warehouse, at the corner of Lipscomb and Commercial streets, blew up on May 25, 1865. The warehouse had 20 tons of gunpowder and numerous shells, and other ammunition. Much of Mobile was devastated by the explosions. (*OR*, 49:1:566–67; 49:2:913; *MSV*, 119; *LLC*, 307.)

Kentucky Brig. Confederate. Length 65 feet. Was scuttled to act as an obstruction by Confederates at the Dog River Bar in Mobile Bay with a load of bricks in 1862. Probably removed in 1871. (Irion, *Mobile Bay Ship Channel, Mobile Harbor,* 35, 36, 58.)

Lecompte. U.S. Side-wheel steamer, 238 tons. Length 176 feet, beam 33 feet, depth 5 feet 6 inches, 3 boilers. Built in 1855 at Louisville. Was burned on March 27, 1861, at Mobile, Ala. (*MSV*, 126, 276; *WPD*, 281.)

Milliner. Confederate. Steamboat. Cargo of cotton, corn, and bacon. Was captured on April 14, 1865, on the Coosa River with the *Augusta* and *Henry J. King* by the Union 4th Ky. Cavalry Regiment during Wilson's Raid. The steamers were taken to Montgomery and were burned. (*OR*, 49:1:352, 497–98.)

USS *Milwaukee.* Union. Double-turret monitor, 970 bulk tons, 1,300 displacement tons. Length 257 or 229 overall feet, beam 57 or 56 feet, depth 6 feet, speed 9 knots, turrets armor 8-inch iron, deck armor 1.5-inch iron. Complement of 127–38, with four 11-inch Dahlgren smoothbores. Laid down in 1862 and launched in 1864 at Carondelet, Mo. Was sunk by a torpedo in the Blakely River within 200 yards of the Union fleet on March 28, 1865, while returning to the fleet after attacking a Confederate transport near Spanish Fort. The torpedo exploded under the vessel, 40 feet from the stern. The ship sank with no loss of life in three minutes with the bow section above water for about an hour. Located within a mile and a half of the lower

Confederate fort on the left bank of the Blakely River. Its guns and valuables were later salvaged by Union divers. (*ORN*, 22:67, 70–71, 73–74, 92, 129; ser. 2, 1:144; *WCWN*, 149; Perry, *Infernal Machines*, 185.)

Monticello. Nationality unknown. Small blockade-runner schooner. Out of Havana, Cuba. Ran ashore 6 to 8 miles east of Fort Morgan on June 26, 1862, and was set afire by the crew. A boat from the USS *Kanawha* boarded the vessel but was driven off by fifty Confederate soldiers firing from shore. (*ORN*, 18:568–69.)

CSS *Muscogee* (CSS *Jackson*). Confederate. Screw ironclad ram. Length 223 feet 6 inches overall, beam 40 or 59 feet, draft 6 feet 6 inches to 7 feet 6 inches, casemate armor 4-inch iron, 2-foot layer of pitch pine. Armed with six Brooke rifled guns (another source—four 7-inch and two 6.4-inch). Laid down in 1862 and launched in 1864 at Columbus, Ga. Was burned at the Columbus, Ga., Navy Yard and set adrift on April 17, 1865, to prevent capture by Union forces under Gen. James Harrison Wilson. Was discovered in the Fort Benning Military Reservation on the Alabama side of the Chattahoochee River in 1960. The wreck was visible at low water with half of the vessel under a 10-foot high bank. Salvaged by local interests. The CSS *Muscogee* is now located in the Civil War Museum at Port Columbus (Ga.). Listed in the National Register of Historic Places. (*OR*, 49:1:344, 352, 365, 384, 392, 482, 485; *ORN*, 22:259; *CWC*, 6-373; *WCWN*, 119; Civil War Museum at Port Columbus Web site.)

CSS *Narcissus* (*Mary Cook*). Union. Screw steam tug, 101 tons, 115 bulk tons. Length 81 feet 6 inches, beam 18 feet 9 inches, draft 6 feet, speed 6–14 miles per hour. Complement of between nineteen and thirty-two, with one 20-pounder Parrott and one 12-pounder smoothbore. Built in 1863 at East Albany, N.Y. Struck a Confederate torpedo on December 7, 1864, while anchored on picket duty at the Dog River Bar in Mobile Bay. The torpedo made a large hole amidships in the starboard side. Was sunk in 9 feet of water within fifteen minutes, with four crewmen scalded. All guns, small arms, and supplies were salvaged. Was raised by Union forces in December 1864. Wrecked again on January 4, 1866, at Egmont Key, Fla. (*ORN*, 21:752–54, 793–94; ser. 2, 1:155; *WCWN*, 119.)

CSS *Nelms*. Confederate. Steamer. May have been lost in Mobile Bay. Outfitted at the Pensacola Navy Yard, Fla., in 1861. (*CWC*, 6-275–76; *DANFS*, 2:552.)

USS *Osage*. Union. Iron-hulled, single-turret monitor, 523 bulk tons. Length 180 feet, beam 45 feet, depth 9 feet, draft 4 feet 6 inches, maximum speed 12 miles per hour, turret armor 6-inch iron, deck armor 2.25-inch iron. Complement of 100–142, with two 11-inch Dahlgren smoothbore guns in the revolving turret and one 12-pounder deck gun. Laid down in 1862 and launched in 1863 at Carondelet, Mo. Was sunk in two fathoms of water by a Confederate torpedo under the bow in the Blakely River, with five crewmen killed and eleven wounded on March 29, 1865, while recharting the river. Was raised and later sold for scrap on November 22, 1867. (*ORN*, ser. 2, 1:167; Miller, *Photographic History*, 6:147; *WCWN*, 149.)

USS *Philippi* (*Ella*). Union. Wooden side-wheel gunboat, 311 bulk tons, 368 gross tons, 124 registered tons. Length 140 or 150 feet, beam 24 or 23 feet, depth 9 feet 10 inches or 8 feet 6 inches. Complement of forty-one, with one 20-pounder Parrott, one 24-pounder howitzer, and two 12-pounder rifled guns. Built in 1863 at Brooklyn, N.Y. Was captured as the blockade-runner *Ella* by the USS *Howquah* on November 10, 1863, off New Inlet, N.C. Used as a dispatch steamer in Adm. David G. Farragut's fleet. Hit in the boiler on August 5, 1864, by a shell from Fort Morgan and immobilized on the West Bank Shoals while attempting to pass Fort Morgan, contrary to orders to remain outside Mobile Bay. The vessel suffered two killed and two wounded. After being disabled, the USS *Philippi* was burned by a small boat from the CSS *Morgan*. Acting Mate James T. Seaver, the USS *Philippi*'s commander, was later court-martialed and dishonorably discharged from the U.S. Navy for disobeying orders and causing his vessel's loss. May have been located by a Clive Cussler survey in 1989. (*OR*, 35:2:224; 39:1:429, 435; *ORN*, 21:505–7, 522, 575, 584, 586, 800, 806; ser. 2, 1:177; *LLC*, 297; NUMA Web site, "Survey of Civil War Ships.")

CSS *Phoenix*. Confederate. Floating ironclad battery, 500 tons. Outfitted as a ram similar to the CSS *Nashville*. Length 250 feet. Armed with 6 guns. Built in 1863–64 at Selma, Ala. Severely damaged when launched in March 1864, and could not be used as a normal warship. Sunk to act as an obstruction on August 7, 1864, at the Dog River Bar and to serve as a battery. A few nights later the vessel was burned and blown up by sailors from the USS *Metacomet* then burned to the waterline by Confederates. In 1985 divers discovered the well preserved vessel. Also investigated by remote sensing for the U.S. Army Corps of Engineers. Archaeological work done in the fall of 1993 by the Florida State University Department of Anthropology and Academic Diving Program. (*OR*, 39:3:794; *ORN*, ser. 2, 1:262; *CWC*, 6-282–83; Irion, *Mobile Bay Ship Channel, Mobile Harbor*, 59; *WCWN*, 235; Florida State University, "Exploration of the *Phoenix* Wreck" Web site.)

USS *Pink* (*Zouave*). Union. Wooden screw steamer, 184 bulk tons. Length 110 feet 4 inches, beam 24 feet 6 inches, depth 7 feet. Complement of between twenty-four and twenty-nine, with two heavy 12-pounder smoothbores and one 30-pounder Parrott. Built in 1863 at Newburgh, N.Y. Ran aground and bilged off Dauphin Island while trying to make the Sand Island Light on September 23, 1865, during a gale. Was raised and later sold. (*ORN*, 22:250–51; ser. 2, 1:179; *MSV*, 236; *WCWN*, 120.)

CSS *Pioneer II* (*American Diver*). Confederate. Submarine. Length 36 feet, beam 3 feet, draft 4 feet, speed 5 knots. Had hand cranks to power the propeller. Complement of five. Built in 1863 at Mobile, Ala., from an old boiler with backing from Horace L. Hunley and James McClintock. Was sunk off Fort Morgan on February 14, 1863, while being towed in rough weather on the way to Fort Morgan to attack the Union fleet. (Bass, *Ships and Shipwrecks of the Americas*, 226; *WCWN*, 221; Cussler and Dirgo, *Sea Hunters*, 183–84; Hicks and Kropf, *Raising the Hunley*, 24–31.)

R. B. Hamilton. Union army. Stern-wheel steam transport, 175 tons. Built in 1858 at Symmes Creek, Ohio. While carrying part of the 3rd Mich. Cavalry Regiment, it struck a Confederate torpedo and sank on May 12, 1865, in Mobile Bay with the loss of thirteen killed and wounded. (*MSV*, 179; Perry, *Infernal Machines*, 188; *WPD*, 382.)

R. B. Taney. U.S. Side-wheel steamer, 301 tons. Built in 1857 at Mobile. Stranded on October 27, 1865, at Mobile. (*MSV*, 180, 291.)

USS Rodolph (Number 48). Union. Stern-wheel tinclad, 217 tons. Complement of sixty, with two 30-pounder Parrotts and four 24-pounder howitzers. Built in 1863 at Cincinnati. Hit a Confederate torpedo 30 feet aft of the bow and sunk in a few minutes in 12 feet of water on April 1, 1865, in the Blakely River with four killed and eleven wounded. Was towing a barge with a machine on board for raising the USS *Milwaukee*, which had sunk on March 28, 1865. The torpedo made a 10-foot diameter hole in the starboard bow. Union divers later salvaged the vessel's guns and valuables. (*OR*, 22:70, 72–74, 129, 132; *ORN*, ser. 2, 1:194; *DANFS*, 2:147; *WCWN*, 178.)

USS Rose (Ai Fitch). Union. Armed steam tug, 96 tons. Length 84 feet, beam 18 feet 2 inches, depth 7 feet 3 inches, speed 8.5 knots. Complement of seventeen, with one 20-pounder Parrott and one 12-pounder smoothbore. Built in 1863 at New Brunswick, N.J. Was sunk in April 1865, by a Confederate torpedo in Mobile Bay with two killed and three wounded. Was raised and continued in service in the U.S. Navy. (*ORN*, ser. 2, 1:195; Scharf, *History of the Confederate Navy*, 767; *DANFS*, 6:158; *WCWN*, 120.)

Saint Mary's (St. Marys) (Genesee) (Nick King). Union. Side-wheel steam transport, 337 tons. Built in 1857 at Wilmington, Del. Originally the Confederate steamer *Saint Mary's*, which was sunk to avoid capture in May 1862 in Florida and later raised by Confederates. Was sunk by the USS *Norwich* on February 9, 1864. Was raised and rebuilt by Union forces. Was destroyed by a Confederate torpedo in April 1864, in the Alabama River. Served in the United States Quartermaster Division as the *Genesee* from 1864 to 1868. Renamed *Nick King* for commercial trade. Sank on June 30, 1874, near Darien, Ga. (*MSV*, 192; *WCWN*, 105; *LLC*, 319.)

Sam Kirkman. Confederate. Stern-wheel steamer, 271 tons. Length 157 feet, beam 36 feet 6 inches, depth 5 feet. Carried a cargo from Fort Henry. Built in 1857 at Paducah, Ky. Was burned in the Tennessee River by Confederates on February 7–8, 1862, at Florence at the foot of Muscle Shoals when the USS *Tyler*, USS *Conestoga*, and *Sam Orr* approached. (*OR*, 7:154; *ORN*, 18:669; 22:821; *CWC*, 6-297; *MSV*, 193, 296; *WPD*, 417.)

USS Sciota. Union. Wooden screw steam two-masted schooner gunboat, 507 bulk tons, 691 displacement tons. Length 158 feet, beam 28 feet, depth 12 feet, draft 7 feet or 9 feet 6 inches. Complement of 65–114, with one 20-pounder Parrott, three 24-pounder howitzers, one 11-inch Dahlgren, and one 12-pounder smoothbore. Built in 1861 at Philadelphia. Was sunk in Louisiana in 1863 and raised. Was sunk in 12 feet of water by a Confederate torpedo on April 14, 1865, in the Blakely River, with four killed and six wounded. Was raised by Union forces on July 7, 1865. Sold by auction on October 25, 1865. (*ORN*, 22:96, 130, 237; ser. 2, 1:203; Miller, *Photographic History*, 6:193; Scharf, *History of the Confederate Navy*, 767; *WCWN*, 49, 53.)

CSS Selma (Florida) (USS Selma). Confederate. Side-wheel gunboat, 320 bulk tons. Length 252 feet, beam 30 feet, draft 6 feet, speed 9 knots. Complement of between sixty-five and ninety-four, with two 9-inch smoothbores, one 8-inch smoothbore, and one 6.4-inch rifled gun, all pivots. Built in 1856 at Mobile. Carrying one hundred extra men on the way to board a blockader at the entrance to Mobile Bay. Hit an iron-pointed pile or snag while crossing the Dog River Bar on February 5, 1863, and sank in eight feet of water. Was raised by Confederates on February 13, 1863, and put back into service. Was captured by Union forces during the Battle of Mobile Bay on August 5, 1864, after losing seven killed and eight wounded. Became the USS *Selma* in Union service. (*ORN*, 19:627; ser. 2, 1:266; *MSV*, 197; *CWC*, 6-300–301, *WCWN*, 86, 236.)

USS Tecumseh. Union. Single-turreted monitor, 1,034 tons. Length 223 feet, beam 43 feet 4 inches, depth 13 feet 4 inches, draft 14 feet loaded / 13 feet 4 inches light, speed 8 knots. Complement of 118, with two 15-inch Dahlgren smoothbores. Launched in 1863 at Jersey City, N.J. Was sunk by a Confederate torpedo in less than 25 seconds, about 500–600 yards from Fort Morgan in Mobile Bay on August 5, 1864, at 7:40 a.m. when Adm. David G. Farragut's Union fleet attacked the Confederate forts at the entrance to Mobile Bay. Cdr. Tunis A. M. Craven and ninety-three crewmen were lost with the ship, while twenty-four survived. Six of the vessel's crew were captured by Confederate soldiers from Fort Morgan after they swam ashore. Union divers examined the wreck a week after it was sunk in 7 fathoms of water with 3 fathoms over the vessel. The USS *Tecumseh*'s anchor has been salvaged. In 1966 the Smithsonian Institution received title to the wreck, but dropped plans to raise it in 1974 after Congress refused to fund the project. Listed in the National Register of Historic Places. East Carolina University archaeologists have surveyed the wreck. (*OR*, 35:2:223–24; 39:1:431–35; 39:2:225–27, 230, 755, 759, 785–86; *ORN*, 21:405, 415–17, 419, 422, 438–40, 442, 445, 465, 489–93, 496, 518–19, 521–22, 532, 542, 567, 569, 575, 579, 581, 597–99, 669, 818; ser. 2, 1:221; Irion, *Mobile Bay Ship Channel, Mobile Harbor,* 13; *WCWN,* 10–11; Naval Historical Center Web site, "USS *Tecumseh.*")

CSS *Time*. Confederate. Side-wheel steamer, 263 tons. Cargo of $100,000 worth of Confederate stores. Built in 1860 at Elizabeth, Pa. Was burned by Confederates and sank on February 7, 1862, in the Tennessee River at Florence with the CSS *Julius* and *Sam Kirkman* when the USS *Tyler,* USS *Conestoga,* and *Sam Orr* steamed upriver. (*ORN,* 22:782, 821–22; *MSV,* 212, 301.)

CSS *Tuscaloosa*. Confederate. Screw ironclad steam ram, 500 tons. Length 152 feet overall, beam 34 feet, depth 10 feet 6 inches, draft 7–8 feet, speed 3 knots. Complement of forty, with one 6.4-inch Brooke rifled gun and possibly four 32-pounder smoothbores. Used as a floating battery. Laid down in 1862 and launched in 1863 at Selma, Ala. Completed in 1864 at Mobile. Was scuttled on April 12, 1865, mid-channel of the Spanish River, 12 miles north of Mobile. Its crew and material were put aboard the CSS *Nashville* and moved upriver. The wreck was located in 1985. (*ORN,* 20:705; 22:95, 139; ser. 2, 1:269; CWC, 6-318; *WCWN,* 207; Hand, "Confederate Ironclads," *Skin Diver,* 140–41.)

***Vernon*.** Confederate. One-mast barge, 113 tons. Length 120 feet, beam 25 feet 6 inches. Built in 1854 at Mobile. Was scuttled by Confederates to serve as an obstruction at

the Dog River Bar in Mobile Bay. (Irion, *Mobile Bay Ship Channel, Mobile Harbor,* 62.)

***Wave*.** Confederate. Sloop. Cargo of 60 sacks and 2 barrels of flour. En route from Mobile to Mississippi City. Was captured on June 27, 1862, and destroyed by the USS *Bohio* after the *Wave*'s cargo was removed. (*ORN,* 18:569.)

***William B. King*.** Confederate. Schooner. Was scuttled to serve as an obstruction at the Dog River Bar at Mobile Bay. Probably removed in 1871. (Irion, *Mobile Bay Ship Channel, Mobile Harbor,* 59; *WCWN,* 233.)

***William Jones*.** Confederate. Length possibly 170 feet. Was scuttled to serve as an obstruction at the Dog River Bar in Mobile Bay. Was probably removed in 1871. (Irion, *Mobile Bay Ship Channel, Mobile Harbor,* 58.)

▷ **VESSELS WITHOUT NAMES**

barge. Confederate. Length 117 feet, beam 26 feet. Capacity of 900 cotton bales. Was scuttled by Confederates to act as obstruction at the Dog River Bar in Mobile Bay. (Irion, *Mobile Bay Ship Channel, Mobile Harbor,* 62.)

launch from USS *Cincinnati*. Union. Sank while dragging for torpedoes on April 14, 1865, in the Blakely River, with three killed. The wreck was raised to within 2 feet of the surface, but the mooring parted, and strain brought the rope to stern, so the launch sank back into the water and was not recovered. (*ORN,* 22:96, 131; Porter, *Naval History,* 786.)

ram. Confederate. Unnamed side-wheel ram under construction. Was destroyed on the stocks at Oven Bluff sometime during the war. (*WCWN,* 209.)

schooner. Confederate. Carried cotton and naval stores. Grounded a mile or so south of Fort Morgan on January 23, 1862, while trying to come out of the eastern Swash Channel. The USS *Huntsville* and USS *R. R. Cuyler* set the schooner afire. (*ORN,* 17:82–83.)

schooner. Confederate. Ran ashore by the USS *Kanawha* in early July 1862. Was burned by the Confederates near Mobile. (*ORN,* 18:669.)

schooner. Confederate. Cargo of cotton. Beached on shoals eastward of the northern point of Sand Island during a gale, on its way out of Mobile Bay. Was destroyed by the crew on December 15, 1862. (*ORN*, 19:412–13.)

schooner. Confederate. Was scuttled to act as an obstruction at the Dog River Bar during the Civil War. (Irion, *Mobile Bay Ship Channel, Mobile Harbor*, 62.)

steamboats. Confederate. Two steamboats. Cargo of cotton, corn, and commissaries. Was burned along with the steamboats *Augusta, Henry J. King,* and *Milliner* on the Coosa River on April 14, 1865, at Montgomery by Wilson's Union raiders. (*OR*, 49:1:352.)

Arkansas

Most of the Civil War shipwrecks in Arkansas, other than those in the Mississippi River, are located in the Arkansas and White rivers. Wrecks on the Mississippi River are found in the Mississippi River section.

Major Arkansas naval battles occurred at DuVall's Bluff on the White River and Arkansas Post on the Arkansas River. No vessels were sunk in any engagements between warships, but several steamboats were captured and destroyed by Confederate shore batteries and guerrilla bands.

Most vessels lost in Arkansas were either destroyed to prevent capture or were snagged in accidents. To block the White River from advancing Union gunboats, the Confederates scuttled the *Eliza G,* CSS *Mary Patterson,* and CSS *Maurepas* at St. Charles on June 16, 1862.

When Union troops raided Van Buren on the Arkansas River on December 28–29, 1862, the Confederate steamers *Arkansas, Era No. 6, Frederick Notrebe, Key West,* and *Rose Douglas* were scuttled or burned. When the Confederates evacuated Little Rock and Union forces occupied the Arkansas capital on September 10, 1863, the Confederates scuttled or burned the steamers *Arkansas, Chester Ashley, Little Rock,* CSS *Pontchartrain,* CSS *St. Francis No. 3,* and *Tahlequah* on the Arkansas River.

Adams. Union. Steamer. Cargo of quartermaster's stores and ammunition. Ran into the steamer *Chippewa* 20 miles below Little Rock on the Arkansas River the night of April 12, 1864, and sank. Part of the cargo was salvaged by Union forces. (*OR*, 34:3:147.)

Ad. Hine (*Ad. Hines*) (*Nugget*). Union. Stern-wheel steam transport, 94 tons. Length 129 feet, beam 24 feet, depth 35 feet, 2 boilers. Built in 1860 at Monongahela City, Pa. Snagged while carrying a cargo from St. Louis on February 18, 1864, on the Arkansas River, 8 miles below Pine Bluff. Sank in 8 feet of water in five minutes. Was raised by the crew. Was later renamed *Nugget*. (*ORN*, 25:775–76, 781–82, 784–85; 26:10; *MSV*, 2; *WPD*, 5.)

Aid. U.S. side-wheel steamer, 60 tons. Built in 1860 at Evansville, Ind. Snagged and sank on January 28, 1861, in the St. Francis River. (*MSV*, 4, 239.)

Arkansas. Confederate. Side-wheel steamer, 115 tons. Cargo of freight. Built in 1832 at Cincinnati. Trapped by low water in the Arkansas River above Lee's Creek Bluff. Part of the vessel's cargo was unloaded. Was burned on Maj. Gen. Thomas C. Hindman's orders on December 28, 1862, to prevent capture by Maj. Gen. James G. Blunt's advancing Union forces. (*OR*, 22:1:167–68, 172; *MSV*, 13.)

Arkansas. Confederate. Stern-wheel steamer, 223 tons. Length 154 feet, beam 33 feet, depth 5 feet, 3 boilers. Built in 1860 at Pittsburgh, Pa. Was burned on the Arkansas River at Little Rock on September 10, 1863, as Gen. Frederick Steele's Union forces approached the capital city. (*MSV*, 13, 242; *WPD*, 29.)

Bracelet. Confederate. Cottonclad side-wheel steamer, 169 tons. Built in 1857 at Louisville. Was burned by Confederates at Little Rock on September 10, 1863, as Gen. Frederick

Steele's Union forces approached the city. Removed in 1906 by the snagboat *C. B. Reese*. (*MSV*, 246; *WPD*, 60.)

Cambridge. Confederate. Stern-wheel steamer, 242 tons. Built in 1856 at Brownsville, Pa. Snagged on February 23, 1862, at Grand Glaise on the White River, with forty-two lives lost. (*MSV*, 28, 248.)

Cedar Rapids. U.S. Stern-wheel steamer, 131 tons. Length 153 feet, beam 25 feet, 2 boilers. Built in 1858 at Freedom, Pa. Snagged on February 12, 1861, at Douglas Landing after salvaging the *A. H. Sevier*. (*EAS*, 274; *WPD*, 75.)

Celeste. Union. Stern-wheel steamer, 79 tons. Snagged at Du-Vall's Bluff in March or April 1865. (*WPD*, 248; *WSTD*, 76.)

Chester Ashley. Confederate. Stern-wheel steamer, 192 tons. Built in 1860 at Cincinnati. Was burned by Confederates on September 10, 1863, at Little Rock as Gen. Frederick Steele's Union army approached the city. (*EAS*, 275.)

Chippewa (New Chippewa). Union. Steamer. Carried a Union escort and Union refugees from Van Buren in the lead of a convoy of four Union steamboats. Grounded on the south side of the Arkansas River on January 17, 1865, at Ivey's Ford, about 14 miles above Clarksville. Confederate forces captured the vessel, two to four cannons, 1 officer, and 29 men of the 50th Ind. Regiment, as well as the vessel's captain, crew, the white refugees, and 40 African Americans. The vessel's upper works were destroyed, but the machinery and hull were in good condition after the attack. The vessel was set afire after the stores were removed by the Confederates. (*OR*, 48:1:12:14–17, 583, 613.)

Des Arc. Union. Side-wheel steamer, 276 tons. Length 205 feet, beam 31 feet, depth 6 feet, 3 boilers. Built in Paducah, Ky. Caught fire on March 22, 1862, probably in the White River at DuVall's Bluff. Was towed across the river and sunk by shelling from the USS *Queen City* to prevent the other nearby steamers from getting set afire. The *Emma No. 2* arrived in Cincinnati on July 12, 1864, with machinery salvaged from the *Des Arc*. (*WPD*, 125.)

Des Moines City. Union. Stern-wheel steamer, 122 tons. Built in 1859 at Pittsburgh, Pa. Snagged on January 1, 1865, in the Arkansas River. (*MSV*, 53, 255; *WPD*, 125.)

Diurnal. Union. Side-wheel steamer, 199 tons. Built in 1850 at Brownsville, Pa. Snagged and burned on September 12, 1863, in the White River at St. Charles. (*ORN*, 25:417; *MSV*, 55, 256; *WPD*, 130.)

Doane (Doan No. 2). Union. Stern-wheel steamer, 250 tons. Cargo of forage and freight. Built in 1863 at Cincinnati. Grounded and broken in two, sinking in six feet of water in the Arkansas River at 2:00 p.m. on November 28, 1864, about 20 miles above Dardanelle and 18 miles east of Clarksville. The vessel's cargo was saved. Also see **Doan No. 2** in Tennessee. (*OR*, 41:4:712–13, 754, 838, 935; *MSV*, 55.)

Doctor Buffington. Union. Side-wheel steamer, 262 tons. Length 176 feet, beam 32 feet, depth 5 feet. Built in 1857 at Cincinnati. Foundered in December 1862, in the White River. (*MSV*, 55, 256; *WPD*, 130.)

Eliza G. Confederate. Steamer. Was scuttled with the CSS *Maurepas* and CSS *Mary Patterson* by Confederates at St. Charles on June 16, 1862, in the White River to block a Union fleet coming upriver. Holes were bored in the vessel to sink it. (*OR*, 13:929–32; *ORN*, 23:166, 168, 200, 202, 205, 379, 693; *CWC*, 6-224.)

Ella. U.S. Stern-wheel steamer, 173 tons. Built in 1854 at Elizabeth, Pa. Snagged on December 13, 1865, at Little Rock on the Arkansas River. (*MSV*, 62, 258.)

Ellwood. U.S. Side-wheel ferry steamer, 21 tons. Built in 1864 at Portsmouth, Ohio. Was sunk in the St. Francis River in the fall, 1864, and raised. (*WPD*, 147.)

Era No. 6 (Era). Confederate. Stern-wheel steamer, 83 tons. Built in 1860 at Pittsburgh, Pa. Was burned after its cargo was removed under orders of Maj. Gen. Thomas C. Hindman on December 27–28, 1862, on the Arkansas River above Van Buren, to prevent its capture by Union troops. (*OR*, 22:1:167–68, 172; *MSV*, 66.)

Frederick Notrebe (Notre). Confederate. Side-wheel steamer, 190 tons. Cargo of corn. Built in 1860 at Cincinnati. Grounded in the Arkansas River one mile below Van Buren. Was captured by Union raiders on December 28, 1862. Was shelled by Confederates and burned by Union forces on December 29, 1862. May have been raised and put into Union service. (*OR*, 22:167–68, 172; *MSV*, 77, 262.)

I Go. Union. Stern-wheel steamer, 104 tons. Built in 1860 at Antiquity, Ohio. Was burned on June 12, 1864, at Arkansas Post on the Arkansas River. (*MSV*, 99, 268.)

J. H. Done. Union. Stern-wheel steamer, 211 tons. Length 155 feet, beam 30 feet, depth 4 feet. Built in 1854 at Shousetown, Pa. Lost at Scotia in 1864 in the upper Arkansas River. (*WPD*, 231.)

Julia Roane. Confederate. Stern-wheel steamer. Length 141 feet, beam 31 feet 1 inch (originally 21 feet 2 inches), depth 4 feet 10 inches. Built in 1859 at California, Pa. Was burned at Little Rock on September 10, 1863. (*WPD*, 261.)

Juliet (*Goldena*) (*USS Juliet*) (*Number 4*). U.S. Stern-wheel steamer, 157 tons. Length 155 feet 6 inches, beam 30 feet 2 inches, depth 5 feet. Built in 1862 at Brownsville, Pa. Former Union tinclad gunboat USS *Juliet* or *Number 4*, which was renamed *Goldena* after Union service. Stranded at the White River Cutoff between the Arkansas River and White River on December 31, 1865. (*MSV*, 118, 273; *WCWN*, 173.)

Key West. Confederate. Stern-wheel steamer, 169 tons. Built in 1857 at Elizabeth, Pa. Was burned on December 27, 1862, after being captured by Union forces at Van Buren on the south side of the Arkansas River opposite Strain's Landing. (*OR*, 22:1:167–68, 172; *MSV*, 121, 274; *WPD*, 271.)

Key West No. 4. Union. Stern-wheel steamer, 91 tons. Built in 1863 at Manchester, Pa. Sank 20 miles below Little Rock in the Arkansas River on April 1, 1864, at Paw Paw Landing due to a snag. (*MSV*, 271.)

Lady Jackson. Union. Stern-wheel steamer, 207 tons. Built in 1860 at Cincinnati. Snagged on October 14, 1863, in the White River. (*MSV*, 123, 275.)

Leon. Union. Stern-wheel steamer, 87 tons. Built in 1859 at Brownsville, Pa. Snagged in March 1864, at Burnum. Some cargo was removed by Union forces. (*OR*, 34:3:40; *MSV*, 126, 276.)

USS Linden (*Tinclad 10*). Union. Side-wheel steamer, 177 tons. Length 154 feet, beam 31 feet, depth 4 feet. Armed with six 24-pounder howitzers. Built in 1860 at Belle Vernon (Pittsburgh), Pa. Was sunk by a snag in the Arkansas River on February 22, 1864, 15 miles above the mouth of the Arkansas River, below Arkansas Post. Reported to be within 400 yards of the snagged *Ad. Hines*. The port bow hit a stump which ripped a 90-foot hole from the bow to the port magazine. Reported to have taken an hour and a half to fill two-thirds full of water. The vessel's guns, paymaster's safe, casemate, shells, and stores were removed by Union forces. The machinery was raised and taken to the Union naval base at Mound City, Ill. (*ORN*, 25:774–83; ser. 2, 1:128; *WCWN*, 173.)

Little Rock. Confederate. Stern-wheel steamer, 183 tons. Built in 1858 at Cincinnati. Was burned by Confederates at Little Rock on the Arkansas River on September 10, 1863, as Gen. Frederick Steele's Union army approached the capital. (*MSV*, 129, 277.)

CSS Mary Patterson. Confederate. Stern-wheel steamer, 105 tons. Built in 1859 at Grand Glaize, Ark. Was scuttled when Confederate forces bored holes in the hull on June 16, 1862, at St. Charles with the CSS *Maurepas* and *Eliza G* on the White River to block a Union fleet of gunboats then ascending the river. (*OR*, 13:929–32; *ORN*, 23:166, 200, 205; *CWC*, 6-268.)

CSS Maurepas (*Grosse Tete*). Confederate. Side-wheel gunboat, 399 tons. Length 180 feet, beam 34 feet, draft 7 feet. Complement of seventy-nine, with five guns, 32-pounders and 24-pounders. Built in 1858 as the *Grosse Tete* at New Albany, Ind. Purchased by Confederates at New Orleans. Sunk along with the CSS *Mary Patterson* and *Eliza G* by Confederates to block the White River below St. Charles on June 16, 1862, after removal of the vessel's guns and supplies. The crew manned shore batteries on the river. Capt. Joseph Fry was wounded and captured during the battle. (*OR*, 13:929–32; *ORN*, 23:166, 168, 200–205; *CWC*, 6-268–69.)

Mill Boy. Union. Stern-wheel steamer, 86 tons. Cargo of stores, forage, and one cannon. Built in 1857 at Brownsville, Pa. as a barge. Converted to a steamer and a floating grist mill in 1860. En route to DuVall's Bluff. During a storm the rope to the vessel's anchor broke, and the vessel drifted into a snag and sank nine miles downstream, after turning upside down on January 31, 1864, on the White River, 9 miles above Jacksonport. Thirty-five tons of Union stores and forage, along with a caisson and gun carriage, were lost, but the cannon was recovered by Union forces. (*OR*, 34:2:241–42; *MSV*, 145, 281; *WPD*, 321–22; *WSTD*, 163.)

Miller (*J. H. Miller*). Union. Stern-wheel steamer transport, 68 tons. Cargo of commissary supplies and mail. Built in 1863 at Hazelton, Ind. Was captured and burned by Confederates on the Arkansas River, 20 miles from Pine Bluff on August 17, 1864. (*MSV*, 105, 270.)

CSS *Pontchartrain* (*Eliza Simmons*) (*Lizzie Simmons*). Confederate. Side-wheel armored gunboat, 454 tons. Length 204 feet, beam 36 feet 6 inches, depth 6 feet 6 inches, draft 10 feet. Carried two 32-pounders and five other guns. Built in 1859 at New Albany, Ind. Two rifled 32-pounders were transferred to Confederate batteries at St. Charles on the White River. Was burned on September 9, 1863, at Little Rock on the Arkansas River by Gen. Sterling Price's command on the approach of Gen. Frederick Steele's Union army. The ammunition exploded on the ship. Part of the vessel's crew was later captured while fighting Union forces. The USS *General Price* destroyed the vessel on September 10, 1863. (*ORN*, ser. 2, 1:263; *CWC*, 6-288; *WCWN*, 245; *WPD*, 291.)

Progress. U.S. Side-wheel steamer, 59 tons. Built in 1862 at Zanesville, Ohio. Was sunk on December 1, 1865, in the Arkansas River with a loss of twenty lives. (*MSV*, 178, 291; *WPD*, 379.)

Quapaw. U.S. Stern-wheel steamer, 245 tons. Length 152 feet, beam 31 feet 11 inches, depth 5 feet 5 inches. Built in 1857 at California, Pa. Snagged in the Arkansas River on February 11, 1861, at Little Rock. (*MSV*, 179, 291; *WPD*, 380.)

USS *Queen City* (*Number 26*) (*Queen City*). Union. Side-wheel tinclad gunboat, 210 or 212 tons. Armor 1.25-inch iron. Complement of sixty-five, with two 30-pounder Parrotts, two 32-pounder smoothbores, four 24-pounder howitzers, and one 12-pounder gun. Built in 1863 at Cincinnati. Attacked by Confederate general Joe Shelby's brigade and four cannons at daylight on June 24, 1864, at Clarendon on the White River about 200 yards from shore. The first or second shot disabled the starboard engine and penetrated the steam pipe. After a twenty-minute fight the boat surrendered, with six killed and nine wounded. The captain's mate and twenty-five crewmen were captured. Ten thousand dollars in greenbacks had been aboard the ship, but most of the money had been removed by a Union paymaster a few days earlier. There is a legend of lost treasure on this wreck, based on the payroll of greenbacks that was removed before the gunboat was captured. Two 24-pounder howitzers were removed by the Confederates, along with fifty small arms, most of the vessel's ammunition, and other supplies. Was burned by the Confederates when the USS *Tyler*, USS *Fawn*, and USS *Naumkegs* approached. Several captured crewmen were later rescued by the Union ships. Two 24-pounder howitzers and one 32-pounder from the USS *Queen City* were later salvaged by the USS *Tyler*. The *Exchange* raised another gun. A total of seven cannons were salvaged, and two were left in the hull by August 9, 1864. Two 24-pounders captured by General Shelby's forces from the vessel were recaptured on June 26, 1864, by Union forces during a skirmish at Pikesville. In 1878 a Captain Kehoe salvaged much of the vessel's machinery using a diving bell, diving suit, and mule-drawn barge and winch system. In 1977 the American Archaeology Division of the University of Missouri–Columbia did a magnetometer survey, and divers found the remains of the hull and iron fittings. This vessel has been located and surveyed by National Park Service archaeologists. (*OR*, 34:1:1044, 1049–51; 34:4:535, 571, 579; 53 [supp.]: 479; *ORN*, 26:418, 423–25, 428–29, 432, 502; *WCWN*, 168; Garrison, May, and Marquardt, "Search for the U.S.S. *Queen City*: Instrument Survey, 1977," Arnold, *Ninth Conference on Underwater Archaeology*, 45–49.)

Rodolph. U.S. Stern-wheel steamer, 249 tons. Built in 1864 at Cincinnati. Snagged in December 1865, on the Arkansas River, 15 miles below Little Rock. (*MSV*, 187, 294.)

Rose Douglas. Confederate. Stern-wheel steamer, 123 tons. Cargo of 4,300 bushels of corn, 6 hogsheads of sugar, and a large amount of molasses. Built in 1860 at Belle Vernon (Pittsburgh), Pa. Was captured on December 28, 1862, on the Arkansas River at Van Buren by Maj. Gen. James G. Blunt's Union forces. Was shelled by the Confederates and burned on December 29, 1862, by Union soldiers, with all the cargo but the corn removed. (*OR,* 22:1:167–68, 171–71; *MSV,* 188, 294.)

St. Francis No. 3. Confederate. Stern-wheel cottonclad steamer, 219 tons. Length 160 feet, beam 29 feet, draft 6 feet. Built in 1853 at Jeffersonville, Ind. Was burned on the Arkansas River on September 10, 1863, at Little Rock as Gen. Frederick Steele's Union army approached. (*CWC,* 6-296; *WCWN,* 248; *EAS,* 289.)

Tahlequah. Confederate. Side-wheel steamer, 92 tons. Built in 1860 at Brownsville, Pa. Was burned by Confeder- ates on September 10, 1863, at Little Rock on the Arkansas River upon the approach of General Steele's Union army. (*MSV,* 208, 300.)

Violet. Confederate. Stern-wheel steamer, 89 tons. Built in 1856 at Brownsville, Pa. Was burned on the Arkansas River at Van Buren on December 27, 1862. (*MSV,* 222, 304.)

William Henry. Confederate. Stern-wheel steamer, 95 tons. Built in 1857 at Paducah, Ky. Snagged on June 2, 1861, on the Arkansas River at Fort Smith. (*MSV,* 231, 307.)

Atlantic Ocean

During the Civil War the Confederate commerce raiders CSS *Alabama,* CSS *Florida,* CSS *Georgia,* CSS *Savannah,* and CSS *Tallahassee* (later renamed CSS *Olustee*) and the tenders CSS *Clarence,* CSS *Archer,* and CSS *Tacony* caused major damage to Union shipping along the Eastern Seaboard as well as off South America. Shipping lanes between Europe and North America were particularly hard hit, and insurance rates skyrocketed. The Confederate commerce raiders were very effective. Many American vessels were redocumented as foreign vessels to avoid destruction if stopped by Confederate raiders.

Ada. Union. Fishing schooner, 69 tons. Was captured and burned by Lt. Charles W. Read and the CSS *Tacony* on June 23, 1863, off New England. (*ORN,* 2:332, 656.)

A. J. Bird. Union. Schooner, 182 tons. Was captured and burned by the CSS *Olustee* on November 3, 1864, off the Delaware capes. (*OR,* ser. 4, 3:1058; *ORN,* 3:836; Scharf, *History of the Confederate Navy,* 814.)

Aldebaran. Union. Schooner. Cargo of flour, provisions, clocks, and desks. En route from New York City to Maraham, Brazil. Was captured near latitude 29° 18' north, longitude 51° 4' west by the CSS *Florida* on March 13, 1863, and destroyed. (*ORN,* 2:648, 671, 677.)

Amazonian. Union. Bark, 480 tons. Cargo of twenty cases of varnish, flasks of oil, and mail. Out of Boston. En route from New York City to Montevideo, Uruguay. Was captured and burned by the CSS *Alabama* on June 2, 1863, at latitude 15° 1' 18" north, longitude 34° 56' 30" west. (*ORN,* 2, 690:747–48; Semmes, *Service Afloat,* 624; Summersell, *Boarding Officer,* 118.)

Anna F. Schmidt. Union. Ship, 784 tons. Cargo of lamps, chinaware, glass, crockery, clothes, medicine, clocks, and sewing machines. Built in 1854 in Kennebunk, Maine. Out of Maine. En route from Boston to San Francisco. Was captured and burned at latitude 25° 27' south, longitude 37° 56' west by the CSS *Alabama* on July 2, 1863, in the South Atlantic. (*ORN,* 2:690, 754; 3:680; Semmes, *Service Afloat,* 631; Summersell, *Boarding Officer,* 124–25.)

Arcade. Union. Schooner. Cargo of staves to exchange for rum and sugar. En route from Portland, Maine, for Pointe-a-Pitre, Guadalupe. Was captured and burned by the CSS *Sumter* on November 26, 1861, at latitude 20° 27' north, longitude 57° 15' west. (*ORN,* 1:646, 726, 744; Semmes, *Service Afloat,* 270.)

Atlantic. U.S. Screw steamer, 1,054 tons. Built in 1864 at Mystic, Conn. Foundered at sea at latitude 36° 3' north, longitude 72° 30' west on October 15, 1865, with forty-eight lives lost. (*MSV*, 15, 243.)

Bold Hunter. Union. Ship. Cargo of 1,025 tons of coal. Out of Boston. En route from Dundee, Scotland, to Calcutta, India. Was captured on October 9, 1863, and burned by the CSS *Georgia* on October 10, 1863, near latitude 19° north, longitude 21° west, off French West Africa. (*ORN*, 2:808–9, 817.)

Byzantium. Union. Clipper ship. Cargo of coal. Bound for New York City from London. Was captured and burned by the newly captured CSS *Tacony* under Confederate lieutenant Charles W. Read on June 21, 1863, near latitude 41° north, longitude 69° 10' west, southeast of Canada and east of New England. (*ORN*, 2:656.)

Clarence (CSS Clarence) (Coquette). Union. Brigantine, 253 tons. Length 114 feet, beam 24 feet, draft 11 feet. Complement of twenty-one, with one 12-pounder howitzer. Cargo of cotton. Built in 1857 at Baltimore. En route from Rio de Janeiro, Brazil, for Baltimore. Was captured on May 6, 1863, by the *Towry*, which was manned by CSS *Florida* crewmen. Lt. Charles W. Read and a Confederate crew then sailed the CSS *Clarence* to Chesapeake Bay but were grounded. They captured three vessels on June 12, 1863, and transferred the crew and gun aboard the *Tacony*. They burned the *Clarence* on the morning of June 25, 1863. (*ORN*, 2:654–56; ser. 2, 1:250; *CWC*, 6-212.)

USS Commodore McDonough. Union. Side-wheel steamer, 532 tons. Length 8 feet 6 inches, speed 8 knots. Carried one 100-pounder rifled gun, one 9-inch Dahlgren smoothbore, two 50-pounder Dahlgrens, and two 24-pounder howitzers. Built in 1862 at New York City. Foundered on August 23, 1865, in the Atlantic Ocean while being towed from New York City to Port Royal, S.C. (*ORN*, ser. 2, 1:62; *WCWN*, 100.)

Commonwealth. Union. Ship, 1,300 tons. Cargo worth $60,000. From New York City. En route to San Francisco. Was captured and burned in the Atlantic Ocean by the CSS *Florida* on April 17, 1863. (*ORN*, 2:649, 672, 679.)

Constitution. Union. Bark. Cargo of coal. From Philadelphia. En route to Shanghai, China. Forty-eight days out of port, the CSS *Georgia* captured the vessel on June 25, 1863. It took two weeks for the crew of the CSS *Georgia* to transfer the badly needed coal by using buckets. The *Constitution* was then used for gunnery practice, set afire, and sunk on July 8, 1863. (*ORN*, 2:408, 814–15; Shomette, *Shipwrecks of the Civil War*, 181–82; Hearn, *Gray Raiders*, 242–43.)

Crenshaw. Union. Schooner, 279 tons. Cargo of grain. From New York City. En route to Glasgow. Was captured and burned by the CSS *Alabama* on October 26, 1862, at latitude 40° 11' 28" north, longitude 64° 32' 15" west, north of Bermuda. (*ORN*, 1:527, 780, 799–800; Semmes, *Service Afloat*, 489–91; Summersell, *Boarding Officer*, 42.)

Crown Point. Union. Ship, 1,098 tons. From New York City. En route to San Francisco. Carried assorted cargo. Was captured and burned in the Atlantic Ocean by the CSS *Florida* on May 13, 1863. (*ORN*, 2:652, 263–64, 680.)

Daniel Trowbridge (Trowbridge). Union. Packet schooner. Cargo of provisions, including lobster, beef, pork, hams, bread, crackers, cheese, flour, milk, fruit, and preserved meats. Out of New Haven, Conn. En route to Demerara, British Guiana. Was captured on October 27, 1861, and burned on October 30, 1861, by the CSS *Sumter* near latitude 16° 40' north, longitude 58° 16' west (another source—17° 54' north, 56° 3' west), northeast of Dominica. The fresh provisions were welcomed by the crew of the CSS *Sumter*, which had been subsisting on bad food. (*ORN*, 1:209, 216, 239, 637, 716–17, 744; Semmes, *Service Afloat*, 226–27; Hearn, *Gray Raiders*, 129.)

D. Godfrey. Union. Bark, 299 tons. Cargo of mess beef and pork. Out of Boston. Was captured and sunk by the CSS *Shenandoah* on November 8, 1864, southwest of the Cape Verde Islands at latitude 4° 42' north, longitude 28° 24' west, after the removal of 220 barrels each of mess beef and pork. (*ORN*, 3:760, 786, 802; Horan, CSS *Shenandoah*, 196; *WCWN*, 214; Shomette, *Civil War Shipwrecks*, 184; Hearn, *Gray Raiders*, 265.)

D. H. Mount. U.S. Screw steamer, 321 tons. Built in 1863 at Bound Brook, N.J. Foundered on October 23, 1865, between Cape Hatteras, N.C., and Jacksonville, Fla., with twenty-four lives lost. (*MSV*, 49, 254.)

Dictator. Union. Ship. Cargo of coal. From New York City. En route to Hong Kong. Was captured by the CSS *Georgia* on April 25, 1864, at latitude 25° 45' north, longitude 23° 15' 30" west. Was burned the next day. (*ORN,* 2:355, 811.)

Ebenezer Dodge. Union. Whaling bark. Out of New Bedford, Mass. En route to the Pacific Ocean. Crew of twenty-two. Leaking badly when captured, at latitude 30° 57' north and longitude 51° 49' west, by the CSS *Sumter* on December 8, 1861, and was burned off the Canary Islands. The vessel's provisions, water, clothing, twelve whale boats, and other small stores were removed to the Confederate raider. (*ORN,* 1:646, 728, 744; Semmes, *Service Afloat,* 278–79.)

Edward. Union. Whaling bark. Was captured and burned on December 4, 1864, by the CSS *Shenandoah* off Tristan de Cunha. (*ORN,* 3:760, 787, 804.)

E. F. Lewis. Union. Schooner, 119 tons. Was captured and destroyed by the CSS *Olustee* on November 3, 1864, off the Delaware capes. (*OR,* ser. 4, 3:1058; *ORN,* 3:836; Scharf, *History of the Confederate Navy,* 814.)

Elizabeth Ann. Union. Fishing schooner, 92 tons. Was captured and burned on June 22, 1863, by the CSS *Tacony* off New England. (*ORN,* 2:332, 656.)

Empress Theresa. Union. Bark, 312 tons. Was captured and burned by the CSS *Olustee* on November 1, 1864, off the Delaware capes. (*OR,* ser. 4, 3:1058; *ORN,* 3:836; Scharf, *History of the Confederate Navy,* 814.)

Flora. British. Side-wheel steamer, 571 gross tons, 359 registered tons. Length 215 feet, beam 25 feet 8 inches, depth 13 feet 6 inches. En route from Halifax, Nova Scotia for Bermuda to be repaired. Built in 1858 at Greenock, Scotland. Foundered at sea on January 11, 1864. (*LLC,* 300.)

George Latimer. Union. Schooner, 198 tons. Cargo of flour, lard, bread, and kerosene. From Baltimore. En route to Pernambuco (Recife), Brazil. Was captured and burned by the CSS *Florida* on May 18, 1864, at latitude 33° 55' north, longitude 55° 13' west. (*ORN,* 3:618, 644.)

Golden Eagle. Union. Ship, 1,121 tons. Cargo of guano. Out of San Francisco. En route from Howland Island to Cork,

Ireland. Was captured and burned by the CSS *Alabama* on February 21, 1863, near latitude 29° 28' north, longitude 44° 58' west. (*ORN,* 2:728–29; Semmes, *Service Afloat,* 579; Summersell, *Boarding Officer,* 88.)

Goodspeed. Union. Bark. From Londonderry, Ireland, to New York City in ballast. Was captured by the CSS *Tacony* and burned off New England on June 21, 1863. (*ORN,* 2:656.)

Hattie. British. Iron side-wheel steamer, 284 gross tons, 203 registered tons. Length 219.4 feet, beam 20 feet 2 inches, depth 8 feet 5 inches. Built in 1864 at Greenock, Scotland. Lost at sea on May 8, 1865. (*LLC,* 303.)

Henrietta. Union. Bark. Cargo of 3,100 whole bundles and 300 half-bundles of flour, 600 kegs of lard, and 75 boxes of candles. En route from New York City to Rio de Janeiro, Brazil. Was captured and burned by the CSS *Florida* on April 23, 1863. (*ORN,* 2:204, 649, 672–73.)

Hoboken. Union. Side-wheel steamer, 530 tons. Built in 1861 at Hoboken, N.J. Was lost on January 1 or 2, 1862, or in February 1862, during the Burnside Expedition to the North Carolina sounds. (*MSV,* 96, 267.)

Jacob Bell. Union. Clipper ship, 1,300 tons. Cargo of 1,380 tons of tea, matting, camphor, chow chow, and 10,000 boxes of firecrackers. Carried forty-one people on board, including two women. En route from Foochow (Fuzhou), China, for New York City. Was captured and burned by the CSS *Florida* on February 13, 1863, at latitude 25° 3' north, longitude 67° west, southwest of Bermuda. (*ORN,* 2:93, 642, 669, 675.)

USS Jacob Bell. Union. Side-wheel steamer, 229 tons. Length 141 feet 3 inches, beam 21 feet, depth 8 feet 1 inch. Complement of forty-nine, with one 8-inch smoothbore, one 32-pounder smoothbore, one 50-pounder rifled gun, and two 12-pounder smoothbores. Built in 1842 at New York City. Decommissioned on May 13, 1865. Foundered at sea en route to New York City while under tow by the USS *Banshee* on November 6, 1865. (*ORN,* 2:1:111; *WCWN,* 85; *DANFS,* 3:483.)

John A. Parks. Union. Ship, 1,047 tons. Cargo of white pine lumber. Out of Hallowell, Maine. En route for Montevideo, Uruguay, and Buenos Aires, Argentina. Was captured, stripped of the cargo, and burned by CSS *Alabama* on March 2, 1863, near latitude 29° 15' north, longitude 38° 20' west. (*ORN*, 2:685, 730–32; Semmes, *Service Afloat*, 284; Summersell, *Boarding Officer*, 93.)

Joseph Park. Union. Brig, 244 tons. Out of Boston. In ballast. Crew of seven. Built in Maine. Six days out of Pernambuco (Recife), Brazil. Was captured by the CSS *Sumter* on September 28, 1861. Its provisions, sails, and cordage were removed. Was burned on September 29, 1861, after being used for target practice. (*ORN*, 1:209, 627, 636–37, 711, 744; Semmes, *Service Afloat*, 220; Hearn, *Gray Raiders*, 28–29.)

Kingfisher. Union. Whaling schooner, 120 tons. Out of Fairhaven, Mass. Length 78 feet 11 inches, beam 21 feet 2 inches, depth 8 feet 1 inch. Manned by twenty-three crewmen, all Portuguese but three or four. Was captured and burned by the CSS *Alabama* on March 23, 1863, after removing nine barrels of beef and pork, and some flour, at latitude 1° 26' south, longitude 26° 30' west, between Africa and Brazil. (*ORN*, 2:203, 685, 734; Semmes, *Service Afloat*, 588; Summersell, *Boarding Officer*, 97–98.)

L. A. Micabar (Macomber) (Micawber). Union. Fishing schooner. Was captured and burned by the CSS *Tacony* on June 20, 1863, off New England at latitude 40° 50' north, longitude 69° 20' west. (*ORN*, 2:656.)

Lizzie M. Stacey. Union. Schooner. Cargo of pine salt and iron. Was captured and burned by the CSS *Shenandoah* on November 13, 1864, near the Equator. (*ORN*, 3:404, 760, 787, 804.)

Mandamis. Union. Bark. Out of Baltimore. Crew of two officers and twelve sailors. Sailing in ballast. Was captured and burned by the CSS *Florida* on September 26, 1864, in the South Atlantic. (Scharf, *History of the Confederate Navy*, 816; Hearn, *Gray Raiders*, 128, 312.)

Marengo. Union. Fishing schooner, 83 or 84 tons. Was captured and burned by the CSS *Tacony* off the New England coast on June 22, 1863. (*ORN*, 2:332, 656; Scharf, *History of the Confederate Navy*, 817.)

Margaret Y. Davis. Union. Schooner, 170 tons. Carried an assorted cargo. Out of New York City. En route from Port Royal, S.C., with seven aboard. Was captured and burned by the CSS *Florida* on July 9, 1864. (*ORN*, 3:623, 645.)

Mark L. Potter. Union. Bark, 389 tons. Crew of thirteen. Cargo of lime bricks and lumber. Out of Bangor, Maine. En route for Key West, Fla. Was captured and burned by the CSS *Chickamauga* on October 30, 1864, one day north of Wilmington, N.C. (*OR*, ser. 4, 3:1058; *ORN*, 3:318, 712.)

Mary Alvina. Union. Brig. Cargo of commissary stores. Out of Boston. En route to New Orleans. Was captured and destroyed by the CSS *Clarence* on June 9, 1863, at latitude 33° 52' north, longitude 74° 6' west. (*ORN*, 2:332, 655.)

M. J. Colcord. Union. Bark. Cargo of provisions. En route from New York City for Cape Town, South Africa. Was captured on March 30, 1863, by the CSS *Florida* and was burned on April 1, 1863. (*ORN*, 2:648, 671.)

Nare. Union. Steamer. Out of New York City. En route to Santa Marta, Venezuela. Sprung a leak and sank in one hour on July 15, 1864. One boat with the captain, the mate, and seven crewmen was rescued by the bark *Sicilian* on July 16. Another boat of crewmen was missing. (*New York Times*, July 25, 1864.)

Nina. Confederate. Side-wheel steamer blockade-runner, 338 bulk tons, 205 registered tons. Length 145 feet, beam 26 feet, depth 9 feet 6 inches. Built in 1848 at Washington, N.J. Foundered in late January 1863 between Nassau, Bahamas, and Charleston, S.C. (*LLC*, 314.)

North America. Union. Chartered by the War Department. Screw steamer, 1,651 tons. En route from New Orleans for New York City. Carried 225 sick and wounded soldiers. Built in 1864 at Philadelphia. Foundered at latitude 31° 10' north, longitude 78° 40' west, on December 22 or 24, 1864, with the loss of 197 people. (*OR*, ser. 3, 5:288; Spence, *List*, 665; *MSV*, 159, 285; Carnahan, *4000 Civil War Battles*, 99.)

Olive Jane. Union. Bark, 360 tons. Cargo of French wine, brandies, canned meats, fruits, and other delicacies. En route from Bordeaux, France, to New York City. Was captured and burned at latitude 29° 28' north, longitude 44° 58' west, by the CSS *Alabama* on February 21, 1863. (*ORN*, 2:685, 728–29; Semmes, *Service Afloat*, 578–79; Summersell, *Boarding Officer*, 86–87.)

Oneida. Union. Merchantman. Cargo of $1 million worth of tea. En route from Shanghai, China, for New York City. Was captured and burned by the CSS *Alabama* on April 24, 1863. (*ORN*, 2:205, 649.)

Palmetto. Union. Schooner, 172 tons. Length 90 feet, beam 24 feet 4 inches, depth 8 feet 1 inch. Cargo of mixed goods. En route from New York City to San Juan, Puerto Rico. Built in 1860 at Trenton, Maine. Was captured and burned on February 3, 1863, after provisions were removed to the CSS *Alabama* at latitude 27° 18' 27" north, longitude 66° 10' west. (*ORN*, 2:685, 726.)

Primero. Union. Screw steamer, 331 tons. Built in 1861 at Brooklyn, N.Y. Was lost on February 18, 1862, between Port Royal, S.C., and New York City. (*MSV*, 178, 291.)

Red Gauntlet. Union. Clipper ship. Cargo of ice, coal, musical instruments, and other goods. Out of Boston. En route to Hong Kong. Was captured and sunk by the CSS *Florida* on June 14, 1863, after the coal was removed. (*ORN*, 2:653; Owsley, *C.S.S. Florida*, 70, 72.)

Ripple. Union. Fishing schooner, 64 tons. Was captured and burned by the CSS *Tacony* on June 22, 1863, off New England.(*ORN*, 2:332, 656.)

Robert Gilfillan. Union. Schooner. Cargo of provisions. En route from Philadelphia to Haiti. Was captured and burned by the CSS *Nashville* on February 26, 1862. (*ORN*, 1:747–48.)

Rockingham. Union. Ship, 979 tons. Cargo of guano from the Chincha Islands. Built in 1858 at Portsmouth, N.H. En route from Callao, Peru, to Cork, Ireland. Was captured on April 22, 1864, by the CSS *Alabama*, which had not captured any other vessel for three months. Used for target practice and then burned near latitude 15° 53' south, longitude 31° 44' west. (*ORN*, 3:53, 55, 681, 671; Semmes, *Service Afloat*, 748–49; Summersell, *Boarding Officer*, 183.)

Rufus Choate. Union. Fishing schooner, 90 tons. Was captured and burned by the CSS *Tacony* off New England on June 22, 1863. (*ORN*, 2:332, 656.)

Shooting Star. Union. Ship, 947 tons. Cargo of 1,500 tons of coal. En route from New York City to Havana, Cuba, or Panama. Was captured and burned on October 31, 1864, by the CSS *Chickamauga* off the northeast coast at latitude 39° 20' north, longitude 70° west. (*ORN*, 3:318, 712.)

Star of Peace. Union. Ship, 840 tons. Cargo of hides and saltpeter for the Union army. Out of Boston. En route from Calcutta, India, to Boston. Was captured and burned by the CSS *Florida* on March 6, 1863. (*ORN*, 2:648, 671, 676.)

Susan. Union. Brig. Cargo of coal. Was captured and scuttled by the CSS *Shenandoah* southwest of the Cape Verde Islands on November 10, 1864. (*ORN*, 3:407, 760, 786, 802.)

Talisman. British. Iron side-wheel steamer, 266 gross tons, 173 registered tons, 359 bulk tons. Length 201 feet 4 inches, beam 24 feet, depth 9 feet 6 inches. Built in 1864 in Greenock, Scotland. Hit the wreck of the CSS *Raleigh* while leaving New Inlet, N.C. on December 18, 1864, and forced to return to Wilmington for repairs. Escaped from Wilmington but sank in a storm on December 29, 1864. (*LLC*, 323.)

Thomas B. Wales. Union. East India Trader, 599 tons. Cargo of jute, linseed, and 1,700 bags of saltpeter. From Boston. En route to Boston from Calcutta, India. Was captured and burned near latitude 29° 15' north, longitude 57° 57' west by the CSS *Alabama* on November 7, 1862. Its passengers included the captain's wife as well as an American former consul, his wife, and his three daughters. The vessel's spars and rigging were removed. (*ORN*, 1:551, 780, 803, 807; 3, 678; Semmes, *Service Afloat*, 494–96; Summersell, *Boarding Officer*, 48–49.)

Vigilant. Union. Ship. In ballast. Crew included 10 African Americans. Armed with a rifled 9-pounder. Out of Bath, Maine. Sailing from New York City to the guano island of Sombrero, West Indies. Was captured and burned by the CSS *Sumter* at latitude 29° 10' north, longitude 57° 22' west, on December 3, 1861. The 9-pounder with ammunition and a chronometer were removed. (*ORN*, 1:646, 727, 744.)

Wanderer. Union. Fishing schooner, 94 tons. Was captured and burned by the CSS *Tacony* under Lt. Charles W. Read on June 23, 1863, off New England. (*ORN*, 2:332, 656.)

Azores

The Azores served as a navigation marker and rest stop for transatlantic voyages, serving both British blockade-runners and Yankee whalers. The CSS *Alabama* raided the waters in 1862, snaring several Yankee whalers and traders. The CSS *Shenandoah* destroyed one vessel near the Azores in 1864.

Alert. Union. Bark, 398 tons. Cargo of 80 boxes of tobacco, clothes, and other goods to trade for sea elephant oil. En route from New London, Conn., for the Navigators' Islands in the South Indian Ocean. Was captured on September 9, 1862, by the CSS *Alabama* at latitude 39° 37' north, longitude 31° 5' west. Some cargo was removed, and the vessel was set afire at 4:00 p.m. Richard Henry Dana Jr., the author of the classic sea adventure *Two Years before the Mast* (1840), served aboard the *Alert* in 1836 on the voyage from San Diego to Boston. (*ORN*, 1:789; Semmes, *Service Afloat*, 435; Summersell, *Boarding Officer*, 19–20, 199; Hearn, *Gray Raiders*, 168.)

Alina. Union. Bark, 574 tons. Cargo of railroad iron. Out of Searsport, Maine. On its maiden voyage. En route to Buenos Aires, Argentina. Was captured and scuttled by the CSS *Shenandoah* due south of the Azores and west of Dakar, Africa, on October 30, 1864. (*ORN*, 3:760, 785, 800: Hearn, *Gray Raiders*, 263–64.)

Altamaha. Union. Whaling brig, 119 burden tons. From New Bedford, Mass. Had a little whale oil aboard. Was captured and burned by the CSS *Alabama* on September 13, 1862, at latitude 40° 34' north, longitude 35° 24' 15" west (another source—35° 9' west) near the Azores. (*ORN*, 1:780, 789; Semmes, *Service Afloat*, 438; Hearn, *Gray Raiders*, 168; Summersell, *Boarding Officer*, 22–24, 199.)

Benjamin Tucker. Union. Whaling ship, 349 tons. Crew of thirty. Cargo of 340 barrels of whale oil. From New Bedford, Mass. Was captured and burned by the CSS *Alabama* on September 14, 1862, near the Azores. The crew was put aboard boats to row to shore. (*ORN*, 1:790; Semmes, *Service Afloat*, 440; Hearn, *Gray Raiders*, 168–69; Summersell, *Boarding Officer*, 22, 24, 199.)

Courser. Union. Whaling schooner, 121 tons. Out of Providencetown, Mass. Was captured on September 16, 1862, by the CSS *Alabama*. Used for target practice and burned four to five miles from Flores, Azores. (*ORN*, 1:790; Semmes, *Service Afloat*, 441; Hearn, *Gray Raiders*, 169.)

Elisha Dunbar. Union. Whaling ship, 257 tons. Out of New Bedford, Mass. Was captured and burned by the CSS *Alabama* near the Azores on September 18, 1862, at latitude 39° 50' north, longitude 35° 25' 45" west. (*ORN*, 1:790–91; Semmes, *Service Afloat*, 444; Hearn, *Gray Raiders*, 170.)

Ocean Rover. Union. Whaling bark, 313 tons. Crew of 36. Cargo of 1,100 barrels of whale oil. From New Bedford, Mass. Was captured by the CSS *Alabama* off Flores, Azores, on September 8, 1862, and burned on September 9, 1862, along with the *Alert* and *Ocean Rover*. The vessel's crew rowed to the Azores in six whale boats. (*ORN*, 1:788–89; Semmes, *Service Afloat*, 431–33, 435; Hearn, *Gray Raiders*, 167–68.)

Ocmulgee. Union. Whaling brig, 454 tons. Crew of 37. Cargo of whale oil and a partially suspended sperm whale on the cutting tackles. Out of Edgartown, Mass. Was captured on September 5, 1862, and was burned the morning of September 6, 1862, by the CSS *Alabama* off the Azores. Some beef, pork, and small stores were removed to the CSS *Alabama*. Its crew used its whale boats to reach the Azores. (*ORN*, 1:787–88; Semmes, *Service Afloat*, 423–25; Hearn, *Gray Raiders*, 165–67.)

Run Her. British. Steamer blockade-runner, 829 gross tons. Length 230 feet, beam 27 feet, depth 14 feet 7 inches. Built in 1865 at London. Lost at Terceira Island on the trip out in 1865. (*LLC*, 319.)

Starlight. Union. Schooner. Out of Boston. En route from Fayal to Boston. Carried a crew of seven and some passengers, including several women. Was captured by the CSS *Alabama* near the Azores on September 5, 1862. The passengers and crew were landed at Santa Cruz on September 6, 1862. The *Alert*, *Starlight*, and *Ocean Rover* were burned with the vessel on September 9, 1862. (*ORN*, 1:788–89; Semmes, *Service Afloat*, 429–30; Hearn, *Gray Raiders*, 167–68.)

Virginia. Union. Whaling ship, 346 tons. From New Bedford, Mass. En route to the Pacific Ocean. Was captured and burned by the CSS *Alabama* on September 17, 1862, near latitude 40° 3' north, longitude 32° 46' 45" west. (*ORN*, 1:790; Semmes, *Service Afloat*, 442; Hearn, *Gray Raiders*, 169.)

Weather Gauge. Union. Whaling ship. Out of Providencetown, Mass. Was captured on September 9, 1862, by the CSS *Alabama*. The crew was landed in their boats on September 11, 1862, and the vessel was burned. (*ORN*, 1:788–89; Semmes, *Service Afloat*, 436; Hearn, *Gray Raiders*, 168.)

Bahamas

The British Bahama Islands had the major blockade-running base of Nassau, where cargoes bound for blockaded Confederate ports were transferred to fast, sleek steamers and small sailboats to sneak through the Union blockade with war material and luxury items. On their return trips from the Confederacy, the blockade-runners carried cotton and other Confederate agricultural products. The treacherous Bahamian reefs were the scene of numerous shipwrecks of blockade-runners and Union blockaders.

USS *Adirondack.* Union. Wooden steam screw sloop, 1,240 tons. Length 207 feet 1 inch, beam 38 feet, depth 16 feet 10 inches, draft aft 10 feet 2 inches, speed 14 knots. Complement of 160, with two 11-inch Dahlgren smoothbores, two 24-pounder Dahlgren smoothbores, and one 12-pounder. Launched in 1862 at the Brooklyn Navy Yard. On August 23, 1862, at 3:55 a.m., the USS *Adirondack* ran aground due to a navigation error on a reef about one mile northeast of Little Bahama Bank outside of Man of War Cay. Cannon, coal, and stores were jettisoned, but the sloop could not be extricated from the reef. Capt. Guert Gansevoort remained aboard the ship for four days before spiking the rest of the guns and throwing them overboard, as the CSS *Florida* was in the area, and he feared capture. Bahamian wreckers tried to claim the ship's stores and five of the ship's crew deserted, joining the wreckers. The captain tried to rent the wreckers' boats and finally bought a schooner for $2,500 to help salvage his vessel.

He ultimately paid $625 for the schooner's use. The crew saved the 24-pounder howitzers and the 12-pounder gun with carriages. The ship's back was broken on the reef. The vessel was set afire by the wreckers, who were probably paid by Confederate agents to destroy it. The wreck is located under 10–25 feet of water with 80 feet of visibility, making it a popular diving site. Steam boilers, machinery, and two 11-inch Dahlgrens were on site. (*ORN*, 1:422–29; 13:293–94, 313; ser. 2, 1:28; *WCWN*, 42; Tzimoulis, "Best of the Bahamas," *Skin Diver*, 61–91; Murphy, "Tropical Shipwrecks," *Skin Diver*, 29.)

Agnes Louisa (Grapeshot). British. Iron side-wheel steamer blockade-runner, 578 gross tons, 434 registered tons. Length 243 feet 10 inches, beam 25 feet, depth 12 feet 6 inches. Built in 1864. Ran onto Hog Island (now called Paradise Island) off Nassau and was thought to have been a total loss on September 4, 1864, while outbound for Charleston, S.C. (*ORN*, 10:477; *LLC*, 286.)

Cecile. Confederate. Side-wheel steamer, 360 bulk tons, 460 gross tons. Length 156 feet, beam 29 feet, depth 8 feet 6 inches. Cargo of eight cannons, ammunition wagons, knapsacks, harness, 2,000 rifle-muskets, 400 barrels of gunpowder for the Confederate navy, 100 powder kegs on the ship's account, and medicine. Built in 1857 at Wilmington, Del. Sank in ten minutes with no loss of life on June 17, 1862, while going through the Northeast Providence Channel on the reefs of Abaco near Abaco Lighthouse and Hole in the Wall. Part of the cargo was salvaged and sold at auction. Confederate agents purchased six cannons at the auction. Made thirteen successful runs of the Union blockade before being wrecked. (*OR*, ser. 4, 1:1174; Horner, *Blockade-Runners*, 188; *MSV*, 31; *LLC*, 292.)

USS *Courier*. Union. Sailing store ship, 556 or 554 tons. Length 135 feet, beam 30 feet, depth 15 feet. Complement of between seventy-five and eight-two, with two 32-pounder smoothbores, two 24-pounder smoothbores, and one rifled 12-pounder. Built in 1858 at Newburyport, Mass. Was grounded on a reef at Abaco Island, about 10 miles south of the Elbow Cay Lighthouse on June 14, 1864. Both cargo and crew were saved. (*ORN*, 17:720–21; 27:591–92, 598; ser. 2, 1:67; *DANFS*, 2:196; *WCWN*, 139.)

***George C. Ross*.** Union. Brig. Cargo of coffee, honey, and logwood. From Port-au-Prince, Haiti, for New York City. Was wrecked on Long Cay in mid-January 1862. (*ORN*, 12:629.)

***Kelpie*.** British. Blockade-runner steamer. Length 191 feet, beam 18 feet, depth 10 feet. Built in 1857 at Glasgow, Scotland. Was sunk while cruising into Nassau Harbor in December 1862. (*LLC*, 307.)

USS *Magnolia* (*Magnolia*). Union. Side-wheel steamer, 843 bulk tons, 1,067 new measurement tons. Length 242 feet 5 inches or 246 feet, beam 33 feet 11 inches or 37 feet, draft 5 feet, depth 11 feet 3 inches or 10 feet 9 inches, speed 8–12 knots. Complement of ninety-five, with four 24-pounders and one 20-pounder Parrott. Built in 1854 in New York City. Was captured as the blockade-runner *Magnolia* on February 19, 1862, at Pass a l'Outre, La., by the USS *Brooklyn* and USS *South Carolina*. Was holed and ran ashore on Man-of-War Key near Great Abaco. Was later raised. Decommissioned on June 10, 1865. Sold at public auction in New York City on July 12, 1865. (*ORN*, ser. 2, 1:131; *WCWN*, 74.)

***Margaret and Jessie* (*Douglas*) (USS *Gettysburg*).** Confederate. Steamer, 732 tons. Cargo of 730 bales of cotton. Carried 16 passengers. En route from Charleston, S.C., to Nassau, Bahamas. Chased by the USS *Rhode Island* and hit by a shell, which killed one aboard. Ran ashore at Eleuthera Island on May 27, 1863, in neutral waters, 25 miles from Nassau. The British island was hit by Union shells. British authorities were enraged at the territorial violation. (*ORN*, 2:235–51.)

***Marion*.** Side-wheel steamer, 900 tons. Built in 1851 at New York City. Stranded at Doubleshot Key on April 4, 1863. (*MSV*, 137, 279.)

***Maryland*.** Nationality unknown. Bark. Cargo of 4,300 bags of coffee. Wrecked on January 30, 1862, at Inagua. (*ORN*, 12:629; Bernath, *Squall across the Atlantic*, 114–16.)

USS *San Jacinto*. Union. Screw steam frigate, 1,567 tons. Length 234 feet, beam 37 feet 9 inches, depth 23 feet 3 inches, draft 16 feet 6 inches, speed 8 knots. Complement of 278, with ten 11-inch Dahlgrens, one 100-pounder Parrott, one 20-pounder Parrott, and three 12-pounders (another source—two 8-inch and four 32-pounders). Laid down in 1847 and launched in 1850 in the Brooklyn Navy Yard. Wrecked on January 1, 1865, at No Name Cay or Turtle Cay near Treasure Cay and Great Abaco Island. Capt. Richard W. Meade salvaged the guns, ammunition, ship's copper, and other items of value. Forty-six crewmen deserted from the vessel, and four were later captured. Bahamian wreckers removed iron, copper, and lead from the wreck as the Bahamian police magistrate would not let Union vessels near the wreck. In August 1865 the Union removed additional material from the wreck. The wreck was sold for $224.61 in Nassau on May 17, 1871. On February 10, 1866, Captain Meade was court-martialed and found guilty of inattention and negligence as well as inefficiency and suspended from rank for three years. Two boilers, a 3-blade propeller, masts, and the stern are located in 20–50 feet of water and are often visited by sport divers. (*ORN*, 22:246; ser. 2, 1:200; Tzimoulis, "Best of the Bahamas," *Skin Diver*, 66; Murphy, "Tropical Shipwrecks," *Skin Diver*, 29; *DANFS*, 6:295–97.)

Bering Sea

The rich whaling waters between Russian Siberia and Russian Alaska were a haven for Yankee whalers during the American Civil War. The safety of this fleet ended when the CSS *Shenandoah* arrived in the Bering Sea with charts taken from a Yankee whaler in the Pacific Ocean. In the spring and summer of 1865 the CSS *Shenandoah* destroyed twenty whaling vessels of the fifty-eight Yankee whalers in the Bering Sea. Most of these whalers were destroyed after Gen. Robert E. Lee had surrendered at Appomattox Court House along with the rest of the Confederate military high command. As the U.S. Civil War ended, a large part of the once mighty New England whaling business suddenly ceased to exist.

Brunswick. Union. Whaler. Carried whale oil. Stove in by an ice flow 20 inches below the starboard bow water line. While being assisted by a whaling fleet of 10 whalers on June 28, 1865, the CSS *Shenandoah* captured and burned the *Brunswick* and most of the Yankee whaling fleet near the Bering Straits Narrows. (*ORN*, 3:791–2, 828–29; Hearn, *Gray Raiders*, 289–90.)

Catharine. Union. Whaling bark, 389 tons. Cargo of whale oil. Out of New Bedford, Mass. Was captured and burned by the CSS *Shenandoah* on June 26, 1865, in the Bering Sea. (*ORN*, 3:790, 792, 828.)

Congress. Union. Whaling bark. Out of New Bedford, Mass. Was captured by the CSS *Shenandoah* with ten other vessels. Was destroyed on June 28, 1865, near the Bering Strait. Master Daniel Wood on the vessel had lost two other vessels over the previous four years. (*ORN*, 3:791–92, 829; Hearn, *Gray Raiders*, 291.)

Covington. Union. Whaling bark, 350 tons. Built in Baltimore. Out of Warren, R.I. Was captured and burned by the CSS *Shenandoah* along with 10 other whalers on June 28, 1865, in East Cape Bay near the Bering Strait Narrows. (*ORN*, 3:791–92, 829.)

Euphrates. Union. Whaling ship, 364 tons. Out of New Bedford, Mass. Was captured and burned on June 22, 1865, by the CSS *Shenandoah* in the Bering Sea near latitude 62° 23' north, longitude 179° 46' east. The vessel's navigation instruments were removed. (*ORN*, 3:790, 792, 825.)

Favorite. Union. Whaling ship. Out of New Haven, Conn. One of the whalers captured and burned by the CSS *Shenandoah* on June 28, 1865, in East Cape Bay in the Bering Strait. (*ORN*, 3:791–92, 828–29.)

General Williams. Union. Ship, 419 tons. Out of New London, Mass. Was captured and burned by the CSS *Shenandoah* near St. Lawrence Island in the Bering Strait on June 25, 1865. (*ORN*, 3:790, 792, 827.)

Gipsey. Union. Whaling ship. Was captured and burned by the CSS *Shenandoah* on June 26, 1865, in the Bering Strait. (*ORN*, 3:791–92, 828.)

Hillman. Union. Whaling ship. Out of New Bedford, Mass. Was captured and burned by the CSS *Shenandoah* on June 28, 1865, in East Cape Bay in the Bering Strait. (*ORN*, 3:791–92, 829.)

Isaac Howland. Union. Whaling ship, 399 tons. Out of New Bedford, Mass. Was captured and burned by the CSS *Shenandoah* on June 28, 1865, in East Cape Bay in the Bering Strait. (*ORN*, 3:791–92, 829.)

Isabella. Union. Whaling bark, 315 tons. Was captured and burned by the CSS *Shenandoah* on June 26, 1865, in the Bering Sea at latitude 64° 21' north, longitude 172° 20' west. (*ORN*, 3:791–92, 828; Hearn, *Gray Raiders*, 289.)

Jireh Swift. Union. Whaling bark, 428 tons. Out of New Bedford, Mass. Was captured and burned in the Bering Sea by the CSS *Shenandoah* on June 22, 1865. (*ORN*, 3:790, 792, 826; Hearn, *Gray Raiders*, 287.)

Martha. Union. Whaling ship. Out of New Bedford, Mass. Was captured and burned by the CSS *Shenandoah* on June 28, 1865, in East Cape Bay in the Bering Sea. (*ORN*, 3:791–92 829; Hearn, *Gray Raiders*, 290–91.)

Nassau. Union. Whaling ship. Out of New Bedford, Mass. Built in 1825. Was captured and burned by the CSS *Shenan-*

doah on June 28, 1865, in East Cape Bay in the Bering Sea. (*ORN,* 3:791–92, 829; Hearn, *Gray Raiders,* 290–91.)

Nimrod. Union. Whaling ship, 340 tons. Cargo of whale oil. Out of New Bedford, Mass. Was captured and burned by the CSS *Shenandoah* near St. Lawrence Island in the Bering Sea on June 26, 1865. The vessel's captain, James Clark, had been in command of the *Ocean Rover,* which had been destroyed by the CSS *Alabama* near the Azores. (*ORN,* 3:790, 792, 828.)

Sophia Thornton. Union. Whaling bark, 426 tons. Out of New Bedford, Mass. Was captured and burned by the CSS *Shenandoah* in the Bering Sea on June 22, 1865, at latitude 62° 40' north, longitude 178° 50' west. (*ORN,* 3:790, 792, 826–27.)

Susan Abigail (Susan and Abigail). Union. Brigantine, 159 tons. Out of San Francisco. Was captured and burned by the CSS *Shenandoah* on June 23, 1865, in the Bering

Sea at latitude 62° 48' north, longitude 179° 4' west. (*ORN,* 3:790, 792, 827.)

Waverly. Union. Whaling bark, 327 tons. Crew of thirty-three. Out of New Bedford, Mass. Was captured amid a dead calm and burned by the CSS *Shenandoah* in the Bering Strait on June 28, 1865, near the Diomede Islands. (*ORN,* 3:791–92, 829.)

William C. Nye. Union. Whaling ship, 389 tons. Cargo of 240 barrels of whale oil. Out of New Bedford, Mass. Was captured and burned by the CSS *Shenandoah* on June 26, 1865, in the Bering Sea. (*ORN,* 3:790–92, 828; Hearn, *Gray Raiders,* 288.)

William Thompson. Union. Whaling ship, 495 tons. Out of New Bedford, Mass. Was captured on June 22, 1865, and burned by the CSS *Shenandoah* the next day, northeast of Cape Narrows in the Bering Sea. (*ORN,* 3:790, 792, 825.)

Bermuda

During the American Civil War, British Bermuda was a major transshipment point and blockade-running port, especially for the Confederate ports of Wilmington, N.C., and Charleston, S.C. British-owned and Confederate-owned blockade-runners crowded the island's harbor waiting for dark moonless nights to run the Union blockade.

Near Bermuda the Confederate raiders CSS *Alabama,* CSS *Florida,* and CSS *Tacony* captured and destroyed several Union vessels. The blockade-runners *Mary Celestia* and *Nola* were wrecked on Bermuda's reefs.

Golconda. Union. Whaling bark, 335 tons. Cargo of 1,800 barrels of whale oil. Out of New Bedford, Mass. En route for New Bedford from Talcahuano, Chile. Was captured by the CSS *Florida* off Florida at latitude 37° 28' north, longitude 72° west. After removing some whale oil, it was torched on July 8, 1864, off Bermuda. (*ORN,* 3:623, 645.)

Harriet Stevens. Union. Bark, 463 tons. Manned by a captain, two mates and six crewmen. Cargo of 285 pounds

of gum opium, shooks, heads, spats, cement, and lumber. Out of Portland, Maine. En route for Cienfuegos, Cuba. Was captured, used for target practice, and burned by the CSS *Florida* on July 1, 1864, southwest of Bermuda at latitude 31° 33' north, longitude 64° 8' west. The opium was removed and sent through the blockade in the blockade-runner *Lillian* for the Confederate Medical Department. (*ORN,* 3:621–22, 645; Stern, *Confederate Navy Pictorial History,* 212–13.)

Levi Starbuck. Union. Whaling ship, 376 tons. Crew of 29. Out of New Bedford, Mass. En route to the Pacific Ocean whaling grounds. Was captured and burned by the CSS *Alabama* on November 2, 1862, off Bermuda near latitude 35° 40' north, longitude 66° west. The stores were removed. (*ORN,* 1:551, 780, 802; Semmes, *Service Afloat,* 493.)

Mary Celestia (Bijou) (Mary Celeste). British. Iron side-wheel steamer, 207 registered tons, 314 gross tons. Length 221 feet, beam 22 feet 1 inch, depth 10 feet 5 inches. Cargo of bacon, rifle-muskets, and ammunition. Built in 1864 at Liverpool, England. Hit a rock and sank in less than eight minutes, just south of Gibbs Lighthouse in 60 feet of water on September 26, 1864, in a sand patch surrounded by coral. This wreck is located at latitude 32° 12' 10" north, longitude 64° 42' 15" west. Extensively dived on and salvaged. Much of the vessel's hull collapsed. The boilers, engines, and paddlewheels remain. Surveyed by East Carolina University and the Bermuda Maritime Museum in 1983 and 1986. (*ORN*, 17:720–21: ser. 2, 1:67; *LLC*, 312; Bass, *Ships and Shipwrecks of the Americas,* 218, 228–29; Watts, "Bermuda and the American Civil War," *International Journal of Nautical Archaeology and Underwater Exploration,* 160–68, 170–71; Watts, "Runners of the Union Blockade," *Archaeology,* 37.)

***Nola* (*Gloria*) (*Montana*) (*Paramount*).** British. Steel-hulled side-wheel steamer, 607 gross tons, 432 registered tons, 750 tons. Length 228 feet 5 inches or 236 feet, beam 25 feet, draft 13 feet 6 inches. Cargo of dry goods from Glasgow, Scotland. Built in 1863 at Greenock, Scotland. Driven ashore on a reef 7 miles northwest of Bermuda in the Western Blue Cut area off Ireland Island on December 30, 1863. The cargo and engines were salvaged. The wreck is located at a depth of 25 feet, with the upper works within 8 feet of the surface. East Carolina University and

Bermuda Maritime University surveyed the wreck in 1985 and 1986. About 70% of the hull structure is exposed. (Robinson and Gould, "Bermuda's Storybook Wreck," *Skin Diver,* 64–65; Bass, *Ships and Shipwrecks of the Americas,* 218, 228–29; *LLC,* 314; Watts, "Bermuda and the American Civil War," *International Journal of Nautical Archaeology and Underwater Exploration,* 160, 164–71; Watts, "Runners of the Union Blockade," *Archaeology,* 35–36.)

Roanoke. Union. Mail steamer, 1,071 tons. Carried $20,000 in specie, some cargo, fifty crewmen and thirty-five passengers. En route from Havana, Cuba, to New York City. Built in 1851 at New York City. Was captured 12 miles off Cuba by two or three Confederates posing as passengers led by Acting Master John C. Braine. One crew member was shot and thrown overboard. The Confederates were reinforced by twenty to thirty men from the *Village Girl.* The Confederates planned to run the blockade but abandoned their plan and burned the *Roanoke* on October 9, 1864, off Bermuda. (*ORN,* 3:229–48; *MSV,* 186.)

William C. Clarke. Union. Brig, 338 tons. Cargo of lumber. Out of Boston. En route from Mathias, Maine, to Mantanzas, Cuba. Was captured and burned by the CSS *Tacony* on June 17, 1864, at latitude 30° north, longitude 62° 40' west. (*ORN,* 3:618, 645.)

Big Sandy River

The Big Sandy River is the dividing line between West Virginia (formerly part of Virginia) and Kentucky.

Fawn. Union. Steamer, 25 tons. Built in 1862 at Pittsburgh, Pa. Was captured and burned by Lt. Col. A. Witcher and the 34th Va. Cavalry Battalion on November 5, 1864, in Buffalo Shoals, Big Sandy River. (*OR,* 43:1:650–51; *MSV,* 72, 260.)

Fawn. Union. Stern-wheel steamer, 36 tons. Built in 1863 at Marietta, Ohio. Was burned on November 11, 1864, in

the Big Sandy River. Could be same vessel as the one cited in the preceding entry. (*MSV,* 72, 260.)

***R. H. Barnum* (*Barnum*).** Union. Stern-wheel steamer, 30 tons. Built in 1862 at Warren, Ohio. Was captured and burned by Lt. Col. A. Witcher and the 34th Va. Cavalry Battalion on November 5, 1864, in Buffalo Shoals near Louisa, Ky. (*OR,* 43:1:650–51; *MSV,* 180, 292.)

Brazil

The Atlantic Ocean off Brazil and the Brazilian island of Fernando de Noronha was hunting ground for the Confederate commerce raiders CSS *Alabama* and CSS *Florida*. Union commerce was interrupted, with three Yankee whalers and a number of Union trading ships destroyed.

Charles Hill. Union. Ship, 699 tons. Length 150 feet, beam 31 feet 1 inch, depth 23 feet. Cargo of 699 tons of salt. Built in 1850 at Newburyport, Mass. Out of Boston. En route from Liverpool, England, to Montevideo, Uruguay. Was captured and burned on March 25, 1863, by the CSS *Alabama* off the Brazilian coast at latitude 1° 23' north, longitude 26° 30' west. (*ORN*, 2:203, 206, 685; 3:679; Semmes, *Service Afloat*, 589–90; Summersell, *Boarding Officer*, 99.)

Dorcas Prince. Union. Ship, 699 tons. Cargo of coal. Built in 1850 at Yarmouth, Mass. Crew of 20. En route from New York City to Shanghai, China. Was captured and burned by the CSS *Alabama* on April 26, 1863, at latitude 7° 37' south, longitude 31° 30' west. (*ORN*, 2:685, 741–42; Semmes, *Service Afloat*, 612; Summersell, *Boarding Officer*, 108; Hearn, *Gray Raiders*, 195.)

Express. Union. Ship, 1,072 tons. Cargo of guano from the Chincha Islands. Out of Boston. En route from Callao, Peru, to Antwerp, Belgium. Was captured and burned on July 6, 1863, by the CSS *Alabama* at latitude 28° 28' south, longitude 30° 7' west. (*ORN*, 3:670, 680; Semmes, *Service Afloat*, 633–35; Summersell, *Boarding Officer*, 126–27; Hearn, *Gray Raiders*, 202.)

Jabez Snow. Union. Ship, 1,074 tons. Cargo of coal Built in 1853 at Newburyport, Mass. Out of Backport, Maine. En route from Cardiff, Wales, for Montevideo, Uruguay, and Calcutta, India. Was captured on May 29, 1863, by the CSS *Alabama* and burned the next day at latitude 13° 25' 11" south, longitude 35° 38' west. (*ORN*, 2:371, 382, 680, 690, 746–47; Summersell, *Boarding Officer*, 117–18.)

Kate Cory. Union. Whaling brig, 132 tons. Out of New Bedford, Mass. Was captured by the CSS *Alabama* on April 15, 1863, at Fernando de Noronha. Taken 4 miles from land on April 17, 1863, and burned. (*ORN*, 2:201, 203–4, 643, 685, 740; Semmes, *Service Afloat*, 604; Summersell, *Boarding Officer*, 106, 210.)

Lafayette. Union. Whaling bark. Out of Westport, Conn. Was captured and burned by the CSS *Alabama* on April 15, 1863, at Fernando de Noronha near latitude 4° 10' south, longitude 32° 10' west (or 32° 26' west). (*ORN*, 2:201, 204, 740; Semmes, *Service Afloat*, 604; Summersell, *Boarding Officer*, 106, 210.)

CSS Lapwing (Lapwig). Union. Bark. Armed with a 12-pounder howitzer. Cargo of coal, tobacco, and provisions. En route from Boston to Batavia (present-day Jakarta), Java, and Singapore. Was captured on March 28, 1863, by the CSS *Florida* and used as a tender. Was burned by Confederates on June 20, 1863, off Rocas Island, about 80 miles west of Fernando de Noronha. (*ORN*, 2:407, 648, 671, 677; *CWC*, 6-260.)

Leighton. Union. Bark. Was capsized in Rio de Janeiro Harbor by a tornado on October 10, 1864. The captain's son drowned. (*New York Times*, Dec. 2, 1864.)

Louisa Hatch. Union. Ship, 853 tons. Cargo of 1,100 tons of Welsh coal for the P & O Steam Navigation Company. Out of Rockland, Maine. En route from Cardiff, Wales, to Point de Galle, Ceylon. Was captured by the CSS *Alabama* on April 4, 1863, and taken to Fernando de Noronha on April 10, where it was anchored within one mile of land. The vessel's coal was removed to the USS *Alabama* when the Confederate tender with coal failed to show up as planned. The *Louisa Hatch* was moved 4 miles from land on April 17, 1863, and was burned. (*ORN*, 2:203–4, 740; Semmes, *Service Afloat*, 594–95, 598, 602, 604; Hearn, *Gray Raiders*, 193–94.)

Nora. Union. Ship. Cargo of salt. Out of Boston. En route from Liverpool, England, to Calcutta, India. Was captured on March 25, 1863, and burned by the CSS *Alabama* off Brazil on March 26, 1863, near latitude 1° 12' 49" south, longitude 26° 32' 45" west. (*ORN*, 2:201, 203, 206–8, 685, 735; Semmes, *Service Afloat*, 589–90.)

Nye. Union. Whaling bark, 211 tons. Crew of 24. Cargo of 425 barrels of sperm whale oil and 75 barrels of whale oil. Out of New Bedford, Mass. Was captured on April 24, 1863, by the CSS *Alabama* and destroyed off Brazil, at latitude 5° 45' 15" south, longitude 31° 53' west. (*ORN*, 2:685, 741; Semmes, *Service Afloat*, 611–12; Hearn, *Gray Raiders*, 194–95.)

Sea Lark. Union. 973 tons bark. Out of New York City. En route from New York City to San Francisco. Was captured and destroyed by the CSS *Alabama* off Brazil on May 3, 1863, at latitude 9°, 39' south, longitude 32° 44' west. (*ORN*, 2:690, 745–46; Semmes, *Service Afloat*, 620–21; Summersell, *Boarding Officer*, 115–16.)

S. Gildersleeve (*Gildersleeve*). Union. Ship, 848 tons. Cargo of English coal for the P&O Steam Navigation Company. Out of New York City. En route from London to Calcutta. Was captured off Bahia by the CSS *Alabama* on May 25, 1863, and burned on March 26, 1863, near latitude 12° 4' south, longitude 35° 10' 45" west. (*ORN*, 2:690, 745–46; Semmes, *Service Afloat*, 620–21; Summersell, *Boarding Officer*, 115–16.)

Talisman. Union. Medium clipper, 1,100 or 1,237 tons. Cargo of coal, four brass 12-pounders, powder, shot, two steam boilers for a steam gunboat, beef, port, and bread. The Taiping Rebellion was raging in China, so the equipment was for a gunboat. En route from New York City to Shanghai, China. Was captured by the CSS *Alabama* on June 5, 1863, at latitude 14° 35' 42" south, longitude 36° 26' 45" west. The CSS *Alabama* transferred several cannons before destroying the vessel. (*ORN*, 2:690, 748–49, 751; Semmes, *Service Afloat*, 624–25; Hearn, *Gray Raiders*, 199.)

Tycoon. Union. Bark, 717 tons. Cargo of general merchandise and clothing. En route from New York City to San Francisco. Was captured by the CSS *Alabama* on April 26, 1864, and burned east of Bahia, Brazil, on April 27, 1864. (*ORN*, 3:53, 672; Shomette, *Civil War Shipwrecks*, 729.)

Union Jack. Union. Bark, 483 tons. En route from Boston to Shanghai, China. Carried six passengers, including Reverend Franklin Wright, an editor and U.S. counsel to Foochow (Fuzhou). Was captured and burned off Brazil by the CSS *Alabama* on May 3, 1863, at latitude 9° 40' south, longitude 32° 30' west. (*ORN*, 2:685, 742–43; Semmes, *Service Afloat*, 612–14; Summersell, *Boarding Officer*, 109.)

California

California was vital to the Union effort in the Civil War as it supplied gold to help fuel the Union economy. Although California was relatively removed from the Civil War battles, pro-Confederate sentiment was strong in some areas of the state. Wrecks along the California coast and inland rivers resulted from fires, storms, boiler explosions, and groundings. The CSS *Shenandoah* had a plan to attack San Francisco, but the Civil War ended before it could be executed.

Acadia. Nationality unknown. Bark. Hit rocks at Trinidad on February 4 (or March 2), 1861. The steam tug *Mary Ann* recovered the *Acadia*'s anchor while looking for the wreck of the *Brother Jonathan* in 1865. (Marshall, *California Shipwrecks*, 163; Jackson, *Doghole Schooners*, 22.)

Ada Hancock (*Milton Willis*). Union. Twin screw steamer, 83 tons. Length 65 feet. Built in 1858 or 1859 at San Francisco. While ferrying sixty passengers and $45,000 to the waiting San Francisco–bound steamer *Senator*, the *Ada Hancock*'s boiler exploded, and it sank on April 27, 1863, in Wilmington Harbor at San Pedro, about 1,000 yards from shore. It took twenty-six lives and injured thirty-seven, of which twenty-three later died. (*MSV*, 145, 281; *New York Times*, May 3, 1863; Marshall, *California Shipwrecks*, 24.)

Aeolus. Union. Brig. Wrecked on January 28, 1863, one and a half miles south of the Humboldt Bay Bar. (Marshall, *California Shipwrecks*, 146; Jackson, *Doghole Schooners*, 22, 33; Gibbs, *Shipwrecks Pacific Ocean*, 274.)

Alcyone (Alcyona). Union. Schooner, 88 tons. Built in 1861. Capsized in a heavy gale at the Noyo River in Noyo Harbor on February 17 (January 12–16), 1863. (Marshall, *California Shipwrecks,* 130; Jackson, *Doghole Schooners,* 32; California State Lands Shipwreck Web site.)

Amazon. Union. Lumber schooner. Came ashore near the entrance of San Francisco Bay at Cliff House on May 14, 1865. Was salvaged. (Marshall, *California Shipwrecks,* 101.)

Anglo American. Wrecked in 1861 at Tomales Bay. (Marshall, *California Shipwrecks,* 120; *MSV,* 10.)

Annie B. Bourne (Hannah B. Bourne). Union. Schooner. Snagged in the Sacramento River at Sutterville (near Sacramento) on August 5, 1862. (California State Lands Commission, *Historical Sites and Shipwrecks along the Sacramento River,* 109; California State Lands Shipwreck Web site.)

Ann Perry. Bark, 348 tons. Length 197 feet, beam 27 feet. Cargo of lumber and 250 sacks of potatoes. Built in 1825. From Puget Sound. Came ashore a few miles south of Cliff House on January 4, 1865, with three aboard drowned. (Gibbs, *Shipwrecks Pacific Ocean,* 275; Marshall, *California Shipwrecks,* 101; California State Lands Shipwreck Web site.)

Aquila. Union. Ship. Just arrived in San Francisco with parts for the Union monitor USS *Comanche,* which was to be built to protect California from Confederate commerce raiders such as the CSS *Shenandoah.* Was sunk by a storm or Confederate agents at Hathaway's Wharf in November 1864, in 37–39 feet of water. Four divers quickly salvaged the parts of the USS *Comanche.* The USS *Comanche* was launched on November 14, 1864, and commissioned on May 24, 1865. The CSS *Shenandoah* planned to attack San Francisco, but the Civil War ended before it reached California waters. (*MSV,* 12; Stern, *Confederate Navy Pictorial History,* 164; Marshall, *California Shipwrecks,* 71–72, 76.)

Beeswing. Union. Schooner. From Monterey, Calif. Wrecked near the Golden Gate, with eight dead, in February 1863. (Marshall, *California Shipwrecks,* 97, 101.)

Bianca. Schooner. Cargo of wood. Ran ashore in December 1861 at Salt Point. (Marshall, *California Shipwrecks,* 120.)

Brother Jonathan (Commodore). Union. Wooden side-wheel steamer, 1,359 tons. Length 220 feet, beam 36 feet. Owned by the California Steam Navigation Co. Carried 120 cabin passengers, 72 steerage passengers, and 50 officers and crew. Cargo of 346 barrels of whiskey, 100 tons of machinery for the Providence Mining Co., mill equipment, $10,000 in Indian treaty funds entrusted to Indian agent William Logan, and $200,000 in currency in a U.S. Army payroll. Also rumored to have $850,000 in gold (1890 value), $140,000 sent by Wells Fargo and Co. and possibly Haskins and Co., and $1 million being carried by a New York businessman to invest in the goldfields. Built in 1851 in New York City. Was reportedly overloaded when it left San Francisco for Fort Vancouver, Washington Territory. Capt. Samuel J. De Wolf said the vessel was overloaded but was told by the company's agent that he must take the *Brother Jonathan* out or the company would find a captain who would. The *Brother Jonathan* dropped cargo off at Crescent City, Calif., and headed out to sea. Unable to make headway in a raging storm, the *Brother Jonathan* turned around 4 miles north of the latitude of Point St. George, about 3 miles above Crescent City, and tried on July 30, 1865, to make the Crescent City Harbor. The fury of the storm forced the *Brother Jonathan* onto Northwest Seal Rock, a ledge just one yard above the water surface at low tide. This ledge is part of St. George's Reef, which is located 8 to 12 miles from Crescent City. Among those drowned was Brig. Gen. George Wright, of the U.S. Army, who was en route to his new command in the Department of Columbia. Also drowned was a colonel of the 9th U.S. Infantry Regiment. Altogether 213 people died; only 11 men, 5 women, and 3 children in one boat survived. Two other lifeboats were launched but were swamped. The vessel then slid off the rocks into 250 feet of water, near St. George's Reef Lighthouse close to the Dragon Channel. The bodies of General Wright and Maj. Ellery W. Eddy, the army paymaster, were recovered. Eddy had a premonition he would die during the trip. Some 170 bodies were recovered, mostly from Pelican Bay, north of Crescent City. Sixteen bodies were recovered between Gold Bluffs and Trinidad. Several bodies were found at the entrances to the Rogue and Smith rivers. Forty-six wreck victims were buried in the Crescent City Cemetery. Its wheelbox floated ashore, and the golden wooden eagle from the wreck is now in the San Francisco Maritime Museum. The wreck's wheel and 40 feet of the upper deck came ashore near Gold Bluff.

The tug *Mary Ann* from San Francisco arrived soon after the wreck but failed to find the *Brother Jonathan* or retrieve any objects or pieces from it. In 1867 William Ireland hunted unsuccessfully for the wreck. In 1869 and 1872 other salvage groups also failed to locate the wreck. There were attempts in the 1890s to pinpoint the wreck by a Mr. Woods and a Captain Gee. In the 1930s a fisherman caught in his net an old almost unrecognizable Francis Patent lifeboat that probably came from the *Brother Jonathan*. The nearly destroyed lifeboat contained a rotting valise under a seat with eleven gold bars weighing 22 pounds. Due to the outlawing of gold ownership at that time, the gold bars were hidden until 1974, when the gold was sold. The wreck of the *Brother Jonathan* was found in 1993 by Deep Sea Research, Inc., using sophisticated equipment and was claimed in court by the treasure-hunting group. The wreck broke in half and rests in two pieces at a depth of about 250 feet off St. George Reef, just southeast of Jonathan Rock near the Dragon Channel. The lower part of the vessel remained intact. Many coins ($5, $10, and $20 gold pieces) and bullion have been removed along with bottles, ceramics, and other material. The vessel was sitting upright on the bottom, much of it buried in the mud. The upper structure has disintegrated over time. Artifacts from the vessel have been exhibited at the Del Norte Count Historical Society. A lawsuit over ownership of the *Brother Jonathan* between California's State Lands Commission and Deep Sea Research went to the U.S. Supreme Court. In a negotiated settlement Deep Sea Research received 80 percent of the material, with the remaining 20 percent to go to the state of California. Coins and gold removed from the vessel have been displayed and sold. About a thousand coins and bars with a value of about $5 million were removed from the wreck. (*OR,* 48:2:1200; Potter, *Treasure Diver's Guide,* 422; *MSV,* 247; Marshall, *California Shipwrecks,* 157–61, 163; Marshall, *Oregon Shipwrecks,* 1–11; Vesiland, *Lost Gold of the Republic,* 255; Wiltse, *Gold Rush Steamers,* 304–6; Hollister, "Revealed: The Phantom Treasure of the *Brother Jonathan*," *Treasure,* 58–61, 65; Riley, "*Brother Jonathan* Search Con-

tinues," *Treasure Diver,* 8–12; Tompkins, *Treasure,* 164–65; California State Lands Shipwreck Web site, "*Brother Jonathan*"; "Deal Allows Salvage Firm to Keep Much of Sunken Ship's Treasure," *Sacramento Bee,* March 19, 1999.)

Cabot. Nationality unknown. Brig. Sank on March 10, 1865, at Mendocino, Calif. (Jackson, *Doghole Schooners,* 22.)

Caroline. Nationality unknown. Schooner, 80 tons. Wrecked in 1863 in Mendocino County. (California State Lands Shipwreck Web site.)

Caroline Reed. Nationality unknown. Was lost in December 1864 between Bellingham, Washington Territory, and San Francisco. Could be off the Oregon or Washington coast. (Marshall, *California Shipwrecks,* 91.)

Charlotte. Union. Schooner. Built in 1861 at Point Arena, Calif. Was lost on February 5, 1865, at the mouth of the Klamath River. Later refloated. (Marshall, *California Shipwrecks,* 163; Jackson, *Doghole Schooners,* 22, 36.)

Cleopatra. Nationality unknown. Bark. Cargo of lumber. En route from the Puget Sound to San Francisco. Burned on July 1, 1861, off the California coast. (Gibbs, *Shipwrecks Pacific Ocean,* 274; Marshall, *California Shipwrecks,* 91.)

Cochief. Union. Schooner, 69 tons. Wrecked on January 30, 1863, or 1865, at Fish Rock, Point Arena. (Marshall, *California Shipwrecks,* 131; Jackson, *Doghole Schooners,* 22, 36.)

Constantine. Nationality unknown. Schooner. Wrecked at Cuffey's Cove in November 1862. (Jackson, *Doghole Schooners,* 36.)

Cuffey's Cove. Nationality unknown. Schooner. Wrecked at Cuffey's Cove in 1861. (Jackson, *Doghole Schooners,* 36.)

Curacao. Nationality unknown. Brig. Went ashore on December 22, 1862. (Marshall, *California Shipwrecks,* 131.)

C. W. Gunnel (G. W. Gunnel). Nationality unknown. Schooner. Was stranded at Point Arena in December 1862. (Marshall, *California Shipwrecks,* 131.)

Dashaway. Nationality unknown. Schooner. En route from Eureka to San Francisco. Was beached at Big Flat in December 1864. Found on January 3, 1865, about 22 miles south of Cape Mendocino, with fourteen dead, including Captain Kelsey, his wife, and child; another couple; and nine crewmen. May also have been stranded on December 30, 1863. (Marshall, *California Shipwrecks,* 146; Jackson, *Doghole Schooners,* 21, 36; California State Lands Shipwreck Web site.)

Dictator. Nationality unknown. Bark. Probably sailed from Hong Kong. Capsized between Puget Sound and San Francisco in January 1862. (Marshall, *California Shipwrecks,* 91.)

Don Leandro. Nationality unknown. Two-masted lumber schooner, 86 tons. Wrecked at Little River on November 17, 1865. Was refloated and wrecked again in 1872 and 1883. (Marshall, *California Shipwrecks,* 131; Jackson, *Doghole Schooners,* 22, 36.)

Eagle. Nationality unknown. Schooner. Was stranded in a gale in May 1865 at Russian Gulch. May also have been stranded in 1863. (Marshall, *California Shipwrecks,* 131; California State Lands Shipwreck Web site.)

Efina Kuyne. Dutch. Galliot. Wrecked in 1862 at Half Moon Bay. (Marshall, *California Shipwrecks,* 49; California State Lands Shipwreck Web site.)

Eliza. Nationality unknown. Wooden barge. Sank in front of the old town of Washington (West Sacramento) on the Yolo County side of the Sacramento River after hitting the *Governor Dana* on December 3, 1864. Part of the cargo floated off. May have been raised. (California State Lands Commission, *Historical Sites and Shipwrecks along the Sacramento River,* 59, 111.)

Elizabeth Buckley. Nationality unknown. Schooner. Cargo of lumber. Stranded with one lost on July 10, 1864, at Point Arena. (Marshall, *California Shipwrecks,* 131; Jackson, *Doghole Schooners,* 22.)

European. Nationality unknown. Wrecked at Tomales Bay in 1861. (Gibbs, *Shipwrecks Pacific Ocean,* 38; Jackson, *Doghole Schooners,* 22, 38; Marshall, *California Shipwrecks,* 121.)

Fabrius. Union. Whaler. Was lost off the California coast in 1861. (Hearn, *Gray Raiders,* 291.)

Far West. Nationality unknown. Two-masted schooner. Was stranded on February 17 (or January 15), 1863, at Rus-

sian Gulch. (Marshall, *California Shipwrecks,* 131; Jackson, *Doghole Schooners,* 22, 39.)

Flying Dragon. Union. Ship, 1,127 tons. Cargo of one thousand tons of coal from Newcastle, New South Wales, Australia. Built in 1853. Sank during a storm near Arch Rock, San Francisco Bay, on the night of January 29, 1862. A tug and soldiers from Fort Alcatraz tried to help, but the vessel rolled over the next morning. In 1877 the vessel was located by dragging in 20 fathoms, 270 yards west of Arch Rock. (Marshall, *California Shipwrecks,* 72, 77; Gibbs, *Shipwrecks Pacific Ocean,* 274.)

Francis Helen (Francis Ellen). Nationality unknown. Schooner. Cargo of railroad ties and pilings. En route from Bells Harbor or Little River. Drifted ashore at Bell's Creek on the reef on the south side of the port entrance in April or on October 6, 1863. (Marshall, *California Shipwrecks,* 131, Jackson, *Doghole Schooners,* 40.)

F. W. Bailey. Nationality unknown. Ship, 711 tons. Length 160 feet, beam 33.3 feet. Built in 1854. En route to Puget Sound to get lumber for Australia. The wind died, and its anchor failed to hold the vessel against the currents outside the San Francisco heads. The *F. W. Bailey* went onto the rocks 3 miles south of Point Lobos on January 8, 1863. Capt. L. R. Dyer and nine members of the crew died. (Marshall, *California Shipwrecks,* 102; Gibbs, *Shipwrecks Pacific Ocean,* 274; California State Lands Shipwreck Web site.)

Galveston. Nationality unknown. Brig. Was stranded on May 21, 1863, at Kents Point, Mendocino. (Marshall, *California Shipwrecks,* 131.)

George Washington. Nationality unknown. Was lost in December 1864 off the northern California coast. (Marshall, *California Shipwrecks,* 92.)

Gina Reed. Nationality unknown. Schooner. Was stranded at Stewart's Point in November 1861. (Marshall, *California Shipwrecks,* 121.)

Goddess. Nationality unknown. Vessel type unknown. Was grounded in 1865 in San Francisco County. (California State Lands Shipwreck Web site.)

Golden State. Nationality unknown. Schooner. Sank at its moorings in Mendocino Bay during a storm on November 17, 1865. (Marshall, *California Shipwrecks*, 131, Jackson, *Doghole Schooners*, 42.)

Gypsy. Union. Stern-wheel steamer, 113 tons. Built in 1850 at Wilmington, Del. Snagged in the Sacramento River, 20 miles below Sacramento, near Lugkin's Ranch, on September 2, 1862. (California State Lands Commission, *Historical Sites and Shipwrecks along the Sacramento River*, 111; *MSV*, 90.)

Hartford. Nationality unknown. Bark. Wrecked in October 1861 or 1864 on the Humboldt Bar. (Marshall, *California Shipwrecks*, 146.)

Helen. Union. Two-mast schooner, 121 or 65 tons. Built in 1863 or 1864 at Point Arena, Calif. Went ashore at Point Arena on November 17, 1865. (Marshall, *California Shipwrecks*, 132; Jackson, *Doghole Schooners*, 22, 43; Gibbs, *West Coast Windjammers*, 146.)

H. T. Clay. Nationality unknown. Schooner. Was stranded in December 1862 in the Noyo River. (Marshall, *California Shipwrecks*, 132.)

Hyack. Nationality unknown. Bark. Wrecked on a reef off Cape Mendocino on April 23, 1863. (Marshall, *California Shipwrecks*, 146.)

Isca. Nationality unknown. Went aground in a storm in San Francisco Bay on November 16, 1863. (Marshall, *California Shipwrecks*, 77.)

J. A. McClennan (J. A. McClelland) (Rainbow). Union. Stern-wheel steamer, 73 tons. Built in 1860 or 1861 at San Francisco. Its boiler blew up while on the Sacramento River, killing twenty-five on August 25, 1861. The boiler landed 350 yards away on shore. The pilot was blown 200 feet into the air. Sank in 15 minutes, 1–3 miles below Knight's Landing. Was salvaged and renamed *Rainbow* before being dismantled in 1873. (California State Lands Commission, *Historical Sites and Shipwrecks along the Sacramento River*, 112; Marshall, *California Shipwrecks*, 77; *MSV*, 104.)

J. E. Murcock. Nationality unknown. Schooner. Was stranded in the Noyo River in December 1862 and possibly in 1864 in Mendocino County. (Marshall, *California Shipwrecks*, 132; California State Lands Shipwreck Web site.)

Jenny Ford. Nationality unknown. Bark, 396 tons. Length 133 feet, beam 30 feet 4 inches. Built in 1854. Was grounded in San Francisco County on January 29, 1864, with one dead. (Marshall, *California Shipwrecks*, 102; California State Lands Shipwreck Web site.)

J. M. Chapman. Union. Schooner, 90 tons. Was captured as a Confederate privateer by the USS *Cyane* in 1863. Part of a Confederate plot to intercept California gold shipments. Was lost in December 1864 between Shoalwater Bay and San Francisco. (Marshall, *California Shipwrecks*, 92.)

Josephine Wilcutt. Union. Schooner, 86 tons. Wrecked at Newport on the Mendocino Coast in April 1863. (Marshall, *California Shipwrecks*, 132; Jackson, *Doghole Schooners*, 46.)

J. R. Whiting (J. R. Whitney). Nationality unknown. Schooner. Was lost in the Noyo River on February 13 (or 16), 1863. Was refloated and repaired. Was lost with seven men without a trace on November 17, 1865, while tied up in Noyo Harbor or Kents Point along the Mendocino coast. (Marshall, *California Shipwrecks*, 132; Jackson, *Doghole Schooners*, 22, 45.)

Julius Pringle. Nationality unknown. Ship. Was lost on September 27, 1863, at Monterey, with one dead. (Marshall, *California Shipwrecks*, 48.)

Kaluna. Nationality unknown. Schooner, 96 tons. Wrecked on Humboldt Bar in January 1862. (Marshall, *California Shipwrecks*, 147; Jackson, *Doghole Schooners*, 46.)

Kate Blackstone (Kate Blakiston). Union. Schooner. Crew of three. Cargo of general merchandise. Out of San Francisco. Capsized at the foot of Sacramento's I Street in the Sacramento River, within 100 feet of the east bank, on June 15, 1865. Two crewmen drowned. The steam engine hoist was salvaged on June 22, 1865. Was probably not raised. (Marshall, *California Shipwrecks*, 77; California State Lands Commission, *Historical Sites and Shipwrecks along the Sacramento River*, 69, 112; *Sacramento Union*, June 12, 20, 22, 1865; *Daily Examiner*, June 19, 1865; California State Lands Shipwreck Web site.)

Maggie Johnston. Nationality unknown. Schooner. Was stranded in 1863 in San Mateo County. (Marshall, *California Shipwrecks,* 48.)

Malabar. Nationality unknown. Schooner. Wrecked in Mendocino in January 1864. (Marshall, *California Shipwrecks,* 132; Jackson, *Doghole Schooners,* 22.)

Marin. Nationality unknown. Schooner. Was lost at Tomales Bay in October 1861. (Marshall, *California Shipwrecks,* 121.)

Mary Ann. Nationality unknown. Steam schooner, 102 tons. Built in 1852. Wrecked on January 28, 1863, one and a half miles south of Humboldt Bar. Was refloated on June 29, 1863. (Marshall, *California Shipwrecks,* 147, Gibbs, *Shipwrecks Pacific Ocean,* 274.)

Maryland. Nationality unknown. Schooner. Lost at Cape Mendocino on October 7, 1862. (Marshall, *California Shipwrecks,* 147; California State Lands Shipwreck Web site.)

Mary Martin. Nationality unknown. Schooner. Stranded in 1863 in San Mateo County. (Marshall, *California Shipwrecks,* 49.)

Merrimac. Union. Screw steam tug, 100 tons. Built in 1862 at San Francisco. Capsized at 12:30 p.m. on February 22, 1863, while trying to cross Humboldt Bar. Thirteen to eighteen aboard were lost. Floated onto the North Spit, bottom up, then floated free on the next high tide and struck again near Bulksport. Was later salvaged. (Marshall, *California Shipwrecks,* 147; Jackson, *Doghole Schooners,* 50; *MSV,* 143; Gibbs, *Shipwrecks Pacific Ocean,* 192–94, 274.)

Metis. Nationality unknown. Schooner. Wrecked in a gale at Casper on November 17, 1865. (Marshall, *California Shipwrecks,* 132; Jackson, *Doghole Schooners,* 21, 50.)

Monitor. Union. Barge. Crew of two. Cargo of thirty tons of hay and a wagon. Constructed from the hull of the steamer *Monitor.* Was burned and sank on July 25, 1864, in the Sacramento River about 2 miles downstream of Rio Vista. The barge was being towed by the steamer *Christina* when the accident occurred. (California State Lands Commission, *Historical Sites and Shipwrecks along the Sacramento River,* 75, 113.)

Monterey. Union. Schooner, 120 tons. Was lost at Point Reyes in November 1861 or 1862. (Marshall, *California Shipwrecks,* 121; California State Lands Shipwreck Web site.)

Mosquito. Union. Barge. Cargo of one hundred cords of wood. Snagged and sank in the Sacramento River below Sacramento's I Street Bridge on July 29, 1864. The wood was salvaged. (California State Lands Commission, *Historical Sites and Shipwrecks along the Sacramento River,* 77, 113; *Sacramento Union,* June 16, 1865.)

Nevada. Union. Side-wheel steamer, 757 tons. Built in 1861 at San Francisco. Snagged in 1863 in Steamboat Slough, upstream of Rio Vista, while racing the steamer *New World.* Ran into a bank of Cache Slough in quicksand and sank, with no lives lost. Part of the wreck was reported to have been visible at the point where Cache Slough and Steamboat Slough meet. (California State Lands Commission, *Historical Sites and Shipwrecks along the Sacramento River,* 83, 113; *MSV,* 154, 284; Marshall, *California Shipwrecks,* 74; Drago, *Steamboaters,* 228; Holden, *Sacramento,* 287; Gibbs, *Shipwrecks Pacific Ocean,* 274.)

Ninus. Nationality unknown. Bark. Was sunk on November 16, 1861, in the Sacramento River below R Street in Sacramento. (California State Lands Commission, *Historical Sites and Shipwrecks along the Sacramento River,* 114.)

Noonday. Union. Clipper ship, 2,000 tons. Length 200 feet, beam 38.5 feet. Built in 1855. Out of Boston. Was lost on January 1 or 2, 1863. The vessel sunk in 40 fathoms when it hit Fanny Rock in the Farallons, which supposedly had risen because of an earthquake. The pilot boat *Relief* rescued the crew. Fanny Rock was renamed Noonday Rock. (Gibbs, *Shipwrecks Pacific Ocean,* 274; Marshall, *California Shipwrecks,* 87, 92; California State Lands Shipwreck Web site.)

Novick (Norvick). Russian navy. Steam corvette. Wrecked on September 26, 1863, 2 miles north of Point Reyes. In November 1863 one rifled brass cannon, four 24-pounders, and several powder chests were removed from the wreck. (Marshall, *California Shipwrecks,* 122; California State Lands Shipwreck Web site; Gibbs, *Shipwrecks Pacific Ocean,* 275.)

O.K. Union. Side-wheel steamer, 43 or 78 tons. Cargo of wood. Built in 1862 at San Lorenzo, Calif. Was burned on the Yolo County side of the Sacramento River across from Sacramento's M Street on July 3, 1865. Was salvaged but was later lost, in 1867 or 1881. (California State Lands Commission, *Historical Sites and Shipwrecks along the Sacramento River,* 87, 114; *MSV,* 160, 286; MacMullen, *Paddle Wheel Days,* 139; *Sacramento Union,* July 3, 1865.)

Paul Pry. Union. Side-wheel steamer, 229, 350, or 330 tons. Built in 1856 or 1859 at San Francisco. Hit a rock at Alcatraz Island in San Francisco Bay and sank on December 22, 1862. Was later salvaged. (Marshall, *California Shipwrecks,* 78; *MSV,* 169; MacMullen, *Paddle Wheel Days,* 139.)

Phoebe Fay. Nationality unknown. Schooner. Wrecked on November 17, 1865, at Little River. Was later salvaged. (Marshall, *California Shipwrecks,* 132; Jackson, *Doghole Schooners,* 22.)

Pike. Nationality unknown. Wooden barge. Snagged in the Sacramento River below Sacramento's I Street Bridge on June 29, 1864. (California State Lands Commission, *Historical Sites and Shipwrecks along the Sacramento River,* 114.)

Polynesia. Union. Clipper ship, 1,084 tons. Built in Boston. Went ashore on South Beach, San Francisco Bay, on March 1, 1862. The crew set the vessel afire. The wreck was later sold at auction. (Gibbs, *Shipwrecks Pacific Ocean,* 274; Marshall, *California Shipwrecks,* 78.)

Relief (Pilot Boat No. 2). Union. Pilot boat. Built in 1845. Capsized in a storm in February 1863 at the breakers at San Francisco Bar. Four crewmen died. (Marshall, *California Shipwrecks,* 97, 103.)

Republic. Union. Steamer. Built in 1855. Was lost in January 1862 at the Golden Gate. (Marshall, *California Shipwrecks,* 103.)

Rosalie. Nationality unknown. Schooner. Was stranded at Point Arena in January 1862. (Marshall, *California Shipwrecks,* 132.)

Sagamore. Nationality unknown. Schooner. Cargo of granite and cobbles. Foundered in a storm 4 miles above Point Pinole on November 26, 1864. One crewman died. (Marshall, *California Shipwrecks,* 79.)

Salinas. Union. Screw steamer, 131 tons. Built in 1861 at San Francisco. Was swamped at the mouth of the Salinas River and ran ashore on October 31, 1861. The cargo was salvaged, and the ship was raised. (*MSV,* 192; Marshall, *California Shipwrecks,* 48.)

Sarah Louise. U.S. Ship. Driven ashore in a storm on November 11, 1865, about 21 miles northwest of Tennessee Cove. (Marshall, *California Shipwrecks,* 122.)

Sea Nymph. Clipper ship, 1,215 tons. Built in 1853. Sank on May 4, 1861, at Point Reyes, with two killed. (Marshall, *California Shipwrecks,* 115–16, 122; California State Lands Shipwreck Web site; Gibbs, *Shipwrecks Pacific Ocean,* 274.)

Senator. Union. Side-wheel steamer, 121 tons. Built in 1846 at Wheeling, Va. (now W. Va.). Wrecked on March 12, 1863, at the entrance to San Pedro Harbor. Was probably raised. (Marshall, *California Shipwrecks,* 28; *MSV,* 197.)

S. F. Blunt. Nationality unknown. Schooner. Became waterlogged at Albion in November 1862. Was later salvaged. (Marshall, *California Shipwrecks,* 132.)

Shawmut. Nationality unknown. Ship. Was lost at Bird Rock in San Francisco in 1863. (Marshall, *California Shipwrecks,* 79.)

Shooting Star. Nationality unknown. Schooner. Built in 1860. Capsized in July 1861 off Bodega Bay. (Marshall, *California Shipwrecks,* 122; California State Lands Shipwreck Web site.)

Sir John Franklin. British. Ship, 999 tons. Cargo of lumber, dry goods, pianos, and two hundred barrels of spirits. Built in 1855. En route from Baltimore to San Francisco. On January 17, 1865, the vessel hit rocks halfway between Pigeon Point and Point Ano Nuevo at Franklin Point. Captain Dupeaux and twelve men were killed, but three survived. The cargo was salvaged. (Marshall, *California Shipwrecks,* 49; *Daily Chronicle,* January 19, 1865; Reinstedt, *Shipwrecks and Sea Monsters,* 21–22.)

Sophie McLane (Sophie McLean). Union. Side-wheel or stern-wheel steamer, 242 tons. Built in 1858 or 1859 at San Francisco. Exploded on October 26, 1864, at the Suisan Bay Wharf, with thirteen dead or missing. The boiler was fabricated from the same batch of iron as the faulty boiler on the *Washoe,* which exploded on September 4 or 5, 1864.

The *Sophie McLane* was later salvaged. (*MSV,* 200, 298; Gibbs, *Shipwrecks Pacific Ocean,* 275; Marshall, *California Shipwrecks,* 79; California State Lands Commission, *Historical Sites and Shipwrecks along the Sacramento River,* 115; California State Lands Shipwreck Web site; MacMullen, *Paddle Wheel Days,* 29.)

Sovereign. Nationality unknown. Schooner. Parted the vessel's moorings at Navarro on December 27, 1862. Was apparently raised. (Marshall, *California Shipwrecks,* 133.)

Sparking Wave. Nationality unknown. Schooner. Was lost in January 1862 between San Francisco and Shoalwater Bay. (Marshall, *California Shipwrecks,* 92.)

Storm Cloud. Nationality unknown. Schooner, 118 tons. Cargo of 150,000 feet of lumber. Lost in a gale while tied up to moorings at Mendocino on November 17, 1865. (Marshall, *California Shipwrecks,* 133; Jackson, *Doghole Schooners,* 42, 51–55.)

Syren. Union. Clipper ship, 1,064 tons. Built in 1851 in Boston. Hit rocks twice at Mile Rock on April 25, 1861, returned to San Francisco harbor, and was beached in the flats with 4 feet of water in the hold. The cargo was unloaded. The ship was later towed to Mare Island, where its repairs cost $15,000. (Marshall, *California Shipwrecks,* 103.)

T. H. Allen. Nationality unknown. Schooner, 48 tons. Short of food and water after being driven northward for ten days in a storm. In desperation the *T. H. Allen* tried to cross Humboldt Bar and wrecked in January 1862. One crewman drowned, but the others were rescued. (Marshall, *California Shipwrecks,* 147; Jackson, *Doghole Schooners,* 55.)

Tongawanda. Nationality unknown. Schooner. Capsized 12 miles north of the San Francisco Heads in April 1862. (Marshall, *California Shipwrecks,* 103.)

Visalia. Union. Screw steamer, 76 tons. Built in 1860 at San Francisco. Was sunk in the Sacramento River at Hayes Bend, 3 miles above Nicholas, by a snag on May 25, 1864. Was probably raised. Abandoned in 1868. (California State Lands Commission, *Historical Sites and Shipwrecks along the Sacramento River,* 116; *MSV,* 222.)

Walcott (Charlotte Francis). Nationality unknown. Brig. Lost on May 18, 1863, at Bowens Landing. (Marshall, *California Shipwrecks,* 122.)

Washoe. Union. Steamer, 385 or 500 tons. Built in 1863 at San Francisco. Owned by the California Navigation & Improvement Co. The boilers overheated and blew up in Steamboat Slough, above the Hog's Back, on September 4 or 5, 1864. Sixteen whites and a score of Chinese died, and thirty-six people were seriously injured. Several of the injured later died in Sacramento. Was raised and repaired a few months later. (*MSV,* 227; Drago, *Steamboaters,* 228–30; Marshall, *California Shipwrecks,* 74, 80; California State Lands Shipwreck Web site; Holden, *Sacramento,* 287–90.)

Wasp. Union. Sloop. Cargo of cobble and bricks. From Freeport, Calif., bound for San Francisco. Hit a snag on January 12, 1865, at night and sank in Steamboat Slough. (Marshall, *California Shipwrecks,* 80; California State Lands Commission, *Historical Sites and Shipwrecks along the Sacramento River,* 105, 117; *Sacramento Union,* January 16, 1865.)

Yosemite. U.S. Steamer, 1,317, 1,319, or 631 tons. Length 283 feet. Carried 350 passengers and nearly a ton of gold and silver. Built in 1863 at San Francisco. The starboard boiler blew up on October 22, 1865, after leaving the wharf at Rio Vista. At least 29 Chinese and 13 to 22 people of European descent died. Another source says 150 died and 50 were injured. The wreck and its contents were raised. The vessel was cut in half, and 35 feet were later added when it returned to commerce. (Drago, *Steamboaters,* 230–31; Holden, *Sacramento,* 290; California State Lands Commission, *Historical Sites and Shipwrecks along the Sacramento River,* 117; Marshall, *California Shipwrecks,* 80; *MSV,* 235; MacMullen, *Paddle Wheel Days,* 30.)

Young America. Union. Side-wheel steamer, 359 or 179 tons. Built in 1854 or 1856 at San Francisco. Snagged on January 13, 1865, 8 miles below Marysville on the Feather River and broke in two. Its cargo and machinery were salvaged. (*MSV,* 235, 308; Marshall, *California Shipwrecks,* 80.)

Canada

British Canada remained neutral during the American Civil War, but blockade-runners used Halifax, Nova Scotia, as a port from which to run the Union blockade. The Confederate commerce raider CSS *Alabama* captured and destroyed six Union vessels off the coast of Canada, and the CSS *Tallahassee* destroyed one Union ship off the Canadian coast.

Anglo Saxon. British. Screw steamer, 1,715 gross tons. Length 283 Feet, beam 35.2 feet, speed 10 knots. Carried 444 passengers and crew and Canadian and U.S. mail. Built in 1856 at Dumbarton. En route from Liverpool, England, for Quebec. Was lost on April 27, 1863, near Cape Race, Newfoundland. Two hundred and fifty-six bodies were recovered from the wreck. (*New York Times,* May 3, 1865; *Harper's Weekly,* May 9, 1863; www.fortunecity.com/littleitaly/amalfi/13/shipa.htm.)

Anson Northup (Pioneer). U.S. Steamer, 100 tons. Built in Lafayette, Minn. Operated on the Red River of the North. Was lost in 1861 at Lower Fort Garry, Manitoba. (*MSV,* 11; *WPD,* 25.)

Brilliant. Union. Ship, 833 tons. Cargo of flour and grain. Built in 1860. From New York City. En route to London. Was captured and burned by the CSS *Alabama* on October 3, 1862, near latitude 40° north, longitude 50° 30' west, on the Newfoundland Banks. The *Emily Farnum* was accompanying the *Brilliant* but was bonded due to a British cargo. (*ORN,* 1:510, 517–19, 780, 792–93; Semmes, *Service Afloat,* 458; Summersell, *Boarding Officer,* 29–30.)

Dunkirk. Union. Brig, 293 tons. Cargo of flour and Portuguese bibles. En route from New York City to Lisbon, Portugal. Was captured and burned by the CSS *Alabama* on October 7, 1862. A deserter from the CSS *Sumter* was among the crew. (*ORN,* 1:527, 780, 793–94; Hearn, *Gray Raiders,* 174–75.)

Greyhound. U.S. Screw steamer, 290 net tons, 583 tons. Length 201 feet 5 inches, beam 22 feet 8 inches, depth 13 feet. Built in 1863 at Greenock, Scotland. Former Confederate vessel. Stranded on November 14, 1865, at Beaver Harbour, Nova Scotia. (*MSV,* 89, 265.)

Lafayette. Union. Bark, 945 tons. Cargo of corn, wheat, pipe staves, and lard. En route from New York City to Belfast, Ireland. Was captured and burned by the CSS *Alabama* on October 23, 1862, at latitude 39° 34' 50" north, longitude 63° 26' west, south of Halifax. (*ORN,* 1:527, 780, 798; ser. 2, 2:353–64, 373; Semmes, *Service Afloat,* 482–88.)

Lamplighter. Union. Bark, 365 tons. Cargo of tobacco. Out of Boston. En route from New York City to Gibraltar. Was captured and burned by the CSS *Alabama* on October 15, 1862, off the coast of Nova Scotia at latitude 41° 32' 47" north, longitude 59° 17' 45" west. (*ORN,* 1:527, 780, 795–96; Hearn, *Gray Raiders,* 175.)

Lauraetta. Union. Bark, 284 tons. Cargo of 1,424 barrels of flour, pipe staves, 225 kegs of nails, and 290 boxes of herring. En route from New York City for the Mediterranean. Was captured and burned by the CSS *Alabama* on October 28, 1862, south of Halifax at latitude 39° 18' 47" north, longitude 67° 35' west, at St. Georges Bank. (*ORN,* 1:527, 780, 801–2; Semmes, *Service Afloat,* 491; Hearn, *Gray Raiders,* 178.)

Manchester. Union. Ship, 1,062 tons. Cargo of grain. From New York City to Liverpool, England. Was captured and burned by the CSS *Alabama* on October 11, 1862, southeast of Nova Scotia at latitude 44° 8' 55" north, longitude 55° 26' west. (*ORN,* 1:527, 780, 794–95; Hearn, *Gray Raiders,* 175.)

Roan. Union. Brig, 127 tons. Was captured and burned by the CSS *Tallahassee* on August 20, 1864, south of Halifax. (*OR,* ser. 4, 3:1057; *ORN,* 3:704; Hearn, *Gray Raiders,* 138.)

Wave Crest. Union. Bark, 409 tons. Cargo of grain. Out of New York City. En route to Cardiff, Wales. Was captured, used for target practice, and then burned by the CSS *Alabama* on October 7, 1862, southeast of Nova Scotia. (*ORN,* 1:780, 793: Hearn, *Gray Raiders,* 174.)

Caribbean Waters

Caribbean waters were utilized by Yankee traders throughout the American Civil War. The Confederate raiders CSS *Alabama*, CSS *Clarence*, CSS *Florida*, and CSS *Sumter* claimed Union victims amid the subtropical Caribbean islands.

Avon. Union. Ship. Cargo of 1,600 tons of guano. En route from Howland Island to Cork, Ireland. Was captured by the CSS *Florida* on March 29, 1864. Used the next day for target practice at latitude 15° 11' north, longitude 34° 25' west, west of Dominica and southeast of Puerto Rico. Fourteen of the vessel's crew enlisted on the Confederate raider. (*ORN*, 2:683; Hearn, *Gray Raiders*, 120.)

Benjamin F. Hoxie (B. F. Hoxie). Union. Clipper. Cargo of logwood and $105,000 in silver bars. Captain Carey of the vessel reported it carried $400,000 in silver bars, 30 tons of silver ore worth $500,000, and $7,000 to $8,000 in gold. Out of Connecticut. En route from the western Mexican coast to Falmouth, England. Was captured by the CSS *Florida* under Cdr. John N. Maffitt in the West Indies on June 16, 1863. The silver bars were removed and the vessel burned. (*ORN*, 2:653; Shomette, *Shipwrecks of the Civil War*, 177; Hearn, *Gray Raiders*, 96.)

Chastelaine (Chastelain). Union. Brig, 293 tons. Out of Boston. En route to Cienfuegos, Cuba, from Basse-Terre, Guadeloupe, in ballast. Was captured and burned by the CSS *Alabama* on January 27, 1863, at latitude 17° 19' 50" north, longitude 72° 21' west, about 5 miles south of Alta Vela or Tall Sail, off Santo Domingo. (*ORN*, 2:170, 685, 725; Semmes, *Service Afloat*, 567; Summersell, *Boarding Officer*, 84.)

Colombo. Union. Out of Boston. Wrecked off Jamaica in early 1863. The hull, spars, and cargo were sold by auction on March 24–25, 1863. (*New York Times*, April 18, 1863.)

Corris Ann. Union. Merchant brig. From Philadelphia. En route to Mantanzas, Cuba. Was captured by the CSS *Florida* under Lt. John N. Maffitt on January 22, 1863, between Cay Piedras and Cay Mono near Cardenas, Cuba.

Was set afire and drifted onto shore inside Cardenas Harbor. (*ORN*, 2:51, 639, 668, 674.)

Estelle (Estella). Union. Brig. Crew of eight. Cargo of sugar, molasses, and honey. En route from Santa Cruz for Boston. Was captured and burned by the CSS *Florida* on January 19, 1863, near latitude 23° 34' north, longitude 83° 50' west, off Dry Tortugas. (*ORN*, 2:48–49, 639, 668, 674.)

General Rusk (Blanche). British. Iron side-wheel steamer, 750 gross tons, 417 bulk tons. Length 200 feet, beam 31 feet, depth 12 feet, draft 5 feet 7 inches. Built in 1857 at Wilmington, Del., as a merchantman. Seized by the state of Texas from the Southern Steamship Line at Galveston in 1861. Converted to a blockade-runner. While en route to Havana, Cuba, on the way to Lavaca, Tex., the USS *Montgomery* chased the *Blanche* to a point where the blockade-runner had anchored, about 300 yards off Marianao Beach, Cuba, 7 to 8 miles from Havana. The local Cuban alcalde, his son, and a Cuban pilot boarded the vessel to escort it into port. Two boats from the USS *Montgomery* approached the blockade-runner, and the *Blanche*'s captain ran his vessel aground. Either the blockade-runner's crew or boarding Union sailors burned the vessel on October 7, 1862. A crewman and the Spanish pilot were captured aboard the vessel, but the rest made it to shore. Strong protests were made by the governments of Great Britain and Spain over the violation of neutral waters by the Union navy. Reparations were paid to Spain by the United States. Cdr. Charles Hunter, captain of the USS *Montgomery*, was later court-martialed, convicted of violating Spanish territorial jurisdiction, and dismissed from the U.S. Navy. (*ORN*, 19:267–79, 300; *DANFS*, 2:525.)

Golden Rocket. Union. Bark, 690 or 607 tons. Out of Bangor or Brewer, Maine. En route from Havana, Cuba, for Cienfuegos. In ballast. Was captured by the CSS *Sumter* off Cape Corrientes, Cuba, and burned 10 to 12 miles west-southwest of the Isle de Pinas on July 3, 1861. (*ORN*, 16:599; Semmes, *Service Afloat*, 127–29; Hearn, *Gray Raiders*, 15.)

Golden Rule (Retribution). U.S. Side-wheel steamer, 2,267 tons. Carried 635 passengers. Built in 1864 at New York City. Stranded on Roncador Reef off the Nicaraguan coast on May 5, 1865. The passengers were stranded for a week before they were rescued. (*MSV,* 86, 629.)

Golden Rule. Union. Bark. Cargo of masts, spars, and rigging for the USS *Bainbridge,* which had lost its equipment in a gale. En route from New York City for Aspinwall, Columbia. Was captured and burned by the CSS *Alabama* off the coast of Haiti on January 26, 1863, at latitude 17° 50' 39" north, longitude 74° 52' 30" west. (*ORN,* 2:685, 724–251; Semmes *Service Afloat,* 565–66; Summersell, *Boarding Officer,* 82–83.)

Parker Cook. Union. Bark, 136 tons. Cargo of provisions. Out of Boston. En route for Aux Cayes on the south side of Santo Domingo. Was captured and burned on November 30, 1862, by the CSS *Alabama* off Cape Rafael, Santo Domingo. Some of the provisions were transferred to the Confederate raider. (*ORN,* 1:780, 808; 3:678; Semmes, *Service Afloat,* 523; Summersell, *Boarding Officer,* 58–59.)

USS *Shepherd Knapp.* Union. Ship, 838 tons. Length 160 feet 10 inches, beam 33 feet 8 inches, depth 22 feet 3 inches, light draft 13 feet. Complement of ninety-three, with eleven guns. Launched in 1856 at New York City. Ran onto a coral reef on the evening of May 18, 1863, near Cape Haitien, Haiti, with 11 feet of water under the vessel at high tide. All usable stores and provisions were salvaged and put on board the Union ship *National Guard.* Unable to be hauled off the reef by the USS *Rhode Island* and USS *Chippewa.* The eleven guns were removed, along with the anchors, chains, and rigging. (*ORN,* 2:196–98; ser. 2, 1:207; *WCWN,* 139–40.)

Windward. Union. Brig. Cargo of sugar. Out of Philadelphia. En route to Portland, Maine, from Matanzas, Cuba. Was captured and burned by the CSS *Clarence* on January 22, 1863, off Cuba. (*ORN,* 2:639, 668, 674.)

Central America

Columbus. Union. Screw steamer, 460 tons. Built in 1848 at Allowaystown, N.J. Was stranded on December 9, 1861, at Punta Remedos, El Salvador. (*MSV,* 42, 252.)

John Hart. Union. Side-wheel steamer, 220 tons. Built in 1847 at New York City. Was stranded on January 26, 1862, in Lake Nicaragua. (*MSV,* 113, 272.)

China

Trade between the United States and China was extensive during the Civil War, with vessels sailing from New York City and San Francisco. A number of American vessels carried on trade in China's inland waters. The *George Sand* and *Phantom* were reportedly wrecked with large shipments of California bullion and specie.

Chekiang. Union. Side-wheel steamer, 1,264 tons. Built in 1862 at New York City. Burned on August 7, 1864, at Hankow. (*MSV,* 34, 249.)

Cortes. Union. Side-wheel steamer, 1,117 tons. Built in 1852 at New York City. Burned on June 17, 1862, at Shanghai. (*MSV,* 46, 253.)

Firecracker. Union. Steamer, 1,040 tons. Built in 1862 at New York City. Foundered on February 2, 1864, 50 miles above Kiukiang. (*MSV,* 74, 261.)

Fohkien. U.S. Side-wheel steamer, 1,947 tons. Built in 1862 at Greenpoint, N.Y. Was stranded on July 13, 1865, 60 miles from Chinhae. (*MSV,* 74, 261.)

General Ward. Union. Screw steamer, 70 tons. Built in 1863 at East Boston, Mass. Exploded on October 21, 1864, at Shanghai, with all but one aboard killed. (*MSV*, 82, 263.)

George Sand. German. Bark. Carried $13 million in California gold and silver bars and specie. Foundered on January 30, 1863, in 60 fathoms on the Praetus Shoals, about 180 miles southwest of Hong Kong. (Potter, *Treasure Diver's Guide*, 407; Rieseberg, *Guide to Buried Treasure*, 125.)

Hankow. U.S. Side-wheel steamer, 725 tons. Built in 1861 in New York City. Burned on July 21, 1865, at Canton (Kuang-chou). (*MSV*, 91, 266.)

John T. Wright. Union. Side-wheel steamer, 369 tons. Built in 1860 at Port Ludlow, Wash. Wrecked in July 1864 at Lanshan Crossing in the Yangtze River. (*MSV*, 116, 273.)

Phantom. Union. Clipper ship. Cargo of $10 million in gold and silver ingots from California. Foundered on September 24, 1862, on the Tankan Shan Reefs. (Potter, *Treasure Diver's Guide*, 407; Rieseberg, *Guide to Buried Treasure*, 25.)

Santa Cruz (USRC General Sherman). Union. Screw steamer, 96 tons. Built in 1856 at New York City. Was lost on February 24, 1862, below Sterling Island in the Yangtze River. (*MSV*, 194, 296.)

Surprise. Union. Side-wheel steamer, 456 tons. Built in 1853 at New York City. Burned after colliding with the *Hu Quang* on May 4, 1863, on the Yangtze River. (*MSV*, 206, 299.)

Connecticut

Commonwealth. U.S. Side-wheel steamer, 1,732 tons. Built in 1855. Burned on December 29, 1865, at Groton, with one killed. (*MSV*, 44, 252.)

East Indies

The East Indies served as a CSS *Alabama* hunting ground for Union vessels.

Contest. Union. Clipper ship, 1,098 tons. Cargo of Japanese goods. Built in 1863 at New York City. Out of New York City. En route from Yokohama, Japan, for New York City. Was captured by the CSS *Alabama* near latitude 25° 45' north, longitude 106° 49' east, off Gaspar Strait on November 11, 1863, and burned in 14 fathoms. (*ORN*, 2:781; 3:681; Semmes, *Service Afloat*, 694–95; Summersell, *Boarding Officer*, 167; Hearn, *Gray Raiders*, 212.)

Highlander. Union. Ship, 1,049 tons. In ballast. Out of Boston. En route from Singapore to British Burma. Was captured and burned by the CSS *Alabama* at the western edge of the Straits of Malacca on December 26, 1863. (*ORN*, 2:581–82, 591, 793; 3:681; Semmes, *Service Afloat*, 720–21.)

Sonora. Union. Ship, 707 tons. Out of Newburyport, Mass. En route from Singapore to British Burma. Was captured and burned by CSS *Alabama* on December 26, 1863, at the western entrance of the Strait of Malacca. Its crew included fourteen men who had been aboard the *Contest*, which the CSS *Alabama* had also taken. (*ORN*, 2:779–80, 793; 3:681; Semmes, *Service Afloat*, 720–21; Summersell, *Boarding Officer*, 169–70.)

Texan Star (Martaban of Maulmain). British. Bark, 799 tons. Cargo of rice. Built in 1858 in Boston. En route to

Singapore. Was captured and burned by CSS *Alabama* in the Strait of Malacca on December 24, 1863, although it was flying a British flag. The *Texan Star* had been transferred from the United States to foreign registry within ten days of its capture. (*ORN*, 2:792, 3:97, 681; Semmes, *Service Afloat*, 716–18; Summersell, *Boarding Officer*, 167–68.)

Winged Racer. Union. Clipper ship, 1,768 tons. Cargo of sugar, china, camphor, hides, and 5,810 bales of Manila hemp. Out of New York City. En route from Manila, Philippines, to New York City. Was captured on November 9, 1863, and burned by the CSS *Alabama* on November 10, 1863, in the Java Sea. Crews from the *Winged Racer* and *Amanda* rowed to shore in boats. (*ORN*, 2:707, 780; 3:681; Semmes, *Service Afloat*, 691–92.)

European Waters

British vessels sailed from Europe to supply the Confederacy with arms and supplies during the American Civil War. Confederate vessels were built in England and Scotland. The most famous Confederate raider, the CSS *Alabama*, met its fate off the French coast.

CSS *Alabama* (290). Confederate. Wooden steam screw sloop, bark-rigged, 1,050 tons. Length 211 feet 6 inches, beam 31 feet 8 inches, depth 17 feet 8 inches loaded, depth aft 15 feet 4 inches, trial speed 12.8 knots, 2 engines. Complement of 24 officers and 120 seamen, with a battery of one 100-pounder, one 68-pounder, and six 32-pounders. Built in 1862 at Liverpool, England, for the Confederate government. Became the most successful Confederate commerce raider, capturing or destroying sixty Union vessels worth more than $6 million. Was sunk by the USS *Kearsarge* on June 19, 1864, off Cherbourg, France, after a one-hour fight. The CSS *Alabama* and USS *Kearsarge* approached to within 900 and 1,200 yards of each other. The CSS *Alabama*'s powder was bad, making its fire against the USS *Kearsarge* ineffective.

The Confederates lost nine killed, twenty-one wounded, and thirteen missing. The USS *Kearsarge* had only three wounded, including one who later died. The English yacht *Deerhound* rescued Capt. Raphael Semmes and forty-one Confederates, including twelve officers, and landed them at Southampton, England. A French fishing boat picked up three Confederate officers and six crewmen, taking them to France. The USS *Kearsarge* captured four officers and about sixty crewmen. The Confederate crewmen were paroled and landed at Cherbourg. Most of the captured crewmen were not Americans. The vessel was discovered by the French navy minesweeper *Circe* in October 1984. It is at a 30° angle on its starboard side in 195 feet of water about 6 miles off the French coast. About 30 percent of the vessel is still intact. A joint French/American expedition investigated the wreck, which has been undergoing salvage since 1988. The U.S. Navy Historical Center signed an agreement with the Association CSS *Alabama* as operator of the investigation for five years. A number of artifacts, including a Blakely cannon, have been recovered under very difficult diving conditions. (*ORN*, 3:57–83; ser. 2, 1:247; 2:631, 813; Lambert, "CSS 'Alabama' Lost and Found," *American History Illustrated*, 32–37; Semmes, *Service Afloat*, 755–84; Guerout, "Wreck of the C.S.S. *Alabama*," *National Geographic*, 66–83; National Historical Center Web site, "Field Work on CSS *Alabama* Site, Summer 1995," "CSS *Alabama*.")

Anglo Saxon. Union. Collier. Cargo of coal from Liverpool, England. Out of New York City. Was captured and burned by the CSS *Florida* on August 21, 1863, off Brest, France. (*ORN*, 2:659–60; Owsley, *C.S.S. Florida*, 76.)

Harvey Birch. Union. Clipper ship, 1,482 tons. In ballast. En route from Le Havre, France, to New York City. Was captured and burned by the CSS *Nashville* on October 19, 1861, near latitude 49° 6' north, longitude 9° 52' west, in the Atlantic Ocean west of France and southwest of England. (*ORN*, 1:221, 230, 746.)

Iona. British. Iron side-wheel steamer blockade-runner, 325 gross tons, 174 registered tons. Length 225 feet 2 inches, beam 20 feet 5 inches, depth 9 feet. Built in 1855 at Govan, Scotland. Collided with the *Chanticleer* and sank in the Firth of Clyde on October 2, 1862. (*LLC*, 305.)

Iona. British. Iron side-wheel steamer blockade-runner, 368 gross tons, 173 registered tons. Length 249 feet 2 inches, beam 25 feet, depth 9 feet 1 inch. Built in 1863 at Govan, Scotland. En route to Nassau, Bahamas. Foundered on February 2, 1864, in the Bristol Channel off Lundy Island, twenty-four hours after leaving Queenstown. Some items from the wreck were recovered in 1983 and sent to the McLean Museum in Greenock, Scotland. (*ORN*, 9:539; *LLC*, 306; "Civil War Relic," *Treasure Search*, 29.)

Lelia. British. Steel side-wheel steamer blockade-runner, 1,100 bulk tons, 430 registered tons, 640 gross tons. Built in 1865 in Liverpool, England. Was lost on January 14, 1865, at the mouth of the Mersey River with Cdr. Arthur Sinclair and Gunner P. C. Cuddy of the Confederate navy. (*LLC*, 308; Shomette, *Civil War Shipwrecks*, 440.)

Matilda. Confederate. Iron twin screw steamer, 390 registered tons. Length 228 feet, beam 25 feet, depth 12 feet. Built in 1864 at Renfrew, Scotland. On April 4, 1864, it sank in the Firth of Clyde on Lundy Island in the Bristol Channel. (*LLC*, 312.)

Neapolitan. Union. Bark, 322 tons. Cargo of dried and fresh fruit and fifty tons of sulfur. Out of Kingston, Mass. En route from Messina to Boston. Was captured and burned by the CSS *Sumter* inside the Strait of Gibraltar in the Mediterranean Sea, within a mile and a half of Ceuta, Morocco, on January 18, 1862. (*ORN*, 1:370–71, 737–38; Semmes, *Service Afloat*, 308; Hearn, *Gray Raiders*, 36–37.)

Florida

During the Civil War Florida's many small harbors and inlets were used for blockade running, while the Union navy employed Key West as the base of its Florida blockade. The British Bahamas and Spanish Cuba were within easy sailing distance from the Florida coast. Many small blockade-runner schooners and sloops were lost in Florida waters because of storms and Union blockaders. In a seven-month period in the St. Johns River, Confederate torpedoes and artillery sank the Union vessels *Alice Price*, USS *Columbine*, *General Hunter*, *Harriet A. Weed*, and *Maple Leaf.* A number of Union vessels were lost on Florida's reefs and in storms.

A. B. Noyes. Union. Barge. Was burned by Confederates on October 16, 1863, in Tampa Bay near Fort Brooke. (*OR*, 28, Pt. 1:735.)

Aid. Confederate. Ship, 100 tons. Was captured inside the Mobile Bar on June 5, 1861, by a three-boat expedition from the USS *Niagara*. Was sunk on August 23, 1861, on the east end of Santa Rosa Island, to block the entrance to Confederate-held Pensacola harbor. (*ORN*, 16:644; *DANFS*, 5:439.)

Alice Price (Alice C. Price). Union army. Side-wheel steam transport, 320 or 238 tons. Built in 1853 at New York City. Was sunk on September 13, 1864, by a Confederate torpedo in the St. Johns River near Mandarin Point. (*OR*, 35:2:225; *MSV*, 6.)

Alicia. Confederate. Schooner. Was captured and destroyed by the USS *Sagamore* on December 5, 1862, in Jupiter Inlet. (*ORN*, 17:334.)

Alvarado. Union. Bark. Cargo of 458 or 454 bales of wool, 58 goatskins, 26 bales of bucha leaves, 290 bales of sheepskins, 20 bales of buckskins, 231 hides, as well as 70 tons of iron, old copper, and tin valued at $70,000. Out of Boston. En route from Cape Town, South Africa, to Boston. Was captured by the Confederate privateer *Jefferson Davis* at latitude 25° 4' north, longitude 50° west. Ran aground on the southeast side of a shoal a mile and a half from the Amelia Island Lighthouse, about one mile from shore. A

Confederate artillery company from Fort Clinch arrived on the beach with two 6-pounders as boats from USS *Jamestown* burned the *Alvarado* to the water's edge on August 5, 1861. (*OR*, 1:347–48; *ORN*, 6:56–58; 9:539; *CWC*, 6-256.)

USS *Amanda*. Union. Sailing bark, 368 tons. Length 117 feet 6 inches, beam 27 feet 9 inches, depth 12 feet 6 inches. Complement of seventy-one, with six 32-pounder smoothbores, one 20-pounder Parrott, and one 12-pound howitzer. Built in 1858 at New York City. Ran ashore after hitting Dog Island during a gale on May 29, 1863, at East Pass, St. George's Sound, about 200–300 yards from shore and 1,200 yards from Dog Island. The USS *Hendrick Hudson* was nearby but offered little assistance. Was burned by its crew to prevent its capture. Was examined on June 1, 1863, about 150 yards from shore in 18 inches of water, broadside to Topsail Bluff. The USS *Somerset* and USS *Hendrick Hudson* raised six 32-pounders, shot, copper, and chains from the hulk. (*ORN*, 17:451–57; 469; ser. 2, 1:33; *WCWN*, 140; Turner, *Navy Grey*, 112.)

***Ancilla*.** Confederate. Schooner, 81 tons. Was destroyed at Cedar Keys on January 16, 1862, by the USS *Hatteras*. (*ORN*, 17:834.)

***Andrew Manderson*.** Union. Coal bark. Wrecked by a gale on May 29, 1863, at Sand Island. (*ORN*, 17:49–50; *SCH*, 336–37.)

***Ann*.** Confederate. Sloop, 3.5 tons. Crew of four. Cargo of salt, coffee, and other goods. Was destroyed by the USS *Gem of the Sea* on December 30, 1862, at Jupiter Inlet. (*ORN*, 17:453, 456.)

USS *Anna* (*Annie*) (*La Criolla*). Union. Schooner, 27 tons. Length 46 feet 2 inches, beam 14.75 feet, depth 4.5 feet, laden draft 5 feet laden. Carried one 12-pounder rifled pivot gun. Built in 1857. Was captured as the blockade-runner *La Criolla* by the USS *Fort Henry* on February 26, 1863, in the Suwannee River. Was refitted as the USS *Anna*, a tender to the Union ordnance ship *Dale*. The USS *Anna* left Key West and was sunk in 15 fathoms of water by an explosion 10 miles northeast by north of Cape Romain in mid-January 1865. On February 5, 1865, the bow was raised out of the water by the USS *Hendrick Hudson*, and all of the aft was gone, except for the aft cabin. (*ORN*, 17:340–41; *SCH*, 376–77.)

***Anna Eliza*.** British. Sloop. Crew of seven. Cargo of 10,000 gallons of turpentine spirits. Out of Nassau, Bahamas. En route from the Santee River, S.C., for Nassau. Was dismasted and waterlogged when found on May 14, 1864, by the Union mortar schooner USS *Sea Foam*, at latitude 34° 35' north, longitude 74° 55' west. (*ORN*, 17:800–801, 807–8; ser. 2, 1:35; *WCWN*, 144.)

***Anna Smith*.** Confederate. Schooner, 198 tons. Cargo of cotton, lumber, and other goods. Was destroyed on June 16, 1862, at Cedar Keys by the USS *Hatteras*. (*ORN*, 17:704–5.)

***Annie*.** Confederate. Sloop. Cargo of cotton. Was captured on April 11, 1863, in the Crystal River by the USS *Sea Bird*, a tender to the USS *Hibiscus*. Was scuttled as unfit to sail to Key West. (*ORN*, 17:49–50; *SCH*, 336–37.)

***Berosa*.** Confederate. Steam transport blockade-runner. Sprang a leak on the St. Marys River and was abandoned on April 8, 1863, at latitude 29° 50' north, longitude 79° 50' west, in the Gulf of Mexico. The crew escaped. (*ORN*, 14:161; *DANFS*, 2:504.)

USS *Bloomer* (*Bloomer*) (*Emma*). Union. Side-wheel steamer, 130 tons. Armed with one 32-pounder smoothbore and one rifled 12-pounder. Built in 1856 at New Albany, Ind. Was captured from the Confederates by a small boat expedition from the USS *Potomac* and the 91st N.Y. Infantry Regiment in the Choctawhatchee River on December 24, 1864. Served as a tender to the USS *Potomac*. Wrecked in June 1865 in East Pass, Santa Rosa Island. Was salvaged and sold on September 22, 1865. (*ORN*, 22:233, 256; ser. 2, 1:46; *WCWN*, 102.)

CSS *Camilla* (*America*) (USS *America*) (*Memphis*). Confederate. Racing yacht, 100 tons, 208 Thames measurement tons. Length 111 feet, beam 24 feet, draft 12 feet. Armed with one rifled 12-pounder and two 24-pounder smoothbores. Built in 1851 at New York City for a racing syndicate. The *America* won the Queen's Cup and became the namesake of the America's Cup yacht race. The Confederates planned to convert the *America* into a swift blockade-runner. The *America* was scuttled in 3 fathoms of water in Haw Creek off the St. Johns River at the head of Dunn's Lake. Only the vessel's port rail was above water. Was raised by the USS *Ottawa* in March 1862. Was renamed USS *America*. Was later moved to the Naval Academy at Annapolis, Md., and in 1873 was sold to private concerns. The Eastern Yacht Club of Marblehead, Mass., presented the vessel to the U.S. Navy in 1921. The *America* collapsed in 1942 under the weight of snow at the U.S. Naval Academy at Annapolis and was scrapped in 1945. (*OR*, 53 [supp.]: 224–25; *ORN*, 12:615, 638–40, 643; *CWC*, 6-269; *WCWN*, 144.)

Caroline Gertrude. Schooner. Cargo of sixty bales of cotton. En route to Havana, Cuba. Was captured by the USS *Stars and Stripes* when the *Caroline Gertrude* ran aground on a bar immediately inside the mouth of the Ocklockonee River, 100 yards from a beach, on December 29, 1863. Union sailors captured thirteen people onboard and removed forty-three bales of cotton. Confederate cavalry appeared on the beach, and a two-hour fight followed in which the Confederate commander was reported killed. Union sailors set the vessel afire before retiring. (*ORN*, 17:617–18.)

USS *Columbine* (*A. H. Schultz*). Union. Side-wheel steam gunboat tug, 133 bulk tons. Length 117 feet, beam 20 feet 7 inches, depth 6 feet 2 inches. Complement of twenty-five, with two 20-pounder Parrott rifles or two 25-pounder Dahlgren smoothbores. Built in 1850 at New York City. While returning from Volusia with 146–48 onboard, including a detachment of 25 soldiers of the 35th U.S. Colored Infantry Regiment, the USS *Columbine* was ambushed on the St. Johns River opposite Horse Landing by four guns of the Milton Artillery under Capt. J. J. Dickison near Palatka on May 23, 1864. Shells cut the wheel ropes, and the USS *Columbine* drifted 200 yards downstream and ran aground. The ship was shelled for one hour before surrendering. The Confederates boarded the wreck in rowboats, stripped the vessel, and burned it. Union losses were 17–20 killed and missing, 5–6 wounded, and 65 captured. Most of the wreck was removed, probably by the U.S. Army Corps of Engineers, in the 1880s. Located about a mile above Saratoga, on the edge of a sand bar on the east side of the St. Johns River. May have been covered and damaged by dredging during the building of

the Cross-Florida Canal in the 1960s. Howard B. Tower found remnants of the wreck in 7 feet of water in 1971 and salvaged a number of artifacts. (*OR*, 35:2:123; *ORN*, 15:440–55; ser. 2, 1:62; Ammen, "Navy in the Civil War," *Confederate Military History*, 149; Keel, *Florida's Trails*, 155; Tower, "U.S.S. *Columbine*: Civil War Wreck Story with a Twist," *Skin Diver*, 54–56, 109; Florida Division of Historical Resources Web site, "U.S. Navy and Confederate Shipwrecks Project.")

Convey. Union. Steamer, 350 tons. Was burned and sank in 12 feet of water in 1864 in Pensacola Bay. The U.S. Army Corps of Engineers had George W. Le Gallais remove most of the wreckage, including the machinery and half its hull, in 1878 and 1879. (*Chief of Engineers Report 1879*, 1:801–2; Broussara, "*Judah*: Sunken Civil War Schooner," *Skin Diver*, 168.)

Cygnet. Confederate. Pilot boat. Was captured by boats from the USS *Sagamore* at Apalachicola on March 30, 1862. Was grounded and burned on a 7-foot bar. (*ORN*, 17:202, 204.)

Delaware. Union. Side-wheel steamer, 616 or 650 tons. Length 225 feet, beam 29 feet, depth 10 feet 6 inches. Was lost inside St. Johns Bar on May 24, 1865. (*OR*, 47:3:580; *MSV*, 53; Lane, *American Paddle Steamboats*, 102–3.)

Director. British. Schooner. Crew of two. Cargo of one barrel of rum and twenty small bags of salt. En route from Nassau, Bahamas, to Peace Creek, Fla. Was captured on September 30, 1863, by the USS *Gem of the Seas* at Punta Rasa at the entrance to the Caloosahatchee River while coming out of Terraceia Creek. Was destroyed as unseaworthy. (*ORN*, 17:560–62.)

Dudley (Pickney). Confederate. Sloop, 57 tons. Cargo of turpentine and rosin. Was destroyed on June 16, 1862, at Cedar Keys by the USS *Hatteras*. (*ORN*, 17:50; *SCH*, 336–37.)

Elizabeth. British. Sloop out of Nassau, Bahamas. Cargo of salt. Ran aground on a bar at the mouth of Jupiter Inlet. Was captured and burned by the USS *Sagamore* on January 28, 1863. (*ORN*, 17:359.)

Emma (Onward). Nationality unknown. Schooner, 70 tons. Was captured on March 23, 1863, at the mouth of the

Ocklockonee River in Apalachee Bay by a Union small boat expedition consisting of a pilot, two officers, and twenty-seven men from the USS *Amanda*. The captured vessel grounded and was attacked by Confederates from shore on March 24, 1863. Union forces burned the vessel 250 yards from shore. One of two Union boats was lost, with one killed and eight wounded in the fight. (*ORN*, 17:390–94; Robinson, *Confederate Privateers*, 241–43.)

Etta. Nationality unknown. Schooner. Crew of two. Was captured by boats from the USS *Sagamore* on March 31, 1864, and destroyed near Cedar Keys after they had searched three days for two other blockade-runners. (*ORN*, 17:676.)

Finland. Nationality unknown. Blockade-runner. Crew of fifteen. Partially dismantled in an entrance to Apalachicola Bay. Was captured by two boats with forty Union seamen from the USS *Montgomery* and three boats from the USS *R. R. Cuyler* on August 26, 1861. Unable to get the captured vessel over St. Vincent's Bar, the *Finland* was burned to the water's edge upon the approach of a Confederate steamer towing a large schooner on August 28, 1861. The Confederates salvaged lifeboats and a few items from the burning wreck. (*ORN*, 16:646–47; Turner, *Navy Grey*, 34–35.)

Florida. Confederate. Sloop. Carried five aboard. Cargo of cotton. Was captured by the USS *Sea Bird*, tender to the USS *Hibiscus*. Was scuttled off Crystal River on April 11, 1865, as unfit to sail to Key West. (*ORN*, 17:834.)

Fortunate. Confederate. Sloop. Cargo of cotton bales and one barrel of turpentine. Was captured and under tow by the USS *Bermuda* near latitude 27° 53' north, longitude 79° 45' west, when it parted the hawser, filled with water, and was lost on May 30, 1864. (*ORN*, 27:677–78.)

Fulton (USS Fulton). Confederate. Side-wheel steamer, 698 tons, 750 bulk tons, 1,200 displacement tons. Length 180 feet or 180 feet 6 inches, beam 34 feet 8–10 inches, draft 10 feet 6 inches, maximum speed 11 knots. Complement of 79–130, with four 8-inch smoothbores and four 32-pounder smoothbores. Formerly a U.S. Navy ship, built

in 1851 at Brooklyn, New York. Was captured by Confederates on January 12, 1861, at the Pensacola Navy Yard. Was destroyed on May 10, 1862, by Confederates after grounding near Pensacola when they abandoned the area to the Union forces. (*ORN*, ser. 2, 1:89; *CWC*, 6-230; *WCWN*, 24.)

General Finegan (Madge). Confederate. Small sloop. Cargo of two barrels of turpentine and five bales of cotton. En route to Havana, Cuba, from Florida's Crystal River. Was captured by two boats from the USS *Ariel*. The cargo was removed. Was destroyed as unseaworthy on May 28, 1864, just north of the Chassahowitzka River near the Homosassa Bay. (*ORN*, 17:709–12.)

General Hunter (Bay Queen) (General Sedgwick) (Jacob H. Vanderbilt). Union army. Transport, 350 or 475 tons. Built as the *Jacob H. Vanderbilt* in 1863 in Jersey City, N.J. Was destroyed by a Confederate torpedo in the St. Johns River on April 16, 1864, at Mandarin Point near where the *Maple Leaf* was sunk. Sank in three to five minutes, with the quartermaster killed and another person wounded. Was raised and first renamed *General Sedgwick* and then *Bay Queen* as a post–Civil War vessel. (*ORN*, 15:314; Scharf, *History of the Confederate Navy*, 763; *MSV*, 80; Perry, *Infernal Machines*, 116.)

George C. Collins. U.S. Screw steamer, 234 tons. Stranded on March 27, 1865, in the St. Johns River. (*MSV*, 83, 263.)

USS G. L. Brockenboro (G. L. Brockenborough). Confederate. Small sloop. Was captured by the USS *Fort McHenry* after being scuttled in the Apalachicola River on October 15, 1862. Put into Union naval service as a tender to the USS *Port Royal* and USS *Somerset*. Its bottom was smashed during a gale on St. George's Sound on May 27, 1863, and the vessel was unable to be raised. (*ORN*, 17:321, 524–25; ser. 2, 1:89; *WCWN*, 145.)

Good Hope. Nationality unknown. Schooner, about 150 tons. Cargo of salt and a few dry goods. Was captured and burned by the USS *Fox* on April 18, 1864, near the mouth of the Homosassa River. (*ORN*, 17:683–84.)

Harriet A. Weed. Union army. Side-wheel steam transport, 210 or 290 tons. Armed with two guns. Built in 1863 at

Newburgh, N.Y. Was sunk by two Confederate torpedoes while towing a schooner and carrying thirteen officers and twenty men of the 3rd U.S. Colored Infantry Regiment on the morning of May 10, 1864, in the St. Johns River at Mandarin Point, near the mouth of Cedar Creek. One officer was blown 20 feet into the air, and five men were killed. It was a total loss. (*OR*, 35:2:88, 123; *ORN*, 15:426–27; Ammen, "Navy in the Civil War," *Confederate Military History*, 148; *MSV*, 92; Scharf, *History of the Confederate Navy*, 763; Perry, *Infernal Machines*, 116.)

Havana (Havanah). Confederate. Screw steamer, 169 tons. Length 115 feet 4 inches, beam 22 feet 6 inches. Carried a remaining cargo of ten tons of lead and cotton. Built in 1855 at Hoboken, N.J. Had already landed most of the cargo and was loading cotton when set afire and abandoned by its crew to prevent its capture by the USS *Isilda*, a tender to the USS *Somerset*, on June 5, 1862, in Deadman's Bay. Union sailors salvaged the jib, anchor, two chain cables, and three lead pigs. (*ORN*, 17:262; Horner, *Blockade-Runners*, 203; Shomette, *Civil War Shipwrecks*, 145; *LLC*, 304.)

Helen. Confederate. Guard boat steamer. Was burned by Confederate troops at Pensacola on May 9, 1862, to prevent its capture. (*OR*, 6:658, 661.)

Helen. Confederate. Sloop. Cargo of corn. Out of Florida's Crystal River. Was captured and destroyed by a small boat expedition from the USS *Lawrence*, USS *Sagamore*, and USS *Fort Henry* on April 2 or 3, 1863, at the mouth of Bayport Harbor. (*ORN*, 17:406–10; *WCWN*, 236; *SCH*, 390–91.)

Ida. Confederate. Schooner. Cargo of liquor. Formerly of Key West. Was run aground by the USS *James S. Chambers* about midway on Sanibel Island, 15 miles south of Charlotte Harbor. Was destroyed to prevent its recapture on March 4, 1863. (*ORN*, 17:379–80.)

Indian River (USS Clyde) (Neptune). Union. Side-wheel steamer, 260 or 294 bulk tons, 250 tons. Length 200 feet 6 inches or 166 feet 8 inches, beam 18 feet 6 inches or 27 feet 6 inches, depth 8 feet or 9 feet 6 inches, speed 9 knots. Built in 1861 at Glasgow, Scotland. Was captured as the blockade-runner *Neptune* on June 14, 1863, by the USS

Lackawanna. Was grounded at the mouth of the Indian River on December 3, 1865. Was probably raised and later lost in 1867. (*MSV*, 101, 269; *LLC*, 313–14; *WCWN*, 81.)

Inez. British. Old leaky schooner, 4 tons. Crew of three. Cargo of fifteen sacks of salt and fourteen pounds of shoe thread. Was captured and destroyed by the USS *Gem of the Sea* off Indian River Inlet on April 18, 1863. (*ORN*, 17:416–17.)

J. Appleton. Union. Schooner, 1,200 tons. Former revenue cutter. Cargo of water. At Egmont Key it parted its cable during a gale on August 15, 1861, near the lighthouse. Was driven ashore 30 feet above the low waterline. The wreck was stripped and burned. (*ORN*, 16:666–68.)

Jefferson Davis (Echo) (Jeff Davis) (Putnam) (Rattlesnake). Confederate. Privateer brig, 187 or 230 tons. Draft 10 feet 6 inches. Complement of seventy to seventy-nine, with old British guns, including two 24- or 18-pounders, two 12-pounders, and a long 18-pounder pivot. Built about 1845 at Baltimore. Out of Charleston, S.C. Formerly the slaver *Echo*, captured in 1853 by the USS *Dolphin* with a cargo of 271 slaves. Grounded on August 18, 1861, on the St. Augustine Bar in a half-gale after a successful voyage from Charleston, S.C., during which the *Jefferson Davis* took nine Union ships in 7 weeks. The guns on the starboard side were thrown overboard, but the crew was unable to refloat the ship. The crew abandoned the vessel, with only the small arms and stores saved. (*ORN*, ser. 2, 1:257; Scharf, *History of the Confederate Navy*, 78; *CWC*, 6-256.)

Judah (William J. Judah). Confederate. Two-mast privateer schooner, 250 tons. Complement of twenty-five. Armed with one pivot gun and four broadside cannons. A blockade-runner from St. John's, Newfoundland. Was captured and set afire while moored at the Pensacola Navy Yard Wharf in front of a two-gun Confederate battery at 3:30 a.m. on September 14, 1861, by one hundred Union sailors and marines in four launches from the USS *Colorado*. The two-gun battery on shore was spiked. Drifted to the middle of Pensacola Bay, burned to the water's edge, and sank opposite Fort Barrancas. The Union expedition lost three killed, including one marine accidentally killed by his own men, and thirteen wounded. The Confederates lost three killed and a number of men wounded. Thought to be located opposite Fort Barrancas near the mouth of Pensacola Bay, mostly under 4–5 feet of shifting sand. This wreck site could be the site of the *Convoy* or another vessel. (*OR*, 6:437–38, 666; *ORN*, 16:670–74; ser. 2, 1:257; *CWC*, 6-328; Porter, *Naval History*, 50–52; Broussara, "*Judah:* Sunken Civil War Schooner," *Skin Diver*, 164–68.)

Kate Dale. Nationality unknown. Sloop. Cargo of cotton. Was captured by a small boat expedition of two acting ensigns and forty seamen from the USS *Tahoma* and two acting ensigns, one assistant engineer, and sixty seamen from the USS *Adela*. Set afire in the Hillsborough River, 2 miles above Tampa on October 16–17, 1863. The Union sailors lost three killed, one mortally wounded, and nine wounded, along with five captured in the fight. The Confederates lost two men captured, along with five captured on the blockade-runner. (*ORN*, 17:570–79.)

Lafayette. Confederate. Sloop. Was captured in St. Andrews Bay by boats from the USS *Pursuit* on April 4, 1862. Sprang a leak and foundered while in tow of the captured steamer *Florida* at sea on the way to Key West. (*ORN*, 17:208–9.)

Laura. Nationality unknown. Stern-wheel steamer, 83 tons. Built in 1855 at Elizabeth, Pa. Was lost in 1862 in Florida. (*MSV*, 125, 275; *WPD*, 278.)

Little Lila (Flushing) (Little Lily) (Nan Nan). British. Blockade-runner steamer, 147 registered tons, 303 bulk tons. Length 156 feet 4 inches, beam 27 feet 2 inches, depth 8 feet 4 inches. Cargo of cotton. Built in 1860 at Brooklyn, N.Y., as the *Flushing*. Was destroyed by the USS *Nita* at the mouth of the East Pass of the Suwannee River on February 24, 1864. Some of the cotton was thrown overboard, and fifty-five bales were recovered. (*ORN*, 17:654–55, 658; Horner, *Blockade-Runners*, 203.)

Madison. Confederate. Side-wheel steamer, 99 tons. Probably built in 1855 at New Albany, Ind. Was scuttled on the rocks at Troy Springs by Capt. James Tucker, the owner, in September 1863. The ship's boilers, cabins, and smokestacks were removed during the Civil War. (Keel, *Florida's Trails*, 33; *MSV*, 133.)

Manderson. Union. Bark. Driven ashore by a gale near West Pass, St. George's Sound, on May 27, 1863. (*ORN*, 17:456.)

Maple Leaf. Union army. Double-stack side-wheel steam transport, 508 tons. Length 181 feet, beam 26 feet 6 inches. Built in the 1850s at Kingston, Ontario. Was sunk by a Confederate torpedo on April 1, 1864, while carrying baggage of the 112th N.Y. Infantry Regiment, 169th N.Y. Infantry Regiment, and the 13th Ind. Infantry Regiment up the St. Johns River. Sank at McIntosh's Point opposite Doctor's Lake, 15 miles above Jacksonville. Four aboard were killed. The smokestacks and upper deck were above water. Was set afire by a company of the 1st Ga. Infantry Regiment and a section of the Fla. Light Artillery the next day. The anchor and some equipment were probably removed during the Civil War. In 1882–83 the wreck was removed to a low-water depth of 19 feet by a U.S. Army Corps of Engineers contractor. In 1984 the wreck was located in 20 feet of water by Keith Holland and Lee Manley. In 1988 the St. Johns Archaeological Expeditions, Inc., received permits to excavate the wreck. East Carolina University assisted. Thousands of articles have been recovered, many of them now displayed at the Jacksonville Museum of Science and History. Some of the objects recovered were loot from Union expeditions. The wreck was designated a National Historic Landmark in 1994. (*OR*, 35:2:47, 397; *ORN*, 15:316; *Annual Report of the Chief of Engineers to the Secretary of War for the Year 1883*, 186, 955; Ammen, "Navy in the Civil War," *Confederate Military History*, 148; Babits, "Exploring a Civil War Sidewheeler," *Archaeology*, 48–50; Towart, "The *Maple Leaf* in Historical Perspective," *Maple Leaf* Shipwreck Web site.)

Mary. British. Sloop, 11 tons. Out of Nassau, Bahamas. Carried five crewmen and five passengers. Cargo of thirty-one bales of cotton. Was captured by boats from the USS *Roebuck* a mile inside Jupiter Inlet. Nine bales of cotton were taken aboard the USS *Roebuck*. A prize crew of one officer and four men put aboard. The sloop ran onto a reef in the Florida Keys while en route to Key West on January 22, 1864. The prize crew and cargo were saved by running the vessel onto the beach. (*ORN*, 17:633, 637.)

Mary. Confederate. Small guard boat steamer. Was burned by Confederate troops at Pensacola on May 9, 1862, to prevent its capture. (*OR*, 6:658, 661.)

Mary Jane. Nationality unknown. Schooner. Ran ashore on a small key's beach near Clearwater Harbor, latitude 28° north, longitude 82° 53' west. Was destroyed by the USS *Tahoma* on June 18, 1863. (*ORN*, 17:477; *Marine Magnetometer Survey . . . Pinellas County, Fla.*, 12–13.)

Mary Nevis. Union. Sloop attached to the USS *Ethan Allen.* Grounded at Bayes Pass. Was stripped then set afire by the Union navy on February 20, 1861. (*ORN*, 17:133.)

Mary Olivia. Confederate. Pilot boat sloop. Was captured by boats from the USS *Sagamore* at Apalachicola on March 30, 1862. Was grounded on a 7 feet deep bar and burned. (*ORN*, 17:202, 204–5.)

Menemon Sanford (Memnorium Sanford). Union. Steamer, 904 tons. Length 244 feet, beam 32 feet 7 inches, depth 12 feet. Built in 1854 at Greenpoint, N.Y. Carried five hundred officers and men of the 156th N.Y. Infantry Regiment. Ran onto Carysfort Reef, on December 10, 1862, at 6:20 a.m., a mile and a half south by west of the lighthouse, bearing south by west and heading south-south-west. The cargo was thrown overboard. The regiment was rescued by the USS *Gemsbok* and *Blackstone* without any loss of life. One company lost 127 rifle muskets with bayonets and its tent poles and pins. The steamer's engine was later salvaged and put into the *George Levy* in 1864. (*OR*, 15:608–9; *ORN*, 1:587; 19:401; *MSV*, 143, 281; Lane, *American Paddle Steamboats*, 110–11.)

USS Merrimac (Merrimac) (Nanis). Union. Iron side-wheel steamer, 684 tons, 634 gross tons, 536 registered tons. Length 230 feet, beam 30 feet, depth 11 feet, loaded draft 8 feet 6 inches, 4 boilers, maximum speed 11.5 knots, average maximum speed 8 knots. Complement of 519, with one 30-pounder Parrott, four 24-pounders, and one 12-pounder. Former Confederate blockade-runner captured by the USS *Iroquois* on July 24, 1863, off New Inlet, N.C. Off the Florida coast, the ship's tiller broke, and its boilers flooded, sinking the vessel on February 15, 1865, at latitude 29° 11' north, longitude 79° 12' west, during a northeast gale. The mail steamer *Morning Star* rescued the crew. (*ORN*, 12:38–41, 43; ser. 2, 1:141; *LLC*, 312.)

Neptune. Confederate. Schooner. Sank in the Hillsborough River near Tampa in 1863. (*ORN*, 17:575.)

New Island. Confederate. Schooner. Was captured with two pilot boats, the *Mary Olive* and *Cygnet*, by boats from the USS *Sagamore* at Apalachicola on March 30, 1862. Was grounded on the bar at 7 feet and burned. (*ORN*, 17:202, 204–5.)

Norman. Union. Schooner. Was captured by Confederates near the Perdido River mouth in November 1863. As the USS *Bermuda* approached it, the *Norman* was run aground by the prize crew and set afire to avoid capture. (*ORN*, 20:675–76.)

Oconee (Everglade) (Savannah) (CSS Savannah). Confederate. Side-wheel steamer, 160, 475, or 486 tons; 406 bulk tons. Length 169 feet 6 inches or 173 feet, beam 30 feet or 28 feet 8 inches, depth 8 feet 6 inches or 8 feet. Crew of forty-three. Cargo of cotton. Built in 1856 at New York City. Formerly the steamer *Everglade*, which was converted to the gunboat CSS *Savannah* with one 32-pounder. Fought at Port Royal and Fort Pulaski, serving as a Confederate receiving ship. Converted to the blockade-runner *Oconee*. Foundered at sea south of St. Catherine's Island, Ga., the night of August 18–19, 1863, after coming out from Savannah during bad weather. One boat with four officers and eleven men was captured by a Union ship off Florida on August 20, 1863. The rest of the crew escaped. (*ORN*, 14:492–93; ser. 2, 1:266; 2:530; *CWC*, 6-298; *DANFS*, 2:564; *MSV*, 68; *LLC*, 319–20.)

O.K. Union. Small sloop. One crewman. En route to St. Marks. Was captured by the USS *Santiago de Cuba* on February 8, 1862, off Cedar Keys. Was swamped en route to the Union blockaders off St. Marks. (*ORN*, 1:356.)

Patriot. British. Schooner. Out of Nassau, Bahamas. Ran ashore 12–15 miles south of Mosquito Inlet. The USS *South Carolina* found the *Patriot* beached, holed, its masts cut down, and stripped of its cargo on August 27, 1862. (*ORN*, 13:253.)

Petee. Confederate. Sloop, 6 tons. Crew of three. Cargo of fifty sacks of salt from Nassau, Bahamas. Out of Savannah. Was destroyed by the USS *Gem of the Sea* while trying to enter the Indian River Inlet on March 10, 1863. (*ORN,* 17:383–84.)

Pilot. Confederate. Schooner. Was burned on October 21, 1862, by the USS *E. B. Hale* off the Florida coast. (*SCH,* 368–69.)

Powerful. Canadian. Wooden side-wheel steamer, 189 bulk tons, 119 registered tons. Length 126 feet, beam 23 feet. Built in 1862 at Quebec. Was grounded and captured by the USS *Fox* after being abandoned by the crew during its first run through the blockade. The captured ship was taking on water and was destroyed on December 20, 1863, at the mouth of a channel of the Suwannee River. The machinery was later destroyed to avoid Confederate salvage. (*ORN,* 17:608–9; *LLC,* 317.)

USS Preble. Union. Wooden sloop, 566 tons. Length 117 feet or 117 feet 7 inches, beam 32 feet or 33 feet 10 inches, depth 15 feet or 15 feet 8 inches, Complement of 150, with four 8-inch smoothbore guns, twelve 30-pounder Parrott rifles, and one 12-pounder. Was laid down in 1838 and launched in 1839 at the Portsmouth, N.H., Navy Yard. Was accidentally destroyed by fire on April 27, 1863, at Pensacola. U.S. Navy divers located what appears to be the wreck in 1963 and recovered some artifacts, including a mast. (*ORN,* ser. 2, 1:184; *WCWN,* 129; Florida Division of Historical Resources Web site, "U.S. Navy and Confederate Shipwrecks Project.")

Rattler. Confederate. Sloop, 66 tons. Was destroyed at Cedar Keys on January 16, 1862, by the USS *Hatteras.* (*ORN,* 17:49–50; *SCH,* 336–37.)

Rebel. Nationality unknown. Schooner. Crew of six. Cargo of salt, liquor, boxes of goods, and one bale of cotton. Was captured by boats from the USS *Roebuck* on February 27, 1864, at Fort Compton on the Indian River. The leaking vessel was destroyed and the cargo sent to Key West. (*ORN,* 17:655, 660.)

Rob Roy. Honduran. Schooner, 66 burden tons. Length 78 feet, beam 22 feet 6 inches, depth 6 feet, draft 13 feet. Crew of six. Cargo of cavalry sabers along with mechanical and farming equipment. Out of British Honduras (Belize). Ran aground and burned on the south side of Deadman's Bay while looking for the mouth of the Suwannee River on March 2, 1865, and being chased by the USS *Fox,* tender to the USS *Stars and Stripes.* The crew was captured, and some of the cargo was removed. (*ORN,* 17:825.)

Saint Mary's (USS *Genesee*) (*Nick King*) (*St. Marys*). Confederate. Side-wheel steamer, 337 tons. Cargo of cotton. Built in 1857 at Wilmington, Del. Sank 5 miles from Jacksonville in McGirt's Creek or Haw Haw Creek in March 1862. Was raised by Confederates but again was sunk by Union forces on February 9, 1864, in Alabama. Was raised again by Union forces, becoming the *Nick King* after the Civil War. (*OR,* 35:2:123; *ORN,* 12:615, 638, 640, 643; *MSV,* 69, 192.)

Sarah Mary. British. Sloop. Out of Nassau, Bahamas. Was captured on June 28, 1864, off Mosquito Inlet by Union forces. Was sunk as unseaworthy after the cargo was removed. (*ORN,* 17, 15:541; *New York Times,* July 23, 1864.)

Scottish Chief. Confederate. Wooden side-wheel steamer, 102 bulk tons. Length 123 feet 9 inches, beam 18 feet, depth 4 feet 9 inches. Cargo of cotton. Built in 1855 at Wilmington, N.C. Was captured and destroyed with the *Kate Dale* in the Hillsborough River, 2 miles above Tampa on October 16–17, 1863, by a Union small boat expedition consisting of five officers and one hundred men from the USS *Tahoma* and USS *Adela.* Two crewmen escaped. A nearby Confederate garrison attacked the Union raiding party. (*ORN,* 17:570–79; *LLC,* 320.)

Sort. British. Schooner, 33 tons. Out of Havana, Cuba. Assorted cargo, including twenty demijohns of liquor. Ran aground on St. Martin's Reef at the mouth of Crystal River by boats from the USS *Honeysuckle* on February 28, 1865. Had previously been captured on December 10, 1864, by the USS *O. H. Lee* off Anclote Keys, Fla., and returned to the British. (*ORN,* 17:824; *LLC,* 117.)

Sparkling Sea. Union. Transport. Carried seventy men of the 25th Battery, N.Y. Light Artillery, and 106 horses from Fort Monroe, Va., bound for Ship Island. Ran onto Ajax Reef on January 9, 1863, about 10 miles north of Carysfort Lighthouse. It was a total wreck by January 18. The horses and some stores were removed by the USS *Sagamore.*

The crew was in mutiny, and some were arrested. (*OR*, 15:231–233; *ORN*, 2:17–18, 272; 17:352.)

CSS *Spray*. Confederate. Steam gunboat tug, 105 tons. Armed with two guns. Possibly built in 1852 at Wilmington, Del. Was sunk by Confederates on the St. Marys River after November 5, 1864. (*ORN*, ser. 2, 1:267, *LLC*, 237.)

***Stag*.** Confederate. Schooner, 200 tons. Was destroyed at Cedar Keys on January 16, 1862, by the USS *Hatteras*. (*ORN*, 17:49; *SCH*, 336–37.)

CSS *Viper*. Confederate. Torpedo boat with a movable spar torpedo on the bow. Built in December 1864 or January 1865 at Columbus, Ga. Was captured by Union cavalry forces during Wilson's Raid in April 1865. While being towed by the *Yucca* from Apalachicola to Key West, the CSS *Viper* started leaking in a storm. The prize crew was removed. Sank at 4:15 p.m. on May 26, 1865, at latitude 20° 12' north, longitude 83° 20' west. (*ORN*, 17:853–54; Taylor, *Navy Grey*, 234, 245–46.)

***Wild Pigeon*.** Nationality unknown. Schooner, 37 tons. Out of Havana, Cuba. En route to Florida. Was struck amidships by the USS *Hendrick Hudson* on March 21, 1864 and sank in three minutes, with one crewman drowned. The remaining crewmen were put ashore 40 miles from Tampa. (*ORN*, 17:670–71; *LLC*, 91.)

***William H. Middleton*.** Confederate. Sloop, 69 tons. Was destroyed at Cedar Keys on January 16, 1862, by the USS *Hatteras*. (*ORN*, 17:49–50; *SCH*, 336–37.)

***Wyfe* (*Nye*).** Confederate. Schooner. Was destroyed at Cedar Keys on January 16, 1862, by the USS *Hatteras*. (*ORN*, 17:49–50; *SCH*, 336–37.)

***Young Racer*.** British. Sloop. Cargo of salt. Was run ashore and destroyed 15 miles north of Jupiter Inlet by boats from the USS *Roebuck* on January 14, 1864. (*ORN*, 17:633–34.)

➤ **VESSELS WITHOUT NAMES**

barge. Confederate. Was sunk with stone across the St. Mark River, a mile and a half below Port Leon. (*ORN*, 17:498, 500.)

schooner. Confederate. Cargo of three hundred bales of cotton. Was burned by Confederates on April 2, 1863, to prevent its capture by a Union small boat expedition from the USS *Lawrence*, USS *Sagamore*, and USS *Fort Henry* in Bayport Harbor. (*ORN*, 17:406–10.)

schooner. Nationality unknown. Cargo of six bales of cotton and one barrel of turpentine. Sank in Indian River Inlet in June 1864. Two cotton bales were salvaged by the USS *Roebuck*'s launch. (*ORN*, 17:730–31.)

schooner. Nationality unknown. Eighty tons. Assorted cargo, including ammunition. Was grounded upon the approach of the USS *Anna* on March 2, 1864. Was burned by the crew in Deadman's Bay. (*ORN*, 17:664.)

schooner. Nationality unknown. Was driven ashore on December 11, 1862, by the USS *Bienville* at St. John's River. (*ORN*, 12:393–94.)

schooner. Nationality unknown. Was with the *Etta* when it was destroyed on March 31, 1864, by a Union small boat expedition from the USS *Sagamore*, which had been searching for three days for two blockade-runners near Cedar Keys. (*ORN*, 17:676.)

vessels. Confederate. A sailboat, launch, and ferry scow were destroyed at Cedar Keys on January 16, 1862, by the USS *Hatteras*. (*ORN*, 17:48–50; *SCH*, 336–37.)

vessels. Confederate. Five fishing smacks were partially laden with goods. Three schooners carried lumber and turpentine. Was captured and destroyed by the USS *Hatteras* at Sea Horse Key and near Cedar Keys on the night of January 16, 1862. May have also been burned by Confederates to avoid capture. (*ORN*, 12:473; *New York Times*, January 27, 1862.)

vessels. Confederate. Some carried cargoes of cotton. Was destroyed by the USS *Beauregard*, USS *Oleander*, and boats from the USS *Sagamore* and USS *Para* at New Smyrna on July 28, 1863. (*ORN*, 17:529–30.)

Georgia

One of the first Confederate ports blockaded by the Union navy was at Savannah. A number of vessels were sunk as obstructions in the Savannah River by both Union and Confederate forces. The CSS *Nashville* was blown up and burned in the Ogeechee River in February 1863 and had extensive salvage operations in the 1970s and 1980s. Several blockade-runners were destroyed or wrecked along the Georgia coast or in its sounds and inlets.

When Maj. Gen. William Tecumseh Sherman's Union army was about to capture Savannah by land, the Confederate Savannah fleet was scuttled and burned to avoid being captured. Among the vessels destroyed were the CSS *Firefly,* CSS *Georgia,* CSS *Milledgeville,* CSS *Savannah,* CSS *Isondiga,* CSS *Water Witch,* and an unfinished ironclad on the stocks. Several of these wrecks have been uncovered in the Savannah River during dredging.

A. B. Thompson. Union. Ship, 980 tons. Draft 19 feet. Built in 1853 at Brunswick, Maine. Was captured by the Confederate privateer *Lady Davis.* Was sunk to act as an obstruction in the Savannah River in late 1861 or early 1862. (*ORN,* 6:182; Spence, *List,* 626–28.)

Annie (***Dolphin***) (***Emma Veleria***). U.S. Iron side-wheel steamer, 357 tons, 129 bulk tons. Length 162 feet or 170 feet 2 inches, beam 21 feet or 21 feet 2 inches, depth 11 feet or 10 feet 6 inches. Built in 1844 in Glasgow, Scotland. Was captured on March 25, 1863, as the British blockade-runner *Dolphin* in the Caribbean by the USS *Wachusett.* Ran ashore on the south side of Fig Island in the Savannah River on October 22, 1865, after hitting a snag. The Coast Wrecking Co. of New York raised the vessel after two hours of pumping. (Spence, *List,* 678; *MSV,* 11; *LLC,* 296.)

Antoinette. British. Schooner. Out of Nassau, Bahamas. Carried a captain and crew of five. En route for Fernandia, Fla. Was run aground on Cumberland Island by the USS *Braziliera* on December 8, 1863. Union ships salvaged the vessel's anchors, chains, sails, and such. (*ORN,* 15:173–74.)

Arletta. British. Schooner of 35–50 tons. Crew of five. Cargo of coffee, whiskey, and alcohol. Out of Nassau, Bahamas.

Was run ashore by the USS *South Carolina* on the south end of Tybee Island the night of March 3–4, 1864. The crew and the boat were captured by a detachment of the 3rd R.I. Artillery Regiment, which was stationed on the island. The coffee was damaged, and the cargo was removed. (*ORN,* 15:354–56.)

Buffalo. Union. Prize sloop. Was captured by the USS *Braziliera* on February 1, 1864. Ran high onto a beach on Ossabaw Island on March 22, 1864, during a storm. (*ORN,* 15:372–74.)

CSS *Chattahoochee.* Confederate. Twin screw ironclad gunboat. Length, 130 or 150 feet, beam 25 or 30 feet, depth 10 feet, draft 7 feet 3 inches or 8 feet, speed 12 knots. Complement of 120, with four 32-pounder rifled guns and one 9-inch smoothbore gun. Built in 1861–62 at the Saffold Navy Yard, Saffold, Ga. The ship's first captain, Cdr. Catesby R. Jones, later commanded the CSS *Virginia* in its battle with the USS *Monitor* at Hampton Roads, Va. Plagued by poor engines that kept the vessel out of combat. Its boilers exploded and the vessel sank, killing nineteen men and wounding others, on May 27, 1863, near Blounts Town, Fla. The Confederates raised the vessel in August 1863, took it to Columbus, Ga., and repaired it with boilers from the wrecked CSS *Raleigh.* In mid-April 1865 the vessel was burned to the water's edge and scuttled in the Chattahoochee River to prevent its capture by Brig. Gen. James Harrison Wilson's Union raiders. The vessel's engines were hit with sledgehammers to wreck them before it sank. The wreck was at Broken Bow Bend, about 13.9 miles below Columbus. Two guns were raised in 1912 during very low water. The vessel was located by the U.S. Army Corps of Engineers in the 1960s. The U.S. Army Corps of Engineers and the Confederate Gunboat Association tried to raise it in 1964. The keel snapped, and only the stern was salvaged. The salvaged 30-feet-long stern section was put in the Civil War Naval Museum at Port Columbus. Later a survey by East Carolina University located about 90 feet of the midship and bow, which is reported to be under 15 feet of water and mud. The wreck is located in the upper portion of the Walter F. George Reservoir. Listed in the National Register of Historic Places. (*OR*, 49, Pt. I:365; *ORN*, 22:258–59; ser. 2, 1:250; 2:530, 752; *CWC*, 6-208, 354; Boozer, "Chattahoochee's Sunken Guns," *True Treasure*, 28, 30; Bass, *Ships and Shipwrecks of the Americas*, 221; Stephenson, "Physical Processes at the C.S.S. *Chattahoochee* Wreck Site," *Proceedings of the Sixteenth Conference on Underwater Archaeology*, 97–99; Civil War Naval Museum at Port Columbus Web site.)

Colonel Long. Confederate. Fishing schooner, 14 tons. Crew of eight. Cargo of one barrel of whiskey, a few bags of arrowroot, and a bag of sponges. Out of Miami. Was captured by the USS *Jamestown* and scuttled off the Georgia coast on September 4, 1861. (*ORN*, 6:166–67; Spence, *List*, 606–7; Shomette, *Civil War Shipwrecks*, 410.)

CSS Columbus. Confederate. Screw steamer, 106 tons. Length 82 feet, beam 19 feet, depth 7 feet 6 inches. Armed with two guns. Built in 1855 at Wilmington, Del. Tender to the CSS *Nashville*. Was burned and sank in the Ogeechee River in 1864, about 5 miles above the wreck of the CSS *Nashville*. In 1888 the vessel's machinery and part of the wreck was removed. In 1890 the wreck was removed to within 10 feet of the water's surface. (*Annual Report of the Chief of Engineers*, 1891, 3:1605; Spence, *List*, 660.)

Comet. U.S. Wooden side-wheel steamer, 496 tons. Length 131 feet, beam 26 feet 3 inches, depth 5 feet 5 inches. Built in 1857 and probably rebuilt in 1865 at Savannah. Snagged and sank in November or December 2, 1865, at Hawkinsville in the Ocmulgee River, with no lives lost. (*MSV*, 42, 252; Spence, *List*, 681–82; *EAS*, 113.)

Cossack. Union. Whaling bark, 254 or 256 tons. Out of New Bedford, Mass. Built in 1836 at Nobleboro, Maine. Carried 250 tons of stone. Was to be sunk as an obstruction. The *Cossack* was beached at Tybee Island to serve as a jetty and wharf for the Union invasion force in early December 1861. (*ORN*, 12:418; ser. 2, 1:67; *DANFS*, 5:430, 433; Spence, *List*, 711.)

Emerald. Union. Ship, 518 tons. Part of the 2nd Stone Fleet. Ran aground on Tybee Island in late December 1861 or early January 1862. (*OR*, 14:378–80; *ORN*, 13:508; *LLC*, 298.)

Emma (Ocean). British. Side-wheel steamer, 460 bulk tons. Length 150 feet, beam 30 feet, depth 9 feet 9 inches. Cargo of cotton and turpentine. Built in 1861 at Charleston, S.C. Ran ashore on the southeast side of Jones Island off Cunningham Point. Was set afire by its crew on August 30, 1862. (*ORN*, 12:510; *DANFS*, 5:435.)

Enoch Dean. Union. Transport, 135 or 194 tons. Length 135 feet 8 inches, beam 25 feet 10 inches, depth 7 feet. Built in 1852 at Keyport, N.J. While carrying African Americans for the Freedmen's Bureau, the vessel hit piles, became grounded, and was set afire on July 10, 1863, at Willstown Bluff in the Pon Pon River, more than 30 miles from the river's mouth. (*OR*, 28:1:194–99; *MSV*, 65.)

CSS Firefly. Confederate. Wooden side-wheel steamer. Complement of fifteen and one gun. Bought by South Carolina in 1861. Was transferred to the Confederate States Navy in May 1861. Used as a tender to the Savannah Squadron. Damaged by fire on November 5, 1862, but appears to have been repaired. Was burned and sank when Savannah fell on December 21, 1864, at Screven's Ferry at the wharf in Savannah. (*OR*, 44:280; *ORN*, 16:483–84; ser. 2, 1:252; Spence, *List*, 626, 663; *CWC*, 6-226.)

General Lee. U.S. Stern-wheel steamer, 250 burden tons. Length 139 feet, beam 27 feet, depth 4 feet 7 inches. Built in 1859 at Jacksonville, Fla. Was used as a Confederate transport until it was captured, with Confederate officers and a woman aboard, on August 10, 1862, by the Union tug *Thomas Foulkes*, which was manned by detachments of the 3rd R.I. Artillery Regiment and 48th N.Y. Infantry Regiment. Sank in the Savannah River below the Savannah City Works, near Hammond, in about 10 feet of water, near Hull & Co.'s wharf in 1865. The wreck was in place in 1890 but was moved by private parties to open a channel. (*Annual Report of the Chief of Engineers 1891*, 3:184, 1603–4; Spence, *List*, 677.)

CSS Georgia (State of Georgia). Confederate. Ironclad floating battery, 500 tons. Length 260 or 250 feet, beam 60 feet. Complement of two hundred, with two 9-inch Dahlgren smoothbores and two 32-pounder smoothbore guns. Built in 1863 at Savannah. The vessel's engine was weak and could barely move it. Was moored as a floating battery northeast of Fort Jackson, near Elba Island, in the Savannah River. The CSS *Georgia* was surrounded by stone-filled cribs. Was burned at its moorings and blown up to avoid being captured on December 21, 1864. Was dynamited in 1866 to help clear channel obstructions, with some 80 tons of railroad iron armor removed. Was discovered in 28 feet of water in about 1968 by the U.S. Army Corps of Engineers next to the Savannah River ship channel. Part of the wreck has been hit by dredges. Some shells and other artifacts were recovered by divers. Part of the wreck is under 2 feet of mud. It has been studied since the 1980s by the U.S. Army Corps of Engineers. Under investigation as part of the Savannah Harbor expansion by the Georgia Ports Authority. Listed in the National Register of Historic Places. (*ORN*, 15:702–3; 16:459, 482, 489–90; ser. 2, 1:254; Granger, *History of the Savannah District*, 11; *Annual Report of the Chief of Engineers 1888*, 1017; *CWC*, 6-238; Anuskiewicz and Garrison, "Underwater Archaeology by Braille—A Study of a Scuttled Confederate Ironclad, C.S.S. *Georgia*," *Twelfth Annual Scientific Diving Symposium*, 1–11; U.S. Army Corps of Engineers, Savannah District, and Georgia Ports Authority, "CSS *Georgia*" Web site; Toner, "Divers Study Long-Sunk Civil War Ship," *Atlanta Journal-Constitution*, July 31, 2003.)

CSS Ida. Confederate. Side-wheel steamer, 77 tons. Used as a dispatch boat, transport, and tow boat. On December 10, 1864, the CSS *Ida* and one Confederate officer, Col. D. L. Clinch of Lt. Gen. William J. Hardee's staff, and twelve men were captured by a party of Union soldiers of the 150th N.Y. Infantry Regiment. The CSS *Ida* was burned at Argyle Island as the Confederate vessels approached. (*OR*, 44:208, 215, 222, 235, 239, 247.)

Iddo Kimball. U.S. Bark. En route from New York City to the Savannah River. Was lost at the Oyster Beds near Fort Pulaski about September 27, 1865. (Spence, *List*, 678.)

CSS Isondiga. Confederate. Steam cottonclad gunboat. Draft 6 feet 7 inches, speed 5 knots. Complement of sixty, with one 9-inch shell gun and one 6.4-inch rifle, and three guns reported on November 5, 1864. Was set afire and blown up at noon on December 20, 1864, above a pontoon bridge near Savannah in the Black River to prevent

its capture by Union forces. (*ORN*, 16:459, 484, 489; ser. 2, 1:256; *CWC*, 6-252.)

Israel R. Snow (Israel L. Snow). U.S. Schooner, 95 tons. Draft 8 feet 6 inches. Cargo of eight hundred bushels of lime and one hundred bushels of potatoes. Built in 1853 at Owlshead, Maine. En route from Rockland, Maine, to Savannah. Was beached on Tybee Island on December 18, 1865, with the cargo on fire and the ship leaking. (Spence, *List*, 682–83.)

Kate L. Bruce. Confederate. Armed schooner, 310 or 270 tons. Draft 10 feet. Was sunk to obstruct the Chattahoochee River below Columbus in December 1864. The *Kate L. Bruce* had been a British blockade-runner. (*ORN*, ser. 2, 1:257; *DANFS*, 2:541.)

Leesburg. U.S. Steamer. Partially loaded with a cargo of cotton. Hit a snag and sank in the Savannah River on June 22, 1865, with two lives lost. (Spence, *List*, 676.)

Lewis. Union. Whaling ship, 308 tons. Purchased at London, Conn. Loaded with stone. Was to be sunk to act as an obstruction. Was run aground at Tybee Island, bilged, and broke up in early December 1861. (*ORN*, 12:418; ser. 2, 1:126; *DANFS*, 5:430, 433.)

Marianna. British. Ship, 1,000 tons. En route from London to Savannah in ballast. Was driven ashore near the second outer buoy of Tybee Bar on November 14, 1865, during a storm. The brig *Rush* rescued the captain and crew. (Spence, *List*, 680.)

Meteor. Union. Ship, 324–25 tons. Draft 15 feet. Built in 1819 at Newburyport, Mass. Carried several hundred tons of stone. Purchased on November 4, 1861, at Mystic, Conn. In early 1862, while on the south edge of the Savannah River Main Channel, the vessel parted the anchor chain inside the bar, bilged, and drifted ashore, breaking up. (*ORN*, 12:418; ser. 2, 1:142; *DANFS*, 5:430, 433; Spence, *List*, 718–19.)

CSS Milledgeville. Confederate. Steam ironclad sloop, 1,000 tons. Length 175 feet, beam 35 feet 3 inches, depth 12 feet, draft 9 feet, armor plate 6 inches. Pierced for a battery of four guns, but none were mounted. Was launched in 1864 at Savannah. Was burned to the water's edge to avoid being captured on December 21, 1864, at Savannah. In 1890 the CSS *Milledgeville* was near the sunken CSS *Robert Habersham*. Parts of the CSS *Milledgeville* were removed in January and February 1896 by a contractor for the U.S. Army Corps of Engineers. (*ORN*, 16:502–3; ser. 2, 1:260; *Chief of Engineers Report 1891*, 3:1602–4; *CWC*, 6-271; *WCWN*, 208.)

CSS *Nashville* (*Rattlesnake*) (*Thomas L. Wragg*). Confederate. Wooden two-mast side-wheel steam privateer, former blockade-runner, 1,221 or 1,220 tons, 1,800 bulk tons. Length 215 feet 6 inches, beam 34 feet 6 inches or 34 feet 9 inches, draft 12 feet, depth 21 feet 9 inches. Complement of 40–130, with two 12-pounders or 6 guns. Built in 1854 at New York City. Ran aground on February 27, 1863, at a bend of the Great Ogeechee River about one mile above and across from Fort McAllister. Was grounded three-quarters of a mile from the USS *Montauk*. The next day the monitor USS *Montauk* came in and shelled the CSS *Nashville* from a distance of 1,200 yards, while the rest of the Union fleet bombarded Fort McAllister. CSS *Nashville* blew up between 9:40 and 9:50 a.m. on February 28, 1863. By 3:00 p.m. the vessel had burned to the water's edge. The wreck's stern was 90 feet from the bank in 28 feet of water with the bow in 13 feet of water, angled 45° from shore. The machinery and part of the wheels were above water. There was some salvage of the wreck between 1866 and 1868 and again in 1888. Divers with the Georgia Historical Society salvaged much of the vessel's machinery and other items between 1956 and 1959 for the Fort McAllister Museum. The U.S. Army Corps of Engineers demolished part of the wreck in the 1950s and 1960s as a navigation hazard. The wreck was extensively worked during the 1970s and 1980s by Dave Topper, Frank Chance, and Paul Chance, who recovered thousands of items and attempted to claim salvage rights. The State of Georgia won a lawsuit over rights to the wreck. Some artifacts are on exhibit at the Fort McAllister Museum, Fort McAllister State Historic Park. (*OR*, 14:217; *ORN*, 13:704–10, 712; ser. 2, 1:261; *Chief of Engineers Report 1891*, Pt. 3:1605; *MSV*, 152; *CWC*, 6-275; Spence, *List*, 632–33; *LLC*, 313; Chance and Topper, *CSS Nashville*, entire book; Bass, *Ships and Shipwrecks of*

the Americas, 220; Georgia Historic Preservation Division Web site; Fort McAllister Web site.)

CSS *Ogeechee* (*CSS Macon*). Confederate. Screw ram. Length 130 or 150 feet, beam 30 or 25 feet, draft 7 feet 3 inches or 8 feet, depth 10 feet, speed 12 knots. Complement of 120, with four 32-pounder smoothbores, one rifled 32-pounder, and one 9-inch smoothbore. Built in 1863 at Savannah. Surrendered to Union forces in May 1865. Was sunk in the Savannah River across from the City Exchange. (*Chief of Engineers Report 1888*, 1017; *CWC*, 6-265; *WCWN*, 218.)

Peter Demill. Union. Bark, 300 tons. Out of New York City. Part of the First Stone Fleet. Purchased in 1861 at New London, Conn. Sank at a jetty and wharf off Tybee Island in early December 1861. (*ORN*, ser. 2, 1:176; *DANFS*, 5:430, 433.)

Petit (*Oliver M. Petit*) (*USS O. M. Petit*) (*Petit M. Smith*). U.S. Side-wheel steam tug, 165 tons. Length 106 feet, beam 24 feet 4 inches, depth 7 feet, draft 6 feet, speed 8 knots. Armed with one 30-pounder and one rifled 20-pounder. Built in 1857 at Williamsburg, N.Y. Was sunk on April 24, 1865, across from the wreck of the *General Lee*. Was raised and returned to service. (Spence, *List*, 674–75; *MSV*, 163.)

Phoenix. Union. Whaling ship, 404 tons. Out of New London, Conn. Was to be used to obstruct the Savannah River Bar or Tybee Island Bar. Lost its rudder, began leaking, and was towed to a beach and sunk as a breakwater off Tybee Island in early December 1861. (*ORN*, 12:418; ser. 2, 1:177; *DANFS*, 5:430, 433; Spence, *List*, 719–20.)

Republic (*USS Mobile*) (*Tennessee*) (*USS Tennessee*). U.S. Wooden hull, iron framed side-wheel steamer, 1,149 or 1,275 bulk tons; 1,500 or 852 tons. Length 210 feet, beam 33 feet 11 inches, draft 12 feet, depth 19 feet. Cargo of $400,000 in gold and silver coins, also freight, including cloth, ceramic religious goods, bottled foodstuffs, chamber pots, dishes, inkwells, slates, shoes, and telescopes. Built in 1854 at Baltimore. En route from New York City for New Orleans as the *Tennessee*. Was captured on April 25, 1862, by Union forces when New Orleans fell. Was commissioned as the USS *Tennessee* on May 2, 1862, with a complement of 217 and two 30-pounders, one rifled 30-pounder, and one rifled 12-pounder. Was renamed USS *Mobile* on September 1, 1864, after the captured Confederate ironclad CSS *Tennessee* became the Union navy ship USS *Tennessee*. Was sold to private interests as the *Republic* on May 12, 1865. Foundered in a hurricane on October 25, 1865, about 100 miles southeast of Savannah, and thirty-four lives were lost. The vessel's three lifeboats and a makeshift raft were recovered with survivors along the East Coast. Was discovered in late July 2003 in about 1,700 feet of water by Odyssey Marine Expeditions, a salvage company led by Greg Stemm and John Morris, in their vessel *Odyssey*. A bottle and piece of wood taken from the wreck were used in a Tampa, Fla., federal court to "arrest" the shipwreck in international waters in order to establish claims for the salvage process. The *Odyssey Explorer* used a remotely operated vehicle (ROV) and salvaged more than fifty thousand rare coins from the wreck by late 2004, including samples of all double eagles ($20 gold pieces) minted between 1850 and 1865 except for an 1856-O. About one-fourth of the specie believed to have been part of the cargo has been recovered. Much of the cargo of consumer items has also been recovered. (*ORN*, ser. 2, 1:221; *MSV*, 231, 307; Vesilind, *Lost Gold of the Republic*, 26–27, 152–57, 185–214, 260–67; Vesilind "Lost Gold Bounty from a Civil War Ship," *National Geographic Magazine*, 108–27.)

CSS *Resolute* (*Ajax*). Confederate. Side-wheel steamer, 322 tons. Complement of seven officers and twenty-eight men. Used as a tender and residence for the crew of the CSS *Savannah*. Collided with the CSS *Macon* on December 12, 1864, about 800 yards from a bluff near a mill at Tweedside on the Savannah River. Ran aground while under fire and hit in the wheel. Was captured and destroyed by Union troops. (*ORN*, 16:486, 489–90; ser. 2, 1:264; Spence, *List*, 659; *WCWN*, 241; *MSV*, 184; *CWC*, 6-292–93.)

CSS *Robert Habersham* (*Haversham*). Confederate. Side-wheel steamer, 173 or 200 tons. Length 135 feet, beam 25 feet. Complement of twenty-five. Built in 1860 at Savannah. Was used to drag the Savannah River. The boiler exploded in the Savannah River at Screven's Ferry in August

1863 with at least eight to ten wounded and possibly all hands killed. The hulk was moved to the Wreck Channel near the fourth spur of Fig Island with the machinery removed. Was permanently removed in January to February 1896 by U.S. Army Corps of Engineers contractor Charles Johnson of Lewes, Del. (*Chief of Engineers Report 1891*, 3:1602–4; *MSV*, 186; Spence, *List*, 645.)

***Santa Clara*.** Union. Brig, 190 tons. Built in 1856 at Eastport, Maine. Was captured by the Confederate privateer *Jefferson Davis*. Was sunk with two other prizes in the Savannah River in November 1861 to block the waterway, probably near Fort Pulaski. (*ORN*, 1:818; *Chief of Engineers Report 1888*, 1017; Spence, *List*, 626.)

***Savannah*.** U.S. Ship. Former Confederate captured during the Civil War and became a Union tinclad. Returned to commerce. Was run into by the steamer *Mayflower* and sank on November 5, 1865, at Hickory Bend in the Savannah River, 28 or 35 miles above Savannah. Was raised and taken to Savannah. (Spence, *List*, 626–27.)

CSS *Savannah*. Confederate. Ironclad steam sloop. Length 150 feet, beam 34 feet, depth 14 feet, draft 12 feet 6 inches, speed 6–7 knots, armor 4 inches iron, 22 inches wood planking. Complement of 27 officers and 154 men, with two 7-inch rifled Brookes and two 6.4-inch rifled Brookes guns. Was launched in 1863 at Savannah. Was burned to prevent its capture on December 21, 1864, in the Savannah River. (*OR*, 44:7, 12, 209, 280, 792, 965; *ORN*, 16:289, 459, 484, 489; ser. 2, 1:266; *DANFS*, 2:565.)

***Sebusticook*.** Union. Ship, 560 or 549 tons. Draft 18 feet. Sunk in 1862 to obstruct the Savannah River. (*DANFS*, 5:430, 433.)

***Silvanus* (*Sylvanus*).** British. Schooner, 9 tons. Crew of nine. Cargo of salt, liquor, and cordage. Out of Nassau, Bahamas. Was chased ashore at Doboy Sound by USS *Huron* after being hit by an 11-inch shell at the waterline on January 2, 1864. The tide came over the vessel, and the crew was captured. (*ORN*, 15:219–21; *SCH*, 424–25.)

***Sophia*.** Union. Schooner. Carried assorted cargo. Sailed from Charleston, S.C. British blockade-runner out of

New Providence, Bahamas. Was captured by the USS *Dan Smith*. Got caught in a storm with the Union prize crew southeast of Cape Henry, Va., with its sails shattered, hull leaking, and the crew short of food, at latitude 36° 35' north, about 200 miles from shore, on May 5, 1863. By May 7, 1863, it had traveled 72 miles farther north. The crew was finally rescued a day later at latitude 38° 30' north, longitude 69° west, by the Italian bark *Aurora* from Messina, en route to New York City. The *Sophia* was left to drift and later was found high and dry and abandoned northeast of Egg Island in Altamaha Sound. (*ORN*, 15:349–50, 354; *WCWN*, 135.)

South America. Union. Bark, 606 tons. Carried 650 tons of stone. Purchased at New Bedford, Mass. Was sunk in early December 1861 off Tybee Island to serve as a jetty and wharf for Union troops. (*ORN*, 12:418; ser. 2, 2:211; *DANFS*, 5:430, 433.)

Standard. Canadian. Brig, 110 tons. Cargo of groceries, medicine, boots, lead, and gun caps. Carried ten people. Out of Windsor, Nova Scotia. Was supposed to be en route to Matamoras, Mexico. In April 1862 it got trapped up the North Newport River off St. Catherine's Island at Mr. Bishop's Landing on Melon Bluff. Was later scuttled at Melon Bluff. (Dickson, "Voyage of Fear and Profit, Part I," *Civil War Times Illustrated*, 14–15; Dickson, "Voyage of Fear and Profit, Part II," *Civil War Times Illustrated*, 32–35.)

Swan. Confederate. Iron screw steamer, 316 tons. Length 135 feet, beam 27 feet, depth 5 feet. Built in 1856 at Wilmington, Del. Was burned and sank at Screven's Ferry at Savannah on December 21, 1864. Was raised in July 1865 and refitted as a passenger and freight steamer. (Spence, *List*, 665.)

Sylph. U.S. Steamer from Hilton Head, N.C. Ran ashore on May 7, 1865, on the Savannah River above and north of Fort Pulaski. Was probably refloated. (Spence, *List*, 675.)

CSS Talomico. Confederate. Side-wheel steamer. Complement of twenty and a battery of two guns. Accidentally sank at Savannah in 1863. (*ORN*, ser. 2, 1:268; *CWC*, 6-311.)

CSS Water Witch (*USS Water Witch*). Union. Side-wheel gunboat, 378 tons. Length 150 feet, beam 23 feet, draft 8 feet 2 inches draft, depth 11 feet 6 inches, speed 7 knots. Complement of 80–55, with one rifled 32-pounder and two 12-pounder howitzers (another source—1864 battery: one rifled 30-pounder, one rifled 12-pounder, and two 12-pounder smoothbores). Built in 1852 at the Washington Navy Yard. Was captured on June 3, 1864, by Lt. Thomas P. Pelot and a force of Confederates from the CSS *Sampson* in Ossabow Sound, about a half-mile north of the mouth of Bradley's River. Lieutenant Pelot was killed in the attack. The Confederates removed the pivot gun, and the vessel remained in the Vernon River at White Bluff until the CSS *Water Witch* was burned on December 19, 1864, to prevent its capture by Union forces. A contract was let between the U.S. government and a contractor in 1866 to raise the vessel. It was probably removed. (*ORN*, 16, 484; 15:468–72; ser. 2, 1:237; Spence, *List*, 660–61; *WCWN*, 24; Chance and Topper, *CSS Nashville*, 100; *CWC*, 6-323.)

William H. Starke. Confederate. Steamer. Cargo of 2,000 bushels of corn and other articles. Sank in the Savannah River on February 3, 1863, in 30 feet of water, 20 miles below Augusta, Ga. (*MSV*, 231, 307; Spence, *List*, 603–4.)

William Jenkins. U.S. Side-wheel steamer, 1,012 or 1,011 tons. Length 209 feet, beam 31 feet 10 inches, depth 15 feet 11 inches, draft 13 feet. Built in 1855 at Baltimore. Caught fire on January 19, 1861, in Savannah at Carlton's Wharf near the gas house. The *William Jenkins* was cut loose from its moorings and moved downstream to the other side of Lamar's Cotton Press. (*MSV*, 231, 307; Spence, *List*, 630.)

➤ VESSELS WITHOUT NAMES

dry dock. Confederate. Floating dry dock. Sank in the middle of Saint Augustus Creek, Thunderbolt River, about a mile from its confluence with the Savannah River. Was removed by the U.S. Army Corps of Engineers in 1880–81 to a depth of 10 feet below low water. (*Annual Report of the Chief of Engineers, 1881*, 1:174–75.)

schooner. Nationality unknown. Cargo of coffee, cigars, blankets, shoes, and other goods. Was run ashore on December 15, 1861, by the USS *Bienville* off St. Andrews and set afire. (*ORN*, 12:402.)

schooner. Nationality unknown. Was destroyed on December 15, 1861, at St. Simon's Bay by the USS *Alabama*. (*ORN,* 12:402, *SCH,* 334–35.)

schooner. Confederate. Was set afire below the Coffee Bluff Confederate battery in the Little Ogeechee River on November 7, 1862, as the USS *Wissahickon* and USS *Dawn* approached. (*ORN,* 13:439–40.)

vessel. Confederate. Was sunk during the Civil War in the Savannah River just upstream of the wreck of the CSS *Ogeechee,* across from the Savannah City Exchange. (*Chief of Engineers Report 1888,* 1017.)

vessel. Confederate. Sank during the Civil War in the Savannah River North Channel, opposite the upper end of Elba Island. Was probably removed by the U.S. Army Corps of Engineers in the 1870s. (*Annual Report for the Fiscal Year Ended June 30, 1872,* 2:653.)

vessels. Confederate. About sixty vessels including those in the previous entry were sunk in the Savannah River below the head of Elba Island by Confederate forces in order to block the channel. The area became known as the "obstructions." Twenty of these wrecks were removed in 1866 by Henry S. Welles, a contractor for the U.S. Army Corps of Engineers. Three vessels and parts of one vessel were removed in 1873 by the U.S. Army Corps of Engineers from the upper end of Elba Island in the Savannah River. (*Chief of Engineers Report 1873,* 69; and *Chief of Engineers Report 1888,* 1017.)

vessels. Confederate. Four hulks were sunk by Confederates with ballast in a narrow channel just below Fort Pulaski in the Savannah River in November 1861 to keep Union vessels from approaching and shelling Fort Pulaski. (*New York Times,* December 10, 1861; *DANFS,* 5:433.)

vessels. Confederate. Two vessels captured by Confederates were sunk with the captured prize *Santa Clara* in the Savannah River in November 1861 to block the waterway, probably near Fort Pulaski. (*ORN,* 1:818; *Chief of Engineers Report 1888,* 1017; Spence, *List,* 626.)

Gulf of Mexico

Blockade-runners used the Gulf of Mexico to travel between Cuba and the Bahamas to Confederate ports at New Orleans and Mobile as well as to small Texas, Louisiana, and Florida ports and harbors.

C. Vanderbilt (*Black Hawk*) (*Black Joker*). British. Side-wheel steamer, 346 bulk tons. Length 170 feet 7 inches, beam 23 feet 4 inches, draft 9 feet. Cargo of coffee, zinc, sheet copper, oil, and pepper. Built in 1837 at New York City. En route to New Orleans from Havana, Cuba. Foundered in the Gulf of Mexico on March 15, 1862. Officially, it was traveling to Matamoras, Mexico. One lifeboat from the vessel was found beached near Pensacola, Fla., by the USS *Maria A. Wood*. The lifeboat contained seventeen people, mostly crew members except for one fifteen-year-old girl and two adult male passengers. (*ORN,* 17:125; 18:86–87, 91, 101, 121; *LLC,* 291.)

Enterprise (*America*). Confederate. Side-wheel steamer, 372 bulk tons. Length 172 feet 2 inches, beam 26 feet 6 inches, draft 8 feet 6 inches. Built in 1852 at Brownsville, Pa. Was lost in a storm in the Gulf of Mexico about March 15, 1862. (*MSV,* 9; *LLC,* 298.)

Pizzaro. Confederate. Steamer, 419 bulk tons. Length 190 feet, beam 25 feet 4 inches, draft 9 feet. Cleared the New Orleans Custom House on December 11, 1861, and vanished. Was probably lost in a storm in the Gulf of Mexico. (*MSV,* 174; *LLC,* 316.)

Soler (*Worcester*). Spanish. Side-wheel steamer, 605 bulk tons. Built in 1841 at New York City as the *Worcester*. En route to Mobile. Was lost in the Gulf of Mexico in mid-June 1863. (*MSV,* 234; *LLC,* 321.)

Swan. Union. Side-wheel steamer, 487 bulk tons. Length 188 feet, beam 36 feet 6 inches, draft 7 feet 7 inches. Foundered on February 19, 1863, between Key West and New Orleans. Formerly a Confederate steamer captured by the USS *Amanda* and USS *Bainbridge* on May 24, 1862. (*MSV,* 300; *LLC,* 322.)

William V. Gillum. Union. Stern-wheel steamer, 70 tons. Cargo of lumber. Built in 1855 at New Albany, Ind. En route from New Orleans to Matamoras, Mexico. Wrecked in the Gulf of Mexico on September 1, 1864. Its officers and crew were picked up a few days later by the Mexican schooner *Cory.* (*WPD,* 490.)

Yorktown. Confederate. Side-wheel steamer, 298 bulk tons. Length 173 feet, beam 28 feet 3 inches, depth 6 feet 6 inches. Sprang a leak after clearing Mobile. Foundered on August 26, 1862. Twenty-six men, aboard two boats, were rescued by the schooner *Annie Clapp,* 72 miles southeast of Ship Island, and were released 10 miles off Mobile Point so they could make their way back to their home port. (*ORN,* 19:238–40; *LLC,* 327.)

Illinois

Illinois is bounded on the west by the Mississippi River, on the south by the Ohio River, and on the east for more than one hundred miles by the Wabash River. These rivers saw many wrecks during the Civil War. Cairo, a major Union naval base, is located at the confluence of the Ohio and Mississippi rivers. Vessels listed as being lost at Cairo may be either in the Ohio River or the Mississippi River. There are separate listings for vessels lost in Lake Michigan, the Mississippi River, and the Ohio River.

Advance. Union. Stern-wheel towboat steamer, 39 tons. Built in 1862 at Franklin, Pa. Snagged on February 6, 1863, in the Wabash River at Hutsonville. (*MSV,* 3, 239.)

Annie Mae. U.S. Side-wheel steamer, 31 tons. Built in 1864 at Reed Landing, Minn. Was burned on August 1, 1865, at Kingston. (*MSV,* 11, 242.)

Dan Pollard. Union. Stern-wheel steamer, 77 tons. Built in 1857 at McKeesport, Pa. Snagged on August 3, 1864, at Cairo. (*MSV,* 50, 254.)

Fannie Fisk. Union. Side-wheel steamer, 97 tons. Built in 1856 at Howard, Wis. Was burned on July 16, 1865, at Cairo. (*MSV,* 70, 260.)

John Gault. Union. Stern-wheel steamer, 198 tons. Built in 1857 at Louisville, Ky. Foundered on March 15, 1862, at Cairo. (*MSV,* 113, 272.)

Minnesota Belle. Union. Side-wheel steamer, 225 tons. Built in 1854 at California, Pa. Snagged on March 28, 1862, in the Illinois River at Liverpool. (*MSV,* 146, 281; *WPD,* 323.)

Indiana

Indiana is bounded on the south by the Ohio River, which contains a number of wrecks. Shipwrecks listed in this section are in the Wabash and Tippecanoe rivers.

Caroline. U.S. Stern-wheel steamer, 122 tons. Built in 1858 at Parkersburg, Va. (now W. Va.). Was sunk by ice on Jan-

uary 1, 1861, in the Wabash River at Terre Haute. (*MSV,* 30, 248.)

Greenville. Union. Stern-wheel steamer, 105 tons. Built in 1857 at Evansville, Ind. Snagged on June 6, 1861, in the Wabash River at Terre Haute. (*MSV,* 89, 265; *WPD,* 199.)

Lady Walton. Union. Stern-wheel steamer, 150 tons. Built in 1858 at Cincinnati. Captured from Confederates on June 6, 1863, by the USS *Tyler* at the mouth of the Red River. Collided with the *Norman* at Warsaw, Ind., in the Tippecanoe River on August 2, 1864, and was lost. (*MSV*, 124, 275; *CWC*, 6-259.)

Union. U.S. Side-wheel steamer, 139 tons. Built in 1857 at Louisville, Ky. Snagged on April 2, 1861, at Clinton in the Wabash River. (*MSV*, 218, 303.)

Indian Ocean

Amanda. Union. Bark, 598 tons. Cargo of hemp and sugar. Out of Bangor, Maine, or Boston. En route from Manila, Philippines, to Queenstown, Ireland. Was captured and burned on November 6, 1863, by CSS *Alabama* in the East Indies or Indian Ocean. (*ORN*, 2:502, 707, 779; 3:681; Semmes, *Service Afloat*, 688–89; Hearn, *Gray Raiders*, 210.)

Delphine. Union. Bark, 705 tons. Cargo of rice. Out of Bangor, Maine. En route for Akyab, Burma from London. Was captured and burned by CSS *Shenandoah* in the Indian Ocean on December 29, 1864. Six of its crew became crewmen on the CSS *Shenandoah*. (*ORN*, 3:760, 787, 807; Shomette, *Civil War Shipwrecks*, 185; Hearn, *Gray Raiders*, 272.)

Emma Jane. Union. Ship, 1,097 tons. Out of Bath, Maine. En route from Bombay, India for Amherst. In ballast after it was unable to get a cargo because of news that a Confederate commerce raider was nearby. Built in 1854 at Bath. Was captured and burned by the CSS *Alabama* on January 14, 1864, off Malabar in the Bay of Bengal at latitude 7° 59' south, longitude 76° 4' 45" east. (*ORN*, 2:630, 795; 3:681; Semmes, *Service Afloat*, 723; Hearn, *Gray Raiders*, 218; Summersell, *Boarding Officer*, 173–74.)

Kentucky

Most Civil War wrecks in Kentucky are located in the Ohio River and Mississippi River sections of this book. Only wrecks in other rivers and streams are found in this section.

Clara Poe. Union. Stern-wheel steamer, 208 tons. Length 149 feet, beam 32 feet, depth 4 feet 9 inches. Built in 1859 at California, Pa. Was burned by Confederates on April 15 or 17, 1865, at Eddyville on the Cumberland River. (*MSV*, 38, 251; *WPD*, 99.)

Ed Air. U.S. Screw steamer, 35 tons. Built in 1863 at Cincinnati. Was stranded on December 1, 1865, at Big Bone. (*MSV*, 60, 257.)

Hanging Rock. Confederate. Stern-wheel steamer, 96 tons. Built in 1859 at Portsmouth, Ohio. Was stranded on November 14, 1861, at Cannelton, Ky. The engine was salvaged and put in the *Minnie*. (*MSV*, 91, 266; *WPD*, 206.)

Henry Fitzhugh. Union. Stern-wheel steamer, 217 tons. Built in 1857 at Cincinnati. Previously sunk at Shawneetown and raised. Laid up at the mouth of the Licking River. On September 5, 1864, the Licking River flooded and overturned the *Henry Fitzhugh*, with the cabin floating free. See in the Ohio River section. (*MSV*, 94, 266; *WPD*, 211.)

J. C. Irwin. Union. Stern-wheel steamer, 145 tons. Built in 1864 at Wyandotte, Ks. and completed in June 1864 at Leavenworth, Ks. The boilers exploded at Big Eddy Towhead, 10 miles above Eddyville on the Cumberland River. Captain Smith, John Elliott Hask, the pilot, the mate, three deckhands, a watchman, and four passengers died. (*WPD*, 230.)

Lebanon No. 2. Union. Stern-wheel steamer, 254 tons. Built in 1862. Snagged on June 24, 1863, at Big Hurricane. (*MSV*, 126, 276; *WPD*, 281.)

Nellie Moore. Union. Stern-wheel steamer, 226 tons. Built in 1863 at Cincinnati. Was stranded on November 25, 1863, at Cumberland Island. (*MSV*, 154, 284.)

▷ **VESSELS WITHOUT NAMES**

wharf boat. Union. Was burned with government stores by Confederates in August 1864 at Owensboro. (*ORN*, 26:532.)

Lake Erie

Lake Erie was a commercial link between Canada and the United States. In 1864 Confederate spies planned to capture the only Union military vessel on Lake Erie, the USS *Michigan,* and free Confederate prisoners in the prisoner-of-war camp on Johnson's Island. Although the Confederates captured and sank the vessels *Island Queen* and *Philo Parsons,* they failed to capture the USS *Michigan.* The Confederate raiders fled to Canada when their plot failed. Other vessels were lost on Lake Erie in accidents and storms.

Amily. Canadian. Screw steamer. Sank in October 1864 off Long Point, Ontario. (*EAS*, 234.)

Belle. Canadian. Schooner. Foundered in November 1864 off Long Point, Ontario. (*EAS*, 236.)

B. F. Bruce. Union. Screw steamer, 168 tons. Built in 1852 at Buffalo, N.Y. Burned in August 1862 at Port Stanley, Ontario. (*MSV*, 16, 244.)

Cataract. Union. Screw steamer, 393 tons. Built in 1852 at Buffalo, N.Y. Burned on June 16, 1861, at Erie, Pa., with four killed. (*MSV*, 31, 248; *EAS*, 238.)

City of Buffalo. Union. Screw steamer, 2,026 tons. Built in 1857 at Buffalo, N.Y. Sank in November 1864 off Long Point, Ontario. Was probably raised but was lost in 1866. (*MSV*, 37, 250; *EAS*, 239.)

Euphrates. Union. Screw steamer, 587 tons. Built in 1856 at Buffalo, N.Y. Was stranded in May 1862 at Sandusky, Ohio. (*MSV*, 67, 259.)

Fox. Union. Steamer, 102 tons. Built in 1851 at Buffalo, N.Y. Burned in October 1863, near Newport, Mich. (*MSV*, 75, 261.)

Illinois. U.S. Screw steamer, 530 tons. Built in 1849 at Buffalo, N.Y. Sank following a collision with the *Dean Richmond* on June 28, 1865, near Pelee Point, Ontario. (*MSV*, 100, 268.)

Island Queen. Union. Side-wheel steamer, 168 or 173 tons. Cargo of 30 tons of pig iron. Built in 1855 at Kelley's Island, Ohio. Carried 125 unarmed passengers and 32 Union soldiers. Captured on September 19, 1864, at Middle Bass Island by Confederate raiders in the *Philo Parsons.* They had planned to capture the USS *Michigan,* the only Union military ship on Lake Erie. The vessel's engineer was shot in the face and 1 passenger was cut with a hatchet. The captured crew and passengers were left on Middle Bass Island. The *Island Queen* was towed to deep water beyond Ballast Island, and sunk on a shoal. Was later raised and converted to a barge. (*OR*, 39:2:427–28; 43:2:128–29, 226–28, 234, 236–37, 239, 244–45; *MSV*, 104; *CWC*, 6-282.)

Ogdensburg. Union. Screw steamer, 352 tons. Built in 1852 at Ohio City, Ohio. Collided with the schooner *Snow Bird* at Fairport, Ohio. on September 30, 1864, and sank. (*MSV*, 161, 286; *EAS*, 257.)

Philo Parsons. Union. Side-wheel steamer, 221 or 222 tons. Carried 40 passengers. Built in 1861 at Algonac, Mich. En route from Detroit to Sandusky. Captured by 18–25

Confederate raiders in civilian clothes on September 19, 1864. The Confederate raiders wanted to capture the USS *Michigan* and free Confederate prisoners at Johnson's Island off Sandusky, Ohio. The Confederates boarded the *Philo Parsons* at Malden, Ontario, and later captured the *Island Queen*. The crew and passengers were put ashore on Fighting Island on September 20, 1864. The Confederate raiders cut the pipes and scuttled the *Philo Parsons* at a dock at Sandwich, Ontario, on September 20, 1864. The Confederates intended to burn the vessel but did not. (*OR*, 43:2:128–29, 226–28, 234–39, 242–45; *MSV*, 172; *CWC*, 6-282.)

Pocahontas. Union. Screw steamer, 426 tons. Built in 1846 at Buffalo, N.Y. Was stranded on May 27, 1862, at Long Point, Ontario. (*MSV*, 175, 290.)

Racine. Union. Screw steamer, 157 tons. Built in 1856 at Cleveland. Was burned on August 10, 1864, at Rondeau, Ontario, with thirteen killed. (*MSV*, 181, 292.)

Return. Schooner. Foundered in 1863 off Long Point, Ontario. (*EAS*, 261.)

William S. Bull. Union. Screw steamer, 16 tons. Built in 1861 at Buffalo, N.Y. Foundered on August 20, 1863, about 40 miles from Erie, Pa. (*MSV*, 232, 307.)

Winslow. Union. Screw steamer, 265 tons. Built in 1862 at Cleveland, Ohio. Collided with another vessel on November 1, 1864, and sunk at Cleveland, Ohio. (*MSV*, 210, 307.)

Lake Huron

The Civil War wrecks on Lake Huron were the result of accidents. Lake Huron was a route of commerce between the United States and Canada.

Kelloha. Union. Side-wheel steamer, 396 tons. Built in 1858 at Newport, Mich. Was stranded on August 22, 1862. (*MSV*, 120, 274.)

Kenosha. Union. Screw steamer, 645 tons. Built in 1856 at Cleveland. Burned on October 26, 1864, at Sarnia, Ontario. (*MSV*, 120, 274.)

Keystone State. Union. Side-wheel steamer, 1,354 tons. Cargo of hardware, crockery, farm implements, glassware, and $3,000–$9,000 in gold in a safe. Built in 1849 at Buffalo, N.Y. Sank at latitude 44° 4' north, longitude 83° west on October 30, 1861. Thought to be located 3–3.5 miles northeast of Port Austin, near Saginaw Bay, Mich. (*MSV*, 121, 274; Nesmith and Potter, *Treasure*, 131.)

Pewabic. Union. Screw steamer, 350 or 738 tons. Cargo of 250–300 tons of copper ingots and ore, $40,000–$50,000 in the safe ($250,000 gold and silver specie according to one story which proved to be false), and 175–80 passengers. Built in 1863 at Cleveland. Sank in upper Lake Huron in 120–80 feet of water with 125 killed when the *Pewabic* was rammed by the *Meteor*, its sister ship, off Thunder Bay near Aplena, Mich., on August 8–9, 1864, at latitude 45° 6' north, longitude 83° 13' west. Currents are extremely treacherous in this area. At least 10 divers have died on this wreck: 1 in 1865, 3 between 1880 and 1884, 1 in 1891, and 5 in a diving bell in 1895. Some copper was reportedly recovered in the early dives. A 1917 salvage attempt recovered 70 tons of copper, beer, clothing, rings, a revolver, gold coins, shoes, and the safe. Some paper money in the safe was Confederate and only $5 was recognizable. (*MSV*, 171, 289; Wrigley, "Treasure Ships of the Great Lakes," *Treasure Search*, 77; Rieseberg, *Guide to Buried Treasure*, 60; Remick, "Treasure Ships of Lake Huron," *True Treasure*, 37–39; Hollister, "Sunken Treasure of the Great Lakes," *Western Treasures*, 25.)

Water Witch. Union. Screw steamer, 369 tons. Carried a mixed cargo. Built in 1862 at Newport, Mich. Sank, with twenty lives lost, in October 1863 at latitude 44° 25' north, longitude 83° 19' west. Thought to be located less than 2 miles off Oscoda, Mich., near Saginaw Bay. (*MSV*, 305; Nesmith and Potter, *Treasure*, 131.)

Lake Michigan

Lake Michigan served as a link between Illinois, Michigan, Wisconsin, and Canada. Wrecks on Lake Michigan resulted from storms and accidents.

Alvin Clark. Union. Two-mast schooner. Length 110 feet. Sank on June 29, 1864, in Green Bay. Found in 1967 in 110 feet of water by Frank Hoffman, of Egg Harbor, Wis. The silt was pumped out, and the vessel was raised by cables on July 29, 1969. No conservation was done on the recovered wreck. It rotted away on shore. In 1995 it was bulldozed and taken to the dump. (Burgess, *Sinkings, Salvages, and Shipwrecks,* 152–53.)

Black Hawk. Union. Brig. Cargo of $4,000 in specie and stained glass. Foundered during a gale in November 1862 off Point Betsie near latitude 44° 42' north, longitude 86° 16' west. (Nesmith and Potter, *Treasure,* 130.)

M. Fannie Stafford. U.S. screw steamer, 42 tons. Built in 1863 at Buffalo, N.Y. Exploded on June 19, 1865, at Chicago. (*MSV,* 133, 278.)

Minnesota. Union. Side-wheel steamer, 749 tons. Built in 1851 at Maumee, Ohio. Was stranded on September 27, 1861, at Green Bay, Wis. (*MSV,* 146, 281.)

Torch Lake. Union. Screw steamer, 20 tons. Built in 1860 at Cleveland. Foundered in November 1864 at Sturgeon Bay, Wis. (*MSV,* 214, 302.)

Lake Superior

Lake Superior had less commerce than the other Great Lakes and had only one major wreck during the Civil War.

Sunbeam. Union. Side-wheel passenger steamer, 398 tons. Cargo of 112 barrels of whiskey and $10,000 in specie. Built in 1861 at Manitowoc, Wis. Foundered during a storm in 22 fathoms on August 28, 1863, off Keweenaw Point, 2 miles east of Copper Harbor or Eagle Harbor, Mich., at latitude 47° 29' north, longitude 87° 47.8' west. (*MSV,* 205, 299; Nesmith and Potter, *Treasure,* 129; Hollister, "Sunken Treasure of the Great Lakes," *Western Treasures,* 23.)

Louisiana

With the great Mississippi River running through it to the Gulf of Mexico, Louisiana was a key state in international and regional trade from the heartland of the United States. The port city of New Orleans became the target of one of the first Union efforts to close a major Confederate port by capturing it. The people of New Orleans hoped that Fort Jackson and Fort St. Philip could hold back the Yankees, as Gen. Andrew "Old Hickory" Jackson had saved New Orleans from capture by the British during the War of 1812.

At the Battle of the Forts, also known as the Battle of New Orleans, Flag Officer David G. Farragut's Union navy easily cut through the boom across the Mississippi River, steamed past the forts, and outfought the Confederate fleet before daylight on April 24, 1862. The victorious Union fleet proceeded up to New Orleans. New Orleans, the greatest Confederate port and largest city, was captured and occupied by the Union navy. During and after the Battle of the Forts, the Confederate vessels

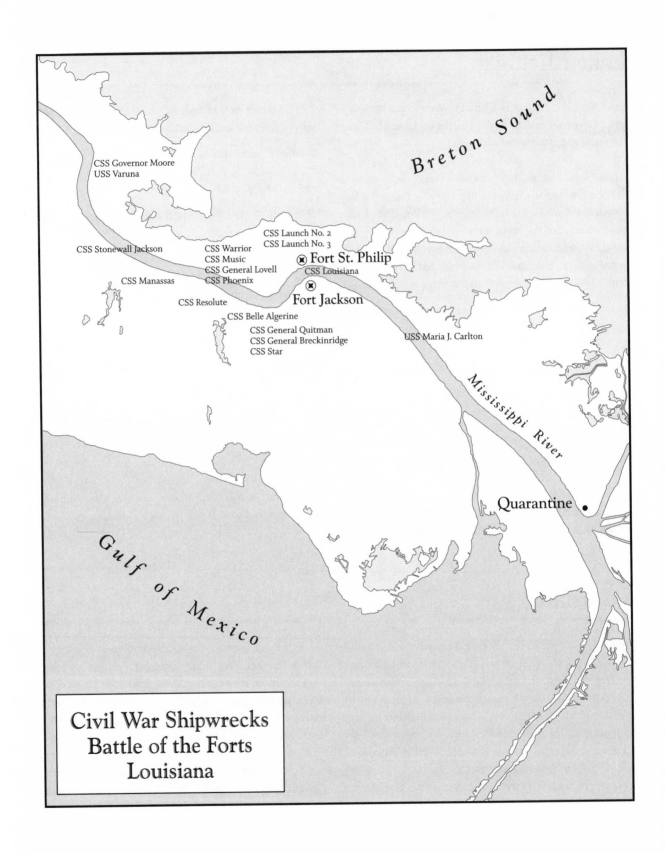

CSS Governor Moore
USS Varuna

Breton Sound

CSS Launch No. 2
CSS Launch No. 3

CSS Stonewall Jackson

CSS Warrior
CSS Music
CSS General Lovell
CSS Phoenix

ⓧ Fort St. Philip

CSS Louisiana

CSS Manassas

CSS Resolute

ⓧ Fort Jackson

CSS Belle Algerine

CSS General Quitman
CSS General Breckinridge
CSS Star

USS Maria J. Carlton

Mississippi River

Quarantine ●

Gulf of Mexico

Civil War Shipwrecks
Battle of the Forts
Louisiana

lost included the CSS *Anglo-Norman*, CSS *Belle Algerine*, CSS *General Breckinridge*, CSS *Carondolet*, CSS *General Quitman*, CSS *Governor Moore*, CSS *Launch No. 2*, CSS *Launch No. 3*, CSS *Louisiana*, CSS *Manassas*, CSS *Mosher*, CSS *Music*, CSS *Pamlico*, CSS *Phoenix*, CSS *Pioneer*, CSS *Resolute*, CSS *Stonewall Jackson*, and CSS *Warrior*. The Union losses, the USS *Maria J. Carlton* and USS *Varuna*, were insignificant.

Confederate vessels fled up the Mississippi River to the Red River, Yazoo River, Big Black River, and other smaller tributaries to escape capture by Flag Officer David G. Farragut's Union fleet. The Mississippi River became a Union waterway, with the Rebel vessels confined to shallow bayous and tributaries. In April 1863 Union forces attacked Confederate troops in Bayou Teche and Bayou Fusilier causing the destruction of the Confederate vessels *Uncle Tommy*, CSS *Hart*, CSS *Darby*, and *Blue Hammock*.

The Red River Expedition in 1864 under Maj. Gen. Nathaniel P. Banks ended in disaster for the Union army at the battles of Mansfield, or Sabine Cross Roads, and Pleasant Hill. Cut off from much of the Union army, the Union fleet in the Red River was forced to fight its way back to the Mississippi River. Construction of wing dams in the Red River at Alexandria enabled the Union fleet to escape the abnormally low water. Union losses in the Red River Campaign included the USS *Champion No. 3*, USS *Champion No. 6*, USS *Covington*, USS *Eastport*, USS *John Warner*, *Pauline*, USS *Signal*, and *Woodford*, while Confederate losses included the *City Belle*, *Countess*, and *New Falls City*.

One of the last Confederate naval actions in the Civil War was the CSS *Webb* escaping from the Red River down the Mississippi River past New Orleans and dozens of Union warships before being scuttled on April 25, 1865. Wrecks in this section include wrecks in the Mississippi River below Louisiana's boundary with Mississippi.

Anglo-American. Union. Steamboat. Was captured and burned on June 18, 1863, by Confederate forces in Col. James P. Major's 2nd Texas Cavalry Brigade while assisting the steamer *Sykes*, which was stuck on a pile in the Bayou Plaquemine. (*OR*, 26:1:46, 191–92, 216, 567–68, 589; *ORN*, 20:235–36, 239–40, 304–6, 309.)

CSS Anglo-Norman. Confederate. Side-wheel steamer, 558 tons. Length 175 feet 2 inches, beam 29 feet 5 inches, draft 9 feet. Complement of thirty-five to eighty, with one 32-pounder and possibly another gun. Built in 1850 at Algiers, La. Burned at New Orleans on April 27, 1862, before the city fell to Flag Officer David G. Farragut. Listed as a Union prize on May 1, 1862, so it may not have been completely destroyed. (*ORN*, 18:249–50, 252; *MSV*, 10, 242; *DANFS*, 2:498.)

USS Antelope (Antelope). Union. Side-wheel tinclad steamer, 173 tons. Length 264 feet, beam 34 feet, draft 3 feet. Armed with two 30-pounder Parrotts on the bow and four 24-pounders broadside. Built in 1853 at New Albany, Ind. Went down the Mississippi River to relieve the USS *Meteor* at Pass a l'Outre on the night of September 23, 1864. Its pumps could not keep up with the vessel's leaks. The USS *Antelope* may also have hit a snag which increased the water influx. Ran ashore on the west bank of the Mississippi River about 7 miles below New Orleans and sank. Was stripped and its guns removed. Was later salvaged and broken up. (*ORN*, 21:658–60; ser. 2, 1:36; *MSV*, 11, 242; *WCWN*, 180.)

Argus. Confederate. Steamer. Used to transport Gen. Dick Taylor's Confederate troops. Captured along with its captain and one crewman by twenty Union sailors from the USS *Osage* on October 7, 1863, while at anchor in the Red River. The vessel was burned when it was unable to cross Red River Bar and enter the Mississippi River. (*ORN*, 25:450–57, 523; *MSV*, 21; *CWC*, 6-198; *WCWN*, 245.)

USS Arizona (Arizona) (Caroline). Union. Iron side-wheel steamer, 632 bulk tons, 959 tons. Length 200 or 201 feet, beam 34 feet, depth 17 feet 6 inches, loaded draft 8 feet. Complement of ninety-eight, with one 30-pounder Parrott, one rifled 12-pounder, and four 32-pounder smoothbores. Built in 1859 at Wilmington, Del. Captured as the blockade-runner *Caroline* on October 28, 1862, by the USS *Montgomery*. Was accidentally burned on the night of February 27, 1865, 38 miles below New Orleans while coming upriver from Southwest Pass. Drifted and lodged on the west bank of Mississippi River. The USS *Arizona*'s boiler exploded, and four crewmen were lost.

Three water tanks and one mast showed above water after the vessel sank. (*ORN,* 22:57–59; ser. 2, 1:38.)

CSS *Arkansas.* Confederate. Screw ironclad, 2,000 tons. Length 165 feet, beam 35 feet, draft 11 feet 6 inches, speed 8 miles per hour. Complement of 120–80, with two 8-inch guns, four 6-inch guns, one 9-inch Dahlgren, and two rifled 32-pounders (according to some sources, six 8-inch and four rifled 50-pounder guns). Launched in May 1862 at Memphis. Completed at Yazoo City, Miss. Its poor engines constantly broke down. Steamed out of the Yazoo River through the Union navy and docked at Vicksburg, where Cdr. Isaac N. Brown was taken off because of illness. Lt. Henry K. Stevens took over as captain. On August 5, 1862, the CSS *Arkansas,* accompanied by the CSS *Webb* and CSS *Music,* sailed down the Mississippi River to assist the Confederates in their attack on Union forces in Baton Rouge. After a long distance battle with the USS *Essex,* USS *Kineo,* and USS *Katahdin,* the CSS *Arkansas* grounded four miles above Baton Rouge. Its engines were broken up with axes. Shells were placed on the deck between its guns. Was set afire and then drifted downstream for an hour before blowing up. Ten members of the CSS *Arkansas'*s crew were captured. In the mid-1960s the citizens of Baton Rouge wanted to raise the wreck when Russell Light claimed to have located it, but this claim proved to be false. In 1981 Clive Cussler found a magnetic anomaly on the west bank of the Mississippi River and an article indicating that in June 1927 a Civil War wreck had been found in the Thompson Gravel Company Pit, a few miles north of Baton Rouge. This location may be the resting place of the CSS *Arkansas.* (*OR,* pp. 15, 14–15; *ORN,* 19:115–25; ser. 2, 1:248; Pratt, *Western Waters,* 230; *WCWN,* 202; Cussler and Drago, *Sea Hunters,* 103–36.)

A. W. Baker. Confederate. Side-wheel steamer, 112 tons. Length 95 feet, beam 25 feet, depth 4 feet 6 inches. Carried some stores aboard after discharging a cargo at Port Hudson. Built in 1856 at Louisville. Was run ashore on February 3, 1863, to allow some Confederate officers to escape by jumping overboard. Was captured by the USS *Queen of the West* below the mouth of the Red River, along with five army captains, two lieutenants, and a number of Confederate citizens, including seven or eight women. Set fire on February 3, 1863, along with the *Moro* and *Berwick Bay* about 15 miles below the mouth of Red River. (*OR,* 24:1:338–39; *ORN,* 24:217, 224–25; *CWC,* 6-189–90.)

Baltic. Confederate. Side-wheel steamer, 604 tons. Built in 1860 at Algiers, La. Burned on May 6, 1861, at Algiers. (*MSV,* 17, 244.)

USS *Barataria* (CSS *Barataria*). Union. Ironclad side-wheel steamer, 52 or 400 tons. Length 125 feet, draft 3 feet 6 inches, armor 1-inch iron. Battery of two guns. Built in 1857 at Barataria, La. Was captured from the Confederates at New Orleans by the Union army in April 1862. Transferred to the Union navy. Hit a snag in 8 feet of water at the mouth of the Amite River in Lake Maurepas on April 7, 1863, with Col. Thomas S. Clark and a company of the 6th Mich. Infantry Regiment onboard. Members of the 1st Miss. Cavalry Regiment fired on the ship, 50–75 yards from the east shore of the Amite River. The vessel's guns were spiked and the foreword gun dumped overboard. Was set afire by the crew and the magazine was blown up. The Union lost one wounded and two killed. The vessel was located and dived on in recent years. (*OR,* 15:291; *ORN,* 20:123–26, 130–31; ser. 2, 1:43; *MSV,* 18; *CWC,* 6-202; Boyd, "Wreck Facts," *Skin Diver,* 14.)

Belfast. Union. steamboat. Was captured and burned at Bayou Plaquemine by Col. James P. Major's 2nd Tex. Cavalry Brigade on June 18, 1863, during a raid that destroyed the Union steamboats *Anglo-American* and *Sykes,* and two steam flatboats. (*OR,* 26:1:46, 191–92, 216, 567–68, 589; *ORN,* 20:235–36, 239–40, 304–6, 309.)

Bella Donna. U.S. Side-wheel steamer, 152 tons. Length 142 feet, beam 32 feet 2 inches, depth 4 feet 10 inches. Built in 1864 at New Orleans. Snagged and sunk in July 1865, 50 miles below Alexandria. (*MSV,* 19, 245; *WPD,* 41.)

CSS Belle Algerine. Confederate. Screw steam tug. Complement of thirty to forty, with possibly one gun. Was accidentally rammed and sunk by CSS *Governor Moore* on the Mississippi River near Fort Jackson and Fort St. Philip on April 24, 1862, then burned. (*OR,* 6:529; *ORN,* 18:249–50, 252, 297; *CWC,* 6-205.)

Belle Creole. Union. Side-wheel steamer. Length 250 feet, beam 36 feet, depth 7 feet. Burned along with nine boats on May 28, 1864, at New Orleans. (*WPD,* 42.)

Berwick Bay. Confederate. Side-wheel steamer, 64 tons. Cargo of 200 barrels of molasses, 10 hogsheads of sugar, 30,000 pounds of flour, and 40 bales of cotton. Built in 1857 at Plaquemine, La. Captured by the USS *Queen of the West* on February 3, 1863, as the *Berwick Bay* came out of the Red River while en route to Port Hudson. Set afire with the *A. W. Baker* and *Moro* about 15 miles below the mouth of Red River. (*OR,* 24:1:338–39; *ORN,* 24:217, 224–25; *CWC,* 6-205; *WCWN,* 246.)

CSS Bienville. Confederate. Side-wheel gunboat. Armed with five 42-pounders. Launched in February 1862 at Bayou St. John, La. Was destroyed near the wreck of the CSS *Oregon* in the Bogue Falaya River by Confederates in April 1862 before its completion following the fall of New Orleans and the approach of Union forces. (*ORN,* 18:253, 287, 830; *Annual Report of the Secretary of War 1871,* 552; *WCWN,* 219; Pearson, *History of New Orleans District,* 201.)

Bio Bio. Union. Side-wheel steamer, 822 tons. Loaded draft 15 feet, speed 6 miles per hour. Built in 1859 at Boston. Burned on March 22, 1863, at New Orleans. (*OR,* 15:1102; *MSV,* 22, 246.)

Black Hawk. Union. Side-wheel steam transport, 26 tons. Built in 1863 at New Orleans. Ambushed by the 1st La. Regiment on November 21, 1863, at Hay Point, a mile below the mouth of Red River. Ran into a bank, destroying the upper works. May not have been destroyed but was seriously damaged. (*OR,* 26:1:455; *MSV,* 22.)

Black Hawk (Black Hawk No. 2). Union. Side-wheel steamer, 57 or 211 tons. Three boilers. Built in 1859 at Cedar Rapids, Iowa. Previously sank and was raised at the mouth of Bee Creek, Missouri River. Was burned on May 28, 1864, at New Orleans, along with eight other steamers. (*WPD,* 54.)

Blue Hammock. Confederate. Side-wheel steamer, 74 tons. Built in 1855 at Plaquemine, La. Was burned on April 17, 1863, at the confluence of the Bayou Teche and Bayou

Fusilier near Breaux Bridge, to prevent its capture. (*OR,* 15:343; *MSV,* 23.)

Capitola. U.S. Side-wheel steamer, 137 tons. Built in 1860 at Wheeling, Va. (now W. Va.). Snagged on November 15, 1865, at Shreveport. (*MSV,* 29, 248.)

CSS Carondolet. Confederate. Side-wheel steamer, 700 tons. Length 200 feet. Armed with five 42-pounders and one rifled 32-pounder. Launched in 1862 at Bayou St. John, La. Was destroyed by Confederates in April 1862, near Lake Pontchartrain, in the Tchefuncte River (other sources—Bogue Falaya River), a mile below Covington, near the Confederate Navy Yard. Covered by sand, the CSS *Carondolet* became a navigation obstruction; it was probably removed by the U.S. Army Corps of Engineers in 1871. (*ORN,* 18:253; ser. 2, 1:249; *Annual Report of the Secretary of War 1871,* 552; *CWC,* 6-207; Pearson *History of New Orleans District,* 201.)

Ceres. Union. Side-wheel steamer, 217 tons. Length 166 feet, beam 37 feet 6 inches, depth 5 feet. Built in 1853 at Jeffersonville, Ind. Exploded on October 9, 1862, at St. Joseph Island with a loss of twelve lives. (*MSV,* 32, 249; *WPD,* 76.)

USS Champion No. 3 (New Champion). Union. Side-wheel steamer tug / pump boat transport, 195 tons. Carried men, women, and children who were former slaves from Red River plantations, along with two pumps and other material from the USS *Eastport.* Attacked by Capt. Florian O. Cornay's St. Mary's Cannoneers La. Artillery and 200 sharpshooters under Lt. Col. J. H. Caudle from the right bank of Red River, 5 miles above the mouth of Cane River on April 26, 1864. A shell exploded in the boiler, killing Captain Stewart, 3 crewmen, and 172 former slaves. Captain Cornay was killed in the battle. Only 15 people aboard the USS *Champion No. 3* survived the scalding. The ship was sunk by Confederates to block the channel. Was later raised by the Confederates. (*OR,* 34:3:449; *ORN,* 26:87–88, 176, 782, 787; Dimitry, *Confederate Military History,* vol. 10: *Louisiana,* 152–53; *MSV,* 32.)

USS Champion No. 5. Union. Side-wheel steamer tug/pump boat, 184 tons. Built in 1863 at Cincinnati. Attacked by Capt. Florian O. Cornay's and Capt. John T. M. Barnes's

St. Mary's Cannoneers La. Artillery four-gun battery with Lt. Col. J. H. Caudle's sharpshooters on Red River on April 26, 1864, 5 miles above the mouth of the Cane River. The pilot was wounded in the pilothouse, and the vessel became disabled and ran into the left bank, across from the battery. The crew abandoned ship, and most were captured. The ship sank with the hurricane deck and boiler deck below water. (*OR*, 34:3:449; *ORN*, 26:81–88, 176, 782, 787; *MSV*, 249.)

Charmer. U.S. Side-wheel steamer, 667 tons. Built in 1859 at Cincinnati. Burned at Lauderdale on February 10, 1861, with five lives lost. May have been salvaged. (*MSV*, 34, 249; *EAS*, 161.)

City Belle. Union. Side-wheel steamer, 153 tons. Length 179 feet, beam 35 feet, depth 5 feet. Often used as a hospital boat. Built in 1855 at Paducah, Ky. While carrying 425–700 men of the 120th Ohio Infantry Regiment on the way to Alexandria, it was ambushed and hit in the boiler on May 3, 1864, about 20–40 miles above Fort De Russy near Snaggy Point on the Red River. Col. Chauncey J. Bassett of the 73rd U.S. Colored Infantry Regiment was killed. One-third of the Ohio regiment was killed, and about 200 soldiers and Captain Tully escaped by jumping overboard and reaching land. (*OR*, 34:1:211, 475, 622; *ORN*, 26:105, 107, 117, 123, 782; Milligan, *Fresh-Water Navy*, 273; *WPD*, 88; *EAS*, 162.)

City Belle. Confederate. Side-wheel steamer, 215 tons. Built in 1854 at Murraysville, Va. Burned on May 5, 1862, at Alexandria in the Red River. (*MSV*, 250; *EAS*, 162.)

Concordia (Conchita). British. Schooner. Was captured by an armed cutter and gig from the USS *Granite City*. Was set afire at the mouth of Calcasieu River at Calcasieu Pass on October 5, 1863. (*ORN*, 19:227 ; 20:612, 613.)

Conqueror. U.S. Side-wheel steamer, 398 tons. Built in 1847 at New Albany, Ind. Burned on May 10, 1861, at New Orleans. (*MSV*, 44, 252.)

Cora Anderson. U.S. Side-wheel steamer, 658 tons. Length 256 feet, beam 39 feet, depth 8 feet, 3 boilers. Built in 1856 at New Albany, Ind. Snagged on June 18, 1861, in Lake Providence. Previously sunk 40 miles above Vicksburg at Eagle Bend on January 22, 1861. (*MSV*, 46, 253; *WPD*, 111.)

Corrine. U.S. Side-wheel steamer, 83 tons. Exploded and was lost, with fifteen killed, on February 28, 1861, at McDonoughville. (*WPD*, 111.)

CSS Countess. Confederate. Side-wheel steamer, 198 tons. Length 150 feet, beam 30 feet, draft 4 feet 9 inches. Built in 1860 at Cincinnati. Used by Maj. Gen. John G. Walker to evacuate Alexandria. Grounded in the Alexandria Falls, Red River while trying to escape the advancing Union fleet. Set afire on March 15, 1864. (*ORN*, 26:31, 164; *CWC*, 6-217; *MSV*, 47.)

USS Covington (Number 25) (Covington No. 2). Union. Tinclad side-wheel steamer, 224 tons. Length 126 feet, beam 37 feet, depth 6 feet 6 inches. Complement of fourteen officers and sixty-two men, with four 24-pounders, two 30-pounder Parrotts, two 50-pounder Dahlgren rifles, and one 12-pounder. Built in 1862 at Cincinnati. Carried Col. Jacob Sharpe of the 156th N.Y. Volunteer Infantry Regiment and Col. William H. Rayner of the 56th Ill. Infantry Regiment. Was ambushed below Alexandria Falls by Confederate batteries in the Red River on May 5, 1864. The escape pipe was hit, its howitzers disabled, and its guns ran out of ammunition. Ran into the Red River's north bank, downstream from Dunn's Bayou. Cotton around the engine was set afire. Five shells hit the hull, and forty to fifty shells riddled the upper works before it sank. The crew spiked the guns before leaving. Nine officers and twenty-three crewmen escaped. (*OR*, 34:1:622–23; *ORN*, 26:112–23, 127, 134, 172, 174, 772, 782; ser. 2, 1:67; Miller, *Photographic History*, 6:230; Pratt, *Western Waters*, 241; *MSV*, 47; *WCWN*, 166.)

Cricket. Confederate. Ship. Was destroyed in April 1863, in Bayou Teche. (Pearson, *History of New Orleans District*, 178.)

CSS Darby. Confederate. Steamer. Armed with three guns, including a 32-pounder brass gun. Used to transport stores, ordnance, and troops. Was burned on April 17, 1863, on Bayou Teche near Bayou Fusilier above Beaux Bridge to prevent its capture. (*OR*, 15:343; *CWC*, 6-218.)

CSS Defiance. Confederate. Side-wheel steam gunboat ram, 544 tons. Length 178 feet, beam 29 feet 5 inches, depth 10 feet 11 inches. Complement of thirty to seventy-five, with one 32-pounder smoothbore pivoted aft and possibly a second gun. Built in 1849 at Cincinnati. Without firing a shot, Capt. John K. Mitchell and his crew abandoned the vessel, cutting the supply pipes and setting it afire on April 28, 1862, at the Battle of the Forts. The captain may have been drunk, as his vessel took no active role in the engagement. (*ORN*, 18:249–50, 252, 297, 309–10, 439; ser. 2, 1:251; *CWC*, 6-220.)

Delphina. Confederate. Schooner. Cargo of 180 bales of Texas cotton. Was destroyed on the night of January 22, 1865, by the USS *Chocora*'s launch and first cutter with 40 men under Lt. Cdr. Richard W. Meade Jr., when coming down the Calcasieu River near Calcasieu Pass. Ran ashore on one-foot-deep flats at low tide near a beach. Unable to escape, the vessel and six crewmen were captured. Eighty cotton bales were thrown overboard, and thirty were recovered by Union vessels at sea on January 23. (*ORN*, 22:19; Porter, *Naval History*, 777–78.)

USS *De Soto* (*De Soto*) (*General Lyon*). Union. Side-wheel steamer, 1,675 bulk tons, 1,200 tons. Length 253 feet, beam 38 feet, depth 26 feet, draft 26 feet, speed 8–11 knots, armor of cotton and iron. Launched in 1860 at Brooklyn, N.Y. Probably was the Confederate steamer *De Soto* captured at Island No. 10 on April 8, 1862. Also called the *General Lyon*. While towing a coal barge, the USS *De Soto* lost a rudder and drifted 15 miles down Red River with Confederate boats nearby. Was burned with the coal barge by Capt. Charles R. Ellet of the *Era No. 5* near Fort Taylor above Gordon's Landing on February 14, 1863, on the Red River. Was raised and later sold on September 30, 1865, at New York City. (*OR*, 24:1:343, 346; 24, Part 3:833; *ORN*, 24:385, 398–400; ser. 2, 1:74; *CWC*, 6-219; *WCWN*, 70–71.)

Dewdrop. Confederate. Schooner. Was towed ashore and burned by the USS *Owasco* in the Mississippi River below New Orleans on April 29, 1862. (*ORN*, 18:384.)

D. H. Blunk. U.S. Stern-wheel steamer, 98 tons. Built in 1863 at Portsmouth, Ohio. Snagged on November 19, 1865, at Brown's Landing. (*MSV*, 49, 254.)

CSS *Diana* (*Diana*). Confederate. Side-wheel ironclad gunboat, 239 tons. Armed with five Parrott guns. Built in 1858 at Brownsville, Pa. Captured by the Union navy gunboat USS *Cayuga* on April 27, 1862. Converted to a Union transport. Recaptured with part of the 12th Conn. and 160th N.Y. Infantry regiments onboard on March 28, 1863, by Confederate batteries on the Atchafalaya River near Bayou Teche and Pattersonville, with six killed, including Acting Master T. L. Peterson, and three wounded in a two-hour battle. Another report says there were four killed, fourteen wounded, and ninety-nine missing. Used by Confederate forces in actions on Bayou Teche and at Camp Bisland under Lt. T. D. Nettles. Capt. O. J. Semmes then took command. A 30-pound Union shell exploded in the engine room, killing two engineers and damaging the engines on April 12, 1863. The damage was repaired, and the CSS *Diana* steamed up to Franklin to support Confederate forces. When Confederate troops retreated, the vessel stayed behind at a burning bridge before being destroyed by Confederate forces in Grand Lake on April 14, 1863, to prevent its capture. Channel clearing by the U.S. Army Corps of Engineers probably removed the CSS *Diana* prior to 1872. (*OR*, 15:290, 297, 389, 390, 392; *ORN*, 20:131, 135; ser. 2, 1:74; *CWC*, 6-220–21; Carnahan, *4000 Civil War Battles*, 111; *EAS*, 165; Pearson, *History of New Orleans District*, 236.)

CSS *Dolly Webb* (*Dollie Webb*) (*Webb*). Confederate. Stern-wheel steamer, 139 tons. Length 125 feet, beam 27 feet, draft 4 feet 6 inches. Complement of up to two hundred, with five guns. Built in 1859 at Wheeling, Va. (now W. Va.). Burned on May 5, 1861, at Algiers but was probably repaired. (*CWC*, 6-222; *WCWN*, 229.)

CSS *Doubloon*. Confederate. Side-wheel steamer, 293 tons. Length 171 feet 10 inches or 165 feet, beam 33 feet or 33 feet 7 inches, draft 5 feet. Built in 1859 at Cincinnati. Was scuttled in Red River in May 1864. Was raised and repaired. (*WCWN*, 246; *WPD*, 132.)

Drover. Confederate. Side-wheel steam ferry, 26 tons. Built in 1862 at Wheeling, Va. (W. Va.). Was probably sunk at Shreveport to block the Red River in May 1864. Was probably raised. (*WPD*, 133.)

USS *Eastport*. Union. Ironclad steam gunboat, 570, 700, or 800 tons. Length 280 feet, beam 43 or 32 feet, draft 6 feet 3 inches. Armed with four 9-inch Dahlgren smoothbores, two rifled 60-pounder Dahlgrens, and two 100-pounder

Parrotts. Built in 1862 at New Albany, Ind. Originally captured from the Confederates while being converted into an ironclad at Cerro Gordo, Tennessee. A Confederate torpedo under the bow shattered its hull eight miles below Grand Ecore on April 15, 1864. The leak was not noticed for several hours and it took five hours to sink. Was refloated two days later by the USS *Champion No. 3* and USS *Champion No. 6*. Was moved 62 miles downstream. Its guns and heavy articles were removed to lighten the vessel because of a falling river. The lightened USS *Eastport* grounded eight times. A determined Lt. Cdr. S. Ledyard Phelps succeeded in refloating his vessel seven times. Was finally grounded in low water, 8 miles below Natchitoches in the Red River. It was so damaged on a bed of logs that it was blown up by 3,000 pounds of gunpowder with seven different explosions, about 1.5 miles above Montgomery and a short distance (20 miles) above the mouth of Cane River on April 26, 1864, after the Union naval force was attacked by fifteen hundred Confederates. Two pumps, parts of the machinery, and guns were removed but were later captured when the USS *Champion No. 5* surrendered to the Confederates. Its armor plating was also removed. The U.S. Army Corps of Engineers located the wreck under about 50–60 feet of sand, silt, and fill by a magnetometer and investigated the wreck in 1995 as part of the Red River navigation project. Some material was recovered. (*OR*, 34:1:190, 206, 403, 585; 34:3:174, 449; *ORN*, 26:62–63, 68–79, 86, 110, 167–70, 781; ser. 2, 1:77; *CWC*, 6-223; Pratt, *Western Waters*, 230; Longmire, "Vicksburg Discovers Civil War 'Treasure,'" *Engineer Update*, 4; Magruder, "Divers Explore Underwater Antiques," *Engineer Update*, 5; Patrick, *Legacy Resource Management Program*.)

Editor. Union. Side-wheel steamer, 246 tons. Built in 1851 at Brownsville, Pa. Burned on May 6, 1861, at Algiers. (*MSV*, 60, 257.)

Edward F. Dix. U.S. Side-wheel steamer, 296 tons. Length 266 feet, beam 40 feet, depth 5 feet 6 inches. Built in 1864 at Madison, Ind. Was burned by Confederate agents on July 15, 1864, at St. Louis on the Mississippi River. Was later repaired. On June 15, 1865, the *Edward F. Dix* ran onto the wreck of the USS *Eastport* and sank on top of the

vessel. Was investigated in 1995 by the U.S. Army Corps of Engineers. (*MSV*, 60, 257; Magruder, "Divers Explore Underwater Antiques," *Engineer Update*, 5; *WPD*, 142.)

Eliza. Confederate. Sloop. Cargo of fifteen hogsheads of sugar. Was captured on or about October 9, 1862, by the USS *Kensington* and destroyed near Calcasieu. (*ORN*, 19:226–27.)

Emma. Union. Side-wheel steamer, 385 tons. Length 211 feet, beam 35 feet, depth 5 feet 6 inches. Cargo of stores. Built in 1856 at Cincinnati. Was captured and burned by a Confederate battery on May 1, 1864 at David's Ferry, 30 miles below Alexandria near Fort De Russy, on the Red River. (*OR*, 34:1:475; 34:3:478, 554; *ORN*, 26:123; *WPD*, 148; *MSV*, 64.)

Emma. U.S. Stern-wheel steamer, 189 tons. Built in 1859 at Freedom, Pa. Snagged on June 20, 1865, at Shreveport. (*MSV*, 64, 258.)

Empire Parish. Union. Side-wheel steamer, 279 tons. Length 170 feet, beam 31–32 feet, depth 6 feet 2 inches. Built in 1859 at New Albany, Pa. Used as a Confederate towboat, flag of truce boat, and dispatch boat before being captured in April 1862. Burned at New Orleans on May 28, 1864, along with eight other steamers. (*CWC*, 6-225; *WCWN*, 232; *WPD*, 151–52.)

Era No. 2. Confederate. Ship. Was destroyed in April 1863 in Bayou Teche. (Pearson, *History of New Orleans District*, 178.)

Falls City. Union. Stern-wheel steamer, 183 tons. Length 155 feet, beam 27 feet, depth 4 feet 6 inches, 3 boilers. Built in 1855 at Wellsville, Ohio. Foundered on April 19, 1864, at Loggy Bayou. Was removed by the U.S. Army Corps of Engineers in 1878–79. (*MSV*, 70, 260; *WPD*, 160.)

Fashion. Confederate. Steamer. Cargo of cotton and turpentine. En route to Havana, Cuba. Was chased onto a reef by the USS *Hatteras* on May 6, 1862. Was set afire by its crew in Berwick Bay to prevent its capture. (*ORN*, 18:462; *WCWN*, 73.)

Fawn. Union. Side-wheel steamer. Length 101 feet, beam 21 feet 2 inches, depth 5 feet 5 inches. Built in 1863 at Jefferson City (New Orleans), La. Was destroyed by fire in New Orleans, along with eight other steamers on May 28, 1864. (*WPD*, 164.)

Flycatcher. Confederate. Screw steamer, 37 tons. Built in 1860 at Manchester, Pa. Was sunk in November 1862 to act as an obstruction in the Atchafalaya River (another source—Bayou Teche) with a schooner just above Cornay's Bridge. (*ORN*, 19:328; *CWC*, 6-229; Pearson, *History of New Orleans District*, 177, 236.)

Fox. Stern-wheel steamer, 74 tons. Built in 1855 at Little Rock, Ark. Was sunk during the Civil War by gunfire above the raft on the Red River. (*MSV*, 261.)

Frolic. Union. Tender. Complement of six. Driven to sea the night of October 17–18, 1861. Drifted, started leaking, and grounded in three feet of water at Southwest Pass after losing all its sails. Was stripped and burned by the USS *South Carolina* after the crew was removed. (*ORN*, 16:733.)

CSS *General Breckinridge* (*R. J. Breckinridge*). Confederate. Side-wheel or stern-wheel ram. Complement of thirty-five to fifty-three, and one 24-pounder. Was set afire by its crew at the Battle of the Forts on April 24, 1862. (*ORN*, 18:249–52, 291, 296, 305–6; Johnson and Buel, *Battles and Leaders of the Civil War*, 2, 75; *CWC*, 6-232; *WCWN*, 227.)

CSS *General Lovell*. Confederate. Side-wheel ram steam tug. Complement of forty to fifty, and one 32-pounder. Built in 1845 at Cincinnati. Was abandoned by its crew and set afire at the Battle of the Forts on April 24, 1862, near Fort Jackson and Fort St. Philip. (*OR*, 6:612; *ORN*, 18:249–52, 291; *WCWN*, 226; *CWC*, 6-233.)

General Pike. Confederate. Side-wheel steamer, 248 tons. Built in 1856 at Cincinnati. Burned on May 6, 1861, at Algiers. (*MSV*, 81, 263; *WPD*, 182.)

CSS *General Quitman* (*Galveston*). Confederate. Side-wheel steamer, 945 or 946 bulk tons. Length 233 feet 3 inches, 230 feet, or 236 feet; beam 34 feet 3 inches, 37 feet 6 inches, or 37 feet; depth 12 feet 3 inches; draft 6 or 9 feet. Complement of thirty-two to ninety; with two 32-pounder

smoothbores. Built in 1857 at New York City. Was set afire by the USS *Varuna* and ran into a riverbank during the Battle of the Forts on April 24, 1862, near Fort Jackson and Fort St. Philip. (*OR*, 6:612; *ORN*, 18:296, 249–50, 252, 291; *CWC*, 6-234; *WCWN*, 229; *LLC*, 301.)

Gertrude. Union. Side-wheel steamer, 70 tons. Length 167 feet, beam 17 feet 7 inches, depth 4 feet 4 inches. Built in 1864 at New Orleans. Foundered on September 21, 1864, at College Point with the loss of six lives. (*MSV*, 85, 264; *WPD*, 187.)

Gipsy. U.S. Side-wheel steamer, 43 tons. Length 87 feet, beam 18 feet, depth 3 feet 6 inches. Built in 1858 at Barnesville, Ohio. Snagged on February 19, 1861, at Black Bayou. (*MSV*, 85, 264; *WPD*, 188.)

Glide No. 3. U.S. Stern-wheel steamer, 225 tons. Length 156 feet, beam 33 feet, 2 boilers. Cargo of 630 bales of cotton. Built in 1864 at Freedom, Pa. Exploded on November 15, 1865, near Shreveport at Madame Roubleau's Plantation. (*MSV*, 86, 264; *WPD*, 189–90.)

Gossamer. Union. Stern-wheel steamer, 144 tons. Length 122 feet 6 inches, beam 23 feet 1 inch, depth 3 feet 4 inches. Built in 1863 at Pittsburgh, Pa. Was burned at Franklin in April 1863, on Bayou Teche under order of General Banks. Was salvaged prior to 1872 and rebuilt. (*MSV*, 87; *WPD*, 193; Pearson, *History of New Orleans District*, 236.)

CSS *Governor Moore* (*Charles Morgan*). Confederate. Schooner-rigged side-wheel steamer, 1,215 tons. Complement of ninety-three and two rifled 32-pounder guns. Built in 1854 and named for the Southern Steam Ship Company's founder, Charles Morgan. Seized in New Orleans in 1862 by Maj. Gen. Mansfield Lovell. During the Battle of the Forts on April 24, 1862, the CSS *Governor Moore* rammed the USS *Varuna* and attacked the USS *Cayuga*. The upper deck was shot away by the USS *Pensacola* and the Union fleet above the forts. Hit by forty or fifty shells. Its colors were shot away three times but rehoisted each time. The captain, pilot, and a seaman set the vessel afire after sixty-four members of the crew were killed. Most of the survivors were captured, although some of them escaped into the swamps. Novelist Clive Cussler reported that in 1981 while remote sensing he had a "hit" on the east bank that he thought was this vessel. Cussler also reported that local boys had used the top of the boiler, which protruded from the bank, as a diving platform. (*ORN*, 18:201, 208, 215, 296, 304–9, 317, 359, 723, 779; *CWC*, 6-241–42; *WCWN*, 229; Pratt, *Western Waters*, 229; Cussler and Dirgo, *Sea Hunters II*, 110.)

CSS *Grand Duke*. Confederate. Cottonclad side-wheel steamer, 508 tons. Length 205 feet, beam 35 feet, draft 7 feet 6 inches, 4 boilers. Armed with one 9-inch and four 8-inch guns. Built in 1859 at Jeffersonville, Ind., with engines from the *Duke*. Was accidentally burned at Shreveport on September 25, 1863. (*CWC*, 6-242; *WPD*, 196.)

Grenada. Confederate. Side-wheel steamer, 217 tons. Length 140 feet, beam 28 feet, depth 6 feet. Built in 1851 at New Albany, Ind. Burned on May 6, 1861, at Algiers. (*MSV*, 89, 265; *WPD*, 200.)

Hannibal. Union. Side-wheel steamer, 497 tons. Length 226 feet, beam 36 feet, depth 7 feet, 4 boilers. Built in 1856 at Belle Vernon, Pa. Snagged and sunk to its guards in October 1863, 5 miles above Donaldsonville. The USS *Champion No. 5* later raised the vessel. (*ORN*, 25:443–44, 461, 519; *MSV*, 92, 266.)

Harry of the West. U.S. Clipper ship, 1,050 tons. Built in 1855. Burned in November 1865, near the mouth of the Mississippi River. (*EAS*, 172.)

CSS *Hart* (*Ed R. Hart*) (*E. J. Hart*). Confederate. Side-wheel steam ironclad, 175 tons. Built in 1860 at Paducah, Ky. Was destroyed on April 14, 1863, to avoid capture by Union ships and troops of Maj. Gen. Nathaniel P. Banks in Grand Lake near Camp Bisland, Bayou Teche. Nearly raised by Confederates in July 1863 but was sunk upon the reappearance of Union gunboats. Used with CSS *J. A. Cotton No. 2*, two other wrecks, and piles to block the channel to navigation. In late 1863 powder charges were set off in the boilers, machinery, and boiler pipes by Union forces when the midships were in nine feet of water. The pieces were then hauled out to open the channel. The channel was cleared by the U.S. Army Corps of Engineers prior to

1872, when the wreck was probably removed. (*OR*, 15:297; ser. 3, 3:978–79; *CWC*, 6-249; *WCWN*, 232; Pearson, *History of New Orleans District*, 236.)

Hastings. Union. Stern-wheel steamer, 191 tons. Built in 1857 at Shousetown, Pa. Was sunk by a snag that tore a hole in the bottom of the vessel on April 23, 1864, at Alexandria. (*OR*, 34, Pt. 3, p. 268; *MSV*, 64, 92; *WPD*, 208.)

Helena. Union. Barge, 33 tons. Was burned by Confederates at 1:00 a.m. on December 11, 1863, on Bayou Bonfouca. (*OR*, 26:2:559; *ORN*, 20:856; 26:453.)

Hope. Union. Side-wheel steamer, 218 tons. Built in 1859 at Cincinnati. Collided with the USS *St. Clair* when strong winds and an eddy drove the vessel into the *Hope* on February 17, 1864, above New Orleans in the Mississippi River. Was later raised. (*ORN*, 25:766–67; *MSV*, 97.)

Huntress (**USS *Huntress***) (**Number 58**). U.S. Stern-wheel steamer, 138 tons (211 tons as naval vessel). Length 131 feet 8 inches, beam 31 feet 3 inches, draft 5 feet. Built in 1862 at New Albany, Ind. Formerly the Union ship USS *Huntress*. Snagged and was lost on December 30, 1865, near Alexandria. (*MSV*, 98, 268; *WCWN*, 172–73.)

Ida May. U.S. Side-wheel steamer, 220 tons. Length 157 feet, beam 32 feet, depth 4 feet 10 inches. Built in 1858 at Freedom, Pa. Altered December 8, 1865, from a stern-wheel to a side-wheel steamer. Wrecked in Red River 100 miles below Shreveport on December 28, 1865. (*MSV*, 99, 268; *WPD*, 220–21.)

Isabel. Confederate. Schooner, 30 tons. Out of Sabine City carrying passengers. Captured and destroyed by USS *Huntsville* on August 13, 1861, at Atchafalaya Bay. (*ORN*, 16:641; *SCH*, 326–27; *WCWN*, 79.)

Isabel (*Isabell*) (*Isabella*) (*Ysabel*). British. Steamer blockade-runner. Cargo of arms and powder. From Havana, Cuba, bound for Galveston. Subjected to two broadsides and small arms fire by the USS *Admiral* and USS *Kineo* before surrendering on the night of May 28, 1864, within 30 miles of Galveston off San Luis Pass. One crewman was badly wounded. Was taken to Southwest Pass and anchored at Quarantine Station, where the *Isabel* sank on June 2, 1864, as a result of leaks caused by the shelling. Slid off the bank into deep water. (*ORN,* 21:305–10; 27:667–68.)

Jackson. Union. Stern-wheel steamer, 84 tons. Built in 1860 at Brownsville, Pa. Burned at New Orleans on April 2, 1864. (*MSV,* 107; *EAS,* 174.)

CSS J. A. Cotton No. 2 (CSS Cotton) (Mary T). Confederate. Side-wheel partial ironclad, 549 tons. Length 229 feet, beam 36 feet, depth 7 feet. Armed with one 32-pounder smoothbore and one rifled 9-pounder, or two 32-pounder smoothbores. Built in 1861 at Jeffersonville, Ind. Shelled January 14, 1863, in Bayou Teche, Berwick Bay, off Brashear City by Union vessels. Fired on by the 8th Vt. Regiment and 75th N.Y. Regiment. Its guns were removed to an earthwork on the west bank of Bayou Teche by Confederates. Lt. H. K. Stevens was killed along with four crewmen. Capt. E. W. Fuller and eight crewmen were wounded. The CSS *J. A. Cotton No. 2,* CSS *Hart,* and two other vessels were sunk and burned on January 15, 1863, off Brashear City to close the channel to the USS *Kinsman,* USS *Estrella,* and USS *Diana* above Patterson. The CSS *J. A. Cotton No. 2* was sunk in 6 feet of water. In late 1863 Union forces used an 80-pound charge of gunpowder and several smaller charges to remove the vessel's stern. Part of the wreck forward of the wheel shaft was removed about 1870. (*OR,* 15:233–37, 1089; 53, supp., 462–63; *ORN,* 19:515–27; ser. 2, 1:251; *CWC,* 6-252; *WCWN,* 230; Pearson, *History of New Orleans District,* 236, 266.)

James Stockman. Union. Schooner. Was captured 1.5 miles from the mouth of the Amite River by forty-five Confederates in four boats under Lieutenant Wilkinson and Lieutenant McDermott of the Confederate States Navy after a half-hour fight in which three Union sailors were wounded. The Confederates had one lieutenant and three soldiers killed, and two soldiers wounded. The schooner surrendered, and the Union prisoners were released. The captured schooner went up Tickfaw River into the Blood River, where its cargo was landed, and the vessel was burned in March 1865. The wreck has been found and dived on in recent years. (*OR,* 48:1:1199, 1201, 1226–27; Boyd, "Wreck Facts," *Skin Diver,* 14.)

J. D. Clarke. Confederate. Side-wheel steamer. Was captured along with Maj. George T. Howard (another source called him Major Howell) and two engineers on April 9, 1863, by the USS *Hartford* on the Mississippi River outside the mouth of Red River. Major Howell was a brother of Gen. Volney E. Howard. Was scuttled on April 10, 1863, after its machinery was removed. (*ORN,* 20:54, 765–66, 810; *CWC,* 6-253.)

CSS J. D. Swain (J. D. Swain). Confederate. Side-wheel steamer, 1,228 tons. Length 50 feet 6 inches, beam 30 feet, depth 6 feet. Built in 1859 at Jeffersonville, Ind. Sank in the East Pearl River below the mouth of McCall's River in 1862. Was raised on April 5, 1864, and removed to Fort Pike by the Union 20th Infantry, Corps d'Afrique. Sold in 1866. (*OR,* 34:1:869–70; *CWC,* 6-253; *WPD,* 230.)

J. H. Russell (Cherokee). Union. Side-wheel steamer, 416 tons. Cargo of 700 bales of cotton, 50 mules, 3,000 sacks of seed, 150 hogs, and 50 cattle. En route to New Orleans. Built in 1850 at New Albany, Ind. as the *Cherokee.* Rebuilt as the *J. H. Russell.* Set afire by Confederate agent Isaac Ayleshire, who boarded the vessel at Baton Rouge. Burned near Plaquemine the night of March 28, 1864. (*MSV,* 34; *WPD,* 231–32.)

Jim Barkman. Confederate. Stern-wheel steamer, 65 tons. Cargo of corn. Built in 1859 at New Albany, Pa. Was burned by the Union 4th and 5th Ill. Cavalry Regiments on February 4, 1865, after ferrying the Union 3rd U.S. Colored Cavalry Regiment across the Ouachita River. (*OR,* 48:1:69, 806, 1404–5; *MSV,* 111.)

John Warner. Union army. Side-wheel transport steamer, 391 tons. Length 220 feet, beam 35 feet, depth 6 feet, 3 boilers. Carried confiscated cotton and about 250 men of the 56th Ohio Infantry Regiment going home on furlough. Built in 1856 at New Albany, Ind. Attacked by Confederate infantry supported by artillery, 20 miles downstream from Alexandria Falls on the Red River near Marksville on May 5, 1864, while under escort of the USS *Signal* and USS *Covington.* One shot cut a steam pipe, 15 shots went through the cabin, four shots went through the pilothouse, and the rudders were disabled. Ran into a bank downstream, about 100 yards from another Confederate battery, and sank at a point opposite Dunn's Bayou. About 34 men of the 56th Ohio Regiment were killed or wounded, and 150 captured in the engagement. The regiment's colonel was wounded and captured. (*OR*, 34:1:211, 623; 34:3:478–79; *ORN*, 26:112–13, 117–20, 122–23, 126, 134, 782; Milligan, *Fresh-Water Navy*, 273–75; *MSV*, 116; *WPD*, 257.)

Joseph H. Toone. Confederate. Schooner. Was captured on October 4, 1861, by the USS *South Carolina*. Was recaptured by the CSS *Manassas*. Was captured again by the Union fleet at Fort Jackson and burned on April 29, 1862. (*ORN*, 16:728, 738–39; 18:383–84; *WCWN*, 81.)

Josephine Truxillo. Union. Schooner, 37 tons. Was burned by Confederates at 4:00 p.m. on December 10, 1863, at Bayou Lacomb for trading with the Union. (*OR*, 26:2:559; *ORN*, 20:856.)

J. P. Smith. Blockade-runner steamer. Reported as "rotten" when captured by the USS *Kinsman* and the steamer *Seger*. Was hard aground when burned on November 7, 1862, in Bayou Cheval, about 9 miles from Grand Lake. (*ORN*, 19:328–29.)

Judah Touro. Confederate. Side-wheel steamer, 332 tons. Length 175 feet, beam 34 feet, depth 6 feet, 4 boilers. Built in 1854 at New Albany, Ind. Was burned at Shreveport about July 5, 1863, to prevent its capture. (*WPD*, 259.)

Julia. Confederate. Schooner, 130 tons. Cargo of cotton. Was forced aground by the USS *Mercedita* at the mouth of the Southeast Pass, Mississippi River, on January 24, 1862, and burned by its crew. (*ORN*, 17:76–78.)

Kate. Union. Schooner. Cargo of 130 tons of coal for the Union navy. En route from New Orleans to Brashear City. Was seized by twenty Confederates, burned in July 1864 across from Lost Island, and sank. (*OR*, 41:2:70–71.)

Kentucky (CSS Kentucky). U.S. Side-wheel steamer, 375 tons. Carried eight hundred paroled Confederate troops. Built in 1856 at Cincinnati. Formerly a Confederate gunboat captured at Memphis on June 6, 1862, and put into Union service. Snagged and sank with the boiler exploding on June 1, 1865, between the mouth of Red River and

Alexandria. Thirty paroled Confederate soldiers died. (*OR*, 52:1 [supp.]: 714; *MSV*, 120; *CWC*, 6-258–59; *WPD*, 269.)

USS Kinsman (CSS Colonel Kinsman) (Gray Cloud). Union. Tinclad side-wheel gunboat, 245 tons. Draft 4 feet. Built in 1854 at Elizabeth, Pa. Formerly a Confederate gunboat captured by the Union army at New Orleans and fitted out by Gen. Ben Butler for river service. Transferred to the Union navy on January 1, 1863. Snagged February 23, 1863, by a log on the starboard side on a bank in Berwick Bay (Atchafalaya River). Ran into 3-feet-deep water on the bow but slid off stern first, sinking in 18 fathoms of water on February 24, 1863, with six men lost. (*OR*, 15:1105; *ORN*, 19:625; ser. 2, 1:122; *CWC*, 97; *WPD*, 197.)

La Crosse. Union. Stern-wheel (screw) steamer, 186 tons. Length 150 feet, beam 29 feet. Built in 1856 at California, Pa. Burned on April 12, 1864, at Egg Bend, La. (*MSV*, 123, 275; *WPD*, 274.)

Landis (Joseph Landis) (Landes). Union. Side-wheel steam transport, 377 tons. Built in 1853 at Cincinnati. Was captured from Confederates on April 28, 1862. Was attacked by the 1st La. Cavalry Regiment with two 12-pounder howitzers and two Napoleons at Magnolia Landing, about 6 miles from Port Hudson on the night of June 16, 1864. Reportedly sank near Baton Rouge. (*OR*, 34:1:1014–15; *ORN*, 26:399–400; *MSV*, 117.)

Launch No. 3. Confederate. Steam launch. Complement of eight to twenty, with one howitzer. Lost in defense of Fort St. Philip and Fort Jackson on April 24, 1862. (*ORN*, 18:249, 252, 260, 291; *CWC*, 6-260.)

Launch No. 6. Confederate. Steam launch. Complement of eight to twenty crewmen, with one howitzer. Was burned and destroyed with the CSS *Louisiana* on April 28, 1862, below Fort St. Philip and Fort Jackson. (*ORN*, 18:249, 252, 260, 291, 299; *CWC*, 6-260–61.)

Laurel Hill. Union. Wharf boat. Leaks caused the boat to sink after drifting down the Mississippi River from Baton Rouge on August 12, 1862. The USS *Kineo*'s rigging was aboard and was salvaged from the wreck's upper deck. (*ORN*, 19:150.)

Lecompte. U.S. Side-wheel steamer, 250 tons. Length 155 feet, beam 32 feet, depth 6 feet 6 inches, 3 boilers. Built in 1856 at Cincinnati. Snagged on April 17, 1864, ten miles above Campti. (*MSV,* 126, 276; *WPD,* 281.)

Lenox. Union. Bark. Was captured and burned by Confederates under Master James Duke on June 8, 1863, in Pass a l'Outre, Mississippi River. (*ORN,* 20:828.)

Lone Star. Union. Steamer. Cargo of sugar. Captured with its crew and 2 passengers by the Terrell Dragoons Miss. Cavalry on the night of November 27, 1862, below Plaquemine. They brought the boat 10 miles down the Mississippi River to a bluff where it was burned. (*OR,* 15:189.)

Louise (Louis d'Or). Confederate. Side-wheel steamer, 343 or 369 tons. Length 180 feet, beam 32 feet, depth 7 feet. Built in 1860 at Cincinnati. Was burned on April 17, 1863, at the confluence of Bayou Teche and Bayou Fusilier near Breaux Bridge before an advancing Union force. (*OR,* 15:343; *MSV,* 131.)

CSS Louisiana. Confederate. Two-paddlewheel ironclad, 1,400 tons. Length 264 feet, beam 62 feet, 4 engines (from steamer *Ingomar*). Complement of two hundred to three hundred, with two rifled 7-inch guns, three 9-inch guns, four 8-inch shell guns, and seven rifled 32-pounders. Construction began at New Orleans in mid-October 1861 but was not completed because of the lack of raw materials. Used as a floating battery. Supposed to have cost about $1 million to build. Mechanics worked day and night on the east bank of the Mississippi River trying to get the vessel's machinery to work. Trapped after the Union fleet passed by on April 24, 1862. Hit by several shells while moored to the riverbank. Was set afire near Fort St. Philip by its crew under order of Capt. John K. Mitchell on April 28, 1862, after Fort St. Philip and Fort Jackson surrendered. Was blown up with 10,000 pounds of gunpowder at 10:45 a.m. near Fort St. Philip's water battery and drifted downstream. One soldier in Fort St. Philip was killed, and one was wounded by fragments from the explosion. In 1981 Clive Cussler used a gradiometer in a swamp of the main river channel and found a wreck directly off Fort St. Philip that he thought was the CSS *Louisiana.* (*ORN,*

18:242, 287–88, 294–302, 309–10, 312–15, 318–20, 369–71, 433, 439; 26:568; ser. 2, 1:258; *CWC,* 6-263–64; Pratt, *Western Waters,* 228; Still, "Confederate Behemoth: The CSS *Louisiana,*" *Civil War Times Illustrated,* 20–25; Cussler and Dirgo, *Sea Hunters II,* 109–10.)

Louisiana Bell (Louisiana Belle). Confederate. Stern-wheel steamer, 89 tons. Built in 1859 at Cincinnati. Burned on June 1, 1862, in the Red River. Was repaired and burned in a wharf fire in New Orleans on May 28, 1864, along with eight steamers. (*MSV,* 131; *EAS,* 178; *WPD,* 296; Pearson, *History of New Orleans District,* 162.)

Majestic. U.S. Stern-wheel steamer, 201 tons. Cargo of 650 cotton bales. Built in 1864 at Cincinnati. Burned on October 22, 1865, at Point Coupee. (*MSV,* 135, 278; *WPD,* 304.)

CSS Manassas (Enoch Train). Confederate. Ironclad ram, 387 bulk tons. Length 143 feet, beam 33 feet, depth 11 feet or 17 feet, with a turtle back deck of 42-inch oak, armor 1.5-inch iron over 12 inches of wood. Able to make only 2.5 miles per hour against the river current. Complement of a captain and thirty-six crewmen, with one 32-pounder carronade. The hull projected about two and one-half feet above water. Originally built in 1855 at Medford, Mass., as the towboat *Enoch Train.* Shelled and holed by Flag Officer David G. Farragut's Union fleet when it attacked the USS *Pensacola,* USS *Mississippi,* and USS *Brooklyn* on April 24, 1862, in the Battle of the Forts. Rammed by the USS *Mississippi.* Its armor was pierced and engine smashed. The crew escaped, running ashore as the vessel slipped off the bank in flames and floated past Union ships, exploded, and sank. Novelist Clive Cussler did a 1981 gradiometer survey that may have indicated this wreck. (*ORN,* 18:302–4, 335–45, 357–58; ser. 2, 1:259; *CWC,* 6-266; Pratt, *Western Waters,* 228; Cussler and Dirgo, *Sea Hunters II,* 108–14.)

USS Maria J. Carlton. Union. Wooden mortar schooner, 178 tons. Length 98 feet, beam 27 feet, depth 7 feet 8 inches. Complement of twenty-eight, with one 13-inch mortar and two rifled 12-pounder howitzers. Built in 1859 at Saybrook, Conn. Sank on April 19, 1862, below Fort St. Philip, above the passes. A Confederate shell hit the magazine deck, tearing a hole in the bottom and injuring two crewmen. On April 25, 1862, the remains of the vessel were destroyed by Union forces. (*ORN*, 18:359, 430; *DANFS*, 4:235; *WCWN*, 137.)

Mark R. Cheek. Union. Side-wheel steamer, 122 tons. Built in 1860 at Madison, Ind. Burned at Ouachita City on March 31, 1865. (*MSV*, 137, 279.)

Martha. Union. Lighthouse tender schooner. Was captured, along with eight crewmen, while two escaped, in Chandeleur Sound near Mason's Keep by a Confederate launch with twenty-two men under Captain Jefferson. Was set afire in August 1864, after being stripped of sails and part of its cargo. (*OR*, 41:2:565–66.)

CSS McRae (Marquis de la Habana). Confederate. Wooden screw steamer; 600 bulk tons; 230, 680, or 830 tons. Length 176 feet, beam 29 feet 6 inches, depth 14 feet. Armed with one 9-inch pivot shell gun or 11-inch Dahlgren pivoted amidships, six 32-pounder smoothbores, and possibly one rifled 6-pounder. Formerly the Mexican rebel bark *Marquis de la Habana*, which was captured on March 7, 1860, by the USS *Saratoga*. Was run ashore by the USS *Iroquois* after three shells hit the CSS *McRae* above the waterline during the Battle of the Forts on April 24, 1862. Cut to pieces, with four killed and seventeen wounded. Lt. Charles W. Read took over from Lt. Thomas B. Huger, who was wounded in the battle. Came upriver under a flag of truce on April 27, 1862, to New Orleans to land wounded Confederates from Fort St. Philip and Fort Jackson. Was leaking badly and unable to steam well, so it was scuttled along the New Orleans City Wharf on April 28, 1862. (*OR*, 6:612; *ORN*, pp. 18, 287, 295, 302, 331–34, 346, 440, 445, 697, 722, 757, 792–93; ser. 2, 1:259; *LLC*, 310.)

Mary Ann. Confederate. Schooner. Was burned by the USS *Kensington* at Calcasieu River in early October 1862. (*ORN*, 19:227.)

Meteor. Union. Side-wheel steamer, 417 tons. Length 233 feet, beam 36 feet, depth 6 feet, 4 boilers. Built in 1857 at Louisville. Lost in a wharf fire at New Orleans on May 28, 1864. (*LLC*, 320.)

Minnehaha (Minnetonka). Union. Side-wheel steamer, 531 tons. Length 236 feet, beam 36 feet 6 inches, depth 6 feet 6 inches. Built in 1857 at Guyandotte, Va. (W. Va.). Burned on May 15, 1865, at New Orleans. (*MSV*, 146, 281; *WPD*, 323.)

CSS Mississippi. Confederate. Three screw ironclad gunboat, 1,400 tons. Length 260 feet, beam 58 feet, draft 12 feet 6 inches, depth 15 feet, speed estimated 14 knots, armor 3.75-inch iron, 16 boilers, designed to carry 20 guns. Launched on April 14, 1862, in Jefferson City, La., upstream from New Orleans. Set afire by Confederate commander Arthur Sinclair and drifted down the Mississippi River from New Orleans on April 26, 1862, and sank. No guns or ammunition were aboard when destroyed. (*ORN*, 18:149, 158, 321, 350–53; ser. 2, 1:260; *CWC*, 6-271; Pratt, *Western Waters*, 228.)

Mist. Union. Steamer. Was captured and burned by twenty Confederate guerrillas under Dick Holland at the foot of Ship Island on October 22, 1863. The captain was a pro-Confederate who claimed more than $17,000 had been taken from him. The captain and ten men were allowed to leave. The pilot said $5,000 Confederate had been stolen from the vessel's safe. (*OR*, 31:1:32–33; *ORN*, 25:521.)

Moro. Confederate. Side-wheel steamer, 132 tons. Length 122 feet, beam 24 feet 10 inches, depth 4 feet 9 inches. Cargo of 110,000 pounds of pork, 500 hogs, and salt. Built in 1858 at Louisville. En route to Port Hudson when captured and burned by the USS *Queen of the West* on February 3, 1863, with the *A. W. Baker* and *Berwick Bay* at the mouth of the Red River. (*OR*, 24:1:338–39; *ORN*, 24:224–25; *CWC*, 6-273; *EAS*, 182; *WCWN*, 248.)

CSS Mosher (C. A. Mosher). Confederate. Screw steam tug, 35, 45, or 49 tons. Complement of forty and one gun. Built in 1857 at Philadelphia for the Southern Steamship Company. Pushed a fire raft up to USS *Hartford* and was sunk with all hands when a Union shell hit its boiler on April 24, 1862, at the Battle of the Forts near Fort St. Philip and Fort Jackson. (*OR*, 6:613; *ORN*, 18:249–50, 252, 268, 270, 291, 295; *MSV*, 27; *CWC*, 6-273.)

CSS *Music.* Confederate. Privateer side-wheel steamer, 273 or 330 tons. Length 172 feet, beam 29 feet, depth 6 feet. Complement of twenty-five to forty, with two 6-pounders. Built in 1857 at Jeffersonville, Ind. A former towboat used as a tender. Was destroyed by Confederates to prevent its capture on April 24, 1862, at the Battle of the Forts. The USS *Kineo* captured the vessel's captain and nine crewmen. May have been salvaged and used on the Red River and Atchafalaya River. (*ORN*, 18:249–50, 252, 268, 270, 291; ser. 2, 1:261; *CWC*, 6-273–74; Pearson, *History of New Orleans District*, 171.)

Newboy. Confederate. Transport. Was destroyed in April 1863 in Bayou Teche. Was removed by the U.S. Army Corps of Engineers prior to 1872. (Pearson, *History of New Orleans District*, 178, 198.)

New Falls City. Confederate. Side-wheel steamer, 880 tons. Length 301 feet 4 inches, beam 39 feet 9 inches, draft 7 feet 7 inches. Built in 1858 at Paducah, Ky. Was sunk on April 5, 1864, by Confederates 30 miles below Springfield Landing at the foot of Scopern's Cutoff, a mile above Loggy Bayou to block the Red River from Union vessels. Its machinery was probably removed, and the vessel was filled with rocks. The ends of the boat rested on each bank with as much as 15 feet onshore, and the vessel was broken down the middle. On the vessel the Confederates left an invitation to the Union forces to attend a ball upriver in Shreveport. While the Union fleet halted its advance at the wreck, news arrived of General Banks's army's defeat at Pleasant Hill and its retreat from the area. Without supporting infantry, R. Adm. David D. Porter's fleet was forced to retreat on April 8, 1864. The wreck was later partly removed as an obstruction by the Confederates. The rest of the wreck was removed by the U.S. Army Corps of Engineers in 1878–79. (*OR*, 34:2:1056, 1068; 34:3:172; *ORN*, 26:51, 60, 164, 169, 786; *Chief of Engineers Report 1879*, 114; *CWC*, 6-276.)

New Orleans. Union. Side-wheel steamer, 198 tons. Length 154 feet, beam 34 feet, depth 4 feet. Burned in a wharf fire at New Orleans on May 28, 1864. (*WPD*, 345.)

CSS *Oregon.* Confederate. Wooden side-wheel gunboat, 532 or 700 tons. Length 216 feet 10 inches, beam 26 feet 6 inches, depth 9 feet 6 inches. Armed with one 8-inch gun, one 32-pounder, and two howitzers. Built in 1846 at New York City for the Mobile Mail Line. Used as a mail boat between New Orleans and Mobile. Was sunk in the Tchefuncte River (other sources—Bogue Falaya River below Covington) by Confederates in late April 1862, to prevent its capture by Union forces and to block a channel. Was removed under contract for the U.S. Army Corps of Engineers in 1872–73. Debris from the wreck was put on the banks and burned with the iron debris removed by the contractor. (*OR*, 6:596, 605; *MSV*, 164; *Annual Report of the Secretary of War 1871*, 552; *Chief of Engineers Report 1873*, 65, 633–34; *WCWN*, 232; Pearson, *History of New Orleans District*, 198, 201.)

Osprey. Confederate. Steamer. Was captured and burned by the USS *Kinsman* along with the *J. P. Smith* in Bayou Cheval, about 9 miles from Grand Lake on November 7 or 9, 1862. The vessel had no wheel, and part of the machinery had been removed. (*ORN*, 19:328–29.)

CSS *Pamlico.* Confederate. Side-wheel steamer, 218 tons. Armed with three 8-inch smoothbores and one 6.4-inch rifled gun (one source says there were two guns on February 27, 1862 so additional guns may have been added before its destruction). Built in 1856 at New York City. Out of New Orleans. Was burned in April 1862 by its officers after the fall of New Orleans, on Lake Pontchartrain, to prevent its capture. (*ORN*, 18:287, 830; ser. 2, 1:262; *MSV*, 167; *CWC*, 6-279–80.)

Panola. U.S. Side-wheel steamer, 89 tons. Length 132 feet, beam 22 feet, depth 3 feet 11 inches. Built in 1863 at Aberdeen, Ohio. Snagged on October 3, 1865, on Grand Bayou or Bayou Goula. (*MSV*, 167, 288; *WPD*, 362.)

Pauline. Confederate. Side-wheel steamer, 135 tons. Built in 1860 at Madison, Ind. Burned at Shreveport on May 3, 1864. (*MSV*, 169, 288.)

CSS *Phoenix.* Confederate. Side-wheel steam tug, 75 tons. Complement of seventy-five. Tender to the CSS *Manassas*. Was destroyed near Fort St. Philip and Fort Jackson on April 24, 1862. (*ORN*, 18:249–50, 252, 291, 297; *CWC*, 6-283.)

Pine Hill. U.S. Stern-wheel steamer, 73 tons. Built in 1864 at Concord, Ky. Snagged in June 1865 at Tucker's Bar on the Red River. (*MSV*, 173, 290.)

CSS *Pioneer*. Confederate. Privateer submarine, 4 tons. Length 20 or 34 feet, beam 3 feet 2 inches to 4 feet, maximum depth 4–6 feet, equipped with a hand crank propeller, speed 2 knots. Complement of two or three and armed with a clockwork torpedo. Built in 1861–62 at New Orleans by machinist James McClintock. One of the financial backers was Horace L. Hunley, who later built and died on the CSS *H. L. Hunley*. The CSS *Pioneer* blew up a schooner in Lake Pontchartrain during the vessel's trials. Accidentally sunk with 3 killed in Bayou St. John several days before the Union troops captured New Orleans. Was scuttled by Confederates in a deep bend of the New Basin Canal between New Orleans and Lake Pontchartrain when Flag Officer David G. Farragut captured New Orleans. In 1863 a "Rebel Submarine Ram" was raised outside of New Orleans near the New Basin Canal. In 1868 a newspaper article reported the CSS *Pioneer* was raised and sold for $43 as scrap metal. A vessel similar to descriptions of the CSS *Pioneer* was discovered in 1878 by boys swimming near Spanish Fort. Was raised in 1907 by a sand barge and given to Camp Nicholls, the Louisiana Home for Confederate Soldiers. Measured in 1926 and found to be hardly 20 feet long. The long spar may have been removed or the recovered vessel may be another version of the CSS *Pioneer*. In 1957 the vessel was transferred to Presbytere Arcade, the Louisiana State Museum in New Orleans. (*ORN*, ser. 2, 1:263; Bass, *Ships and Shipwrecks of the Americas*, 226; Scharf, *History of the Confederate Navy*, 761; *CWC*, 6-285–86, 380; Stern, *Confederate Navy Pictorial History*, 174–75; Cussler and Dirgo, *Sea Hunters*, 183; Hicks and Kropt, *Raising the Hunley*, 13–14, 23–24, 254.)

Planet. Union. Side-wheel steamer, 604 tons. Built in 1856 at Cincinnati. Was stranded in the Mississippi River on February 1, 1864, at College Point. (*MSV*, 174, 290.)

Planter No. 2. Union. Side-wheel steamer, 58 tons. Built in 1860 at Baresville, Ohio. Crashed into a New Orleans dock on July 8, 1864. (*WPD*, 374.)

Pushmataha. Sloop. Cargo of rum, claret, and French gunpowder. In company with another schooner when chased by the USS *Cayuga* off the Calcasieu River on October 7, 1863. While trying to enter the Mermentau River it ran aground, three-quarters of a mile from a beach. A Union boarding party found a burning match on a keg of gunpowder. One Union sailor threw the match overboard, saving the boarding party. The *Pushmataha* was stripped of all but two kegs of gunpowder and blown up. (*ORN*, 20:614–15.)

USS *Queen of the West* (CSS *Queen of the West*). Union. Side-wheel cottonclad ram, 212 or 406 tons. Length 180 or 181 feet, beam 37 feet 6 inches or 37 feet, depth 8 feet. Complement of 120, with one 30-pounder, one 20-pounder, and three 12-pounder howitzers. Built in 1854 at Cincinnati. Purchased by the Union army in 1862. Was captured by Confederates at Fort De Russy, La., on the Red River on February 14, 1863. Was raised by the Confederates and helped force the surrender of the USS *Indianola* on February 24, 1863. Chased by the USS *Clifton*, USS *Estrella*, and USS *Calhoun* on the Atchafalaya River. Disabled on Grand Lake by shells from the USS *Estrella*, USS *Calhoun*, and USS *Arizona* on April 14, 1863, with 90 of the Confederate crew rescued and 26 killed. Drifted two to three miles down the lake, grounded, and its magazine blew up. Union forces salvaged one 30-pounder Parrott, one 20-pounder Parrott, and three brass 12-pounders. (*OR*, 15:297; 24:3:259; *ORN*, 20:134–39; 24:412, 437, 515; ser. 2, 1:187; *CWC*, 6-289; Melton, "From Vicksburg to Port Hudson," *Civil War Times Illustrated*, 26–37.)

CSS *Resolute* (*Orizaba*). Confederate. Side-wheel gunboat ram, 630 bulk tons. Length 210 feet, beam 30 feet, depth 10 feet 6 inches, draft 6 feet. Complement of thirty-six to forty, with two 32-pounders. Built in 1858 at Brooklyn, N.Y. Ran ashore on the west bank a mile above Fort Jackson during the Battle of the Forts on April 24, 1862. Ten men under Lt. T. Arnold from the CSS *McRae* boarded the vessel, hauled down its white flag, and attempted to refloat the vessel while under Union fire. Several Union shells hit it. Was set afire on April 26, 1862, to prevent its capture. (*ORN*, 18:249–50, 252, 296, 445; *CWC*, 6-292; *LLC*, 315.)

Reub White. U.S. Side-wheel steamer, 110 tons. Length 104 feet, beam 27 feet, depth 3 feet 9 inches. Built in 1856 at Murraysville, Va. (now W. Va.). Was stranded on February 3, 1861, in the Harvey Canal. (*ORN,* 20:406–7.)

Revenge. Confederate. Schooner, 20 tons. Cargo of 18 hogsheads of sugar, 200 hides, and mineral salt. Out of New Orleans. Was captured and destroyed by boats from the USS *Owasco* and USS *Cayuga* on July 21–22, 1863, several miles above the Calcasieu Pass Bar. (*ORN,* 20:406–7.)

Rinaldo. Confederate. Small steamer. Was captured by the Union 17th Wis. Infantry (Mounted) Regiment under Col. A. G. Malloy and burned on September 1–2, 1863, at Trinity. (*OR,* 26:1:273–74, 278; *ORN,* 25:400.)

Robert Fulton (Fulton). Confederate. Side-wheel steamer, 158 tons. Length 137 feet, beam 29 feet, depth 4 feet 4 inches. Cargo of stores. Built in 1860 at California, Pa. Was captured with the *Argus* near the mouth of Red River on October 7, 1863, by a boat crew of twenty men from the USS *Osage.* Also captured were six crewmen and 1st Lt. J. M. Avery, aide to Confederate general Richard Taylor, who was to use the boat to transport Confederate troops. Burned when the Union crew could not pass a shoal to get out of the Red River into the Mississippi River. (*ORN,* 25:450–57, 523; *CWC,* 6-294; *MSV,* 77, 262; *WPD,* 398.)

Robert McClelland (Pickens). Union. Revenue cutter schooner. Length 100 feet. Built in 1853 at Somerset, Mass. Taken into Confederate service and renamed *Pickens.* Was burned on April 25, 1862, at Algiers to prevent Union capture upon the fall of New Orleans. (Scharf, *History of the Confederate Navy,* 767; *MSV,* 91.)

Rose Hambleton (Hamilton) (Rose Hamilton). Union. Side-wheel steamer, 529 tons. Built in 1863 at Brooklyn, N.Y. Carried the 3rd Mich. Cavalry Regiment from New Orleans when it hit a torpedo in April 1865, in the Lauren Gap Channel. Lost thirteen killed and wounded. Was probably raised. (*OR,* 15:499; *ORN,* ser. 2, 1:265; *WCWN,* 192.)

R. W. Powell. Confederate. Side-wheel steamer, 349 tons. Built in 1855 at New Albany, Ind. Snagged on August 20, 1861, at Plaquemine. (*MSV,* 180, 292.)

Sarah Bladen. Union. Schooner, 43 tons. Was burned by Confederate troops at 4:00 a.m. on December 11, 1863, on Bayou Bonfouca for trading with the Union. (*OR,* 26:2:559; *ORN,* 20:856.)

USS Sciota. Union. Wooden screw steam two-mast schooner gunboat, 507 bulk tons, 691 displacement tons. Length 158 feet, beam 28 feet, draft 7 feet or 9 feet 6 inches. Complement of 65–114, with one 11-inch smoothbore, two 24-pounder smoothbores, and one rifled 20-pounder. Built in 1861 at Philadelphia. Sank in a collision with the USS *Antona* in the Mississippi River, 68 miles below New Orleans, north of the Quarantine, at 3:00 a.m. on July 14, 1863. Was raised in August 1863, and returned to service. Later sank and was raised in the Blakely River, Ala. Sold by auction on October 25, 1865. (*ORN,* 20:388, 391, 396, 485; *WCWN,* 49–50, 53.)

USS Signal No. 2 (Number 8). Union. Wooden sternwheel gunboat, 190 tons. Length 157 feet, beam 30 feet, depth 4 feet 4 inches, draft 1 foot 10 inches. Complement of fifty, with two 32-pounders, two 24-pounder howitzers, and two rifled 12-pounder Dahlgrens. Built in 1862 at Wheeling, Va. (now W. Va.). Was captured and sunk by Confederates on the Red River on May 5, 1864, downstream from Dunn's Bayou, 20 miles below Alexandria while with the USS *Covington* and *John Warner.* Hit thirty-eight times in four minutes by Confederate batteries. Lost twenty-five killed and thirteen wounded, with seven of the wounded captured and later paroled. Continued fighting for a half-hour after the USS *Covington* was lost. Act. Vol. Lt. Edward Morgan, commander of the USS *Signal No. 2,* was probably captured, but some of the vessel's crew escaped. Drifted downstream, grounded, and was set afire but would not burn. Finally sank in the middle of the river. Confederates removed its guns. Pilot Perry Wilkes was later awarded the Medal of Honor for his actions during the battle. (*OR,* 34:1:589, 623; 34:3:449; *ORN,* 26:127, 134, 172; ser. 2, 1:208–9; Miller, *Photographic History,* 6:230; *WCWN,* 178; Pratt, *Western Waters,* 240–41.)

Southerner. Union. Side-wheel steamer, 393 tons. Length 240 feet, beam 34 feet, depth 6 feet. Built in 1853 at Jeffersonville, Ind. Collided and sank on July 21, 1862, at College Point. Was probably raised. (*MSV*, 201, 298; *WPD*, 430.)

Star. U.S. Stern-wheel steamer, 94 tons. Built in 1864 at New Albany, Ind. Burned in July 1865, at Red Bayou. (*MSV*, 202, 298; *EAS*, 192.)

CSS *Star*. Confederate. Tug, 250 or 420 tons. Length 158 feet, beam 27 feet, depth 11 feet. Complement of forty to eighty, with possibly two guns. Built in 1840 at New Albany, Ind. Chartered from the Southern Steamship Company in New Orleans. Used as a telegraph station. Its engines were removed to the *Mohican*. Was destroyed to prevent its capture near Fort Jackson and Fort St. Philip on April 24, 1862. (*ORN*, 18:249–50, 252, 270, 291, 297; *CWC*, 6-304; *WSTD*, 211.)

Stepheny. Union. Barge, 26 tons. Was burned by Confederates for trading with the Union on December 10, 1863, on Bayou Lacomb. (*OR*, 26, Pt. 2, p. 559; *ORN*, 20:856.)

CSS *Stevens*. Confederate. Unfinished gunboat. Was destroyed 2 miles below New Iberia on April 13, 1863, on the approach of a Union force. (*OR*, 15:393.)

CSS *Stonewall Jackson* (*Yankee*). Confederate. Side-wheel ram tug, 297 or 299 tons. Complement of thirty to seventy-five, with one 32-pounder gun and one 24-pounder smoothbore, or two pivot 32-pounders or 8-inch guns. Built as the *Yankee* in 1849 at Cincinnati. At the Battle of the Forts, the vessel rammed the USS *Varuna* after the CSS *General Moore* hit the vessel. The USS *Varuna* gave the CSS *Stonewall Jackson* a broadside and the USS *Oneida* chased the vessel ashore. Became beached and burned near the Chalmette Battery on the Mississippi River on April 24, 1862. (*OR*, 52 [supp.]: 40; *ORN*, 18:210–12, 249, 251–52, 296, 305–9, 338–39; ser. 2, 1:257; *MSV*, 234; *CWC*, 6-253–54; Pratt, *Western Waters*, 227.)

USS *Sumter* (CSS *General Sumter*) (*Junius Beebe*). Union. Side-wheel steam ironclad, 400 or 525 tons. Length 182 feet, beam 28 feet 4 inches, depth 10 feet 8 inches. Armed with two 32-pounders. Built in 1853 as the towboat *Junius Beebe* at Algiers, La. Was captured by the Union fleet on June 6, 1862, at the Battle of Memphis.

Grounded downriver and abandoned off Bayou Sara on August 14–15, 1862. Was burned by Confederates, with the machinery stripped for spare parts by both sides. (*ORN*, 19:159, 165; ser. 2, 1:216; *CWC*, 6-236–37; *WSTD*, 213.)

Sykes (*Lorenzo A. Sykes*). Union. Steamer, 163 tons. Built in 1862 at Stanton Island, N.Y. Stuck on a pile in Bayou Plaquemine. Was captured and burned on June 18, 1863, along with the *Anglo-American* by Confederate colonel James P. Majors's 2nd Texas Cavalry Brigade. (*OR*, 26:1:46, 191–92, 216, 567–68, 589; *ORN*, 20:235–36, 239–40, 304–6, 309; *MSV*, 130, 277.)

Tallahassee. Confederate. Steamboat. Was towed ashore and burned on April 29, 1862, by the USS *Owasco* on the Mississippi River below New Orleans. (*ORN*, 18:384.)

Tecumseh. Union. Side-wheel steamer, 418 tons. Length 177 feet, beam 32 feet, depth 7 feet, 4 boilers. Built in 1852 at Cincinnati. Lost on December 1, 1863, at West Baton Rouge. (*MSV*, 209, 300; *WPD*, 445.)

Telegram. U.S. Stern-wheel steamer, 205 tons. Length 158 feet, beam 31 feet, depth 4 feet 6 inches. Built in 1858 at Cincinnati. Burned on May 6, 1861, at Algiers. (*MSV*, 209, 300; *WPD*, 445.)

Texana. Union. Bark. Was boarded and burned by Confederate guerrillas on the captured Union tug *Boston* on June 8, 1863, off Pass a l'Outre. (*ORN*, 20:828.)

Texas. Confederate. Wooden side-wheel steamer, 1,223 bulk tons. Length 216 feet, beam 34 feet 6 inches, depth 16 feet 10 inches. Built in 1852 at New York City. Possibly converted from a blockade-runner to a gunboat. Was destroyed at the Battle of the Forts on April 24, 1862. (*LLC*, 323.)

Time and Tide. Union. Stern-wheel steamer, 130 tons. Built in 1853 at Freedom, Pa. Burned on May 28, 1864, at New Orleans. (*MSV*, 212, 301.)

CSS *Tuscarora*. Confederate. Side-wheel steamer. Armed with one 8-inch Columbiad and one rifled 32-pounder. Accidentally burned at New Orleans in January 1862. (*ORN*, ser. 2, 1:270.)

T. W. Roberts. Union. Side-wheel steamer, 288 tons. Length 158 feet, beam 32 feet, depth 6 feet 1 inch. Built in 1860 in New Albany, Ind. Was destroyed in Shreveport in 1863 to prevent its capture. (*WPD*, 443.)

Uncle Tommy. Confederate. Steamboat. Was burned on April 17, 1863, at the junction of Bayou Teche and Bayou Fusilier near Breaux Bridge on the advance of a Union force. (*OR*, 15:343.)

USS *Varuna.* Union. Screw steam sloop or corvette, 1,247 or 1,300 tons. Length 218 feet, beam 34 feet 8 inches. Complement of 157, with eight 8-inch smoothbore guns and two 30-pounder Parrotts. Launched in 1861 at Mystic, Conn. Hit by the rams CSS *Governor Moore* and CSS *Stonewall Jackson* on April 24, 1862, while running past Fort St. Philip and Fort Jackson. Sank up to the forecastle on the east bank of the Mississippi River above the Quarantine, stern on the bank. The USS *Varuna* lost 3 killed and 12 wounded. Parts of the wreck were visible in 1885. Novelist Clive Cussler reported a gradiometer hit in 1981 on the east bank where the USS *Varuna* was thought to have sunk. (*ORN*, 18:178–80, 201, 208–15, 296, 305–9, 359, 754, 769, 779–80, 796; ser. 2, 1:231; *MSV*, 220; *WCWN*, 81; Cussler and Dirgo, *Sea Hunters II*, 110.)

Venango. Union. Stern-wheel steamer, 120 tons. Built in 1858 at California, Pa. Sank in August 1862, at Scuffletown Bar loaded with freight for the Cumberland River. Was raised and later burned on December 31, 1864, at Pilcher Point. (*MSV*, 220, 303; *WPD*, 466–67.)

Victoria. U.S. Stern-wheel steamer, 23 tons. Built in 1863 at New Orleans. Lost on November 29, 1865, at New Orleans. (*MSV*, 221, 304.)

Victoria. Confederate. Side-wheel steamer, 487 bulk tons. Length 180 feet, depth 9 feet 7 inches. Cargo of ammunition. Built in 1859 at Mystic, Conn. Sister ship to the USS *Arizona.* Was run into Atchafalaya Bay on November 14, 1862, set afire, and blown up off Last Island. (*LLC*, 325.)

Wanderer. U.S. Side-wheel steamer, 36 tons. Built in 1860 at Pascagoula, Miss. Was stranded on November 24, 1865, at Gretna. (*MSV*, 225, 305.)

CSS *Warrior.* Confederate. Side-wheel cottonclad ram. Armor 4-inch oak, bow armor 1-inch iron. Complement of forty, with one 32-pounder and possibly two other guns. Was run ashore and set afire above Fort St. Philip on April 24, 1862, during the Battle of the Forts after being hit by a broadside from the USS *Brooklyn* and disabled. (*ORN*, 18:249–52, 263, 270, 291, 296, 305; *CWC*, 6-322; *WCWN*, 228.)

Washington. Confederate. Brig. Length 91 feet 2 inches, beam 22 feet 1 inch. Complement of seventeen, with one 42-pounder. Launched in 1837 at Baltimore, Md. A U.S. revenue cutter seized by Confederate forces in 1861 in New Orleans. Was scuttled on April 25, 1862, at the New Orleans docks as Flag Officer David G. Farragut's Union fleet arrived to take possession of the city. (*WCWN*, 232; *Century War Book*, 109.)

CSS *Webb* (*William H. Webb*). Confederate. Iron and wood side-wheel ram, 655 tons, 656 bulk tons. Length 195 or 206 or 190 feet, beam 31 feet 6 inches or 32 feet or 31 feet, depth 12 feet 6 inches to 13 feet, draft 9 feet 6 inches, speed 15–22 knots. Complement of two hundred, with two 12-pounder howitzers, one 4-inch rifled gun, one 30-pounder Parrott, and two iron 12-pounders secured from Gen. Edmund Kirby Smith's command. Outfitted with a spar torpedo and five torpedoes. Built in 1856 by William H. Webb at New York City. Constructed for ocean work and used as an eastern icebreaker before being sold to New Orleans merchants. Originally a privateer that operated in the Mississippi River and captured three Union merchant vessels carrying oil. Escaped to Shreveport when New Orleans fell to Union forces. On April 23, 1865, under the command of Lt. Charles W. Read, the CSS *Webb* ran the Union blockade of the Red River, passed Union vessels at Baton Rouge, and passed the Union fleet at New Orleans. Ran into the left bank of the Mississippi River, 20–24 miles below New Orleans, at Bonnet Carre on April 24, 1865, to escape capture by the USS *Richmond* and USS *Hollyhock.* Was hit by three shells and burned with 217 bales of cotton. At least forty-five crewmen were reported killed, with eight officers and twenty-six men captured. The U.S. Navy contracted Spencer Field and a diving bell boat company in New Orleans on April 26,

1865, to salvage the wreck with half of the proceeds going to the United States. Was probably salvaged. (*OR*, 48:1:203–7; *ORN*, 22:141–70; 27:155–59; ser. 2, 1:271; *CWC*, 6-323, 6-329; *WCWN*, 231; *WPD*, 488.)

William M. Morrison. Confederate. Side-wheel steamer, 662 tons. Built in 1856 at Cincinnati. Set afire and adrift at New Orleans on April 25, 1862, as Flag Officer David G. Farragut's Union fleet approached. Ran into the ferry boat at Canal Street. Was salvaged and may have been renamed *Alice V.* (*ORN*, ser. 2, 1:504–5, 761–62; *WPD*, 12–13, 489.)

Woodford. Union. Side-wheel hospital steamer, 487 tons. Built in 1856 at Louisville. Part of the Marine Brigade. Wrecked and sank on March 28, 1864, on rocks while going over Alexandria Falls on Red River. (*OR*, 34:3:19, 36; *ORN*, 26:39, 774, 781; *MSV*, 235.)

➤ VESSELS WITHOUT NAMES

barge. Union. Carrying coal under tow by the USS *De Soto* when the USS *De Soto* lost a rudder and drifted 15 miles down the Red River with Confederate boats nearby. Was burned with the USS *De Soto* by Capt. Charles R. Ellet of the *Era No. 5* near Fort Taylor above Gordon's Landing on February 14, 1863, on the Red River. (*OR*, 24:1:343, 346; 24, 3:833; *ORN*, 24:385, 398–400; ser. 2, 1:74; *CWC*, 6-219; *WCWN*, 70–71.)

barges. Union. Two coal barges were sunk in the lower part of Alexandria Falls on the Red River to raise the river stage so Adm. David D. Porter's fleet could escape downstream in May 1863. (*ORA*, pl. 53, no. 2.)

bark. Confederate. Cargo of about four hundred bales of cotton. Ran aground with the *Julia* at the mouth of the Mississippi River at Southeast Pass the night of January 23, 1862, by the USS *Mercedita*. Probably from New Orleans. The USS *Vincennes* sent a launch, which fired shells with its 12-pounder howitzer at the bark on January 24, 1862. Lt. Cdr. Samuel Marcy was mortally wounded on the launch by the gun's recoil when a bolt came lose. He died on January 29. (*ORN*, 17:76–79.)

brig. Confederate. Cargo of cotton. Was burned on April 28, 1862, at Fort Livingston to prevent its capture by approaching Union ships. (*ORN*, 18:397.)

schooner. Confederate. Blown up by the Confederate submarine CSS *Pioneer* during its trials in 1862 in Lake Pontchartrain. (Bass, *Ships and Shipwrecks of the Americas*, 226; Scharf, *History of the Confederate Navy*, 761; *CWC*, 6-285–86, 380; Stern, *Confederate Navy Pictorial History*, 174–75; Cussler and Dirgo, *Sea Hunters*, 183.)

schooner. Confederate. Blown up in the Calcasieu River on October 7, 1863, by the USS *Cayuga*. (*ORN*, 20:614–15.)

schooner. Confederate. Loaded with bricks. Was sunk with the *Flycatcher* to block the Bayou Teche channel above Cornays Bridge in November 1862. Was probably removed by the U.S. Army Corps of Engineers in 1872. (*ORN*, 19:328; Pearson, *History of New Orleans District*, 177, 236.)

steamers. Confederate. Two steamers were burned on July 13, 1863, during an expedition by the USS *Rattler* and USS *Manitou* in the Little Red River. Possibly the *James Thompson* and *Fort Hindman*. (*ORN*, 25:263–64.)

steam flatboats. Union. Two steam flatboats were captured and burned by Confederate colonel James P. Major's 2nd Tex. Cavalry Brigade on June 18, 1863, in Bayou Plaquemine along with the steamboats *Anglo-American*, *Belfast*, and *Sykes*. (*OR*, 26:1:46, 191–92, 216, 567–68, 589; *ORN*, 20:235–36, 239–40, 304–6, 309.)

vessels. Confederate. Undetermined number. Some were set afire, some drifted down the Mississippi River from New Orleans, as Flag Officer David G. Farragut's Union fleet advanced upriver after passing Fort St. Philip and Fort Jackson. Between 6:00 and 7:30 a.m. on April 25, 1862, three burning Confederate vessels drifted down from New Orleans and passed the USS *Brooklyn*, which was coming upstream. Other steamboats carrying cotton were burned at the New Orleans wharves. (*ORN*, 18:760; Dimitry, *Confederate Military History*, vol. 10: *Louisiana*, 47.)

The USS *Cairo* was sunk by two Confederate torpedoes on December 12, 1862, in the Yazoo River. It was raised in 1964 and was later put on display at the Vicksburg National Military Park as a partially reconstructed ironclad.

COURTESY U.S. NAVY.

A Confederate fleet of nine vessels was scuttled in the Mississippi River at Island No. 10 in March–April 1862. Many of the vessels were raised by Union forces and became supply vessels. The CSS *Red Rover* became a Union hospital ship. *Harper's Weekly,* 1862.

COURTESY U.S. NAVY.

Photo from 1863 of the City Class ironclads USS *Baron de Kalb* (formerly USS *St. Louis*), USS *Cincinnati,* and USS *Mound City.* The USS *Baron de Kalb* was sunk by two Confederate torpedoes on July 13, 1863, in the Yazoo River, two miles below Yazoo City, Miss. The USS *Cincinnati* was sunk on May 10, 1862, at Plum Point, Tenn., in the Mississippi River by the CSS *General Bragg.* It was raised by Union forces and was sunk by Confederate batteries at Vicksburg, Miss., on May 27, 1863. The USS *Cincinnati* was refloated again and survived the Civil War.

COURTESY U.S. NAVY.

At the Battle of Memphis, Tenn., on the Mississippi River on June 6, 1862, the Union fleet destroyed six Confederate cottonclad gunboats.

The USS *Monitor* sank in an Atlantic Ocean storm off Cape Hatteras, N.C., on December 30, 1862. This is a mosaic of photographs taken in 1974 showing the USS *Monitor* upside down with part of its novel revolving turret visible in the lower left-hand area.

COURTESY U.S. NAVY.

The Battle of the Forts below New Orleans, La., on April 24, 1862. A Confederate fleet of more than sixteen vessels
was destroyed by the Union fleet, which lost only two vessels. From *Virtue*.

COURTESY U.S. NAVY.

The commerce raider CSS *Florida* torched the clipper *Jacob Bell* in the Atlantic Ocean, southwest of Bermuda, on February 13, 1863. The CSS *Florida* was captured in Brazil and was scuttled by Union forces in Hampton Roads, Va., near where the USS *Cumberland* and USS *Congress* were sunk. *Harper's Weekly,* January–June 1863, p. 189.

Union schooners scuttled in the James River, Va., to block the Confederate Richmond Fleet.

The double-turret USS *Keokuk* sank on April 8, 1863, off Morris Island, S.C., after being hit by ninety shells from Confederate cannon the previous day during the Union attack on Charleston Harbor forts. *Harper's Weekly,* 1863.

COURTESY U.S. NAVY.

While moored at Vicksburg, Miss., the CSS *Vicksburg* was shelled and rammed by the USS *Queen of the West* on February 3, 1863. The CSS *Vicksburg* was totally burned and destroyed on March 29, 1863. The USS *Queen of the West* was sunk on February 14, 1863, at Fort De Russy, La., and raised by the Confederates. The CSS *Queen of the West* was destroyed on April 14, 1863, on Grand Lake, La., by Union ships. *Harper's Weekly,* 1863.

COURTESY U.S. NAVY.

Wreck of the blockade-runner *Celt* at the Bowman's Jetty, near Fort Moultrie, Charleston Harbor, S.C. The *Celt* ran aground the night of February 14, 1865, just four days before Charleston was abandoned by the Confederates.

A Confederate "David," or torpedo boat, at Charleston, S.C. Note the damage on the forward half of the vessel. The Davids were scuttled when the Confederates prepared to abandon Charleston. Several were raised by Union forces.

COURTESY U.S. NAVY.

The tug USS *Bazely* was sunk by a Confederate torpedo in the Roanoke River while assisting the USS *Otsego*, which had been sunk by two torpedoes on December 9–10, 1864. *Harper's Weekly*, January 21, 1865.

COURTESY U.S. NAVY.

A painting of the Battle of Mobile Bay, Ala., as the Union fleet passes Fort Morgan and the USS *Tecumseh* is sunk by a Confederate torpedo. The CSS *Gaines* and USS *Philippi* were also sunk.

COURTESY U.S. NAVY.

The Union flagship USS *Black Hawk* was accidentally burned on April 22, 1865, in the Ohio River near Cairo, Ill.

The CSS *H. L. Hunley* sank the USS *Housatonic* off Charleston, S.C., and was the first submarine to sink an enemy warship in combat. While en route back to Charleston it sank on February 17, 1864. It was raised in 2000 and is now on exhibit.

COURTESY U.S. NAVY.

Maine

Maine was isolated from Confederate attacks until the CSS *Tallahassee* and CSS *Archer* captured and destroyed Union vessels in Yankee waters. The capture of the USS *Caleb Cushing* by Confederate raiders sent shock waves throughout New England, shifting Union vessels from blockade duty off southern ports to the New England coast.

USS *Caleb Cushing*. Union. Revenue cutter, 153 tons. Length 100 feet 4 inches, depth 8 feet 8 inches, draft 9 feet 7 inches. Armed with one 32-pounder and one 12-pounder Dahlgren. Built in 1853 at Somer, Mass. Boarded at the Portland docks at 1:30 a.m. on June 27, 1863, by Confederate lieutenant Charles W. Read of the CSS *Florida* on the captured vessel *Archer,* which had earlier been taken by the CSS *Florida.* First Lieutenant Dudley Davenport and his crew were put in chains. The vessel slowly sailed out the harbor after being pulled by two rowboats. The captured vessel was chased by two large side-wheel steamers, the *Casco* and the *Forest City,* the propeller steamer *Chesapeake,* and a tug. The twenty Union crewmen were set loose in a boat. The captured USS *Caleb Cushing* fired eight 32-pounder rounds but ran out of ammunition because they did not find the other 90 rounds on the vessel. The Confederate crew surrendered and set the vessel afire. The USS *Caleb Cushing* blew up at sea about midnight on June 27, 1863, 20 miles east of Portland. (*OR,* 27:3:369; *ORN,* 2:654, 656–57; ser. 2, 1:249; *CWC,* 6-207; Miller, *Civil War Sea Battles,* 178–82; *WCWN,* 192.)

Etta Caroline. Union. Fishing schooner, 39 tons. Cargo of wood. Out of Portland, Maine. Was captured and scuttled by the CSS *Tallahassee* under Cdr. John Taylor Wood off the Maine coast on August 15, 1864. (*OR,* ser. 4, 3:1057; *ORN,* 3:703; Shingleton, *John Taylor Wood,* 207.)

Floral Wreath. Union. Schooner, 54 tons. Cargo of wood. Out of Georgetown, Maine. En route from Bridgeport for C. H. Island. Was captured and scuttled by the CSS *Tallahassee* off the Maine coast on August 15, 1864. (*OR,* ser. 4, 3:1057; *ORN,* 3:703; *Naval Records Group 45, M101, Subject File of the Confederate States Navy.*)

Howard. Union. Schooner, 148 tons. Cargo of coal. Out of New York City. En route from Bridgeport, Cape Breton Island, Canada, to New York City. Was captured and scuttled by the CSS *Tallahassee* off Maine on August 15, 1864. (*OR,* ser. 4, 3:1057; *ORN,* 3:703.)

James Littlefield. Union. Ship, 547 tons. Cargo of coal. Out of Bangor, Maine. En route from Cardiff, Wales, to New York City. Was captured and burned by the CSS *Tallahassee* off the Maine coast on August 14, 1864. (*OR,* ser. 4, 3:1057; *ORN,* 3:703.)

Josiah Achorn. Union. Schooner, 123 tons. In ballast. Out of Rockland, Maine. En route for Lingan from Portland, Maine. Was captured and destroyed off the Maine coast by the CSS *Tallahassee* on August 17, 1864. (*OR,* ser. 4, 3:1057; *ORN,* 3:704.)

Leopard. Union. Schooner, 74 tons. Cargo of wood. From Cornwallis, Nova Scotia, Canada. En route to Boston. Was captured and burned off the Maine coast by the CSS *Tallahassee* on August 16, 1864. (*OR,* ser. 4, 3:1057; *ORN,* 3:704.)

Magnolia. Union. Fishing schooner, 35 tons. Out of Friendship, Maine. Was captured and burned by the CSS *Tallahassee* off the Maine coast on August 16, 1864. (*ORN,* 3:704; *Naval Records Group 45, M101, Subject File of the Confederate States Navy;* Owsley, *C.S.S. Florida,* 134–35.)

Mary A. Howes. Union. Schooner, 61 tons. Was captured and scuttled by the CSS *Tallahassee* off the Maine coast on August 15, 1864. (*OR,* ser. 4, 3:1057; *ORN,* 3:703.)

North America. Union. Fishing schooner, 87 tons. Out of New London, Conn. Was captured and scuttled by the CSS *Tallahassee* off the Maine coast on August 17, 1864. (*OR,* ser. 4, 3:1057; *ORN,* 3:704; *MSV,* 159.)

P. C. Alexander. Union. Bark, 283 tons. In ballast. En route from New York City to Pictou, Nova Scotia. Was captured and burned by the CSS *Tallahassee* off the Maine coast on August 16, 1864. (*OR,* ser. 4, 3:1057; *ORN,* 3, 704.)

Pearl. Union. Fishing schooner, 42 tons. Out of Friendship, Maine. Was captured and burned by the CSS *Tallahassee* off the Maine coast on August 16, 1864. (*OR*, ser. 4, 3:1057; *ORN*, 3:704.)

Piedmont (Potomac). Union. Screw steamer, 448 tons. Built in 1853 at Glouchester, N.J. Burned on January 6, 1865, at Cape Elizabeth, Maine, with four lives lost. (*MSV*, 173, 289.)

Restless. Union. Fishing schooner, 50 tons. Out of Boothbay, Maine. Was captured and burned by the CSS *Tallahassee* off the Maine coast on August 15, 1864. (*OR*, ser. 4, 3:1057; *ORN*, 3:703.)

Sarah Louise (Louisa). Union. Schooner, 81 tons. Cargo of wood. Out of Jonesport, Maine. Was captured and burned by the CSS *Tallahassee* off the Maine coast on August 16, 1864. (*OR*, ser. 4, 3:1057; *ORN*, 3:704.)

Tacony (CSS Florida No. 2). Union. Bark, 296 bulk tons. Draft 12 feet. Armed with one 12-pounder howitzer. Built in 1856 at Newcastle, Del. Was captured by Lt. Charles W. Read of the CSS *Florida* in the captured brig *Clarence* on June 12, 1863. Used by Confederate sailors to capture fifteen Union vessels. Burned on the morning of June 25, 1863, after the Confederate crew transferred to the CSS *Archer* off the Maine coast. (*ORN*, 2:656; *CWC*, 6-309.)

Maryland

The many inlets along the Chesapeake Bay and Atlantic coast of Maryland were used by smugglers to transfer supplies purchased in the north to Confederate Virginia. Confederate boat raids in Maryland waters captured and destroyed the *Knickerbocker*. The CSS *Florida* captured and destroyed the *Electric Spark, General Berry,* and *Zelinda* on July 10, 1864, off the Maryland coast.

Columbia. Confederate. Schooner. Used for smuggling and raiding. Was burned to the water's edge by a Union small boat expedition on October 12, 1863, at Ape's Hole near the head of Pocomoke Sound, about 15 miles from Drummondtown. (*OR*, 29:1:212.)

Curlew. Union. Screw steamer, 343 tons. Built in 1856 at Newtown, N.Y. Collided with the *Louisiana* on November 5, 1863, and sank near Point Lookout. (*MSV*, 49, 254.)

Electric Spark. Union. Side-wheel mail steamer, 810 tons. Draft 19 feet, top speed 12 knots. Cargo of assorted merchandise, dry goods, shoes, boots, fine provisions, wines and liquors, $12,000 worth of postage stamps, mail, as well as an Adams Express chest containing $1,305 in U.S. greenbacks, $219 in gold specie, $328 in New Orleans bank notes, and $132 in New Orleans City notes. Built in 1864 at Philadelphia. En route from New York City to Havana, Cuba. Was captured by the CSS *Florida* and scuttled when its seacocks were opened and pipes cut on July 10, 1864, off the Md. coast. The Adams Express chest was removed and the mail was thrown overboard. During the capture a Confederate boat was swamped and one Confederate crewman drowned. (*ORN*, 3:103, 107, 109, 624, 646; *MSV*, 61, 254.)

Favorite. Confederate. Schooner. Was captured by the USS *Yankee*, USS *Resolute*, and three boats from the USS *Pawnee* in the Yeocomico River on July 14, 1861. Accidentally ran into another vessel or the vessel's pumps were not kept pumping as the *Favorite* sank off Piney Point on July 18, 1861. (*ORN*, 4:577–78.)

General Berry. Union chartered. Bark, 469 or 1,197 tons. Cargo of 1,166 hay bales and 36 straw bales. Out of Kennebunk, Maine. En route to Fort Monroe, Va. Was captured and burned by the CSS *Florida* on July 10, 1864, near latitude 37° 33' north, longitude 74° 20' west, about 35 miles offshore of Maryland. (*ORN*, 3:623, 645.)

Kettle Bottom light ship. Union. Burned at Kettle Bottom Shoals, in the Potomac River on April 26, 1861. (Shomette, *Shipwrecks on the Chesapeake*, 253.)

Knickerbocker. Union. Side-wheel steamer, 858 tons. Built in 1843 at New York City. Stranded between Fleet's Points and Smith's Point, in eight to 10 feet of water on January 4, 1865. Confederate guerrillas tried to burn the steamer, but the USS *Mercury* chased them off. A second Confederate attack succeeded in capturing and burning the *Knickerbocker* in fog on February 15, 1865. The USS *Mercury* fired some shots during the incident. The wreck has been dived on by Washington, D.C., and Baltimore scuba divers with some salvage. (*ORN*, 5:508–10; *MSV*, 122, 274.)

Passenger. Union. Sloop. Out of Baltimore. Capsized in the Potomac River on the morning of June 30, 1861. The USS *Reliance* rescued one person. (*ORN*, 4:556.)

Somerset. Nationality unknown. Blockade-runner schooner. Was burned by the USS *Resolute* on June 8, 1861, off Bretons Bay in the Potomac River. (*ORN*, 4:507; Shomette, *Shipwrecks on the Chesapeake,* 253; *WCWN*, 120.)

USS Tigress. Union. Steam tug. Launched in August 1861. Was run down by the steamer *State of Maine* and sank on September 10, 1862, in the Potomac River off Indian Head. Was later raised and sold. (*ORN*, 4:668, 732; ser. 2, 1:223–24; *WCWN*, 121.)

USS Tulip (Chih Kiang). Union. Screw steam tug, 240 bulk tons, 183 burden tons. Length 97 feet 3 inches or 93 feet 3 inches or 101 feet 4 inches, beam 21 feet 9 inches, depth 9 feet 6 inches, loaded draft 8 feet. Complement of 43–69, with one 20-pounder Parrott, two 24-pounders, and two 12-pounders. Built in 1862 at Brooklyn, N.Y., as the lighthouse tender *Chih Kiang* for use in China. A defective boiler on the vessel blew up on November 11, 1864, off Piney Point near Ragged Point, Va. Sank in about 60 feet of water within three minutes, with forty-nine killed. The Union army tug *Hudson* brought ten survivors ashore, but two of them died within hours. Three others may have died later. There were sixty-nine officers and men aboard at the time of the explosion. The wreck has been visited by scuba divers and the guns are reported to have been raised. The wreck was investigated by funding from the U.S. Naval Historical Center and a Maryland Department of Housing and Community Development initiative called The Maryland Maritime Archaeology Program. Some artifacts, including navigational instruments, were salvaged in the 1960s and given to the U.S. Navy in 1994. (*ORN*, ser. 2, 1:226; Shomette, *Shipwrecks on the Chesapeake,* 162–65; *WCWN*, 104; Morr, "Been Blown to Atoms," *Naval History,* 34–36; Thompson, "Legacy of a Fourth-Rate Steam Screw," *Naval History,* 36–39.)

Zelinda. Union. Bark, 559 tons. In ballast. Out of Eastport, Maine. En route from Matanzas, Cuba to Philadelphia. Was captured by the CSS *Florida* and burned on July 10, 1864, 35 miles off the Maryland coast. (*ORN*, 3:623, 645.)

➤ **VESSELS WITHOUT NAMES**

vessels. Confederate. Six small boats and two scows. Was burned by a launch from the USS *Satellite* along the Maryland shore on August 28, 1861. (*ORN*, 4:768.)

Massachusetts

Most vessels lost off the Massachusetts coast sank as a result of accidents. The Confederate commerce raider CSS *Tallahassee* destroyed the Union bark *Glenavon* off the coast.

Gazelle. Union. Schooner. Cargo of coal. Out of Providencetown. En route to Portsmouth, N.H. Hit a rock off Thatcher Island and sank on July 23, 1864. Its crew was rescued. (*New York Times,* July 26, 1864.)

Glasgow. British. Ship. Burned on July 31, 1865, off Nantucket Island. (*EAS,* 37.)

Glenavon. Union. Bark, 789 tons. Cargo of iron. En route to Greenock, Scotland, from New York City. Was captured and burned by the CSS *Tallahassee* off the coast on August 13, 1864. (*ORN*, 3:148, 152, 703.)

USS *Howell Cobb.* Union. Revenue cutter. Length 63 feet. Built in 1857 at Milan, Ohio. Wrecked off Cape Ann on December 27, 1861, but was refloated. (*WCWN*, 192.)

Maritana. British. Ship, 991 tons. Lost on November 3, 1861, at latitude 42° 19' 47" north, longitude 70° 52' 54" west, at Shag Rocks, Broad Sound, near Boston. (*EAS*, 62.)

Nathaniel Cogswell. Nationality unknown. Bark. Lost on November 3, 1861, off Scituate. (*EAS*, 62.)

Newton. U.S. Ship, 699 tons. Lost on December 25, 1865, off Nantucket Island. (*EAS*, 70.)

Swordfish. Nationality unknown. Brig. Lost on Toddy Rocks in December 1864. (*EAS*, 89.)

Walpole. Union. Side-wheel steamer, 145 tons. Built in 1854 at Philadelphia. Stranded on April 7, 1863, at Minot Ledge with two lives lost. (*MSV*, 225, 305.)

Mexico

American vessels traveled along the coasts of Mexico and up the Colorado River Delta to transport goods and machinery to the Arizona mines and to carry gold and silver from mining areas. The western Mexican coast was also the vital route in transferring California gold to New York City and Union ports in the east. A California gold steamer, the *Golden Gate,* was lost on the Mexican west coast in an accident.

Explorer. Union. Barge. Originally a stern-wheel steamer. Length 54 feet, beam 13 feet, draft 3 feet. Built at Philadelphia. The steamer was cut into pieces, transported by mule across Panama, shipped by boat up the western coast of Central America and Mexico, and then reassembled in 1857 at Robinson's, Mexico. The steam engine filled one-third of the vessel. The engine and boiler were removed in 1858 and the *Explorer* was converted to a barge. The barge was sunk in 1864 by a Colorado River flood which tore the vessel from its moorings at Pilot Knob, near Yuma, Ariz. In 1929 the vessel's hull was found by surveyors in the Colorado River Delta, 40 miles below Yuma and 4 miles inland from the present Colorado River at latitude 32° 20' north, longitude 114° 56' west. The hull, ribs, and parts of the transom were excavated and measured by Godfrey Sykes of Tucson in 1930. (Lingenfelter, *Steamboats of the Colorado River,* 162–63; "Ancient Steamboat Sleeps in Swamp," *Treasure,* 40.)

Golden Gate. Union. Side-wheel steamer, 2,067 tons. Owned by the Pacific Mail Steamship Company. Carried 242 passengers, 96 crewmen, and a cargo of $1,577,760 in gold bullion and specie, and possibly $2,000,000 in gold dust and nuggets from the California goldfields. Built in 1851 at New York City. En route from San Francisco. Caught fire between the forward smokestack and the cabin galley on July 27, 1862, at 4:45 p.m. while 3.5 miles offshore and 15 miles north of Manzanillo in a heavy fog. Ran ashore about 5:00 p.m. amid huge breakers. By 9:00 p.m. the steamer broke apart, with the bow and stern coming ashore. Killed in the wreck were between 176–198 passengers and crewmen. About 100 survivors, including 5 children and 1 woman, walked over land toward Manzanillo and were rescued by boats from the steamer *St. Louis* and the Manzanillo custom boat. By morning only the bed-plate, wheels, and attachments were visible. Located about a half-mile offshore in 6 fathoms of water. In 1900 Duncan Johnston of Providence, R.I., recovered about $10,000 in gold. About $1 million in gold was later recovered by various divers. (*ORN*, 3:361; *MSV*, 86, 264; Wiltse, *Gold Rush Steamers,* 291–98; Rieseberg, *Guide to Buried Treasure,* 70.)

Smoker. British. Iron steamer. Cargo of eighty bales of cotton just loaded from the blockade-runner *Sarah,* when the *Smoker* was stranded on a beach near Tampico. Was declared a total loss in September 1863. (*ORN,* 20:595.)

Victoria. Union. Barge converted to a four-mast schooner. Used as a store ship at the mouth of the Colorado River. Towed to Port Famine Slough and burned in 1863 or 1864. (Lingenfelter, *Steamboats of the Colorado River,* 43–44.)

Michigan

This section notes vessels lost in Michigan rivers and tributaries, and possibly part of the Great Lakes, between 1861 and 1865. All were victims of accidents. Other wrecks off Michigan in the Great Lakes are listed by lake.

Charles Mears. Union. Screw steamer, 272 tons. Built in 1856 at Cleveland, Ohio. Burned on August 7, 1864, at Muskegon. (*EAS,* 238; *MSV,* 33, 249.)

General Taylor. Union. Screw steamer, 462 tons. Built in 1848 at Buffalo, N.Y. Stranded in October 1862 at Sleeping Bear Point. (*MSV,* 82, 263.)

Globe. U.S. Screw steamer, 313 tons. Built in 1846 at Maumee, Ohio. Burned on the Tittabawas River in 1865 near Saginaw. Was later returned to service. (*MSV,* 82; *EAS,* 245.)

Julius D. Morton. Union. Side-wheel steamer, 472 tons. Built in 1848 at Monroe, Mich. Burned on April 8, 1863, in the St. Clair River. (*MSV,* 118, 273.)

May Flower. U.S. Screw steamer, 57 tons. Built in 1864 at Muskegon, Mich. Lost in the Detroit River on November 11, 1865. (*MSV,* 141, 280.)

Nile. Union. Screw steamer, 650 tons. Built in 1852 at Cleveland, Ohio. Exploded, with thirteen killed, at Detroit on May 21, 1864. (*MSV,* 158, 285.)

P. F. Barton (Pliny F. Barton). U.S. Screw steamer, 40 tons. Built in 1853 at Buffalo, N.Y. Burned in May 1865 on the St. Clair River. (*MSV,* 166, 288.)

Pilot. Union. Screw steamer, 77 tons. Built in 1853 at Buffalo, N.Y. Burned in November 1865 at Algonac. (*MSV,* 173, 290.)

Pontiac. Union. Side-wheel steamer, 68 tons. Built in 1853 at Grand Rapids, Mich. Blew up, killing three, in May 1864 at Grand Haven. (*MSV,* 176, 290.)

Stockman. U.S. Screw steamer, 81 tons. Built in 1853 at Cleveland, Ohio. Burned in August 1865 at Bear Creek. (*MSV,* 204, 298.)

Tom Cochrane. Union. Screw steamer, 14 tons. Built in 1861 at Buffalo, N.Y. Stranded in October 1862 at Sturgeon Point. (*MSV,* 213, 302.)

Union. U.S. Side-wheel steamer, 116 tons. Built in 1855 at Port Huron, Mich. Burned on December 30, 1865, at Detroit. (*MSV,* 218, 303.)

Minnesota

Between 1861 and 1865 accidents claimed a few vessels in Minnesota.

Fanny Harris. Union. Stern-wheel steamer, 159 tons. Built in 1855 at Brownsville, Pa. Was sunk by ice at Point Douglas on December 29, 1862. (*MSV,* 71, 260.)

John Rumsey. Union. Steamer, 39 tons. Built in 1862 at Waubeck, Wis. Lost in 1864 at St. Paul. (*MSV,* 115, 272.)

New Ulm Belle. Union. Stern-wheel steamer, 50 tons. Built in 1862 at St. Paul, Minn. Snagged in August 1862 on the Minnesota River. (*MSV,* 156, 285.)

Mississippi

With the loss of Memphis and New Orleans to Union forces in 1862, the remaining Confederate vessels on the Mississippi River fled up the southern rivers feeding into the Mississippi River. Some vessels escaped up the Yazoo River and found refuge at Yazoo City. Several Union expeditions up the Yazoo River forced the Confederates to scuttle vessels at various points in the Mississippi Delta region on the Yazoo River, Tallahatchie River, and other streams.

In one of the Union expeditions the USS *Cairo* became the first vessel to be sunk by a torpedo or mine. The USS *Cairo* was raised in 1964 and is exhibited in a partially reconstructed state at the Vicksburg National Military Park. Its salvaged artifacts are exhibited in The USS *Cairo* Museum in the park.

Many of the other vessels sunk in Mississippi were removed by the U.S. Army Corps of Engineers after the Civil War as threats to navigation. The wrecks of several vessels are still visible at extremely low water. Vessels that sank in the Mississippi portion of the Mississippi River are in the Mississippi River section.

Advocate. Confederate. Fishing schooner. Crew of four. Was captured on December 1, 1861, by the USS *New London*. Was scuttled on January 1, 1862, in Petit Bois Channel to act as an obstruction between the Gulf of Mexico and the Mississippi Sound. (*ORN*, 16:817; *DANFS*, 5:439.)

Alonzo Child (Child). Confederate. Side-wheel steamer, 493 tons. Length 236 feet, beam 38 feet, depth 7 feet. Built in 1857 at Jeffersonville, Ind. Purchased for $35,000 by the Confederacy. Shot to pieces by the USS *Baron de Kalb* at Snyder's Bluff on the Yazoo River in May 1863. Was sunk to block the Yazoo River channel at Haynes' Bluff. The engines were salvaged and later put into the CSS *Tennessee* at Mobile. The *Alonzo Child* was raised and put into Union service as a receiving ship. (*ORN*, 25:326, 393; *CWC*, 6-196; *WPD*, 16; War Department, Record Group 109, Vessel Papers.)

Arcadia (Acadia). Confederate. Side-wheel steamer, 343 tons. Length 188 feet, beam 35 feet, depth 7 feet. Built in 1860 at Jeffersonville, Ind. Was scuttled and burned in the Yazoo River about a mile below the mouth of the Yalobusha River or about a mile below Greenwood on July 17, 1863. In 1864 the upper works of the vessel were reported to be above water. Was probably removed by the U.S. Army Corps of Engineers between 1878 and 1879. (*ORN*, 25:133, 756; *Chief of Engineers Report 1873*, 483; *Executive Documents, HR, Forty-fifth Congress, 1878–79*, 628; *MSV*, 2, 239; *WPD*, 4.)

Argo. Confederate. Stern-wheel steamer, 99 tons. Length 136 feet, beam 21 feet, depth 4 feet. Built in 1856 at Freedom, Pa. Burned before May 25, 1863, in a small bayou 75 miles up the Sunflower River. (*OR*, 24:3:372; *ORN*, 25:134, 136; *MSV*, 12; *CWC*, 6-198; *WCWN*, 245.)

Argosy. Confederate. Steamer. Was destroyed in the Sunflower River in mid-1863 to prevent its capture by Union forces. (*ORN*, 25:136; *CWC*, 6-198.)

CSS Arrow. Confederate. Screw steamer. Armed with one 32-pounder. Was burned in the West Pearl River on June 4, 1862, by Confederates to prevent its capture. (*CWC*, 6-200; *WCWN*, 229.)

USS Baron De Kalb (USS St. Louis). Union. Ironclad steam gunboat, 512 tons. Length 172 feet, beam 51 feet 2 inches, draft 6 feet, speed 9 miles per hour, casemate armor 2.25-inch iron, pilothouse armor 1.25-inch iron. Complement of 175–200, with two 30-pounder Parrotts, two 9-inch smoothbores, six 32-pounders, and three 8-inch rifled guns. Built by James B. Eads in 1861 at Carondelet (now part of St. Louis), Mo. Was sunk in 15–20 feet of water in fifteen minutes by two Confederate torpedoes, one at the bow and one at the stern, on July 13, 1863, in the Yazoo River, 2 miles below Yazoo City and a half-mile downriver from a Confederate battery. The guns, stores, and part of the machinery were salvaged, along with iron and part of the hull, during the Civil War. The wreck was then blown up. In 1873 the wreck was still in place and has not been removed. The wreckage was last seen during low water in the 1950s. (*OR*, 24:3:512, 520, 572, 1014, 1035; *ORN*, 20:393–94, 400; 25:282–87, 289–91; ser. 2, 1:42;

Chief of Engineers Report 1873, 483; *Chief of Engineers Report 1874,* 366; *WCWN,* 153; Gordon Cotton of Vicksburg, pers. comm.)

CSS *Ben McCulloch.* Confederate. Stern-wheel steamer, 80 tons. Length 100 feet, beam 22 feet, draft 13 feet 9 inches. Built in 1860 at Cincinnati. Was burned by Confederates to prevent its capture in July 1863 in Tchula Lake. Repaired and returned to service after the war. (Shomette, *Civil War Shipwrecks,* 230; *CWC,* 6-205; *EAS,* 158; *MSV,* 21; *WCWN,* 246.)

CSS *B. P. Cheney (Milton Brown).* Confederate. Side-wheel steamer, 247 tons. Built in 1859 at Cincinnati. Burned at Yazoo City on July 14, 1863. (*CWC,* 6-208; *MSV,* 17.)

USS *Cairo.* Union. Ironclad gunboat, 512 tons. Length 175 feet, beam 51 feet 2 inches, draft 6 feet, speed 8 knots. Complement of 175, with one 30-pounder Parrott, three 42-pounder rifled guns, six 32-pounders, and two 9-inch smoothbores. Built by James B. Eads in 1861 at Mound City, Ill. Sank within twelve minutes in 40 feet of water on December 12, 1862, by two Confederate torpedoes in the Yazoo River 4 miles below Snyder's Bluff. The top of its smokestacks were above water and were removed by the USS *Queen of the West* to conceal the wreck's location. Bags, hammocks, and other floating items were recovered. In 1956 the wreck was found by National Park Service historian Edwin C. Bearss; National Park Service maintenance man Don Jacks; and geologist Warren Grabau. After many false starts, the vessel was raised in 1964 and taken to Pascagoula, Miss., where it deteriorated in the hot Gulf sun from 1965–77 while awaiting restoration funds. Finally, Congress granted funds to restore and exhibit the USS *Cairo.* The vessel was partially restored and is on display with a museum containing artifacts in the Vicksburg National Military Park. Hundreds of recovered items, such as rubber combs, pumps, knives, forks, shells, and other material are now exhibited in the USS *Cairo* Museum. (*ORN,* 23:544–56, 580; 25:141, 282; *DANFS,* 2, 9; *Chief of Engineers Report 1874,* 365; *CWC,* 6-347; 349–53; Bearss, *Hardluck Ironclad; WCWN,* 151; McGrath, "Preservation of the U.S.S. *Cairo,*" *Eleventh Annual Conference,* 96–106.)

Capitol. Confederate. Side-wheel steamer, 488 or 499 tons. Length 224 feet, beam 32 feet, depth 6 feet or 6 feet 6 inches, 6 boilers. Built in 1854 or 1855 at Jeffersonville, Ind. Partially burned on June 28, 1862. Was later scuttled in July 1862 in the Yazoo River, a half-mile below Liverpool Landing. Its engines and machinery were removed and transferred to Selma, Ala., and later to Mobile. Some equipment was put on the CSS *Arkansas.* Part of the wreck was removed in 1873 by the U.S. Army Corps of Engineers. The shaft was removed by the U.S. Army Corps of Engineers in 1876 and dropped in a bar off the main channel. (Mills, *Of Men and Rivers,* 51; *Chief of Engineers Report 1873,* 483; *Chief of Engineers Report 1874,* 366; *Chief of Engineers Report 1876,* 1:78; *MSV,* 29; *WPD,* 71.)

CSS *Charm.* Confederate. Side-wheel transport steamer, 223 tons. Built in 1860 at Cincinnati. Lashed to the *Paul Jones* and scuttled by Confederates on May 17, 1863, in the Big Black River. Found in 1962 due to bank erosion. Visible in 1965 and 1989 because of low water. Portions of a paddle wheel are located in the Grand Gulf Military Park, just west of Port Gibson. (*CWC,* 6-280; *EAS,* 161; *WCWN,* 246.)

Clyde (Glyde). Union. Probably stern-wheel steamer, 25 tons. Built in 1862 at Portsmouth, Ohio. Lost in 1864 in the Yazoo River. Was removed by the U.S. Army Corps of Engineers between 1878 and 1879. (*Executive Documents, HR, Forty-fifth Congress, 1878–79,* 628; *MSV,* 40.)

Cotton Plant (Flora Temple). Confederate. Side-wheel steamer. Length 158 feet, beam 30 feet, depth 4 feet. Built in 1858 in Monongahela, Pa., as the *Flora Temple.* Renamed *Cotton Plant.* The vessel's boilers exploded on the Sunflower River at Lake George on July 24, 1863. Found by Union forces 17.7 miles up the Sunflower River in Lake George with its smokestacks above water. (*ORN,* 25:134, 286; *WPD,* 113, 167.)

Cotton Plant. Confederate. Side-wheel steamer, 59 tons. Cargo of cotton. Built in 1859 at Rochester, Pa. Was burned and abandoned in the Tallahatchie River by its crew on July 23–24, 1863, to prevent its capture by the Union. Appears to be a different vessel than the preceding one but could be the same. (*OR,* 24:3:1016; *CWC,* 6-216; *DANFS,* 2:512; *WCWN,* 246; *MSV,* 73, 261; *WPD,* 113.)

Deer Island. Confederate. Schooner. Cargo of twenty barrels and thirty bags of flour, and thirteen tierces of rice. En route from Mobile for Biloxi, Miss. Chased by the USS *Bohio* and scuttled by the Confederates on May 13, 1862, in Mississippi Sound off Petit Bois. The owner, the captain, and two crewmen were captured and twelve bags of flour were removed. (*ORN*, 18:496.)

Delight. Confederate. Fishing schooner. Owned by New Orleans residents. Crew of four. Carried a Rebel pass, Rebel flag, and a U.S. flag when captured with the sloop *Express* on December 9, 1861, off the Cat Island Passage, Miss. by the USS *New London*. Was sunk to act as a Union obstruction in the Petit Bois Channel between the Gulf of Mexico and Mississippi Sound on January 7, 1862. (*ORN*, 16:817; *CWC*, 6-220.)

De Soto. U.S. Side-wheel steamer, 104 gross tons. Built in 1859 at Wellsville, Ohio. Exploded on December 9, 1865, at Pascagoula, with eleven killed. Was probably repaired. (*MSV*, 53, 255; *WPD*, 126.)

CSS *Dew Drop*. Confederate. Side-wheel steamer, 184 tons. Cargo of commissary stores. Built in 1858 at Cincinnati. Was burned to the water's edge and sank on May 30 or 25, 1863, in the Quiver River, 15 miles below Greenwood to block the channel. Act. Lt. G. W. Brown led a Union force that completed the vessel's destruction. The wreckage was visible in 1959. (*OR*, 24:3:372; *ORN*, 25:134, 136; *CWC*, 6-220; *WCWN*, 246; *MSV*, 54; *WPD*, 126.)

Dot. Confederate. Steam transport. Ferried Confederate supplies up the Big Black River. Was stripped of its machinery and sunk at the road crossing on the Big Black River to serve as a bridge for fleeing Confederate troops heading for Vicksburg on May 17, 1863. Torched and burned to the water's edge by retreating Confederates. (National Park Service historian, pers. comm.)

CSS *Edward J. Gay*. Confederate. Side-wheel steamer, 823 tons. Length 277 feet, beam 39 feet, draft 8 feet 6 inches. Built in 1859 at St. Louis. Was scuttled by Confederates in the Yalobusha River about July 13, 1863. In February 1864 the wreck was reported to have had its decks just above water. (*ORN*, 25:286, 756; *CWC*, 6-223; *WCWN*, 246; *MSV*, 60; *WPD*, 142.)

Emma Bett. Confederate. Stern-wheel steamer, 79 tons. Built in 1858 at Pittsburgh, Pa. Was captured by three boats from the USS *Forest Rose* and USS *Linden* and set afire in the Quiver River near the Sunflower River on May 30, 1863. (*ORN*, 25:134, 286; *CWC*, 6-224; *MSV*, 64; *WPD*, 149.)

Express. Confederate. Fishing sloop. Crew of four. Was captured with the schooner *Delight* off Cat Island Passage on December 9, 1861, by the USS *New London*. Was probably filled with sand and scuttled on January 7, 1862, to block the Petit Bois Channel between the Mississippi Sound and the Gulf of Mexico. (*ORN*, 16:817; *DANFS*, 5:440; *CWC*, 6-225.)

Fall City (Falls City). Confederate. Side-wheel steamer, 642 tons. Length 308 feet, beam 36 feet, depth 6 feet 6 inches, 5 boilers. Built in 1853 at Louisville. Sank during the Civil War. Located near Snyder's Bluff on the Yazoo River. (*Chief of Engineers Report 1874*, 365; *MSV*, 70; *WPD*, 160.)

Ferd Kennett (Ferd Kennet). Confederate. Side-wheel steamer, 591 tons. Length 238 feet, beam 40 feet 6 inches, depth 6 feet 6 inches. Built in 1861 at St. Louis. Seized by Confederates in May 1861 for use as a transport. Was burned and sunk by Confederates on July 17, 1863, at the mouth of the Yalobusha River near Greenwood. Part of the wreck was removed by the U.S. Army Corps of Engineers in 1900 and 1901. (*ORN*, 25:286, 320; *CWC*, 6-226; *Chief of Engineers 1901*, 2048; *WCWN*, 246; *MSV*, 72; *WPD*, 165.)

Fox (A. J. Whitmore) (Fanny) (Strike) (Washington Potts). Confederate. Steam tug, 432 bulk tons or gross tons. Length 180 feet, beam 28 feet, depth 8 feet 11 inches. Carried an assorted cargo. Built in 1857 in New York City. En route from Havana, Cuba for Mobile or Pascagoula, Miss. Was previously captured by the Union in Berwick Bay in May 1862. Used as a towboat, transport, dispatch boat, and then a private tow boat. Recaptured by a Confederate raiding party of fourteen under Acting Master George C. Andrews of the Confederate navy at a coal yard at Pass a l'Outre on April 12, 1863. Converted to a blockade-runner. Chased aground in Horn Island Pass near Pascagoula by the USS *Genesee*, USS *Jackson*, and USS *Calhoun*. Was burned to the water's edge by its crew to prevent its capture on September 12–13, 1863. The cargo and engine were destroyed. (*OR*, 26:2:244, 52:2:531; *ORN*, 17:551–53; 20:141, 583–85, 809; *LLC*, 285, 299; Horner, *Blockade-Runners*, 203.)

Freestone (*Free Stone*). U.S. Side-wheel steamer, 150 tons. Built in 1858 at Cincinnati. Its hull was constructed at Murrysville, Va. Snagged on September 27, 1865, a quarter-mile below Piney Bayou at Yazoo City. Was probably removed by the U.S. Army Corps of Engineers in the 1870s. (*Chief of Engineers Report 1874*, 366; *MSV*, 77, 262; *WPD*, 173–74.)

Garonne. Confederate. Sloop, 14 tons. Cargo of 165 small bales of tobacco. Was captured by boats from the USS *Santee* on December 30, 1861, off the Galveston Bar, Tex. after a 6-mile chase. Was scuttled to act as a Union obstruction on January 7, 1862, to block the Petit Bois Channel between Mississippi Sound and the Gulf of Mexico. (*ORN*, 17:86–87.)

CSS *General Clark*. Confederate. Side-wheel steamer, 214 tons. Length 182 feet, beam 28 feet 4 inches, depth 10 feet 8 inches. Built in 1819 at Silver Creek, Ind. Set afire, turned adrift, and sank on June 26, 1862, at Liverpool Landing on the Yazoo River. (*ORN*, 23:242–43; *MSV*, 80.)

CSS *General Earl Van Dorn*. Confederate. Side-wheel steam cottonclad ram. Armed with one 32-pounder. Built in 1853 at Algiers, La. Set afire by Confederates at Liverpool Landing and drifted down the Yazoo River on June 26, 1862, toward Union vessels. Blown up "terribly." Was removed by the U.S. Army Corps of Engineers in 1878–79. (*OR*, 15:515; 52:1 [supp.]: 40; *ORN*, 23:242–43; ser. 2, 1:253; *Executive Documents, HR, Forty-fifth Congress, 1878–79*, 628; *WPD*, 180.)

CSS *General Polk* (*Ed Howard*) (*Howard*). Confederate. Side-wheel steam gunboat, 390 tons. Length 280 feet, beam 35 feet, draft 8 feet. Armed with six or seven guns (another source—two rifled 32-pounders and one 32-pounder smoothbore). Built in 1852 at New Albany, Ind. Purchased by Confederates in 1861 at New Orleans. Set afire and drifted toward Union vessels on June 26, 1862, at Liverpool Landing in the Yazoo River. Was removed by the U.S. Army Corps of Engineers in 1878–79.

(*OR*, 15:515; 52:1 [supp.]: 40; *ORN*, 23:242–43; ser. 2, 1:253; Pratt, *Western Waters*, 227; *Executive Documents, HR, Forty-fifth Congress, 1878–79*, 628; *WCWN*, 244; *MSV*, 60; *WPD*, 140.)

Golden Age. Confederate. Side-wheel steamer. Length 180 feet, beam 32 feet, depth 6 feet 6 inches. Built in 1858 at Pittsburgh, Pa. Was sunk with the *R. J. Lockland, John Walsh*, and *Scotland* to act as an obstruction in the Yazoo River in May 1863 about 15 miles below Fort Pemberton to block advancing Union vessels. The Union forces burned the vessel above the waterline. Was removed by the U.S. Corps of Engineers in 1878–79. (*OR*, 24:3:372; *ORN*, 25:133; *CWC*, 6-241; *Chief of Engineers Report 1873*, 483; *Executive Documents, HR, Forty-fifth Congress, 1878–79*, 628; *MSV*, 86; *WPD*, 190.)

Hartford City. Confederate. Side-wheel towboat steamer, 150 tons. Built in 1856 at McKeesport, Pa. Was burned by Confederates to prevent its capture on July 24–25, 1863, in the Yazoo River. (*OR*, 24:3:1016; *CWC*, 6-249–50; *WCWN*, 247; *MSV*, 92; *WSTD*, 93.)

H. D. Mears (*Meares*). Confederate. Side-wheel steamer, 338 tons. Length 214 feet, beam 34 feet, depth 5 feet 6 inches, 5 boilers. Built in 1860 at Wheeling, Va. (W. Va.). Was scuttled by Confederates in the Sunflower River on July 25, 1863, to escape capture by a Union fleet. (*ORN*, 25:286; *CWC*, 6-244; *MSV*, 90; *WCWN*, 247; *EAS*, 171; *WPD*, 203.)

CSS Hope. Confederate. Side-wheel steamer, 193 tons. Length 128 feet, beam 34 feet, depth 5 feet. Built in 1855 at Louisville. Was burned by Confederates on July 24, 1863, at Eagle Bend near Fort Pemberton near the Yazoo River. Was probably removed by the U.S. Army Corps of Engineers in the 1870s. (*OR*, 24:3:1016; *ORN*, 25:286; *Chief of Engineers Report 1873*, 483; *Chief of Engineers Report 1874*, 366; *MSV*, 97; *WCWN*, 247; *WPD*, 217.)

Idaho. Union. Screw steamer, 522 tons. Built in 1864 at Mystic, Conn. Collided with the steamer *Poland* on June 3, 1865, and sank with the loss of ten to twelve lives. (*Daily Examiner*, June 19, 1865; *Executive Documents, HR, Forty-fifth Congress, 1878–79*, 678; *MSV*, 100.)

CSS *Ivy* (*El Paraguay*) (*New Orleans*) (*Roger Williams*) (*W. H. Ivy*). Confederate. Side-wheel steamer, 447 bulk tons, 454 tons. Length 191 feet, beam 28 feet, depth 9 feet. Complement of sixty, with one rifled 8-inch gun (another source—one rifled 32-pounder) and two 24-pounder brass howitzers. Built in 1857 at Brooklyn, N.Y. Was later converted to a privateer by Confederates. Was sunk by Confederates with other steamers in the Yazoo River near Liverpool Landing in May 1863 to block approaching Union vessels. Union forces burned the above-water portions of the vessel when they were unable to get around the wrecks. The wrecking boat *Travis Wright* removed part of the wreck in November 1873. The remaining hulk was removed by the U.S. Army Corps of Engineers in 1878–79. (*ORN*, 25:133, 765; ser. 2, 1:256; *CWC*, 6-252; *Chief of Engineers Report 1873*, 483; *Executive Documents, HR, Forty-fifth Congress, 1878–79*, 628; *WCWN*, 229; *MSV*, 187; Pratt, *Western Waters*, 227; *WPD*, 228.)

CSS *J. F. Pargoud* (*J. Frank Paragoud*). Confederate. Stern-wheel or side-wheel steamer, 338 or 522 tons. Length 219 feet, beam 36 feet 6 inches, depth 7 feet. Built in 1860 at Jeffersonville, Ind. Was scuttled 3 miles from Greenwood on the Yazoo River adjacent to Fort Pemberton on May 13, 1863, and burned on July 14, 1863, to prevent capture by Rear Adm. David D. Porter's Union fleet. (*OR*, 24:1:389; 24:3:302, 668; *ORN*, 25:283, 286; *Chief of Engineers Report 1874*, 365; *CWC*, 6-280; *MSV*, 187; *WPD*, 238.)

John Walsh. Confederate. Side-wheel steamer, 809 tons. Length 275 feet, beam 38 feet, depth 18 feet. Built in 1858 at Cincinnati. Was sunk with the *Golden Age, Scotland,* and *R. J. Lockland* and later burned to the water's edge in the Yazoo River, 15 miles below Greenwood, opposite Southworth's Landing, to block the river and close the Tallahatchie River and Yalobusha River to advancing Union vessels. Was burned in May 1863 by Union forces from the USS *Forest Rose,* USS *Linden,* and USS *Petrel.* (*OR*, 24:1:380, 389; 243:372; *ORN*, 25:286; *CWC*, 6-257; *Chief of Engineers Report 1873*, 483; *Chief of Engineers Report 1874*, 365; *EAS*, 176; *MSV*, 116; *WPD*, 256–57.)

USS *Lily* (*Jessie*) (*Jessie Benton*). Union. Screw towboat steamer, 50 tons. Built in 1862 at St. Louis. Transferred to the Union navy from the Union army in 1862. Was sunk in 10 fathoms after colliding with the USS *Choctaw* during an attack on Drumgould's Bluff on the Yazoo River on April 28, 1863. The cook was below and drowned. Vessel was probably later raised. (*ORN*, 24:585–86, 644; ser. 2, 1:128; *WSTD*, 122.)

CSS *Livingston*. Confederate. Side-wheel steamer. Length 180 feet, beam 40 feet, depth 9 feet or 9 feet 9 inches. Armed with two rifled 30-pounders and four shell guns (another source—six rifled 32-pounders. Built in 1861 at New Orleans as a ferryboat. Set afire and floated down the Yazoo River toward the Union fleet at the raft at Liverpool Landing on June 26, 1862. (*OR*, 15:515; 52:1 [supp.]: 40; *ORN*, ser. 2, 1:258; *CWC*, 6-262–63; Pratt, *Western Waters*, 227–28; *WCWN*, 245; *WPD*, 290.)

Luella. Union. Stern-wheel steamer, 135 tons. Carried a company of the 29th Iowa Infantry Regiment in the White River Expedition. Probably built in 1860 at New Haven, Mo. Sank in March 1863 on the Tallahatchie River. The Iowa company lost all its arms and supplies. (*OR*, 24:144; *WPD*, 298.)

CSS *Magenta*. Confederate. Side-wheel steamer, 782 tons. Length 265 feet, beam 40 feet, depth 8 feet 6 inches, 8 boilers. Cargo of cotton. Built in 1861 at New Albany, Ind. Was burned on the Yazoo River about 5 miles above Yazoo City on May 24–31, 1863, to prevent its capture by Union gunboats. Was probably removed by the U.S. Army Corps of Engineers in the 1870s. (*ORN*, 25:133, 283, 286; *Chief of Engineers Report 1873*, 483; *Chief of Engineers Report 1874*, 366; *CWC*, 6-265; *MSV*, 133; *WPD*, 302.)

CSS *Magnolia*. Confederate. Side-wheel steamer, 824 tons. Length 258 feet, beam 44 feet, depth 7 feet 6 inches, 5 boilers. Cargo of cotton. Built in 1859 at New Albany, Ind. Was burned 4–5 miles above Yazoo City on July 14, 1863, as Rear Adm. David D. Porter's Union gunboats approached. Was probably removed by the U.S. Army Corps of Engineers in the 1870s. (*OR*, 24:2:668; *ORN*, 24:284, 541; 25:283, 286; *Chief of Engineers Report 1874*, 366; *CWC*, 6-265–66; *MSV*, 134; *WPD*, 303–4.)

Mary Crane. Union. Stern-wheel steamer, 111 tons. Hull built at Madison, Ill. Completed in 1862 at Evansville, Ind. Burned on January 8, 1863, on Lake Cormorant. Its machinery was salvaged and taken to Louisville in September 1863. (*MSV,* 139, 280; *WPD,* 311.)

CSS *Mary E. Keene* (*Mary Keene*). Confederate. Side-wheel steamer, 659 tons. Length 238 feet, beam 38 feet, depth 7 feet 8 inches, 5 boilers. Built in 1860 at New Albany, Ind. Was scuttled on July 14, 1863, at the foot of French Bend near Yazoo City (also reported as being 2 miles below Greenwood) to prevent capture by approaching Union gunboats. Burned on July 24, 1863. Part of the wreck was removed by the U.S. Army Corps of Engineers snagboat *John R. Meigs* in 1879–80 and 1897–98. The U.S. Army Corps of Engineers snagboat *Columbia* removed part of the wreck's wheel in 1897–99. (*ORN,* 25:286; *Chief of Engineers Report 1873,* 483; *Chief of Engineers Report 1874,* 366; *Chief of Engineers Report 1880,* 2:1310; *Chief of Engineers Report 1898,* 1620; *Chief of Engineers Report 1901,* 2519–20; *CWC,* 6-268; *MSV,* 139; *WPD,* 312.)

Mist. Union. Steamer. Was burned by 20 Confederate guerrillas under Dick Holland near Ship Island in the Mississippi Gulf at 3:00 p.m. on October 22, 1863. The vessel's captain was pro-Confederate and claimed $17,000 had been taken from him. The captain and ten men were allowed to leave. The pilot claimed $5,000 Confederate had been taken from the safe. (*OR,* 31:1:32, 780; *ORN,* 25:521.)

CSS *Mobile.* Confederate. Wooden 3-mast screw steamer, 250, 282, 283, or 1,000 tons. Ready for railroad iron plating. Length 150 feet. Armed with three 32-pounder smoothbores, one rifled 32-pounder, one 8-inch smoothbore, and probably one additional gun. Built in 1860 at Philadelphia. Ran the blockade in 1861 and 1862. Burned by Confederates 2 miles (also reported as 15 miles) below Yazoo City on May 20–21, 1863, while being converted to an ironclad gunboat. Was probably removed by the U.S. Army Corps of Engineers in the 1870s. (*ORN,* 25:8; ser. 2, 1:260; *Chief of Engineers Report 1873,* 483; *Chief of Engineers Report 1874,* 366; *CWC,* 6-271–72; Pratt, *Western Waters,* 230; *WCWN,* 230; *MSV,* 147.)

Natchez. Confederate. Side-wheel steamer, 714 tons. Length 270 feet, beam 34 feet, depth 8 feet, 6 boilers. Built in 1854 at Cincinnati. Burned at Castleman on April 4, 1863. (*ORN,* 25:286; *MSV,* 152, 283; *WPD,* 337.)

CSS *Natchez.* Confederate. Side-wheel cottonclad steam gunboat, 800 tons. Length 273 feet, beam 38 feet, depth 8 feet. Built in 1860 at Cincinnati. Was burned by Confederates on March 13, 1863, a mile below Burtonia (Bertonia) Landing, about 25 miles above Yazoo City when Union gunboats advanced. Its machinery was salvaged after the Civil War. Was probably removed by the U.S. Army Corps of Engineers in the 1870s. (*OR,* 24:3:746; *ORN,* 24:541; *CWC,* 6-275; *Chief of Engineers Report 1873,* 483; *Chief of Engineers Report 1874,* 366; *MSV,* 152; *WPD,* 337.)

Osceola. Confederate. Sloop. Crew of two. Was captured by the USS *New London* on December 9, 1861, off Cat Island. Was probably filled with sand and scuttled on January 7, 1862, to block the Petit Bois Channel, between the Mississippi Sound and the Gulf of Mexico. (*ORN,* 16:817; *CWC,* 6-278.)

CSS *Paul Jones.* Confederate. Side-wheel steamer and store boat, 353 tons. Length 172 feet, beam 34 feet, depth 6 feet 6 inches. Built in 1855 at McKeesport, Pa. Transported Confederate supplies up the Big Black River. Lashed to the *Charm* and sunk on May 17, 1863, in the Big Black River. The wreck was visited by divers in 1962 and was exposed in low water in 1965 and 1988. Some artifacts have been removed. (*OR,* 52:1 [supp.]: 40; *CWC,* 6-280–81; *MSV,* 169; *WPD,* 364.)

Paul Pry. Confederate. Ship. Wrecked 2 miles above the mouth of the Big Sunflower River (62 miles above Yazoo City) during the Civil War. Was probably removed in the 1870s by the U.S. Army Corps of Engineers. (*Chief of Engineers Report 1873,* 483; *Chief of Engineers Report 1874,* 366.)

USS *Petrel* (*Duchess*) (*Number 5*). Union. Stern-wheel tinclad gunboat, 226 tons. Complement of more than 66 with eight 24-pounder howitzers. Built in 1862 at Brownsville, Pa., with machinery from the *Jacob Poe.* Was captured by Confederate sharpshooters and two 10-pounder Parrotts on the Yazoo River 3–4 miles above Yazoo City on April 22, 1864, when its boilers and steam pipes were hit by shells. Had four wounded, two killed, and Acting Master Thomas McElroy and the pilot captured. At least nine African-American crewmen were missing. The USS *Prairie Bird* was nearby but did not come to the aid of the USS *Petrel*. The Confederates removed the USS *Petrel*'s stores and guns then burned the vessel. Was removed by the U.S. Army Corps of Engineers in 1878–79. (*ORN*, 26:246–59, 267, 280, 286; ser. 2, 1:176; *Executive Documents, HR, Forty-fifth Congress, 1878–79*, 628; Pratt, *Western Waters*, 240.)

CSS *Peytona*. Confederate. Side-wheel steamer, 685 tons. Length 256 or 268 feet, beam 33 feet, depth 8 feet, 5 boilers. Built in 1859 at New Albany, Ind. Tender to the ironclad CSS *Mississippi* at New Orleans. Was burned and scuttled in the Yazoo River at Eureka Landing (Eureka Plantation), about 24 miles above Yazoo City near Satartia on July 14, 1863, by Cdr. Isaac N. Brown to prevent its capture by Adm. David D. Porter's Union gunboats. (*OR*, 24:2:668; *ORN*, 25:283, 286; *Chief of Engineers Report 1873*, 483; *Chief of Engineers Report 1874*, 366; *CWC*, 6-282; *MSV*, 171; *WPD*, 369.)

***Poland*.** U.S. Stern-wheel steamer, 161 tons. Built in 1857 at Elizabeth, Pa. Collided with the steamer *Idaho* and sank on June 3, 1865, in the Yazoo River, with twelve killed. (*Daily Examiner*, June 21, 1865; *MSV*, 175, 290; *WPD*, 375.)

CSS *Prince of Wales*. Confederate. Side-wheel transport steamer, 572 tons. Length 248 feet, beam 40 feet, depth 7 feet. Built in 1860 at Cincinnati. Was burned near Yazoo City opposite Andrews' Landing on July 14, 1863, to prevent its capture by Adm. David D. Porter's Union gunboats. (*ORN*, 25:283, 286; *Chief of Engineers Report 1874*, 365; *CWC*, 6-289; *MSV*, 178; *WPD*, 378.)

***R. E. Hill*.** U.S. Stern-wheel steamer, 103 tons. Length 128 feet, beam 22 feet, depth 4 feet. Built in 1863 at Warsaw, Ill. Snagged on August 26, 1865, at the Oxbow at Greenwood, with nineteen killed. (*MSV*, 180, 292; *WPD*, 383.)

CSS *Republic*. Confederate. Side-wheel steamer, 689 tons. Length 249 feet, beam 40 feet, depth 7 feet 4 inches. Built in 1855 at Jeffersonville, Ind. While being converted into a ram similar to the CSS *Arkansas*, the CSS *Republic* was burned on May 20–21, 1863, 2 miles below Yazoo City at the navy yard. (*ORN*, 25:8; *Chief of Engineers Report 1873*, 483; *Chief of Engineers Report 1874*, 365; *EAS*, 188; Pratt, *Western Waters*, 230; *WCWN*, 248; *WPD*, 391.)

***R. J. Lockland* (*R. J. Lackland*).** Confederate. Side-wheel steamer, 710 tons. Length 265 feet, beam 40 feet, depth 7 feet. Built in 1857 at Cincinnati. Was scuttled along with the *Golden Age, Scotland,* and *John Walsh* in the Yazoo River, 15 miles below Greenwood and burned on May 22, 1863, to block the channel as Union gunboats approached. (*ORN*, 25:133, 286; *Executive Documents, HR, Forty-fifth Congress, 1878–79*, 628; *DANFS*, 2:559; *WPD*, 384.)

CSS *St. Mary* (*Alexandria*) (USS *Alexandria*) (USS *Sidewheeler No. 40*). Confederate. Side-wheel steamer, 60 tons. Length 89 feet 9 inches, beam 15 feet, depth 4 feet, 1 boiler and engine. Armed with two guns. Burned in the Yazoo River in July 1863. Was raised by Union forces. (*ORN*, 2, 1:265; *WCWN*, 165, 245.)

CSS *St. Philip* (*San Juan*) (*Star of the West*). Confederate. Side-wheel steamer, 1,172 tons. Length 228 feet 3 inches, beam 32 feet 10 inches, depth 24 feet 6 inches, speed 11.5 knots. Armed with two 68-pounders and four 32-pounders. Built in 1852 as the *San Juan* at Greenpoint, N.Y. As the *Star of the West,* it sailed between New York City and the east coast of Central America. Chartered by the federal government to reinforce Fort Sumter, S.C., in January 1861. Confederate batteries in Charleston Harbor fired the first cannon shots of the Civil War at the *Star of the West,* driving it off. On April 17, 1861, the CSS *General Rusk* captured the vessel. Renamed CSS *St. Philip*. Was sunk to act as an obstruction in the Tallahatchie River to help anchor a raft at Fort Pemberton on March 10, 1863. Pieces of the vessel's machinery and iron were removed by the U.S. Army Corps of Engineers in 1876–97. The vessel was visible in 1951 and is listed in the National Register of Historic Places. (*OR*, 24:1:380, 389; 24:2:680; *ORN*, 24:266, 284, 295–96, 302, 541, 671; 25:133; *Chief of Engineers Report 1879*, 116; *Chief of Engineers Report 1880*, 2:1310; *Chief of Engineers Report 1897*, 308, 1933; *CWC*, 6-296–97; Mills, *Of Men and Rivers*, 51; *WPD*, 432.)

***Scotland*.** Confederate. Side-wheel transport steamer, 567 tons. Length 225 feet, beam 38 feet, depth 7 feet 6 inches, 4 boilers. Built in 1855 at Jeffersonville, Ind. Was scuttled by Confederates along with the *Golden Age, R. J. Lockland,* and *John Walsh* on May 22, 1863, in the Yazoo River, 15 miles below Greenwood and opposite Southworth's Landing. Union forces burned the above-water portions of the vessel. (*OR*, 24:3:372; *ORN*, 25:133, 136, 756; *Chief of Engineers Report 1873*, 483; *Chief of Engineers Report 1874*, 365; *CWC*, 6-299; *EAS*, 190; *WPD*, 421.)

CSS *Sharp* (*J. M. Sharp*). Confederate. Side-wheel transport steamer and dispatch boat, 218 tons. Length 147 feet, beam 29 feet, depth 6 feet 6 inches. Built in 1859 at Jeffersonville, Ind. Was burned to prevent its capture in the Yalobusha River in early February 1864. Was raised and rebuilt as the *J. M. Sharp* in 1865. (*ORN*, 25:136, 756; *CWC*, 6-301; *WCWN*, 249; *MSV*, 106; *WPD*, 233.)

***Thirty-fifth Parallel* (*Parallel*).** Confederate. Side-wheel steamer, 419 tons. Protected by cotton bales. Built in 1859 at Cincinnati. Ran into trees and was disabled in the narrow Tallahatchie River on March 10, 1863, when the USS *Chillicothe* and USS *Baron De Kalb* approached. Burned on March 13, 1863. (*OR*, 24:1:397; *ORN*, 25:286; *CWC*, 6-315; *WCWN*, 249; *MSV*, 210; *WPD*, 450.)

▷ **VESSELS WITHOUT NAMES**

ironclad. Confederate. Twin screw side-wheel ram. Length 310 feet, beam 70 feet, armor 4.5-inch iron, 4 engines. Designed along the lines of the CSS *Louisiana*. Was burned in the stocks at Yazoo City to prevent its capture on May 20–21, 1863. (*ORN*, 25:8; Pratt, *Western Waters*, 133, 230; *WCWN*, 209.)

steamer. Confederate. Possibly the *Hine* or *Beaufort*, is located downstream of the wrecks of the *Dot*, *Charm*, and *Paul Jones* in the Big Black River. Probably sank on May 17, 1863. (Vicksburg National Park Service ranger, pers. comm.)

vessels. Confederate. Six large ships, three large flatboats were captured and destroyed by a Union small boat expedition from the USS *Cowslip* and USS *Vincennes* on June 2, 1864, in Biloxi Bay. (*ORN*, 21:792.)

Mississippi River

Domination of the Mississippi River was a major Union objective in the West. By occupying the Mississippi River, the Confederacy would be divided, and Texas beef and other supplies would be cut off from the Confederate armies in the East. Union riverboats under the command of Flag Officer Andrew H. Foote, then Flag Officer Charles H. Davis, and finally Rear Adm. David D. Porter steamed southward from Cairo, Ill., while Rear Adm. David G. Farragut's deep-water ships steamed northward from occupied New Orleans.

Confederate vessels the *Admiral*, CSS *Grampus*, *L. B. Winchester*, CSS *John Simonds*, CSS *Kanawha Valley*, CSS *Mohawk*, CSS *Red River*, *Yazoo*, and the floating battery CSS *New Orleans* were trapped and scuttled at Island No. 10 in March–April 1862. Another Confederate fleet was destroyed at the Battle of Memphis on June 6, 1862, with the loss of the cottonclad gunboats the CSS *Colonel Lovell*, CSS *General Beauregard*, CSS *General Bragg*, CSS *General M. Jeff Thompson*, CSS *General Sterling Price*, and CSS *General Sumter*.

As the Confederate steamboats abandoned the Mississippi River for smaller rivers and streams, Confederate strongholds fell at Grand Gulf, Mississippi; Port Hudson, Louisiana; and Vicksburg, Mississippi. The Union fleets were united, and the Mississippi River became a lifeline to supply Union troops attacking and occupying the Confederacy's heartland.

Confederate spies continually set Union steamboats on fire with bombs and incendiaries. At St. Louis Confederate agents burned the Union steamers the *Cherokee*, *Edward F. Dix*, *Glasgow*, *Northerner*, *Sunshine*, and *Welcome* on July 5, 1863; and the *Imperial*, *Hiawatha*, *Jesse K. Bell*, and *Post Boy* on September 13, 1863. The *Ruth*, with a Union army payroll of $2.6 million destined for Maj. Gen.

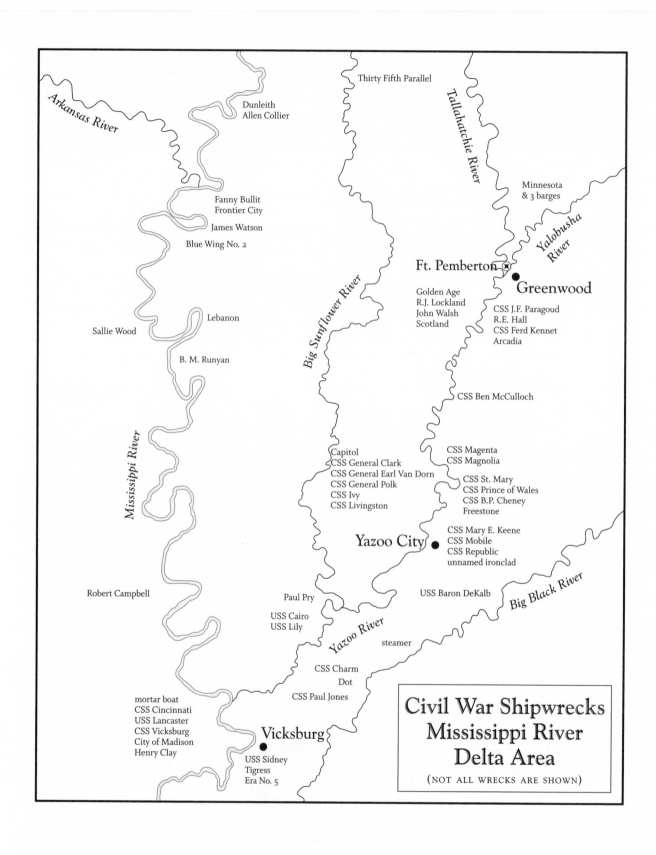

Arkansas River

Thirty Fifth Parallel

Tallahatchie River

Dunleith
Allen Collier

Minnesota
& 3 barges

Fanny Bullit
Frontier City

Yalobusha River

James Watson

Blue Wing No. 2

Ft. Pemberton ⊗ ● Greenwood

Golden Age
R.J. Lockland
John Walsh
Scotland

CSS J.F. Paragoud
R.E. Hall
CSS Ferd Kennet
Arcadia

Lebanon

Sallie Wood

Big Sunflower River

B. M. Runyan

CSS Ben McCulloch

Mississippi River

Capitol
CSS General Clark
CSS General Earl Van Dorn
CSS General Polk
CSS Ivy
CSS Livingston

CSS Magenta
CSS Magnolia

CSS St. Mary
CSS Prince of Wales
CSS B.P. Cheney
Freestone

Yazoo City ●

CSS Mary E. Keene
CSS Mobile
CSS Republic
unnamed ironclad

Robert Campbell

Paul Pry

USS Baron DeKalb

Big Black River

USS Cairo
USS Lily

Yazoo River

steamer

CSS Charm
Dot

CSS Paul Jones

mortar boat
CSS Cincinnati
USS Lancaster
CSS Vicksburg
City of Madison
Henry Clay

Vicksburg ●

USS Sidney
Tigress
Era No. 5

Civil War Shipwrecks
Mississippi River
Delta Area

(NOT ALL WRECKS ARE SHOWN)

Ulysses S. Grant's army at Vicksburg, was destroyed just below Cairo, Ill., by a fire set by Confederate agents.

Confederate guerrillas fired on Union steamers and sometimes captured and burned them, often within sight of Union gunboats and camps. A number of vessels were snagged during the Civil War and were lost or damaged as a result, as the removal of obstacles from the waterways had low priority.

Acacia Cottage (Acacia) (W. H. Langley). Union. Stern-wheel steamer, 109 or 100 tons. Length 145 feet, beam 28 feet, depth 3 feet 6 inches. Built in 1857 at California, Pa. Length 128 feet, beam 23 feet, depth 4 feet. Built in Fraziers Landing Ohio, as the *W. H. Langley*. Its engines were from the *Fannie Malone.* Was captured from Confederates near Memphis on June 6, 1862, after the Battle of Memphis. Snagged and sank on August 21, 1862, about 25 miles above Helena, Ark., with the loss of about 100–140 lives. (*ORN*, 23:379; *WCWN*, 245; *MSV*, 2, 239; *WPD*, 4, 496.)

Admiral. Confederate. Stern-wheel steamer, 244 tons. Length 161 feet, beam 26 feet, 3 boilers. Built in 1853 at McKeesport, Pa. Was scuttled by Confederates near Island No. 10 on April 5, 1862. (*ORN*, 22:757; 23:379; *MSV*, 2, 239; *WPD*, 6.)

Alhambra. Union. Stern-wheel steamer, 187 tons. Built in 1852 at McKeesport, Pa. Burned in 1863 at Commerce, Mo. May have been salvaged. (*MSV*, 6, 240; *WPD*, 11.)

Allen Collier. Union. Stern-wheel steamer, 133 tons. Built in 1860 at Cincinnati. The steamer's captain disobeyed orders not to land to pick up cotton without a Union gunboat escort, so the *Allen Collier* was captured and burned by forty or fifty of Col. Milton Montgomery's guerrillas at Bolivar or Whitworth's Landing on November 7, 1863, opposite and a mile above Laconia, Ark. The USS *Eastport* was anchored less than a half-mile away. Acting Master Lyman Bartholomew, who was the captain of the USS *Eastport*, three African Americans, and a boy rowed to the vessel and were captured by Confederates. The boy escaped. (*OR*, 31:1:36; 32:1:178, 183; *ORN*, 25:535–37; *MSV*, 240; *WPD*, 14.)

Alliance. Union. Stern-wheel steamer, 136 tons. Length 144 feet, beam 27 feet 2 inches, depth 3 feet 11 inches. Built in 1852 at Shousetown, Pa. Stranded on April 17, 1863, on Devil Island, near Cape Girardeau, Mo. Was probably salvaged. (*MSV*, 7, 240; *WPD*, 15.)

Arago. Union. Side-wheel steamer, 268 tons. Length 176 feet, beam 33 feet, depth 6 feet, 3 boilers. Cargo of lime. Built in 1860 at Brownsville, Pa. Was sunk by ice and caught fire at Commerce, Mo., at Dog Tooth Bend on February 6, 1865. Its engines were from the *F. X. Aubrey*. (*MSV*, 12, 242; *WPD*, 26.)

Augustus McDowell. Union. Side-wheel steamer, 451 tons. Built in 1860 at St. Louis. Burned on October 27, 1862, at St. Louis. (*MSV*, 16, 243; *WPD*, 33.)

Badger State. Union. Stern-wheel steamer, 127 tons. Length 140 feet, beam 28 feet, depth 3 feet 6 inches. Built in 1852 at California, Pa. Stranded on December 14, 1862, at Chain of Rocks, 12 miles above St. Louis. (*MSV*, 17, 244; *WPD*, 36.)

Belle Creole. Union. Stern-wheel steamer, 206 tons. Length 190 feet, beam 33 feet, depth 7 feet 6 inches. Built in 1856 at Moundsville, Va. (W. Va.). Snagged at Plum Point, Tenn. on February 1, 1864, with one life lost. Was probably raised. (*MSV*, 19, 245; *WPD*, 41.)

Ben Stickney. U.S Side-wheel steamer, 889 tons. Length 285 feet, beam 40 feet, depth 8 feet, 5 boilers. The *Ben Stickney*'s hull was built at Cannelton, Ind., and completed in 1864 at New Albany, Ind. The machinery was from the *Bostonia* and then from the *James Guthrie*. Snagged on November 16, 1865, at Island No. 18. In 1867 the U.S. Army Corps of Engineers reported the wreck between Island No. 20 and Island No. 21. (*Chief of Engineers Report 1867*, 392; *MSV*, 21, 245; *WPD*, 49.)

Blue Wing No. 2. Union. Side-wheel steamer, 170 tons. Length 150 feet, beam 30 feet, depth 6 feet 6 inches, 3 boilers. Built in 1860 at Jeffersonville, Ind. Originally seized by Union forces from the Confederates. Was captured 8 miles below Napoleon, Ark., at Cypress Bend after being shelled by Confederate artillery. The vessel had no military guard, so it surrendered, was towed, and then burned by Confederates on December 28, 1862, after its cargo was removed. (*OR*, 22:1:218, 886; *ORN*, 26:485; *Chief of Engineers Report 1867*, 391; *MSV*, 16, 244; *WPD*, 55–56.)

B. M. Runyan. Union army. Side-wheel transport steamer, 443 tons. Length 230 feet, beam 34 feet, depth 6 feet 6 inches, 4 boilers. Carried 500 Union soldiers and civilians. Built in 1857 or 1858 at Cincinnati. Sank in shallow water below Alton, Ill., in December 1862. Was raised and repaired in St. Louis in 1864. Snagged at the foot of Island No. 84 near Skipwith's Landing, Miss. and Gaines Landing, Ark. on July 21, 1864. About 70–150 men died. The USS *Prairie Bird* rescued 350. The cabin parted from the hull and sank in a sandbar at American Cutoff. The U.S. Army Corps of Engineers reported the wreck as a navigation hazard in 1867. (*OR*, 41:4:309; *ORN*, 26:485; *Chief of Engineers Report 1867*, 391; *MSV*, 23; *WPD*, 35–36.)

Brilliant. U.S. Side-wheel steamer, 440 tons. Length 241 feet, beam 35 feet, depth 5 feet 7 inches. Built in 1863 at Cincinnati. Burned on October 16, 1865, at New Madrid, Mo., when an oil lamp exploded. Sixty-five people escaped to shore. (*MSV*, 24, 247; *WPD*, 61–62.)

Calypso. U.S. Side-wheel steamer, 245 tons. Length 193 feet, beam 30 feet, depth 5 feet, 2 boilers. Built in 1863 at Wellsville, Ohio. Was sunk by ice on December 16, 1865, at St. Louis. (*MSV*, 28, 247; *WPD*, 69.)

Carrier. U.S. Side-wheel steamer, 345 tons. Length 215 feet, beam 33 feet. Built in 1855 at Jeffersonville, Ind. Sank at Island No. 25 in the Mississippi River on February 21, 1861. Was raised and later sank in the Missouri River at St. Charles on August 12, 1861. (*WPD*, 74.)

Catahoula. Union. Side-wheel steamer, 227 tons. Length 137 feet, beam 33 feet, depth 5 feet. Built in 1858 at Murraysville, Va. (W. Va.). Was burned with the *Chancellor* and *Forest Queen* on October 4, 1863, by Confederate agents in St. Louis. (*OR*, 48:2:195; *MSV*, 30, 248; *WPD*, 75.)

Champion. Union. Side-wheel steamer, 676 tons. Built in 1858 at Cincinnati. Was burned by Confederate agents on August 21, 1863, at Memphis, Tenn., with one killed. (*OR*, 48:2:195; *MSV*, 32, 249; *WPD*, 77.)

Chancellor. Union. Side-wheel steamer, 392 tons. Built in 1856 at New Albany, Ind. Was burned with the *Catahoula* and *Forest Queen* by Confederate agents on October 4, 1863, at St. Louis. (*OR*, 48:2:195; *MSV*, 32, 249; *WPD*, 78.)

Cherokee. Union. Stern-wheel steamer, 261 tons. Built in 1864 at Monongahela, Pa. Burned on July 15, 1864, at St. Louis, along with the *Edward F. Dix, Glasgow, Northerner, Sunshine,* and *Welcome,* at the levee. (*OR*, 41:2:209; *MSV*, 34, 249; *WPD*, 83.)

USS Cincinnati. Union. Ironclad, 512 tons. Length 175 feet, beam 51 feet 2 inches, draft 6 feet, speed 9 miles per hour. Complement of 175, with three 8-inch Dahlgren smoothbores, six 32-pounders, two rifled 42-pounders, and one 12-pounder boat howitzer. Built in 1861 at Carondelet, Mo. Sank the first time on May 10, 1862, with thirty-five killed and wounded at Plum Point, 4 miles above Fort Pillow, when rammed by CSS *General Bragg* in 11 feet of water. Only the pilothouse, chimneys, and jack staffs were above water. Was raised a few days later and refitted. Sank for a second time when hit below the waterline on the stern on May 27, 1863, by shells from Vicksburg's batteries, especially those on Wyman's Hill. Steamed a mile and a half upstream, ran ashore, and was secured to the bank. Sank bow down in 3 fathoms of water and stern up with the upper deck above water and its flag flying within range of a Confederate battery. Lost five killed, fourteen wounded, and fifteen drowned or missing. Three of the dead were with the 58th Ohio Infantry Regiment. The Confederates set the vessel on fire on May 30, 1863. Was raised on August 16, 1863, refitted, and put in service again. Was sold on November 29, 1865. (*OR*, 24:3:354, 358, 926, 937; 52:1 [supp.]: 38–39; *ORN*, 23:4, 5, 19, 20; 25:37–44, 56, 109, 141, 218, 370–71, 384; ser. 2, 1:58; Miller, *Photographic History,* 1:185; 6:149; *WCWN*, 150–51.)

City of Madison. Union. Side-wheel steamer, 419 tons. Cargo of ammunition, Built in 1860 at Madison, Ind. Exploded in September 1863 in a fire caused by Confederate agents near Vicksburg, Miss., with 156 killed, although another report claimed 63 died. (*OR*, 48:2:195; *MSV*, 37, 250; *WPD*, 93–94.)

Clara Bell (Clarabell). Union. Side-wheel steamer, 200 tons. Length 139 feet, beam 28 feet, depth 5 feet 6 inches. Built in 1860 at Louisville. While under guard by four companies of the 6th Mich. Heavy Artillery, the *Clara Bell* was attacked by a Confederate battery on the White River on July 24, 1864, at Caroline Landing, Miss. Hit by thirty shells and had thirteen men wounded. Landed above Caroline Landing to undergo repairs, but Confederates pursued the vessel to Louisiana Bend, where a shell set it afire. (*OR*, 41:1:87–88; *EAS*, 162; *WPD*, 100.)

Clara Eames. Union. Stern-wheel transport steamer, 105 tons. Cargo of cotton. Built in 1862 at Wacouta, Minn. Ambushed about 3.5 miles below Columbia, Ark., by Confederate brigadier general John Marmaduke's brigade of Burbridge's, Jeffers's, and Kitchen's regiments and artillery. The boiler was penetrated by a shell and seventeen additional shells hit the boat. Ran ashore and surrendered on the morning of May 30, 1864. The Confederates took fifteen white and seven African-American prisoners, and burned the boat to the water's edge at Smith's Plantation, about four miles above Sunnyside. (*OR*, 34:1:949, 951–52; *ORN*, 26:339, 406, 804, 806; *MSV*, 38.)

CSS *Colonel Lovell* (*Hercules*). Confederate. Side-wheel cottonclad steam ram, 371 or 521 tons. Length 162 feet, beam 30 feet 10 inches, draft 11 feet. Armed with one 32- or 64-pounder (another source—four guns). Built in 1845 or 1852 at Cincinnati. During the Battle of Memphis on June 6, 1862, its engines malfunctioned. Rammed by the USS *Queen of the West* and the USS *Monarch* and almost cut in two. Sank off Beale Street in the middle of the Mississippi River up to the hurricane deck, with Capt. J. C. Delaney and six or seven of the crew saved. (*OR*, 10:1:913; 52:1 [supp.]: 39–40; *ORN*, 23:120, 133, 140, 379, 685; ser. 2, 1:251; *MSV*, 95.)

Columbia. Union. Screw tug steamer, 44 tons. Built in 1863 at Peninsula, Ohio. Burned on March 30, 1864, at Memphis. (*MSV*, 42, 252.)

USS *Conestoga* (*J. M. Convers*). Union. Side-wheel timberclad steamer, 672 tons. Speed 12 miles per hour, armor 5 feet wood. Armed with two rifled 30-pounder Dahlgrens, one 30-pounder Parrott, three 32-pounders, and one 12-pounder smoothbore. Built in 1859 at Brownsville, Pa. as the coal barge tow boat *J. M. Convers*. Part of the Union army's Western Flotilla before being transferred to the Union navy. Sank on March 8, 1864, in less than four minutes after a night collision with the ram USS *General Price* about 10 miles below Grand Gulf at Boudurant

Point. Only the top of the wheelhouse was visible above water. Two were drowned in the accident. Was raised on September 27, 1865, near Bruinsburg, Miss., with its stores and machinery. (*ORN*, 26:18–20; ser. 2, 1:65; Miller, *Photographic History*, 1:189; Pratt, *Western Waters*, 191, 231; *DANFS*, 2:161; *WTBD*, 46; *WCWN*, 158.)

Continental. Union. Side-wheel steamer. Length 282 feet, beam 41 feet, depth 8 feet 6 inches, 4 boilers. Built in 1862 at Pittsburgh, Pa. Hit the wreck of the *James Montgomery* in early December 1864 and sank at Devil's Island above Cape Girardeau, Mo. Was later raised. (*WPD*, 109, 241.)

Dan. Union. Side-wheel steamer, 112 tons. Armed with one 20-pounder Parrott and one 12-pounder howitzer. Built in 1858 at Calcasieu, La. Was captured from the Confederates by a small boat expedition from the USS *Kensington* in October 1862. Sank in February 1863 in the Mississippi River while in Union service. (*ORN*, 2, 1:71; *CWC*, 6-218.)

Darling. U.S. Side-wheel steamer. Length 180 feet, beam 37 feet, 4 boilers. Built in 1863 in McKeesport, Pa. Sank at Plum Point in December 1865. Was later raised. (*WPD*, 120.)

Denmark. Union. Side-wheel steamer, 283 tons. Length 171 feet, beam 34 feet, depth 5 feet 4 inches. Built in 1856 at Shousetown (Pittsburgh), Pa. Snagged on October 8, 1862, at Atlas Island below Keokuk, Iowa. (*MSV*, 53, 255; *WPD*, 125.)

Diligent. Union. Side-wheel steamer, 140 tons. Built in 1859 at Louisville. Snagged on January 10, 1865, upstream from Helena, Ark. (*OR*, 48:1:35; *MSV*, 55, 256; *WPD*, 129.)

Dunleith. Union. Stern-wheel steamer, 155 tons. Hull built at Shousetown, Pa., and completed in 1856 at Pittsburgh, Pa. Snagged on October 31, 1864, at Island No. 67. (*MSV*, 57, 256; *WPD*, 134.)

Edward F. Dix. Union. Side-wheel steamer. Length 266 feet, beam 40 feet, depth 5 feet 6 inches. Built in 1864 at Madison, Ind. Was burned on July 15, 1864, by Confederate agents along with the *Glasgow, Northerner, Sunshine, Cherokee,* and *Welcome* at the St. Louis levee at 4:00 a.m. Was repaired and later lost on the Red River after hitting the wreck of the USS *Eastport*. (*OR*, 41:2:209; *MSV*, 112; *WPD*, 142.)

Elvira. Union. Side-wheel steamer, 222 tons. Length 172 feet, beam 26 feet, depth 3 feet 6 inches. Built in 1851 at Brownsville, Pa. Snagged on October 11, 1863, below St. Louis, at the foot of Widow Beard's Island. (*Chief of Engineers Report 1867,* 387; *MSV,* 63, 258; *WPD,* 147.)

Empress. Union. Side-wheel steamer, 854 tons. Built in 1861 at Madison, Ind. Was burned on October 28, 1864, at Island No. 34 by Gen. Nathan Bedford Forrest's Confederate cavalry. Also was reported to have hit a snag and broke in two. The wreck was reported present in 1867 but was not considered a navigation hazard due to the Mississippi River's channel change. (*OR,* 39:1:589; *MSV,* 65, 258; *Chief of Engineers Report 1867,* 392; *WPD,* 152.)

E. M. Ryland. Union. Side-wheel steamer, 267 tons. Built in 1857 at Brownsville, Pa. Burned on October 8, 1861, at St. Louis. (*MSV,* 58, 256; *WPD,* 136.)

Enterprise. U.S. Side-wheel steamer, 26 tons. Built in 1861 at Warsaw, Minn. Snagged on October 8, 1865, below Red Wing, Minn. (*MSV,* 65, 259; *WPD,* 153.)

Era No. 5. Union. Stern-wheel steamer, 115 tons. Shallow draft. Built in 1860 at Pittsburgh, Pa. Was captured from the Confederates on February 14, 1863, 15 miles above the mouth of the Big Black River by the USS *Indianola.* Was dismantled with machinery detached, scattered, and sunk in the middle of the Mississippi River below Vicksburg on orders of Maj. Gen. Ulysses S. Grant on February 28, 1863. (*OR,* 24:3:76–77; *ORN,* 24:396; *MSV,* 66; *WPD,* 154.)

Era No. 7 (Indianola). Union. Stern-wheel steamer. Built in 1859 at Freedom, Pa. Snagged on February 24, 1863, 20 miles below Warrenton, Miss. (*WPD,* 154.)

Estrella. Union. Side-wheel steamer, 414 tons. Length 205 feet, beam 35 feet, draft 6 feet. Built in 1862 at Shousetown, Pa. Burned on October 27, 1862, at St. Louis. (*MSV,* 67, 259; *WPD,* 154.)

Eugene. Union. Side-wheel steamer, 298 tons. Length 183 feet, beam 32 feet, depth 5 feet 6 inches. Built in 1860 at Parkersburg, Va. (W. Va.). Snagged on the wreck of the *Eliza* on November 1 or 14, 1862, at Plum Point, Tenn., near Osceola and Fort Pillow, with fifteen lost. (*MSV,* 67, 259; *WPD,* 155.)

Evansville. Union. Stern-wheel steamer, 155 tons. Built in 1854 at West Brownsville, Pa. Snagged on January 28, 1864, at Memphis. (*MSV,* 67, 259; *WPD,* 156.)

Fanny Bullitt. Union. Side-wheel steamer, 438 tons. Length 245 feet, beam 35 feet, depth 7 feet. Built in 1854 at Jeffersonville, Ind. Snagged on March 15, 1864, at Napoleon, Ark. The *Fanny Bullitt* Towhead formed at the wreck site. (*MSV,* 71, 260; *WPD,* 162.)

Fanny McBurney (Fanny McBurnie). Union. Stern-wheel steamer, 207 ton. Built in 1860 at Cincinnati. Stranded on December 6, 1863, at Island No. 34. (*MSV,* 71, 260; *WPD,* 163; *WTBD,* 200.)

Forest Queen. Union. Side-wheel steamer, 419 tons. Built in 1858 at Madison, Ind. Was burned by Confederate agents on October 4, 1863, at St. Louis, along with the *Chancellor* and *Catahoula.* (*OR,* 48:2:195; *MSV,* 74, 261; *WPD,* 169.)

Fort Wayne. U.S. Stern-wheel steamer, 321 tons. Length 148 feet, beam 41 feet, depth 6 feet. Built in 1857 at California, Pa. Sank in February 1861 at Island No. 16 and was raised. (*WPD,* 170.)

Frank Steel (Frank Steele). Union. Side-wheel steamer, 136 tons. Length 175 feet, beam 28 feet. Built in 1857 at Hampton, Ky. Exploded on June 2, 1864, at La Crosse, Wis., with two killed. (*MSV,* 76, 261; *WPD,* 172.)

Frontier City. U.S. Stern-wheel steamer, 144 tons. Cargo of salvaged goods from the *Cedar Rapids* and *A. H. Sevier.* Built in 1860 at Pittsburgh, Pa. Snagged at Napoleon, Ark., at the head of Smith's Cut-off near the mouth of the Arkansas River on January 4, 1861. (*MSV,* 77, 262; *WPD,* 174.)

CSS *General Beauregard* (*Ocean*). Confederate. Side-wheel cottonclad steam ram, 454 tons. Length 161 feet 10 inches, beam 30 feet, draft 10 feet. Armed with possibly four 8-inch guns and one 42-pounder. Built in 1847 at Algiers, La. During the Battle of Memphis on June 6, 1862, the vessel accidentally rammed the CSS *General Sterling Price* and was hulled by shells from the USS *Monarch.* Shells from the USS *Benton* hit its boilers. Was floated a quarter-mile downstream and sunk up to its Texas deck on a bar in 20 feet of water on the Arkansas side of the river. One crewman was killed, three were wounded, and the rest of the crew was captured. Some damaged cotton was later recovered. The side-wheel steamer *Platt Valley* was snagged and sunk by this wreck in 1867. (*OR,* 52:1 [supp.]: 40; *ORN,* 23:118, 120–21, 123–25, 135–36, 140, 143, 196, 379, 685; *CWC,* 6-230–31; *MSV,* 161; *WPD,* 179.)

CSS *General Bragg* (USS *General Bragg*) (*Mexico*). Confederate. Side-wheel steamer, 840 or 1,043 tons. Length 208 feet, beam 32 feet 8 inches, depth 15 feet, draft 12 feet, speed 10 knots. Armed with one 30-pounder rifle, one 32-pounder, and one rifled 12-pounder. Built in 1851 at New York City. Damaged on May 10, 1862, by the USS *Cincinnati* during the Battle of Plum Point above Memphis. Repaired by the Confederates. Sank during the Battle of Memphis on June 6, 1862, when it ran ashore below Memphis. Union forces raised the vessel, but it later sank in 11 feet of water. Renamed USS *General Bragg* after being raised and repaired by Union forces. (Miller, *Photographic History,* 6:83; *CWC,* 6-231–32; *MSV,* 144; *WPD,* 179.)

CSS *General M. Jeff Thompson*. Confederate. Side-wheel steam cottonclad ram. Armed with one gun. Ran aground on June 6, 1862, during the Battle of Memphis opposite President's Island below Memphis by its crew after being heavily damaged. Burned to the water's edge, and its magazine blew up. The damaged cotton was later removed. Half-buried on shore and half-sunk in water. Partially removed in 1867. (*OR,* 52:1:39–40; 10:1:907; *ORN,* 23:118, 120, 123, 136; ser. 2, 2:53; *Chief of Engineers Report 1867,* 386–87, 392; *CWC,* 6-233–34; *WCWN,* 227.)

CSS *General Sterling Price* (*Laurent Millandon*) (USS *General Price*). Confederate. Steam ram, 483 or 633 tons. Length 182 feet, beam 30 feet, depth 9 feet 3 inches, draft 13 feet, speed 12 miles per hour. Complement of seventy-seven, with one 64-pounder gun. Built in 1856 as the *Laurent Millandon* at Cincinnati. Was accidentally sunk by the CSS *General Beauregard* during the Battle of Memphis on June 6, 1862, on the Arkansas side of the river across from Memphis Bluffs near the grounded USS *Queen of the West,* which captured the vessel's surviving crew. The port wheel and wheelhouse were carried away. Was raised by the USS *Champion* and USS *Judge Terrence* on June 15, 1862. Renamed USS *General Price* in Union service. (*OR,* 10:1:908; 52:1 [supp.]: 40; *ORN,* 23:55–56, 142–43, 208; ser. 2, 1:254; *CWC,* 6-235–36; *WCWN,* 227.)

CSS *General Sumter* (*Julius Beebee*) (USS *Sumter*). Confederate. Side-wheel steam gunboat, 400 or 524 tons. Length 182 feet, beam 28 feet 4 inches, depth 10 feet 8 inches. Built in 1853 as the towboat *Junius Beebe* at Algiers, La. Ran aground on the Arkansas side during the Battle of Memphis on June 6, 1862. The vessel was raised and became the USS *Sumter* in Union service. See **USS *Sumter*** in Louisiana for information on a later sinking. (*ORN,* ser. 2, 1:216, 254; *CWC,* 6-236–37; *WCWN,* 162, 227.)

***Geneva*.** U.S. Stern-wheel steamer, 127 tons. Built in 1863 at Brownsville, Pa. Was sunk by ice on December 16, 1865, at St. Louis. (*MSV,* 83, 263; *WPD,* 184.)

***George Sturgess*.** Union. Screw tug, 47 tons. Towed two barges loaded with commissary stores and hay. Built in 1863 at Chicago, Ill. Attempted to run past Vicksburg on the night of May 3, 1863, when hit in the boiler by shells from the Confederate water batteries and set afire along with the two barges it was towing. (*OR,* 24:1:687–88; *MSV,* 84.)

***Gladiator*.** Union. Side-wheel steamer, 425 tons. Length 27 feet, beam 34 feet, depth 5 feet 10 inches. Construction was started at Belle Vernon but completed in 1857 at McKeesport or Pittsburgh, Pa. Stranded on August 14, 1864, at Willard, 65.6 miles above Cairo. (*MSV,* 85, 264; *WPD,* 188.)

***Glasgow*.** Union. Side-wheel steamer, 340 tons. Built in 1862 at New Albany, Ind. Was burned by Confederate agents at the St. Louis levee at 4:00 a.m. on July 15, 1864, along with five other steamboats. Was rebuilt later. (*OR,* 41:2:209; *MSV,* 84; *WPD,* 188.)

USS *Glide*. Union. Stern-wheel tinclad gunboat, 137 tons. Crew of eight European Americans and thirty African Americans, with six 24-pounder howitzers. Built in 1862 at Shousetown, Pa. Accidentally burned on February 7, 1863, a mile below Cairo, Ill., while being refitted. Cast off and floated downstream 1–2 miles below to the Ky., side near Fort Holt. Burned to the water's edge in 5 feet of water. Some shells aboard exploded, but the vessel's magazines did not explode. Two African Americans were killed. Guns, shells, anchors, chains, iron plates, and machinery were salvaged by Union forces. (*ORN*, 24:305–10, 354–55, 417; ser. 2, 1:96; *WCWN*, 172.)

Gordon Grant (Gurdon Grant). Union. Screw steamer, 41 tons. Built in 1855 at Philadelphia. Burned on June 6, 1862, at Fort Pillow, Tenn. (*MSV*, 90, 265.)

CSS Grampus. Confederate. Stern-wheel towboat steamer, 100 tons. Built in 1857 at Brownsville, Pa. (another source— 221 tons, built in 1850 at Freedom, Pa.). Was scuttled below Island No. 10 on April 7, 1862, when the Confederate forces surrendered. Was raised by Union forces and used as a receiving ship. Was lost in 1865 at an unknown location. Its engines were used in the *Mittie Stephens*. There is much confusion over several *Grampus* vessels, so some of this data might be incorrect. (*ORN*, 22:721 725; 23:107, 379; *WPD*, 195; *WSTD*, 86.)

Grampus No. 2. Union. Stern-wheel or side-wheel gunboat, 352 tons. Armed with two brass 12-pounders. Built in 1856 at McKeesport, Pa. Was captured on January 11, 1863, at Wolf Creek by Capt. J. H. McGehee's Ark. Cavalry Company, just off the wharf at Memphis. Ran 5 miles above Memphis to Mound City, Ark. Was set afire and turned loose in the Mississippi River with five coal barges and sank. (*OR*, 8:674; 22:1:232–33; *ORN*, 24:134–36, 696; *CWC*, 6-242; *MSV*, 88, 265; *WPD*, 195.)

Grey Eagle. Union. Side-wheel steamer, 382 tons. Length 250 feet, beam 35 feet, depth 5 feet, 4 boilers. Built in 1857 at Cincinnati. Hit a bridge on May 9, 1861, at Rock Island, Ill. (*MSV*, 89, 265; *WPD*, 200.)

Hannibal City. Union. Side-wheel steamer, 563 tons. Built in 1858 at Madison, Ind. Snagged on September 4, 1862, 8 miles below Louisiana, Mo. Its machinery was salvaged and put on the *J. H. Johnson*. (*MSV*, 92, 266; *WPD*, 206.)

H. D. Bacon. Union. Side-wheel steamer, 370 tons. Built in 1860 at Louisville. Was burned on October 27, 1862, at St. Louis, along with the *T. L. McGill, Estrella, A. McDowell,* and *W. H. Russell*. (*MSV*, 90, 265; *WPD*, 203.)

Henry Ames. Union. Side-wheel steamer, 777 tons. Length 260 feet 8 inches, beam 22 feet 5 inches, depth 7 feet 7 inches. Built in 1864 at Carondelet, Mo. Snagged about 7 miles above Cairo, Ill., on July 30, 1864. Was later raised. (*WPD*, 211.)

Henry Chouteau. Union. Side-wheel steamer, 623 or 633 tons. Length 263 feet, beam 35 feet, depth 7 feet, 6 boilers. Built in 1853 at Cincinnati. Burned on September 26, 1863, at Columbus, Ky. The hull was salvaged and used as a wharf boat at Natchez, Miss. (*MSV*, 94, 266; *WPD*, 211.)

Henry Clay. Union army. Side-wheel steamer, 257 tons. Length 181 feet, beam 31 feet. Used as a transport protected by cotton and hay bales. Cargo of 50,000 rations and oats. Built in 1858 at McKeesport, Pa. Ran past the Confederate Vicksburg batteries on the night of April 16, 1863, with Adm. David D. Porter's fleet. Hit in the stern, caught fire, and burned to the water's edge while floating downstream past New Carthage. Its crew escaped without loss of life. A barge it was towing with Union soldiers was cut loose. (*OR*, 24:1:517; 24:3:200–201, 208; *ORN*, 23, 409; *MSV*, 94, 266; *WPD*, 211.)

Henry S. Dickerson. Union. Screw steamer, 57 tons. Built in 1863 at Chicago, Ill. Exploded on October 6, 1864, at St. Louis with five killed. (*MSV*, 94, 267.)

Hercules. Union. Stern-wheel steam tug, 151 tons. Built in 1854 at McKeesport, Pa. Was captured with seven coal barges in fog near Hopefield, Ark., opposite Memphis, on February 17, 1863, by Capt. J. H. McGehee's Ark. Cavalry Company. One of the crew was killed. Union gunboats in Memphis shelled and sank the captured *Hercules* and one coal barge. The *Hercules* was burned to the waters edge by the guerrillas. Was probably later raised. The village of Hopefield, Ark., was burned by the 63rd Ill. Infantry Regiment in retaliation. (*OR*, 22:1:230–33; 243:78; *MSV*, 95, 267.)

Hiawatha. Union. Side-wheel steamer, 767 tons. Length 250 feet, beam 41 feet. Built in 1856 at Elizabeth, Pa. Was burned by Confederate agents, along with the *Imperial* and *Post Boy*, on September 13, 1863, at St. Louis. (*OR*, 48:2:195; *MSV*:95, 267; *WPD*, 214.)

Horizon (John C. Fremont). Union. Stern-wheel steamer, 315 tons. Length 215 feet, beam 41 feet. Built in 1854 at California, Pa. While transporting Company G, 2nd Ill. Light Artillery, it collided with the *Moderator* and sank the night of April 30, 1863, at Bruinsburg, Miss., taking sixty horses and several men down with the vessel. The *Horizon* was running without lights past Confederate batteries at night. The USS *Louisville* raised three gun carriages on May 26, 1863, and salvaged the six field pieces later with divers. (*OR*, 24:1:634, 643; *ORN*, 25:45–46; *MSV*, 112, 272; *WPD*, 217.)

Imperial. Union. Side-wheel steamer, 907 tons. Built in 1858 at Jeffersonville, Ind. Used as a Union hospital boat. Was burned on September 13, 1863, at St. Louis, along with the *Jesse K. Bell, Hiawatha,* and *Post Boy.* (*OR*, 48:2:195; *MSV*, 100, 269; *WPD*, 223.)

USS Indianola. Union. Side-wheel and screw steam ironclad ram, 511 tons. Length 174 or 175 feet, beam 52 feet 4 inches or 50 feet, draft 6 feet or 7 feet 8 inches, speed 6 knots, 5 boilers. Complement of about 110, with two 11-inch Dahlgren smoothbores foreword, two 9-inch Dahlgren smoothbores aft, and seven 24-pounders. Launched in 1862 at Cincinnati. Seized by Union major general Lewis Wallace for the protection of Cincinnati. Converted to a ram in 1862. Reduced to a sinking condition by the CSS *Queen of the West*, CSS *Webb*, and CSS *Dr. Beaty* and ran aground on February 24, 1863, in 10 feet of water on the La. side, opposite the head of Palmyra Island near the Joe Davis Plantation. Union losses were ninety captured, seven African Americans captured, one killed, one wounded, and seven missing. The CSS *Queen of the West* had two killed and four wounded and the CSS *Webb* had one wounded. The Confederates recovered the wine and liquor aboard and salvaged the vessel.

The USS *Indianola* was sunk again when a dummy Union ironclad was sent downriver on February 26, 1863. A Confederate force of one hundred men salvaged two 11-inch guns and one 9-inch gun. One 11-inch gun was burst on the deck and a 9-inch gun was lost in the river while attempting to load it on a boat. The Confederates threw two 6-pounder guns overboard and burst three guns. The woodwork was burned off the deck, the case-

mate was blown apart, but the hull and machinery were intact. Twenty-five Confederates were later captured on Palmyra Island while salvaging the wreck. The wreck was 2 feet under water. Six months later a sandbar formed around it. Union forces cleaned mud out of the interior, digging a trench on June 18, 1863, with thirty-seven African Americans working on the wreck. One 9-inch gun was salvaged and the boat was caulked up waiting for high water to float the vessel. On December 11, 1863, a force of sixty Confederates under Major Bradford came to destroy the wreck but were driven off by the USS *Carondolet*. The hulk was raised by Union forces on January 5, 1865, and sold on November 29, 1865. (*OR*, 24:1:361–71; 24:3:70–71, 77, 97–98, 646–47, 656; *ORN*, 24:398, 400–412, 543–44, 572; 25:141, 172, 182, 218, 624; ser. 2, 1:107; Miller, *Photographic History*, 1:250; 6, 71; *WCWN*, 155; *WPD*, 224.)

Jacob Musselman. Union. Stern-wheel steam transport, 144 tons. Built in 1860 at Paducah, Ky. Was captured on January 6, 1863, by Confederate guerrilla Capt. J. H. McGehee's Ark. Cavalry opposite Memphis. Ran into Bradley's Landing, Ark., 15 miles above Memphis, and was destroyed along with a flatboat after taking off the cargo. (*OR*, 22:1:233; *ORN*, 24:134–37; *CWC*, 6-254; *MSV*, 107, 270.)

James Montgomery. Union. Side-wheel steamer, 536 tons. Length 270 feet, beam 36 feet, depth 7 feet 6 inches, 6 boilers. Built in 1856 at New Albany, Ind. Snagged on December 11, 1861, at Devil's Island near Cape Girardeau, Mo. In 1867 the U.S. Army Corps of Engineers identified the wreck as a hazard with barely enough room for boats to pass. The wreck sank the *Continental* in 1864 and the *Paragon* in 1868. U.S. snag boats probably removed the wreck in September 1931. (*Chief of Engineers Report 1867*, 388; *MSV*, 109, 271; *WPD*, 241, 362.)

James Watson. Union. Stern-wheel steamer, 200 tons. Built in 1863 at Cincinnati. Carried a Union cargo, an Adams Express cargo, and eighty-six Union soldiers. Burned on March 2, 1865, at Island No. 76 (now Lake Whittington) near Caulk Neck Cutoff, with thirty-five killed, including twenty soldiers, three women, two children, five male passengers, and deckhands. (*MSV*, 109, 271; *WPD*, 242.)

James White. Union. Side-wheel steamer, 662 tons. Length 240 feet, beam 40 feet, depth 7 feet, 4 boilers. Built in 1864 at Cincinnati. Snagged and sank in 13 feet of water on November 5, 1864, at Island No. 10, with fifteen killed. In 1867 the U.S. Army Corps of Engineers considered the wreck a navigation hazard. (*Chief of Engineers Report 1867,* 388; *MSV,* 109, 271; *WPD,* 242–43.)

Jesse K. Bell. Union. Side-wheel steamer, 325 tons. Length 255 feet, beam 40 feet, depth 6 feet, 3 boilers. Built in 1856 at Cincinnati. Was burned by Confederate agents at St. Louis on September 13, 1863, along with the *Hiawatha, Imperial,* and *Post Boy.* (*OR,* 48:2:195; *MSV,* 111, 271; *WPD,* 246.)

John A. Fisher. Union. Stern-wheel steamer, 122 tons. Built in 1859 at Louisville. Snagged on October 27, 1864, at Carroll Island below St. Louis. (*MSV,* 112, 272; *WPD,* 249.)

John J. Roe. Union. Side-wheel steamer, 691 tons. Length 270 feet, beam 40 feet, depth 8 feet, 3 boilers. Built in 1856 at Cincinnati. Snagged on September 12, 1864, above New Madrid, Mo., while carrying the 2nd Wis. Cavalry Regiment, which lost 165 horses. Sank up to the roof. (*MSV,* 114, 272; *WPD,* 252.)

CSS *John Simonds.* Confederate. Side-wheel steamer, 1,024 tons. Length 295 feet, beam 40 feet 6 inches, depth 8 feet. Hull built in 1852 at Freedom, Pa. Completed at Pittsburgh, Pa. Was scuttled by Confederates with the *Winchester* in a chute near Island No. 10 on April 6, 1862, to block the chute. (*CWC,* 6-257; *WCWN,* 247; *WPD,* 255.)

John Swasy. Union. Stern-wheel steamer, 236 tons. Length 157 feet, beam 33 feet, depth 5 feet, 2 boilers. Built in 1864 at Cincinnati. Snagged above Cape Girardeau, Mo., at Devil's Island on August 31, 1864. (*Chief of Engineers Report 1867,* 388; *MSV,* 116, 272; *WPD,* 255.)

Joseph Pierce. U.S. Side-wheel steamer, 533 tons. Length 260 feet, beam 36 feet, depth 6 feet, 4 engines. Its hull was built at Freedom, Pa. Completed in 1864 at Pittsburgh, Pa. Exploded on July 31, 1865, at Palmyra Landing, with twelve killed. (*MSV,* 117, 273; *WPD,* 258.)

CSS *Kanawha* (*Kanawha Valley No. 2*). Confederate. Stern-wheel steamer, 147 tons. Used as a watch boat and hospital boat. Built in 1860 at Wheeling, Va. (W. Va.). Was scuttled by Confederates behind Island No. 10 on April 6, 1862. (*MSV,* 119, 273; *WCWN,* 247; *WPD,* 263.)

Keystone. U.S. Side-wheel steamer, 69 tons. Built in 1839 at Pittsburgh, Pa. Was burned on June 24, 1861, at Arkansas City, Ark. (*MSV,* 121, 274.)

Key West No. 2. Union. Stern-wheel steamer, 206 tons. Built in 1860 at Pittsburgh, Pa. Snagged on October 26, 1863, at Chester, Ill., probably at Key West Point. (*Chief of Engineers Report 1867,* 388; *MSV,* 121, 274; *WPD,* 271.)

LaClede. Union. Stern-wheel steamer, 179 tons. Length 152 feet, beam 29 feet 6 inches, depth 4 feet 4 inches. Built in 1855 at California, Pa. Stranded on November 19, 1862, at Chester, Ill. (*MSV,* 123, 275; *WPD,* 274.)

Lady Jane. Union. Steamer, 40 tons. Built in 1857 at Berlin, Wis. Hit a bridge and sank on April 19, 1865, at Rock Island, Ill., with one killed. (*MSV,* 123, 275.)

Lake City. Union. Stern-wheel steamer, 171 tons. Built in 1857 at Brownsville, Pa. Ran aground on White's Riffle below Neville Island. Sank when a towboat tried to free it. Was burned by Capt. J. M. McGehee's Confederate guerrillas on December 8, 1862, at Carson Landing, Ark. (*MSV,* 124, 275; *WPD,* 276.)

USS *Lancaster* (USS *Kosciusko*) (USS *Lancaster No. 3*). Union army. Side-wheel steam ram, 257, 350, or 375 tons. Length 176 feet, beam 30 feet, depth 5 feet 6 inches. Armed with one 24-pounder howitzer. Built in 1855 at Cincinnati. Called a "rotten boat." Only a skeleton crew and part of Ellet's Marine Brigade were aboard when it challenged the Vicksburg batteries on March 25, 1863. The boilers were hit and blown up by a 10-inch shell. Steam filled the boat. Started sinking after taking a shot in the stern about three-quarters of a mile down from the head of De Soto Point. Ran into a bank on fire. Sank 2 miles below Vicksburg. One man drowned, the pilot lost a foot, and three men were wounded. Lt. Col. John Alexander Ellet and his crew escaped in two yawls. (*OR,* 24:1:473, 476, 477; *ORN,* 20:20–23, 30; 23:277, 406–7; 24:515, 541; ser. 2, 1:124; Pratt, *Western Waters,* 236; *WCWN,* 161; *WPD,* 277–78.)

Lancaster No. 4. Union. Side-wheel steamer, 218 tons. Built in 1861 at Cincinnati. Snagged on November 18, 1864, below Portland, Mo., and sank in 10 feet of water. (*MSV,* 124, 275; *WPD,* 278.)

La Salle. Union. Stern-wheel steamer, 196 tons. Built in 1860 at Freedom, Pa. Snagged in late September or August 1864 at Cape Girardeau, Mo., between Devil's Island and the Illinois banks. Sank up to the boiler deck. (*MSV,* 123, 275; *WPD,* 274.)

Laurel (Erebus). Union army. Screw tug, 50 tons. Length 60 feet, beam 14 feet, draft 6 feet, speed 6 miles per hour average. Built in 1862 at St. Louis. Was accidentally burned to the waterline within a half-mile of Craighead Point, 3,800 yards above Fort Pillow, Tenn., on April 14, 1862. The crew was rescued. Transferred to the Union navy on September 30, 1862. Was raised. Was sold on August 17, 1865, at Mound City, Ill. (*ORN,* 23:676; ser. 2, 1:125; *MSV,* 125; *WCWN,* 183.)

Lavina Logan. Union. Stern-wheel steamer, 145 tons. Built in 1861 at Parkersburg, Va. (W. Va.). Used as a transport and powder boat. Lost in the Mississippi River on September 23, 1864. (*MSV,* 125; *WPD,* 280.)

L. B. Winchester (Winchester). Confederate. Side-wheel steamer, 180 tons. Built in 1851 at Freedom, Pa. Was scuttled by Confederate engineers on March 16, 1862, near Island No. 10 in the Wash Channel to block it. On April 7, 1862, Acting Master E. W. Wheelock and H. A. Glassford with pilots of *Mortar Boat No. 7* and *Mortar Boat No. 8* boarded the partially submerged vessel and burned it to the water's edge. The wreck was discovered more than a hundred years later by the New Madrid Historical Society in Winchester Chute. (*ORN,* 22:771; 26:804; *CWC,* 6-325; *WPD,* 491; *EAS,* 177.)

Lebanon. Union. Side-wheel transport steamer, 225 tons. Cargo of goods and stores. Built in 1855 at Brownsville, Pa. Attacked about 10 miles below Greenville. A shell cut a steamline. Was captured on May 25, 1864, near Ford's Landing by a Confederate yawl with forty men under the command of Capt. John W. Jacobs, 4th Mo. Regiment. Burned with its cargo on May 27, 1864, at Greenville, Miss. (*OR,* 34:1:951; *MSV,* 126, 276; *WPD,* 281.)

CSS Little Rebel (USS Little Rebel) (R. E. & A. N. Watson) (R. & J. Watson) (Spy). Confederate. Screw towboat steamer, 151 tons. Deeply laden draft 12 feet, 2 boilers. Later, as a Union vessel, it carried between two and four cannons. Built in 1859 at Belle Vernon, Pa. The Confederates acquired the vessel in the spring 1861. On June 6, 1862, at the Battle of Memphis, a Union shell hit its steam chest, and it was beached on the west bank by the USS *Monarch.* It was salvaged by Union forces and put into naval service. (*ORN,* 23:118, 120, 123, 136, 140, 684–85; ser. 2, 1:128; *WSTD,* 146, 185.)

Luzerne. Union. Side-wheel steamer, 179 or 180 tons. Built in 1852 at Brownsville, Pa. Was sunk by ice on January 28, 1864, at Crawfords Landing, Miss. (*ORN,* 26:806; *MSV,* 132, 278; *WPD,* 299.)

Majestic. Union. Side-wheel steamer, 648 tons. Built in 1863 at Shousetown, Pa. Burned on May 6, 1863, at Island No. 8 near Hickman, Ky. (*OR,* ser. 3, 3:406; *MSV,* 135, 278; *WPD,* 304.)

Mariner. Union. Stern-wheel steamer, 193 tons. Length 180 feet, beam 33 feet, depth 6 feet. Cargo of coal. Built in 1856 at Belle Vernon, Pa. Ran aground in June 1864. Became high and dry on a sandbar near the mouth of the St. Francis River above Helena, Ark. Lt. or Capt. A. C. McCoy and fourteen Confederates of Brig. Gen. Joe Shelby's command robbed the ten crewmen. Captain Collin and his crew were allowed to leave. Vessel was burned on July 4, 1864. (*OR,* 41:2:42–43, 992, 996; *ORN,* 26:808; *WPD,* 308.)

Mars. U.S. Side-wheel steamer, 329 tons. Length 180 feet, beam 34 feet, 3 boilers. Built in 1856 at Cincinnati. Was captured from Confederates on April 7, 1862, at Island No. 10. Snagged and sank on July 7–8, 1865, at Cogswell Island, Mo., opposite the mouth of the Fishing River. (*CWC,* 6-268; *WCWN,* 248; *WPD,* 309.)

Mercury. Union. Stern-wheel steamer, 184 tons. Built in 1862 at Brownsville, Pa. Collided in May 1865 with the *Hard Times* at Harrison's Landing below St. Louis. Was beached and sank. Was later raised. (*WPD,* 319.)

Metropolitan. U.S. Side-wheel steamer, 313 tons. Built in 1856 at McKeesport, Pa. Reportedly was sunk by ice at St. Louis on December 16, 1865. (*MSV,* 144, *WPD,* 321.)

Mingo. Union army. Stern-wheel ram, 228 or 300 tons. Length 170 feet, beam 29 feet, depth 5 feet, maximum speed 12 knots, average speed 7 knots. Armed with one 24-pounder howitzer. Built in 1856 at Cincinnati. Modified in 1859 at California, Pa. Used as a transport. Converted to an Ellet ram. Accidentally sank in November 1862 off Cape Girardeau, Mo. (*ORN*, ser. 11, 1:144; *WCWN*, 161; *WTBD*, 163.)

Minnesota. Union. Stern-wheel steam towboat, 142 tons. Built in 1857 at California, Pa. While towing two barges with coal and one barge with sutler's stores, the *Minnesota* and the barges were captured and destroyed by Confederates on May 3, 1863, at Argyle Landing, three miles above Greenville. (*ORN*, 24:637–40, 696; *MSV*, 146, 281; *WPD*, 323.)

USS *Mississippi.* Union. Side-wheel steam frigate, 1,692 or 1,732 tons. Length 225 or 229 feet, beam 40 feet, depth 23 feet 6 inches or 22 feet 9 inches. Complement of 300, with one 10-inch Dahlgren pivot smoothbore, nineteen 8-inch guns, and one rifled 20-pounder Parrott. Laid down in 1839 on the Philadelphia Navy Yard, Pa., and commissioned in 1841. Comm. Matthew C. Perry's flagship in the Mexican War and the opening of Japan. Flagship of the East Gulf Blockading Squadron. On the night of March 14–15, 1863, it grounded opposite Port Hudson on a spit and was shelled by three Confederate batteries. One of the Union officers aboard was Lt. George Dewey, a future hero of the Spanish-American War. The small guns were thrown overboard, the engine was destroyed, the crew was put ashore, and the vessel was set afire by volunteers. Floated off the shoal about 3:00 a.m. and drifted downstream through the Union fleet past Profit's Island, exploding at 4:30 p.m. May have sunk in 80–110 feet deep water. During the engagement it lost 1 officer killed, 3 seamen missing, 52 seamen killed and wounded, 8 marines killed and wounded, and 47 crewmen captured by Confederates. Twenty-two officers, 179 seamen, and 32 marines were rescued. May have been located by a State of Louisiana magnetometer survey. Clive Cussler believes the USS *Mississippi* is under the Solitude Point Swamp, about three-quarters of a mile west of the present west bank of the Mississippi River channel, below Springfield Landing. In 1999 Cussler funded a helicopter geophysical aeromag-netic survey which had a very large reading at that location. (*ORN*, 19:680–85; ser. 2, 1:146; Hewitt, *Port Hudson,* 88–93; Cussler and Dirgo, *Sea Hunters II,* 116–33.)

Moderator. Union. Stern-wheel steamer, 231 tons. Built in 1856 at Brownsville, Pa. Was sunk by ice at St. Louis on January 28, 1864. (*MSV*, 147, 282; *WPD*, 327.)

CSS *Mohawk.* Confederate. Stern-wheel steamer, 100 tons. Built in 1860 at Elizabeth, Pa. Was scuttled by Confederates at Island No. 10 on April 7, 1862. (*ORN*, 22:725, 742, 757; 23:379; *MSV*, 147.)

USS *Monarch* (*Monarch*). Union army. Side-wheel ram, 406 tons. Built in 1853 at Fulton (Cincinnati), Ohio. Sank on March 5, 1861, at Louisville. Was later raised. Was converted into an Ellet ram. Was laid up below St. Louis after July 1863. Was sunk by ice in December 1864, and broken up. (*WCWN*, 161; *WPD*, 328–29.)

USS *Mound City.* Union. Ironclad, 512 tons. Length 175 feet overall, beam 51 feet 2 inches, depth 5 feet, speed 9 miles per hour. Complement of 175, with three 8-inch shell guns, six 32-pounders, and four rifled 42-pounders. Built in 1861 at Mound City, Ill. Was holed by the CSS *General Earl Van Dorn,* with the bow nearly wrenched off during the Battle of Plum Point Bend near Fort Pillow, Tenn., on May 10, 1862. Ran into a bank and sank. The USS *Champion* raised the vessel. (*OR*, 10:1:889; *ORN*, 23:14, 17–21, 23, 28, 52, 56, 92–93, 95; *WCWN*, 151.)

USS *Nettle* (*Wonder*). Union. Side-wheel steam tug, 50 tons. Built in 1862 at St. Louis. Originally a Union army tug. Ran into by a Union ironclad and sank on October 20, 1865, in the Mississippi River. (*ORN*, ser. 2, 1:158; *WCWN*, 184; *WSTD*, 172.)

CSS *New Orleans* (*Pelican Floating Dock*). Confederate. Floating battery. Two small boilers fitted with connections to scald boarders. Armed with seventeen 8-inch, one 9-inch, and two rifled 32-pounders. Fitted out in 1861 in New Orleans or Algiers, La., from the Pelican Floating Dock. Was scuttled with its guns aboard and set adrift on March 12, 1862, at Island No. 10. Ran aground in shoal water at New Madrid, Mo. Was captured by Union forces. Used as a Union floating dock for repairing vessels. Confederates burned the vessel in August or September 1863 at Walnut Bend. (*ORN*, 22:725; 25:381–82, 397; ser. 2, 1:261; *CWC*, 6-276–77.)

Niagara. U.S. Side-wheel steamer, 797 tons. Built in 1864 at Cincinnati. Collided with the *Post Boy* on November 20, 1865, above Helena, Ark., at the mouth of the St. Francis River, with seventy-five killed. The steamer carried many African-American soldiers returning home. Reported by the U.S. Army Corps of Engineers in 1867 to be near Island No. 34, but was not a navigation hazard due to a shifted channel. (*Chief of Engineers Report 1867*, 391; *MSV*, 157, 285; *WPD*, 347.)

Northerner. Union, Side-wheel steamer, 332 tons. Length 210 feet, beam 33 feet, depth 5 feet 6 inches. Built in 1859 at Elizabeth, Pa. Was burned by Confederate agents at St. Louis, along with the steamers *Cherokee, Edward F. Dix, Glasgow, Sunshine,* and *Welcome,* on July 15, 1864. (*OR*, 41:2:209; *MSV*, 160, 286; *WPD*, 350.)

Odd Fellow. Union. Side-wheel steamer, 70 tons. Built in 1862 at Wheeling, Va. (W. Va.). Was sunk by ice on January 1 or 6, 1865, at Columbus, Ky. (*MSV*, 161, 286; *WPD*, 352.)

Omaha. U.S. Side-wheel steamer, 307 tons. Length 206 feet, beam 30 feet, depth 5 feet, 3 boilers. Built in 1856 at Madison, Ind. Was sunk by ice on December 16, 1865, at St. Louis. (*MSV*, 163, 287; *WPD*, 355.)

Orient. Union. Stern-wheel steamer, 222 tons. Length 154 feet, beam 33 feet, depth 4 feet 10 inches, 3 boilers. Built in 1862 at California, Pa. Snagged and was lost at Commerce, Mo., on February 17, 1864, with fourteen killed. (*WPD*, 357.)

USS Paw Paw (Fanny) (Number 31) (St. Charles). Union. Center-wheel gunboat, 175 tons. Length 120 feet, beam 34 feet, draft 6 feet, speed 4 miles per hour. Armed with two 30-pounders and six 24-pounders. Built in 1862 at St. Louis. Hit a snag on August 6, 1863, while backing out from a riverbank and sank within fifteen minutes in the lower end of Walnut Bend on Hardings Point, Ark. Everything was removed by the USS *Covington.* Was later raised by the USS *Champion No. 5* and repaired. (*ORN*, 25:344–46, 368, 414; *WCWN*, 180.)

Platte Valley. Union. Side-wheel steamer. Length 220 feet, beam 33 feet, depth 5 feet, 3 boilers. Built in 1857 at Jeffersonville, Ind. Sank at Devil's Island near St. Louis in September 1864. Was later raised. (*WPD*, 374.)

Post Boy. Union. Side-wheel steamer, 348 tons. Length 215 feet, beam 33 feet, depth 5 feet 6 inches. Built in 1859 at Elizabeth, Pa. Was burned by Confederate agents at St. Louis on September 13, 1863, along with the *Imperial, Jesse K. Bell,* and *Hiawatha.* (*OR*, 48:2:195; *MSV*, 177, 291; *WPD*, 376.)

CSS Prince. Confederate. Side-wheel transport steamer, 223 tons. Built in 1859 at Cincinnati. Snagged near Island No. 10 and Hickman, Ky., on February 27, 1862, with the loss of seventy-four lives. (*ORN*, 23:379; *CWC*, 6-289; *MSV*, 178; *WPD*, 378.)

USS Rattler (Florence Miller) (Tinclad No. 1). Union. Wooden stern-wheel steamer, 165 tons. Armed with two 30-pounder Parrotts and six 24-pounders. Built in 1862 at Cincinnati. Parted its cables, hit a snag, bilged, and sank within five minutes on December 30, 1864, near Grand Gulf, Miss., with most of its arms and supplies. The vessel's commander was ill, so the executive officer was in charge. The *Magnet* failed to save the vessel but rescued the crew. Two 30-pounder Parrotts were spiked and the *Magnet* removed the 24-pounders. One of the vessel's crew deserted to the Confederates. The USS *Forest Rose* later removed other items from the wreck, which was set afire by Confederates, with its upper works destroyed. (*ORN;* 26:769–71, 802; 27:204; ser. 2, 1:189; *WPD*, 168.)

Red Fox. Confederate. Stern-wheel steamer, 78 tons. Built in 1855 at Brownsville, Pa. Sank in late 1861 at Island No. 10. (*MSV*, 182, 292.)

CSS Red Rover (USS Red Rover). Confederate. Side-wheel steamer, 625 tons. Length 256 feet, beam 40 feet 11 inches, depth 8 feet, speed 8 knots, 5 boilers. As a Union hospital boat it had a complement of forty-seven and a medical staff of thirty. Built in 1857 at Louisville. Used as a barracks for the crew of the CSS *New Orleans.* Hit by a shell fragment and began leaking near Island No. 10. Was scuttled behind Island No. 10 on April 3, 1862. Was raised by Union forces and converted to the Mississippi Squadron hospital ship, becoming the first hospital ship in the U.S. Navy. (*OR*, ser. 3, 2:833; *ORN*, 22:725; *CWC*, 6-291–92; *MSV*, 182; *WPD*, 389–90.)

Roanoke. U.S. Stern-wheel steamer, 266 tons. Length 156 feet, beam 32 feet 2 inches, depth 5 feet 10 inches. Built in 1864 at California, Pa. Wrecked on December 17, 1865, near Commerce, Mo. The wreck was removed by the *Underwriter*. (*WPD*, 394.)

Robert Campbell Jr. Union. Side-wheel steamer, 421 tons. Length 226 feet, beam 41 feet, depth 6 feet. Built in 1860 at Jeffersonville, Ind. Burned on September 28, 1863, near Milliken's Bend, La. Was set afire by Confederate guerrilla Isaac Elshire, who posed as a passenger. A total of twenty-two died, including a number of Union soldiers. The *General Anderson* helped save some passengers. (*OR*, 48:2:195; *ORN*, 25:442; *MSV*, 186, 293; *WPD*, 395.)

Robert Emmert (Robert Emmet). Union. Stern-wheel steamer, 178 tons. Built in 1864 at Memphis. Snagged on November 3, 1864, at De Witt, Mo., near St. Aubert's Island. (*MSV*, 186, 293; *WPD*, 398.)

Rosalie. U.S. Stern-wheel steamer, 158 tons. Built in 1854 at Brownsville, Pa. Was sunk by ice on December 16, 1865, at St. Louis. (*MSV*, 188, 294; *WPD*, 402.)

Rowena. Union. Side-wheel steamer, 435 tons. Length 225 feet, beam 33 feet 6 inches, depth 6 feet, 4 boilers. Built in 1858 at Elizabeth, Pa. Snagged on April 18, 1863, at Devil's Island or Buffalo Island just above Cape Girardeau, Mo. Another account said the vessel burned on May 13, 1863. (*ORN*, 24:587; *Chief of Engineers Report 1867*, 389; *MSV*, 189, 294; *WPD*, 403.)

Ruby. U.S. Side-wheel ferry steamer, 78 tons. Built in 1859 at Cincinnati. Foundered in December 1865 on the Mississippi River. (*MSV*, 189, 294; *WPD*, 405.)

Ruth. Union. Side-wheel steamer, 702 tons. Length 270 feet, beam 46 feet, depth 8 feet. Carried a $2.6 million Union army payroll in United States notes and eight paymasters and their clerks bound for the Union army at Vicksburg, Miss. Also carried stores along with thirty-one guards of Company I, 9th Wis. Infantry Regiment.

Built in 1862 at St. Louis. Was burned by Confederate agents on the night of August 5, 1863, between Cairo, Ill., and Columbus, Ky., at Lucas Bend, 4 miles below Norfolk, Mo. One of the agents was said to have been Robert Louden. The vessel was engulfed within five minutes and continued to burn for five hours, sinking in 18 feet of water. Thirty lives were lost, including five Union guards and three clerks. Union salvage divers recovered only pieces of the bank notes. The *Ruth* was blown up with gunpowder on October 19, 1863, to prevent others from trying to recover any remaining payroll. (*OR*, 24:3:580; *Daily Illinois State Journal* [Springfield], Aug. 6 and 8, 1863; *H.R. 38th Cong., 1st sess., Report No. 123*, June 21, 1864; *WPD*, 405.)

Sallie Wood. Union. Side-wheel or stern-wheel transport steamer, 256 tons. Length 160 feet, beam 31 feet. Built in 1860 at Paducah, Ky. Originally a Confederate vessel captured by the USS *Conestoga* on the Tennessee River at Chickasaw, Ala., on February 8, 1862. Ambushed at Island No. 82 near Argyle Landing or Caroline Point on July 21, 1862. A shell hit the vessel's steam drum, forcing it ashore. The Confederates captured 32 aboard, removed everything of value, and burned it. Several local citizens in the area were later arrested for burning the vessel and stealing articles from it. A bell, chain, and other articles were recovered from their homes and farms. In 1865 the vessel was reported as covered by sand with only a flange in sight. (*OR*, 17:2:140; *ORN*, 19:57; 24:212–13, 428–29; 27:293–94; *MSV*, 198; *WPD*, 415.)

Sam Gaty. Union. Side-wheel steamer, 294 tons. Length 210 feet, beam 36 feet, 3 boilers. While carrying 307 soldiers, 37 wagons, horses, and other government property, the *Sam Gaty* sank in the Mississippi River above Skipwirth's Landing at Island No. 92 in September or on October 1, 1863. Was later raised. (*ORN*, 25:442; Milligan, *Fresh-Water Navy*, 141–42; *WPD*, 416–17.)

Shingiss. Union. Stern-wheel steamer, 185 tons. Carried sick and wounded sailors to the Mound City Hospital. Built in 1854 at California, Pa. Hit a snag on July 9, 1862, and sank 7 miles below Fort Pillow, Tenn. Was raised on July 13, 1862, by Union divers. (*ORN*, 23:255, 257; *MSV*, 198.)

USS *Sidney C. Jones*. Union. Sailing mortar schooner, 245 tons. Length 98 feet, beam 27 feet, draft 7 feet 8 inches. Complement of thirty-six, with one 13-inch mortar, two 32-pounder guns, and two heavy 12-pounder smoothbores. Built in 1856 at East Haddam, Conn. Blown up and burned on July 15, 1862, after grounding in a few feet of water because the CSS *Arkansas* came downriver from Vicksburg, Miss. (*ORN*, 19:27–36, 712; ser. 2, 1:208; *WCWN*, 138.)

***Silver Wave*.** Union. Stern-wheel steamer, 245 tons. Length 159 feet, beam 35 feet, depth 5 feet. Built in 1854 at Glasgow, Pa. Sank at Columbus, Ky., in November 1863. Was later raised. (*WPD*, 427–28.)

***Sioux City*.** U.S. Side-wheel steamer, 379 tons. Length 218 feet, beam 33 feet, depth 5 feet 10 inches, 3 boilers. Built in 1857 at Cincinnati. Foundered on December 6, 1865, at St. Louis. Was later raised. (*MSV*, 199, 298; *WPD*, 428.)

***Stephen Bayard*.** Union. Stern-wheel steamer, 155 tons. Built in 1851 at West Elizabeth, Pa. Burned on March 6, 1865, at Memphis. (*MSV*, 203, 298; *WPD*, 433.)

***Stephen Decatur*.** Union. Side-wheel steamer, 308 tons. Built at Belle Vernon, Pa. Sank at Devil's Island below St. Louis between 1862 and 1865. Was later raised. (*WPD*, 433–34.)

***Sultana*.** Union. Side-wheel steamer, 660 tons. Length 260 feet, beam 45 feet, depth 17 feet. Authorized for only 76 cabin passengers and 300 deck passengers but carried citizen passengers, 2 companies of guards, and about 1,866–2,400 Union former prisoners of war onboard as well as a cargo of 90 cases of wine, 100 hogsheads, 100,000 pounds of sugar, and 70 to 100 horses and mules. While heavily overloaded one of the vessel's three boilers blew up at 2:00 a.m. on April 27, 1865, at Hen and Chicken islands across from Tagleman's Landing, about 10 miles above Memphis. The burning wreck drifted 2 to 3 miles downstream and sank after 8:00 a.m. Between 1,238 and 1,647 people were killed, probably the greatest loss of life in a shipping accident along inland waterways. There were 800 survivors, of whom 300 later died of their wounds. Reportedly found in the 1970s by Jerry Potter and San Oliver under a soybean field in the Mound City Chute near Mound City, Ark. (*OR*, 48:1:210–26; Dixon, "Aboard the *Sultana*," *Civil War Times Illustrated*, 38–39; Levstick, "*Sultana* Disaster," *Civil War Times Illustrated*, 18–24; Potter, "*Sultana* Disaster: Conspiracy of Greed," *Blue & Gray Magazine*, 8–24, 54–59; *WPD*, 436.)

***Sunshine*.** Union. Side-wheel steamer, 354 tons. Built in 1860 at Elizabeth, Pa. Was burned by Confederate agents on July 15, 1864, at 4:00 a.m., along with the *Cherokee*, *Glasgow*, *Northerner*, *Edward F. Dix*, and *Welcome*, at St. Louis. (*OR*, 41:2:209; *MSV*, 205, 299; *WPD*, 437–38.)

***Swallow*.** Union. Stern-wheel steamer, 190 tons. Length 153 feet, beam 29 feet 6 inches, depth 4 feet 8 inches. Built in 1854 at California, Pa. Ran ashore 22 miles below Memphis. Unable to be refloated after ten to twelve days. Burned on August 19, 1862, at Glover, Miss. (*ORN*, 23:307; *WPD*, 439.)

CSS *Tennessee*. Confederate. CSS *Arkansas* Class steam ironclad ram, 2,000 tons. Length 165 feet, beam 35 feet, draft 11 feet 6 inches, speed 8 knots. Designed for a complement of two hundred, with six guns. Was framed and being planked when burned at the stocks of the Confederate navy yard on June 6, 1862, by Confederates after the Battle of Memphis to avoid capture. (*ORN*, ser. 2, 1:268, 782; *CWC*, 6-311–12.)

***Thomas J. Patten*.** Union. Stern-wheel steamer, 118 tons. Built in 1860 at Bellaire, Ohio. Burned on January 25, 1864, at Walker's Bend below Memphis. (*MSV*, 211, 301; *WPD*, 451.)

***Tigress*.** Union army. Side-wheel steamer, 321 tons. Built in 1858 at Cincinnati. Hit by thirty-five shells the night of April 22–23, 1863, while passing the Confederate Vicksburg batteries. Grounded 3.5 miles below Vicksburg, Miss. Hit by fourteen shells. One made a four-foot hole. Broke in half and sank at Brown and Johnson's Plantation. The crew and passengers were rescued by the *J. W. Cheeseman*. Its smokestacks and wheelhouse were above water. (*OR*, 24:1:564–65; *ORN*, 24:604, 630–31; *EAS*, 194; *WPD*, 455.)

***T. L. McGill*.** Union. Side-wheel steamer, 598 tons. Length 238 feet, beam 36 feet, depth 4 feet 7 inches, 4 boilers. Burned at St. Louis at the big wharf fire on October 27, 1862. (*WPD*, 441.)

CSS *Tuscarora*. Confederate. Side-wheel gunboat. Armed with one rifled 32-pounder and one 8-inch Columbiad. Built in 1861 at Philadelphia. A fire was discovered forward under the wheelhouse, and it ran ashore on November 23, 1861, 15 miles below Memphis. The magazine blew up seven minutes later near Harbert's Plantation, setting the plantation's slave quarters on fire. Its crew was saved. (*ORN*, 22:804; *CWC*, 6-318.)

Tycoon. U.S. Side-wheel steamer, 332 tons. Cargo of 1,595 bales of cotton. Built in 1860 at Brownsville, Pa. Burned on October 9, 1865, at Tiptonville, Tenn. (*MSV*, 216; *WPD*, 461.)

Universe. Union. Side-wheel steamer, 399 tons. Length 180 feet, beam 35 feet, depth 7 feet, 3 boilers. Built in 1857 at Cincinnati. Snagged on October 30, 1864, at Plum Point, Tenn., with seventeen killed. A diving bell was sent to the site, so some salvage is likely. (*MSV*, 219, 303; *WPD*, 465.)

CSS _Vicksburg_ (_City of Vicksburg_). Confederate. Side-wheel steamer, 635 tons. Length 244 feet 6 inches, beam 36 feet, depth 7 feet 6 inches, 5 boilers. Built in 1857 at New Albany, Ind. While tied up to shore at Vicksburg, the CSS *Vicksburg* was shelled and rammed on February 2, 1863, by the USS *Queen of the West*. Set afire, holed, and later burned as a hulk on March 29, 1863. Its machinery was removed and taken to Mobile. (*OR*, 24:3:698; *CWC*, 6-319; *MSV*, 220; *WPD*, 468.)

W. A. Moffitt. U.S. Side-wheel steamer, 553 tons. Built in 1865 at Metropolis, Ill. Burned on November 17, 1865, at St. Louis. (*MSV*, 223, 304; *WPD*, 473.)

Welcome. Union. Stern-wheel steamer, 499 tons. Length 214 feet, beam 36 feet 2 inches, depth 6 feet. Built in 1863 at Shousetown, Pa. Was burned by Confederate agents at the St. Louis levee on July 15, 1864, at 4:00 a.m., along with five other steamboats. The wreck was towed to the Ill., shore and sold in August 1864. Was later returned to service. (*OR*, 41:2:209; *MSV*, 227; *WPD*, 483.)

Whiteman. Union. Transport steamer. Carried dead and wounded from the Battle of Baton Rouge and a cargo of sutler's stores. The body of Brig. Gen. Thomas Williams was aboard. Accidentally ran into by the USS *Oneida* and sank in the Mississippi River with all hands on August 7,

1862, near Donaldsonville, La. The Confederates salvaged some sutler's stores. (*OR*, 15:1124.)

William H. Russell. Union. Side-wheel steamer, 405 tons. Length 204 feet, beam 34 feet, depth 5 feet 6 inches, 4 boilers. Built in 1856 at Madison, Ind. Burned at St. Louis on October 27, 1862. Its machinery went to the *T. L. McGill*. (*WPD*, 488.)

William L. Ewing. Union. Side-wheel steamer, 335 tons. Length 181 feet, beam 32 feet, depth 5 feet 6 inches, 3 boilers. Built in 1856 at New Albany, Ind. Stranded on November 25, 1864, at Hardscrabble, St. Louis, opposite Tilly's. The wreck later sank another vessel that ran into it. Its machinery was salvaged and went to the *Des Arc*. (*Chief of Engineers Report 1867*, 387; *MSV*, 231, 307; *WPD*, 489.)

W. I. Maclay. Union. Stern-wheel steamer, 245 tons. Length 159 feet, beam 33 feet, depth 5 feet 6 inches, 3 boilers. Built in 1856 at Brownsville, Pa. Snagged on October 19, 1861, below St. Louis. (*MSV*, 223, 304; *WPD*, 475.)

Wyaconda. U.S. Side-wheel steamer, 239 tons. Built in 1864 at La Grange, Mo. Burned on July 14, 1865, at St. Genevieve, Mo., with one killed. (*MSV*, 234, 308; *WPD*, 492.)

Yazoo. Confederate. Side-wheel steamboat, 371 tons. Built in 1860 at Jeffersonville, Ind. Left behind by Confederates on the evacuation of Island No. 10. Was captured by Union forces and sank on April 7, 1862, by order of Flag Officer Andrew R. Foote. (*CWC*, 6-326; *MSV*, 235; *WPD*, 492–93.)

▷ VESSELS WITHOUT NAMES

barge. Union. A barge with a cargo of coal was sunk off Point Pleasant before December 2, 1863. (*ORN*, 25:613.)

barge. Union. One barge with a cargo of coal. Was captured along with the steamboat *Hercules* and six other coal barges in fog near Hopefield, Ark., opposite Memphis, on February 17, 1863, by Capt. J. H. McGehee's Ark. Cavalry Company. Union gunboats in Memphis shelled and sank the captured *Hercules* and one coal barge. The village of Hopefield, Ark., was burned by the 63rd Ill. Infantry Regiment in retaliation. (*OR*, 22:1:230–33; 24:3:78; *MSV*, 95, 267.)

barges. Union. Five barges with cargoes of coal and the *Grampus No. 2* were captured on January 11, 1863, at Wolf Creek by Capt. J. H. McGehee's Ark. Cavalry Company, just off the wharf at Memphis. Ran 5 miles above Memphis to Mound City, Ark. Was set afire and turned loose in the Mississippi River and sank. (*OR*, 8:674; 22:1:232–33; *ORN*, 24:134–36, 696; *CWC*, 6-242; *MSV*, 88, 265; *WPD*, 195.)

barges. Union. Two barges loaded with commissary stores and hay attempted to run past Vicksburg on the night of May 3, 1863, when their tow boat, the *George Sturgess,* was hit in the boiler by shells from the Confederate water batteries. The tow boat and the barges were set afire by the shells. (*OR*, 24:1:687–88; *MSV*, 84.)

barges. Union. Two barges with cargoes of coal and one barge with sutler's stores were being towed by the *Minnesota* when captured and destroyed by Confederates on May 3, 1863, at Argyle Landing, 3 miles above Greenville. (*ORN*, 24:637–40, 696; *MSV*, 146, 281; *WPD*, 323.)

floating dry dock. Union. Formerly the CSS *New Orleans* or *Pelican Floating Dock.* Fitted out in 1861 in New Or-leans or Algiers, La., from the Pelican Floating Dock as a floating battery. Was scuttled with its guns aboard and set adrift on March 12, 1862, at Island No. 10. Ran aground in shoal water at New Madrid, Mo. Was captured by Union forces. Used as a Union floating dock for repairing vessels. At Walnut Bend, Confederates burned the vessel in August or September 1863. See **CSS *New Orleans***. (*ORN*, 22:725; 25:381–82, 397; ser. 2, 1:261; *CWC*, 6-276–77.)

mortar boat. Union. Towed by the USS *Petrel* when it capsized and sank on October 24, 1863, at the upper mouth of the canal near Vicksburg, Miss. (*ORN*, 25:518–19.)

transports. Union. Col. Colton Greene's brigade shelled three Union transports at Daniel Session's plantation coming upriver. One careened over and was hauled to the bank. Two were disabled and set afire by the shelling on May 24, 1864. (*OR*, 34:1:951; *ORN*, 26:803, 805–7.)

wharf boat. Union. Cargo of eleven thousand sacks of grain. Sank on February 13, 1865, at Memphis. (*New York Times,* February 19, 1864.)

Missouri River and Tributaries

The Missouri River was a major transportation route from St. Louis, Missouri, and the Mississippi River to the Great Plains and the newly opened Montana gold fields. During Confederate major general Sterling Price's invasion of Missouri in 1864, his forces captured and burned the *West Wind* on the Missouri River.

The Missouri River was the supply line for Brig. Gen. Alfred Sully's Northwest Expedition, which was sent to punish the Sioux for Indian massacres in Minnesota and their resistance to white settlement. The treacherous snags of the Missouri River claimed many steamboats, including the *Bertrand,* which sank in 1865 and was fully excavated of its contents in 1968–69.

Adriatic. Union. Stern-wheel steamer. Length 200 feet, beam 45 feet, depth 6 feet 6 inches, 4 engines. Built in 1854 at Shousetown, Pa. Sank at the head of Palmyra Bend on March 28, 1865. Was raised and converted to a barge. (*WPD*, 6.)

Belle Peoria. Union. Side-wheel steamer. Length 180 feet, beam 32 feet. Built at Monongahela, Pa. Rebuilt in 1862 after burning in 1860. Wrecked at Fort Buford. Ran onto a bar near Acrow's Trading Post, 5 miles above the Cheyenne River in October 1864. Wrecked by ice in spring 1865. The pilothouse was deposited in the prairie and gave the area the name Peoria Bottoms. (*WPD*, 45.)

Bertrand. Union. Stern-wheel steamer, 251 tons. Length 161 feet, beam 32 feet 9 inches, depth 5 feet 2 inches, light draft 1 feet 6 inches. Cargo of food, five thousand barrels of whiskey, clothes, agricultural goods, mining supplies, more than one hundred earthenware carboys of mercury, machinery, and ammunition for Union army 12-pounder howitzers. Built in 1864 at Wheeling, W. Va., with machinery salvaged from the *A. J. Sweeney*. En route to Montana Territory mining districts. Snagged on April 1, 1865, sinking within five to ten minutes in 8 feet of water near present Blair, Neb., in the De Soto Bend of the Missouri River in what is now the De Soto National Wildlife Refuge. Most of the valuable machinery, mercury, and whiskey were salvaged within six weeks of sinking as were goods from the wreck of the *Cora II*, located several hundred feet upstream. Found in 1968 by Jesse Pursell and Sam Corbino with a magnetometer. Salvaged in 1968–69 under a contract that gave 60 percent to the U.S. government and 40 percent to the salvagers. More than a million articles and nine carboys of mercury were recovered from the vessel, which was buried under 27 feet of silt and sand. A museum exhibiting the artifacts is located in the De Soto National Wildlife Refuge. The wreck was covered up in place after the excavation. Listed in the National Register of Historic Places. (*Bertrand* Pamphlet; Petsche, *Steamboat Bertrand*, 164; *Chief of Engineers Report 1897*, 6:3874; *WPD*, 2, 51; Haydon, "Sunken Treasure Every Five Miles," *Saga*, 20; Bass, *Ships and Shipwrecks of the Americas*, 199–205.)

Black Hawk No. 2 (Black Hawk). Union. Side-wheel steamer, 57 or 211 tons. Built in 1859 at Cedar Rapids, Iowa. Snagged and sank in 1862 in the Missouri River at the mouth of Bee Creek, 2 miles below Weston, Mo. The boat and cargo were a total loss, but no lives were lost. (*Chief of Engineers Report 1897*, 6:3875; *MSV*, 22, 246; *WPD*, 54.)

Carrier. Union. Side-wheel steamer, 345 tons. Length 215 feet, beam 33 feet. Built in 1855 at Jeffersonville, Ind. Had been previously snagged in the Missouri River in 1858. Sank in the Mississippi River on February 21, 1861. Snagged on August 12, 1861, at St. Charles, Mo. (*MSV*, 30, 248; *WPD*, 74.)

Chippewa. Union. Side-wheel steamer, 173 tons. Length 100 feet, beam 30 feet, 3 boilers. Built in 1857 at Belle Vernon, Pa. While en route for the mountains with a cargo that included gunpowder, it caught fire in May 1861. Drunken deckhands tipped over a candle after tapping some whiskey barrels. The fire was discovered at suppertime on a Sunday evening. The flaming vessel was run ashore, and the passengers fled the boat. The vessel turned and drifted about a mile downstream, blowing up about 15 miles be-

low Poplar River, Dakota Territory (now Mont.). (*Chief of Engineers Report 1897*, 6:3876; *MSV*, 35, 250; *WPD*, 86.)

Cora II (Cora) (Cora No. 2). Union. Stern-wheel steamboat, 215 tons. Cargo of stores and ordnance for Brig. Gen. Alfred Sully's expedition. Built in 1864 at Cincinnati. En route to Fort Benton. Sank on May 1 or 4, 1865, near Fort Calhoun and De Soto, just above the site of the *Bertrand* wreck. The boilers and engines were salvaged by insurers about six weeks after sinking. (*OR*, 48:2:558; *Chief of Engineers Report 1897*, 6:3877; Petsche, *Steamboat Bertrand*, 17, 27; *WPD*, 110.)

Dacotah. Union. Side-wheel steamer, 90 tons. Built in 1858 at Freedom, Pa. Operated by the St. Louis & Hannibal Railroad. Foundered in a tornado on April 15, 1862, at St. Joseph, Mo., with the loss of four lives. (*MSV*, 50, 254; *WPD*, 118.)

Deer Lodge. U.S. Stern-wheel steamer. Length 165 feet, beam 35 feet, depth 5 feet, 3 boilers. Built in 1865 at Belle Vernon, Pa. Snagged and sank in 1865, 12 miles below St. Joseph, Mo. Was later raised. (*WPD*, 122.)

Denmark. Union. Side-wheel steamer, 283 tons. Its hull was built at Shousetown, Pa. Completed in 1856 at Pittsburgh, Pa. Snagged on October 8, 1862, at Atlas Island below Keokuk, Iowa. (*MSV*, 53, 255; *WPD*, 125.)

Emilie No. 2. Union. Side-wheel steamer. Wrecked by wind at St. Joseph in 1865. The hull floated down the Missouri River and sank at Atchison, Kan. It was the first side-wheel steamer to land at Fort Benton. (*Chief of Engineers Report 1897*, 6:3880.)

E. O. Stanard (A. E. Stanard) (Stanard). Union. Side-wheel steamer, 281 tons. Cargo of stores for Brig. Gen. Alfred Sully's expedition. Built in 1865 at Metropolis, Ill. Snagged on May 13, 1865, at De Soto Bend on the Missouri River. (*OR*, 48:2:558; *MSV*, 58, 256.)

Florence. Union. Steamer, 399 tons. Length 200 feet, beam 34 feet, 3 boilers. Built in 1857 at Elizabeth, Pa. Snagged on March 29, 1864, near Atchison, Kan. (*MSV*, 261; *WPD*, 167.)

General McNeil. Nationality unknown. Stern-wheel steamer. Sank during the 1860s at Howards Bend on a snag. (*Chief of Engineers Report 1897*, 6:3881.)

Gus Linn (Colonel Gus Linn) (Col. Gus Lynn). Union. Stern-wheel or side-wheel steamer, 83 tons. Length 132 feet, beam 25 feet 8 inches, depth 2 feet 10 inches . Built in 1859 at California, Pa. Snagged in 1865 in Upper Chatillion Bend or Henry Bend off Turston County, Neb., not far from Sioux City, Iowa. The boat and cargo were a total loss. (*OR*, 41:1:147; *Chief of Engineers Report 1897*, 6:3882; *MSV*, 41, 251; *WPD*, 104.)

Island City. Union. Stern-wheel steamer, 139 tons. Length 140 feet, beam 30 feet. Cargo of corn for the Northwestern Indian Expedition. Built in 1863 at Port Byron, Ill. Snagged on July 25, 1864, near present Fort Union, N.D., across from the site of Fort Buford. The machinery was salvaged and taken to St. Louis and put on the *Belle of Peoria*. (*OR*, 41:1:147; *Chief of Engineers Report 1897*, 6:3883; *MSV*, 103, 269; *WPD*, 227.)

J. G. Morrow. Union. Side-wheel ferry steamer, 163 tons. Built in 1861 at Brownsville, Pa. Snagged on September 1, 1861, at St. Joseph, Mo. (*MSV*, 105, 270; *WPD*, 231.)

John Bell. Union. Stern-wheel steamer, 209 tons. Carried Union government supplies. Built in 1855 at Louisville. Snagged on September 24 or 28, 1863, at St. Charles, Mo. Possibly opposite the foot of Howards Bend near the rocks. (*Chief of Engineers Report 1897*, 6:3883; *MSV*, 112, 272; *WPD*, 250.)

Julia. Union. Steamer. Cargo of eight thousand bushels of corn for Brig. Gen. Alfred Sully's expedition. Sank on May 21, 1865, about 10 miles below Sioux City, Iowa. May have been raised. (*OR*, 48:2:558.)

Lancaster. Union. Side-wheel steamer. Sank in 1865 at Smiths Island or Portland Bend after hitting a snag. (*Chief of Engineers Report 1868*, 657; *Chief of Engineers Report 1897*, 6:3884.)

Louisa. Union. Side-wheel steamer, 250 tons. Length 130 feet. Cargo of hemp. Sank in 1864 at South Point, Mo., when its cargo caught fire and the boat was scuttled. Was not raised due to rising water. (*Chief of Engineers Report 1868*, 657; *Chief of Engineers Report 1897*, 6:3884.)

Louisville. Union. Stern-wheel steamer, 288 tons. Length 180 feet, beam 33 feet, 2 boilers. Built in 1863 at Wheel-

ing, W. Va. While en route for the Yellowstone area, it was sunk by a snag in April or May 1864, at Pratts Cutoff or Louisville Bend between present Sioux City and Fort Randall, S.D. (*Chief of Engineers Report 1868*, 657; *Chief of Engineers Report 1897*, 6:3884; *MSV*, 131; *WPD*, 296.)

Magenta. Union. Side-wheel steamer, 424 tons. Length 215 feet, beam 35 feet, 2 boilers. Built in 1863 at Mound City, Ill. Snagged on May 22, 1863, at a bend of the Missouri River below De Witt, Mo., on its first or second trip. Both boat and cargo were a total loss, but no lives were lost. (*Chief of Engineers Report 1897*, 6:3884; *MSV*, 134, 278.)

Mars. U.S. Side-wheel steamer, 55 tons. Length 180 feet, beam 34 feet. Built in 1862 at Cleveland, Ohio. Hit a snag and sank in May 1865, at Cogswell Landing across from the mouth of the Fishing River. (*Chief of Engineers Report 1897*, 6:3885; *MSV*, 137.)

Mary Lou. Union. Steamer. Cargo of two thousand barrels of whiskey and ten thousand bottles of whiskey. Lost in 1864 south of Omaha, Neb. (Lowry, "Treasures of the Big Muddy," *True Treasure*, 49.)

Orion. Union. Stern-wheel steamer, 138 tons. Built in 1851 at Wheeling, Va. (W. Va.). Snagged in 1864 at Eureka Landing, Mo. (*Chief of Engineers Report 1897*, 6:3887; *MSV*, 165.)

Portsmouth. U.S. Stern-wheel steamer. Length 160 feet, beam 32 feet. Snagged in 1861 about 3 miles below Weston, Mo., at the mouth of Bee Creek. (*Chief of Engineers Report 1897*, 6:3888.)

Rialto. Union. Stern-wheel steamer. Sank in about 1864 at the mouth of Bee Creek, about 2 miles below Weston, Mo. (*Chief of Engineers Report 1897*, 6:3888.)

Sallie List. Union. Stern-wheel steamer, 212 tons. Built in 1860 at Elizabeth, Pa. Snagged 5 miles above Kickapoo, Kan., on May 5, 1863. Was raised and returned to service. (*WPD*, 415.)

Silver Lake. Union. Stern-wheel steamer. 70 tons. Built in 1858 at Wellsville, Ohio. Burned in the Osage River, Mo., on September 3, 1862. May have been raised. (*MSV*, 99, 297.)

Spread Eagle. Union. Side-wheel steamer, 389 tons. Built in 1857 at Brownsville, Pa. Snagged on March 20, 1864, at

Pickney Bend or Washington, Mo. (*Chief of Engineers Report 1897*, 6:3889; *MSV*, 202, 298.)

Tempest. U.S. Stern-wheel steamer, 364 tons. Built in 1863 at Pittsburgh, Pa. Snagged in about 1865 at Upper Bonhomme Island about 28 miles upstream of present Yankton, S.D. (*Chief of Engineers Report 1897*, 6:3890; *WPD*, 448.)

Twilight. U.S. Side-wheel steamer, 230 tons. Length 180 feet, beam 32 feet. Built in 1865 at St. Louis. Snagged going upriver on September 10, 1865, across the mouth of Fire Creek, a quarter-mile above Napoleon. In 1897 part of the cargo was reported to have been salvaged. In 2001 the wreck site was dewatered by twenty wells, and the hull, two steam engines, paddle wheels, and many other artifacts were recovered. About 90,000 cubic yards of material were removed from the wreck site. A varied cargo was recovered in the modern excavation and was restored at St. Charles, Mo. (*Chief of Engineers Report 1897*, 6:3890; *WPD*, 448; *MSV*, 216, 302; Petsche, *Steamboat Bertrand*, 118; "The Steamboat *Twilight*," www.lostreasure.com/pressrelease/Sage%Marketing-12-Jul-01.cfm.)

West Wind. Union. Side-wheel steamer, 350 tons. Length 210 feet, beam 33 feet, depth 5 feet 8 inches, 3 boilers. Built in 1860 at Elizabeth, Pa. Landed six companies of the Union 43rd Mo. Infantry Regiment at Glasgow, Mo. The Union troops were attacked by Confederates under Gen. John B. Clarke and Brig. Gen. Joe Shelby of Maj. Gen. Sterling Price's army. Confederate artillery fire disabled the *West Wind* and the Union troops surrendered. Confederates burned the *West Wind* on October 16 or 17, 1864, before leaving Glasgow. (*OR*, 41:1:430–32, 434; *Chief of Engineers Report 1897*, 6:3392; *MSV*, 228, 306; *WPD*, 484.)

New Jersey

The area off Sandy Hook was along the shipping routes to and from New York City and became a favorite hunting ground for Confederate commerce raiders. The CSS *Tallahassee* destroyed the *A. Richards*, *Carrie Estelle*, *William Bell*, and *Sarah A. Boyce* on August 11, 1864, as it raided the Union Atlantic Coast. The Union schooner *Billow* was reported as having been sunk by the Confederate commerce raider CSS *Tallahassee* on August 12, 1863, off the New Jersey coast but was recovered by the USS *Grand Gulf*. The CSS *Tallahassee* was renamed the CSS *Olustee* in September–October 1864, after being refitted at Wilmington, North Carolina. The CSS *Olustee* destroyed the *Arcole*, *T. D. Wagner*, and *Vapor* off Sandy Hook on November 2–3, 1864. Other vessels were lost off the New Jersey coast because of accidents and storms.

Admiral Du Pont (Angelina) (Anglia) (Anglica). U.S. Side-wheel steamer, 210 bulk tons, 473 gross tons, 201 registered tons, 750 tons. Length 195 feet, beam 28 feet, depth 12 feet 6 inches. Cargo of government supplies. Built in 1847 at West Ham, England. En route from New York City to Fort Monroe, Va. Was the former British blockade-runner *Anglia* captured by the USS *Flag* in Bull's Bay, S.C., on October 27, 1862. Collided with the British vessel *Stodacona* off Cape May on June 8, 1865, and sank, with the loss of fifty to twenty crew members. (*OR*, ser. 3, 5:288; *Daily Examiner*, June 21, 1865; *MSV*, 3, 239; *LLC*, 288.)

Arcole. Union. Ship, 663 tons. Captured and burned by the CSS *Olustee* on November 3, 1864, off Sandy Hook. (*OR*, ser. 4, 3:1058; *ORN*, 3:836; Scharf, *History of the Confederate Navy*, 814.)

A. Richards. Union. Brig, 274 tons. Cargo of coal. Out of Glace Bay, Cape Breton Island, Canada. En route to New York City. Was captured and burned by the CSS *Tallahassee* on August 11, 1864, off Sandy Hook. (*ORN*, 3:137, 703.)

Carrie Estelle. Union. Schooner, 218 tons. Cargo of logs. Was captured and burned by the CSS *Tallahassee* on August 11, 1864, about 80 miles off Sandy Hook. (*ORN*, 3:137, 703.)

Idaho. U.S. Screw steamer, 522 tons. Built in 1864 at Mystic, Conn. Was stranded on December 23, 1865, at Barnegat. (*MSV*, 100, 268.)

Isabel (*Ella Warley*). Union. Side-wheel steamer, 1,115 tons. Length 220 feet, beam 33 feet, depth 21 feet. Built in 1848 at Baltimore. Captured as the *Ella Warley* by the USS *Santiago de Cuba* on April 24–25, 1862. Collided with the *North Star* on February 9, 1863, at sea off the New Jersey coast, with four killed. (*MSV*, 103, 269; *LLC*, 297.)

Locust Point. Union. Screw steamer, 462 tons. Built in 1853 at Philadelphia. Collided with the *Mantanzas* off Absecon, with seventeen killed on July 3, 1864. (*MSV*, 130, 277.)

USS *Picket Boat No. 2.* Union. Screw steam torpedo boat. Length 30–40 feet, beam 9 feet 6 inches, depth 4 feet 6 inches. Built at Boston. Sank in September 1864 on rocks near Bergen Point while en route from New York City to Hampton Roads, Va. Was raised and sent to Philadelphia. See **USS *Picket Boat No. 2*** in Virginia for a later sinking. (*ORN*, 10:483.)

Sarah A. Boyce. Union. Schooner, 382 tons. Out of Egg Harbor, N.J. Captured and burned by the CSS *Tallahassee* within 80 miles of Sandy Hook on August 11, 1864. (*ORN*,

3:137, 142, 703; *Naval Records Group 45, M101, Subject File of the Confederate States Navy*.)

Seagull. Union. Ship. Cargo of oysters. Came ashore on Brigantine Beach near Atlantic City on March 11, 1864. Was full of water and without a crew. (*New York Times*, March 14, 1865.)

T. D. Wagner. Union. Brig. Captured and burned by the CSS *Olustee* on November 3, 1864, near Sandy Hook. (*OR*, ser. 4, 3:1058; *ORN*, 3:836; Semmes, *Service Afloat*, 494–96; Summersell, *Boarding Officer*, 48–49.)

Vapor (*Napor*). Union. Schooner, 312 tons. Captured and burned by the CSS *Olustee* on November 3, 1864, off Sandy Hook. (*OR*, ser. 4, 3:1058; *ORN*, 3:836.)

William Bell (*Number 24*). Union. Pilot boat. Manned by a captain and crew of six. Captured and burned by the CSS *Tallahassee*, 90 miles east southeast off Sandy Hook or 35 miles southeast of Fire Island on August 11, 1864. (*ORN*, 3:144–45, 703; *New York Times*, August 15, 1864.)

New York

During the Civil War the Confederate commerce raiders CSS *Chickamauga*, CSS *Florida*, and CSS *Tallahassee* (CSS *Olustee*) captured and burned nine Yankee vessels in crowded shipping lanes off New York Harbor. Several other ships were lost as a result of collisions with other vessels, running aground, and exploding.

Adriatic. Union. Ship, 989 tons. Carried 170 emigrants. En route from London to New York City. Was captured by the CSS *Tallahassee* and burned on August 12, 1864, 35 miles off Montauk Point. (*OR*, ser. 4, 3:1057; *ORN*, 3:145; Shingleton, *John Taylor Wood*, 130, 207.)

Arrow (*Broadway*) (*George Washington*). U.S. Side-wheel steamer, 290 tons. Built in 1837 at New York City. Exploded off 13th Street (Haverstraw) in New York City on August 5–6, 1865, with five killed. (*MSV*, 14, 243; *EAS*, 10.)

Atlantic. Union. Schooner, 156 tons. Out of Addison. En route to New York City. Captured and burned by the CSS *Tallahassee* on August 12, 1864, off the New York coast. (*ORN*, 3:703.)

Augusta. U.S. Side-wheel steamer, 218 tons. Built in 1838 at New York City. Stranded in September 1863 at Hell Gate, New York City. (*MSV*, 15, 243.)

Bay State. Union. Bark, 200 tons. Cargo of wood. Out of Boston. En route from Alexandria to New York City. Burned by the CSS *Tallahassee* on August 11, 1864. (*ORN*, 3:137, 142, 703.)

Berkshire. Union. Steamer, 649 tons. Built in 1864 at Athens, N.Y. Burned on June 8, 1864, at Poughkeepsie with a loss of thirty-five lives. (*MSV*, 21, 245.)

Charity. Confederate. Schooner, 127 tons. Carried assorted cargo. En route from Alexandria, Va., to New York

City. Wrecked on Long Island after capture by the USS *Stars and Stripes* on December 15, 1861. (*ORN*, 6:480–81; *SCH*, 334–35.)

Emma L. Hall. Union. Bark, 492 tons. Cargo of sugar and molasses. En route from Cardenas, Cuba to New York City. Captured and burned by the CSS *Chickamauga* within 50 miles of New York City on October 31, 1864. (*OR*, ser. 4, 3:1058.)

Francis Skiddy (General Taylor). Union. Side-wheel steamer, 1,183 or 1,235 tons. Length 332 feet, beam 38 feet. Built in 1851 at New York City. Stranded on a ledge on November 25, 1864, 4 miles south of Albany on the Hudson River, near Staats Landing or Staat's Dock. The engine was removed and put in the new vessel *Dean Richmond*. (*MSV*, 76, 261; Lane, *American Paddle Steamboats*, 94, 95.)

Isaac Newton. Union. Side-wheel steamer, 1,332 tons. Built in 1846 at New York City. Exploded on December 6, 1863, at Fort Washington with nine killed. (*MSV*, 103, 269.)

James Funk (Pilot Boat No. 22 of New York). Union. Pilot boat, 121 tons. Captured on August 11, 1864, by the CSS *Tallahassee* off Montauk Point and burned. (*ORN*, 3:703; *CWC*, 6-6-254.)

Lammont Du Pont. Union. Schooner, 194 tons. Cargo of coal. Out of Wilmington, Del. En route from Cow Bay, Cape Breton, Canada, for New York City. Captured and burned by the CSS *Tallahassee* within 60 miles of New York City on August 13, 1864. (*ORN*, 3:703.)

Neptune (Allegany) (USS Neptune). U.S. Screw steamer, 1,244 tons. Length 209 feet 6 inches or 203 feet 6 inches, beam 35 feet 6 inches, depth 14 feet. Built in 1863 at New York City. Formerly the Union vessel USS *Neptune*. Was stranded in a fog on December 5, 1865, off Long Island. (*MSV*, 164, 284; *WCWN*, 79.)

Oregon. Union. Side-wheel steamer, 1,004 tons. Built in 1845 at New York City. Collided with the *City of Boston* on October 22, 1863, at New York City. (*MSV*, 164, 287.)

Rienzi. Union. Whaling schooner. Cargo of whale oil. Out of Provincetown, R.I. Captured and burned by the CSS *Florida* within 50 miles of New York City on July 8, 1863. (*ORN*, 2:653.)

Scioto. Union. Screw steamer, 389 tons. Built in 1848 at Huron, Ohio. Collided with the *Arctic* on September 2, 1864, and sank at Dunkirk. (*MSV*, 196, 297.)

Spokane. Union. Schooner, 126 tons. Cargo of lumber. Out of Fremont. En route from Calais, France to New York City. Captured and burned by the CSS *Tallahassee* off the New York coast on August 12, 1864. (*ORN*, 3:703.)

William B. Nash. Union. Brig. Cargo of 650,000 pounds of lard. Out of New York City. Captured and burned by the CSS *Florida* on July 8, 1863, off New York City. (*ORN*, 2:653.)

William J. Romer. Union. Pilot schooner. Wrecked during the Civil War on a submerged rock on what is now known as Romer Shoals in New York Harbor. One pilot died in the wreck. (Morris and Quinn, *Shipwrecks in New York*, 21.)

North Carolina

The North Carolina sounds were the objective of one of the first Union invasions of the Confederacy in August 1861 and February 1862. To impede the Union invasion fleet, lighthouses along the North Carolina Atlantic coast were abandoned, and light ships were sunk or removed by the Confederates. The treacherous Atlantic coast, known as a graveyard for ships, became more hazardous for commercial and military ships. Vessels were also scuttled to block portions of the Pamlico Sound and the Neuse River.

In January 1862 fierce Atlantic storms sank the Union vessels the *Grapeshot*, *City of New York*, *Pocahontas*, and *Union* from Brig. Gen. Ambrose Everett Burnside's invasion fleet. Storms also sank the USS *Monitor* on December 31, 1862, off Cape Hatteras. The wreck of the USS *Monitor* has been located and is now a marine preserve.

Union forces quickly captured isolated barrier islands along the North Carolina coast and expanded their operations into the sounds and inlets, capturing Roanoke Island.

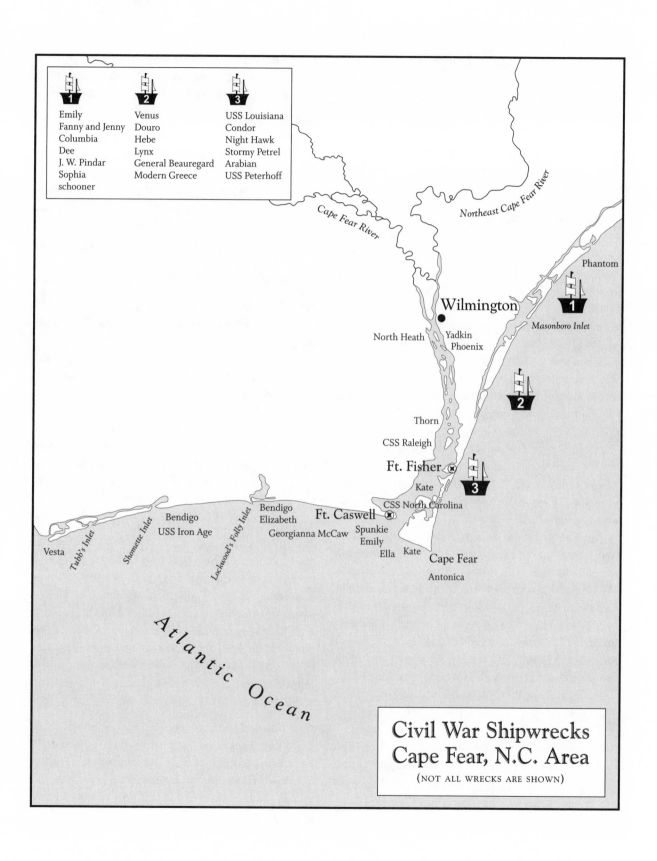

Emily
Fanny and Jenny
Columbia
Dee
J. W. Pindar
Sophia
schooner

Venus
Douro
Hebe
Lynx
General Beauregard
Modern Greece

USS Louisiana
Condor
Night Hawk
Stormy Petrel
Arabian
USS Peterhoff

Cape Fear River

Northeast Cape Fear River

Phantom

Masonboro Inlet

Wilmington

North Heath

Yadkin
Phoenix

Thorn

CSS Raleigh

Ft. Fisher

Kate

CSS North Carolina

Bendigo
Elizabeth

Ft. Caswell

Bendigo
USS Iron Age

Georgianna McCaw

Spunkie
Emily

Shanette Inlet

Lockwood's Folly Inlet

Ella

Kate

Cape Fear

Tubb's Inlet

Vesta

Antonica

Atlantic Ocean

Civil War Shipwrecks
Cape Fear, N.C. Area
(NOT ALL WRECKS ARE SHOWN)

On February 10, 1862, a Confederate fleet was attacked at Elizabeth City, and the CSS *Appomattox*, CSS *Black Warrior*, CSS *Fanny*, CSS *Forrest*, CSS *M. C. Etheridge*, CSS *Sea Bird*, and a schooner were destroyed with no Union vessel loss.

Wilmington became the major Confederate port because the Cape Fear River had several entrances to the Atlantic Ocean. Blockade-runners from Canada, Bermuda, the Bahamas, and Cuba regularly sailed into and out of the Cape Fear River. The entrances to the Cape Fear River were guarded by Confederate Fort Fisher and Fort Caswell, a number of Confederate batteries, as well as a Confederate fleet of ironclads and gunboats. Supplies were moved from Wilmington to Confederate forces throughout the Confederacy, especially to Gen. Robert E. Lee's Army of Northern Virginia.

The area around Wilmington has the greatest concentration of wrecks from the American Civil War and now is an archaeological preserve. Among the wrecks of note are the *Arabian*, *Bendigo*, *The Dare*, *Douro*, *Elizabeth*, *Ella*, *General Beauregard*, *Georgiana C. McCaw*, USS *Iron Age*, USS *Louisiana*, *Modern Greece*, *Nutfield*, USS *Peterhoff*, *Phantom*, *Ranger*, *Sophia*, *Stormy Petrel*, and *Venus*. Several blockade-runners, including the *Annie*, *Armstrong*, *Badge*, and *Kate* (*G. T. Watson*), were reported as destroyed but were in fact just temporarily grounded and were later refloated.

The CSS *Arctic*, CSS *Raleigh*, and CSS *North Carolina* were sunk in the Cape Fear River. The CSS *Albemarle* sank the USS *Southfield* in the Roanoke River, but Lt. William B. Cushing sank the CSS *Albemarle* during a daring night torpedo boat raid. The ironclad CSS *Neuse* was scuttled in 1865. Several unfinished Confederate ironclads were scuttled in the Tar River in 1863 and in the Cape Fear River at the end of the Civil War. When Wilmington fell to Union troops in February 1865, the Confederates scuttled the CSS *Chickamauga*, the CSS *Caswell*, and the ironclad CSS *Wilmington*.

Actor. Confederate. Schooner. Was sunk by the USS *Ceres* in the Pamlico River on March 6, 1862. Was later raised. (Pleasants, *Vessels Destroyed or Captured*, 2; *SCH*, 340–41; *WCWN*, 96.)

A. C. Williams. Confederate. Schooner. Was scuttled to act as an obstruction on January 19, 1862, below Weir's Point, Roanoke Island. (*ORN*, 6:787; *CWC*, 6-6-333.)

Adelaide. Confederate. Schooner. Cargo of 600 barrels of turpentine, 36 bales of cotton, and some tobacco. En route from Wilmington for Halifax, Nova Scotia. Ran aground on October 21–22, 1862, by the USS *Ellis* under Lt. William Barker Cushing. Was set afire by its crew and abandoned, but Union sailors boarded the vessel and put out the fire. The USS *Ellis* tried to tow the vessel, but the draft was several feet too shallow, so the *Adelaide* kept running aground. The *Adelaide* was finally destroyed about a mile north of New Topsail Inlet. (*ORN*, 8:151–52, 242; 11:385.)

Agnes E. Fry (Roe). British. Side-wheel steamer, 559 gross tons, 350 tons. Length 236 feet 7 inches, beam 25 feet 3 inches, depth 13 feet 6 inches. Built in 1864 at Greenock, Scotland. Renamed after Confederate lieutenant Joseph Fry's wife. The USS *Monticello* chased the *Agnes E. Fry* aground on December 27, 1864, about 4 miles from Fort Campbell and about 2 miles southwest of Fort Caswell, 4 miles below the Western Bar. Located about 20 yards from the low-water mark in the sand beyond the wreck of the *Georgiana McCaw*. Most of the cargo and the vessel's machinery were salvaged.(*OR*, 42:3:1326, 1328, 1344–45, 1358; *ORN*, 11:385, 627, 725, 788; Horner, *Blockade-Runners*, 227; *LLC*, 286.)

Albemarle. Union. Stern-wheel cargo steamer, 183 tons. Built in 1855 at Wheeling, Va. (W. Va.). Captured on March 25, 1862, off New Bern by the USS *Delaware*, with eleven crewmen captured and two drowned. As a Union transport evacuating wounded, it accidentally hit piles on March 31, 1862, in the New Bern Harbor and immediately sank. The crew, wounded, sick, prisoners, and stores were removed. On April 4, 1862, the *Albemarle* was destroyed by the USS *Louisiana*. Was probably raised and put back into Union service as an ordnance ship. (*ORN*, 7:174–75, 703; *CWC*, 6-6-193; *MSV*, 5.)

CSS Albemarle. Confederate. Twin screw ironclad ram, 2,000 tons. Length 158 feet, beam 35 feet 3 inches, depth 8 feet 2 inches, draft 9 feet, armor 2-inch iron, 2 engines, 2 boilers. Armed with two 6.4-inch pivot guns. Was sunk by a Union torpedo boat and thirteen volunteers under

Lt. William Barker Cushing on the night of October 28, 1864, above Plymouth in the Roanoke River in 8 feet of water under heavy fire from Confederates guarding the boat. One Union sailor and Lieutenant Cushing escaped, but the other eleven Union sailors were captured. The Confederates blew up the forward and top sections of the CSS *Albemarle,* making a 6-foot diameter hole, but the vessel's works were above water. Was raised in February 19, 1865, by Union forces and towed northward. Arrived at the Norfolk Navy Yard on April 27, 1865. Was sold on October 11, 1867. (*ORN,* 10:611–17, 619–24; 12:9, 22, 75, 128; ser. 2, 1:247; Miller, *Photographic History,* 6:87; *CWC,* 6-6-193; Elliott, *Albemarle,* 251–62, 272–76.)

Alexander. Nationality unknown. Schooner. Wrecked off Wilmington in 1862. (Pleasants, *Vessels Destroyed or Captured,* 3.)

Alexander Cooper. Confederate. Schooner. Burned at anchor on August 22–23, 1863, by two boats under Lt. William Barker Cushing from the USS *Shokokon* at the sea beach about 6 miles up New Topsail Inlet, close to Confederate saltworks, by a wharf. Three Confederate soldiers were captured during the expedition. (*ORN,* 9:176–78; Porter, *Naval History,* 428.)

Alice Webb. Nationality unknown. Schooner. Carried assorted cargo. Beached on or prior to November 3, 1863, inside of Bogue Inlet. The cargo was recovered by Confederates. (*OR,* 29:2:452–53; *ORN,* 9:780.)

USS *Alligator.* Union. First Union submarine. Length 47 feet, beam 4 feet 6 inches, depth 6 feet, powered by 16 folded oars pulled by its crew. Complement of seventeen. Carried two spar torpedoes. Built in Philadelphia. Launched on April 30, 1862. While under tow by the USS *Sumpter* to Port Royal, S.C., from the Washington Navy Yard the vessel was cut adrift during a storm off Cape Hatteras and lost on April 2, 1863. (*ORN,* ser. 2, 1:32; Christley, "Alligator, the North's Underwater Threat," *Civil War Times Illustrated,* 26–31; Stern, *Confederate Navy Pictorial History,* 173; Bass, *Ships and Shipwrecks of the Americas,* 226.)

Alpha. U.S. Screw steamer, 107 tons. Built in 1858 at Brooklyn, N.Y. Exploded in Albemarle Sound on October 7, 1865. (*MSV,* 8, 241.)

Amelia. Nationality unknown. Schooner. Cargo of cotton. En route from Port Royal, S.C., to Philadelphia. Captured by the USS *Flag* while coming out of Charleston, S.C., on the night of May 8, 1863. Was lost off Cape Hatteras on May 15, 1863, in a gale as a result of leaks caused by a collision while under tow with by the prize steamer *Cherokee.* The British schooner *Halitia* rescued the crew. (*ORN,* 14:182–84.)

Ann Marie (Anna). British. Schooner, 80 tons. Out of Nassau, Bahamas. Was chased ashore by the USS *Monticello* on November 18, 1862, southwest of Shallotte Inlet in 4 fathoms of water. Sank west of the wreck *Ariel.* Some of the cargo was unloaded. The vessel bilged, broke up, and was set afire. (*ORN,* 8:218–19, 814.)

Antonica (Herald). British. Side-wheel steamer, 563 tons. Cargo of 1,200 bales of cotton, $1,200 cash, liquor, dry goods, general provisions, and clothing. En route for Wilmington. Grounded on December 20, 1863, when going inshore of the USS *State of Georgia,* USS *Connecticut,* and USS *Governor Buckingham* at 3:00 a.m. on the western side of Frying Pan Shoals, 3 miles from Bald Head, 3 miles from Confederate batteries on Smith's Island, and 3.5 miles south of Cape Fear. The crew took to the boats, and forty-two were taken prisoner. Several days later the vessel broke apart. Part of the cargo was salvaged by Union forces along with $1,200, part of which was Confederate money. The Union tug *Violet* grounded for more than two days after trying to refloat the vessel. (*ORN,* 9:362–67, 775, 781; Horner, *Blockade-Runners,* 140, 216–17.)

Aphrodite. Union. Chartered screw steamer, 1,098 tons. Carried 510 Union navy recruits from New York to join the Atlantic and Gulf Squadrons. Built in 1864 at Mystic, Conn. At 5:00 a.m. on October 31, 1864, the vessel grounded on a shoal in Core Sound, 12 miles north northeast of Cape Lookout. The USS *Keystone State* and USS *Shokokon* arrived on November 4, 1864, rescued the crew and sailors, and removed the cargo. The ship bilged and broke in two. Its anchors, cables, and other parts were salvaged. (*ORN,* 10:523–24, 531; *MSV,* 12, 242.)

CSS *Appomattox (Empire).* Confederate. Side-wheel steam tug, 90 tons. Armed with one howitzer and one bow gun.

Built in 1846 at Grand Rapids, Mich. Tried to enter the Dismal Swamp Canal on February 10, 1862, after the destruction of the Confederate fleet at Elizabeth City, but the vessel's beam was a few inches too wide to go through the lock. Set afire and blown up to prevent capture. (*ORN*, ser. 2, 1:248; *MSV*, 64; *CWC*, 6-224–25; Horner, *Blockade-Runners*, 113–26.)

Arabian. Canadian. Side-wheel steamer, 263 registered tons. Length 174 feet, beam 24 feet, depth 18 feet 4 inches. Cargo of cotton. Built in 1851 at Niagara, Ontario. Turned back by the USS *Iron Age* and USS *Shenandoah* while exiting the Cape Fear River at night on September 15, 1863, and ran aground north of Corncake Inlet at the entrance of the Cape Fear River, about one mile below Fort Fisher at Kure Beach. Its machinery and paddlewheel are located above the sandy bottom in 20 feet of water. Listed in the National Register of Historic Places as part of an archaeological district. (*ORN*, 9:211, 214, 216, 221, 228, 248; *Federal Register*, December 4, 1990, 50141–42; Bright, "Wrecked Blockade Runners of the Lower Cape Fear," *Historical Archaeology*, 129; *LLC*, 288.)

CSS Arctic. Confederate. Iron plated floating battery, 500 tons. Armed with three guns. Converted from a light ship in 1863 at Wilmington, N.C. Served as a receiving ship for Flag Officer Robert F. Pinkney's North Carolina Defense Force. Its machinery was removed in late 1862 and put in the CSS *Virginia II* at Richmond, Va. Was scuttled by the Confederates in the Cape Fear River below Wilmington on December 24, 1864, to obstruct the channel at the "Rips." (*OR*, 18:863; 42:3:1302; *ORN*, 11:787; ser. 2, 1:248; *ORA*, pl. 68, no. 7; *CWC*, 6-198; *WCWN*, 237.)

Ariel. British, Schooner, 80 tons. Cargo of salt, lard, flour, and sugar. En route from Halifax, Nova Scotia. Chased ashore by USS *Monticello* on November 18, 1862, at Shallotte Inlet. Some goods were unloaded from the wreck. The USS *Monticello* pursued the *Ann Maria* ashore and set the *Ariel* afire the next day. (*ORN*, 8:218–19.)

USS Aster (Alice). Union. Wooden screw steam tug, 285 bulk tons. Length 122 feet 6 inches, beam 23 feet, depth 10–12 feet. Complement of thirty, with one 30-pounder Parrott and two smoothbore 12-pounders. Launched in 1864 at Wilmington, Del. Grounded while chasing the blockade-runner *Annie*. The tug USS *Berberry* was unable to pull the USS *Aster* off. The *Annie* was refloated by the Confederates and made it safely into Wilmington, while the Union vessels were heavily shelled by Confederate shore batteries. To avoid capture, the USS *Aster* was burned on October 8, 1864, on Caroline Shoals off New Inlet near the wrecks of the *Night Hawk* and *Condor*. The wreck is usually sanded over except for a four-blade propeller and part of its machinery. Now under 20 feet of water. Listed in the National Register of Historic Places as part of an archaeological district. (*ORN*, 10:541–46; ser. 2, 1:40; *Federal Register*, December 4, 1990, 50143; Horner, *Blockade-Runners*, 63–65; Bright, "Wrecked Blockade Runners of the Lower Cape Fear," *Historical Archaeology*,129.)

USS Bainbridge. Union. Brig, 259 tons. Length 100 feet, beam 25 feet, depth 11 feet 6 inches, draft 13 feet 7 inches, maximum speed 11 knots, average speed 6 knots. Complement of one hundred, with six 32-pounders and one rifled 12-pounder. Launched in 1842 at Boston. Capsized and sank off Cape Hatteras on August 21, 1863, with all lost but a cook and one crewman, who climbed into a boat. The crazed cook jumped off the boat and drowned. The *South Boston* rescued the lone crewman forty-eight hours later. (*ORN*, 14:514; ser. 2, 1:42.)

USS Bazely (USS Beta) (J. E. Bazely) (Picket Boat No. 2) (Tug No. 2). Union. Tug, 50 tons. Length 70 feet, beam 16 feet, depth 6 feet 7 inches, draft 7 feet, maximum speed 10 knots, average speed 8 knots. Complement of fourteen. Built in 1863 at Gloucester, N.J. Sank on December 9–10, 1864, when it hit a torpedo a few yards off the wrecked USS *Otsego* in the Roanoke River, just below Jamestown Bluff. The USS *Bazely* lost two killed. (*ORN*, 11:161, 177; ser. 2, 1:43; *WCWN*, 114; Ammen, "Navy in the Civil War," *Confederate Military History*, 214.)

Bendigo (Milly). Confederate. Iron side-wheel steamer, 178 registered tons. Length 162 feet 1 inch, beam 20 feet 1 inch, depth 10 feet 11 inches. Ran aground west of the entrance of Lockwood's Folly Inlet on January 2–3, 1864, when the pilot saw the wreck of the *Elizabeth* and thought it was a Union blockader. Found by the USS *Fahkee* when the *Bendigo* was set afire by Confederates. The Union sailors were unable to refloat the *Bendigo,* but the USS *Iron Age* grounded and was blown up to prevent its capture. The *Bendigo* was shelled by the USS *Iron Age,* USS *Fort Jackson,* USS *Montgomery,* and USS *Daylight.* Now buried in the sand except for the top of the boilers and paddlewheels. Listed in the National Register of Historic Places as part of an archaeological district. (*ORN,* 9:385–86, 396–401; *Federal Register,* December 4, 1990, 50142; Porter, *Naval History,*471; Bright, "Wrecked Blockade Runners of the Lower Cape Fear," *Historical Archaeology,* 129; *LLC,* 290.)

Black Squall. Nationality unknown. Brig. Was lost on April 8, 1861, at Ocracoke Inlet. (Stick, *Graveyard of the Atlantic,* 247.)

CSS Black Warrior. Confederate. Schooner. Cargo of naval stores and provisions. Armed with two 32-pounders. Moored off Fort Cobb at Elizabeth City when abandoned and burned by Confederates on February 10, 1862, as a Union fleet attacked. The crew escaped through the marshes of the Pasquotank River. Its machinery was destroyed, but its guns may have been salvaged. (*ORN,* 6:607; ser. 2, 1:249; *CWC,* 6-206; Ammen, "Navy in the Civil War," *Confederate Military History,* 184–85.)

Bombshell. Union army. Transport tug. Length 90 or 96 feet, draft 3 feet 6 inches. Complement of thirty-seven, with three howitzers and one 20-pounder. Sank in 20 feet of water at the Plymouth dock by a Confederate battery on April 18, 1864. Was raised by the Confederates. Recaptured by Union forces on May 5, 1864. (*OR,* 33:298, 305, 960; *ORN,* 6:472; 9:637, 644–45; ser. 2, 1:249; *CWC,* 6-206.)

B. T. Martin. Union. Brig. Cargo of 40 barrels of potatoes, a complete sugar mill, and 3 large iron tanks. Out of Boston. En route from Philadelphia to Havana, Cuba. Captured by the Confederate privateer *York* 110 miles east of Cape Hatteras. Beached on July 24, 1864, 20–30 miles north of Cape Hatteras near Chicamacomico. The Confederates began unloading cargo and stripping the vessel, but the USS *Union* appeared and Confederates burned the ship and its cargo on July 28, 1864. (*ORN,* 1:59–60; 6:41; ser. 2, 2:160.)

Caldwell. Confederate. Stern-wheel steamer, 51 tons. Built in 1859 at Fayetteville, N.C. Burned at Fayetteville on March 14, 1865. (*MSV,* 28, 247.)

C. A. Nicholas. Confederate. One of two barges grounded by Confederates on Croatan Sound on Roanoke Island, filled with mud, and made into a fort with seven guns. The makeshift fort was destroyed by the USS *Southfield* in February 1862. (*ORN,* 6:571.)

Cantilabria. French. Frigate, 2,500 tons. Ran onto a bar in a gale off Cape Hatteras. The crew abandoned the vessel, which burned and blew up on November 8, 1861. (*New York Times,* November 12, 1861.)

Cape Fear (Flora) (Hart) (Virginia). Confederate. Iron twin screw transport steamer, 434 bulk tons. Length 161 feet 4 inches, beam 22 feet 6 inches, depth 12 feet 5 inches. Built in 1862 at London. Served as the blockade-runner *Flora* from December 1862 to September 1863. Purchased by the Confederate States in October 1863. Renamed *Cape Fear.* Was scuttled by Confederates on January 17, 1865, in the Cape Fear River near Smithfield after the *Cape Fear* evacuated Confederate troops from Fort Holmes to Smithville. (*OR,* 46:2:1088; Stick, *Graveyard of the Atlantic,* 248.)

Caroline Virginia. Confederate. Schooner. Wrecked off New Bern on March 14, 1862. (Pleasants, *Vessels Destroyed or Captured,* 3.)

Carter. Confederate. Schooner. Was scuttled by the CSS *Ellis* in Croatan Sound off Roanoke Island below Weir's Point on January 21, 1862. (*ORN,* 6:788; *CWC,* 6-333.)

CSS Caswell. Confederate. Wooden side-wheel tender. Complement of thirty-two. Served as a tender at Wilmington. Burned to prevent its capture when Wilmington fell on February 22, 1865. (*ORN,* ser. 2, 1:250; *CWC,* 6-208.)

Charity. Confederate. Schooner, 128 tons. Cargo of salt, sugar, coffee, shoes, and general cargo. Out of Providence, R.I. Supposed to have been trading with Alexandria, Va. Wrecked when chased by the USS *Stars and Stripes* at Hatteras Inlet on December 15, 1861. (*ORN,* 6:480–81; *WCWN,* 94; Pleasants, *Vessels Destroyed or Captured,* 1.)

Chatham. Confederate. Side-wheel steamer, 57 tons. Built in 1850 at New Bern, N.C. Burned by Confederates to prevent capture at New Bern on March 14, 1862. (*MSV,* 34.)

CSS Chickamauga (Edith). Confederate. Double screw steamer, 531 displacement tons, 370 gross tons, 239 registered tons, 586 tons. Length 175 feet, beam 25 feet, depth 15 feet, draft 7 feet 9 inches, speed 13.4 knots. Complement of 120, with one rifled 12-pounder, one 64-pounder pivot gun, and two 32-pounder pivots (another source– one 84-pounder, two 24-pounders, and two 32-pounders). Built in 1863 at London. Formerly the blockade-runner *Edith,* which was sold to the Confederacy and commissioned in September 1864. As a commerce raider, the CSS *Chickamauga* captured seven Union vessels, destroying five and bonding two. After the fall of Wilmington to Union forces, the CSS *Chickamauga* went up the Cape Fear River and two of its guns were placed on a bluff commanding the river. Was sunk by Confederates to block the channel on February 25, 1865, at Gray's Point, 50 miles above the Wilmington. The river current moved the vessel to the side of the river. Other Confederate steamers were also burned at Gray's Point. (*OR,* 47:2:643, 791; *ORN,* 12:57, 63, 71; ser. 2, 1:250; *CWC,* 6-211; *WCWN,* 210; *LLC,* 297.)

City of New York. Union. Screw transport steamer, 574 tons. Cargo of $200,000 worth of ordnance, including 400 barrels of gunpowder, 1,600 rifle muskets, 800 shells, tents, and hand grenades. Built in 1852 at Hoboken, N.J. Went ashore on January 13, 1862, at the entrance to Hatteras Inlet. Part of Burnside's expedition that was to attack Roanoke Island. Some of its cargo floated onto Hatteras Inlet. All of the crew were saved after hanging onto the rigging for forty-two hours. (*OR,* 9:355; *Charleston Mercury,* February 3, 1862; *MSV,* 37, 250.)

Clarendon. Confederate. Screw steam ferryboat, 143 tons. Used as a dispatch boat and transport. Built in 1860 at Portsmouth, Va. Seized by Union forces on March 14, 1865, at Fayetteville and burned. (*CWC,* 6-212; *MSV,* 38.)

Cleopatra. French. Frigate. Burned to the water's edge off Cape Hatteras in November 1862 with no loss of life. (*ORN,* 12:292.)

Colonel Hill (*General Hill*). Confederate. Steamer. Boarded and burned with the *Governor Morehead* in the Tar River near Tarsboro on July 20, 1863, by the 12th N.Y. Cavalry Regiment of General John G. Foster's expedition. (*OR,* 27:2:964, 973; 29:2:71; *ORN,* 9:164–65; *CWC,* 6-213.)

USS *Columbia* (*Columbia*). Union. Iron screw steamer, 503 tons. Length 168 feet, beam 25 feet, depth 14 feet. Complement of one hundred, with six smoothbore 24-pounders and one 30-pounder Parrott. Built in 1862 at Dumbarton, Scotland. Originally a blockade-runner captured on August 3, 1862, by the USS *Santiago de Cuba* off Florida. Wrecked at Masonboro Inlet on a bar in 8 feet of water within a crescent shaped breaker on January 14, 1863, while on a night patrol under inexperienced Lt. Joseph P. Couthouy. Located 3 miles from a beach and 4–5 miles southwest of Masonboro. Struck by a gale on January 15, 1863. The USS *Penobscot* rescued thirty men from the wreck during the storm on January 15–16, but a Confederate battery drove it off. The crew spiked and threw its guns overboard. A 30-pounder Parrott saved by the USS *Penobscot* was lost overboard on February 3, 1863. Surrendered to the Confederates, who stripped and burned the vessel. Probably now buried by sand. (*ORN,* 8:422–37, 499; ser. 2, 1:62; Bright, "Wrecked Blockade Runners of the Lower Cape Fear," *Historical Archaeology,* 129; *WCWN,* 88.)

Condor. British and possibly Confederate. Iron side-wheel steamer, 285, 300, or 446 tons. Length 270 feet, beam 24 feet, draft 7 feet, speed 14–18 knots. Crew of forty to fifty. Ran aground near the wreck of the *Night Hawk* on October 1, 1864, at 4:00 a.m. near New Inlet, 400 yards from shore. The *Condor*'s pilot thought the wreck of the *Night Hawk* was a Union blockader, so the *Condor* was run aground near the wreck of the CSS *Raleigh*. Rose O'Neal Greenhow, a noted Confederate spy and author, was aboard on a Confederate mission. She drowned when her lifeboat capsized in rough weather. She had sewn Confederate dispatches and eight hundred gold sovereigns into her petticoat. The money was the royalty proceeds of her book. She was afraid of being imprisoned or executed as a spy if captured by Union forces. Some three hundred gold sovereigns were stolen from her body and later turned over to authorities by a guilty Confederate guard. The Confederates salvaged most of the *Condor*'s supplies. The wreck is on New Inlet Bar in about 15 feet of water, listing to port, with paddlewheels and machinery intact, but partially sanded in. Listed in the National Register of Historic

Places as part of an archaeological district. (*ORN*, 11:745; ser. 2, 3:1253, 1258; Horner, *Blockade-Runners*, 54–66; *Federal Register*, December 4, 1990, 50142; Bright, "Wrecked Blockade Runners of the Lower Cape Fear," *Historical Archaeology*,129; *WCWN*, 222; *LLC*, 294.)

Constitution. U.S. Screw steamer, 944 tons. Built in 1863 at Mystic, Conn. Stranded on December 12, 1865, at Cape Lookout with forty lost. (*MSV*, 45, 253.)

USS *Crocus* (*Solomon Thomas*). Union. Screw steam tug, 122 or 129 tons. Length 79 feet, beam 18 feet 6 inches, depth 9 feet 3 inches, draft 7 feet 6 inches, speed 7.5 knots. Armed with two guns. Built in 1863 at Mystic, Conn. Ran aground and wrecked on August 17, 1863, at Bodie Island with no loss of life. (*ORN*, 9:162–63; ser. 2, 1:68; *MSV*, 200; *WCWN*, 115–16.)

CSS *Curlew*. Confederate. Side-wheel steam tug, 236 or 260 tons. Length 150 feet, draft 4 feet 6 inches, speed 12 knots. Armed with one 32-pounder or two guns. Built in 1856 at Wilmington, Del. Ran ashore off Fort Forrest and sank off the northwest end of Roanoke Island in Croatan Sound on February 7, 1862. A 100-pounder Union shell went through the vessel's magazine and drove the hull's iron plate off the vessel. Was burned and blown up by Confederates on February 8, 1862. (*OR*, 9:185; *ORN*, 6:590, 594; ser. 2, 1:251; *MSV*, 49; *CWC*, 6-217.)

Dare, The. British. Side-wheel steamer, 311 gross tons, 179 registered tons. Length 211 feet 8 inches, beam 23 feet 1 inch, depth 9 feet 5 inches. Carried a small cargo. Built at Glasgow, Scotland. Discovered by Union blockaders at 6:45 a.m., chased, and forced aground in fog at 1:00 p.m. by the USS *Aries* and USS *Montgomery*. Burned by the crew a little north of North Inlet off Lockwood Folly near Georgetown on January 7, 1864. The crew escaped. Two Union boats overturned and 25 officers and men were captured by Confederate troops on the beach. The Union sailors set it afire in three places and shells later went through the vessel's machinery. (*ORN*, 9:388–93, 409–10; *ORN*, 15:224; Porter, *Naval History*, 471; *LLC*, 323.)

"David." Confederate. Torpedo boat. Built in 1864 or 1865 in Charleston, S.C. Captured there. While being transported by the USS *Mingoe* the "David" was lost in a storm off Cape Hatteras on June 6, 1865. (*ORN*, 16:344; Perry, *Infernal Machines*, 171.)

Dee (*Aurora*). Confederate. Twin screw iron steamer, 215 registered tons, 200 tons. Length 165 feet, beam 23 feet, depth 13 feet. Cargo of bacon, liquor, coffee, guns, 200 lead ingots, and ammunition. Built in 1863 at London. En route from Hamilton, Bermuda, on its second trip through the Union blockade. Hit a shoal at 3:30 a.m. a mile south of Masonboro Inlet on February 6, 1864. Sailors from the USS *Niphon* boarded the vessel and threw 170 lead pigs overboard on February 7, 1864, to lighten the ship to tow the vessel off. Grounded again across from Mr. Thomas Hansley's plantation and burned. (*OR*, 33:1228; *ORN*, 9:467–68; Horner, *Blockade-Runners*, 220; Porter, *Naval History*, 472; Shomette, *Civil War Shipwrecks*, 414.)

Dolly. Confederate. Steamer. Seized by the Union navy in Roanoke River area near Edwards Ferry in May 1865. On May 27, 1865, the *Dolly* was reported sunk in a canal with a lighter of iron plates. (*ORN*, 12:165; *CWC*, 6-222.)

Douro. Confederate. Iron screw steamer, 180 tons. Crew of twenty-two. Cargo of 20 tierces of tobacco, 279 boxes of tobacco, 550 cotton bales, turpentine, and rosin. Coming out of Wilmington on its third trip. Captured on March 9, 1863, by the USS *Quaker City*, condemned, and later sold. Resumed blockade-running under its original name. Passed through New Inlet at 9:30 p.m. on October 11, 1863, and was chased by the USS *Nansemond* after crossing the bar. Ran aground at full speed above Fort Fisher and the wreck of the *Hebe*, in the surf zone, not far from the wreck of the *Venus*. Boarded by Union sailors who captured two officers, two crewmen, and one passenger. Burned with little of the cargo salvaged. Was raised in part by the Union and sold. Remains of the vessel are reported in 10 feet water. Listed in the National Register of Historic Places as part of an archaeological district. (*ORN*, 8:593; 9:232–33; *Federal Register*, December 4, 1990, 50142; Horner, *Blockade-Runners*, 214.)

E. H. Herbert. Union. Steam tug. Out of Baltimore. Part of the Burnside Expedition. Turned back from Hatteras

Inlet as a result of a disabled engine. Sank near New Inlet on February 7, 1862. The crew was rescued by the schooner *William H. Mailler,* with no loss of life. (*New York Times,* February 10, 1862.)

Elizabeth (Atlantic). Confederate. Wooden side-wheel steamer, 623–60 tons. Length 217 feet, beam 27 feet 6 inches, depth 10 feet 6 inches. Carried a military cargo. Built in 1852 at New York City. Grounded and burned on September 24, 1863, at the east edge of Lockwood's Folly Inlet, about 12 miles from Fort Caswell. A few engine parts are exposed under 15 feet of water. Listed in the National Register of Historic Places as part of an archaeological district. (*ORN,* 9:234; *Federal Register,* December 4, 1990, 50142; *MSV,* 15; *CWC,* 6-201; Stick, *Graveyard of the Atlantic,* 247; Bright, "Wrecked Blockade Runners of the Lower Cape Fear," *Historical Archaeology,* 129; *LLC,* 289.)

Ella. Confederate. Iron side-wheel steamer blockade-runner, 1,165 displacement tons, 634 gross tons, 404 registered tons. Length 225 feet, beam 28 feet, depth 13 feet. Cargo of twenty-three cases of rifle muskets, various munitions, and Holland gin. Built in 1864 at Dumbarton, Scotland. Chased ashore by the USS *Emma* and USS *Pequot* on December 3, 1864. Ran aground about one and a third miles offshore of Fort Holmes, opposite the Mound Battery in 2.25–3 fathoms on Marshall Shoal offshore 250 yards from a beach southeast of Cape Fear. Hit by at least forty shells from six Union vessels and Confederate shore batteries. The Confederates salvaged little cargo, except some gin. On December 5, 1864, a Union small boat expedition burned the *Ella.* Located in 9 feet of water with its boilers, machinery, and starboard paddlewheels intact. The midsection is upright, stern listing to port, and bow 90° to starboard. In the 1960s several 105-pound Whitworth shells were recovered as well as bottles, pins, nails, buttons, and other artifacts. Listed in the National Register of Historic Places as part of an archaeological district. (*ORN,* 11:126–27, 134; Horner, *Blockade-Runners,* 75–92, 214; *CWC,* 6-342; Shomette, *Civil War Shipwrecks,* 416; Bright, "Wrecked Blockade Runners of the Lower Cape Fear," *Historical Archaeology,* 129; *Federal Register,* December 4, 1990, 50142; *LLC,* 297.)

Ellen. Confederate. Schooner. Tried to run into the Bald Head Channel on June 26, 1862, but was run ashore by Union blockaders. The USS *Victoria* towed the *Ellen* off, but it sank. (*ORN,* 7:720.)

USS Ellis (CSS Ellis). Union. Iron side-wheel steamer, 100 tons. Draft 6 feet. Complement of twenty-eight, with one 80-pounder pivot gun and one 12-pounder rifled howitzer. Purchased by North Carolina in 1861 for the Confederacy. Captured from the Confederates at Elizabeth City on February 10, 1862. Ran aground about 500 yards from a bluff at the shallows and a narrow location called the "Rock" on November 24, 1862, some 40 miles west of Beaufort and about 5 miles up the New Inlet River during an attack on Jacksonville. The USS *Ellis* missed the channel while under the command of Lt. William Barker Cushing. One 12-pounder, small arms, ammunition and valuables were carried off by the crew on November 25, 1862, in a captured schooner. The crew blew up the USS *Ellis* and set it afire. The USS *Ellis* was also holed by a Confederate battery. The Confederates later salvaged some ammunition, small arms, and the other howitzer. (*OR,* 18:34; *ORN,* 8:230–33; ser. 2, 1:78, 252; *CWC,* 6-224; Ammen, "Navy in the Civil War," *Confederate Military History,* 194–95; *WCWN,* 122.)

Emily. Schooner. Cargo of salt. Ran aground near Fort Caswell on June 25, 1862, by the USS *Mount Vernon,* USS *Mystic,* and USS *Victoria.* Was set afire by a Union boat and later reboarded by its crew. The Union boats returned and the vessel's crew again fled to shore. Towed by Union vessels and burned to the water's edge in deep water. (*ORN,* 7:504–5.)

Emily of London (Emily). British. Screw steamer, 253 registered tons, 355 gross tons. Length 181 feet, beam 22 feet 5 inches, depth 12 feet 1 inch. Cargo from Bermuda of salt, gunpowder, and war materials. Built in 1863 at Renfrew, Scotland. Sank about 300 yards above the wreck of the *Dee* on February 9–10, 1864, north of Masonboro Inlet, a half-mile north of the wreck of *Fanny and Jenny* near Wrightsville Beach. The crew escaped and the vessel was boarded by Union sailors from the USS *Florida.* The USS *Florida* was hit by four Confederate shells, and one Union boarder was injured. The *Emily of London* was set afire and blew up. (*ORN*, 9:473–75; Daly, *Aboard the USS Florida*, 150–53; Porter, *Naval History*, 472; *LLC*, 298.)

Emma Tuttle. Schooner. Cargo of rosin. Burned by the USS *Mount Vernon* 7 miles southeast of Fort Fisher on November 20, 1862. (*ORN*, 8:226.)

CSS *Equator.* Confederate. Wooden side-wheel or screw steam tug, 64 tons. Armed with one gun. Built in 1854 at Philadelphia. Burned by Confederates in the Cape Fear River in January 1865 to prevent its capture. (*ORN*, ser. 2, 1:252; *CWC*, 6-225; *WCWN*, 239.)

***Etta* (*Retribution*) (*Uncle Ben*).** Confederate. Screw steamer, 155 tons. Armed with one gun. Built in 1856 at Buffalo, N.Y. Chartered in April 1861 by the Union government to reinforce Fort Sumter in Charleston Harbor, S.C. Violent storms forced the vessel to Wilmington, where the Confederates seized the vessel. The engines were removed for the CSS *North Carolina*. Became the privateer schooner *Retribution*. Renamed *Etta* and lost off Cape Hatteras in 1865. (*MSV*, 217; *CWC*, 6-318.)

CSS *Fanny* (*Fanny*). Confederate. Screw or side-wheel steam iron tug. Complement of forty-nine with a long 32-pounder and a 8-pounder. Flagship of the Confederate Elizabeth City Fleet. Originally a Union army steamer *Fanny* with quartermaster and commissary stores for the 20th Ind. Regiment, forty-seven soldiers, two officers, and one African American. The vessel and all aboard were captured on October 1, 1861, by the CSS *Curlew*, CSS *Raleigh*, and CSS *Junaluska* at Loggerhead Inlet, N.C. The CSS *Fanny* was run aground by the USS *Lockwood* near Fort Cobb and set afire on February 10, 1862. Twenty stands of arms were captured and the vessel's machinery was destroyed by the USS *Valley City*, which also salvaged the 32-pounder. (*ORN*, 6:277–78, 615–16, 622–23, 646; ser. 2, 1:252; *CWC*, 6-226; Ammen, "Navy in the Civil War," *Confederate Military History*, 184; *EAS*, 119.)

***Fanny and Jenny* (*General Banks*) (*Scotia*).** British. Iron side-wheel steamer, 497 or 727 bulk tons. Cargo of liquor, bacon, gunpowder, a jeweled sword worth $2,500 (1864 value) from British sympathizers for Gen. Robert E. Lee, and a rumored gold shipment. Built in 1847 at Blackwell, England. Out of Nassau, Bahamas. First ran the blockade as the *Scotia* but was captured by the USS *Restless* and sold as a prize. Returned to blockade-running as the *Fanny and Jenny*. Burned by a boarding party from the USS *Florida* on February 10, 1864, after grounding near Masonboro Inlet. The paymaster drowned while trying to land on the beach. The vessel was under Captain Coxetter, the former captain of the Confederate privateer *Jeff Davis*, who was branded a pirate by the Union government. Coxetter took Lee's sword in the boat and was reported to have said before the boat capsized, "I have got to go to hell anyhow and I might as well go now as any time." Coxetter survived. Twenty-five members of the crew were captured on the vessel. Union sailors were chased off the ship by a Confederate Whitworth battery on shore, which shelled the vessel. The Union boarding party removed a Confederate flag, spyglass, chronometer, sextant, and charts. The vessel was set afire and exploded several times. In the surf zone off Wrightsville Beach. Was visible at low tide until Hurricane Hazel in August 1955. The wreck is located perpendicular to shore, partly under the north end of a pier with one of the pier's pilings driven through the bow. (*ORN*, 9:473–76; Horner, *Blockade-Runners*, 221–22; Daly, *Aboard the USS Florida*, 152–53; *MSV*, 79; Shomette, *Civil War Shipwrecks*, 420–21; *LLC*, 299.)

Fanny Lewis. Nationality unknown. Brig, 273 tons. Wrecked in 1864 off Fort Fisher. (*ORN*, 8:484–85.)

Florie. Confederate. Iron side-wheel steamer, 349 gross tons, 215 registered tons. Length 222 feet 5 inches, beam 23 feet 6 inches, depth 9 feet 7 inches. Built in 1863 at Glasgow, Scotland. Was lost on September 10, 1864, on the Cape Fear River Bar after running onto a wreck. (*ORN*, 10:504, 601; *LLC*, 300.)

CSS *Forrest* (*Edwards*). Confederate. Steam tug. Armed with two guns. Burned on February 10, 1862, at the Elizabeth City wharves while under repair for damage suffered three days earlier at the Battle of Roanoke Island. (*ORN*, 6:622; ser. 2, 1:253; *CWC*, 6-229.)

***Frying Pan Shoals* light ship.** Confederate. Gun ports were cut in preparation to arm the vessel with eight guns.

Located in the Cape Fear River near Fort Caswell when destroyed by a gig and cutter with two officers and twenty men from the USS *Mount Vernon* on December 31, 1862. (*ORN*, 6:493; Soley, "Blockade and the Cruisers," *Confederate Military History*, 7:158–59.)

General Beauregard **(*Havelock*)**. Confederate. Iron screw steamer, 629 gross tons, 339 registered tons, 824 tons. Length 223 feet 2 inches, beam 26 feet 2 inches, depth 14 feet 3 inches. Complement of forty-seven. Cargo of cotton, turpentine, and possibly Confederate gold in a strongbox. Built in 1858 at Govan, Scotland. En route to England. Grounded near Battery Gatlin off Carolina Beach in the surf 2 miles north of Fort Fisher on December 11, 1863. A Confederate battery of Whitworth guns shelled and hit four Union gunboats that approached. Burned to prevent capture between Flag Pond Hill and Dick's Bay, about 3 miles above New Inlet. Now sanded over in 15 feet of water by a sand renourishment project with the paddle-wheel hubs above the surface at low tide. Made sixteen runs through the Union blockade. Listed in the National Register of Historic Places as part of an archaeological district. (*ORN*, 9:354–55; 10:504; *Federal Register*, December 4, 1990, 50142; Horner, *Blockade-Runners*, 161–72; Bright, "Wrecked Blockade Runners of the Lower Cape Fear," *Historical Archaeology*, 129; *LLC*, 304.)

General Lyon. Union army. Screw steamer, 1,026 tons. Built in 1864 at East Haddam, Conn. Was lost in a gale while under charter on March 25, 1865, off Cape Hatteras with the loss of four hundred lives. (*OR*, ser. 3, 5:228; *MSV*, 81, 263.)

General Whiting **(*Rafael*)**. Confederate. Steamer, 816 gross tons, 425 registered tons. Length 199 feet 6 inches, beam 30 feet, depth 19 feet 1 inch. Burned amidships and the machinery had been stripped when its hull was recovered in April 1865 near Wilmington. (*ORN*, 12:118; *LLC*, 302.)

Georges Creek. Union. Screw steamer, 448 tons. Built in 1853 at Philadelphia. Foundered on August 22, 1863, off Cape Hatteras. (*MSV*, 84, 264.)

Georgiana C. McCaw **(*Dundalk*)**. British. Side-wheel steamer, 373 registered tons, 700 tons. Maximum speed 12.5 knots. Cargo of 60 tons of weapons and ammunition.

Reportedly carried gold from Nassau, Bahamas, on board. Grounded on the morning of June 2, 1864, off Western Bar near Cape Fear. Shelled by the USS *Victoria* and burned by a boarding party. Forty-three passengers and crew, or twenty-nine crew and three passengers, were captured and four escaped. The Union boarding party took two chronometers, a barometer, a sextant, and a marine clock. The wreck was later boarded by Confederates. Located a quarter-mile west and directly under the fire of Fort Caswell with the Bay Light Batteries one mile west. Sank in 10 feet of water about 2 miles west of Cape Fear River Inlet. Now deeply buried by sand under 6 feet of water. (*ORN*, 10:114–15; Horner, *Blockade-Runners*, 222; Bright, "Wrecked Blockade Runners of the Lower Cape Fear," *Historical Archaeology*, 129; *LLC*, 302.)

G. O. Bigelow. British. Schooner, 90 tons. En route from Bermuda. Crew of fifteen. Cargo of 40 tons of salt. Captured without papers by the Union transport *Fulton* on December 9, 1863, at 8:45 a.m. A prize crew of five was put on the *G. O. Bigelow* and the vessel's crew was transferred to the *Fulton*. Towed and two more crewmen were put onboard. Found to be leaking water so it was cut loose on December 10, 1863, and the original crew put back on. Discovered aground without a cargo at the entrance to Bear Inlet by the USS *Mount Vernon* and USS *New Berne*. Was scuttled by Confederates and set afire on December 17, 1863. (*ORN*, 9:341–44, 780.)

Golden Liner. Blockade-runner. Was lost on April 12, 1863, in the Cape Fear River. (Stick, *Graveyard of the Atlantic*, 247.)

Governor Morehead. Confederate. Iron stern-wheel steamer. Draft 20 inches. Used as a tow boat and transport. Was destroyed with the *Colonel Hill* by Union forces under Brig. Gen. Edward E. Potter on July 20, 1863, at Tarboro. (*OR*, 27:2:964, 965, 973; 29:2:71; *ORN*, 9:164; *CWC*, 6-242.)

Grapeshot. Union army. Chartered transport. Length 96 feet. Armed with two Dahlgren rifled guns, two 12-pounder mountain howitzers. Cargo of hay and oats for the Burnside Expedition. Formerly a canal boat. Parted the hawser while under tow and ran ashore by a storm 14 miles above Cape Hatteras on January 13–16, 1862. (*ORN*, 6:472; *Charleston Mercury*, February 3, 1862.)

Hebe. British. Iron twin screw steamer. Length 165 feet, beam 23 feet, depth 13 feet 6 inches, draft 10 feet. Cargo of coffee, medicine, clothing, and quartermaster's supplies. Built in 1863 at London, England. Ran aground in the early morning of August 18, 1863, in seven feet of water by the USS *Niphon* and USS *Shokokon* on Federal Point along a narrow low beach about one and three-quarters miles from Camp Wyatt and 8 miles north of New Inlet in a northeastern gale. The captain and crew escaped in boats and most of the cargo was landed. Three Union boats capsized while trying to board the *Hebe* and fifteen Union sailors were captured, but four of them later escaped. A two-gun Whitworth battery shelled Union ships near the wreck. On August 20, 1863, six Union ships shelled the wreck of the *Hebe.* On August 23 the Confederate Whitworth battery was disabled and one Whitworth and one Armstrong gun were captured by a Union raiding party from the USS *James Adger* and USS *Minnesota* under cover of the USS *Niphon,* USS *Stockton,* and USS *Western World.* The *Hebe*'s boiler and machinery were destroyed by shelling. Now sanded up much of the time under 22 feet of water. The bow, boiler, and stern have been exposed at times by tides. Listed in the National Register of Historic Places as part of an archaeological district. (*OR,* 29:1:77–78; 53, Supp.:93; *ORN,* 9:165–68; *Federal Register,* December 4, 1990, 50143; Porter, *Naval History,* 427–28; Soley, "Blockade and the Cruisers," *Confederate Military History,* 162; Horner, *Blockade-Runners,* 211–12; Bright, "Wrecked Blockade Runners of the Lower Cape Fear," *Historical Archaeology,* 129; *LLC,* 304.)

Industry. British. Schooner, 200 tons. Cargo of salt. Ran ashore about five miles north of New Topsail Inlet on February 1, 1863, within 100 yards of a beach by the USS *Mount Vernon.* Set afire by the crew and scuttled by Union ships in three fathoms of water. (*ORN,* 8:499; *WCWN,* 93.)

USS *Iron Age.* Union. Wooden, brass sheathed screw steamer, 424 tons. Length 144 feet, beam 25 feet, draft 12 feet 6 inches. Complement of 107, with three 30-pounder Dahlgrens and six 8-inch Dahlgren smoothbores. Built in 1862 at Kennebunk, Maine. While trying to refloat the blockade-runner *Bendigo* the USS *Iron Age* grounded. Mistakenly set afire and blown up by its crew off Lock-wood's Folly Inlet on January 11, 1864, after the USS *Minnesota* and USS *Governor Buckingham* could not refloat the vessel after several guns were thrown overboard. The Confederates later salvaged at least one gun. Located on the eastern edge of Lockwood's Folly Channel. Only the vessel's bottom, 4-blade propellers, shaft, machinery, and the boiler are above sand in 12 feet of water. Studied by archaeologists for the U.S. Army Corps of Engineers in 1973. Listed in the National Register of Historic Places as part of an archaeological district. (*ORN,* 9:396–401, 437; ser. 2, 1:109; Bright, "Wrecked Blockade Runners of the Lower Cape Fear," *Historical Archaeology,* 129; *MSV,* 102; Bass, *Ships and Shipwrecks of the Americas,* 223–24; *Federal Register,* December 4, 1990, 50143; Porter, *Naval History,* 471; *WCWN,* 92.)

USS *Isaac N. Seymour* (*I. N. Seymour*) (*Magnolia*) (*Tulip*). Union. Wooden side-wheel steam gunboat, 133 or 140 tons. Length 100 feet, beam 19 feet, depth 7 feet 6 inches, loaded draft 6 feet 6 inches, average speed 5 knots. Armed with one 20-pounder Parrott and one 12-pounder Parrott. Built in 1860 at Keyport, N.J. Hit a submerged anchor left by the Union army vessel *Louisiana* off Hatteras and sank on February 20, 1863. Was later raised. Hit the riverbank of the Neuse River, about 3 miles above New Bern, and sank within an hour on August 24, 1863, in 7.5–9.5 feet of water. Salvaged, raised, and returned to active service. Sold on June 20, 1865. (*ORN,* 6:657; 7:671–72, 685; 8:82–83, 102; ser. 2, 1:106; *WCWN,* 97.)

J. J. Crittenden. Confederate. Schooner. Captured on April 10, 1862, off Newbegan Creek by the USS *Whitehead.* Probably scuttled full of sand as an obstruction in the Currituck, or "Breaches," lock of the Albemarle and Chesapeake Canal. (*ORN,* 7:736; *DANFS,* 5:440.)

Josephine. Confederate. Schooner. Was scuttled by Confederates on January 21, 1862, below Weir's Point off Roanoke Island. (*CWC,* 6-333.)

J. W. Pindar. Schooner. Cargo of salt. Forced ashore by the USS *Cambridge* the morning of November 17, 1862, about 12 miles northeast of Fort Fisher, just below Masonboro Inlet. A boatload of sailors was swamped, but reached the *J. W. Pindar* and set it afire. Twenty-five to thirty men of the 3rd N.C. Cavalry Regiment arrived and captured Master W. H. Maies, two officers, and ten men from the Union boarding party. (*ORN*, 8:214–15, 226.)

Kate (Lenora) (Lenore) (Lucy C. Chomea). Confederate. Schooner. Cargo of salt. Chased ashore in the surf zone by the USS *Mount Vernon* and USS *Fernandia* on April 2, 1862, near Lockwood's Folly Inlet. The crew set the ship afire and left. Union sailors boarded the vessel and extinguished the fire, but they were unable to refloat the *Kate*. Confederates on shore fired on the vessel, so the Union boarding party took off some salt and set the *Kate* afire. Was later shelled by the Union fleet. The *Kate* appears to have been refloated but hit a snag on the Cape Fear River Bar on November 18, 1862, and sank. The vessel's cargo was saved. (*ORN*, 7:196–97; *WCWN*, 140; *LLC*, 307.)

USS Lavender (Mayflower). Union. Wooden screw steam tug, 169 or 173 tons. Length 112 feet, beam 22 feet, depth 7 feet 6 inches. Complement of twenty-three, with two rifled 12-pounders and two 24-pounder howitzers. Built in 1864 at Philadelphia. Formerly the blockade-runner *Mayflower*, which was captured in January 1864 by the USS *Union* near Tampa Bay, Fla. While en route from the Delaware Capes to Charleston, S.C., the USS *Lavender* grounded on the Cape Lookout Shoals in a storm on June 12, 1864. Boats from the vessel were swamped, and four crewmen drowned while trying to reach shore. On June 15 five more crewmen died of exposure and exhaustion. The *John Farron* arrived and saved the remaining crew. Between nine and fourteen sailors died. (*ORN*, 10:200–201; *MSV*, 141.)

Linwood. Union. Bark. Draft 15 feet. Crew of thirteen. Cargo of coffee. Out of New York City. En route from Rio de Janeiro, Brazil for New York City. Wrecked on July 16, 1861, 6 miles north of Hatteras Inlet and 400 feet from a beach when the Confederates removed the lights and buoys along the coast. (*ORN*, 6:67, 78–79.)

Lizzie. British. Sloop, 41 tons. Cargo of blankets, sheet tin, arrowroot, soda ash, and caustic acid. Out of Nassau, Bahamas. Captured by the USS *Peterhoff* off Wilmington on August 1, 1862. Its crew was captured. The vessel was destroyed when it was rated unseaworthy. (*ORN*, 7:612.)

Louisa. Confederate. Schooner, 200 tons. Cargo of coffee. Out of Wilmington, N.C. Ran onto a reef by the USS *Penguin* and capsized on August 10, 1861, near the lighthouse, about 3 miles south of Fort Fisher. The surf quickly broke over the vessel. (*ORN*, 6:86.)

Louisiana. Union army. Chartered steamer. Length 300 feet. Built in 1852. Part of the Burnside Expedition. Grounded on Hatteras Inlet Bar on January 14, 1862, and later refloated. Grounded again on January 23, 1862, in a gale after the *New Brunswick* collided with the *Louisiana* and carried off its anchor. May have been refloated. (*Charleston Mercury*, February 3, 1862.)

USS Louisiana. Union. Three-masted iron side-wheel steamer, 295 bulk tons, 438 displacement tons. Length 143 feet 2 inches, beam 27 feet 3 inches, depth 8 feet 1 inch, draft 8 feet 6 inches. Built in 1860 at Wilmington, Del. Loaded with 180 tons of gunpowder, towed by the USS *Wilderness*, and floated within 400 yards of Fort Fisher. The 90-minute fuse failed, but a fire had been set in a stack of pinewood in an open cabin which finally caused 20 percent of the gunpowder aboard to blow up at 1:40 a.m. on December 24, 1864, with no damage to Fort Fisher. Col. William Lamb, commander of Fort Fisher, heard the explosion, but thought another blockade-runner had run aground. The vessel's remains are reported to be under 20 feet of water. Listed in the National Register of Historic Places as part of an archaeological district. (*ORN*, 11:207–45; ser. 2, 1:129; *Federal Register*, December 4, 1990, 50143; Chaitin, *Coastal War*, 159–61; Scharf, *History of the Confederate Navy*, 766; *MSV*, 131.)

Lydia and Martha. Confederate. Schooner. Was scuttled at the second barricade by Confederates on February 1, 1862, below Weir's Point, Roanoke Island. (*ORN*, 6:789; *CWC*, 6-333.)

Lydia Francis. Union. Brig. Cargo of sugar. En route from Cuba to New York City. Wrecked at Hatteras Cove on May 6, 1861. (*ORN*, 6:78.)

Lynnhaven. Confederate. Cargo of 4,500 bushels of corn. Captured along with a schooner by the USS *Delaware* near Elizabeth City on February 10, 1862. Was scuttled on

February 14, 1862, along with the schooner at the mouth of the Albemarle and Chesapeake Canal which connected the North River and Currituck Sound. (*ORN*, 1:130; *DANFS*, 5:440.)

Lynx. British. Iron side-wheel steamer, 372 gross tons, 233 registered tons. Length 220 feet, beam 24 feet, depth 11 feet 6 inches, maximum speed 10 knots. Cargo of 600 cotton bales and $50,000 in Confederate government gold and bonds. Built in 1864 at Liverpool, England. En route for Bermuda. Chased by the USS *Niphon*, USS *Governor Buckingham*, and USS *Howquah* when crossing New Inlet Bar on September 26, 1864. Eight 100-pound and 30-pound shells hit the paddlebox and other areas, slowing the *Lynx*. Ran aground near Half Moon Battery, 5 miles above Fort Fisher and set afire by the crew. The ship's purser saved the gold and bonds. Union vessels continued shelling the ship, wounding one and killing one. Some cotton from the vessel was recovered from the ocean. The wreck is often sanded in. (*ORN*, 10:478–79; 3:710; Horner, *Blockade-Runners*, 224; *CWC*, 6-264–65; Bright, "Wrecked Blockade Runners of the Lower Cape Fear," *Historical Archaeology*, 129; *LLC*, 310; Boyd, "Top 10 Wrecks of the East Coast," *Skin Diver*, 22–23.)

USS *Madgie*. Union. Wooden screw steamer, 218 or 220 tons. Length 122 feet 10 inches, beam 22 feet 7 inches, depth 8 feet 5 inches. Armed with one 30-pounder, one 20-pounder Parrott, two 24-pounder howitzers, and one 12-pounder smoothbore. Built in 1858 at Philadelphia. While being towed by the USS *Fahkee* from off station at Charleston, S.C, it took on water and sank on October 11–12, 1863, in 18 fathoms about 12 miles southeast of Frying Pan Shoals. (*ORN*, 15:34–35; ser. 2, 1:131; *MSV*, 133.)

Mars. Blockade-runner. Ran ashore on October 20, 1863. (Daly, *Aboard the USS* Florida, 104.)

Mary A. Schindler. Union. Schooner. In ballast. En route from Port Royal, S.C., to Philadelphia. Was captured and burned by the CSS *Clarence* under Lt. Charles W. Read off Cape Hatteras on June 12, 1863, after it answered their fake distress signal. (*ORN*, 2:273, 354, 656; Owsley, *C.S.S. Florida*, 81.)

Mary E. Pindar. Confederate. Schooner. Out of Edenton, N.C. Captured by the USS *Gemsbok* on September 22, 1862. Was lost at sea en route to Hampton Roads, Va., on February 12, 1863, near Federal Point. (*ORN*, 6:641.)

CSS *M. C. Etheridge*. Confederate. Schooner, 144 tons. Length 92 feet, beam 24 feet, draft 7 feet. Armed with two guns. Cargo of naval stores. Built in 1859 at Plymouth, N.C. Attacked by the USS *Whitehead* on February 10, 1862, in the Pasquotank River. Set afire by Confederates to prevent capture. Was scuttled by its Union captors when they could not extinguish the fire. The vessel's books and papers were removed. (*ORN*, 6:617–18; *CWC*, 6-265.)

Minquas (Minquass). Union. Side-wheel steamer, 160 tons. Built in 1864 at Wilmington, Del. The *Minquas* and two barges with quartermaster and commissary supplies were captured and burned on the Neuse River on April 7, 1865, by Company A, 67th N.C. Regiment. (*OR*, 47:1:1134; 47:3:160; *MSV*, 146, 282.)

Modern Greece. British. Iron screw steamer, 753 or 1,000 tons. Length 210 feet, beam 29 feet, depth 17 feet 2 inches. Cargo of brandy, rifled cannons, 4 brass smoothbore cannons, 7,000 Enfield rifle muskets, 1,000 tons of gunpowder, various military equipment, liquor, clothing, and a civilian cargo. Built in 1854 at Stock-on-Tees, England. Registered destination was Tampico, Mexico, but was heading into Wilmington. Was hit nine times by shells and chased ashore by the USS *Cambridge* and USS *Stars and Stripes* on June 27, 1864. Sank in 40 feet of water about 200 yards offshore, about a half-mile north of the Mound Battery on Federal Point near New Inlet. The passengers and their property were put safely ashore. The Confederates salvaged six rifled 12-pounder Whitworth cannons, five hundred stands of arms, powder, lead, surgeons kits, salt, boots, shoes, clothes, a couple of barrels of clothes, and the vessel's steam engine. The company that owned the vessel went bankrupt as a result of the wreck. The rifled Whitworths increased the range of the Confederate shore batteries from 2.5–4 miles, causing many Union vessels to anchor further offshore, thus saving many blockade-runners from Union capture. After the 1962 Good Friday storm, the formerly sanded-in wreck was exposed and rediscovered by eleven navy divers from the Naval Ordnance School at Indian Head, Md., while on a holiday dive. By 1963 more than 11,500 artifacts, including about 1,770 rifle muskets, shells, sheets of tinned steel, bayonets, bullet molds, along with tons of lead pigs, were recovered by U.S. Navy divers and the North Carolina Department of Archives and History for the Fort Fisher Historic Site Museum (Kure Beach, N.C.). Items salvaged from the *Modern Greece* are in the Cape Fear River Museum at Wilmington; North Carolina Museum of History; the Smithsonian Institution; Naval Historical Center; Mariner's Museum (Newport News, Va.). The large two-blade 12-foot diameter propeller and part of the hull are intact under 16 feet of water. Listed in the National Register of Historic Places as part of an archaeological district. (*OR,* 18:415; 51:2:584–85; *ORN,* 7:514–18; Bright, "Wrecked Blockade Runners of the Lower Cape Fear," *Historical Archaeology,* 129; *LLC,* 313; Horner, *Blockade-Runners,* 204; Bright, *Blockade Runner Modern Greece,*1–23; Bass, *Ships and Shipwrecks of the Americas,* 216–17.)

USS *Monitor.* Union. First monitor, 766 bulk tons, 987 displacement tons. Length 176 or 172 feet, beam 41 feet 6 inches, draft 11 feet 4 inches or 10 feet 6 inches, speed 9 knots. Complement of forty-nine, with two 11-inch Dahlgrens. Built in 1862 at Greenpoint, N.Y. Became famous in its battle with the CSS *Virginia* in Hampton Roads, Va., on March 9, 1862. Sank while under tow by the USS *Rhode Island* in a storm off Cape Hatteras at 1:00 a.m. on December 31, 1862, with four officers and twelve seamen drowned. Located about 18 miles southeast of the Hatteras Lighthouse, 15 miles from the Diamonds Lighthouse, in 220–30 feet of water. The wreck was depth charged during World War II as a suspected German sub. The turret was under the port stern of the upside down wreck. Discovered in 1973. On January 30, 1975, the wreck was made a National Marine Sanctuary under U.S. Department of Commerce jurisdiction under the Marine Protection Research and Sanctuaries Act of 1972. The wreck site is now called the Monitor National Sanctuary. Numerous scientific dives have been made on the wreck. In 1987 the vessel's 1,500-pound anchor was recovered. Artifacts recovered from the wreck are at the Mariner's Museum (Newport News, Va.), and the U.S. Naval Academy at Annapolis. Listed in the National Register of Historic Places and designated a National Historic Landmark. In 1991 a fishing boat anchor accidentally knocked off the skeg. The hull is deteriorating and falling in. Those involved in preserving the vessel are seriously considering raising all or part of it to save it from further deterioration. Salvage continues. In 1998 its 3-ton, 9-foot-long propeller and shaft were removed. The revolving turret and cannon inside were recovered in 2002. National Oceanic and Atmospheric Administration, the University of North Carolina at Wilmington, East Carolina University, the Mariner's Museum, and others have been involved in the recoveries. (*ORN,* 8:340–59; ser. 2, 1:148; Miller *Photographic History,* 6:159; Newton, "How We Found the *Monitor,*" *National Geographic Society,* 48–51; Boyd, "Raise the Monitor," *Skin Diver,* 18–21; Hoehling, *Thunder at Hampton Roads,* all of book; Bass, *Ships and Shipwrecks of the Americas,* 210–14; *Federal Register,* December 4, 1990, 50144; Boyd, "Diving Down to Dixie," *Gold!* 42–47; Hubinger, "Can We Ever Raise the *Monitor?*" *Civil War Times Illustrated,* 38–48; Marx, *Search for Sunken Treasure,* 168–71; *Monitor* National Marine Sanctuary Web site.)

Mystic. Union. Side-wheel steamer, 154 tons. Built in 1852 at New London, Conn. Was burned by the 67th N.C. Regiment on April 5, 1865, near Maple Cypress on the Neuse River. (*OR,* 47:1:1134; *MSV,* 151.)

CSS *Neuse.* Confederate. Twin screw steam sloop, 376 tons. Length 150 feet, 158 feet, 152 feet overall, 139 feet between foreside of stern to aftside of rudder post; beam 34 or 40 feet; draft 7–9 feet; bow ram 6 feet. Complement of 150, with two 6.4-inch or 8-inch guns. Built in 1863 at White Hall Landing, N.C. Received minor damage from a December 13, 1862, Union attack and was transferred to Kinston without armor plating. On March 10, 1865, it was again threatened by Union forces at Kinston. The Confederates blew up the ram and set the vessel afire, causing an 8-foot diameter hole in the port side, which sunk the vessel. Local people salvaged items from time to time from the wreck at Gunboat Bend. In 1961 local citizens began salvaging the vessel after raising funds. A cofferdam was built around the wreck, but it collapsed in 1962. In 1963 the lower hull was removed and put on the riverbank. In 1964 the recovered hull was moved by cutting it into three sections to meet road restrictions during highway transport. The gunboat hull was put on display in 1964 at the Governor Richard Caswell Memorial in Kinston. The State of North Carolina built a cover over the CSS *Neuse* in 1969 and the museum is now known as the CSS *Neuse* State Historic Site. (*OR*, 47:2:789, 1367; *ORN*, 12:67, 76; ser. 2, 1:261; Calhoun, "Question of Wood and Time," *Naval History*, 49; Martin, "North Carolina's Ironclad," *Naval History*, 45–50; *CWC*, 6-374–79: *CWN*, 205.)

CSS North Carolina. Confederate. Screw ironclad sloop, 600 tons. Length 150 feet between foreside of stern to aftside of rudder post and 172 feet 6 inches overall, beam 32 feet, depth 14 feet, draft 12 feet, armor 4-inch iron and 22-inch wood. Complement of 150–80, with two 6.4-inch Brooke guns and two smoothbores. Launched in 1863 at Wilmington, N.C. The engines were from the *Uncle Ben.* Sank when its worm-eaten hull gave way on September 27, 1864, off Smithville, 3 miles up the Cape Fear River from the old inlet. (*ORN*, 10:509; *CWC*, 6-277; *WCWN*, 205.)

North Heath. British. Iron side-wheel steamer, 541 gross tons, 343 registered tons. Length 229 feet 11 inches, beam 25 feet, depth 13 feet 5 inches. Built at London in 1864. Damaged upon entering Wilmington in October 1864. Was sunk to act as an obstruction on January 15, 1865, in the Cape Fear River near Fort Strong or Fort Lee. The upper works were removed by salvagers. In 17–20 feet of water. Was removed to within 7 feet of the surface by the U.S. Army Corps of Engineers in 1887. (*OR*, 42:3:1288; *ORN*, 11:785–86; *ORA*, pl. 68, no. 7; *Chief of Engineers Report 1887*, 1047; Stick, *Graveyard of the Atlantic*, 248; *LLC*, 314.)

Nutfield. British. Side-wheel steamer, 531 gross tons, 402 registered tons, 450 or 750 tons. Length 224.2 feet, beam 26.6 feet, depth 12.6 feet, speed 12–13 knots. Cargo of munitions, quinine, Enfield rifle muskets, eight Whitworth rifled guns, lead, and other goods. Built in 1863 at London. En route from Bermuda. Chased by the USS *Sassacus* at 7:00 a.m. on February 4, 1864. The crew threw lead, cannons, and other cargo overboard to lighten the vessel, but it ran onto a bar north of New River Inlet at 12:45 p.m.

on February 5, 1863. Abandoned with one boat capsized and all on the boat lost but the purser, who was saved by Union sailors. Union sailors boarded the vessel on February 5 and removed six hundred rifle muskets, swords, some quinine, and compasses before leaving. The USS *Sassacus* and USS *Florida* shelled the vessel, making it a total wreck. (*ORN*, 9:459–61; Porter, *Naval History*, 472; *LLC*, 314.)

Oriental. Union. Screw steel transport, 1,202 tons. Built in 1861 at Philadelphia. Was lost on May 8, 1862, at Bodie Island, north of Oregon Inlet. (*MSV*, 164, 287; Quinn, *Shipwrecks along the Atlantic Coast*, 2, 106.)

USS Otsego. Union. Side-wheel schooner, 974 tons. Length 205 feet, beam 35 feet, depth 11 feet 6 inches, loaded draft 9 feet, maximum speed 14 knots. Complement of 145, with two 100-pounder Parrotts, four 9-inch Dahlgrens, and two 24-pounders. Laid down in 1862 at New York City. The vessel's torpedo net had two torpedoes caught in it when a torpedo exploded on the port side under the wheel at 9:15 p.m. in the Roanoke River off Jamestown Bluff. Ten minutes later a second torpedo fired electrically from the bank was set off under the foremast. Sank in thirteen minutes in 2.5 fathoms with the top three feet underwater. The USS *Bazely* came to aid the USS *Otsego*, but the vessel also hit a torpedo and sank. Was blown up on December 9, 1864, to prevent Confederate salvage. A number of the guns were salvaged by Union forces. Was removed in 1873 by a contractor for the U.S. Army Corps of Engineers. (*ORN*, 11:162–65; ser. 2, 1:168; Scharf, *History of the Confederate Navy*, 766; Ammen, "Navy in the Civil War," *Confederate Military History*, 214; *Chief of Engineers Report 1873*, 76; *WCWN*, 63.)

Pathfinder. British. Schooner. Cargo of salt, boots, shoes, cutlery, olive oil, liquor, and other goods. Out of Nassau, Bahamas. Grounded 2 miles west of the Little River Inlet when chased by the USS *Penobscot*. The crew abandoned the vessel and set it afire on November 2, 1862, to prevent its capture. Two Union boats capsized, but the sailors boarded the ship, put out the fire, and later set the *Pathfinder* afire after they were unable to refloat the vessel. (*ORN*, 8:175, 190; *EAS*, 139.)

Pearl. Nationality unknown. Schooner. Cargo of turpentine, rosin, and shingles. En route from Wilmington to Nassau, Bahamas. Captured by the USS *Chocura* at latitude 33° 38' north, longitude 78° 19' west on November 19, 1862. Taken in tow but was leaking so it was set afire and abandoned on November 20. The USS *Mount Vernon* later found the vessel and took it in tow, but the *Pearl* capsized and sank. (*ORN,* 8:220–21.)

Peerless. Union. Transport steamer, 690 tons. Crew of 26. Cargo of stores and cattle for the Port Royal invasion. Sank on October 31, 1861, along the Hatteras coast. The USS *Mohican* rescued the crew. (*OR,* 6:186; *ORN,* 12:257–58, 260, 288; *New York Times,* November 13, 1861.)

Pelteway. Confederate. Steamer. Was scuttled by Confederates on January 17, 1865, at Smithville in the Cape Fear River. (*OR,* 46:2:1088.)

USS *Peterhoff* (*Peterhoff*). Union. Iron screw steamer, 800 bulk tons, 819 gross registered tons. Length 210 or 220 feet, beam 28 feet, draft 19 feet, depth 15 feet. Complement of 124, with six or seven guns. Launched in 1861 at Sunderland, England. Formerly the British blockade-runner *Peterhoff,* which was captured by the USS *Vanderbilt* on February 25, 1863, off St. Thomas, Virgin Islands. Was accidentally rammed by the USS *Monticello* on the starboard side in front of the engine room on March 9, 1864, while on patrol. Sank 3 miles south of Battle Acre in a northwest position in 35 feet of water within thirty minutes. Had a 30-pounder Parrott on the forecastle and a howitzer on the quarterdeck, which were spiked and thrown overboard. Union vessels cut away the masts. There was 10 feet of water above the spar deck, and only the smokestack was out of the water. Located just south of New Inlet and Sheep Head Rock, about a mile offshore, and about a mile and half off Corn Cake Inlet. Divers recovered two 32-pounders in 1963. Several more cannons were salvaged later. The bow is located 15 feet above the bottom, upright and part of the wreck is in 30 feet of water. The wreck is generally in good condition. Listed in the National Register of Historic Places as part of an archaeological district. (*ORN,* 9:535–38, 781; ser. 2, 1:176; *Federal Register,* December 4, 1990, 50144; Horner, *Blockade-Runners,* 173–80; Bright,

"Wrecked Blockade Runners of the Lower Cape Fear," *Historical Archaeology,* 129; *WCWN,* 80.)

Pevensey. British. Iron side-wheel steamer, 483, 500, or 543 tons. Crew of thirty-five. Cargo of arms, blankets, clothing, cloth, shoes, lead, bacon, etc. En route from Bermuda bound for Wilmington. The Union supply ship USS *New Berne* spotted the vessel and gave chase. Ran aground on Bogue Banks, about 7 miles west of Beaufort, 9 miles west of Fort Macon at the end of what became Iron Steamer Pier, 5 miles west of Atlantic Beach on June 9, 1864. Thirty-four crewmen were captured by Union troops from Fort Macon. The second officer on board was captured by a boat from the USS *New Berne.* The crew blew up the vessel and set it afire. The superstructure was above water for years. (*ORN,* 27:700; Shomette, *Civil War Shipwrecks,* 451–52; *LLC,* 316.)

Phantom. Confederate. Steel screw steamer, 322 gross tons, 266 registered tons, 500 tons. Length 190 feet or 192 feet 11 inches, beam 22 feet, draft 8 feet 6 inches, depth 13 feet 4 inches or 12 feet 4 inches, speed 18 knots. Crew of thirty-three. Cargo of arms, 9 cases of whiskey, 2 cases of gin, 200 pigs of lead, 3 cannons, 50 cases of Austrian rifle muskets, and other Confederate government stores. Built in 1863 at Liverpool, England. En route from Bermuda. Grounded 200–250 yards off New Topsail Inlet to prevent capture by the USS *Connecticut* on September 23, 1863, and set afire. A strongbox with $45,000 in gold supposedly fell over the ship's side. One Union sailor was killed by Confederate snipers while on shore destroying the vessel's lifeboats. Destroyed by the USS *Connecticut* in 32 feet of water after recovering 16 cases of rifle muskets and other goods. The Confederates also salvaged some of the goods, machinery, food, and whiskey. Shelled by the Union fleet and later broke in half. Located in 15 feet of water and has often been dived on. Listed in the National Register of Historic Places as part of an archaeological district. (*ORN,* 9:214, 222, 773–74; *Federal Register,* December 4, 1990, 50143; Horner, *Blockade-Runners,* 39–53; *CWC,* 6-282; *LLC,* 316.)

Picket (James E. Winslow) (Launch No. 5) (USS Picket) (Picket Boat No. 5). Union army. Screw steam gunboat.

Length 45 feet, beam 9 feet 6 inches. Armed with a 12-pounder. An iron barge converted to a gunboat. Hit by shells and blown up off Washington on September 6, 1862. Capt. Sylvester D. Nicoll and nineteen men were killed. The rest of the crew were taken aboard the USS *Louisiana*. The ordnance and machinery were removed and the vessel was burned by Union forces. In 1973 the wreck was discovered by local divers and the site was surveyed and sampled by the North Carolina Office of Archives and History, the Beaufort County (N.C.) Historical Society, and local divers. The iron hull is intact. (*ORN*, 8:6–7; Hill, *Confederate Military History*, vol. 4: *North Carolina*, 142; Bass, *Ships and Shipwrecks of the Americas*, 224.)

Pocahontas. Union. Army-chartered side-wheel steamer, 428 tons. Cargo of 113 horses with 80 crewmen and soldiers. Built in 1828 at Baltimore. En route for Roanoke Island. Beached by a storm 20 yards offshore and broken into three parts, forty-five minutes later. Floated ashore 20 miles north of Cape Hatteras on January 18, 1862. Ninety horses were lost. (*ORN*, 6:583; *Charleston Mercury*, February 3, 1862; *MSV*, 175, 290; Bass, *Ships and Shipwrecks of the Americas*, 224.)

Prony (Catinat). French navy. Side-wheel steam corvette. Armed with six 30-pounders. Ran onto a bar off Ocracoke Inlet one mile from the beach on November 5, 1861. The French were angry because they believed Union vessels did not try to assist them. The CSS *Winslow* grounded trying to come to the French crew's aid. (*ORN*, 6:397–405, 418, 742; *New York Times*, November 12, 1861.)

Quincy. Union. Screw steamer, 396 tons. Built in 1857 at Buffalo, N.Y. Foundered on December 20, 1863, at Cape Hatteras with sixteen killed. (*MSV*, 179, 291.)

Quinnebaug (Quinebaugh). Union army. Transport screw steamer, 186 tons. Loaded with Union troops going home. Built in 1844 at Norwich, Conn. Left Beaufort on July 20, 1865, at 7:30 a.m. and hit a reef about 8:45 a.m. off Shackleford Banks. Lost twenty-five men, with the rest rescued by the Union army tug *Goliath*, ship *Benjamin Adams*, and the USS *Corwin* of the Coast Survey. (*ORN*, 12:170–71; *MSV*, 179, 291.)

CSS *Raleigh*. Confederate. Ironclad sloop. Length 172 feet 6 inches overall or 150 feet, beam 32 feet, depth 14 feet, draft 12–14 feet. Complement of 180–88, with two 6.4-inch Brooke rifled guns and two 4.6-inch smoothbore rifles. Built 1863–64 at Wilmington, N.C. Grounded and the hull broke on the Wilmington Bar "Rip" after engaging Union blockaders off New Inlet on May 7, 1864. All its armor, guns, and engines were salvaged. Burned by Confederates with nothing showing above the water. Listed in the National Register of Historic Places. (*ORN*, 10:24–25; *Federal Register*, December 4, 1990, 50143; *CWC*, 6-290; Porter, *Naval History*, 479; Daly, *Aboard the USS* Florida, 68.)

Ranger. British. Iron side-wheel steamer, 500 tons. Cargo of ammunition and arms, including Austrian rifle muskets. Due to bad weather and the Frying Pans Light being out, the vessel put passengers and baggage ashore at Murrell's Inlet at midnight, and then headed for the bar at Fort Caswell. Forced ashore on January 11, 1864, by the USS *Daylight* and USS *Aries*, supported by the USS *Minnesota* and USS *Governor Buckingham*, a mile west of Lockwood's Folly Inlet in 20 feet of water about 200 feet off Holden Beach. Confederate fire kept Union sailors off the ship and killed one sailor as Union sailors attempted to put out fires and haul the vessel off. Union ships shelled the *Ranger* repeatedly. Some rifle muskets were later salvaged by Confederates. The boilers are visible at low tide in 20 feet of water. Much of the vessel's plates have fallen in, but most of the machinery is intact. Some rifle muskets have been recovered by divers. Listed in the National Register of Historic Places as part of an archaeological district. (*ORN*, 9:402; *Federal Register*, December 4, 1990, 50143; Horner, *Blockade-Runners*, 218; *LLC*, 317; Bright, "Wrecked Blockade Runners of the Lower Cape Fear," *Historical Archaeology*, 129.)

R. B. Forbes. Union. Screw steam tug, 329 bulk tons. Length 121 feet, beam 25 feet 6 inches, draft 12 feet 3 inches, speed 11 knots. Complement of fifty-one, with two 32-pounder guns and one rifled 30-pounder. Built in 1845 at Boston. Wrecked in a storm near Nag's Head on February 25, 1862, on the Currituck Banks about 4 miles south of Currituck Inlet, 10–16 miles south of Cape Charles. Its propellers were embedded and broken. Burned and destroyed by its crew to prevent Confederate capture. The USS *Young America* recovered small arms, chronometers, and spy glasses. (*ORN,* 6:156–57, 664–65, 673; 18:93; *MSV,* 179; *WCWN,* 105–6.)

Rio. Confederate. Schooner. Was scuttled off Weir's Point, Roanoke Island, on January 28, 1862. (*ORN,* 6:788; *CWC,* 6-333.)

***Royal Shoal* light ship.** Nationality unknown. Sank in the Neuse River and raised by the wrecking steamer *Dirigo* in 1862. (*ORN,* 8:117–18.)

Scuppernong. Confederate. Steamer. Cargo of oak timbers for building a steamer. Destroyed by a fire set by Union sailors in boats from the USS *Commodore Perry* below a bridge at Indian Town on June 9, 1862. (*ORN,* 7:487, 701.)

Sea Bird. Union. Schooner. Cargo of more than 50 tons of navy coal. Captured and burned in the Neuse River on May 22, 1863, by Confederate guerrillas from Whitford's band. The Union army steamer *Allison* found the *Sea Bird* afire and also helped destroy the vessel. (*ORN,* 9:38–39.)

CSS *Sea Bird.* Confederate. Side-wheel steam gunboat, 202 tons. Complement of forty-two, with one 32-pounder smoothbore and one 30-pounder. Built in 1854 at Keyport, N.J. Flagship of Confederate Flag Officer William F. Lynch at Elizabeth City. Was rammed by the USS *Commodore Perry* at Elizabeth City on February 10, 1862, and sank, with the loss of two killed and four wounded. The crew was captured. The USS *Valley City* destroyed the vessel's machinery. (*ORN,* 6:596, 607, 622, 646; *CWC,* 6-299–300.)

***Sereta* (*Laura*) (*Soleta*).** Nationality unknown. Schooner, 30 tons. Cargo of salt and fruit. Grounded and abandoned by the crew. Burned by boats from the USS *Penobscot* and USS *State of Georgia* on June 8, 1862, in Shallotte Inlet. (*ORN,* 7:467; Pleasants, *Vessels Destroyed or Captured,* 4.)

USS *Shokokon* (*Clifton*) (*Lone Star*). Union. Side-wheel steamer, 700 or 709 tons. Length 181 feet 7 inches, beam 32 feet, draft 8 feet 6 inches, depth 13 feet, average speed 6 knots. Complement of 120, with two 9-inch smoothbores, two 30-pounder Parrotts, and four smoothbore

24-pounders. Built in 1862 at Greenpoint, N.Y. Wrecked 6 miles up New Top Sail Inlet near the shore and a wharf. Was raised and later sold at auction in New York on October 25, 1865. Renamed *Lone Star* as a merchant ship. (*ORN,* ser. 2, 1:208; *MSV,* 139; *WCWN,* 101.)

Sophia. British. Bark, 375 tons. Cargo of three brass rifled fieldpieces, salt, soda ash, saltpeter, small arms, and ammunition. Ran ashore on November 4, 1862, by the USS *Mount Vernon* about 3.5 miles west of Masonboro Inlet. Burned to the water's edge by Union boarding parties. Five members of the *Sophia*'s crew were captured. Three Union officers and eighteen Union sailors in three boats were washed ashore and captured by Confederates. The wreck is now scattered over a wide area of the sea floor. Among the scattered fragments are field carriages and parts. (*ORN,* 8:193–99, 226; Horner, *Blockade-Runners,* 206.)

Southern Star. Confederate. Schooner. In ballast. Was scuttled by Confederates on January 31, 1862, off Weir's Point, Roanoke Island. (*ORN,* 6:788; *CWC,* 6-333.)

USS *Southfield.* Union. Double-ender side-wheel steam ferryboat, 750 or 751 tons. Length 200 feet, beam 34 feet, depth 11 feet 8 inches, draft 6 feet 6 inches, speed 12 knots. Complement of sixty-one, with one 100-pounder Parrott, five Dahlgren smoothbores, and a 12-pounder howitzer. Was rammed by the CSS *Albemarle* on April 19, 1864, in the Roanoke River off Plymouth in 22 feet of water northeast of the Coneby Redoubt. Sank up to the hurricane deck in three minutes. Seven officers and forty-two crewmen were rescued; the rest drowned. The Confederates raised two 11-inch Dahlgrens and one 100-pounder Parrott for the defense of Plymouth. The Confederates tried but failed to raise the vessel. Was removed by a U.S. Army Corps of Engineers contractor in 1873. (*OR,* 33:298, 938; *ORN,* 9:638–46; 10:640–41; ser. 2, 1:212; *Chief of Engineers Report 1873,* 76; *MSV,* 201; *WCWN,* 102.)

Spray. Union. Schooner. Manned by a captain and 5 crewmen. Cargo of army coal. Out of Egg Harbor, N.J. En route from Fort Monroe, Va., for Beaufort, S.C. Ran aground on February 27, 1865, on shoals about 10–11 miles south southeast of Cape Lookout. The crew was rescued by the USS *Rhode Island* on March 2, 1865. (*ORN,* 12:61; 27:711.)

Spuell and Moss. Confederate. Schooner. Was scuttled on January 26, 1862, at the "barricade" off Weir's Point, Roanoke Island. (*ORN*, 6:788.)

Spunkie. British. Iron side-wheel steamer, 166 gross tons, 81 registered tons. Length 191 feet 4 inches, beam 18 feet 2 inches, draft 7 feet 7 inches. Cargo of blankets, shoes, and provisions. Built in 1857 in Glasgow (Patrick), Scotland. Ran ashore just west of Fort Caswell on February 9, 1864. Found by the USS *Quaker City* and two Union tugs, which tried to refloat the *Spunkie,* but it broke in half due to heavy surf. (*ORN*, 9:473; 10:504; *LLC*, 321.)

Stormy Petrel. British. Iron side-wheel steamer, 220 registered tons. Length 225 feet, beam 25 feet, draft 11 feet 6 inches. Cargo of arms, ammunition, and other items. Built in 1864 at Renfrew, Scotland. Driven ashore by the USS *Kansas* on December 7, 1864, off New Inlet and Smith Island, a mile below Fort Fisher on the South Breakers. Ripped open by the fluke of a submerged anchor of a blockaderunner behind Fort Fisher. A gale broke the vessel up a few days later. Little salvaged except for two boatloads of clothes. Located under 20 feet of water. Listed in the National Register of Historic Places as part of an archaeological district. (*ORN*, 11:195, 745; *Federal Register,* December 4, 1990, 50143; Horner, *Blockade-Runners,* 227; *LLC*, 322.)

USS *Sumter* (USS *Sumpter*) (*Atlanta*) (*Parker Vein*). Union. Wooden screw steamer, 460 bulk tons. Length 163 feet, beam 24 feet 4 inches, draft 11 feet 9 inches. Complement of 64–90, with one 12-pounder Parrott and four 32-pounders. Launched in 1853 at Philadelphia. Carried an iron pay chest with $2,070 when it collided with the Union army transport steamer *General Meigs* on June 24, 1863, at 12:45 a.m. Sank in twenty minutes with the forward section shattered. The *General Meigs* left the scene. The bow was underwater within five minutes. The schooner *Jamestown* rescued the ship's officers and crew. All the crew's effects and the pay chest were lost. Sank 8.5 miles south-southwest of the Smith Island Lighthouse in 7 fathoms of water with the masthead out of water. (*ORN*, 9:88–91; ser. 2, 1:216.)

Thorn. Union army. Screw transport steamer, 403 tons. Built in 1862 at Mystic, Conn. Blown up by a Confederate torpedo and sank in two minutes with no loss of life in the Cape Fear River on March 4, 1865, just below Fort Anderson. Was probably removed January 3–June 27, 1893, by the suction dredge *Woodbury* at the entrance of the Cape Fear River to 13.5 feet. (*OR*, 47:3:729; *Chief of Engineers Report 1893*, 183; *MSV*, 212, 301.)

Tripleet. Confederate. Schooner. Was scuttled at the "barricade" off Weir's Point, Roanoke Island, on January 29, 1862. (*ORN*, 6:788.)

Twilight. U.S. Screw steamer, 644 tons. Built in 1865 at Mystic, Conn. Stranded on November 14, 1865, in the Cape Fear River. (*MSV*, 216, 302.)

USS *Underwriter*. Union. Side-wheel steam gunboat, 341 bulk tons, 325 tons. Length 185 or 170 feet, beam 23 feet 7 inches, depth 8 feet 1 inch. Complement of 12 officers and 40 sailors to 69 crewmen, with two 8-inch guns, one rifled 30-pounder, and one 12-pounder rifle. Built in 1862 at Brooklyn, N.Y. Anchored off a battery near Foster's Wharf on the Neuse River downstream from Fort Stevens near New Bern on the night of February 2, 1864. Captured after a 15-minute fight by 250 Confederates in two launches and twelve boats led by Cdr. John Taylor Wood. Among the crew Acting Master Jacob Westerveht and 8 Union crewmen were killed, 20 were wounded, and 26 were captured. The officers and crew were taken off in boats. The vessel was stripped, set afire, and blown up while under fire from Union-held Fort Anderson. Six Confederates were captured and several wounded when the USS *Underwriter* was set afire. Six weeks later the hull and the rest of the vessel were judged unsalvageable. (*OR*, 33:50, 56, 58, 94, 511–12, 573, 1145; *ORN*, 9:439–45, 449; ser. 2, 1:228; Porter, *Naval History,* 471–72; *WCWN*, 87; Boyd, "Wreck Facts," *Skin Diver,* 32; Shingleton, *John Taylor Wood,* 110–15.)

Union. Union. Side-wheel transport steamer, 149 tons. Crew of seventy-three. Cargo of rifle muskets, horses, gun carriages, and musket powder for the Port Royal invasion. Built in 1861 at Augusta, Maine. Ran onto a beach and broke in two on the night of November 1–2, 1861, in a storm 8 miles east of Bogue Inlet and 16 miles from Fort Macon. The crew and 15 horses were captured by Confederates along with some supplies. (*OR*, 6:186, 310; 51:2:369; *ORN*, 6:416; *MSV*, 218.)

Union. Union. Stern-wheel transport steamer, 139 tons. Cargo of rifle muskets and gunpowder. Built in 1857 at Louisville. En route from Hilton Head to Beaufort, S.C., for Port Royal. While in a sinking condition with the stern-wheel breaking up, the crew was rescued by the USS *Maratanza*. The *Union* was set afire. Two 11-inch shells were fired into the vessel from the USS *Maratanza* and USS *Sacramento* at 3:00 p.m. on April 2, 1863. Sank a half-mile off New Inlet. (*ORN*, 8:703–4.)

Venus. British. Iron side-wheel steamer, 365 tons. Length 265 feet or 159 feet 2 inches, beam 17 feet 1 inch, draft 8 feet 8 inches. Crew of thirty-three. Cargo of 600 cases of rifle muskets, three hundred boxes of cartridges, lead, dry goods, bacon, coffee, one hundred gallons of rum, and various medicines as well as a model of a railroad. Built in 1862 at Govan, Scotland. En route from Nassau. Was shelled and burned by the USS *Niphon*, USS *Nansemond*, and USS *Iron Age* on October 21, 1863, about one to one and a half miles north of Gatlin's Battery, between Flag Pond Hill and Dick's Bay, near the wrecks of the *Hebe*, *Douro*, and *Lynx*. Was hit four times by shells, lost a plate, and was taking on water when grounded while making 14 knots. One crewman was killed by a shell. Union sailors boarded the *Venus*, but could not refloat the vessel so they blew up the boilers and set it afire. Some gold and other articles were taken off by Union sailors. The captain and twenty-two crewmen were captured. The wreck is usually sanded in. (*ORN*, 9:248–50; Soley, "Blockade and the Cruisers," *Confederate Military History*, 162; Horner, *Blockade-Runners*, 215–16; Bright, "Wrecked Blockade Runners of the Lower Cape Fear," *Historical Archaeology*, 129; *LLC*, 325.)

Vesta (Vestra). British. Double propeller steamer, 262 registered tons, 500 tons. Length 165 feet, beam 23 feet, depth 13 feet. Cargo of 1,000 pairs of shoes, 21 bales of blankets, 96 bales of cloth, clothes, a new uniform for Gen. Robert E. Lee, paper, and stationery. Built in 1863 at London, England. Ran aground on January 11, 1864, west of the wreck of the *Ranger*, about four miles below and westward of Tubb's Inlet and Little River Inlet. Was four feet out of the water when burned. The wreck was found by the USS *Aries*. The

Vesta's captain and pilot were reported by a correspondent from the *Richmond Dispatch* to be falling down drunk when the vessel wrecked. Two anchors have been salvaged from the hulk. Vesta Pier at Sunset Beach was built over the *Vesta*'s boiler. (*ORN*, 9:402; Horner, *Blockade-Runners*, 217–218; Spence, *List*, 651; Porter, *Naval History*, 471; *LLC*, 325.)

USS Violet (Lilac) (Martha). Union. Wooden steam screw tug, 146 bulk tons, 166 tons. Length 85 feet, beam 19 feet 9 inches, depth 11 feet. Complement of twenty, with one 24-pounder and two rifled 12-pounders. Built in 1862 at Brooklyn, N.Y. Ran aground in six to nine feet of water on the Western Bar, Cape Fear River on August 7, 1864. The USS *Vicksburg* was unable to get the USS *Violet* refloated. One rifled 12-pounder was spiked in the forecastle, one rifled gun was thrown overboard, and the 24-pounder was put over the magazine on August 8, 1864. At 2:30 a.m. the magazine with 200 pounds of gunpowder blew up. Was probably removed to 22 feet below mean sea level by the U.S. Army Corps of Engineers in 1893. (*ORN*, 10:343–44; ser. 2, 1:233; *Chief of Engineers Report 1893*, 183; *WCWN*, 121–22.)

Volant. Nationality unknown. Brig. Was lost in September 1862 at New Inlet. (Stick, *Graveyard of the Atlantic*, 247.)

Wild Dayrell. Spanish. Iron side-wheel steamer, 320 gross tons, 440 tons. Length 215 feet, beam 20 feet, depth 10 feet 11 inches. Cargo of blankets, provisions, and supplies worth $200,000. Built in 1863 at Liverpool, England. En route from Nassau, Bahamas. Ran aground on February 2, 1864, near New Topsail Inlet and Stump Inlet. Almost half of the cargo was unloaded before it was burned on February 3, 1864, by the USS *Sassacus* and USS *Florida* when Union sailors were unable to refloat the *Wild Dayrell* off the bar. The Union boarding party and vessels were shelled by Confederate batteries. Now sanded in under 10 feet of water at Rich Inlet near Figure 8 Island. Also known as the "Rich Inlet Wreck." Listed in the National Register of Historic Places as part of an archaeological district. (*ORN*, 9:437–38; Horner, *Blockade-Runners*, 219; Bright, "Wrecked Blockade Runners of the Lower Cape Fear," *Historical*

Archaeology, 129; Daly, *Aboard the USS* Florida, 140–46; *Federal Register*, December 4, 1990, 50143; *LLC*, 326.)

CSS *Wilmington*. Confederate. Ironclad steam gunboat. Length 224 feet, beam 42 feet 6 inches, depth 12 feet, draft 9 feet 6 inches, 2 engines, 4 boilers. Armed with two guns. Built 1863–64 at Wilmington, N.C. Destroyed upon the evacuation of Wilmington in February 1865. (*CWC*, 6-325; *WCWN*, 209.)

CSS *Winslow* (*Joseph E. Coffee*) (*Warren Winslow*). Confederate. Side-wheel steamer, 207 tons. Armed with one 32-pounder and one rifled 6-pounder brass gun. Built in 1846 at New York City. On November 7, 1861, the CSS *Winslow* hit a sunken hulk while on the way to aid the grounded French corvette *Prony* at the entrance to Ocracoke Inlet at latitude 38° 28' north, longitude 74° 68' 42" west. The CSS *Winslow* was set afire by the crew to avoid capture. (*ORN*, ser. 2, 1:272; *CWC*, 6-325; *EAS*, 128.)

CSS *Yadkin*. Confederate. Wooden screw steam gunboat, 300 tons. Armed with one or two guns. Built in 1863–64 at Wilmington, N.C. Was scuttled by the Confederates to act as an obstruction in the Cape Fear River off the CSS *Arctic* near Fort Campbell in February 1865. (*ORN*, 11:754; ser. 2, 1:272; *CWC*, 6-326.)

York. Nationality unknown. Blockade-runner, 800 tons. Cargo of wrought iron. Out of Dublin, Ireland. Ran ashore on January 16, 1862, by the USS *Albatross* east of Bogue Inlet. Set afire by six boats from the USS *Albatross* while the USS *Albatross* and USS *Gemsbok* provided covering shellfire. (*OR*, 9:422; *ORN*, 6:520; *ORA*, pl. 68, no. 7.)

York (*Florida*). Confederate. Privateer schooner, 68 tons, 72 tons. Complement of thirty, with one rifled 8-pounder and one 6-pounder gun. Out of Norfolk, Va. Ran ashore on August 9, 1861, by the USS *Union*. Burned to the water's edge by the crew on Cape Hatteras near the lighthouse near New Inlet. The vessel's guns were thrown overboard. (*ORN*, 1:60–61, 818–19; ser. 2, 1:272.)

Zenith. Confederate. Vessel. Was scuttled on January 27, 1862, by Confederates off Weir's Point, Roanoke Island. (*ORN*, 6:788.)

USS *Zouave* (*Marshall Nye*). Union. Screw steam gunboat, 127 or 203 tons. Length 95 feet, beam 20 feet 10 inches, draft 9 feet, maximum speed 14 knots, average speed 10 knots. Armed with two 30-pounder Parrotts (one 30-pounder and two 12-pounder rifles). Built in 1854 at Hoboken, N.J. Probably converted to a gunboat in 1861 at Albany, N.Y. Driven into shallow water onto its own anchor and sank after crossing a bar in Hatteras Inlet on January 14, 1862. The cargo was saved. Was raised and continued in Union service. Was sold at public auction on July 12, 1865. (*ORN*, 6:472, 582; ser. 2, 1:246; *Charleston Mercury*, February 3, 1862; *MSV*, 137, 279; *WCWN*, 122.)

▷ **VESSELS WITHOUT NAMES**

barge. Confederate. One of two barges grounded by Confederates on Croatan Sound on Roanoke Island, filled with mud, and made into a fort with seven guns. The makeshift fort was destroyed by the USS *Southfield* in February 1862. (*ORN*, 6:571.)

barge. Union. Part of the Burnside Expedition. Sank on the outer Hatteras Bar in a gale in early January 1862. (*Charleston Mercury*, February 3, 1862.)

barges. Nationalities unknown. The *Minquas* and two barges with quartermaster and commissary supplies were captured and burned on April 7, 1865, by Company A, 67th N.C. Regiment on the Neuse River. (*OR*, 47:1:1134, 47:3:160; *MSV*, 146, 282.)

brig. British. Chased ashore by the USS *Daylight* near Fort Fisher on the foggy morning of November 17, 1862. The USS *Daylight*'s second cutter and dingy could not get near the brig because of bad weather and shelling from Fort Fisher and Confederate shore batteries. (*ORN*, 8:216–17, 226.)

brig. Confederate. Length 100 feet. Was sunk as an obstruction 3 miles below New Bern on the Neuse River early in 1862 as part of the Fort Point blockade. (*Chief of Engineers Report 1879*, 93, 704, 706.)

brig. Confederate. Was sunk to act as obstructions in a 12-foot-deep channel in the Neuse River, about 3 miles above New Bern. (*ORN*, 11:618.)

cutter from USS *Shawmut*. Union. Was blown up by a torpedo in the Cape Fear River on February 20, 1865, when the Confederates sent 200 floating torpedoes downstream from Wilmington. Two members of the cutter's crew were killed, and two were wounded. (*ORN*, 12:44; Scharf, *History of the Confederate Navy*, 767; Perry, *Infernal Machines*, 200.)

floating battery. Confederate. Length 20 feet, beam 20 feet, height 8 feet, armor 1.5-foot iron, with 6-inch-thick oak on two sides. Armed with a total of six guns on three sides. Anchored 8 miles above Plymouth on the Roanoke River in 2.5–3 fathoms with 2–3 feet of casemate above water. Was sunk by a drifting Confederate torpedo and burned on April 8, 1865, by a launch from the USS *Iosco* and a cutter from the USS *Mattabesett*. Located at Gray's Fisher. Was removed in 1873 under a contract with the U.S. Army Corps of Engineers. (*ORN*, 12:107–8, 116; *Chief of Engineers Report 1873*, 76.)

gunboat. Confederate. Under construction and unfinished. Burned on the stocks at Elizabeth City on February 10, 1862, by Union forces. (*ORN*, 6:608, 620–21.)

ironclad. Confederate. Length 139 feet, beam 34 feet, draft 15 feet. To mount four guns. Under construction and unfinished. Was destroyed by Confederates on the stocks at Edwards Ferry on April 7, 1865. (*ORN*, 11:755; 12:116; *WCWN*, 205; Elliott, *Ironclad of the Roanoke*, 270.)

ironclad. Confederate. Similar in design to the CSS *Virginia II*. Laid down at Tarboro and was known as the "Tar River Ironclad." Under construction and unfinished. The vessel's frame was destroyed by the 3rd N.Y. Cavalry Regiment in Maj. Gen. John G. Foster's expedition on July 20, 1863. (*OR*, 27:2:964–65; *ORN*, 9:164–65; 12:288, 291–93, 828; Still, *Iron Afloat*, 156; *WCWN*, 209.)

lighters. Confederate. Two lighters were sunk by Confederates on February 14, 1862, abreast of Fort Caswell, 100 yards from shore, to block the channel. (*ORN*, 6:646.)

schooner. Confederate. Was burned at the Elizabeth City wharves on February 10, 1862, after the town's capture by the victorious Union fleet. (*ORN*, 6:608, 618, 620–21; Ammen, "Navy in the Civil War," *Confederate Military History*, 185.)

schooner. Confederate. Was burned in Topsail Inlet on August 22, 1863, by Union sailors. (*OR*, 29:2:671.)

schooner. Confederate. Was captured along with the *Lynnhaven* by the USS *Delaware* near Elizabeth City on February 10, 1862. Was scuttled on February 14, 1862, along with the *Lynnhaven* at the mouth of the Albemarle and Chesapeake Canal, which connected the North River and Currituck Sound. (*ORN*, 1:130; *DANFS*, 5:440.)

schooner. Confederate. Was sunk to act as obstructions in a 12-foot deep channel in the Neuse River, about 3 miles above New Bern. (*ORN*, 11:618.)

schooner. Nationality unknown. Found wrecked on July 6, 1862, by the USS *Monticello* after its cargo was removed at Deep River Inlet. (*ORN*, 7:720.)

schooner. Nationality unknown. Cargo of cotton and turpentine. Was burned by Confederates on November 23, 1862, about 5 miles from the New Inlet River mouth when the USS *Ellis* approached. (*OR*, 8:231.)

schooner. Nationality unknown. Cargo of salt. Ran ashore on September 26, 1862, near a bluff with a Confederate battery and camp near New Inlet and Fort Fisher. The USS *Mystic* shelled the wreck. (*ORN*, 8:92–96.)

schooner. Nationality unknown. Cargo of salt and leather. Out of Bermuda. Burned on March 25, 1864, at Morehead City near Bear Inlet by Union forces under Col. James Jourdan, including the USS *Britannia* and two hundred men of the 158th N.Y. Infantry Regiment. (*OR*, 33:257–58.)

schooner. Nationality unknown. Heavily loaded with supplies. Ran ashore by the USS *Daylight* on January 21, 1863, a little west of Stump Inlet. Hit 20–25 times by Union shellfire. (*ORN*, 8:468.)

schooner. Nationality unknown. Ran ashore and destroyed by the USS *Mount Vernon* and USS *Daylight* off New Inlet on November 5, 1862, near the wreck of the *Sophia*. (*ORN*, 8:199.)

schooner. Union. Cargo of coal. Part of the Burnside Expedition. Was grounded on Hatteras Bar in a gale in early 1862. (*Charleston Mercury*, February 3, 1862.)

schooners. Confederate. Three schooners were scuttled to block the Roanoke River upon the destruction of the CSS *Albemarle* by Lt. William Barker Cushing in October 1864. (*ORN*, 10:612.)

schooners. Confederate. Two schooners were captured and burned by the Union army transport *Ella May* and sailors from the USS *Louisiana* and USS *Ceres* on June 16, 1864, near the mouth of the Pamlico River. (*ORN*, 10:154.)

schooners. Nationalities unknown. Seven schooners sunk in the Roanoke River during the Civil War. Were removed by the U.S. Army Corps of Engineers in 1873. (*Chief of Engineers Report 1873*, 76.)

schooners. Union. Filled with stone. Were sunk to block the inlet at Ocracoke Island on November 14, 1861. (*ORN*, 6:428.)

schooners. Union. Two schooners loaded with stone to be sunk to block North Carolina inlets. Were sunk by a storm on October 1, 1861, en route to Hatteras Inlet. (*ORN*, 6:279–80.)

steamer. Confederate. Burned by Confederates at New Berne prior to Union capture of the town on March 14, 1862. (*ORN*, 7:109, 111.)

store ship or light boat. Confederate. Was burned on September 16, 1861, by the USS *Fanny* and a party of Union sailors when the vessel grounded off an abandoned Confederate fort on Beacon Island at Ocracoke Inlet, one mile from Portsmouth. (*ORN*, 6:225.)

torpedo boats. Confederate. Two torpedo boats built at Wilmington, N.C., were destroyed in the great cotton fire at Wilmington in April 1864. One was cigar shaped. (Scharf, *History of the Confederate Navy*, 417.)

transport. Union. Cargo of commissary stores. Burned by Company A, 67th N.C. Regiment, on April 5, 1865, near Cowpen Landing on the Neuse River. (*OR*, 47:1:1134.)

vessel. Confederate. Possibly a floating battery. Launched at Edwards Ferry, N.C., on the Roanoke River. Under construction and unfinished. Set afire and adrift at Hamilton in March or April 1865 and was sunk by Confederate torpedoes. May have sunk below Jamestown in 2.5–3 fathoms of water in the middle of the Roanoke River. Portions of the vessel above the water were burned on April 10, 1865, by the USS *Iosco*. (*WCWN*, 209; Elliott, *Ironclad of the Roanoke*, 271.)

vessel. Nationality unknown. Wrecked in Pamlico Sound at Swan Point near Washington sometime during the war. (*ORN*, 8:674.)

vessel. Union. Was captured by the Confederate privateer *Florida* on July 22, 1861. Ran aground at Nag's Read to prevent its recapture by a Union ship. (*OR*, 4:587.)

vessels. Confederate. One vessel was sunk on each side of the wreck of the USS *Southfield* in the Roanoke River, downstream of Plymouth to block the river sometime during the war. (*ORN*, 11:12–13.)

Ohio River

The Ohio River was the major route of commerce to the Mississippi River from southern Illinois, Indiana, Ohio, Pennsylvania, and West Virginia. Vessels on the Ohio River supplied Union troops and commissary goods for the Union forces invading the Confederacy. The Ohio River served as an obstacle to keep Confederate forces from the Union states on its north bank. Gen. John Hunt Morgan's Confederate cavalry crossed the Ohio River in July 1863 and destroyed the Union steamboat *Alice Dean*. Accidents claimed many steamboats during the Civil War period. Confederate agents set fire to a Union wharf boat at Mound City, Ill., and may have caused other "accidents" to Union steamboats on the Ohio River.

Advance. Union. Stern-wheel towboat steamer, 96 tons. Built in 1857 at California, Pa. Exploded when passing

Barnes Warehouse on January 26, 1862, above New Mata-moros, Ohio, with the loss of three. The boiler flew 300 feet into an orchard. The vessel's pilot was killed, and Captain Stewart was injured. (*MSV*, 3, 239; *WTBD*, 7.)

Alice Dean. Union. Side-wheel steamer, 411 tons. Built in 1863 at Cincinnati. Captured and burned by Gen. John Hunt Morgan's Confederate forces in the captured *John T. McCombs* on July 7, 1863, at Brandenburg, Ky., after ferrying his troops across the Ohio River to invade Indiana. Burned near the Ind. bank between Morvin's Landing and Mauckport. Its machinery was salvaged in the fall of 1863. (*OR*, 23:1:659, 709–10; *ORN*, 25:240; *MSV*, 6, 240; *WPD*, 12.)

Alice Dean. Union. Side-wheel steamer, 394 tons. Built in Cincinnati. Hit a bank on March 25, 1864, about 10 miles below Cincinnati and sank with 12 feet of water over the stern. The passengers and cargo were taken off by the *Jennie Hubbs* and *Lady Pike*. Was later raised. (*WPD*, 12.)

Andy Fulton. Union. Side-wheel steamer, 146 tons. Length 125 feet, beam 27 feet, depth 4 feet 11 inches. Built in 1858 or 1859 at Freedom, Pa. Burned on July 29, 1861, at Carrolton, Ky. (*MSV*, 10, 241.)

Arizona. Union. Stern-wheel steamer. Length 155 feet, beam 35 feet, depth 5 feet 6 inches, 3 boilers. Built in 1857 at Belle Vernon, Pa. In mid-January 1862 it hit an abutment at the Louisville landing and sank to the roof. Was raised a month later. (*WPD*, 29.)

USS Black Hawk (New Uncle Sam) (Uncle Sam). Union. Side-wheel steam tinclad, 572 or 902 tons. Length 227 feet 6 inches, beam 45 feet 6 inches or 38 feet, depth 8 feet, draft 6 or 7 feet. Armed with eight 32-pounders, two 30-pounder Parrott rifles, and two 12-pounder rifles (another source—two 30-pounder Parrott rifles, two 12-pounder Parrott rifles, two heavy 12-pounder Parrott rifles, two Union repeating guns, and one B&R gun). Built in 1857 at New Albany, Ind. Flagship of 1st Rear Adm. David D. Porter and Act. Rear Adm. Samuel Phillips Lee. The magazine accidentally caught fire and blew up, sinking the USS *Black Hawk* 3 miles above Cairo, Ill., on April 22, 1865. The *Tempest* helped save most of the crew. Four men were lost along with the squadron records. The *Peerless* and *Huntsville* later hit the wreck and sank. The USS

Black Hawk was raised and later sold by Dalson Wrecking Company in April 1867. (*ORN*, 27:154, 159, 171; ser. 2, 1:46; Miller, *Photographic History*, 6:225; *WPD*, 54.)

Boston. Union. Side-wheel steamer, 395 tons. Built in 1856 at Cincinnati. Burned on July 25, 1863, at Moore's Bar near Portsmouth, Ohio. (*MSV*, 24, 246; *WPD*, 59.)

Bostona No. 2. U.S. Side-wheel steamer, 304 tons. Length 240 feet. Built in 1860 at Cincinnati. Snagged on October 17, 1865, at Craigs Bar above Carrollton and below Cincinnati. Was raised and taken to Cincinnati. (*MSV*, 246; *WPD*, 60.)

Brown Dick. Union. Stern-wheel steamer, 55 tons. Length 95 feet, beam 19 feet, depth 3 feet 6 inches. Built in 1855 at McKeesport, Pa. Burned on November 23, 1862, at Wheeling, Va. (W. Va.), while being dismantled. Floated downstream. Its machinery was salvaged and used on the *W. H. Harrison*. (*MSV*, 25, 247; *WPD*, 62.)

Burd Levi. U.S. Stern-wheel steamer, 205 tons. Built in 1864 at New Albany, Ind. Exploded on May 19, 1865, at West Franklin, Ind., with five killed. (*MSV*, 247; *WPD*, 64.)

Captain John Brickell. Union. Stern-wheel steamer, 188 tons. Built in 1863 at Freedom, Pa. Ran into a flatboat and then ran ashore on Ohio side and sank to the boiler deck on November 11, 1863, at West Columbia, W. Va. Was raised and taken to Cincinnati. (*MSV*, 29, 248; *WPD*, 71.)

Castle Garden. Union. Stern-wheel steamer, 161 tons. Built in 1853 at Mckeesport, Pa. Stranded on July 25, 1862, at Mound City, Ill. (*MSV*, 31, 248; *WPD*, 75.)

Charlie Potwan. Union. Stern-wheel steamer, 52 tons. Cargo of slack coal. Built at Zanesville, Ohio. En route from Coalport for Ashland, Ky. On November 28, 1864, swells from the *Diamond* and *Coal Hill* caused the vessel to fill and turn over at Eight Mile Island above Point Pleasant. The cabin separated from the hull and floated downstream. There was no loss of life. (*WPD*, 81.)

Colonna. Union. Stern-wheel steamer, 102 tons. Built in 1859 at Brownsville, Pa. Burned on December 1, 1863, at Newburg, Ind. (*MSV*, 41, 252; *WPD*, 104.)

Commodore Perry. Union. Stern-wheel steamer, 193 tons. Built in 1857 at Freedom, Pa. Exploded on August 2, 1862, at the Louisville wharf, with three killed. (*MSV*, 43, 252; *WPD*, 107.)

Cordelia Ann. Union. Stern-wheel steamer. Length 110 feet, beam 24 feet 1 inch, depth 3 feet. Built in 1862 at Paducah, Ky. Snagged below Grandview, Ind., in low water the summer of 1864. Was later raised. (*WPD*, 111.)

Courier. Union. Stern-wheel steamer, 258 tons. Length 168 feet, beam 30 feet, depth 5 feet 6 inches. Built in 1857 at Wheeling, Va. (W. Va.). Burned on August 22, 1864, at the mouth of the Cache River between Cairo and Mound City, Ill., while putting stores on the steamer *Volunteer*. Most of the *Courier*'s cargo was lost. (*ORN*, 26:516; *MSV*, 47, 253; *WPD*, 113.)

Daniel G. Taylor. Union. Side-wheel steamer, 543 tons. Length 240 feet, beam 38 feet, 4 boilers. Built in 1855. Named after the mayor of St. Louis. Burned, with one killed, on February 5, 1864, at Louisville by Confederate partisans who infiltrated the Union occupied city. Its machinery was removed in mid-February 1864. (*MSV*, 50, 254; *WPD*, 120.)

Decotah. Union. Stern-wheel steamer, 230 tons. Built in 1858 at Belle Vernon, Pa. Burned while under repair on March 25, 1864, on the Marine Ways by Gen. Nathan Bedford Forrest's Confederate troops at Paducah, Ky., during a raid that captured much of the city. (*OR*, 32:1:607; *ORN*, 26:199; *MSV*, 52, 255; *WPD*, 122.)

Dick Fulton. Union. Side-wheel steamer, 66 tons. Built in 1857 at Elizabeth, Pa. Sank following a collision with the *Hawkeye* on February 5, 1864, at Point Pittsburgh, with its engineer killed. Was raised and rebuilt. (*WTBD*, 56.)

Dr. Kane. Union. Stern-wheel steamer, 191 tons. Built in 1857 at Brownsville, Pa. Snagged and sunk in deep water, 300 yards below Cairo's public wharf. (*WPD*, 131.)

Echo No. 2. U.S. Stern-wheel steamer. Length 145 feet, beam 26 feet, depth 4 feet. Built in 1863 at California, Pa. While carrying 300 soldiers of the 13th and 41st Ohio Veteran Volunteer Regiments, the vessel hit the prow of the USS *Oneida* in late June 1865 near Cairo. One soldier, ten horses, thirteen mules, and rations were lost. The pilot, Wilson Dunn, was beaten by the soldiers as a result of the accident. (*WPD*, 138.)

Economy. Union. Stern-wheel steamer, 197 or 200 tons. Length 155 feet, beam 30 feet 6 inches, depth 4 feet 6 inches. Built in 1857 at Shousetown, Pa. Was lost on October 17, 1862. (*MSV*, 60, 257; *WPD*, 140.)

Equality. Union. Stern-wheel steamer, 90 tons. Built in 1860 at Paducah, Ky. Snagged on May 11, 1861, at Golconda, Ill. (*MSV*, 66, 259; *WPD*, 153.)

Eunice. Union. Stern-wheel steamer, 231 tons. Built in 1855 at Brownsville, Pa. On April 24, 1862, it collided with *Commodore Perry* near Ashland, Ky., and sank, with no injuries. Was later raised. (*WPD*, 107, 155.)

Express. U.S. Side-wheel steamer, 224 tons. Carried the 32nd Ill. Infantry Regiment. Built in 1862 at Wheeling, Va. (W. Va.). En route from Parkersburg, W. Va., to Louisville. Sank on June 11, 1865, near Manchester, Ohio. No lives were lost. Was raised and returned to service. (*OR*, 47:1:103; *MSV*, 69; *WPD*, 158.)

George Albree. U.S. Stern-wheel towboat steamer, 181 tons. Built in 1854 at Brownsville, Pa. Burned on September 9, 1865, at the Monongahela Wharf in Pittsburgh, Pa. The fire spread to the *River Queen* and *Julia No. 2*. The hull of the *George Albree* was taken to the Allegheny River and used for firewood. (*MSV*, 83, 263; *WTBD*, 81–82.)

Grey Fox. Union. Stern-wheel steamer, 70 tons. Built in 1857 at Brownsville, Pa. Was sunk by ice on January 19, 1864, at Louisville. (*MSV*, 89, 265.)

Henry Fitzhugh. Union. Stern-wheel steamer, 217 tons. Built in 1857 at Cincinnati. Hit ice on January 22, 1864, near Shawneetown, Ill., and sank. Was later raised. (*WPD*, 211.)

Highland Chief. Union. Stern-wheel steamer, 342 tons. Built in 1864 at Cincinnati. Sank in a collision with the *Major Anderson* on August 18, 1864, two miles above Vevay, Ind., with five killed. Its engines were later removed. (*MSV*, 96, 267; *WPD*, 215.)

Idaho. Union. Side-wheel steamer. Length 99 feet 5 inches, beam 17 feet, depth 3 feet 5 inches. Built in 1862 at Melrose, Wis. Was accidentally sunk by a gunboat in April 1864 in the Ohio River. Was later raised. (*WPD*, 221.)

Jennie Hubbs (Empire). Union. Stern-wheel steamer, 220 tons. Built in 1863 at Cincinnati. Sank in November 1864 at falls near New Albany, Ind. Was raised and later renamed *Empire*. (*WPD*, 245.)

Jo Jacques. Union. Stern-wheel steamer, 34 tons. Built in 1856 at Lodi, Tenn. Sank after colliding with the *General Anderson* on April 5, 1864, at Metropolis, Ill. (*MSV*, 112, 272.)

Kaskaskia. Union. Side-wheel steamer, 49 tons. Built in 1859 at Cincinnati. Sank in the Grand Chain on February 20, 1864. (*WPD*, 263.)

Katie. Union. Stern-wheel steamer, 180 tons. Built in 1864 at Elizabeth, Pa. Collided with the *Des Moines* on November 22, 1864, at Diamond Island and sank in nine minutes, with one killed. (*MSV*, 120, 274; *WPD*, 267.)

Maid of the Mist. Union. Side-wheel steamer, 40 tons. Built in 1859 at Evansville, Ind. Foundered on September 18, 1861, at Evansville. (*MSV*, 134, 278; *WPD*, 304.)

Malta. Union. Stern-wheel steamer, 33 tons. Built in 1864 at Marietta, Ohio. Sank on March 30, 1865, at Marietta. Was later raised. (*WPD*, 305.)

Medora. Union. Stern-wheel steamer, 101 tons. Built in 1856 at Brownsville, Pa. Burned on July 20, 1861, at Jeffersonville, Ind. (*MSV*, 142, 281; *WPD*, 318.)

Melrose. U.S. Stern-wheel steamer, 177 tons. Built in 1856 at Monongahela, Pa. Collided with the *Pacific* and sank on January 29, 1861, at Shawneetown, Ill. (*WPD*, 318–19.)

Monarch (USS Monarch). U.S. Side-wheel steamer, 406 tons. Built in 1853 at Fulton (Cincinnati), Ohio. Sank en route to New Orleans on March 5, 1861. Salvaged and converted into the Union army ram *Monarch,* which was sunk by ice while laid up in the Mississippi River below St. Louis in December 1864. See **USS Monarch** in the Mississippi River section. (*MSV*, 148; *WPD*, 328–29; *WCWN*, 161.)

Nettie Hartupee. Union. Stern-wheel steamer, 81 tons. Built in 1863 at Allegheny, Pa. Burned on March 2, 1865, at Pomeroy, Ohio. (*MSV*, 154, 284; *WPD*, 342.)

Nimrod. U.S. Stern-wheel steamer, 30 tons. Built in 1865 at Pittsburgh, Pa. Exploded on September 22, 1865, with five killed at Pittsburgh, Pa. (*MSV*, 158, 285; *WPD*, 348.)

Nymph. Union. Stern-wheel steamer, 35 tons. Built in 1862 at Portsmouth, Ohio. Stranded on December 1, 1864, at Louisville. (*MSV*, 160, 286; *WPD*, 351.)

Oil City. Union. Stern-wheel steamer, 59 or 106.75 tons. Built in 1863 at Wellsburg, Va. Hit a sunken coal barge at Wheeling the night of March 30, 1865, which ripped open its bottom. The cabin separated. The hull and machinery were salvaged. (*WPD*, 354; *WSTD*, 174.)

Olive. Union. Stern-wheel steamer, 220 tons. Length 157 feet, beam 32 feet, depth 4 feet 10 inches. Built in 1863 at California, Pa. In June 1864 coal oil aboard caught fire so the vessel was sunk at Buffington Island to put out the flames. Was later raised. On June 28, 1865, the *Olive* snagged at Golconda, Ill., with seven killed. (*WPD*, 354.)

Peerless. U.S. Side-wheel steamer, 227 tons. Length 182 feet, beam 34 feet, depth 5 feet 10 inches. Built in 1864 at Cincinnati. Hit the wreck of the USS *Black Hawk,* turned over, and caught fire on December 15, 1865, 3 miles above Cairo, Ill. (*MSV*, 169, 288; *WPD*, 365.)

Prioress. Union. Side-wheel steamer, 393 tons. Built in 1859 at Cincinnati. Burned on April 16, 1863, at Cincinnati, with one killed. Its machinery was salvaged and put on the *C. T. Dumont*. (*MSV*, 178, 291; *WPD*, 379.)

Reliance. Union. Stern-wheel steamer, 156 tons. Built in 1855 at Cincinnati. Snagged in December 1862 near Steubenville, Ohio. (*MSV*, 183, 292; *WPD*, 391.)

River Queen. U.S. Stern-wheel steamer. Length 250 feet, beam 30 feet. The hull was built below Warren, Pa. Set afire by the vessel's engineer while being completed on September 10, 1865, at the Monongahela Wharf in Pittsburgh, Pa. (*WPD*, 394.)

Robert Lee. Union. Stern-wheel steamer, 68 tons. Built in 1860 at Allegheny, Pa. Burned on February 5, 1864, at Louisville, with three lost. (*MSV*, 186, 294; *WPD*, 383.)

Science No. 2. Union. Stern-wheel steamer, 116 tons. Length 135 feet, beam 26 feet 7 inches, depth 3 feet 10 inches. Sank up to the boiler deck at Pomeroy, Ohio, in February 1862. (*WPD*, 420.)

Sunnyside (Sunny Side). Union. Side-wheel steamer, 330 tons. Cargo of 1,130 bales of cotton. Built in 1860 at Brownsville, Pa. Burned on November 13, 1863, at Pomeroy, Ohio, near Island No. 16 with 30–40 killed. (*OR,* 31:3:180; *New York Times,* November 29, 1863; *MSV,* 205, 299; *WPD,* 437.)

Tempest. Union. Stern-wheel steamer, 63 tons. Built in 1856. Was sunk by ice on March 28, 1864, at Cincinnati. Was probably raised. (*MSV,* 210, 300; *WPD,* 448.)

Thistle. Union. Stern-wheel towboat steamer, 210 tons. Built in 1863 at Belle Vernon, Pa. Snagged on July 31, 1864, near Big Hurricane Island. (*MSV,* 210, 301; *WPD,* 450.)

Thomas Scott. Union. Stern-wheel steamer, 149 tons. Built in 1856 at Freedom, Pa. Snagged in the Ohio River on July 13, 1863, above Warsaw, Ky. (*MSV,* 212, 301; *WPD,* 451.)

Tiger. Union. Propeller towboat steamer, 97.6 tons. Built in Pittsburgh, Pa. En route with a barge of hay from North Bend, Ohio, to Cincinnati. In June 1864 it hit Kirby's Rock and sank. (*WTBD,* 219.)

Undine. Union. Side-wheel steamer, 158 tons. Built in 1859 at Brownsville, Pa. Sank in January 1864 after hitting ice at New London, Ind., near Payne Hollow, Ky. The cabin separated from the hull and went over the falls at Louisville. (*WPD,* 463.)

➤ **VESSELS WITHOUT NAMES**

barges. Union. Two barges. Cargo of coal. Sank near Smithland, Ky., during the Civil War. The USS *Rose* either salvaged or destroyed the wrecks. (*ORN,* 27:275–76.)

wharf boat. Union. Was burned and blown up at Mound City, Ill., by Confederate agents on the evening of June 1, 1864. The wharf boat contained reserve supplies and ammunition for Adm. David D. Porter's fleet. Losses were about $500,000, including $200,000 in Navy Paymaster Boggs's safe. The paymaster was burned and nearly suffocated while trying to save the funds. (*OR,* 48:2:195; *New York Times,* June 4, 1864; Scharf, *History of the Confederate Navy,* 763.)

Oklahoma

J. R. Williams. Union. Stern-wheel steamer. Cargo of 16,000 pounds of bacon, 150 barrels of flour, clothes, and other supplies with a Union guard of 2nd Lt. Horace A. B. Cook and twenty-four men of the 12th Kan. Cavalry Regiment. En route from Fort Smith, Ark., for Fort Gibson (also called Fort Blunt), Cherokee Nation. Ambushed on June 15, 1864, by a Confederate three-gun battery and Col. Stand Watie's Indian Brigade at Pheasant Bluff on the Arkansas River near the present town of Tamaha on the Arkansas River. The steamer's captain and Lieutenant Hudson, quartermaster of 14th Kan. Cavalry, took a yawl and crossed the river. Confederate artillery sent shells into the upper works and smokestacks, killing two and wounding several on the vessel, and killing two on shore. Became grounded on the opposite side from the battery and captured by the Confederates. Some Union troops were captured, but most escaped. Moved to a sandbar on the south side of the Arkansas River, where Confederates unloaded as much booty as they could carry. Some of the goods were deposited on the sandbar, but the river suddenly rose and floated them away. The boat was set afire and drifted downstream. (*OR,* 34:1:1011–13.)

Oregon

The coast of Oregon claimed a number of wrecked vessels during the Civil War period while transporting cargo along the Pacific coast.

Annie Doyle (Doyle). Nationality unknown. Schooner. Wrecked on Yaquina Bar on March 11, 1865. (Marshall, *Oregon Shipwrecks,* 73; Gibbs, *Shipwrecks Pacific Ocean,* 275.)

Baltimore. Union. Schooner. Wrecked in 1861, about six-tenths of a mile northwest of the Cape Arago Light, at latitude 43° 21' 3" north, longitude 124° 23' west. Wrecked at Tunnel Point in the area later called Baltimore Rocks. (Gibbs, *Shipwrecks Pacific Ocean,* 274; Marshall, *Oregon Shipwrecks,* 43.)

Blanco. Union. Brig, 284 registered tons, 170 tons. Length 125 feet. Built in 1858–60 at North Bend, Ore. Capsized off the Siletz River in 1864. The crew disappeared. The hull washed ashore at the mouth of the Siletz River, was burned, and all the iron and material salvaged by Indians. At an Indian village five zinc sheets, two nail kegs, an oilskin coat, a calico dress, seven pairs of garters, two pairs of boots, rope, and sail were found. It was rumored the survivors were killed by Indians. (Gibbs, *Shipwrecks Pacific Ocean,* 141, 275; Gibbs, *Windjammers,* 138.)

Brandt. Nationality unknown. Vessel. Was lost on October 19 or November 26, 1864, at Yaquina Bay or off Ediz Hook, Wash. (Gibbs, *Shipwrecks Pacific Ocean,* 275.)

Carrie Ladd. Union. Stern-wheel steamer, 128 tons. Length 126 feet, beam 24.4 feet, depth 4.6 feet. Built in 1858 at Oregon City, Ore. Sank on June 3, 1862, about 18 miles below the Cascades. (Gibbs, *Shipwrecks Pacific Ocean,* 274; Marshall, *Oregon Shipwrecks,* 204.)

Cornelia Terry. Nationality unknown. Vessel. Was lost on October 19, 1864, at Yaquina Bay. (Gibbs, *Shipwrecks Pacific Ocean,* 275.)

Cyclops. Nationality unknown. Schooner. En route from San Francisco to Coquille, Ore. Wrecked in the spring of 1862 on Coos Bay Bar. Another source says it was lost in 1858. Only two cross-cut saws and one plow were salvaged from the vessel. (Gibbs, *Shipwrecks Pacific Ocean,* 273; Marshall, *Oregon Shipwrecks,* 73.)

Energy. Nationality unknown. Brig. Was lost in 1862 at Coos Bay Bar. One sailor survived the wreck. (Marshall, *Oregon Shipwrecks,* 44.)

Industry. Union. Bark, 300 tons. Built in 1862 at Stockton, Maine. Became grounded on the southwest shore of the Middle Sands at the Columbia River entrance on March 15, 1865, with a loss of seventeen lives. The survivors carved their name on Shark Rock, which is preserved in the Columbia River Maritime Museum. (Gibbs, *Shipwrecks Pacific Ocean,* 275; Gibbs, *Pacific Graveyard,* 260; Marshall, *Oregon Shipwrecks,* 130.)

James Clinton. U.S. Stern-wheel steamer, 105 tons. Length 90 feet. Built in 1856 at Canemah, Ore. Burned on April 23, 1861, when a fire in a warehouse and flour mills on the Linn side of Oregon City spread to the vessel. (*MSV,* 108, 270; Marshall, *Oregon Shipwrecks,* 207; Mills, *Stern-wheelers Up Columbia,* 196.)

Noyo. Union. Schooner, 95 tons. Cargo of lime. Built in 1861 in Eureka, Calif. Went ashore on Coos Bay Bar and then burned to the water's edge in 1864. The captain and two crewmen were washed overboard but were saved. (Jackson, *Doghole Schooners,* 51.)

Ork. Nationality unknown. Vessel. Was lost on November 24, 1864, at the Umpqua River Bar. (Gibbs, *Shipwrecks Pacific Ocean,* 275.)

Pacific. Union. Steamer. Hit Coffin Rock and ran ashore in July 1861. Was salvaged. (Gibbs, *Shipwrecks Pacific Ocean,* 274; Marshall, *Oregon Shipwrecks,* 209.)

S. D. Lewis. Union. Brig. Became grounded on Clatsop Spit at the entrance to the Columbia River on March 16, 1865, and was dashed to pieces with no loss of life. (Gibbs, *Pacific Graveyard,* 277; Gibbs, *Shipwrecks Pacific Ocean,* 275; Marshall, *Oregon Shipwrecks,* 133.)

Woodpecker (Barkenteen). British. Schooner, 300 tons. Cargo of flour, general freight, and 104 head of cattle. En route from the Columbia River to Victoria, British Columbia. Ran aground on Clatsop Spit on May 10, 1861, with no loss of life. The cargo was thrown overboard when the vessel took on water. The crew abandoned the ship, and only one cow made it ashore. (Gibbs, *Pacific Graveyard,* 286; Gibbs, *Shipwrecks Pacific Ocean,* 274; Marshall, *Oregon Shipwrecks,* 134.)

Pacific Area

The Civil War extended into the Pacific Ocean and the adjacent areas. Yankee commerce ranged worldwide, as did the Confederate commerce raiders CSS *Alabama* and CSS *Shenandoah* as they searched for Yankee prey. The CSS *Shenandoah* burned four Yankee whalers at Ponape Island on April 3, 1865, and then used a captured chart to locate Yankee whalers in the Bering Sea.

Abigail. Union. Whaling bark. Cargo of whale oil and a large quantity of liquor. Out of New Bedford, Mass. Crew of thirty-five. Was captured on May 27, 1865, and burned on May 28, 1865, by the CSS *Shenandoah* near Shantarsky Island in the northwest Sea of Okhotsk, latitude 57° 7' north, longitude 153° 1' east. Fourteen of the captured seamen joined the CSS *Shenandoah,* and many crewmen got drunk from the liquor that was seized. (*ORN,* 3:789, 792; 822–23, Hearn, *Gray Raiders,* 284–85.)

Edward Carey. Union. Whaling ship. Out of San Francisco. Was captured at Lea Harbor, Ponape Island, Eastern Carolines, on April 1, 1865, by the CSS *Shenandoah* and was burned, along with the *Hector, Harvest,* and *Pearl* on April 3, 1865. (*ORN,* 3:588, 788, 792; Hearn, *Gray Raiders,* 283.)

Harvest. Union. Whaling bark. Out of Honolulu, Hawaii. Was captured, grounded, and set afire in Lea Harbor, Ponape Island, Eastern Carolines, by the CSS *Shenandoah* on April 3, 1865. The vessel had Union flags, an American register, and a Yankee captain. Charts taken by the Confederates led the CSS *Shenandoah* to whaling fleets in the Bering Sea. (*ORN,* 3:588, 788, 792, 817–19.)

Hector. Union. Whaling bark. Out of New Bedford, Mass. Was captured, grounded, and burned, along with the *Edward Carey, Harvest,* and *Pearl,* by CSS *Shenandoah* on April 3, 1865, at Lea Harbor, Ponape Island, Eastern Carolines. (*ORN,* 3:588, 788, 792, 817–19; Hearn, *Gray Raiders,* 282–83.)

Pearl. Union. Whaling bark. Out of New London, Conn. Was captured and drawn onto a reef, stripped, and burned on April 3, 1865, by the CSS *Shenandoah* in Lea Harbor, Ponape Island, Eastern Carolines. (*ORN,* 3:588, 788–89, 792, 817–18; Hearn, *Gray Raiders,* 282–83.)

Polar Star. Union. Whaler. Wrecked in 1861 or 1862 in the Sea of Okhotsk. (Hearn, *Gray Raiders,* 291.)

Princeza. British. Schooner. Carried $140,000 in U.S. gold bullion and specie. Foundered on March 15, 1863, in shallow water off the north end of Moreton Island, off Redcliffe, Queensland, Australia. (Rieseberg, *Guide to Buried Treasure,* 133.)

Pennsylvania

J. D. James. Union. Stern-wheel towboat steamer. Length 80 feet, beam 16 feet. Built in 1861 at Warren, Pa. Sank 7 miles above Oil City in the Allegheny River and raised in May–June 1862. (*WTBD,* 111.)

May. Union. Side-wheel steamer, 43 tons. Built in 1848 at Philadelphia. Collided with the *Major Reybold* on August 27, 1861, at Philadelphia. (*MSV,* 141, 280.)

Messenger. Union. Steamer, 254 tons. Length 154 feet, beam 35 feet, depth 5 feet 2 inches. Built in 1855 at Belle Vernon, Pa. Was stranded on December 7, 1861, at Rochester. (*MSV,* 281, *WPD,* 320.)

William Barnhill. Union. Stern-wheel towboat steamer, 149.47 tons. Built in Birmingham (South Pittsburgh), Pa.

Hit an old canal aqueduct on the Allegheny River near Pittsburgh in mid-March 1864 and sank while towing barges carrying empty oil barrels. Turned over below a lock on the Monogahela River. Was raised with its machinery going in the *Seven Seas.* (*WSTB,* 239.)

Rhode Island

Rhode Island's wrecks occurred mainly as a result of accidents along its Atlantic coast. The CSS *Chickamauga* captured and destroyed two Union vessels off Block Island.

Ameilia. Union. Schooner. Was lost on April 30, 1864, near Point Judith. (*EAS,* 7.)

Angler. British. Schooner. Cargo of coffee and logwood. Was lost on Block Island in March 1865. (*Chief of Engineers Report 1868,* 803.)

Boundary. U.S. Schooner. Cargo of lumber. Was lost on April 8, 1861, on Block Island. (*Chief of Engineers Report 1868,* 803.)

Commodore. Union. Steamer. Was lost on August 9, 1863, south of Point Judith. (*EAS,* 22.)

Eagle's Wing. Union. Steamer, 409 tons. Built in 1854 at New York City. Burned on July 24, 1861, off Pawtuxet. (*MSV,* 257.)

Ellen Forrest. U.S. Schooner. Was lost on Block Island on December 21, 1865. (*Chief of Engineers Report 1868,* 803.)

Goodspeed. Union. Schooner, 283 tons. Out of Philadelphia. Was captured and burned by CSS *Chickamauga* on November 1, 1864, off Block Island. (*OR,* ser. 4, 3:1058; *ORN,* 3:323, 712.)

Grecian. Nationality unknown. Schooner. In ballast. Was lost on Block Island on February 21, 1861. (*Chief of Engineers Report 1868,* 803.)

Henry. British. Brig. Carried assorted cargo. Was lost on Block Island on October 10, 1864. (*Chief of Engineers Report 1868,* 803.)

Independence. Union. Schooner. Was lost on June 20, 1862, north of Point Judith. (*EAS,* 45.)

Manelett. British. Schooner. Cargo of coal. Was lost on Block Island in July 1862. (*Chief of Engineers Report 1868,* 803.)

Mary E. Thompson. U.S. Brig. Cargo of hides, wool, and cotton. Was lost on Block Island on December 21, 1865. (*Chief of Engineers Report 1868,* 803.)

M. H. Sheldon. Union. Schooner. Cargo of coal. Was lost on Block Island on September 28, 1861. (*Chief of Engineers Report 1868,* 803.)

Norman. Union. Schooner. Cargo of coal. Was lost on Block Island on November 30, 1861. (*Chief of Engineers Report 1868,* 803.)

Otter Rock. Union. Schooner, 91 tons. Cargo of potatoes. Was captured and scuttled by CSS *Chickamauga* on November 1, 1864, off Brock Island. (*OR,* ser. 4, 3:1058; *ORN,* 3:712.)

Randal S. Smith. Union. Schooner. Cargo of coal. Was lost on Block Island on July 11, 1861. (*Chief of Engineers Report 1868,* 803.)

South Carolina

Charleston Harbor and its channels to the Atlantic Ocean contain most of South Carolina's Civil War shipwrecks. When the Confederates prepared to capture Union-held Fort Sumter in the spring of 1861, the Confederates sank a number of vessels to block part of Charleston's channels from Union warships. Eight months after the Union surrender of Fort Sumter, the Union sent several fleets of old whalers and ships to Charleston loaded with stone and scuttled them in the Main Ship Channel and Maffitt's Channel in an attempt to close Charleston Harbor to blockade-runners. The First Stone Fleet was sunk December 19–20, 1861, and the Second Stone Fleet was sunk January 25–26, 1862. Strong currents and shifting sands caused the channels to change, making the use of scuttled vessels to block Charleston Harbor a futile effort.

Numerous blockade-runners were lost trying to enter and exit Charleston during the blockade. Among the wrecked blockade-runners of note are the *Beatrice, Celt, Constance Decima, Flora, Georgiana, Mary Bowers, Minho, Presto, Prince Albert, Ruby,* and *Stonewall Jackson.* Narrow limited channels caused the wreck of the *Georgiana* to hole and sink the blockade-runners *Constance Decima, Norseman,* and *Mary Bowers.* Wrecks also sank the blockade-runners *Minho, Prince Albert,* and *Rose.* The blockade-runner *Havelock* was grounded on February 25 and June 10, 1863, but was refloated both times and was later lost as the *General Beauregard* off the North Carolina coast.

The Union ironclads USS *Keokuk,* USS *Patapsco,* and USS *Weehawken* were sunk during the long siege of Charleston. The first sinking of an enemy ship by a submarine occurred at the entrance to Charleston Harbor, where the blockader USS *Housatonic* was sunk by the CSS *H. L. Hunley* using a spar torpedo. The CSS *H. L. Hunley* also sank after it attacked.

When Gen. William Tecumseh Sherman's Union army cut the railroads and roads to Charleston, the city was abandoned on February 17–18, 1865, and the once mighty Confederate Charleston fleet was sunk or blown up. The Confederate vessels that were scuttled included the ironclads CSS *Charleston,* CSS *Chicora,* CSS *Columbia,* and CSS *Palmetto State;* the schooner CSS *Indian Chief;* and a number of special torpedo boats, or "Davids." Many Charleston Harbor wrecks were removed or moved by the U.S. Army Corps of Engineers in the years following the Civil War. Salvage of artifacts at Charleston has been under way for several years on the wrecks of numerous blockade-runners. In South Carolina's inland waters and sounds the Union ships the *Boston, George Washington,* USS *Dai Ching,* and *Governor Milton* were sunk by gunfire, and a number of Confederate vessels were scuttled.

Alice Provost. Union. Bark, 476 tons. Depth 12 feet. Cargo of 700 tons of coal. Built in 1856 at Westerly, R.I. En route from Philadelphia for Port Royal, S.C. Went ashore while coming into Port Royal on December 12, 1863. The USS *Vermont* rescued the vessel's crew. (*ORN,* 15:177.)

Amazon. Union. Whaling bark, 318 or 319 tons. Depth 14 feet. Built in 1815 at Berkley, Mass. Out of Fairhaven, Mass. Part of the First Stone Fleet. Scuttled with 325 tons of stone about 3 miles southeast of Morris Island in the Main Shipping Channel, Charleston Harbor, on December 19–20, 1861. (*ORN,* 2:418, 421; ser. 2, 1:34; *DANFS,* 5:430, 433; Spence, *List,* 710–11.)

America. Union. Whaling ship, 418 tons. Out of New Bedford, Mass. Part of the First Stone Fleet. Originally an India Merchantman that made a record run of eighty-nine days from Boston to Calcutta, India, in 1833 via the Cape of Good Hope, a trip of 14,550–15,000 miles. Became a whaler in 1836. Scuttled about 3 miles southeast of Morris Island in the Main Ship Channel, Charleston Harbor, on December 19–20, 1861. (*ORN,* 12:421, 511; ser. 2, 1:34; *DANFS,* 5:432–33.)

American. Union. Whaling bark, 275 or 329 tons. Draft 15 feet. Built in 1822 at New York City. Out of Edgartown or New Bedford, Mass. Part of the First Stone Fleet. Was sunk with 300 tons of stone about 3 miles southeast of Morris Island, Charleston Harbor, on December 19–20, 1861. (*ORN,* 12:418, 421; ser. 2, 1:34; *DANFS,* 5:430, 433; Spence, *List,* 711–12.)

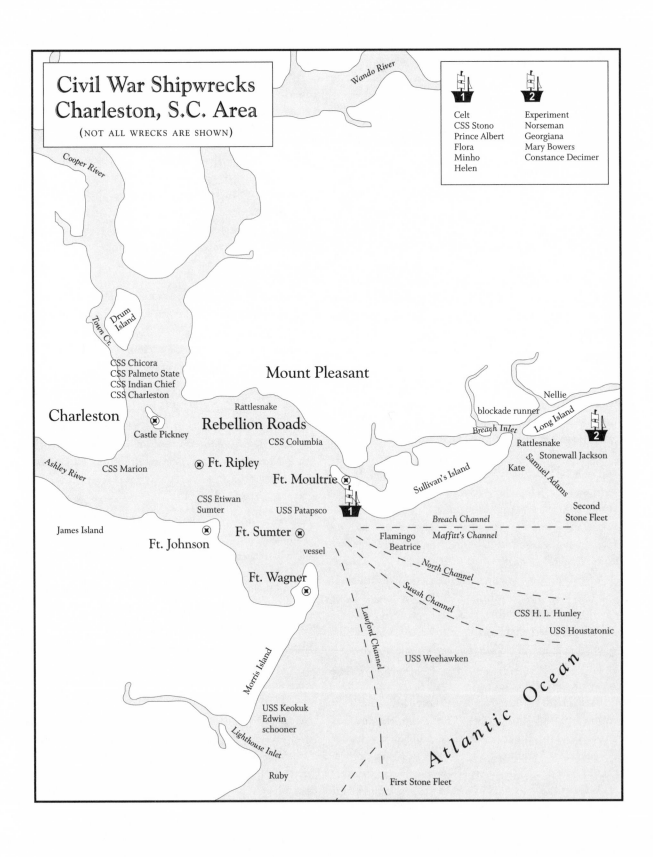

Civil War Shipwrecks
Charleston, S.C. Area
(NOT ALL WRECKS ARE SHOWN)

1	Celt	**2**	Experiment
	CSS Stono		Norseman
	Prince Albert		Georgiana
	Flora		Mary Bowers
	Minho		Constance Decimer
	Helen		

Wando River

Cooper River

Town Cr.

Drum Island

CSS Chicora
CSS Palmeto State
CSS Indian Chief
CSS Charleston

Charleston

Castle Pickney

Ashley River

CSS Marion

James Island

Ft. Johnson

Rattlesnake

Rebellion Roads

CSS Columbia

Ft. Ripley

CSS Etiwan
Sumter

Ft. Sumter

vessel

Ft. Wagner

Mount Pleasant

Ft. Moultrie

USS Patapsco

1

Sullivan's Island

Breach Inlet

blockade runner

Nellie

Long Island

Rattlesnake

Kate

Stonewall Jackson

Samuel Adams

2

Second
Stone Fleet

Breach Channel

Maffitt's Channel

Flamingo
Beatrice

North Channel

Swash Channel

CSS H. L. Hunley

USS Houstatonic

Lawford Channel

USS Weehawken

Morris Island

USS Keokuk
Edwin
schooner

Lighthouse Inlet

Ruby

First Stone Fleet

Atlantic Ocean

Antoinette. Schooner. Was destroyed by Union forces about April 26, 1863, at Murray's Inlet. (Spence, *List,* 640.)

Archer. Union. Whaling ship, 321 tons. Draft 14 feet. Built in 1836 at Philadelphia. Out of New Bedford, Mass. Part of the First Stone Fleet. Loaded with 300 tons of stone. Scuttled 3 miles southeast of Morris Island, Charleston Harbor, on December 19–20, 1861. (*ORN,* 12:418, 421; ser. 2, 1:34; *DANFS,* 5:430, 433; Spence, *List,* 710.)

Beatrice. British. Iron screw steamer, 342 gross tons, 274 registered tons. Length 167 feet 6 inches, beam 24 feet 1 inch, draft 6 feet 8 inches, depth 12 feet, maximum speed 14 knots. Crew of thirty-five. Cargo included twenty 120-pound Whitworth shells. Built in 1863 at Greenock, Scotland. En route from Nassau, Bahamas, to Charleston from the south via the Sullivan's Island Channel. Was hit by Union shells and grounded on Drunken Dick Shoal near midnight on November 29, 1864, not far from the wreck of the *Flamingo.* Was boarded by several boatloads of Union sailors and burned with no salvage. Captain Randle, the pilot, and five crewmen escaped, but thirty crewmen were captured. A Union diver visited the ship in 1865. It was removed to a mean low-water depth of 15 feet by Benjamin Maillefert for the U.S. Army Corps of Engineers in 1871–73. Sanded in to 9.5–11 feet below the water surface. Identified by E. Lee Spence in 1967. (*ORN,* 16:112–14, 354; *Chief of Engineers Report 1872,* 652; *Chief of Engineers Report 1873,* 68; Moore, *Lowcountry Engineers,* 61; Spence, *List,* 658; *LLC,* 290.)

Bogota. Union. Merchantman, 300 tons. Part of the Second Charleston Stone Fleet. Filled with stone scuttled on January 25–26, 1862, in Maffitt's Channel close to the shore of Sullivan's Island, Charleston Harbor. (*DANFS,* 5:432, 436.)

Boston. Union army. Side-wheel transport steamer, 574, 590, or 630 tons. Length 215 feet, beam 28 or 29 feet, depth 9 feet or 9 feet 10 inches or 10 feet 6 inches. Carried three hundred men of Col. James Montgomery's 34th U.S. Colored Infantry Regiment, ninety cavalrymen, and sixty horses. Built in 1850 at New York City. Grounded on May 25, 1864, about midnight in the Ashepoo River while being escorted by the USS *Dai Ching* with seven or eight lives lost at Chapman's Fort, above Ashepoo Ferry.

Was abandoned and set on fire on May 26, 1864, after being hit by seventy or eighty shells. Its machinery, safe, and anchors were removed in 1866 by a salvage group. Was discovered by Howard Tower in 1979 and excavated by the Institute of Archeology and Anthropology at the University of South Carolina from 1981 to 1984. Thousands of artifacts were recovered, including hardtack biscuits, buttons, and brass cavalry saber handles. (*ORN,* 15:458–61; Lane, *American Paddle Steamboats,* 92–93; Spence, "Civil War Shipwrecks," *Argosy Treasure 77 Annual,* 90; Tower, "Civil War Wreck Salvaged," *Treasure Found,* 30; Tower, "Relics Abound on Excavated Civil War Vessel," *Lost Treasure,* 26–29; Spence, *List,* 653–54.)

Celia. British. Schooner. Cargo of turpentine. Out of Nassau, Bahamas. Was shelled and set on fire by a landing party from the USS *Nipsic* during a raid on Murrell's Inlet on January 2, 1865. (*ORN,* 15:154–57, 159.)

Celt (Colt) (Sylph). Confederate. Side-wheel steamer. Length 160 feet, beam 25 feet, depth 9 feet. Cargo of cotton on its fourth trip through the blockade. Built in 1862–63 at Charleston, S.C. Ran aground the night of February 14, 1865, on Sullivan's Island opposite Battery Rutledge and Fort Moultrie on the east side of Bowman's Jetty while trying to leave Charleston. Seized by the USS *Catskill* when the Union occupied the city on February 18, 1865. Broken up and 190 bales of cotton were removed. After the Civil War the wreck was removed to 15 feet below low tide by U.S. Army Corps of Engineers contractors. (*ORN,* 16:246, 256, 369; *Chief of Engineers Report 1873,* 68; Miller, *Photographic History,* 6:106; Horner, *Blockade-Runners,* 228; Spence, *List,* 669–70; *LLC,* 292.)

CSS Charleston. Confederate. Steam ironclad, 600 tons. Length 167 or 180 feet or 189 feet overall, beam 34 feet, depth 14 feet, draft 12.5 feet, speed 6 knots. Complement of 150, with four Brooke rifled guns and two 9-inch smoothbores. Called the "Ladies' Ironclad" and "Ladies' Gunboat" because the vessel was built in 1862–63 at Charleston, S.C., with money raised from ladies' bazaars. The Confederates stripped, burned, and blew up the CSS *Charleston* with 20 tons of gunpowder on February 17–18, 1865, in the Cooper River while anchored below the Drum Island Pleasant

Ferry Wharf. Removed to 12 feet below mean low-water depth in 1871–72 by Benjamin Maillefert for the U.S. Army Corps of Engineers. Probably was completely removed by later dredging. (*OR*, 47:1:1019; *ORN*, 16:372; ser. 2, 1:250; *Chief of Engineers Report 1873*, 652; *CWC*, 6-208; Ammen, "Navy in the Civil War," *Confederate Military History*, 156–57; *WCWN*, 207.)

Chase. British. Schooner, 20 tons. Out of Nassau, Bahamas. Was run ashore on April 26, 1862, on Raccoon Key or Romain Light, about the middle of the key, in Bull's Bay by the USS *Onward*. Could not be refloated, so it was burned a few days later. (*ORN*, 12:781, 795.)

CSS Chicora. Confederate. Ironclad sloop ram, 3,500 tons. Length 172 feet 6 inches overall or 150 feet, beam 34 or 35 feet, depth 14 feet, draft 12 feet. Complement of 150, with two 9-inch Dahlgrens and four 32-pounders (another source—two 9-inch smoothbore shell guns and two 6-inch Brooke rifled guns). Launched in 1862 at Charleston, S.C. Stripped, burned, and blown up by Confederates on February 18, 1865, in Charleston Harbor up the Cooper River below Drum's Island off Marshall's Wharf. A few inches of casemate were visible at low tide. Part of the wreck was removed to a mean low-water depth of 12 feet by Benjamin Maillefert for the U.S. Army Corps of Engineers in 1872. In 1929 the U.S. Army Corps of Engineers' dredge hit part of the remaining wreck while dredging. Probably was completely removed by dredging. (*ORN*, 16:372, 459; ser. 2, 1:250; *Chief of Engineers Report 1873*, 651–52; Miller, *Photographic History*, 6:239; Porter, *Naval History*, 765; *WCWN*, 205; Moore, *Lowcountry Engineers*, 31, 61.)

CSS Columbia. Confederate. Screw ram, 3,500 tons. Length 189 or 216 feet or 218 feet overall, casemate length 75 or 65 feet; beam 51 feet 2–4 inches or 49 feet; depth 13 feet or 13 feet 6 inches; draft 15 feet or 13 feet 6 inches; armor 6-inch iron; 3 propellers. Complement of fifty and pierced for eight or six guns. The newly launched vessel was wrecked accidentally on rocks or a sunken wreck and broke its back near Fort Moultrie on January 12, 1865. The guns and some armor plating were removed. Was raised and repaired by Union forces on April 26, 1865. Was towed to Hampton Roads by the USS *Vanderbilt* on May 25, 1865.

(*OR*, 35:2:288; *ORN*, 16:372; ser. 2, 1:251; *CWC*, 6-214; Porter, *Naval History*, 765; Ammen, "Navy in the Civil War," *Confederate Military History*, 156–57; *WCWN*, 208.)

Constance Decima (Constance). British. Side-wheel steamer, 345 bulk tons, 163 registered tons, 140 tons. Length 201 feet 5 inches, beam 20 feet 2 inches, depth 9 feet 5 inches, draft 6 feet. Crew of twenty-nine. Cargo of weapons and possibly some gold to buy cotton. En route from Nova Scotia for Charleston. Hit the wreck of the *Georgiana* and sank on October 6, 1864, a mile out and 2 miles east of Breach Inlet in 15 feet to 35 fathoms of water, 640–80 yards from the site of the wrecks of the *Georgiana* and *Mary Bowers*. Lee Spence dived on and identified the wreck in 1967. (*ORN*, 16:8, 9; Horner, *Blockade-Runners*, 228; Spence, "Civil War Shipwrecks," 37–38; *LLC*, 294; Spence, *List*, 657.)

Courier. Union. Whaling ship, 381 tons. Draft 16 feet. Built in 1817 in New York City. Out of New Bedford, Mass. Part of the First Stone Fleet. Scuttled with 360 tons of stone 3 miles southeast of Morris Island in the Main Channel on December 19–20, 1861. (*ORN*, 12:418; ser. 2, 1:67; *DANFS*, 5:430, 433; Spence, *List*, 712.)

USS Dai Ching. Union. Three-masted screw steam gunboat, 520 bulk tons, 729 tons. Length 170.5 feet or 175 feet 2 inches, beam 29 feet 4–8 inches, depth 11 feet or 14 feet 10 inches, draft 9.5 feet, maximum speed 6 knots, average speed 4 knots. Complement of eighty-three, with four 24-pounder smoothbores, two 20-pounder Parrotts, and one 100-pounder Parrott rifle. Built in 1862 at New York City for China. Grounded in the Combahee River on January 26, 1865, near a three-gun Confederate battery, while en route to Tar Bluff. The pilot left the wheel and went below as the shelling started. It was shelled for seven hours, while the tug USS *Clover* parted a line trying to pull the vessel off then offered no further assistance. The USS *Dai Ching* had three officers and six men wounded. As the tide fell, the vessel settled so only the 100-pounder Parrott rifle could return fire. At 3:00 p.m. the 100-pounder Parrott rifle was put out of action. Hit thirty times, with its guns disabled and machinery wrecked. Set afire, and four or five crewmen were captured by Confederates, but the rest reached the USS *Clover*. Was removed in 1906 by the U.S. Navy. A marsh island, Gunboat Island, later formed at the wreck site. (*OR*, 47:2:151, 156; *ORN*, 16:198–200, 215; ser. 2, 1:70; Tower, "*Dai Ching*," *Skin Diver*, 54–57, 68–69; Ammen, "Navy in the Civil War," *Confederate Military History*, 155; *WCWN*, 88; Spence, *List*, 668–69.)

Davids Nos. 1 to 5, 7, 8. Confederate. Torpedo boats. Length 60 feet. Length with torpedo spar 64 feet, beam 5 feet 6 inches, speed 5 knots. Built in 1863–65 in Charleston, S.C. Scuttled by Confederates at the end of the war in Charleston Harbor. Three Davids were raised from the Cooper River, repaired, and removed after the Union occupation of Charleston. One went to the U.S. Military Academy. A second was shipped aboard the USS *Mingoe* and lost off Cape Hatteras. The third was called the *Midge*, had a length of 30 feet, beam of 12 feet, and was built in 1864 at Charleston, S.C. The *Midge* was sent to the Brooklyn Navy Yard but was later broken up. (*ORN*, 16:339, 344, 387; *WCWN*, 219; Spence, *List*, 26; Perry, *Infernal Machines*, 170–72.)

Dove. Union. Whaling bark, 146 or 151 tons. Built at Newbury, Mass. Part of the Second Stone Fleet. Scuttled by the Union on January 25–26, 1862, in Maffitt's Channel, Charleston Harbor. (*ORN*, 12:510; ser. 2, 1:75; *DANFS*, 5:432, 436; Spence, *List*, 712–13.)

CSS Eagle. Confederate. Receiving ship. Scuttled February 17–18, 1865, at the foot of Tradd Street in Charleston. (Moore, *Lowcountry Engineers*, 61.)

Edisto. Confederate. Sloop. Cargo of sixteen hundred bushels of rice. Was sunk by boats from the USS *Restless* in Bull's Bay on February 14, 1862. (*ORN*, 12:547–50.)

Edwin. Schooner. Cargo of sundries. En route to Charleston from Nassau, Bahamas. Was run ashore by the USS *Alabama* near a battery near Lighthouse Inlet on Morris Island, on May 8, 1862. Some cargo was carried ashore by Col. L. M. Hatch's Coast Rangers on Morris Island. (*ORN*, 12:800–801; Spence, *List*, 623.)

Elizabeth. Confederate. Schooner. Cargo of eighteen hundred bushels of rice. Was sunk by boats from the USS *Restless* on February 14, 1862, at Bull's Bay. (*ORN*, 12:547–50.)

Empire. Union. Brig. Partly loaded with cotton. Was lost on the North Edisto bar on March 26, 1862. (*ORN*, 12:676.)

CSS Etiwan (Etowan) (Ettiwan) (St. Helena). Confederate. Side-wheel steamer, 132 tons. Built in 1834 at Charleston, S.C. A torpedo drifted from its moorings in the ship channel in Charleston Harbor and exploded against the CSS *Etiwan* on April 4 (or 6 or 7), 1863, and was run ashore near Fort Johnson. Raised and later wrecked on June 7, 1864, in Charleston Harbor off Fort Johnson. Raised and refitted by the U.S. Army. Employed by the Quartermaster Department to help clear Charleston Harbor of wrecks and obstacles. Became the *St. Helena* in 1867. (*ORN*, 13:823; 16:388, 412; Scharf, *History of the Confederate Navy*, 757; *CWC*, 6-225; Perry, *Infernal Machines*, 52; Spence, *List*, 636.)

Faith. Union. Bark. Cargo of 500 tons of coal for the Union Charleston Squadron. Out of Philadelphia. Ran ashore and bilged off Port Royal inside Martin's Industry on August 8, 1863. (*ORN*, 14:431; 27:526–29.)

Fannie Lehr (Burnside). U.S. Side-wheel steamer, 306 or 435 tons. Length 130 feet, beam 22.5 feet, depth 8 feet. Built in 1863 at Baltimore. Formerly the Union Quartermaster Department vessel *Burnside*. Ran into a snag and was beached 5 miles above Purrysburg on November 19, 1865. Raised by the Coast Wrecking Company of New York. (*MSV*, 70; Spence, *List*, 680–81.)

Flamingo. Confederate. Three-stacked, 2-mast, sloop rigged, side-wheel steamer, 283, 284, or 446 tons. Length 270 feet, beam 24 feet, draft 7 feet, speed 15–16 knots. Crew of 45–50. Built in 1864 at Govan, Scotland. Ran aground on October 23, 1864, between Bowman's Jetty and Drunken Dick Shoal off Sullivan's Island near Battery Rutledge in Charleston Harbor. Does not appear to have sank. Was running the blockade in 1865 and survived the Civil War. (*ORN*, 10:476; *CWC*, 6-227, 342; *WCWN*, 222; *LLC*, 299; Spence, *List*, 658.)

Flora (Anna). British. Iron side-wheel steamer, 437 tons. Length 200+ feet. Crew of thirty-nine. Assorted cargo. Made thirteen successful runs through the Union blockade. Ran aground while being chased by Union picket launches and the USS *Wamsutta* on the night of October 22, 1864. Was grounded opposite Battery Rutledge on Drunken Dick Shoal, on the south side of Maffitt's Channel off Fort Moultrie, 2,700 yards from Fort Putnam, 2,600 yards from Battery Chatfield, and 3,500 yards from Fort Strong. Was shelled by Union monitors and the Morris Island batteries. Hit by at least ninety-eight shells. (*ORN,* 16:29–32, 34, 37, 357; Horner, *Blockade-Runners,* 226; *CWC,* 6-343; *LLC,* 300; Spence, *List,* 657.)

Fortune. Union. Whaling bark, 291–92 or 310 tons. Draft 14 feet. Built in 1822 at Amesbury, Mass. Out of New London, Conn. Flagship of the New London part of the First Stone Fleet. Scuttled off Morris Island in the Main Channel of Charleston Harbor on December 19–20, 1861. (*ORN,* 12:418, 421; *DANFS,* 5:430–33; Spence, *List,* 713.)

CSS General Clinch (Clinch). Confederate. Side-wheel steamer, 256 bulk tons. Length 131 feet, beam 24 feet, depth 8 feet 7 inches. Armed with two brass guns. Built in 1839 in Charleston, S.C. Acquired by South Carolina in 1861. Sank in Charleston Harbor and was probably raised before October 1864. Was converted to a blockade-runner. Was run into Nassau, Bahamas, on November 3, 1864. Spent the rest of the Civil War there. (*CWC,* 6-232–33; *LLC,* 301; *MSV,* 80.)

George Chisholm (Chisholm). Schooner. Destroyed by Union forces at Murrell's Inlet on April 26, 1863. (Spence, *List,* 640; *MSV,* 85.)

George Washington. Confederate. Schooner. Cargo of thirty-two hundred bushels of rice, fifty bushels of corn, and twenty bushels of rice meal. Was captured on March 27, 1862, by boats from the USS *Restless* near the Cape Romain Light and the Santee River in Bull's Bay. Was scuttled and set afire by the Union sailors. (*ORN,* 12:666–68.)

George Washington. Union. Army-chartered side-wheel transport steamer, 243 tons. Armed with two 24-pounder brass howitzers and one 20-pounder James rifle foreword. Built in 1851 at New York City. Manned by thirty-four men and four officers in Company A, 3rd R. I. Artillery. Grounded and ambushed on April 9, 1863, by two guns from the Nelson Light Artillery and four guns of the Beaufort Volunteer Artillery, supported by six companies of the 48th N.C. Infantry Regiment and part of the 11th S.C. Infantry Regiment in the Coosaw River, one mile east of the Port Royal Ferry near Chisolm's Island. Hit in the rudder and a shell exploded in the magazine. Burned to the waterline. Sank in 4 feet of water at the edge of a marsh about 500 yards from shore, above a brickyard at Brickyard Point. A white flag was raised. Abandoned by the crew and Union soldiers after losing two killed, ten wounded, and two missing. The Confederates raised one 24-pounder howitzer, several Enfield rifle muskets, a bell, and an anchor. Union forces later salvaged the other 24-pounder howitzer. (*OR,* 14:280–86; 53:4–5; *ORN,* 14:115–19; *MSV,* 84, 264; Higginson, *Army Life in a Black Regiment,* 142–43.)

George W. Coffee. Confederate. Side-wheel steam ferry, 177 tons. Built in 1848 at Jersey City, N.J. Operated at Mount Pleasant. Sunk on October 29, 1861, by possible Union sympathizers. Was later raised with the aid of a steam pump. (*MSV,* 85; Spence, *List,* 608.)

Georgiana (Louisiana). Confederate. Brig-rigged screw steamer, 519 gross tons, 407 registered tons, 580 tons. Length 205 feet 7 inches, beam 25 feet 2 inches, depth 14 feet 11 inches, draft 14 feet. Carried 140 people. Large cargo of merchandise, ammunition, two Whitworth rifled cannons, four rifled Blakely cannons, ten to fourteen other cannons, ten thousand Enfield rifle muskets, swords, and military supplies, along with $90,000 in gold on the ship's account. Built in 1862 at Glasgow, Scotland, as the *Louisiana.* Spotted by the USS *America* and chased by the USS *Wissahickon* in Maffitt's Channel. The *Georgiana* was commanded by British Royal Navy captain A. B. Davidison, who was acting in a civilian capacity although still on half-pay in the Royal Navy. Captain Davidison flashed a white flag to surrender to the Union ship and then dashed ashore at full speed, running aground on the early morning of March 19, 1863. The crew and passengers escaped. Sailors from the USS *Wissahickon* boarded the *Georgiana* but could not refloat it. After removing cargo at daylight, it was set afire. It burned for several days with numerous explosions. Located 3.5 miles east of Breach Inlet at latitude 32° 49.5' north, longitude 79° 49.9' west, a mile from shore off the Isle of Palms in 14 feet of water. The blockade-runners *Norseman, Mary Bowers,* and *Constance Decima* all hit the wreck of the *Georgiana* and subsequently sank. May have been partially salvaged in the 1870s. E. Lee Spence recorded the site in January 1968. A number of groups under the supervision of the State Archaeologist and the Institute of Archeology and Anthropology of the University of South Carolina excavated thousands of items from the wreck. In recent years divers have recovered two 2.9-inch guns, Blakely shells, bullets, china, and other items. The recovered guns are now at the Fort Jackson Museum at Columbia, S.C. The boiler is only 5 feet below the water surface. Part of the cargo was probably washed away by currents. (*ORN*, 13:772–73; *CWC*, 6-240–41; Spence, "Civil War Shipwrecks," *Argosy Treasure Hunting 77 Annual,* 35–37; Rooney, "Wreck of the Georgiana," *Skin Diver,* 80–87; Spence, "South Carolina's Fabulous Underwater Treasures," *Treasure,* 75–77; Horner, *Blockade-Runners,* 207–9; Spence, *List,* 47–55, 634–35, 722–36; *LLC,* 111–12, 302.)

Golden Liner. British. Large schooner. Cargo of flour, brandy, sugar, and coffee. Out of Halifax, Nova Scotia. Was captured and burned by the USS *Monticello* and boats from the USS *Matthew Vassar* at Murrell's Inlet on April 27, 1863. (*ORN*, 8:828–29; 14:191; *LLC,* 302; Spence, *List,* 640.)

Governor. Union. Side-wheel steamer, 644 tons. Carried Maj. John G. Reynolds and the Union Marine Battalion of 385 men among its 650 passengers. Cargo of 19,000 rounds of ammunition. Built in 1846 at New York City. En route to Port Royal, S.C., from the north. Lost its bracing in a storm at 11:00 a.m. on November 1, 1861, then lost its rudder. Its smokestack overturned while it was being towed by the USS *Isaac Smith* on November 2–3, 1861. The USS *Sabine* saved 10,000 rounds of ammunition and rescued all the passengers and crew, except for 6 who fell into the water while leaping between the vessels. The bark *Young Rover* was standing by to assist. Has been heavily salvaged by divers. (*ORN*, 12:232–46; *New York Times,* November 12, 1861; *MSV,* 87, 263; Miller, *Civil War Sea Battles,* 40–46.)

Governor Milton. Union. Tug. Armed with two 12-pounder Armstrong rifled guns. Manned by a section of the 1st Conn. Battery and a squad of the 1st S.C. Colored Infantry Regiment (later became the 33rd U.S. Colored Regiment) under Maj. John D. Strong. Was disabled on July 10, 1864, on the South Edisto River while trying to burn the railroad bridge of the Charleston & Savannah Railway. With the *Enoch Dean* and *John Adams.* The expedition halted at the mouth of the river at a line of piles near Will Town (Wiltown), about 20 miles from the sea. The *Governor Milton's* guns were thrown overboard and the vessel burned. The guns were later salvaged by the Confederates and used in defense of Charleston Harbor, where the 33rd U.S. Colored Infantry later recovered them from a Confederate fort on James Island. (*ORN*, 13:359–61, 364, 366; Higginson, *Army Life in a Black Regiment,* 165–75; Spence, *List,* 630.)

Governor Troup. U.S. Wooden side-wheel steamer, 155 tons. Length 122 feet 6 inches, beam 25 feet, depth 5 feet 6 inches. Carried more than two hundred crewmen and passengers. Cargo of three hundred bales of cotton. Built in 1859 at Dublin, Ga. Ran into the South Carolina bank of the Savannah River below Augusta, Ga., with forty killed and the mail lost, on May 29, 1865. (*OR,* 47:3:633; *MSV,* 88, 265; Spence, *List,* 675–76.)

USS Harvest Moon. Union. Side-wheel steam gunboat, 546 tons. Length 193 feet, beam 29 feet, depth 10 feet, draft 8 feet, maximum speed 15 miles per hour, average speed 9 miles per hour. Armed with one 20-pounder Parrott, four 24-pounder howitzers, and one 12-pounder rifled gun. Built in 1862–63 at Portland, Maine. Rear Adm. John Dahlgren's flagship. Sank in Winyah Bay in the Swash Channel about 3 miles southeast of Battery White in 2.5 fathoms of water in five minutes by a torpedo that blew up between the main hatch and wardroom bulkhead on March 1, 1865. One crewman was killed, and Rear Adm. Dahlgren saw the bulkheads of his quarters collapse. The crew was removed to the USS *Nipsic.* Was stripped of the valuable machinery and abandoned on April 20, 1865. The State of South Carolina had plans to raise the vessel as a Civil War monument. (*ORN*, 16:282–84; ser. 2, 1:99; *CWC,* 6-365.)

Helen (Juno). Confederate. Steamer, 185 registered tons. Cargo of cotton. Built in 1860 at Glasgow, Scotland. En route from Charleston to Nassau, Bahamas. Used as a Confederate gunboat until March 1864. Was lost in a gale on Bowman Jetty on March 10, 1864, with all but one lost. Was removed from Bowman Jetty in 1873 by Benjamin Maillefert for the U.S. Army Corps of Engineers. (*ORN,* 9:802; ser. 2, 2:745; *Chief of Engineers Report 1874, 4; LLC,* 306; Spence, *List,* 651.)

Herald. Union. Whaling ship, 274 tons. Draft 15 feet. Built in 1807 at Salem, Mass. Out of New Bedford, Mass. Was scuttled with 240 tons of stone as part of the First Stone Fleet off Morris Island, Charleston Harbor, on December 19–20, 1861. (*ORN,* 12:418, 421; ser. 2, 1:101; *DANFS,* 5:430, 433; Spence, *List,* 715–16.)

CSS H. L. Hunley. Confederate. Submarine, 7.5 tons. Length 39 feet 6 inches, beam 3 feet 10-inch, speed 2.5–4 miles per hour, depth 4 feet 3-inch. Complement of eight. Built from steam boilers in the spring of 1863 at Mobile. Taken by rail to Charleston, S.C. Five crewmen drowned in Charleston Harbor on August 29, 1863, off James Island at the Fort Johnson wharf when it accidentally submerged with its hatches open in 42 feet of water. Was quickly raised. Horace L. Hunley and seven crewmen drowned when human error and mechanical defects caused the submarine to sink during another trial run in 56 feet of water on October 15, 1863, in Charleston Harbor. Raised and called the "Iron Coffin" because of its sinkings with loss of crews. It was the first submarine to sink an enemy warship in battle. On February 17, 1864, the CSS *H. L. Hunley* rammed a spar torpedo into the USS *Housatonic* and sank the Union warship. The CSS *H. L. Hunley* sank on the way back to Charleston with its commander, Lt. George E. Dixon of the 21st Ala. Volunteer Regiment, and its crew.

Some mistakenly believed the submarine jammed the nose into the hole made by the torpedo and sank. Union sailors dragged the area for 500 yards around the USS *Housatonic* but failed to find the CSS *H. L. Hunley.* After the war some erroneous report said it was about 100 feet from the USS *Housatonic,* with bow toward the USS *Housatonic.* Probably sank due to the hatch being open on its trip back to Charleston when a large wave hit. Originally thought by some to have been removed by Benjamin Maillefert for the U.S. Army Corps of Engineers along with the USS *Housatonic* in 1872–73. P. T. Barnum offered $100,000 for the recovery of the submarine. Searches were made for the vessel in 1876. Clive Cussler's National Underwater and Marine Association (NUMA) with the University of South Carolina and the Institute of Archaeology and Anthropology discovered the vessel in Maffitt's Channel on May 3, 1995, off Sullivan's Island after years of searching. The submarine was in 28 feet of water with 3 feet of silt over it. It was tilted at a 45° angle about 4 miles outside of Charleston. There was some controversy regarding its prior discovery by E. Lee Spence. On June 13, 2000, divers recovered the vessel's 17-foot long iron pole, which had carried its torpedo. Raised on August 7, 2000, amid much fanfare by the work boat *Karlissa B.* Straps were used to lift the vessel out of the mud. The South Carolina Institute of Archaeology and Anthropology, the U.S. National Park Service, and the nonprofit Friends of the *Hunley* were involved. About $17 million from public donations, the State of South Carolina, U.S. Department of Defense, and others were used to recover and restore the submarine. Hauled into Charleston to a lab in the old U.S. Navy Yard at the Warren Lasch Conservation Center. The submarine was conserved, explored, and the crewmen's remains were removed in 2001. Among the items recovered was Lt. George E. Dixon's lucky 1860 $20 gold piece, which had been given to him by his girlfriend, Queenie Bennett of Mobile. The gold piece had deflected a bullet at the Battle of Shiloh and probably saved Dixon's life. A Union dog tag from Ezra Chamberlin of the 7th Conn. Regiment was also found in the submarine. Many had toured the sub in the lab, and a permanent exhibition will be set up. The recovered crew was buried amid much ceremony. (*ORN,* 15:334–38; *Chief of Engineers Report 1873,* 68, 731; Scharf, *History of the Confederate Navy,* 761; *CWC,* 6-244–46; Shugg, "Prophet of the Deep: The *H. L. Hunley,*" *Civil War Times Illustrated,* 4–10, 44–47; Keatts and Farr, *Dive into History,* 26–34; Spence, *List,* 56–60; Wilkinson, "Peripatetic Coffin: Civil War Submarine," *Ocean,* 13–17; Cussler and Dirgo, *Sea Hunters,* 185–221; Chase, "In Search of the CSS *Hunley,*" *Blue & Gray Magazine,* 24–26,

28; Shipwrecks.com Web site, Hunley rebuttal; S.C. Institute of Archaeology and Anthropology, "*Hunley* Update," Web site; Naval Historical Center, "*H. L. Hunley*," Web site; Civil War @ Charleston Web site, "C.S.S. *Hunley* Submarine Recovery Information.")

USS *Housatonic.* Union. Steam sloop-of-war, 1,240 tons. Length 207 feet, beam 38 feet, draft 9 feet 7 inches. Complement of 160, with one 100-pounder Parrott rifle, three 30-pounder Parrotts, one 11-inch Dahlgren smoothbore, four 32-pounders, and one 12-pounder. Laid down in 1861 at the Boston Navy Yard. Was sunk by the Confederate submarine CSS *H. L. Hunley* on February 17, 1864, when rammed by a spar torpedo below the water line, forward of the mizzenmast. Sunk in 27 feet of water in four minutes stern first, upright, with the spar deck 15 feet underwater at latitude 32° 43.1' north, longitude 79° 46.5' west, 5.5 miles east southeast of Fort Sumter, off Breach Inlet, with five crewmen lost. The surviving crewmen climbed up the ship's rigging and were rescued by Union ships. Divers examined the wreck on February 20, 1864, and reported part of the spar deck blown off. The Union divers reported that the guns and other equipment could be recovered by a derrick boat and divers. Union divers again examined the wreck in November 1864 and reported the vessel had settled in 5 feet of sand, with mud and sand forming around the vessel. The cabin and bulkheads aft and the mainmast were demolished, and the propeller shaft was broken. Mostly removed by Benjamin Maillefert in 1873–74 under a contract with the U.S. Army Corps of Engineers. One of the vessel's salvaged boilers was moved to Charleston. Removed to within a 20.5 feet mean low-water depth. In 1908 William Virden salvaged about four tons of iron from the wreck for the U.S. Army Corps of Engineers. E. Lee Spence reported locating the wreck in November 1970. Remains reported to include the hull and a boiler were located by a survey funded by Clive Cussler in the summers of 1980 and 1981. Additional remote sensing was done in 1996. Buried in 4 to 8 feet of sediment. Test excavations and recovery of some small artifacts were made in 1999 by the National Park Service, National Historical Center, and South Carolina Institute of Archaeology and Anthropology, along with the U.S. Geological Survey, Coastal Carolina University, and the South Carolina Department of Natural Resources. (*ORN*, 15:327–38; 16:427; ser. 2, 1:104; *Chief of Engineers Report 1872*, 652; *Chief of Engineers Report 1873*, 727–28; Bass, *Ships and Shipwrecks of the Americas*, 227, 230; Spence, *List*, 652; Cussler and Dirgo, *Sea Hunters*, 196, 209; National Park Service Submerged Resources Web site.)

Huntress. Confederate. Ship. Was sunk by Confederates to block Skull Creek on November 6, 1861. (Spence, *List*, 612.)

CSS *Indian Chief.* Confederate. Schooner receiving ship. Involved in torpedo operations. Burned by the Confederates before the evacuation of Charleston on February 18, 1865, in Town Creek in Charleston Harbor. Removed with dynamite and a clamshell bucket during 1929 dredging operations. (*ORN*, ser. 2, 1:257; *CWC*, 6-251; Moore, *Lowcountry Engineers*, 61.)

John Randolph. Confederate. Transport, 122, 155, or 177 tons. Length 100 or 108 feet, beam 22 feet, depth 7–9 feet, draft 2 feet 9 inches. Built at Birkenhead, England. Sent in pieces to Savannah, where the vessel was assembled in 1834. Wrecked on Sullivan's Island on January 20, 1865. (Spence, *List*, 667–68.)

Joseph. Confederate. Brig. Burned by Confederates in the Waccamaw River when Union gunboats were near Georgetown on May 21–22, 1862. (Spence, *List*, 623.)

Jubilee. Union. Merchantman bark, 233 tons. Out of Portland, Maine. Scuttled with stone. Part of the Second Stone Fleet in Maffitt's Channel near Sullivan's Island, Charleston Harbor, on January 25–26, 1862. (*ORN*, 12:511; ser. 2, 1:257; *DANFS*, 5:432, 436.)

Kate. Nationality unknown. Schooner. Was run ashore by the USS *Augusta*. Shelled in a storm by the USS *Pocahontas* and the pilot boat *Blunt* near Breach Inlet under Battery Beauregard at the east end of Sullivan's Island on May 25, 1862. The cargo was landed by Confederates who waded to the vessel at low tide. (*ORN*, 13:30–32, 38–39, 44–45.)

Kensington. Union. Ship, 357 or 400 tons. Draft 15 feet. Out of New Bedford, Mass. Part of the First Stone Fleet. Scuttled with 350 tons of stones about 3 miles southeast of Morris Island in the Main Channel, Charleston Harbor, on December 19–20, 1861. (*ORN*, 12:421; ser. 2, 1:119; *DANFS*, 5:430, 433; Spence, *List*, 716; Cussler and Dirgo, *Sea Hunters II*, 160–62, 164.)

USS *Keokuk* (*Moodna*). Union. Tower ironclad, 677 tons. Length 159 feet 6 inches, beam 36 feet, depth 13 feet 6 inches. Complement of ninety-two, with two 11-inch guns. Built at New York City as the *Moodna* and launched on December 6, 1862. Hit ninety times by Confederate shells with nineteen hits at or below the water line on April 7, 1863, while attacking Confederate forts in Charleston Harbor. Was sunk the next morning off Fort Shaw, 1,300 yards off the south end of Morris Island in 13 feet of water outside the bar, with no loss of life. The vessel's smokestacks and casemate were above water. At high tide the vessel was in 18 feet of water. The casemate tops were unbolted and removed by Confederates at night, and the two guns along with Union flags and three officer swords were salvaged in April and early May 1863. One gun went to Fort Sumter and much of the salvaged equipment went to the CSS *Chicora*. One gun is now mounted in the White Point Gardens at the Charleston Battery. Removed to 15 feet depth by Benjamin Maillefert in 1873–74 for the U.S. Army Corps of Engineers. E. Lee Spence reported locating the vessel with a magnetometer in 1971. In 1981 Clive Cussler found the wreck under 4–6 feet of mud off the old Morris Island Lighthouse. A 2001 resurvey of the site found 6 feet of silt in 16 feet of water over about 130 feet of vessel. (*ORN*, 14:106–10, 242–43; ser. 2, 1:120; *Chief of Engineers Report 1873*, 68, 727–28; *Chief of Engineers Report 1874*, 4; Cussler and Dirgo, *Sea Hunters*, 207; Spence, *List*, 637.)

USS *Kingfisher*. Union. Wooden sailing bark, 451 tons. Length 121 feet 4 inches, beam 28 feet 8 inches, depth 14 feet 4 inches. Complement of ninety-seven, with four 8-inch Dahlgren smoothbores, one 20-pounder rifle, and one light 12-pounder. Built in 1857 at Fairhaven, Maine. Ran aground March 28, 1864, on a shoal on the Combahee Bank in St. Helena Sound near the south end of Otter Island, 600–800 yards from a buoy in 2–3 fathoms. One report said it was located off the southeastern point of Otter Island. Took on water and keeled over so the star-

board guns were underwater. Was abandoned on April 5, 1864. The *Mountain Home*, USS *O. M. Petit*, USS *Oleander*, and USS *Dai Ching* salvaged the vessel's guns and stores. (*ORN*, 15:383–88; *DANFS*, 3:651; *WCWN*, 142.)

CSS *Lady Davis* (CSS *Gray*) (*James Gray*). Confederate. Screw steamer. Built in 1858 at Philadelphia. Was sunk with the *Huntress* and other light boats to block Skull Creek on November 6, 1861. Its engine was put in the ironclad CSS *Palmetto State*. Was probably raised and captured as a hulk in February 18, 1865. (*ORN*, ser. 2, 1:255, 258; Spence, *List*, 612; *MSV*, 108.)

L. C. *Richmond*. Union. Ship, 341, 350, or 383 tons. Draft 15 feet. Built in 1834 at Bristol, Conn. Out of New Bedford, Mass. Part of the First Stone Fleet. Scuttled with 300 tons of stones in the Main Channel about 3 miles southeast of Morris Island, Charleston Harbor, on December 19–20, 1861. (*ORN*, 12:418, 421; ser. 2, 1:123; *DANFS*, 5:430, 433; Spence, *List*, 717.)

Leonidas. Union. Bark, 231 or 320 tons. Draft 12 feet. Built in 1806 or 1826 at Scituate (Charlestown), Mass. Out of New Bedford, Mass. Part of the First Stone Fleet. Scuttled with 200 tons of stone about 3 miles southeast of Morris Island on December 19–20, 1861. (*ORN*, 12:418, 421; ser. 2, 1:126; *DANFS*, 5:430, 433; Spence, *List*, 716.)

Liverpool. British. Blockade-runner, 150–80 tons. Out of Nassau, New Providence, Bahamas. Ran ashore on April 10, 1862, outside the point of North Inlet, and set afire. The USS *Keystone* found the wreck. (*ORN*, 12:676–77, 679.)

Lotus. Union. Schooner. Crew of five and four passengers. Cargo of sutler's stores and a shipment by Adams Express Company. Out of Boston. En route from New York City for Port Royal, S.C. Ran ashore the night of January 15, 1865, on North Shore Beach, near Winyah Bay. While the USS *Sebago* was trying to refloat the vessel, it was driven farther onto the beach. Part of the cargo was thrown overboard; the rest was saved. (*ORN*, 13:512–13, 657.)

Majestic. Union, Ship, 297 tons. Out of New Bedford, Mass. Part of the Second Stone Fleet. Was scuttled in Maffitt's Channel, Charleston Harbor, on January 25–26, 1862. (*ORN*, 12:511; ser. 2, 1:132; *DANFS*, 5:436.)

Manigault. Confederate. Steam scow. At a partially constructed Confederate battery at Vincent's Creek on Morris Island or James Island. Hit by Union shells, with one killed and the boiler damaged on July 12, 1863. Was burned by Union forces the next day. (*OR*, 28:1:371, 577; *ORN*, 14:719; *Charleston Mercury*, July 25, 1863.)

Marcia. Union. Merchant bark, 343 tons. Out of Portland, Maine. Part of the Charleston Stone Fleet. Struck bottom and sank while crossing Port Royal Bar on January 7, 1862. (*ORN*, ser. 2, 1:134; *DANFS*, 5:432, 435.)

Margaret Scott. Union. Bark, 330 tons. Out of New Bedford, Mass. Part of the Second Stone Fleet. Scuttled in Maffitt's Channel, Charleston Harbor, on January 25–26, 1862. (*ORN*, 12:511; ser. 2, 1:135; *DANFS*, 5:432, 436.)

Maria Theresa. Union. Whaling ship, 330 tons. Draft 16 feet. Built in 1807 at New York City. Out of New Bedford, Mass. Part of the First Stone Fleet. Was scuttled with 320 tons of stone in the Main Ship Channel at Charleston, southeast of Morris Island, on December 19–20, 1861. (*ORN*, 12:418, 421; ser. 2, 1:135; *DANFS*, 5:430, 433; Spence, *List*, 718.)

CSS Marion. Confederate. Side-wheel transport steamer, 258 tons. Length 132 feet, beam 30 feet, depth 7 feet 2 inches. Built in 1850 at Charleston, S.C. Drifted onto a torpedo it had earlier positioned, and the bottom of its hull blew out. Sank in thirty seconds on the night of April 6, 1863, off Charleston in 30 feet of water at the mouth of the Ashley River near the mouth of Wappoo Creek. Capt. John Flyor was killed, and the ship's machinery was destroyed. (*ORN*, 16:402; *CWC*, 6-268; *MSV*, 137; Perry, *Infernal Machines*, 52; Scharf, *History of the Confederate Navy*, 757; Spence, *List*, 635.)

Mary Bowers. British. Iron side-wheel steamer, 750 bulk tons, 220 registered tons, 500 or 680 tons. Length 211 feet, beam 25 feet, depth 10 feet 6 inches. Crew of fifty. Cargo of coal and assorted merchandise. Built in Renfrew, Scotland. Out of Bermuda on its second voyage. Struck the wreck of the *Georgiana* on August 30 or September 1, 1864, and sank on top of the wreck. One fourteen- to sixteen-year old boy was left aboard and was later taken off by Union boarders, along with two dredge anchors, a binnacle, compasses, signal flags, and some liquor. The vessel sank three to 4 miles from shore off Isle of Palms, east of Breach Inlet. The sides of the ship flattened and the cargo washed outside of the ship. Originally the boiler was within 3.5 feet of the surface. Now at a depth of 14 feet. There has been salvage by divers. (*ORN*, 15:658–59; 16:8, 34, 37; *LLC*, 312; Spence, "Civil War Wrecks," *Argosy Treasure Hunting 77 Annual*. 37–38; Horner, *Blockade-Runners*, 223; Spence, *List*, 656.)

Mary Louisa (*Mary Louise*). Confederate. Sloop. Cargo of two thousand bushels of rice and one hundred bushels of corn. Captured on the Santee River near Cape Romain by boats from the USS *Restless* on March 27, 1862, and set afire. (*ORN*, 12:666–68.)

Mechanic. Union. Whaling ship, 335 tons. Out of Newport, R.I. Part of the Second Stone Fleet. Was scuttled in Maffitt's Channel, Charleston Harbor, on January 25–26, 1862. (*ORN*, 12:510; ser. 2, 1:140; *DANFS*, 5:432, 436.)

Messenger. Union. Whaling bark, 216 tons. Out of Salem, Mass. Part of the Second Stone Fleet. Scuttled in Maffitt's Channel, Charleston Harbor, on January 25–26, 1862. (*ORN*, 12:510; ser. 2, 1:142; *DANFS*, 5:432, 436.)

Minho. British. Iron screw steamer, 400 gross tons, 253 registered tons. Length 175 feet or 175 feet 3 inches, beam 22 feet, depth 13 feet 6 inches. Cargo of rifle muskets and swords. Built in 1854 at Paisley, Scotland. Made four successful trips through the blockade before running aground on the night of October 20, 1862, on a wreck on Drunken Dick Shoal while being chased by the USS *Flambeau*. Rolled over on its side. Part of the cargo was removed by Confederates, including 43 cases of rifles and 518 cavalry swords. In 1865 Union divers reported the wreck sanded in. Part of the wreck was probably removed by the U.S. Army Corps of Engineers in 1875, near the wrecks of the CSS *Stono* and *Prince Albert*. E. Lee Spence located the wreck in 1965 and 1966 at Bowman's Jetty. Howard Tower, Larry Tipping, and Mike Zafoot excavated the wreck under a license from South Carolina. Thousands of Enfield bullets, several large boxes of Enfield rifle muskets and swords, along with thousands of percussion caps were recovered. (*ORN*, 13:395–97; 16:354; *Chief of Engineers Report*

1875, 2:28; Tower, "Civil War Wreck Salvaged," *Treasure Found*, 28–33, 61; Boyd, "Wreck Facts," *Skin Diver*, 43–44; *LLC*, 312; Spence, *List*, 624.)

Nellie (Nelly) (Governor Dudley) (Catawba). Confederate. Wooden hull side-wheel steamer. Length 177 feet, beam 24 feet, depth 10 feet. Cargo of medicines and merchandise. Built in 1838 at Wilmington, Del. En route from Nassau, Bahamas. Was fired at by a Union schooner on May 25, 1862, off Dewee Island and run ashore on the south end of North Island or the Isle of Palms. Most of the cargo and the machinery were saved, as the vessel was high and dry at low tide. The vessel's owners sold it for $1,700. (*ORN*, 13:142; *LLC*, 313.)

Newburyport. Union. Whaling ship, 341 tons. Out of Gloucester, Mass. Part of the Second Stone Fleet. Scuttled with stone in Maffitt's Channel, Charleston Harbor, on January 25–26, 1862. (*ORN*, 12:510; ser. 2, 1:158; *DANFS*, 5:432, 436.)

New England. Union. Whaling ship, 336 or 368 tons. Out of New London, Conn. Part of the Second Stone Fleet. Scuttled with stone in Maffitt's Channel, Charleston Harbor, on January 25–26, 1862. (*ORN*, 12:510; ser. 2, 1:158; *DANFS*, 5:432.)

Noble. Union. Whaling bark, 274 tons. Out of Sag Harbor, N.Y. Part of the Second Stone Fleet. Scuttled with stone in Maffitt's Channel, Charleston Harbor, on January 25–26, 1862. (*ORN*, 12:511; ser. 2, 1:162; *DANFS*, 5:432, 436.)

Norseman. British. Three-masted screw steamer, 49 or 197 tons. Cargo of cotton and possible gold. Hit the wreck of the *Georgiana* at high tide and sunk in 8–12 feet of water in Maffitt's Channel off the Isle of Pines near current 39th Street on May 19, 1863. (*ORN*, 13:755; 14:207–8; Spence, "Civil War Shipwrecks," *Argosy Treasure 77 Annual*, 36; *LLC*, 314.)

Osceola. Union. Oak-hulled screw steamer, 177 tons. Length 117 feet 8 inches, beam 22 feet, depth 7 feet 4 inches, draft 7 feet. Cargo of potatoes, vegetables, horses, and thirty-nine cattle. Built in 1848 at Brooklyn, N.Y. En route to Port Royal, S.C. Was stranded during a gale on November 2, 1861, at Day Breaker off North Island, near Georgetown. (*OR*, 6:186; *ORN*, 12:288, 292; *EAS*, 138; *MSV*, 165, 287.)

Osiris (Orsini). Confederate. Wooden two-mast side-wheel steamer, 145 or 183 tons. Length 134 feet 4 inches, beam 20 feet 4 inches, depth 7 feet. Built in 1838 at New York City. Used by the Confederate Quartermaster Department as a ferryboat between Charleston, Castle Pickney, and Sullivan's Island. Set on fire by a "Yankee sympathizer" during the Civil War. An African-American man attached to the vessel was arrested. (*MSV*, 165; Spence, *List*, 608.)

CSS Palmetto State. Confederate. Ironclad ram, 2,500 tons. Length 175 overall feet or 150 feet, beam 34 or 35 feet, depth 14 feet, draft 12 feet, speed 6 knots, armor 4-inch iron. Complement of 180, with ten 7-inch rifled guns (another source—two rifled 7-inch guns and two 9-inch smoothbores). Built in 1862 at Charleston, S.C. Was stripped, burned, and blown up by the Confederates on February 17–18, 1865, at a wharf up the Cooper River. Removed to a depth of 12 feet mean low water by Benjamin Maillefert for the U.S. Army Corps of Engineers at the mouth of Town Creek in 1871–72. Also hit in 1929 while dredging Town Creek. Probably completely removed by dredging. (*ORN*, 16:372; ser. 2, 1:262; Spence, "Civil War Shipwrecks," *Argosy Treasure 77 Annual*, 90; *Chief of Engineers Report 1872*, 2:652; Ammen, "Navy in the Civil War," *Confederate Military History*, 157; *WCWN*, 205; *CWC*, 6-279.)

USS Patapsco. Union. Wood and iron screw monitor with a single turret, 844 bulk tons, 1,335 displacement tons. Length 200 feet, beam 46 feet, depth 11 feet 6 inches, draft 12 feet, speed 6 knots. Complement of 67–105, with one 150-pounder Parrott, one 15-inch Dahlgren-smoothbore, one 12-pounder smoothbore, and one rifled 12-pounder. Built in 1862 at Wilmington, Del. Was sunk by a Confederate torpedo with sixty-two officers and crewmen killed on the night of January 15–16, 1864, while trying to protect Union boats removing Confederate torpedoes between Fort Sumter and Fort Moultrie. Only those on deck, two men in the windless rooms, three men in the berth deck, one man in the turret, and almost all in the fire room escaped. Sank in 5 fathoms of water near the line of obstructions, almost 800 yards east of Fort Sumter at latitude 32° 45.2' north, longitude 79° 51.8' west. The tip of the smokestack was above water. The pilothouse was removed by wreckers and found buried in 10 feet of mud near the wreck. Benjamin Maillefert removed the wreck to 25 feet below the water surface for the U.S. Army Corps of Engineers. Shells, with the powder still dry, were found in the vessel even after 10 years underwater. Blown up by gunpowder into 25-foot sections and removed. It took about thirty-five days of diving over ten months in 1873 to remove portions of the wreck. The remains of the wreck protrude 8 to 10 feet above the bottom and were examined during the summer 1981 by Clive Cussler's group, NUMA. Sank in about 40 feet of water in the channel off Fort Moultrie. (*OR*, 47:1:1068, 1135; *ORN*, 16:171–75, 178; ser. 2, 1:170–71; *Chief of Engineers Report 1872*, 652; *Chief of Engineers Report 1873*, 68, 728–29; Scharf, *History of the Confederate Navy*, 766; "N.O.A.A. Wreck List," *Treasure Quest*, 79; Spence, *List*, 666–67; Cussler and Dirgo, *Sea Hunters*, 207–8; Cussler and Dirgo, *Sea Hunters II*, 163.)

CSS *Pee Dee* (*Pee Dee*). Confederate. Wooden twin-screw gunboat. Length 170 feet, beam 26 feet, depth 10 feet, speed 9 knots. Complement of ninety-one, with one rifled 7-inch gun, one rifled 6.4-inch gun, and one 9-inch smoothbore (another source—two 3-inch pivot guns). Built at Mars Bluff near Marion Court House, S.C., with two engines brought by a blockade-runner from England in 1862. Destroyed 110 miles above Georgetown, just below the railroad bridge on the west side of the Great Pee Dee River, upon the evacuation of Charleston on February 17–18, 1865. In 1926 the Ellison Capers and Maxcy Gregg Florence chapters of the United Daughters of the Confederacy salvaged the vessel's propellers. In 1954 the rest of the vessel was salvaged and put in the Border Tourist Center in Dillon County, S.C. Was allowed to rust away. Is buried in the I-95 overpass fill at a place called South of the Border. (*ORN*, ser. 2, 1:262; *CWC*, 6-281; Cussler and Dirgo, *Sea Hunters*, 207–8; Spence, *List*, 673.)

CSS *Pee Dee No. 2*. Confederate. Steamer. Under construction in 1864. Was destroyed near Mars Bluff in the Pee Dee River at the end of the Civil War. (*ORN*, 15:732–33; ser. 2, 2:757.)

CSS *Pee Dee No. 3*. Confederate. Torpedo boat. Under construction in 1864. Was destroyed near Mars Bluff in the Pee Dee River at the end of the Civil War. (*ORN*, 15:732–33; ser. 2, 2:757.)

Petrel (Eclipse) (William Aiken). Confederate. Privateer, 82 tons. Armed with two guns. Was the Charleston boat *Eclipse*. After 1856 it was the U.S. revenue cutter *William Aiken*. Taken over by South Carolina in December 1860. Turned over to the Confederate States Navy and sold to a group who converted it to a privateer. On July 28, 1861, it fired three shots at the 52-gun frigate USS *St. Lawrence* off Charleston, mistaking the Union frigate for a Yankee merchantman. An 8-inch shell from the USS *St. Lawrence* sunk the *Petrel* in thirty minutes, with four killed and thirty-six captured at latitude 32° 30' north, longitude 79° 9' west. The crew members were tried for piracy by the Union but were later treated as prisoners of war. (*ORN*, 6:61–63; ser. 2, 1:247; *CWC*, 6-281–82; Spence, *List*, 606.)

Potomac. Union. Whaling ship, 350 or 356 tons. Depth 14 feet. Built in 1841 at Rochester, Mass. Out of Nantucket, Mass. Scuttled with 350 tons of stone in the Main Ship Channel, Charleston Harbor, on December 19–20, 1861. (*ORN*, 12:418, 421; ser. 2, 1:183; *DANFS*, 5:430, 433; Spence, *List*, 719.)

Presto (Fergus). British. Side-wheel steamer, 552 gross tons, 164 registered tons. Length 210 feet, beam 23 feet, depth 9 feet 6 inches. Cargo of stores, liquor, blankets, bacon, ham, and other goods. Built in 1863 at Glasgow, Scotland. Out of Nassau, Bahamas. Hit the wreck of the *Minho* on February 2, 1864, and forced aground in 6–7 feet of water off Fort Moultrie on Sullivan's Island, opposite Battery Rutledge. Shelled and set afire on February 2–3, 1864, by the USS *Lehigh*, USS *Passaic*, USS *Catskill*, and USS *Nahant* as well as Battery Gregg and Fort Strong. Confederate troops got hold of liquor onboard and had a grand drunk. Was located in 1967 by E. Lee Spence. (*OR*, 35:2:40; *ORN*, 15:262–66; Spence, *List*, 761; *LLC*, 317.)

Prince Albert. British. Iron side-wheel steamer, 132 gross tons, 94 registered tons. Length 138 feet 1 inch, beam 16 feet 8 inches, depth 7 feet. Cargo of lead pigs and medicine. Built in 1849 at Dumbarton, Scotland. While entering Charleston Harbor on August 9, 1864, it hit the wreck of the *Minho* and sank on Drunken Dick Shoal at Bowman's

Jetty. Was shelled and set afire by the USS *Catskill* and Morris Island Union batteries. Visited by Union divers in 1865. Located near wrecks of the *Minho* and CSS *Stono*. Part of the wreck was removed in the 1870s while Bowman's Jetty was being repaired. Was salvaged by Howard Tower, Larry Tipping, and Mike Zafoot under state license. (*ORN*, 15:624; 16:34, 37, 354; Horner, *Blockade-Runners*, 149; Boyd, "Wreck Facts," *Skin Diver*, 43–44; Tower, "Civil War Wreck Salvaged," *Treasure Found*, 30; *LLC*, 317; Spence, *List*, 656.)

Prince of Wales. British. Schooner. Cargo of a thousand sacks of salt, some fruit, and sundries. Out of Nassau, Bahamas. Boats from the bark USS *Gem of the Seas* and USS *James Adger* captured the vessel on December 24, 1861. Was set afire by its crew on the breakers on the northern end of North Island. Was refloated by the Union but was grounded again at the breakers. Union sailors burned it when Confederate riflemen forced them from the vessel. Was removed by Benjamin Maillefert for the U.S. Army Corps of Engineers in 1873. (*ORN*, 12:428–30; *Chief of Engineers Report 1874*, 4.)

Queen of the Wave (Wave Queen). British. Screw steamer, 775 bulk tons. Length 180 feet, beam 30 feet, depth 12 feet 6 inches. Cargo of 3,200 tin sheets, 20-ounce bottles of quinine, 23-ounce bottles of morphine, 15 pounds of opium, calico, and 12 reams of printing paper. Built in 1861 at Glasgow, Scotland. Was run ashore by the USS *Conemaugh* near the mouth of the North Santee on February 24, 1863. The crew left after setting it afire. Seven Confederates were later captured on the vessel by a boat from the USS *Conemaugh* on February 25. Was broken in half and blown up on March 7, 1863. (*ORN*, 13:687–90; Spence, *List*, 634.)

Raccoon. British. Side-wheel steamer, 159 registered tons. Length 201 feet 2 inches, beam 21 feet 5 inches, depth 9 feet. Cargo of at least 5 tons of lead. En route from Nassau, Bahamas, for Charleston. Chased onto Drunken Dick Shoal off Sullivan's Island on June 19, 1863. Was burned to avoid capture. Shelled by the USS *New Ironsides*. Reportedly located by magnetometer by Clive Cussler and NUMA in the summer of 1981. (*ORN*, 14:367; Horner, *Blockade-Runners*, 317; Spence, *List*, 645; Ammen, "Navy in the Civil War," *Confederate Military History*, 146.)

Rattlesnake. British. Twin screw iron steamer, 529 gross tons, 269 registered tons. Length 201 feet 9 inches, beam 24 feet 5 inches, depth 12 feet 6 inches. Built at London in 1864. Was run aground by the USS *Wamsutta* and USS *Potomska* in 6–7 feet of water a short distance east of Breach Inlet while trying to enter Charleston Harbor on January 4, 1865. Was burned and abandoned. (*ORN*, 16:354; *SCH*, 454–55; *LLC*, 317.)

Rebecca Sims (Rebecca Ann). Union. Whaling ship, 400 tons. Draft 16 feet. Built in 1807 at Philadelphia. Out of Fairhaven, Mass. Part of the First Stone Fleet. Scuttled with 425 tons of stone to act as an obstruction in the Main Ship Channel, Charleston Harbor, on December 19–20, 1861. (*ORN*, 12:418, 421; ser. 2, 1:189; *DANFS*, 5:430, 433.)

Revere. Nationality unknown. Schooner. Burned off Beaufort on September 10, 1862. (Pleasants, *Vessels Destroyed or Captured*, 1.)

Robert B. Howlett. Union. Schooner, 120 or 246 tons. Length 106 feet 6 inches, beam 27 feet, depth 9 feet 7 inches, draft 9 feet. Built in 1860 in Matthews County, Va. Wrecked on North Bar or Charleston Bar during a hurricane on December 9, 1864. One survivor was rescued by the *Eliza Hancox*, and two men died. (Spence, *List*, 659.)

Robin Hood. Union. Ship, 395 or 400 tons. Draft 15 feet. Built in 1824 at South Boston, Mass. Out of Mystic, Conn. Part of the First Stone Fleet. Scuttled in the Main Ship Channel, Charleston Harbor, on December 19–20, 1861. (*ORN*, 12:418, 421; ser. 2, 1:193; *DANFS*, 5:430, 433; Spence, *List*, 721.)

Rose (Rose of London). British. Side-wheel steamer, 67 registered tons. Length 125 feet 4 inches, beam 18 feet 8 inches, depth 12 feet. Crew of twenty. Cargo of liquor and stores. Out of London. En route from Nassau, Bahamas. Was chased ashore onto another wreck and buildings near Georgetown on the south end of Pawley's Island by the USS *Wamsutta* on June 2, 1864. Most of the cargo was unloaded by the Confederates before the *Rose* was set afire by Union forces. (*ORN*, 15:467–68, 513, 517; *LLC*, 318; Spence, *List*, 655.)

Rover. Nationality unknown. Schooner. Ran ashore on October 11, 1863, at Murrell's Inlet. The cargo was removed by Confederates. On October 17, 1863, a Union expedition of seventeen men attempted to destroy the cargo but were defeated, with ten men captured by Company B, 21st Ga. Cavalry Regiment. The vessel was burned. (*OR*, 28:1:736–37; *ORN*, 15:59.)

Ruby. British. Side-wheel iron steamer, 400 tons. Length 177 feet 5 inches, beam 17 feet 1 inch, depth 8 feet 4 inches, draft 7 feet. Crew of twenty-two. Carried general cargo and government property. Built in 1864 at Renfrew, Scotland. En route to Nassau, Bahamas. Was run ashore at Lighthouse Inlet on June 10–11, 1863, by the USS *Memphis*, USS *Stettin*, and USS *Ottawa* near the Lawford Channel on the north end of Folly Island. Burned fore and aft. Left high and dry at low water. Confederate fire kept most of the Union boarding parties away and chased away those who landed. The Confederates dismantled the vessel's machinery. Its iron plates were removed and used for sandbag lining braces by Union troops. The Confederates carried off much of the cargo, although some cargo was salvaged by Union troops on Morris Island. E. Lee Spence found the wreck in 1966 at the entrance to Lighthouse Inlet. (*OR*, 14:319; 28:2:539–40; *ORN*, 14:301; Horner, *Blockade-Runners*, 210–11; *LLC*, 318.)

Samuel Adams. Nationality unknown. Schooner. Cargo of salt, candles, soap, olive oil, rum, and other goods. Was chased ashore by Union vessels on April 12, 1862, on the western end of the Isle of Palms. (Spence, *List*, 622.)

Sarah. British. Schooner, 100 tons. Carried assorted cargo. Out of Nassau, Bahamas. Was run ashore by the USS *Onward* and burned by the crew at the entrance of Bull's Bay on May 1, 1862. (*ORN*, 12:737, 800.)

Sarah Mary. British. Sloop, 15 tons. Cargo of nine bales of cotton. Out of Nassau, Bahamas. Was captured off Mosquito Inlet, Fla., by the Union schooner *Norfolk Packet* on June 26, 1864. Sailed for Port Royal, S.C., but became grounded on a beach at the mouth of Horse Island Creek. (*ORN*, 15:540–41.)

Sir Robert Peel. Nationality unknown. Schooner. Carried a valuable cargo. Was chased ashore by Union steamers in early April 1862. Was burned by its crew. (Spence, *List*, 622.)

Steam Launch No. 3. U.S. Ship. Wrecked on St. Helena Shoals before June 8, 1865, while attached to the fleet at Port Royal. (*ORN*, 16:343.)

Stephen Young. Union. Merchant brig, 200 tons. Out of Boston. Part of the Second Stone Fleet. Scuttled in Maffitt's Channel, Charleston Harbor, on January 25–26, 1862. (*ORN*, 12:511; ser. 2, 1:214; *DANFS*, 5:432, 436.)

Stonewall Jackson (Leopard). British. Side-wheel two-mast steamer, 824 bulk tons, 1,230 displacement tons, 691 gross tons, 435 registered tons, 862 or 872 tons. Length 223 feet 9 inches or 222 feet, beam 27 feet or 27 feet 1 inch, depth 14 feet 7 inches. Crew and passengers of fifty-four. Cargo of rifled guns, two hundred barrels of saltpeter, forty thousand shoes, tin ingots, lead ingots, copper ingots, and ammunition. Built in 1857 at Dumbarton, Scotland. En route from Nassau, Bahamas. On its ninth trip through the blockade. Hit by several shells from the USS *Flag*, USS *Huron*, and USS *Blunt* below the waterline. Grounded in the Rattlesnake Channel or North Channel on April 11, 1863, one and a half miles from the Breach Inlet Battery on Sullivan's Island, a half-mile from a beach. The crew and passengers took to the boats, reaching Battery Marshall with the mail and passengers' effects. Set afire by the USS *Flag* and USS *Huron* at daylight on April 12. High and dry at low tide. Its machinery and most of the cargo were salvaged. E. Lee Spence reported the wreck in 1965 at low water, buried under 6th Street on the Isle of Pines. Clive Cussler thinks the vessel is under a beach and did some rough trenching there in 1981. (*OR*, 14:286; *ORN*, 14:126, 155; *LLC*, 308; Horner, *Blockade-Runners*, 209; Cussler and Dirgo, *Sea Hunters*, 209–10; Spence, *List*, 638.)

CSS Stono (USS Isaac Smith). Confederate. Wooden screw steamer, 453 bulk tons, 382 tons. Length 171 feet 6 inches, beam 31 feet 4 inches, depth 9 feet, draft 7 feet. Complement of fifty-six as a Union vessel, with one 30-pounder and eight 8-inch guns when Union. Cargo of cotton to run the blockade. Built in 1861 at Brooklyn, N.Y. Captured on January 30, 1863, while scouting up the Stono River. Renamed CSS *Stono*. Chased by the USS *Wissahickon* and wrecked on Bowman's Jetty near Fort Moultrie on June 5, 1863. Was burned when the Confederates evacuated Charleston. Mostly removed in 1873–74 by Benjamin Maillefert for the U.S. Army Corps of Engineers. Was located near the wrecks of the *Minho* and *Prince Albert*. Was salvaged under South Carolina license by Howard Tower, Larry Tipping, and Mike Zafoot. (*ORN*, 13:561–71; 14:494; ser. 2, 1:267; 2:530; *MSV*, 103; *CWC*, 6-306; Boyd, "Wreck Facts," *Skin Diver*, 43–44; Tower, "Civil War Wreck Salvaged," *Treasure Found*, 30; *WCWN*, 238; Spence, *List*, 642.)

Sumter. Nationality unknown. Employed by the Confederate army. Probably a side-wheel steamer, 212 tons. Built in 1860 at New Albany, Ind. Was accidentally sunk by Confederate shelling on August 31, 1863, when it failed to show a signal light at night and was mistaken for a Union ship. Was shelled by Fort Wagner and Battery Gregg while coming into Charleston Harbor with the 20th S.C. Regiment, 23rd S.C. Regiment, and Capt. Matthew's Artillery Company. One shell hulled the *Sumter*, which hit a shoal at the end of Fort Sumter and sank in two hours, with at least forty killed, one wounded, and eight missing. More than six hundred officers and men were saved by barges from Fort Sumter and nearby Confederate gunboats. Most of the Confederate equipment aboard was lost. The vessel was used for target practice. (*OR*, 28:1:687–712; *ORN*, 14:755–56; ser. 2, 1:268; *CWC*, 6-308; *MSV*, 205.)

Tenedos. Union. Merchant bark, 245 or 300 tons. Draft 12 feet. Out of New London, Conn. Part of the First Stone Fleet. Scuttled in the Main Channel, Charleston Harbor, on December 20, 1861. (*ORN*, 12:418, 421; ser. 2, 1:221; *DANFS*, 5:430, 433.)

Theodore Stoney. Confederate. Schooner, 54 tons. Cargo of twenty-five hundred bushels of rice. Was captured and burned by boats from the bark USS *Restless* on February 14, 1862, at Bull's Bay. (*ORN*, 12:547–50; *WCWN*, 142.)

Thomas F. Secor. Union. Chartered wooden ship, 210 tons. Built in 1846 at New York City. Burned at Seabrook's Landing at Hilton Head in May 1863. (Spence, *List*, 641.)

Thomas Martin. U.S. Schooner. Cargo of lumber. Out of New York City. En route to Charleston, S.C. Sprang a leak in a storm on October 23, 1865, between Cape Lookout and Frying Pan Shoals. The cargo was thrown overboard, the foremast went overboard, and the mainmast broke.

After seven days the wreck drifted ashore at Folly Island, north of Georgetown. (Spence, *List*, 679.)

Thomas Watson. Nationality unknown. Sailing ship. Cargo of salt, blankets, flannels and other dry goods. En route from London for Wilmington, N.C. Ran ashore on the northeastern side of Stono Reef in 7 feet of water, 1.5 miles from a Confederate battery and 1.5–2 miles from a beach on October 15, 1861. Was abandoned by its crew. A 9-pounder and cannonballs were dumped overboard, and some of the dry goods were taken off by the crew of the USS *Roanoke* before the *Eby* burned the vessel. (*ORN*, 6:324–28.)

Timor. Union. Ship, 289 tons. Out of New London, Conn. Part of the Second Stone Fleet. Scuttled in Maffitt's Channel, Charleston Harbor, on January 25–26, 1862. (*ORN*, 12:418; *DANFS*, 5:433, 436.)

Tropic (CSS Huntress). Confederate. Side-wheel steamer, 500 bulk tons, 333 registered tons, 323 tons. Length 230 or 225 feet, beam 24 feet 6 inches or 23 feet, draft 6 feet 6 inches, speed 16–20 knots. Originally armed with one to three guns. Cargo of turpentine and 326 bales of cotton. Built in 1838 at New York City. Served as a Boston to Portland, Maine, mail packet. Purchased for the State of Georgia in March 1861. Believed to have been the first vessel to raise the Confederate flag on an ocean. Sold in October 1862. Converted to the blockade-runner *Tropic*. Accidentally burned on January 18, 1863, off Charleston. The USS *Quaker City* rescued its passengers and crew. (*ORN*, ser. 2, 1:256; 3:874; *CWC*, 6-251; *MSV*, 98; *WCWN*, 240; *LLC*, 324; Spence, *List*, 629.)

Wandoo (Wando). Nationality unknown. Schooner. Cargo of eighteen hundred bushels of rice. Captured and sunk by boats from the bark USS *Restless* on February 14, 1862, at Bull's Bay. (*ORN*, 12:547–48.)

USS Weehawken. Union. Single-turreted monitor, 844 bulk tons, 1,335 displacement tons. Length 200 feet, beam 46 feet, depth 11 feet 6 inches, speed 5 knots. Complement of seventy-two to ninety-one, with one 15-inch Dahlgren smoothbore and one 11-inch Dahlgren smoothbore. Launched in 1863 at Jersey City, N.J. Overloaded with ammunition. Sank during a gale on December 6, 1863, in five minutes when water flowed through the deck hatch, turret, and plating loosened by many hits from Confederate batteries. Was lost with four engineers and twenty-seven crewmen. Located at latitude 32° 43' north, longitude 79° 50.9' west, just off the Beacon House on Morris Island. Its smokestack was above water. Divers inspected the vessel and found it on soft mud. Removed to a low-water depth of 20 feet for the U.S. Army Corps of Engineers in 1872–73 by Benjamin Maillefert, who took off 130 tons of iron. In 1981 Clive Cussler and NUMA reported the wreck off Morris Island under 8 feet of silt. (*ORN*, 15:161–70; ser. 2, 1:238; *Chief of Engineers Report 1872*, 652; *Chief of Engineers Report 1873*, 68, 727–28; Wegner, "*Weehawken*'s 'Fearful Accident,'" *Civil War Times Illustrated*, 4–9, 46–47; Cussler and Dirgo, *Sea Hunters*, 207.)

Whistling Wind. Union. Bark, 350 tons. Draft 12 feet. Cargo of coal. En route from Philadelphia to New Orleans. Captured and burned on June 6, 1863, by the CSS *Clarence* east of Cape Romain at latitude 33° 39' north, longitude 71° 29' west. (*ORN*, 2:324, 332, 354, 656.)

Wildcat. Nationality unknown. Schooner. Grounded about December 22, 1862, in the Atlantic Ocean, possibly near the Ashepoo River. (*ORN*, 13:486.)

William Lee. Union. Whaling ship, 311 tons. Out of Newport, R.I. Part of the First Stone Fleet. Scuttled on December 19–20, 1861, in the Main Channel, Charleston Harbor. (*ORN*, 12:510; ser. 2, 1:241; *DANFS*, 5:432–33.)

Winfield Scott. Union army. Transport steamer. Wrecked in Skull Creek near Port Royal Sound in January 1862. Also reported as lost at Dawfuskie Island in February 1862. (*DANFS*, 5:432, 433.)

➤ VESSELS WITHOUT NAMES

brig. Union. Cargo of cotton, furniture, and loot stolen from South Carolina plantations and residences on Edisto Island. Ran ashore on Edisto Island on April 9, 1862. (Spence, *List*, 621.)

ironclads. Confederate. Two unfinished ironclads. Length 175 feet, beam 35 feet 3 inches, depth 9 feet. Were burned by Confederates on February 18, 1865, at Charleston when the city was abandoned to Union forces. One was launched in 1864 and the other was still on the stocks. Both were awaiting plating and engines. (*ORN*, 16:372; *WCWN*, 208.)

light boats. Confederate. Were sunk by Confederates with the CSS *Lady Davis* and *Huntress* on November 6, 1861, to block Skull Creek. (Spence, *List*, 612.)

light ships. Confederate. Two light ships were set afire by Confederates about 3 miles below Beaufort on November 7, 1861. (*OR*, 6:29.)

schooner. Confederate. Cargo of furniture. Captured with the *Lynnhaven* by the USS *Delaware* near Elizabeth City on February 10, 1862. Scuttled on February 14, 1862, along with the *Lynnhaven* at the mouth of the Albemarle and Chesapeake Canal, which connected the North River and Currituck Sound. (*ORN*, 1:130; *DANFS*, 5:440.)

schooner. Confederate. Cargo of salt. Burned in a creek near Magnolia Beach by Union landing party on April 28, 1863. (Spence, *List*, 641.)

schooner. Confederate. Cargo of turpentine. Was run aground and destroyed at Murrell's Inlet by the USS *Nipsic* on January 1, 1864. (*ORN*, 15:156.)

schooner. Confederate. Name defaced. Cargo of rice and about six hundred bushels of cornmeal. Was set on fire in the Santee River by Union sailors from the USS *Restless* on March 28–29, 1862, when the schooner *Lydia and Mary* was removed. (*ORN*, 12:681.)

schooner. Nationality unknown. Small schooner. Was sunk to act as an obstruction during the Civil War in the Ashepoo River, a few miles below the Charleston & Savannah Railroad. Was removed in 1873 by the U.S. Army Corps of Engineers. (*Chief of Engineers Report 1873*, 733.)

schooner. Nationality unknown. Was destroyed on May 12, 1863, by the USS *Conemaugh* and other Union vessels at Murrell's Inlet. (*ORN*, 14:191.)

schooner. Nationality unknown. Was run aground by USS *Alabama* on May 8, 1862, at Lighthouse Inlet. (*New York Times*, May 17, 1862.)

schooner. Confederate. Was set afire on December 27, 1864, while grounded by the USS *Monticello* in Murrell's Inlet. (Spence, *List*, 641.)

schooners. Confederate. Were sunk to block Skull Creek before December 7, 1863. (*ORN*, 15:171.)

ships. Confederate. Four old ships were gifts of Savannah for Charleston. They were loaded with granite used for construction of the Charleston Custom House and sunk in the Main Ship Channel near Fort Sumter in early 1861, to block Union large draft ships from bringing supplies to Fort Sumter. By October 1861 vessels of less than 16 feet draft could pass the obstructed area. (*ORN*, 27:414.)

sloop. British. Cargo of cotton and turpentine. Ran ashore on the beach in front of Fort Moultrie on Sullivan's Island on November 5, 1864. Was shelled by the USS *Patapsco* and set afire after being hit three times. (*ORN*, 16:42; Spence, *List*, 658.)

sloop. Nationality unknown. Carried five men. Capsized off Seabrook Island in a squall in June 1865. The *U.S. Grant* rescued the men. (Spence, *List*, 676.)

vessel. Nationality unknown. Old and worthless. Burned without a cargo while aground on a shoal at Bull's Bay on February 14, 1863, by the USS *Restless*. (*ORN*, 12:547–48.)

vessel. Nationality unknown. Wooden. Wrecked near Fort Sumter during the Civil War. Removed to a depth of 7 feet below mean low water after the Civil War by the U.S. Army Corps of Engineers. (*Chief of Engineers Report 1873*, 68.)

vessels. Confederate. Included a tender. Length 128 feet, beam 22 feet. Burned and sunk with the CSS *Pee Dee* about March 15, 1865, to prevent their capture above the railroad bridge on the Pee Dee River. (Spence, *List*, 673.)

vessels. Nationalities unknown. Three unnamed vessels were sunk in the Stono River near Church Flats during the Civil War. One wreck was removed by Joel Griffen for the U.S. Army Corps of Engineers in 1872–73. (*Chief of Engineers Report 1873*, 732.)

Tennessee

The Union navy and army entered the interior of the Confederate heartland through Tennessee. Raids by Confederate cavalry against Union steamers and gunboats on the Cumberland and Tennessee rivers caused significant Union losses. Confederate major general Joseph Wheeler's cavalry burned the Union steamers *Charter*, *Parthenia*, *Trio*, and *W. H. Sidell* on the Cumberland River on January 13, 1863. On April 8, 1863, Confederate forces under Lt. Col. Thomas G. Woodward captured and burned the *R.C.M. Lovell* and *Saxonia* on the Cumberland River. Brig. Gen. Hylan B. Lyon's brigade of Forrest's command burned the Union steamers *Ben South*, *Echo*, and *Thomas E. Tutt*, an unnamed steamer, and two barges on December 9, 1864, on the Cumberland River.

The most successful Confederate raider was Lt. Gen. Nathan Bedford Forrest. Between October 29 and November 4, 1864, Forrest's cavalry and artillery attacked Union steamers and gunboats on the Tennessee River. Forrest's men captured and destroyed the *Mazeppa*, the *Anna*,

two barges, and the *J. W. Cheeseman* before attacking the trapped Union fleet at the Union supply depot at Johnsonville, Tennessee. The panicked Union forces scuttled and burned the gunboats USS *Elfin*, USS *Key West*, USS *Tawah*, and USS *Undine*; the steamers *Arcola*, *Aurora*, *Doan No. 4*, *Goody Friends*, *J. B. Ford*, *Mountaineer*, and *Venus*; and twelve barges at Johnsonville. The Union supply depot and docks were also torched.

A. J. Sweeney. Union. Stern-wheel steamer, 244 tons. Cargo of seven thousand sacks of corn and twenty-eight horses. Built in 1863 at Wheeling, Va. (W. Va.). Burned on the Cumberland River on March 9, 1864, after hitting a bridge pier at Clarksville with no loss of human life. Was raised and towed to Wheeling and dismantled. The machinery went to the *Bertrand*. (*MSV*, 1, 239; *WPD*, 2.)

Anna. Union. Side-wheel steamer, 110 tons. Built in 1860 at Cincinnati. Passed Lt. Gen. Nathan Bedford Forrest's batteries at Paris Landing on the Tennessee River but was so damaged by the shelling that the *Anna* sank on October 30, 1864, before reaching Paducah, Ky. (*OR*, 39:1:869, 870; *ORN*, 26:682–84; *MSV*, 10, 242; *WPD*, 23.)

CSS *Appleton Belle*. Confederate. Stern-wheel or side-wheel steamer, 103 tons. Built in 1856 at West Newton, Pa. Scuttled with the CSS *Samuel Orr* and *Lynn Boyd* at the mouth of Duck River near Paris on the morning of February 7, 1862. (*OR*, 7:864; *ORN*, 22:782, 821; *CWC*, 6-197; *WCWN*, 245.)

Arcola. Union. Stern-wheel steamer, 203 tons. Length 156 feet, beam 32 feet, depth 4 feet 6 inches. The hull was built at Belle Vernon, Pa. Completed in 1863 at Pittsburgh, Pa. Burned at Johnsonville on November 4, 1864, during Lt. Gen. Nathan Bedford Forrest's raid. (*OR*, 39:1:864; 49:1:747–49; 52:1 [supp.]: 123–24; *MSV*, 12; *WPD*, 26.)

Atalanta. Union. Stern-wheel steamer, 141 tons. Built in 1853 at Wheeling, Va. (W. Va.). Hit a bridge at Clarksville on the Cumberland River on March 2, 1863, and the cabin parted from the hull. (*MSV*, 15, 243; *WPD*, 32.)

Aurora. Union. Screw transport steamer, 331 tons. Length 151 feet, beam 43 feet, depth 6 feet, 4 boilers. Built in 1857 at Brownsville, Pa. Was burned with five other transports and twelve barges at Johnsonville on November 4, 1864, during Lt. Gen. Nathan Bedford Forrest's raid. (*OR*, 39:1:589–90; 49:1:747–49; 52:1 [supp.]: 123–24; *MSV*, 16, 243; *WPD*, 33.)

Baton Rouge. Union. Stern-wheel steamer, 65 tons. Built in 1860 at Mason City, Va. (W. Va.). Burned in June 1861 on the Tennessee River. (*MSV*, 18, 244.)

Ben South. Union. Side-wheel steamer, 176 tons. Built in 1860 at New Albany, Pa. Was captured by Gen. Hylan B. Lyon's brigade on December 9, 1864, and burned with three other steamers and two barges at Cumberland City, 20 miles below Nashville on the Cumberland River. (*OR*, 45:2:145; *ORN*, 26:661, 664; *MSV*, 21; *WPD*, 49.)

Callie. Union. Steamer, 129 tons. Built in 1862 at St. Louis. Burned on August 18, 1862, by a reported five hundred Confederates under Capt. Philip D. Roddey at the Duck River while tied up to the bank, changing cargoes. Cap-

tain Roddey was the former commander of the Confederate steamer *Julius H. Smith,* which had been burned to prevent capture by Union forces. (*OR*, 17:1:34; 17:2:202; 45:2:145, 153; *MSV*, 28, 247; Robinson, *Confederate Privateers*, 189.)

Celeste. Union. Barge. Scuttled and burned on November 4, 1864, near Johnsonville on the Tennessee River with eleven other barges to prevent their capture by Lt. Gen. Nathan Bedford Forrest's cavalry. (*OR*, 39:1:589–90, 875; 49:1:747–49; 52:1 [supp.]: 123–24; *ORN*, 26:622–23, 683, 687.)

Charles Miller. Union. Stern-wheel steamer, 93 tons. Built in 1860 at Elizabeth, Pa. Foundered on March 23, 1865, on the Cumberland River and sank about 12 miles below Nashville, with two lost. (*MSV*, 33, 249; *WPD*, 80.)

Charter. Union. Stern-wheel steamer, 114 tons. Cargo of commissary stores. Built in 1856 at Paducah, Ky. Burned by Maj. Gen. Joseph Wheeler's cavalry brigade on January 13, 1863, on the Nashville side of the Cumberland River, 5 miles from Harpeth Shoals. (*OR*, 20:1:982–83; ser. 2, 5:182; *MSV*, 34, 249; *WPD*, 82.)

Chickamauga. Union. Barge. Was scuttled and burned on November 4, 1864, near Johnsonville on the Tennessee River with eleven other barges to prevent their capture by Lt. Gen. Nathan Bedford Forrest's cavalry. (*OR*, 39:1:589–90, 875; 49:1:747–49; 52:1 [supp.]: 123–24; *ORN*, 26:622–23, 683, 687.)

Chippewa Valley. Union. Stern-wheel steamer, 101 tons. Built in 1860 at Eau Claire, Wis. Was snagged in the Cumberland River, 5 miles below Gallatin Landing, on April 30, 1864. (*MSV*, 35, 250; *WPD*, 87.)

David Hughes. Union army. Chartered light draft steamer. Carried government supplies, while the barge carried stores. Was captured and burned by Confederate guerrillas on October 31, 1864, about 15 miles above Clarksville on the Cumberland River. (*OR*, 39:1:864; 39:3:583; *ORN*, 26:604–5.)

Doan No. 2 (Doane No. 2) (Doane). Union. Stern-wheel transport steamer, 250 tons. Built in 1863 at Cincinnati. Burned on November 4, 1864, at Johnsonville during Lt.

Gen. Nathan Bedford Forrest's raid. May have been repaired and later sunk in Arkansas as the barge *Doane*. (*OR*, 39:1:589–90, 875; 49:1:747–49; 52:1 [supp.]: 123–24; *MSV*, 55, 256; *WPD*, 130.)

Duke. Union. Stern-wheel transport steamer, 123 tons. Length 125 feet, beam 26 feet, depth 4 feet. Built in 1862 at New Albany, Ind. Burned on November 4, 1864, in the Cumberland River. (*OR*, 39:1:589–90, 875; 49:1:747–49; *MSV*, 55, 256; *WPD*, 134.)

Eagle Coal Co. Union. Barge. Scuttled and burned on November 4, 1864, near Johnsonville on the Tennessee River with eleven other barges to prevent their capture by Lt. Gen. Nathan Bedford Forrest's cavalry. (*OR*, 39:1:589–90, 875; 49:1:747–49; 52:1 [supp.]: 123–24; *ORN*, 26:622–23, 683, 687.)

Echo. Union. Stern-wheel towboat steamer, 100 tons. Length 147 feet, beam 22 feet, depth 3 feet 2 inches. Built in 1858 at California, Pa. Was captured and burned by Gen. Hylan B. Lyon on December 10, 1864, with three other steamers and two barges in the Cumberland River near Cumberland City. (*OR*, 45:2:145, 153; *MSV*, 59, 257; *WPD*, 138.)

Eclipse. Union. Stern-wheel steamer, 223 tons. Built in 1862 at Elizabeth, Pa. On January 27, 1865, the boiler exploded in the Tennessee River near Johnsonville, with 27 Union soldiers killed, 113 others killed, and a total of 78 injured. Captain Vohris said he had notified the U.S. Quartermaster Division that the boilers were leaking and unsafe and had asked for repairs. (*OR*, 52:1 [supp.]: 714; *MSV*, 60, 257; *WPD*, 140.)

USS Elfin (Number 52) (Oriole) (W. C. Mann). Union. Tinclad steam gunboat, 192 tons. Length 155 feet, beam 31 feet, depth 4 feet 4 inches. Complement of fifty, with eight 24-pounder howitzers. Built in 1863 at Cincinnati. Was scuttled and burned on November 4, 1864, at Johnsonville on the Tennessee River to prevent its capture by Lt. Gen. Nathan Bedford Forrest. Most of the vessel's valuable articles were recovered in August 1865, by the USS *Kate* under Act. Vol. Lt. G. W. Rogers. (*OR*, 39:1:860–67; 52:1 [supp.]: 123–24; *ORN*, 26:609–14, 628, 683, 687; 27:375–76; ser. 2, 1:77; *WCWN*, 165, 171; Pratt, *Western Waters*, 44; *WPD*, 474.)

Ellwood. Union. Side-wheel steamer, 171 tons. Length 114 feet, beam 31 feet, depth 3 feet. Built in 1860 at De Pere, Wis. Burned on April 16, 1865, in the Hatchie River. (*MSV*, 63, 258; *WPD*, 147.)

Goody Friends. Union. Stern-wheel transport steamer, 195 tons. Built in 1857 at Brownsville, Pa. Burned at Johnsonville on November 4, 1864, by Union forces during Lt. Gen. Nathan Bedford Forrest's raid. (*OR*, 39:1:589–90, 875; 49:1:747–49; 52:1 [supp.]: 123–24; *MSV*, 87, 264; *WPD*, 192–93.)

Highlander. U.S. Stern-wheel steamer, 241 tons. Built in 1864 at Wheeling, W. Va. Hit ice and sank on December 16, 1865, at Johnsonville. (*MSV*, 96, 267; *WPD*, 215.)

CSS James Johnson (James Johnston). Confederate. Side-wheel steamer, 525 tons. Built in 1856 at Jeffersonville, Ind. Purchased at Nashville in 1861 by Confederates. Was being converted into a gunboat when burned by Confederates on February 23, 1862, on the Cumberland River at Nashville to avoid capture by Union forces. (*CWC*, 6-225; *MSV*, 108; *WCWN*, 244; *WPD*, 240.)

CSS James Woods (James Wood). Confederate. Side-wheel steamer, 585 tons. Length 257 feet, beam 37 feet, depth 7 feet. Built in 1860 at Jeffersonville, Ind. To be converted to a gunboat. Was destroyed by Confederates on the Cumberland River at Nashville in February 23, 1862, to prevent its capture by Union forces. (*CWC*, 6-255; *WCWN*, 244; *WPD*, 243.)

J. B. Ford. Union. Transport steamer, 197 tons. Built in 1857 at Moundsville, Va. (W. Va.). Burned by Union forces at Johnsonville on November 4, 1864, during Lt. Gen. Nathan Bedford Forrest's raid. (*OR*, 39:1:589–90, 875; 49:1:747–49; 52:1 [supp.]: 123–24; *MSV*, 104; *WPD*, 243.)

J. H. Doane. Union. Barge. Scuttled and burned on November 4, 1864, near Johnsonville on the Tennessee River with eleven other barges to prevent their capture by Lt. Gen. Nathan Bedford Forrest's cavalry. (*OR*, 39:1:589–90, 875; 49:1:747–49; 52:1 [supp.]: 123–24; *ORN*, 26:622–23, 683, 687.)

Josephine. Union. Barge. Scuttled and burned on November 4, 1864, near Johnsonville on the Tennessee River with eleven other barges to prevent their capture by Lt. Gen. Nathan Bedford Forrest's cavalry. (*OR*, 39:1:589–90, 875; 49:1:747–49; 52:1 [supp.]: 123–24; *ORN*, 26:622–23, 683, 687.)

J. W. Cheeseman. Union. Stern-wheel transport steamer, 215 tons. Length 165 feet, beam 33 feet, depth 5 feet 6 inches. Cargo of commissary stores and furniture. Built in 1856 at Cincinnati. Was captured with the crew on October 30, 1864, by Lt. Gen. Nathan Bedford Forrest's men near Paris Landing and White Oak Island in the Tennessee River after a shell cut the steam line. The cargo was unloaded and the steamer was burned by Forrest's soldiers on November 3, 1864, below Johnsonville. (*OR*, 39:1:872–74; 52:1 [supp.]: 121–22; *ORN*, 26:603–5, 620–21, 624, 682, 685–86; *MSV*, 107; *WPD*, 237; *EAS*, 282.)

Kentucky. Union. Barge. Was scuttled and burned on November 4, 1864, near Johnsonville on the Tennessee River with eleven other barges to prevent their capture by Lt. Gen. Nathan Bedford Forrest's cavalry. (*OR*, 39:1:589–90, 875; 49:1:747–49; 52:1 [supp.]: 123–24; *ORN*, 26:622–23, 683, 687.)

USS Key West (*Abeona*) (*Key West No. 3*) (*Number 32*). Union. Stern-wheel tinclad, 207 tons. Length 156 feet, beam 32 feet, depth 4 feet 6 inches. Armed with six 24-pounder howitzers, two 24-pounder guns, and one rifled 12-pounder. Built in 1862 at California, Pa. Fought Lt. Gen. Nathan Bedford Forrest's battery of 20-pounder Parrotts above Reynoldsburg and hit by nineteen shells, with ten through the upper works, seven through the deck, and two in the hull. Was run aground and burned by the Union crew to prevent its capture on November 4, 1864, in the Tennessee River off Johnsonville. One 12-pounder brass rifled gun was salvaged in June 1865 by the USS *Forest Rose* under Act. Vol. Lt. George W. Rogers. (*OR*, 39:1:859, 860–67; *ORN*, 26:609–26, 628; 27:283–84; ser. 2, 1:121; *WCWN*, 165, 173; Pratt, *Western Waters*, 242; *MSV*, 121; *WPD*, 271.)

CSS Lynn Boyd (*Linn Boyd*). Confederate. Stern-wheel or side-wheel steamer, 227 tons. Built in 1859 at Paducah, Ky. Burned on the Tennessee River at the mouth of Duck River near Paris on the early morning of February 7, 1862, to avoid capture. (*OR*, 7:864; *ORN*, 22:782, 821; *CWC*, 6-264; *WCWN*, 247; *MSV*, 128; *WPD*, 287; *EAS*, 284.)

Mazeppa. Union. Stern-wheel steamer transport, 184 tons. Built in 1864 at Cincinnati. Towed barges with 700 tons of freight, including flour, shoes, blankets, arms, hardtack, clothing, and other goods. En route from Cincinnati. On October 29, 1864, Lt. Gen. Nathan Bedford Forrest's batteries at Paris Landing, upriver from Fort Heiman, Ky., shelled the vessel. After three rounds the boat became unmanageable, and the crew abandoned it on the west bank of the river. Most of the guns and ammunition were removed and taken away in wagons. The *Mazeppa* and two barges were burned 2 miles above and across from Fort Henry when Union gunboats approached that night. Might be located on the Kentucky side of the river. (*OR*, 39:1:860, 863, 870; 39:3:583; 52:1 [supp.]: 121; *ORN*, 26:620, 624, 684; *MSV*, 142, 280; Longacre, *Mounted Raids of the Civil War*, 291–92; *WPD*, 318.)

Minnetonka (*Minatonka*). Union. Stern-wheel steamboat, 158 tons. Length 141 feet, beam 26 feet 7 inches, depth 4 feet 6 inches. Built in 1857 at California, Pa. Was captured and burned on the Cumberland River at Nashville on February 26, 1862, by Confederates under Capt. John Hunt Morgan to prevent its recapture by Union forces. (*OR*, 7:433; *MSV*, 146, 282; *WPD*, 323.)

Mountaineer. Union. Stern-wheel transport steamer, 211 tons. Built in 1864 at Cairo, Ill. Was burned by Union forces at Johnsonville on November 4, 1864, during Lt. Gen. Nathan Bedford Forrest's raid. (*OR*, 39:1:589–90, 875; 49:1:747–49; 52:1 [supp.]: 123–24; *MSV*, 150, 283; *WPD*, 334.)

CSS Muscle (*Cerro Gordo*). Confederate. Stern-wheel steamer, 125 tons. Cargo of lumber. Built in 1856 at Allegheny, Pa. Was captured by the USS *Conestoga*, USS *Tyler*, and USS *Lexington* on February 8, 1862, along with the *Sallie Wood*. While under tow, the CSS *Muscle* developed a leak on the Tennessee River downriver from Cerro Gordo and sank near the crossing. (*OR*, 7:154–56; *ORN*, 22:572–73; *WCWN*, 248; *MSV*, 151.)

Neptune. Union. Stern-wheel steamer, 211 tons. Length 150 feet, beam 39 feet 6 inches, depth 4 feet. Built in 1857 at California, Pa. Hit a bridge on March 19, 1862, on the Cumberland River at Clarksville. (*MSV*, 154, 284; *WPD*, 342.)

Paint Rock. Confederate. Steamer. Was scuttled by Confederates when Maj. Gen. Braxton Bragg evacuated Chattanooga in 1862. Might have sunk in Alabama. Was raised and later lost in the same area. (*WPD*, 361.)

Parthenia. Union. Stern-wheel transport steamer, 261 tons. Built in 1862 at Freedom, Pa. Was captured by Maj. Gen. Joseph Wheeler's cavalry brigade at the head of Harpeth Shoals on the Cumberland River on January 13, 1863. Was burned on January 14 along with the *Trio* and the *W. H. Sidell* after the passengers were robbed. The vessel's owners later collected $32,500 from the U.S. government. (*OR*, 20:1:980–81; ser. 2, 5:183, 285; *MSV*, 168, 288; *WPD*, 363.)

R.C.M. Lovell. Union. Stern-wheel steamer, 45 tons. Cargo of sutler's stores for the Union army. Built in 1861 at Elizabeth, Pa. Was captured and destroyed above Clarksville on the Cumberland River on April 8, 1863, by twelve hundred Confederates and two cannons under Lt. Col. Thomas G. Woodward of the 2nd Ky. Cavalry Regiment. Eight African Americans and the captain of the *R.C.M. Lovell* were executed. (*MSV*, 180, 291.)

Saint Louis. Union. Stern-wheel steamer, 191 tons. Cargo of Union stores. Built in 1855 at West Brownsville, Pa. En route for Nashville. Was burned on July 18, 1864, by Confederate guerrillas at Sailor's Rest on the Cumberland River above Fort Donelson. (*New York Times*, July 21, 1864; *MSV*, 192, 295; *WPD*, 412.)

St. Paul. Union. Steamer. Was captured on the Hatchie River on April 16, 1865, by Confederate guerrillas led by a man whose real name was Wilcox but who was also called Luxton and who posed as Bill Forrest, brother of Maj. Gen. Nathan Bedford Forrest. They killed one deckhand on the *St. Paul.* Joining some of William Clark Quantrill's guerrillas, they captured the *Anna Everton* and *Sylph.* The *St. Paul* was burned at Morgan's Landing, about 40 miles from the mouth of the Hatchie River. Wilcox was captured and hung by order of Union colonel Embury D. Osband. (*ORN*, 27:146.)

CSS *Samuel Orr* (*Robert J. Young*) (*Sam Orr*). Confederate. Stern-wheel steamer, 179 tons, 256.94 tons. Length 150 feet or 152 feet 6 inches, beam 29 feet, depth 5 feet. Built in 1861 at New Albany, Ind., as a packet. Used as a hospital boat on the Tennessee River. Upon the fall of Fort Henry the CSS *Samuel Orr* was burned February 7, 1862, at the mouth of the Duck River to prevent its capture by Union gunboats. Raised in 1865, and later rebuilt as the *Robert J. Young* in 1875. (*OR*, 7:864; *ORN*, 22:565, 572, 581; *CWC*, 6-297; *WCWN*, 249; *WPD*, 417.)

Saxonia. Union. Screw steamer, 60 tons. Cargo of Union sutler's stores. Built in 1863. Was captured and destroyed on the Cumberland River on April 8, 1863, by twelve hundred Confederates and two cannons under Lt. Col. Thomas G. Woodward of the 2nd Ky. Cavalry near Clarksville. (*MSV*, 196, 296.)

Silver Cloud No. 2. Union. Stern-wheel steamer, 287 tons. Length 156 feet, beam 33 feet, depth 5 feet 6 inches. Cargo of government supplies. Hit a rock on the Cumberland River on May 9, 1864. Sank with water 10 inches over the main deck. Raised the next day. (*WPD*, 425–26.)

Skylark. Union. Side-wheel steamer, 371 tons. Built in 1858 at Brownsville, Pa. Was captured on the Duck River while tied up to a bank changing cargoes and burned on August 18, 1862, between Waggoner's and Walker's Landing, Tennessee River by five hundred Confederates led by captains Dougherty, Gilliam, and Napier, along with steamboat Capt. Philip D. Roddey, formerly captain of the Confederate boat *Julius H. Smith.* (*OR*, 17:1:34; 17:2:202; *MSV*, 199, 298; *WPD*, 428–29.)

CSS *Slidell*. Confederate. Gunboat. Armed with eight guns. Built in 1862 at New Orleans. Was lost before February 6, 1863, on the Tennessee River. (*CWC*, 6-302; *WCWN*, 249.)

USS *Tawah* (*Collier*) (*Ebenezer*) (*Number 29*). Union. Wooden side-wheel steam tinclad, 108 tons. Length 114 feet, beam 33 feet, depth 3 feet 9 inches. Was armed with two 30-pounder Parrotts, four 24-pounder howitzers, two 24-pounders, and two 12-pounder howitzers. Built in 1859 at Brownsville, Pa. Engaged Lt. Gen. Nathan Bedford Forrest's batteries above Reynoldsburg when the starboard Parrott was disabled by a Confederate shell. Was scuttled and burned by the Union in the Tennessee River on November 4, 1864, to prevent its capture near Johnsonville.

Shells aboard did not fit the vessel's guns. Four 24-pounder howitzers and two 12-pounders were salvaged in June 1865 by Union forces. Many articles were recovered by Act. Vol. G. W. Rogers of the USS *Kate* in August 1865. Tentatively identified by 1994 and 1995 archaeological surveys for the State of Tennessee. (*OR*, 39:3:630; 52:1 [supp.]: 121–24; *ORN*, 26:609–14, 617–24, 683, 686; 27:275–76, 283–84; ser. 2, 1:220; *MSV*, 59; *WCWN*, 169; Pratt, *Western Waters*, 243; *WPD*, 138, 445.)

Thomas E. Tutt. Union. Side-wheel steamer, 351 tons. Length 200 feet, beam 35 feet, depth 5 feet 6 inches, four boilers. Cargo of six thousand sacks of government oats and troops. Built in 1855 at Cincinnati. Was captured and burned on December 9, 1864, at Cumberland City by Gen. Hylan Lyon, along with three other steamers and two barges, after being used to ferry three thousand Confederates across the Cumberland River. The crew was paroled. (*OR*, 45:2:140, 145, 153; *ORN*, 26:661, 664; *MSV*, 211, 301; *WPD*, 450.)

T. H. U. S. 57. Union. Barge. Scuttled and burned on November 4, 1864, near Johnsonville on the Tennessee River with eleven other barges to prevent their capture by Lt. Gen. Nathan Bedford Forrest's cavalry. (*OR*, 39:1:589–90, 875; 49:1:747–49; 52:1 [supp.]: 123–24; *ORN*, 26:622–23, 683, 687.)

Trio. Union. Stern-wheel hospital steamer, 150 tons. Carried four hundred wounded Union soldiers and some cotton. Built in 1858 at Louisville. Was captured at Harpeth Shoals on the Cumberland River, 30 miles from Nashville by Maj. Gen. Joseph Wheeler's cavalry brigade and burned with the *Parthenia* and *W. H. Sidell* on January 13, 1863. (*OR*, 20:1:980–81; ser. 2, 5:183, 285; *MSV*, 215, 302; *WPD*, 459.)

USS *Undine* (*Ben Gaylord*) (*Kate*) (*Number 55*). Union. Stern-wheel steam tinclad, 158 tons, 179 tons. Armed with eight 24-pounder howitzers. Built in 1859 at Cincinnati. Was trapped below Johnsonville on the Tennessee River and captured by Lt. Gen. Nathan Bedford Forrest's men on October 30, 1864, near Paris Landing. The Union crew lost two killed and eight wounded. The rest of the crew fled to Pine Bluff. The vessel was then manned by For-

rest's Confederates with Capt. Frank Gracey of the 3rd Ky. Cavalry Regiment, a former Cumberland River steamboat pilot, serving as the captain. Burned on November 4, 1864, by Confederates to prevent its capture near Reynoldsburg Island, below Johnsonville after being shot up by Union gunboats. The two 24-pounder howitzers were recovered in June 1865. All articles of value were salvaged by the USS *Kate* in August 1865 by Act. Lt. G. W. Rogers. The *Victor No. 4* may have been built from the salvaged *Undine*. (*OR*, 39:1:860–67, 872–74; 52:1 [supp.]: 121–24; *ORN*, 26:489–91, 598–605, 620–21, 627, 683, 706; 27:275–76, 284; ser. 2, 1:229; Pratt, *Western Waters*, 246; *WCWN*, 179; *MSV*, 217, 303; *WPD*, 463.)

U.S. No. 22. Union. Barge. Was scuttled and burned on November 4, 1864, near Johnsonville on the Tennessee River with eleven other barges to prevent their capture by Lt. Gen. Nathan Bedford Forrest's cavalry. (*OR*, 39:1:589–90, 875; 49:1:747–49; 52:1 [supp.]: 123–24; *ORN*, 26:622–23, 683, 687.)

U.S. No. 44. Union. Barge. Was scuttled and burned on November 4, 1864, near Johnsonville on the Tennessee River with eleven other barges to prevent their capture by Lt. Gen. Nathan Bedford Forrest's cavalry. (*OR*, 39:1:589–90, 875; 49:1:747–49; 52:1 [supp.]: 123–24; *ORN*, 26:622–23, 683, 687.)

Venus. Union. Stern-wheel steam transport, 235 tons. Built in 1863 at Carondelet, Mo. Was captured near Paris Landing with a party of recruits for the 34th N.J. Volunteer Regiment by Lt. Gen. Nathan Bedford Forrest's cavalry on October 30, 1864. The *Venus*'s captain and two men of the 34th N.J. Regiment were killed, and seven were wounded, with one officer and ten men captured. Two empty barges with the *Venus* were destroyed. Two 20-pounder Parrotts and supplies from the captured *Mazeppa* were put aboard the *Venus* by the Confederates. The Confederate vessel was captained by Lt. Col. William A. Dawson of the 15th Tenn. Cavalry Regiment. Union vessels drove the *Venus* ashore, where it was abandoned on the western side of the river. Was recaptured by the USS *Tawah* at Johnsonville. Two guns and ammunition were removed along with 100 boxes of shoes, 2 bales of blankets, 576 boxes of hard bread, and other goods. The Confederate crew lost three killed and six wounded. Was burned on November 4, 1864, at Johnsonville by Union forces to avoid capture. (*OR*, 39:1:589, 860–69, 872–74; *ORN*, 26:603–5, 610–13, 624, 626, 682, 686; Forrest, *Gunboats and Cavalry*, 11; Longacre, *Mounted Raids of the Civil War*, 293–94, 297–98; *MSV*, 220, 303; *WPD*, 467.)

Volunteer. U.S. Stern-wheel steamer, 106 tons. Built in 1863 at Cincinnati. Was stranded in July 1865 in the Cumberland River. (*MSV*, 223, 304; *WPD*, 473.)

W. B. Terry. Union. Stern-wheel transport steamer, 175 tons. Armed dispatch boat with two 6-pounder Parrotts. Cargo of coal. Carried two officers; a seventeen-man African-American crew; sixteen soldiers, including ten men of the 81st Ohio. Infantry Regiment; and 5 passengers. Built in 1856 at Belle Vernon, Pa. Was captured at Paducah, Ky., on August 21, 1861, by the USS *Lexington* for trafficking with the Confederacy and flying a Confederate flag. Left Paducah on August 30, 1862. En route to Union gunboats at Hamburg, Tenn. Was captured by about two hundred Confederates, who dumped the coal overboard to lighten the vessel. One male passenger, one female passenger, one gunner, and one African American were wounded. The officers, soldiers, passengers, and crew were paroled. Master Leonard G. Klinck, the steamer's commander, was reportedly a Confederate sympathizer. Hauled over rocks and used to ferry Confederate troops across the Tennessee River. Was grounded 20 feet from shore under a bluff in two feet of water at the foot of the Duck River Sucks while going up the Tennessee River. Stripped of its furniture and burned on August 31, 1862. (*OR*, 17:1:52–53; 20:202; *ORN*, 23:332; *WPD*, 474.)

Whale No. 8. Union. Barge. Was scuttled and burned on November 4, 1864, near Johnsonville on the Tennessee River with eleven other barges to prevent their capture by Lt. Gen. Nathan Bedford Forrest's cavalry. (*OR*, 39:1:589–90, 875; 49:1:747–49; 52:1 [supp.]: 123–24; *ORN*, 26:622–23, 683, 687.)

W. H. Sidell. Union. Converted ferryboat tinclad. Was captured on the Cumberland River on January 13, 1863, by Maj. Gen. Joseph Wheeler's cavalry at the head of Harpeth

Shoals without a fight when the tinclad's pilot deserted the wheel. Its guns and ammunition were thrown overboard. William Van Dorn, the vessel's captain, was captured and held, while the rest of the crew was paroled. Was burned with the *Trio* and *Parthenia*. The starboard guns were later salvaged by Union forces on April 15, 1863. (*OR*, 20:1:981, 983; 23:2:240; *ORN*, 24:19, 81.)

▷ VESSELS WITHOUT NAMES

barge. Union army. Carried stores. Captured and burned by Confederate guerrillas with the steamer *David Hughes* on October 31, 1864, about 15 miles above Clarksville on the Cumberland River. (*OR*, 39:1:864; 39:3:583; *ORN*, 26:604–5.)

barge or boat. Union. Cargo of Union provisions and hay. Burned near Dover by Maj. Gen. Joseph Wheeler's forces on February 4, 1863, during an attack on Fort Donelson. (*OR*, 23:39–41.)

barges. Confederate. Filled with rock. Were scuttled in the Cumberland River near Fort Donelson on October 30, 1861, to prevent Union gunboats from passing the Fort Donelson water batteries. (Shomette, *Civil War Shipwrecks*, 396.)

barges. Union. Two barges. Carried seven hundred tons of freight, including flour, shoes, blankets, arms, hardtack, clothing, and other goods. En route from Cincinnati and under tow by the steamer *Mazeppa*. On October 29, 1864, Lt. Gen. Nathan Bedford Forrest's batteries at Paris Landing, upriver from Fort Heiman, Ky., shelled them. After three rounds the *Mazeppa* became unmanageable, and the crew abandoned it on the west bank of the river. The *Mazeppa* and two barges were burned 2 miles above and across from Fort Henry when Union gunboats approached that night. Could be located on the Kentucky side of the river. (*OR*, 39:1:860, 863, 870; 39:3:583; 52:1 [supp.]: 121; *ORN*, 26:620, 624, 684; *MSV*, 142, 280.)

barges. Union. Two barges. Were captured and burned with a steamer, the *Thomas E. Tutt*, *Ben South*, and *Echo* at Cumberland City on the Cumberland River by Gen. Hylan B. Lyon on December 9, 1864. (*ORN*, 26:661, 664.)

barges. Union. Two empty barges. Were captured near Paris Landing with the *Venus* on October 30, 1864, by Lt.

Gen. Nathan Bedford Forrest's cavalry. Two barges with the *Venus* were destroyed. (*OR*, 39:1:589, 860–69, 872–74; *ORN*, 26:603–5, 610–13, 624, 626, 682, 686.)

barges. Union. Two unnamed barges. Were scuttled and burned with ten other barges on November 4, 1864, near Johnsonville on the Tennessee River to prevent their capture by Lt. Gen. Nathan Bedford Forrest's cavalry. (*OR*, 39:1:589–90, 875; 49:1:747–49; 52:1 [supp.]: 123–24; *ORN*, 26:622–23, 683, 687.)

steamer. Union. Was captured and burned with two barges, the *Thomas E. Tutt, Ben South,* and *Echo* at Cumberland City on the Cumberland River by Gen. Hylan B. Lyon on December 9, 1864. (*ORN*, 26:661, 664.)

Texas

Texas has a long Gulf of Mexico coastline fronted by barrier sea islands. During the Civil War Texas's small ports included Pass Cavallo, Corpus Christi, and Velasco, but the major port was Galveston. These ports were the destination of blockade-runners from Mexico, Cuba, and the British Bahamas. The Union blockade was maintained principally by small coastal vessels. Union forces occupied Galveston and various portions of the Texas coast from time to time.

On the early morning of January 1, 1863, a makeshift Confederate naval and army force attacked the port of Galveston, captured the USS *Harriet Lane,* and caused the USS *Westfield* to be blown up, while the Confederates lost the tug *Neptune Camp* in the engagement. The blockader USS *Hatteras* was sunk by the Confederate commerce raider CSS *Alabama* off Galveston on January 11, 1863.

A. B. (A. Bee). Confederate. Steamer. Ran aground in a narrow 2-foot deep channel leading to Nueces Bay near Corpus Christi. As the USS *Arthur* approached, it was burned to the water's edge on August 17, 1862, by Confederates to prevent its capture. (*ORN*, 19:152, 302.)

Acadia. Canadian. Wooden side-wheel steamer, 738 bulk tons. Length 211 feet 11 inches, beam 31 feet 1 inch, draft 12 feet 6 inches. Built in 1864 at Sorel, Quebec. Wrecked on February 5–6, 1865, about 6 miles east northeast of Velasco while attempting to run into Velasco. Some cargo was salvaged. Was shelled by the USS *Virginia,* which was unable to land a boat to burn the *Acadia* due to rough water. Was partially salvaged by Confederates. Archaeologist Wendell E. Pierce investigated the wreck and a report was published in 1974. (*ORN*, 22:32, 124; Arnold, *Marine Magnetometer Survey,* 13; *LLC*, 216, 285.)

Alice and Mary. Nationality unknown. Ship. Wrecked in 1863 off the Texas coast. (Arnold, "Underwater Cultural Resource Management," *Proceedings of the Eleventh Conference,* 91.)

America. British. Schooner. Cargo of fifty-one bales of cotton. En route from Corpus Christi. Was captured with the captain and crew on August 27, 1863, by the bark USS *William G. Anderson* off the Texas coast. Towed by the USS *William G. Anderson* but capsized between midnight and 4:00 a.m. on August 28, 1863. The Union prize crew of five was taken off. Fourteen cotton bales from the wreck were recovered. Act. Vol. Lt. Frederic S. Hill personally sold bales of cotton and shipped them to Boston. He was later court-martialed and reprimanded for the unauthorized sale of the confiscated cotton. Hill had noted the cotton in the logbook but then erased the notation. (*ORN*, 20:486–89.)

Anna Dale. Confederate. Privateer schooner, 70 tons. Armed with one pivot 12-pounder Dahlgren howitzer. A boat from the USS *Pinola* boarded the anchored *Anna Dale* at a wharf under a Confederate battery at Pass Cavallo on February 18, 1865. In the battle nine Confederates were killed. The captured *Anna Dale* set sail, became grounded, and was set afire. (*ORN*, 22:42–45; *CWC*, 6-197; Porter, *Naval History,* 779–80.)

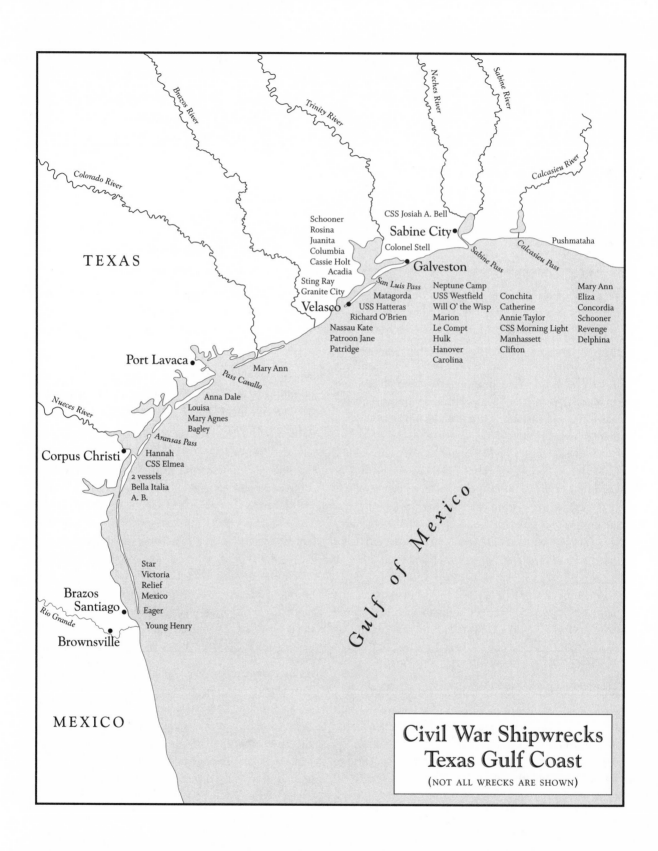

TEXAS

Brazos River

Trinity River

Neches River

Sabine River

Colorado River

Calcasieu River

Schooner
Rosina
Juanita
Columbia
Cassie Holt
Acadia
Sting Ray
Granite City

CSS Josiah A. Bell

Sabine City

Colonel Stell

Galveston

Pushmataha

Calcasieu Pass

Sabine Pass

San Luis Pass

Velasco

Matagorda
USS Hatteras
Richard O'Brien
Nassau Kate
Patroon Jane
Patridge

Neptune Camp
USS Westfield
Will O' the Wisp
Marion
Le Compt
Hulk
Hanover
Carolina

Conchita
Catherine
Annie Taylor
CSS Morning Light
Manhassett
Clifton

Mary Ann
Eliza
Concordia
Schooner
Revenge
Delphina

Port Lavaca

Pass Cavallo

Mary Ann

Nueces River

Anna Dale
Louisa
Mary Agnes
Bagley

Aransas Pass

Corpus Christi

Hannah
CSS Elmea
2 vessels
Bella Italia
A. B.

Gulf of Mexico

Star
Victoria
Relief
Mexico
Eager
Young Henry

Brazos
Santiago

Rio Grande

Brownsville

MEXICO

Civil War Shipwrecks
Texas Gulf Coast
(NOT ALL WRECKS ARE SHOWN)

Annie Taylor (Anna Taylor) (Soledad Cos). Union. Steamer. Wrecked at Sabine Pass on December 10, 1861, with a lieutenant and nine Union men captured by Confederates. Could be in Louisiana. (*ORN,* 17:33, 42, 86; *New York Times,* December 14, 1861.)

Bagley (Bagaley) (William Bagaley) (William Bagley). Union army. Side-wheel steamer, 396 bulk tons. Length 173 feet, beam 32 feet 9 inches, draft 7 feet 6 inches. Built in 1854 at Belle Vernon, Pa. Former blockade-runner captured by USS *De Soto,* USS *Kennebec,* and USS *Ossipee* on July 18, 1863. Sank on November 18, 1863, at Aransas Pass. (*ORN,* 20:397–98, 647–48; *ORA,* pl. 43, no. 8; *MSV,* 230; *LLC,* 327.)

Belle Italia. Confederate. Sloop or schooner. Sunk on July 10, 1862, at Lamar when the USS *Arthur* approached. Later raised and placed as an obstruction in the Corpus Christi Ship Channel. Raised on August 15, 1862, and put back into service. (*OR,* 34:2:1063–64; *ORN,* 19:201–2, 780–81; *WCWN,* 140.)

Benjamin Delano. U.S. Brig. Cargo of forage. Driven ashore during a three-day gale at Galveston in June 1865. (*OR,* 48:2:1041.)

Blossom. Nationality unknown. Ship. Wrecked in 1863 off the Texas coast. (Arnold, "Underwater Cultural Resource Management," *Proceedings of the Eleventh Conference,* 91.)

Breaker. Confederate. Schooner. Was destroyed in Nueces Bay by Confederates on August 12, 1862, as the USS *Arthur* and USS *Corypheus* approached. (*OR,* 9:622; *ORN,* 19:151; Porter, *Naval History,* 346; *WCWN,* 140.)

Casimer Castro (Castro). U.S. Army. Chartered screw steamer, 128 tons. Was seized at Matamoras, Mexico from Confederate owners. Was sunk at the Brazos Bar in November 1865 but was later raised. (*MSV,* 31.)

Carolina (Rosita) (Union). British. Side-wheel steamer, 238 bulk tons, 115 gross tons, 52 registered tons. Length 128 feet, beam 23 feet 11 inches, depth 13 feet. Built as the tug *Union* in 1861 at Philadelphia. Captured by the USS *Huntsville* on May 19, 1863. Converted to the blockade-runner *Rosita* in 1864. The *Rosita* was captured by the Union transport *Western Metropolis* on March 28, 1864, in the Gulf of Mexico and sold as a prize. Was renamed *Carolina* and put back into blockade-running. Ran aground while leaving Galveston on July 7, 1864. (*LLC,* 292, 318, 324–25.)

Cassie Holt (Catherine Holt). Confederate. Sloop. Cargo of twenty-five bales of cotton. Was run aground on February 29, 1864, by the USS *Virginia* inside Galveston Island at San Luis Pass. The USS *Virginia* was unable to burn the vessel. (*ORN,* 21:119.)

Catherine. Nationality unknown. Schooner. Stranded while attempting to run the Union blockade at Sabine. Was burned by the crew. Could be off the Louisiana coast. (*ORN,* 19:480.)

Clifton (USS Clifton). Confederate. Side-wheel steamer, 892 bulk tons. Length 210 feet, beam 40 feet, depth 13 feet 4 inches, draft 7 feet 6 inches. Cargo of cotton. Built in 1861 at Brooklyn, N.Y. Originally a ferryboat. Captured and converted into a Union gunboat with a complement of 121 and armed with four 32-pounders, two 9-inch smoothbores, and one rifled 30-pounder. Captured by Confederates at Sabine Pass, Tex. on September 8, 1863. Ran aground on the west side of the channel at the Sabine Pass Bar and burned on March 21, 1864, while trying to escape through the Union blockade. The cotton was thrown overboard. (*OR,* 41:3:964; *ORN,* 21:158–61; ser. 2, 1:59; *LLC,* 186–87, 294: *WCWN,* 99, 233; Ships of the Texas Marine Department Web site.)

Colonel Stell (Colonel Stelle) (J. D. Stell) (J. D. Stelle). Confederate. Side-wheel steamer, 198 tons. Length 138 feet, beam 24 feet, depth 4 feet 8 inches. Built in 1860 at Pittsburgh, Pa. Confederate transport in the Galveston area. Accidentally sank off Pelican Island in Galveston Bay on February 10, 1864. Was quickly raised by the Confederates. (*CWC,* 6-214; *MSV,* 41.)

Columbia. Confederate. Schooner. Crew of seven. Cargo of cotton. Out of Galveston bound for Kingston, Jamaica. Was captured on April 5, 1862, and destroyed the next day by a boat from USS *Montgomery* near Fort San Luis, San Luis Pass. (*ORN,* 18:104–8.)

Conchita. Confederate. Schooner. Was captured and burned in October 1862 near Calcasieu and Sabine Pass. Could possibly be off the Louisiana coast. (*ORN*, 19:227; *SCH*, 370–71.)

Denbigh. British. Side-wheel iron steamer, 250 gross tons, 162 registered tons. Length 182 feet, beam 22 feet, depth 8 feet 5 inches. Built in 1860 at Birkenhead, England. While arriving in Galveston from Havana, Cuba, it grounded on May 23–24, 1865, on Bird Key Spit near Bolivar Point in 12 feet of water while being chased by the USS *Fort Jackson*, USS *Cornubia*, and USS *Princess Royal*. Part of the cargo was plundered by a mob in the chaos caused at end of the Civil War. Was boarded by a party the next day from the USS *Kennebec* and USS *Seminole* and burned. One Union seaman was killed accidentally when his gun discharged. The *Denbigh* made more than twenty-four trips through the Union blockade before being the last blockade-runner destroyed. Located near Fort Travis. At extremely low tide, the side-wheels and part of the vessel are visible. Investigated by Texas A&M University's Institute of Nautical Archaeology. (*ORN*, 22:197, 224; Horner, *Blockade-Runners*, 203; Daly, *Aboard the USS* Florida, 224; "The *Denbigh* Project: Archaeology of a Confederate Blockade Runner," Texas A&M Institute of Nautical Archaeology Web site; *LLC*, 296.)

Eager. Confederate. Schooner. Cargo of assorted merchandise. Burned at a wharf near the customhouse at Point Isabel near Brazos Santiago on the morning of May 30, 1863, when launches from USS *Brooklyn* approached. (*OR*, 26:1:185; *ORN*, 20:281.)

CSS Elmea (Elma) (Major Minter). Confederate. Armed sloop or schooner. Ran ashore in a channel of Nueces Bay across from Corpus Cristi on August 11, 1862. Was burned the next day by Confederates to prevent its capture by USS *Arthur*. (*OR*, 9:618; *ORN*, 19:151, 302, 783; *CWC*, 6-224; *WCWN*, 235.)

Emily. Nationality unknown. Schooner. Ran on beach below Port Velasco on March 21 or 22, 1864. Quickly filled with sand and water, but its rigging and cargo were saved by the Confederates. (*OR*, 34:1:653; 34:2:1076; *ORN*, 21:152, 883.)

Express (Experiment). Confederate. Schooner. Cargo of 31 bales of cotton. En route from Galveston to Tampico,

Mexico. Was captured on May 3, 1864, by the USS *Virginia*. The vessel was considered unseaworthy, so the cargo was removed and the vessel torched. (*ORN*, 21:238, 273, 814.)

Frederick the Great. Nationality unknown. Schooner. Cargo of gunpowder, lead, caps, rope, liquor, and other goods. Out of Havana, Cuba. Ran ashore near the mouth of Caney River the night of February 2, 1864, to escape capture by Union boats from the USS *Queen*. The cargo was salvaged by the 2nd Tex. Infantry Regiment from a nearby fort. (*OR*, 53 [supp.]: 961; *ORN*, 21:44.)

Gillum. Union. Steamer. En route from New Orleans to Matamoras, Mexico when wrecked. Nine men of the vessel were picked up in a boat on September 3, 1864, by the USS *Circassian* off Sabine Pass. The schooner *Cora* picked up the rest of the crew. (*ORN*, 27:683.)

Granite City (City of Dundee) (USS Granite City) (Three Marys). Confederate. Side-wheel iron steamer, 400 bulk tons, 315 burden tons, 450 gross tons, 463 British gross registered tons. Length 160 feet, beam 23 feet, depth 9 feet 2 inches, draft 5 feet 6 inches. Launched in 1862 at Dumbarton, Scotland. Captured by the USS *Tioga* as a blockade-runner off Eleuthera Island, Bahamas, on March 22, 1863. Converted to a Union warship. The USS *Granite City* was captured on May 6, 1864, by Confederate batteries at Calcasieu Pass, La. The blockade-runner *Granite City* was chased ashore by the USS *Penguin* on January 20–21, 1865, off Velasco. (*CWC*, 6-243; *WCWN*, 82; *LLC*, 303.)

Hannah. Confederate. Armed schooner. Ran aground while attempting to go over a 4-foot high reef or bank into Nueces Bay, 7 miles above Corpus Christi. The USS *Corypheus* anchored 400 yards offshore and landed a party. The Confederates set the *Hannah* afire on August 12, 1862, to prevent the vessel from being captured. (*OR*, 9:618; *ORN*, 19:151, 302, 783; *CWC*, 6-247.)

Hanover. Confederate. Schooner. Chased ashore near Galveston and burned by boats from USS *Owasco* and USS *Katahdin* on May 10, 1863. (*ORN*, 20:177.)

USS Hatteras (St. Marys). Union. Bark rigged wooden side-wheel steam gunboat, 1,126 bulk tons. Length 210 feet, beam 34 feet, depth 18 feet, speed 13 knots. Complement of 18 officers and 108 men, with one 12-pounder howitzer, one 20-pounder, two 30-pounder Parrotts, and four 32-pounder smoothbores. Built in 1861 at Wilmington, Del. Was sunk 19 miles off Galveston in the Gulf of Mexico by Capt. Raphael Semmes's CSS *Alabama* after a fifteen-minute engagement on January 11, 1863. The battle took place at a distance of 25–100 yards. The USS *Hatteras* was holed, its engines disabled with the walking beams shot away, and was afire in two places. Its guns were thrown overboard. The crew lost 2 killed, 5 wounded, and 103 captured, including Lt. Cdr. Homer C. Blake. The CSS *Alabama* had 2 wounded crewmen. The USS *Brooklyn* discovered the masthead of the USS *Hatteras* on January 12, 1863, in 9.5 fathoms about 20 miles south of the Galveston Light. In 1976 the wreck was found by Houston scuba divers under the mud at a depth of 55 feet, about 14 miles offshore. The divers recovered a few artifacts from the site and filed claim on the vessel in district court in a civil lawsuit, *Hatteras, Inc. v. the U.S.S.* Hatteras, in 1978. The U.S. Navy seized the salvaged material from the divers and won a court case that set precedent that the U.S. government continues to own all government shipwrecked vessels due to sovereign immunity. Remote sensing and monitoring has been done by the Texas Historical Commission and the U.S. Minerals Management Service, along with Texas A&M University's Institute of Nautical Archaeology. The wreck is under about 3 feet of sediment, with part of the steam engine and paddlewheels above the sediment. The site is listed as a Texas State Archaeological Landmark and is in the National Register of Historic Places. (*ORN*, 2:18–23, 684; 19:506–9, 512, 582; ser. 2, 1:100; Delaney, "At Semmes' Hand," *Civil War Times Illustrated*, 22–27; Delaney, "Raising the *Hatteras*," *Civil War Times Illustrated*, 28–29; Semmes, *Service Afloat*, 542–50; *Federal Register*, December 4, 1990, 50145; Arnold, *Marine Magnetometer Survey*, 13; Arnold and Anuskiewicz, "USS *Hatteras*: Site Monitoring and Mapping," *Underwater Archaeology Proceedings*, 82–87; Minerals Management Service Web site.)

I. W. Hancox. Union. Steam tug. Was lost in late 1862 off the Texas Coast. (*OR*, 26:1:829.)

Jane. British. Schooner. Out of New Providence, Bahamas. Was destroyed by its crew to prevent its capture by USS *Tennessee* on October 12, 1863, off the Brazos River. The *Jane* blew up and the explosion was heard 30 miles away in Galveston. (*ORN*, 20:632.)

CSS *John F. Carr*. Confederate. Cottonclad gunboat, 200 tons. Draft 2 feet 6 inches. Armed with two guns. Ran ashore high and dry after shelling a Union force. Confederates set the vessel afire to prevent capture on December 30, 1863, at the Matagorda Peninsula. Hauled onto a bank at Lynchburg by Union forces to prevent it from sinking into deeper water. Later appeared to have been put back into Confederate service. Possibly again wrecked in Matagorda Bay in early 1864. (*OR*, 26:1:480–83; 48:2:1121; *ORN*, 20:743; *WCWN*, 234.)

CSS *Josiah A. Bell* (*J. A. Bell*). Confederate. Side-wheel cottonclad gunboat, 412 tons. Length 171 feet, beam 30 feet, draft 4 feet 6 inches, depth 6 feet 8 inches. Complement of thirty-five, with one 24-pounder and one 12-pounder howitzer. Built in 1853 at Jeffersonville, Ind. Operated off Sabine Pass from 1863 to 1864. Was scuttled in 1865, possibly in Sabine Lake. (*ORN*, 19:394; ser. 2, 1:257; Ships of the Texas Marine Department Web site, 5; *MSV*, 105; *WCWN*, 234.)

Juanita. Mexican. Schooner. Out of Matamoras, Mexico. Carried five passengers and a crew on its way from Matamoras, Mexico. Captured by USS *Virginia*. A Union prize crew of six was put aboard, but the prize crew got drunk and the schooner was wrecked inside the line of breakers toward the beach at San Luis Pass on April 11, 1864. The prize crew was captured by Confederates. Shelled by Union vessels and hit by one projectile on April 12, 1864. (*ORN*, 21:174–82.)

Juliana. French. Sloop. Seized by the Union navy at Galveston and sunk in 1863 by the USS *Owasco*. (*ORN*, 20:639)

Kate. Union. Schooner. Was lost at Brazos Pass on October 31, 1863. (*ORN*, 20:648; *ORA*, pl. 43, no. 8.)

***Lecompt* (*Lecompte*).** Confederate. Army chartered schooner. Was captured by the USS *Westfield* and USS *Clifton* in October 1862. Was recaptured by Confederates at Galveston on January 1, 1863. Was grounded on Bird Key Spit or Bolivar Point Beach in Galveston Bay on

May 24, 1865, while being chased by the USS *Cornubia*. Was set afire by Union forces, bilged, and lost its rudder. The schooner's 24-pounder howitzer was thrown overboard. Ten rifle muskets were taken off the wreck. (*ORN,* 22:197–98; *CWC,* 6-261; *WCWN,* 235.)

Lizzie Baron. Confederate. Schooner. Sank near a beach off Lamar in February 1864. (*OR,* 34:1:135.)

Lone Star. Confederate. Schooner. Was burned by boats from USS *Rachel Seaman* and USS *Kensington* in Taylor's Bayou on October 15, 1862. (*ORN,* 19:228.)

Louisa. Schooner. Wrecked in a southeast gale on the night of November 24, 1864. Was found grounded on a bar at the mouth of the San Bernard River by the USS *Chocura*. (*ORN,* 21:755; *WCWN,* 51.)

Louisa. Confederate. Schooner. Cargo of baggage, cordage, wines, and crockery. Was sunk by shells from USS *Penobscot* in shallow water at Aransas Pass on February 16, 1865. Burned on February 18, 1865, by Union forces. (*ORN,* 22:53.)

Manhassett (Manhasset). Union. Supply schooner. Cargo of coal. On September 19, 1863, a heavy gale washed the schooner ashore 7 miles southwest of Sabine Pass, where it broke up. The vessel was out of the water. The crew was captured by Confederate forces. (*ORN,* 20:626, 841.)

Marion (Marian). Confederate. Schooner, 12–18 tons. Cargo of salt and iron bars. Was captured by USS *Aroostook* off Velasco on March 12, 1864. Leaking so badly that the sails, rigging, and cargo were removed and the *Marion* was sunk in 4.5 fathoms off Galveston on March 14, 1864. (*ORN,* 21:136, 142, 780, 810.)

Mary Agnes. Confederate. Schooner. Cargo of baggage, cordage, wines, and crockery. Was chased ashore by USS *Penobscot* on February 16, 1865, in shallow water off Aransas Pass and burned by Union forces two days later. (*ORN,* 22:53.)

Mary Ann. Confederate. Schooner. Cargo of cotton. En route from Calcasieu. La., for Tampico, Mexico when captured by USS *Antona* on November 26, 1863, and destroyed. (*ORN,* 19:227; *SCH,* 420–21; *WCWN,* 87.)

Mary Ann. Confederate. Sloop. Cargo of twenty-one cotton bales. Out of Galveston. Was chased ashore at Pass Cavallo and destroyed by the USS *Itasca* after the removal of its cargo on December 8, 1864. The masts and beams were cut off, and the vessel was last seen underwater. (*ORN,* 21:756, 777.)

Mary Hill. U.S. Side-wheel steamer, 234 tons. Draft 2 feet. Armed with one 24-pounder and one 12-pounder. Built in 1859 at Smithfield, Tex. Was used as a Confederate cotton-clad gunboat, transport, and guard ship during the Civil War. Was lost by snagging in the Trinity River on November 22, 1865. (Ships of the Texas Marine Department Web site, 6; *MSV,* 139.)

Matagorda (Alice). Confederate. Side-wheel steamer, 616 bulk tons, 1,250 gross tons. Length 220 feet, beam 30 feet, draft 10 feet 6 inches. Cargo of cotton. Built in 1858 at Wilmington, Del. En route from Galveston to San Luis. Was driven ashore off Galveston Island, 7 miles northeast of San Luis Pass on July 7, 1864, only three hours after leaving Galveston. The USS *Kanawha* and USS *Penguin* shelled men trying to salvage the wrecked vessel on July 8, 1864. Two boats from the USS *Penguin* and one from the USS *Kanawha* boarded it and set it afire. Was salvaged by the Confederates. Was later captured by the USS *Magnolia* on September 10, 1864. (*ORN,* 21:364–65, 781–82; 27:679.)

Matilda. Confederate. Schooner. Wrecked in 1863 at Matagorda Bay. (*SCH,* 424–25.)

Mexico. Union. Side-wheel steamer, 120 tons. Built in 1859 at Wheeling, Va. (W. Va.). Burned on March 18, 1865, at Point Isabel. (*MSV,* 144, 281; *WPD,* 321.)

Monte Christo. Confederate. Schooner. Burned by Confederates to prevent its capture by the USS *Arthur* on July 10, 1862, at Lamar. (*ORN,* 18:672, 856; 19:302.)

CSS Morning Light (USS Morning Light). Union. Sloop, 937 or 938 tons. Length 172 feet, beam 34 feet 3 inches, draft 19 feet, depth 24 feet. Complement of 120, with eight 24-pounders and one rifled Butler gun. The USS *Morning Light* was captured by the CSS *Josiah H. Bell* and CSS *Uncle Ben,* which were manned by troops from Pyron's 2nd Tex. Cavalry Regiment, Liken's Tex. Battalion, and Cook's

1st Tex. Heavy Artillery at Sabine Pass on January 21, 1863, with one killed and nine wounded. The CSS *Morning Light* burned and sank on January 23, 1863, in 10–25 feet of water on the outer edge of the Sabine Pass Bar when the vessel could not cross and the USS *New London* and USS *Cayuga* approached. Located about 4 miles northwest of a lighthouse. Some guns were removed by the Confederates and the vessel's anchor salvaged by the Union. (*ORN,* 19:553–72; ser. 2, 1:151, 260; *WCWN,* 139.)

Morning Star II. Nationality unknown. Side-wheel steamboat, 198 tons. Built in 1858 at Belle Vernon, Pa. Burned in 1863 by Confederates off the Texas coast. (*MSV,* 149; *EAS,* 182.)

Nassau. Union. Chartered side-wheel or screw steam tug, 518 tons. Speed 6 miles per hour. Built in 1851 at New York City. Sunk on November 5, 1863, at Brazos Pass. (*OR,* 26:1:410; *ORA,* pl. 43, no. 8; *MSV,* 152.)

***Neptune Camp* (*Camp*) (*Neptune*).** Confederate. Cotton-clad wooden steam tug. Complement of two hundred Confederate soldiers, with one rifled 68-pounder and one 24-pounder. Nine cannons had earlier been removed from the *Neptune Camp.* Used as a transport. Attacked the USS *Harriet Lane* on January 1, 1863, in Galveston Harbor during the Confederate recapture of the port. The 24-pounder burst on the second firing. Confederate soldiers from the *Neptune Camp* and CSS *Bayou City* boarded the USS *Harriet Lane* and captured it. The *Neptune Camp*'s bow was damaged when it rammed the USS *Harriet Lane* and one Union shell went through the *Neptune Camp*'s hull, sinking it off the end of Galveston Island on a shoal in eight feet of water. The Confederates lost eight killed and twenty wounded. Three of the wounded later died. (*OR,* 15:202–3, 215–16; *ORN,* 19:468–69, 475; *CWC,* 6-276; *WCWN,* 234.)

Orizaba. U.S. Ship, 630 bulk tons. Not the *Orizaba,* which was converted to the CSS *Resolute.* Stranded on June 15, 1865, at Liberty. (*WCWN,* 232; *MSV,* 165.)

Patridge. Union. Schooner. Was lost at Brazos Pass on November 5, 1863. (*ORA,* pl. 43, no. 8.)

***Patroon* (USS *Patroon*).** U.S. Screw steamer, 183 bulk tons, 237 tons. Length 113 feet, beam 22 feet 5 inches, draft 7 feet. Built in 1859 at Philadelphia. Was decommissioned

on November 18, 1862, and sold on December 30, 1862. Was then sold to the War Department on December 8, 1863. Sunk at Brazos on November 10, 1865. (*OR,* ser. 3, 4:915; *WCWN,* 105; *MSV,* 168.)

Reindeer. Confederate. Schooner, 4 tons. Crew of three. Cargo of sixteen bags of salt. En route to Galveston. Was captured and sunk by the USS *Sam Houston* and USS *Dart* off San Luis Pass on October 3, 1861. (*ORN,* 16:734.)

Relief. Union. Schooner. Out of Chester, Pa. Burned at Point Isabel by Confederates on May 29, 1863. (*ORN,* 20:758.)

Richard O'Brien. British. Schooner. Cargo of $2,000 worth of rum, sugar, and medicines. En route from Jamaica to Matamoras, Mexico. Was run aground about 17 miles southwest of Galveston and 6 miles east of Velasco on July 4, 1862, by the USS *Rhode Island.* About one-half of the cargo was taken ashore by Confederate soldiers. Six coils of rigging and some medical stores were salvaged by Union sailors before they burned the ship as a heavy squall approached. (*OR,* 9:609–10; *ORN,* 27:449–52, 704.)

***Rosalie* (*Rosa Lee*).** Confederate. Schooner. Burned in the Gulf of Mexico off the Texas coast in December 1863. (*ORN,* 20:741.)

Rosina. Confederate. Sloop. Was run ashore on April 13, 1864, by the USS *Virginia* off San Luis Pass. Two Union boats boarded the vessel on April 15, taking out the mast, rigging, and an anchor. Was set afire by Union shells. (*ORN,* 21:195.)

Star. Confederate. Schooner. In charge of the Point Isabel customhouse. Was captured by a shore party of eighty-seven men from the USS *Brooklyn* under Lt. Cdr. Chester Hatfield at Point Isabel near Brazos Santiago on May 30, 1863. Was run aground and burned. (*ORN,* 20:281.)

Sting Ray. British. Schooner. Out of Havana, Cuba. Was captured by the USS *Kineo* on May 22, 1864. A prize crew consisting of Acting Ensign Paul Borner and seven sailors was put aboard. The prize crew obtained liquor from the captured crew and got drunk, running the ship ashore 2 miles west of Velasco. Five members of the Union prize crew were captured by a company of the 13th Tex. Infantry Regiment. (*OR,* 34:1:943–44; *ORN,* 21:296.)

Stonewall. Confederate. Schooner. Burned by boats from the USS *Rachel Seaman* and USS *Kensington* in Taylor's Bayou on October 15, 1862. (*ORN*, 19:228.)

Tom Hicks. Confederate. Schooner, 27 tons. Cargo of lumber. Out of Calcasieu, La. En route to Port Lavaca. Was captured and destroyed by the USS *South Carolina* on July 9, 1861, off Galveston. (*ORN*, 16:578, 595; *WCWN*, 80–81.)

Union. Union. Side-wheel steamer, 227 tons. Speed 6 miles per hour. Was stranded on October 31, 1863, in the Gulf of Mexico off Texas. Was probably salvaged and sold in 1865. (*ORN*, 20:648; *ORA*, pl. 43, no. 8; *MSV*, 218, 303.)

Victoria. Confederate. Sloop, 100 tons. En route from Jamaica. Carried assorted cargo. Was captured by Lt. Cdr. Chester Hatfield and eighty-seven men in four boats from the USS *Brooklyn* at Point Isabel near Brazos Santiago on May 30, 1863. Was run aground and set afire by Union sailors. (*OR*, 26:1:485.)

USS Westfield. Union. Side-wheel steamer, 891 bulk tons. Length 215 feet, beam 35 feet, depth 13 feet 6 inches. Complement of 116, with one 100-pounder Parrott, one 9-inch Dahlgren smoothbore, and four 8-inch smoothbores. Built in 1861 at New York City. Grounded off Pelican Island in Galveston Harbor during the Confederate recapture of Galveston on the early morning of January 1, 1863. Cdr. William B. Renshaw set fire to the USS *Westfield* to prevent its capture by the *Neptune Camp* and CSS *Bayou City* which had just captured the USS *Harriet Lane*. Its magazines blew up prematurely, killing Commander Renshaw, four officers, and six sailors. The Confederates later recovered six cannons and raised the forged steel shafts of the ship, which were converted into gun barrels. (*OR*, 34:4:62; *ORN*, 19:441, 450–51, 464, 466, 663, 745; 24:243; ser. 2 1:238; *CWC*, 6-214; Barr, "Texas Coastal Defense, 1861–1865," *Southwestern Historical Quarterly*, 1–31; *MSV*, 228; *WCWN*, 102.)

Will O' the Wisp. British. Iron side-wheel steamer, 511 bulk tons, 117 registered tons. Length 210 feet, beam 23 feet, depth 10 feet. Cargo of provisions and small arms. Built in 1863 at Renfrew, Scotland. Chased ashore by Union ships and riddled by shelling on February 9–10, 1865, a few miles southwest of Galveston, 1,000 yards from the 12-foot depth line. Some of the cargo of guns was landed by Confederates. Was boarded by Union sailors in five boats from the USS *Princess Royal* and USS *Antona* and set afire. The hold quickly filled with sand, and the wheelhouse was above water. The engine was taken apart, and some of the machinery was removed by Confederates. Has been magnetometer surveyed by Texas A&M University. (*ORN*, 22:33–37; Horner *Blockade-Runners*, 203; Porter, *Naval History*, 779; *LLC*, 216–17, 327: Anuskiewicz, "Marine Archaeology," *Proceedings: Seventh Annual Gulf of Mexico Transfer Meeting*, 234.)

Young Harry. Union. Brig. Cargo of four hundred barrels of flour, clothes, and other goods. En route for Matamoras, Mexico. Wrecked in Texas waters, 6 miles from the mouth of the Rio Grande in March 1863. The crew was captured by Confederates and paroled. (*OR*, 15:1012–13.)

▷ VESSELS WITHOUT NAMES

hulk. Nationality unknown. Was sunk by Confederates in the channel between the fort at the end of town and the town of Galveston in 1861. (*ORN*, 16:812.)

schooner. Confederate. 60–70 tons. Was chased ashore and wrecked on November 13, 1861, by the USS *Sam Houston* at San Luis Bar. (*ORN*, 16:768.)

schooner. Confederate. Cargo of cement. Scuttled in July 1862 in Aransas Bay to block the channel to Union vessels. (*OR*, 9:612.)

schooner. Confederate. Cargo of cotton. Was destroyed by USS *Estrella* on March 28, 1864, at Matagorda Bay. (*ORN*, 21:162.)

schooner. Confederate. 100 tons. Possibly the *Carrie Mair*. En route to Matagorda. Chased ashore and destroyed on November 29, 1864, by the USS *Itasca* about 5 miles northward and eastward of De Crow's Point. (*ORN*, 21:745; *WCWN*, 52.)

schooners. Confederate. Two schooners. Cargoes of cotton. Anchored at Corpus Christi, behind Mustang Island, waiting to leave on July 8, 1863, when the USS *Sciota* appeared. The two schooners sailed up the bay and grounded, enabling Union boats from the USS *Sciota* to burn them. (*ORN*, 20:384.)

schooners. Nationalities unknown. Two schooners. Were lost on October 15, 1861, alongside the Galveston wharf in a storm. (*ORN*, 16:862.)

schooners. Union. Two schooners. Foundered in the Gulf of Mexico off Texas on October 31, 1863, in a storm. The *Kate* may have been one of the schooners. (*ORA*, pl. 43, no. 8.)

sloop. Confederate. Was forced ashore and destroyed by the USS *Kanawha* near Caney Creek on December 28, 1864. (*ORN*, 21:755.)

vessel. Confederate. Cargo of Mexican blankets, salt, and sundries. Out of Tampico, Mexico. Beached by a storm on December 29, 1863, 5 miles from the mouth of the San Bernard River. (*OR*, 26:1:485; *ORN*, 20:758.)

vessel. Nationality unknown. Was chased ashore near the mouth of the Caney River, near Velasco, on September 22, 1863, by a Union schooner. Was set afire by its crew. A skirmish occurred between Union sailors and Confederates onshore. (*OR*, 26:2:263.)

vessels. Confederate. Two vessels. Along with the *Belle Italia*. Loaded with stone. Were sunk in the Corpus Christi "dugout" channel connecting Aransas Bay and Corpus Christi Bay. The vessels were removed by the USS *Corypheus* on August 12, 1862. (*ORN*, 19:151.)

Virginia

During the Civil War there were many waterborne engagements and vessels sunk off the shores of Virginia, the heart of the Confederacy. While abandoning the Gosport Navy Yard at Norfolk on April 20–21, 1861, the Union navy sank and burned the USS *Columbia*, USS *Columbus*, USS *Delaware*, USS *Dolphin*, USS *Germantown*, USS *Merrimack*, USS *New York*, USS *Plymouth*, USS *Raritan*, and USS *Pennsylvania* to prevent their capture by Confederate Virginia forces. The Confederates raised the USS *Plymouth* and USS *Germantown* as well as the USS *Merrimack*, which was converted into the ironclad ram CSS *Virginia*.

The CSS *Virginia* attacked the Union fleet at Hampton Roads on March 8, 1862, sinking the USS *Cumberland* and USS *Congress*. The appearance of the USS *Monitor* on March 9, 1862, and the resulting battle, which ended in a draw, saved the Union fleet in Hampton Roads. On May 10, 1862, the Confederates abandoned Norfolk and the Gosport Navy Yard, scuttling or burning the CSS *Virginia*, CSS *Germantown*, CSS *Plymouth*, CSS *Confederate States*, CSS *Jesup*, CSS *Norfolk*, CSS *Portsmouth*, and *William Seldon*. The Confederate raider CSS *Florida* was scuttled by secret orders on November 28, 1864, at Hampton Roads, in order to end an international incident caused by the capture of the vessel in a neutral port in violation of international law.

Numerous vessels were sunk in the James River, York River, and other rivers and streams that empty into the Chesapeake Bay. Some vessels were sunk to block Union or Confederate ships, while others were destroyed by raiders from both sides throughout the war. John Taylor Wood became legendary for capturing Union vessels in the Chesapeake Bay area. Wood's raiders captured and destroyed the *Alleghany, Coquette, Francis Elmor, Golden Rod, Harriet de Ford,* USS *Reliance,* USS *Satellite, Titan,* and several other Union vessels. Confederate torpedoes sank several Union vessels, including the *Commodore Jones,* and accidentally sank the Confederate vessels *A. H. Schultz* and *Allison.*

On the night of April 2–3, 1865, as Richmond was being abandoned by President Jefferson Davis and the Confederate government, the Confederate James River Fleet—consisting of the CSS *Beaufort,* CSS *Fredericksburg,* CSS *Hampton,* CSS *Nansemond,* CSS *Richmond,* CSS *Roanoke,* CSS *Shrapnel,* CSS *Torpedo,* and CSS *Virginia II*—was blown up and sank in the James River near Drewry's Bluff. The Confederate navy training ship, the CSS *Patrick Henry,* was destroyed at Richmond's Rocketts Navy Yard. As soon as the Civil War ended, with the United States seeking to return to prosperity, some of the wrecks from the James River Fleet were cleared away so that the James River could resume commercial navigation.

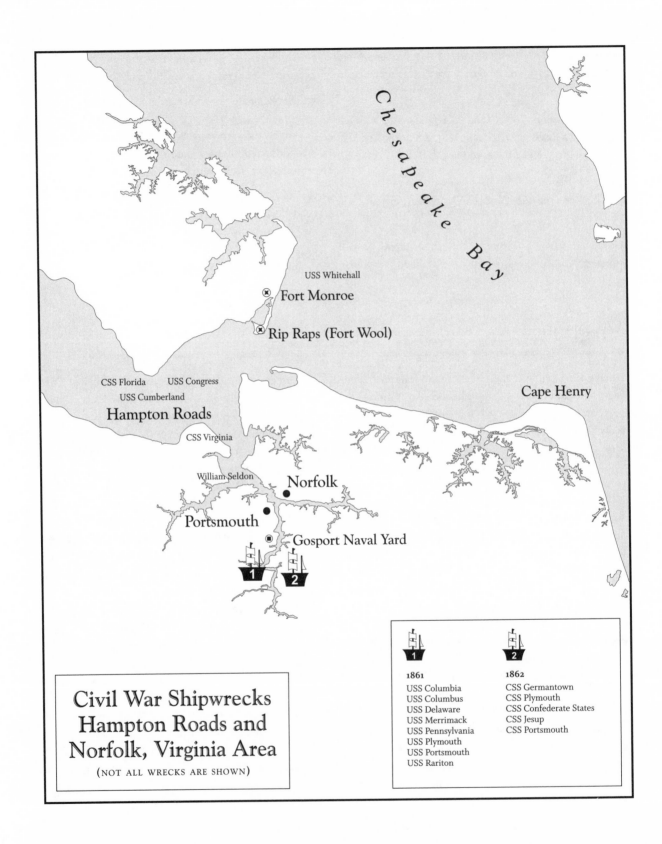

Chesapeake Bay

USS Whitehall
⊗ Fort Monroe

⊗ Rip Raps (Fort Wool)

CSS Florida   USS Congress
USS Cumberland

Hampton Roads

Cape Henry

CSS Virginia

William Seldon

Norfolk

Portsmouth

Gosport Naval Yard

1

2

1861
USS Columbia
USS Columbus
USS Delaware
USS Merrimack
USS Pennsylvania
USS Plymouth
USS Portsmouth
USS Rariton

1862
CSS Germantown
CSS Plymouth
CSS Confederate States
CSS Jesup
CSS Portsmouth

Civil War Shipwrecks
Hampton Roads and
Norfolk, Virginia Area
(NOT ALL WRECKS ARE SHOWN)

Ada. Confederate. Schooner, 120 tons. Cargo of wood. Out of Baltimore. Ran aground on November 6, 1861, 5–6 miles from the mouth of the Curatona Branch of the Rappahannock River or on Corrotoman Creek, 26 miles from the mouth of the Rappahannock River. Was burned by a Union small boat expedition from the USS *Rescue*, including Midshipman William Barker Cushing, three other officers, and thirty sailors. One Union sailor was wounded by ambush when returning from the raid. (*ORN*, 6:407–8, 422, 423, 690–91.)

Agnes. Union. Screw steamer, 299 tons. Built in 1852 at Greenpoint, N.Y. Burned in Virginia waters on June 19, 1862. (*OR*, 11:3:262; *MSV*, 239.)

CSS A. H. Schultz (Schultz). Confederate. Side-wheel steamer, 164 tons. Built in 1849 or 1850 in New York City. Used as a flag of truce ship to transport exchanged prisoners of war from Varina Landing on the James River to other points. On a return trip without prisoners on February 19, 1865, the vessel hit a floating Confederate torpedo, which had broken loose just below the barricades at Drewry's Bluff above Cox's Landing at Bishop's Bluff, 60 yards from the south bank, near Chaffin's Bluff. Sank in five minutes with two African-American firemen and two guards killed. (*OR*, 46:2:646; *ORN*, 12:186; Scharf, *History of the Confederate Navy*, 767; *CWC*, 6-299; *WCWN*, 243.)

Albion. Norwegian. Bark. Wrecked 25 miles below Cape Henry. The cargo may have been salvaged in mid-May 1861. (*ORN*, 4:387.)

Alert. Confederate. Ship. Was scuttled in the Pamunkey River by Confederates near Bassett's Landing on May 17, 1862. (*ORN*, 7:379–82.)

USS Alert (A. C. Powell) (USS Watch). Union. Tug, 90 bulk tons. Length 62 feet, beam 17 feet, draft 6 feet 5 inches. Complement of eighteen, with one 24-pounder smoothbore. Built in 1861 at Syracuse, N.Y. Was burned and sank at a wharf at the Gosport Navy Yard on May 31, 1863. Was raised and returned to Union service as the USS *Watch* on February 2, 1865. (*ORN*, 9:53; ser. 2, 1:237; *WCWN*, 113.)

Alleghany (Alleghanian). Union. Ship, 1,120 or 1,400 tons. Cargo of guano. Out of Baltimore. Crew of twenty-five.

En route to London. Was captured by Lt. John Taylor Wood and three boats with about twenty men and was burned 5–12 miles outside of the mouth of the Rappahannock River off Gwun's Island on October 29–30, 1862, while anchored in 30 fathoms. The fire was put out by the USS *Crusader* and USS *T. A. Wood*. At 10:00 p.m. three Confederate boats under Lieutenant Wood reboarded the vessel and set it afire again as its crew fled in two boats. (*ORN*, 5:138–41; 8:161–68; ser. 2, 3:167; *New York Times*, February 21, 1865; Shingleton, *John Taylor Wood*, 66–67.)

Alliance. Union. Large schooner. Cargo of sutler's stores worth $200,000. En route to Port Royal, S.C. Was captured in Chesapeake Bay by Confederates in small boats under Acting Master John Y. Beall from two Confederate privateers. Grounded on September 23, 1863, in Old Haven Creek or Milford Haven when the prize crew missed the mouth of the Piankatank River. More than $10,000 worth of cargo was landed before the schooner was burned upon the approach of a Union ship. (*ORN*, 9:203–9; *CWC*, 6-196.)

Amazon. Confederate. Schooner. Purchased for $1,600 by the Confederacy. Was sunk on May 10, 1862, to act as an obstruction at Warmick Bar, James River. (*War Department Collection of Confederate Records, Record Group 109, Vessel Papers.*)

American Coaster. Confederate. Ship. Was burned by Confederates between May 5 and 10, 1862, at Cooke Island on the Pamunkey River. (*ORN*, 7:379–82.)

Ann Bell. Confederate. Ship. Was scuttled by Confederates to act as an obstruction near Bassett's Landing on the Pamunkey River on May 17, 1862, to block Union vessels. (*ORN*, 7:379–82; *CWC*, 6-332.)

Arctic. Confederate. Schooner. Was captured with the schooner *Sarah* in the eastern branch of the Great Yeocomico or Wicomico Creek by the USS *Satellite*. Was burned by the USS *Thomas Freeborn* on May 28, 1863, after its sails were removed. (*ORN*, 5:85, 277.)

CSS Beaufort (Caledonia) (Roanoke). Confederate. Iron steam tug, 85 or 90 tons. Length 85 feet, beam 17 feet 5 inches, depth 6 feet 11 inches. Armed with two guns, including a rifled 32-pounder pivot forward. Built in 1854 at Wilmington, Del. Tender of the CSS *Virginia*. Was scuttled at Drewry's Bluff on April 2–3, 1865. Was raised and taken into the Union navy. Was sold on September 15, 1865. Became the merchant vessel *Roanoke*. (*ORN*, ser. 2, 1:249; *CWC*, 6-204; *WCWN*, 243.)

CSS *Beauregard*. Confederate. Schooner. Used to transport coal for the CSS *Virginia*. Was captured and burned by Union forces off Ragged Island at 2:00 a.m. on May 4, 1862, as the vessel carried coal from City Point to Norfolk. Was removed by Benjamin Maillefert under a U.S. Army Corps of Engineers contract in 1871–72. (*ORN*, 7:785; *Chief of Engineers Report* 1870, 73; *Chief of Engineers Report 1872*, 690.)

Ben Bolt. Confederate. Barge. Was captured and destroyed by two cutters from the USS *Mahaska* on February 24, 1863, at Back Creek, York River. (*ORN*, 8:567.)

Betsey Richards. Confederate. Ship. Was scuttled by Confederates to act as an obstruction at Bassett's Landing on the Pamunkey River on May 17, 1862. (*ORN*, 7:379–82; *CWC*, 6-332.)

USS *Brandywine*. Union. Frigate, 1,708 or 1,726 tons. Length 175 feet, beam 45 feet, depth 14 feet 5 inches, draft 22 feet, speed 13 knots. Complement of four hundred, with 44 guns. Laid down in September 1821 and launched in 1825 at Washington, D.C. Used as a store ship. Caught fire on September 3, 1864, while at the Gosport Navy Yard. The conflagration started in the paint locker in the forward hold and gutted the vessel by fire. Was raised on March 26, 1867. (*ORN*, ser. 2, 1:47; *WCWN*, 127–28.)

Buckskin. Union. Sloop. Out of Alexandria. Was captured by Confederate guerrillas. Was recaptured by the USS *Anacostia* on November 7, 1864, and burned on Chopawamsic Creek. (*ORN*, 5:492.)

California. Confederate. Schooner. Was burned by Confederates and sunk to act as an obstruction at Cumberland Landing on the Pamunkey River on May 5–10, 1862. (*ORN*, 7:379–80, 382; *CWC*, 6-332.)

Caroline Anderson. Union. Schooner. Burned on May 23, 1863. The USS *Coeur de Lion* rescued the crew and saved

some rigging and stores. The USS *Coeur de Lion* fired sixteen shells and scuttled the hulk. (*ORN*, 5:273.)

Caroline Baker. Confederate. Schooner. Was burned by Confederates and sunk to act as an obstruction at Cumberland Landing on the Pamunkey River on May 5–10, 1862. (*ORN*, 7:379–80, 382; *CWC*, 6-332.)

Cataline. Union. Side-wheel steamer, 391 tons. Built in 1845 at New York City. Burned on July 2, 1861, at Fort Monroe. (*MSV*, 31, 248.)

Champion. Confederate. Sloop. Cargo of muskets and army stores. Destroyed with the CSS *General Scott* on May 4, 1862, to prevent its capture by the USS *Corwin*, about 9 miles above Gloucester Point, York River. (*ORN*, 7:320.)

Charity. Confederate. Schooner. Was captured and destroyed by boats from the USS *Coeur de Lion* and USS *Eureka* on May 27, 1863, at Piney Point on the Yeocomico River. (*ORN*, 5:581.)

Charles Henry. Confederate. Schooner. Was burned by a gig from the USS *Jacob Bell* and USS *Currituck* on February 24, 1864. (*ORN*, 5:592.)

Christiana Kean. Union. Schooner. Out of New Jersey. Grounded, boarded, and set afire on June 15, 1861, by 30–40 Confederates in row boats off Machodoc Creek on the Potomac River, below Mathias Point opposite Cedar Point, a half-mile from shore in five feet of water. (*ORN*, 4:516–17, 533.)

Claudio. Confederate. Ship. Seized by Confederate general Joseph E. Johnson's forces. Used as a transport. Was scuttled to act as an obstruction in the Pamunkey River at White House by Confederates on May 5–10, 1862. (*ORN*, 7:379–82; *CWC*, 6-332.)

Colonel Satterly. Union. Schooner. Loaded with sand, gravel, and stone. Was sunk by the Union army to act as an obstruction June 27, 1864, in Trent's Reach, James River. Was probably raised by Benjamin Maillefert in April 1865. (*ORN*, 10:212, 464; 12:138; *DANFS*, 5:441, 425.)

USS *Columbia*. Union. Sailing frigate, 1,708 or 1,726 tons. Length 175 feet, beam 45 feet, depth 14 feet 4 inches, draft 22 feet 4 inches, maximum speed 12 knots. Complement of four hundred, with 44–50 guns. Laid down in 1825 and launched in 1836 at the Washington Navy Yard. Had been in the ordinary since 1855. Was burned to the water's edge by Union sailors in the Gosport Navy Yard on April 20–21, 1861. Was raised and sold on October 10, 1867. (*ORN*, 4:306; ser. 2, 1:62; *WCWN*, 127–28.)

USS *Columbus*. Union. Ship of the line, 2,480 bulk tons. Length 191 feet 10 inches, beam 52 feet, depth 21 feet 10 inches, draft 25 feet 8 inches, maximum speed 12.5 knots. Complement of 780, with 74 guns. Commenced in 1816 and launched on March 1, 1819, at the Washington Navy Yard. Burned to the floorheads on April 20–21, 1861, at the Gosport Navy Yard. (*ORN*, 4:306; ser. 2, 1:62; *WCWN*, 125.)

USS *Commodore Jones*. Union. Side-wheel gunboat, 542 bulk tons. Length 154 feet, beam 32 feet 6 inches, depth 11 feet 8 inches, maximum speed 12 knots. Complement of 88–103, with one 9-inch Dahlgren, one 50-pounder Dahlgren, two 30-pounder Parrotts, and three 24-pounder smoothbores. Converted from a ferryboat in 1863 at New York City. Was blown to pieces, with forty officers and men killed (total casualties numbered sixty-nine), in the James River by a 2,000-pound torpedo triggered by a galvanic battery by three Confederates in an on-shore pit about midnight on May 6, 1864. The torpedo was missed by Union dragging operations. One of the Confederates ashore who triggered the torpedo was killed, and the other two were captured by Union soldiers. Sank 250 feet from shore, near the Confederate Point batteries just across Four Mile Creek off Jones Point opposite Sturgeontown at Deep Bottom. In 1985 Underwater Archaeological Joint Ventures found a magnetic anomaly in the area, but metal probes failed to hit anything. (*OR*, 36:2:524; *ORN*, 10:10–15; ser. 2, 1:63; Scharf, *History of the Confederate Navy*, 763; *WCWN*, 100; Margolin, "Endangered Legacy," Grier and Winter, *Look to the Earth*, 95–96; Porter, *Naval History*, 474.)

USS *Congress*. Union. Frigate, 1,867 or 1,869 tons. Length 179 feet, beam 47 feet 8 inches, depth 22 feet 6–10 inches, draft 22 feet 6 inches. Complement of 434–80, with forty 32-pounders and ten 8-inch Dahlgrens. Laid down in 1839 and launched in 1841 at Portsmouth, N.H. Grounded during the Battle of Hampton Roads on March 8, 1862, near Newport News, just above Signal Point while the CSS *Virginia* and Confederate ships shelled it and set it afire. Struck its colors to surrender in order to prevent further loss of life. An officer from the CSS *Virginia* tried to board the USS *Congress* to burn it but was driven back by fire from shore and the USS *Zouave*. The CSS *Virginia* resumed firing and the USS *Congress*'s magazine exploded, with 136 members of its crew killed. Its stern was near the Signal Point Batteries, offshore 500 yards and burned to the water's edge. Part of the hull was raised and taken to Gosport Navy Yard and later sold. (*OR*, 9:2, 5, 8–10; 51:1:58–59; *ORN*, 9:4–5, 8, 10, 15, 21, 23–24, 29–30, 32–36, 38, 41–42, 44–46, 48, 50, 52–54, 65–67, 69–71, 74, 82, 87, 92, 126; ser. 2, 1:65; 3:363; *WCWN*, 128.)

***Coquette*.** Union. Schooner, 50 tons. Crew of two. Cargo of coal. Seized by Lt. John Taylor Wood on the night of August 24–25, 1863, at the mouth of the Rappahannock River in the captured USS *Satellite*. Was towed to Port Royal, Va., stripped, and destroyed on August 31, 1863. (*ORN*, 5:344–45.)

USS *Cumberland*. Union. Sloop, 1,708 or 1,726 tons. Length 175 feet, beam 45 feet, depth 22 feet 4 inches, draft 21 feet. Complement of 376–400, with one 10-inch smoothbore, one rifled 70-pounder, and twenty-two 9-inch smoothbores. Built in 1825 at Charles Town Navy Yard, Mass., and launched in 1842. The paymaster was reported to have had $40,000 on board. On March 8, 1862, during the Battle of Hampton Roads the CSS *Virginia*'s ram broke off in the USS *Cumberland* after it was rammed twice. The CSS *Virginia* shelled the USS *Cumberland* until it sank in 50 feet of water with 121 dead. Sank perpendicular to shore, 800 yards off Camp Butler with the deck underwater. Union navy divers viewed the sunken ship in May 1862 with an idea of raising it. Part of the anchor was dredged up later and is now in Confederate Museum in Richmond. In 1875 a Detroit salvage company reportedly recovered the safe rumored to contain $40,000 in gold coins and raised it. Only $25–$30 was reportedly in the safe. In 1980 and 1981 novelist Clive Cussler's National Underwater and Marine Agency (NUMA) in conjunction with the Virginia Research Center for Archaeology, and Underwater Joint Ventures located the wreck with the aid

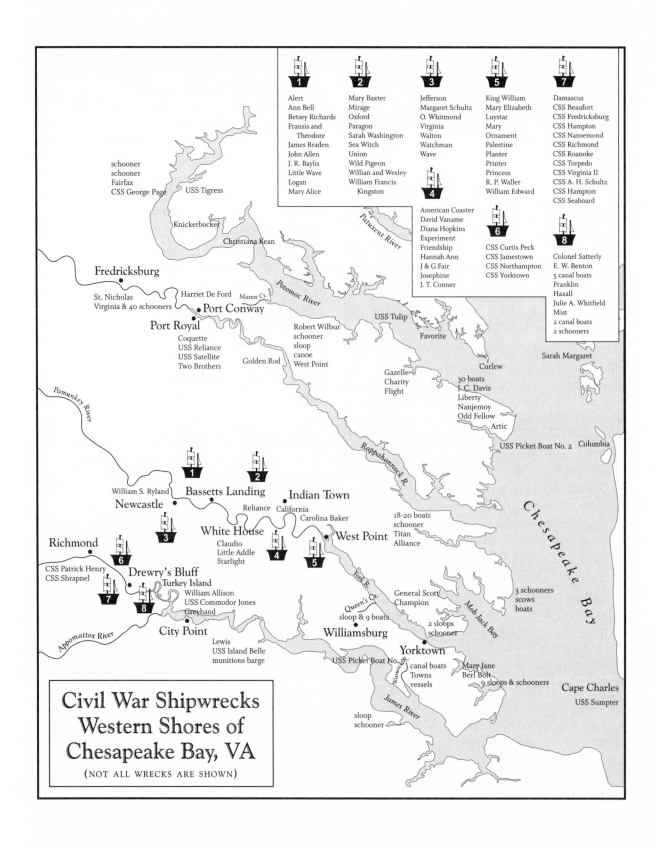

Civil War Shipwrecks Western Shores of Chesapeake Bay, VA

(NOT ALL WRECKS ARE SHOWN)

of clammer Wilbur Riley. The wreck is buried in 40 feet of water in the James River off Pier C at Newport News. Riley had retrieved a brass sword hilt and handle four to five years earlier. Divers found timbers rising above the mud and recovered a number of artifacts, including the ship's bronze bell. Listed as eligible for the National Register of Historic Places. Relics were taken by divers for antique dealers. In 1990 the FBI raided a museum and relic dealers, seizing artifacts recovered from the vessel. A court decision upheld stiff penalties for looting historic wrecks. (*OR,* 9:2, 5, 8; 51:1:58–59; *ORN,* 7:20–23, 140, 186, 403, 420; 9:3, 4, 15–20, 22–23, 26, 29; 32–37, 40–42, 44, 50–52, 54, 61, 65–66, 68–70, 73, 74, 82, 87, 92, 126, 155, 186; ser. 2, 1:69; Cussler and Dirgo, *Sea Hunters,* 89, 94–100.)

CSS *Curtis Peck.* Confederate. Side-wheel steamer, 446 tons. Built in 1842 at New York City. Was sunk in mid-May 1862 along with the steamers *Jamestown* and *Northampton* to obstruct the James River below Drewry's Bluff. (*ORN,* 10:466; *CWC,* 6-217; *WCWN,* 243.)

Damascus. Confederate. Ship. Was sunk in September 1862 to block the James River near Drewry's Bluff. (*ORN,* 10:466; *CWC,* 6-217.)

David Vaname. Confederate. Schooner. Destroyed by Confederates on May 5–10, 1862, in the Pamunkey River off Cooke's Island. (*ORN,* 7:379–80, 382; *CWC,* 6-332.)

D. C. Pearce. Union. Bark. Was taken and sunk in May 1861 to obstruct the channel at Norfolk. (*ORN,* 5:632.)

USS *Delaware.* Union. Ship of the line, 2,633 bulk tons. Length 196 feet 3–4 inches, beam 53 feet, depth 22 feet, draft 26 feet 2 inches. Complement of 820, with 84 guns. Laid down in 1817 and launched in 1820 at Norfolk, Va. Burned on the night of April 20–21, 1861, at the Gosport Navy Yard, Norfolk in the ordinary. Was later raised. (*ORN,* 4:294, 306; ser. 2, 1:73.)

Diana Hopkins. Confederate. Schooner. Destroyed by Confederates on May 5–10, 1862, in the Pamunkey River off Cooke's Island. (*ORN,* 7:379–80, 382; *CWC,* 6-332.)

USS *Dolphin.* Union. Brig, 224 tons. Length 88 feet, beam 25 feet, depth 11 feet, draft 13 feet. Complement of eighty, with three 11-inch smoothbores and one 9-inch smooth-

bore in 1859. Laid down in 1836 at Brooklyn, N.Y. Burned and sank on April 20–21, 1861, in the Gosport Navy Yard. (*ORN,* 4:306; ser. 2, 1:74; *WCWN,* 134.)

CSS *Drewry.* Confederate. Wooden gunboat, 166 tons. Length 106 feet, beam 21 feet, depth 8 feet, draft 5 feet. Armed with one rifled 6.4-inch gun and one rifled 7-inch gun. Grounded on January 23, 1865, 400 yards downriver from the Trent's Reach obstructions of the James River and 1,500 yards above Battery Parsons. Its magazine was blown up by shells from Fort McPherson and the 1st Conn. Heavy Artillery on the morning of January 24, 1865. Was going to help the CSS *Scorpion,* which had been damaged and drifted down to the obstructions. Two members of the crew were lost, but the rest abandoned ship ten minutes before the magazine blew up. (*OR,* 46:1:165–68; *ORN,* 11:659, 661, 665, 667–76, 679, 684, 687–90, 693–94; *CWC,* 6-223.)

Elma. Union. Schooner. En route from New York City to Baltimore. Carried assorted cargo. Burned in the East River after passing the USS *Crusader* on February 18, 1863. (*ORN,* 8:566–67, 578; Shomette, *Shipwrecks on the Chesapeake,* 255.)

E. W. Benton. Union. Schooner. Loaded with sand, gravel, and stone. Was sunk by the Union army to act as an obstruction about June 27, 1864, at Trent's Reach, James River. Was probably removed by Benjamin Maillefert in April 1865. (*ORN,* 10:211, 464; 12:138; *DANFS,* 5:44, 437.)

Experiment. Confederate. Schooner. Was scuttled at Cooke's Island on the Pamunkey River on May 5–10, 1862. (*ORN,* 7, 379–80, 382; *CWC,* 6-332.)

Fairfax. Confederate. Ship. Was burned by Confederates next to the CSS *George Page* on Quantico Creek in early March 1862. (Scharf, *History of the Confederate Navy,* 106.)

Fair Haven. Union. Screw steamer, 474 tons. Built in 1862 at Fair Haven, Conn. Stranded on April 1, 1864, at Cape Henry. (*MSV,* 69, 259.)

Fawn. Union. Steam mail boat. Out of Norfolk. Was captured and burned by James B. Hopkins and thirty-five Confederate guerrillas and sailors from the CSS *Albemarle* on September 9, 1864, at the Currituck Bridge in the Dismal Swamp Canal. One person was killed, and several were wounded. One lieutenant colonel, two majors, one first lieutenant from the 103rd Pa. Volunteer Infantry Regiment, eight men of the 23rd Mass. Infantry Regiment, some civilians, and the *Fawn's* crew were captured. (*OR,* 42:1:956–57; *ORN,* 10:457, 736–37.)

Flight. Confederate. Schooner. Was burned on the Yeocomico River by boats from the USS *Coeur de Lion* and USS *Eureka* on May 27, 1863. (*ORN,* 5:581.)

CSS *Florida* (*Oreto*) (CSS *Manassas*). Confederate. Wooden screw steam sloop, 700 bulk tons, 410 gross tons. Length 191 or 192 feet, beam 27 feet 2 inches, depth 14 feet, draft 13 feet, speed 9.5 knots, speed with sails 12 knots. Complement of 146–52, with six 6-inch Blakely rifled guns, two 7-inch Blakely rifled guns, and one rifled 12-pounder. Launched in 1862 at Liverpool, England, for the Confederate government. Outfitted near Nassau, Bahamas, and commissioned as the CSS *Florida* on August 4, 1863. When half of the crew was on shore leave in the neutral port of Bahia, Brazil, the CSS *Florida* was captured in a night attack on October 6, 1864, under Cdr. Napoleon Collins of the USS *Wachusett* and towed to Hampton Roads. The CSS *Florida* took thirty-eight Union vessels before being captured. If its tenders are included, there was a total of sixty Union vessels captured by it, of which forty-six were destroyed, thirteen bonded, and one recaptured. Much embarrassment over the Union violation of Brazilian neutrality was saved when the captured CSS *Florida* was rammed by the transport *Alliance*, which destroyed the CSS *Florida's* cathead, rigging, jib boom, figurehead, hammock nettings, and bumpkin. Officially sank after a collision with the Union troop transport *Alliance* on November 19, 1864, making 5 inches of water per hour due to a gash in the hull. The CSS *Florida's* sea cocks were actually opened and the CSS *Florida* sank foremost on November 28, 1864, in the James River below Newport News in 63 feet of water with the masts above water. Commander Collins was later court-martialed and ordered dismissed from the navy but was in fact promoted, and the court-martial was overturned. Collins retired in 1874 as a rear admiral in the U.S. Navy. The wreck was found by Clive Cussler's NUMA and the Virginia Research Center for Archaeology in 1980 off Horne Brothers Shipyard

in an area of poor visibility and strong currents. The U.S. Navy recovered some artifacts, including ammunition boxes with round shot and Enfield bullets. Partially buried under the river bottom. The wreck has been damaged by looting. Brass portholes from the vessel were melted down to make belt buckles. In 1990 FBI agents raided a small museum and relic dealer, seizing artifacts taken from the wreck. (*ORN,* 3:274–85; *Federal Register,* December 4, 1990, 50145; *CWC,* 6-228–29; Owsley, *C.S.S. Florida;* Miller, *Civil War Sea Fights,* 138–44; Bass, *Ships and Shipwrecks of the Americas,* 219–20; Cussler and Dirgo, *Sea Hunters,* 90–100.)

Flying Cloud. Confederate. Sloop. Out of Baltimore. Ran into Tabb's Creek and sunk after unloading its cargo in May 1863. The USS *Anacostia* and USS *Primrose* recovered sails and rigging from the wreck an June 2, 1863. (*ORN,* 5:282–83, 606–7.)

Francis and Theodore. Confederate. Ship. Was burned by Confederates at Bassett's Landing in the Pamunkey River on May 17, 1862. (*ORN,* 7:379–82; *CWC,* 6-332.)

Francis Elmor (Frances Elmore). Union. Transport schooner. Crew of seven. Cargo of hay. Was captured and burned off Popes Creek in the Potomac River on October 7–8, 1862, by a Confederate boarding party led by Lt. John Taylor Wood. The crew was later released. (*ORN,* 5:118–19, 346; Shingleton, *John Taylor Wood,* 64–65.)

Franklin. Confederate. Bark. Was sunk about June 27, 1864, to act as an obstacle in Trent's Reach, James River. Was probably removed by Benjamin Maillefert for the U.S. Army Corps of Engineers in April 1865. (*ORN,* 10:211, 464; 12:138.)

CSS *Fredericksburg*. Confederate. Twin screw steam ironclad ram, 2,500 tons. Length 170 feet 2 inches or 175 feet or 188 overall feet, beam 34 feet or 40 feet 3 inches, draft 9 feet 6 inches or 11 feet, armor 4-inch iron. Complement of 150, with four rifled 6-inch guns (another source—one 11-inch smoothbore, one rifled 8-inch gun, and two rifled 6.4-inch guns). Built in 1862–November 1863, at Richmond, Va. Was scuttled at Drewry's Bluff in the James River on April 2–3, 1865. Partially removed in 1871–72 by Benjamin Maillefert for the U.S. Army Corps of Engineers. Large portions of the wreck remain buried in the riverbank. (*ORN*, ser. 2, 1:253; *Annual Report of the Secretary of War 1871*, 73; *Chief of Engineers Report 1872*, 690; *CWC*, 6-185, 229; *WCWN*, 209.)

Friendship. Confederate. Schooner. Was sunk by Confederates on May 5–10, 1862, at Cooke's Island to act as an obstruction in the Pamunkey River. (*ORN*, 7:379–80, 782; *CWC*, 6-332.)

CSS *Gallego.* Confederate. Schooner. Length 144 feet, beam 30 feet, depth 15 feet. Sank in the Graveyard Reach of the James River in late 1864. Was raised on the night of January 18, 1865, and probably later scuttled. Was removed by Benjamin Maillefert under a U.S. Army Corps of Engineers contract in 1871–72. (*ORN*, 10:763; 11:761, 763, 783, 793, 797, 800; *Annual Report of the Secretary of War 1871*, 73; *Chief of Engineers Report 1872*, 690.)

Gazelle. Confederate. Schooner. Was burned by boats from the USS *Coeur de Lion* and USS *Eureka* on May 27, 1863, at Piney Point on the Yeocomico River. (*ORN*, 5:581.)

CSS *General Scott.* Confederate. Steamer. Carried Confederate military supplies. Also used as a guard boat. Was burned with the sloop *Champion* by Confederates to prevent its capture on May 4, 1862, in the York River. The crew escaped ashore. (*ORN*, 7:320.)

CSS *George Page* (*City of Richmond*). Confederate. Side-wheel steamer, 410 tons. Length 128 feet, beam 26 feet, depth 7 feet. Armed with two guns. Built in 1853 in Washington, D.C. Used by the Union army as a transport. Was seized by Confederates in Aquia Creek in May 1861. Was destroyed in Quantico Creek on March 9, 1862, when the Confederate Evansport and Shipping Port batteries were abandoned. (*ORN*, 5:23, 25; ser. 2, 1:254; *CWC*, 6-237.)

USS *Germantown* (CSS *Germantown*). Union. Sailing sloop, 942 tons. Length 150 feet, beam 36 feet or 36 feet 9 inches, draft 17 feet or 17 feet 3 inches, speed 12 knots. Complement of 210, with 20 guns. Laid down in 1843 and launched in 1846 at Philadelphia. Burned to the bulwarks on April 20–21, 1861, in the Gosport Navy Yard. Raised by Confederates in June 1861. In May 1862 the vessel was filled with sand and sank in the Elizabeth River to protect Norfolk from Union advances. Raised on April 22, 1863. Sold at Norfolk on February 8, 1864. (*ORN*, 4:295, 306; 5:806; ser. 2, 1:94, 254; *CWC*, 6-241; *WCWN*, 132.)

Glen Cove. Confederate. Side-wheel steamer, 504 tons. Built in 1854 at New York City. Ran up the James River and destroyed by fire on May 4, 1861. (*ORN*, 5:748; *MSV*, 86.)

Golden Rod. Union. Transport schooner. Draft 11 feet. Cargo of coal. En route from Baltimore for Maine. Seized by Lt. John Taylor Wood in the captured USS *Satellite* on August 25, 1863, at the mouth of the Rappahannock River. Stripped and burned at Urbana upon the approach of Union vessels. (*ORN*, 5:344–45.)

Gratitude. Confederate. Schooner. Was burned by a gig from the USS *Jacob Bell* and USS *Currituck* on February 24, 1864. (*ORN*, 5:592.)

Greenland. Union. Bark, 549 tons. Crew of fourteen. Cargo of coal. Out of Brunswick, Maine. Towed by the tug *America* en route from Philadelphia to Pensacola, Fla. The *America* cast off the *Greenland* as the CSS *Florida* approached. The *Greenland* was captured, burned, and sunk on July 9, 1864, by the CSS *Florida* near latitude 36° 43' north, longitude 74° 11' west. The USS *Dawn* removed the *Greenland*'s masts on September 3, 1864. (*ORN*, 10:429; Owsley, *C.S.S. Florida*, 126–27.)

Greyhound. Union. Side-wheel steamer, 380, 400, or 900 tons. Built in 1863 in Liverpool, England. Used as Gen. Benjamin Butler's headquarters boat. Butler was entertaining Adm. David Dixon Porter and Gen. Robert C. Schenck, in preparation for a meeting with the Union assistant secretary, when the *Greyhound* was blown up by a Confederate bomb disguised as a lump of coal in the coal bunkers on November 27, 1864. Butler lost his horses when the ship sank 5 or 6 miles below Bermuda Hundred in the James River. Often confused with the blockade-runner *Greyhound*, which sank off Nova Scotia in 1865, and the blockade-runner *Greyhound*, which was captured by the USS *Connecticut* with Confederate spy Belle Boyd aboard on May 10, 1864, in North Carolina waters. (*MSV*, 89, 265; *CWC*, 6-243–44; Scharf, *History of the Confederate Navy*, 762; Perry, *Infernal Machines*, 137–38.)

CSS *Hampton*. Confederate. Wooden screw steam gunboat, 80 or 166 tons. Length 106 feet, beam 21 feet, depth 5 feet, draft 8 feet. Complement of 166, with two 8-inch pivot guns, one forward and one aft. Built in 1862 at the Norfolk Navy Yard. Was scuttled on April 2, 1865, at Drewry's Bluff on the James River. (*ORN*, ser. 2, 1:255; *CWC*, 6-246–47.)

***Hannah Ann*.** Confederate. Schooner. Was scuttled on May 5–10, 1862, at Cooke's Island in the Pamunkey River. (*ORN*, 7:379–80, 382; *CWC*, 6-332.)

***Harriet De Ford*.** Union. Screw steamer, 149 tons. En route from Patuxent to Baltimore. Built in 1864 at Baltimore. Was captured on April 4, 1865, at Fair Haven, 30 miles below Annapolis, Md., on the east side of Chesapeake Bay by a party of twenty-eight men and two officers of the 5th Va. Cavalry Regiment, led by Capt. Thaddeus Fitzhugh and Lt. John Taylor Wood. Sailed up the Rappahannock River as far as they could on April 7, 1865, and arrived at 2:00 a.m. at Dimer's Creek near Indian Creek. The Confederates took off the brass pivot gun and burned the vessel to the water's edge. The boiler and machinery were shelled by the USS *Thomas Freeborn*. Several African Americans aboard were taken to Kilmarnock and sold as slaves at auction. (*OR*, 46:1:1305–7; 3:588–90, 591–92, 616; *ORN*, 5:541–45; 12:105; *MSV*, 92 266.)

***Haxall*.** Union. Schooner. Filled with sand, gravel, and stone. Was scuttled by the Union army about June 27, 1864, to block Trent's Reach, James River. (*ORN*, 10:211, 464; *DANFS*, 5:437, 441.)

USS *Henry Andrew*. Union. One-mast screw steamer, 177 tons. Length 150 feet, beam 26 feet, depth 7 feet 6 inches. Complement of forty-nine, with two 32-pounders and one 20-pounder Parrott. Built in 1847 at New York City. Originally a 249 tons sailing brig barge, converted to a steamer in 1859. While en route to New York City from Port Royal, S.C., to be repaired, the USS *Henry Andrew* ran aground 15 miles south of Cape Henry on August 24, 1862, during a gale with no loss of life. The vessel's ordnance, stores, paymaster items, stores, guns, ammunition, powder, and a 20-pounder Parrott were removed. Two cannons may have been left aboard. (*ORN*, 7:674–75; ser. 2, 1:101; *MSV*, 94.)

CSS *Hornet*. Confederate. Wooden screw steam torpedo boat. Length 46 feet, beam 6 feet 3 inches, depth 3 feet 9 inches, one 18-foot spar torpedo. Built in 1864 at Richmond, Va. Sank on January 26, 1865, after colliding with the Confederate flag of truce steamer *William Allison* in the James River, drowning a lieutenant. (*ORN*, 12:185–86; *CWC*, 6-251; *WCWN*, 219.)

USS *Island Belle*. Union. Side-wheel steam tug, 123 bulk tons. Length 100 feet, beam 20 feet 4 inches, depth 6 feet 7 inches. Complement of twenty-four, with one 32-pounder and one rifled 12-pounder. Built in 1855 at Keyport, N.J. Ran aground on Gilliam's Bar in the Appomattox River near City Point on June 28–29, 1862, while on a mission to destroy the railroad bridge at Petersburg. The vessel's master was reportedly drunk and burned the vessel to prevent its capture. (*ORN*, ser. 2, 1:110; *WCWN*, 123.)

***James Braden*.** Confederate. Ship. Was scuttled by Confederates near Bassett's Landing in the Pamunkey River on May 17, 1862. (*ORN*, 7:379–82; *CWC*, 6-332.)

CSS *Jamestown* (*Thomas Jefferson*). Confederate. Side-wheel steam gunboat, 1,300 bulk tons. Length 240 feet 3 inches, beam 33 feet 6 inches, depth 23 feet 5 inches. Armed with two guns. A passenger steamer built in 1852 at New York City. Seized by Confederates from the New York & Virginia Steamship Co. Was scuttled on May 14–15, 1862, in the James River at Drewry's Bluff to block the river. A 1972 gradiometer survey by NUMA and Underwater Archaeological Joint Ventures located few anomalies at where it sank. Was probably removed after the war. (*OR*, 11:1:636; 11:3:178–79; *ORN*, ser. 2, 1:257, 269; 10:466; *Annual Report of the Secretary of War 1871*, 73; Hoehling, *Thunder at Hampton Roads*, 84; *CWC*, 6-255; Margolin, "Endangered Legacy," Grier and Winter, *Look to the Earth*, 90–95.)

***J & G Fair*.** Confederate. Ship. Was scuttled by Confederates at Cooke's Landing on the Pamunkey River on May 5–10, 1862. (*ORN*, 7:379–81, 382; *CWC*, 6-332.)

***Jane Wright*.** Union. Sloop. En route from Washington, D.C., to St. Mary's County after delivering a cargo of oysters, fruit, and other goods. Was scuttled, although the vessel had a Union pass, on August 16, 1861, at Smith Point by the USS *Yankee* to prevent its use by Confederates in a rumored invasion of Maryland. (*ORN*, 4:616–17.)

J. C. Davis. Union. Barge. One of four barges that broke loose in Cornfield Harbor, Md., the night of January 20, 1863. The next day it floated to the Coan River, where it was captured by Confederates along with the *Liberty*. Was plundered and the men aboard robbed. The crew fled into the woods. The barge was run aground by the USS *Dan Smith* 7 miles up the Coan River and burned on January 22, 1863. (*ORN*, 5:216–17.)

Jefferson. Confederate. Transport. Was burned by Confederates to prevent its capture on May 17, 1862, near New Castle in the Pamunkey River. (*ORN*, 7:379–82; *CWC*, 6-332.)

Jemima. Confederate. Schooner, 50 tons. Its cargo had already been landed. Was captured and destroyed with another schooner by a Union expedition of thirty-six men from the USS *Crusader* in Milford Haven in the York River on March 14–15, 1863. (*ORN*, 8:611; *WCWN*, 88.)

Jenny Lind. Confederate. Steamer. Was scuttled at Garlick's Landing in the Pamunkey River on May 5–10, 1862. (*ORN*, 7:379–82; *CWC*, 6-332.)

CSS *Jesup* (*General Jesup*). Confederate. Screw steam gunboat. Designed for a complement of thirty. Built by contributions raised by the "ladies" of Norfolk. The vessel needed new boilers and was under construction when it was partially destroyed as Norfolk was evacuated by the Confederates in May 1862. Was rebuilt and put into Union service as a Union army vessel. (*OR*, 17:393, 404, 476.)

John Allen. Confederate. Schooner. Was seized by Confederates and scuttled to act as an obstruction on May 17, 1862, near Bassett's Landing in the Pamunkey River. (*ORN*, 7:379–82; *CWC*, 6-332.)

John B. White. Union army. Screw steam tug, 39 tons. Built in 1857 at Buffalo, N.Y. Was captured from Confederates on May 8, 1862, and placed in Union service. Was sunk by a Confederate torpedo on January 1, 1864. (*MSV*, 112; *WCWN*, 243.)

John Roach. Confederate. Ship. Was sunk by Confederates in late 1862 to obstruct the James River near Drewry's Bluff. (*ORN*, 10:466; *CWC*, 6-257.)

Josephine. Confederate. Schooner. Was scuttled and burned by Confederates to act as an obstruction at Cooke's Island on the Pamunkey River on May 6–10, 1862. (*ORN*, 7:379–82; *CWC*, 6-332.)

J. R. Baylis. Confederate. Ship. Sank near Bassett's Landing in the Pamunkey River on May 17, 1862. (*ORN*, 7:379–82; *CWC*, 6-332.)

J. T. Connor. Confederate. Ship. Was scuttled by Confederates to act as an obstruction on May 5–10, 1862, at Cooke's Island in the Pamunkey River. (*ORN*, 7:379–81, 382; *CWC*, 6-332.)

***Julie A. Whitford* (*Julia A. Whitfield*).** Union. Schooner. Loaded with sand, gravel, and stone. Was scuttled by the Union army June 27, 1864, in Trent's Reach of the James River to block the Confederate fleet. Was probably removed by Benjamin Maillefert for the U.S. Army Corps of Engineers in April 1865. (*ORN*, 10:211, 464; *DANFS*, 5:437, 441.)

Julia Baker. Union. Schooner. Robbed and set afire by Confederate guerrillas on March 11, 1864, with $2,500 taken and five men captured near Chuckatuck Creek. (*ORN*, 9:548.)

Kingston. Union. Government-chartered side-wheel steamer, 200 tons. Out of Philadelphia. Carried twelve men and two women aboard. Captured and burned on July 24, 1864, by forty Confederates after grounding near Smith's Point on the Virginia shore of Chesapeake Bay on the Diamond Marshes. (*ORN*, 5:469–70.)

King William. Confederate. Ship. Was scuttled by Confederates as an obstruction on May 5–10, 1862, at Cooke's Island on the Pamunkey River. (*ORN*, 7:379–80, 382; *CWC*, 6-332.)

L. and R. Smith. Union. Schooner. Cargo of 353 tons of coal. Sank on the morning of November 25, 1864, about 21 miles east of Cape Henry. (*ORN*, 11:95.)

Lewis. Union. Canal boat. Used as a supply vessel. Blown up in the James River at Lt. Gen. Ulysses S. Grant's supply depot at City Point (now Hopewell) by a time bomb placed by Confederate Secret Service agents John Maxwell and R. K. Dillard. The City Point Explosion on August 9, 1864, destroyed more than $2 million in Union supplies, sank three barges, killed at least 80, and wounded 125. (*OR*, 42:1:17, 954–56; 46:3:1250; Perry, *Infernal Machines*, 133.)

Liberty. Union. Barge. One of four barges towed by the steam tug *Atlantic*. Broke free with the barge *J. C. Davis* the night of January 20, 1863, while anchored at Cornfield Harbor. Grounded in the Coan River and captured by Confederates on January 21, 1863, in the captured barge *J. C. Davis*. The crew was robbed. The barge was taken 4 miles up the Coan River and burned on January 21, 1863. The crew fled into the woods, and the USS *Dan Smith* rescued them. (*ORN*, 5:216–17.)

Little Addie. Confederate. Ship. Seized by Confederate general Joseph E. Johnston's forces and used as a transport. Was scuttled by Confederates on May 5–10, 1862, in the Pamunkey River near White House. (*ORN*, 7:379–82; *CWC*, 6-332.)

Little Magruder. Confederate. Small steamer. Destroyed along with a ferryboat, two sloops, a large scow, two barges, and four pontoon boats at White House on January 7, 1863, by a Union expedition consisting of the USS *Mahaska*, USS *Commodore Perry*, and army tug *May Queen* with three hundred soldiers of the 5th Pa. Cavalry Regiment, 6th N.Y. Cavalry Regiment, and 115th N.Y. Infantry Regiment. (*OR*, 18:124; *ORN*, 8:409–11.)

Little Wave. Confederate. Ship. Was scuttled by Confederates to act as an obstruction on May 17, 1862, at Bassett's Landing in the Pamunkey River. (*ORN*, 7:378–82; *CWC*, 6-332.)

Lizzie Freeman (Resolute). Union. Tugboat, 76 tons. Built in 1864 at Wilmington, Del. Was destroyed off Pagan Creek by a Confederate torpedo boat in December 1864. Was probably raised. (*OR*, 46:2:467; *ORN*, 12:11; *MSV*, 129.)

Logan. Confederate. Side-wheel iron transport steamer, 296 or 514 tons. Length 160 feet, beam 26 feet, depth 7 feet 6 inches. Built in 1855 at Wilmington, Del. Was burned by Confederates on May 17, 1862, at Bassett's Landing, 25 miles above White House on the Pamunkey River upon the approach of Union ships. (*ORN*, 7:378; *CWC*, 6-263; *MSV*, 130.)

Louisa Reed. Union. Schooner. Out of New York City. Was captured and burned by Confederates, possibly in the lower Potomac River. Found by the USS *Wachusett* on July 26, 1862. (*ORN*, 7:735.)

Marens. Nationality unknown. Brig. Sank in the James River. Removed by Benjamin Maillefert under a U.S. Army Corps of Engineers contract in 1871. (*Annual Report of the Secretary of War 1871*, 73.)

Margaret Schultz. Confederate. Ship. Was burned by Confederates to prevent its capture on May 17, 1862, at Newcastle on the Pamunkey River. (*ORN*, 7:379–82; *CWC*, 6-332.)

Marie Banks. Union. Schooner. Cargo of 364 coils of rigging for the Union shipyard at Fort Monroe. Went ashore 3 miles southeast of Cape Henry on February 3, 1863. (*ORN*, 8:515, 517, 524.)

Martha Washington. Confederate. Schooner. Was burned on October 11, 1861, by two launches from the USS *Union*, USS *Rescue*, USS *Resolute*, and USS *Satellite* at Dumfries. (*ORN*, 4:709–10, 768; Shomette, *Shipwrecks on the Chesapeake*, 253.)

Mary Alice. Confederate. Ship. Was scuttled by Confederates on May 17, 1862, at Bassett's Landing in the Pamunkey River as an obstruction. (*ORN*, 7:378–82; *CWC*, 6-332.)

Mary Baxter. Confederate. Ship. Was scuttled by Confederates to act as an obstruction on May 17, 1862, at Bassett's Landing in the Pamunkey River. (*ORN*, 7:378–82; *CWC*, 6-332.)

Mary Elizabeth. Confederate. Ship. Was destroyed by Confederates to prevent the vessel's capture on May 5–10, 1862, at Cooke's Island in the Pamunkey River. (*ORN*, 7:378–82; *CWC*, 6-332.)

Mary Jane. Confederate. Sloop, 30 tons. Was burned by two cutters from the USS *Mahaska* on February 24, 1863, up Back Creek, York River, near the Paqnosin River. (*ORN*, 8:567.)

Mary Luyster. Confederate. Ship. Was scuttled to act as an obstruction on May 5–10, 1862, at Cooke's Island in the Pamunkey River. (*ORN*, 7:379–80, 382; *CWC*, 6-332.)

Mary Willis. Confederate. Schooner. Cargo of wood. Hit below the waterline by shells from a Union battery at Boyd's Hole on December 22, 1861. Ran onto the flats. (*ORN*, 5:14.)

USS *Merrimack* (CSS *Virginia*). Union. Screw frigate, 3,200 bulk tons, 4,636 displacement tons. Length 300 feet overall, 275 feet between the perpendiculars, 257 feet 9 inches on the waterline; beam 38 feet 6 inches or 51 feet 4 inches; depth 27 feet 6 inches; draft 24 feet 3 inches loaded; speed 9 knots. Complement of 519, with fourteen 8-inch, two 10-inch, and twenty-four 9-inch smoothbore cannons. Laid down in 1854 and launched in 1855 at Charles Town Navy Yard, Mass. Burned and sank on April 20–21, 1861, at the Gosport Navy Yard. Was salvaged by Confederates and converted into the ironclad CSS *Virginia* (see **CSS Virginia**), which destroyed two Union warships on March 8, 1862. (*ORN*, 4:295, 306; ser. 2, 1:141–42; *WCWN*, 27.)

Mirage. Confederate. Ship. Was scuttled by Confederates to act as an obstruction on May 17, 1862, at Bassett's Landing in the Pamunkey River. (*ORN*, 7:378–82; *CWC*, 6-333.)

Mist. Confederate. Schooner. Loaded with sand, gravel, and stone. Was scuttled about June 27, 1864, in Trent's Reach, James River to block the Confederate squadron. Was probably removed by Benjamin Maillefert for the U.S. Army Corps of Engineers in April 1865. (*ORN*, 10:211, 464; 12:138; *DANFS*, 5:437, 441.)

Nanjemoy. Confederate. Ship. Out of Baltimore. Used as a blockade-runner. The cargo was removed and vessel half-sunk in the Coan River. Was raised as a prize by the USS *Yankee* on July 15, 1863. (*ORN*, 5:300–301.)

CSS *Nansemond*. Confederate. Wooden twin screw steam gunboat, 80 or 166 tons. Length 106 feet, beam 21 feet, depth 8 feet, draft 5 feet. Armed with two 8-inch guns (another source—one 9-inch smoothbore and one 32-pounder). Built in 1862 at the Gosport Navy Yard, Norfolk. Was scuttled on April 2–3, 1865, at Drewry's Bluff in the James River. Was probably removed after the Civil War. (*ORN*, 12:101, 124; ser. 2, 1:261; *CWC*, 6-300–303; *WCWN*, 218.)

USS *New York*. Union. Ship of the line, 2,633 tons. Laid down in 1820 at the Gosport Navy Yard. Unfinished. Burned on the stocks on April 20–21, 1861, at the Gosport Navy Yard. Sold in 1888 at the New York Navy Yard with the purchaser to break it up. (*ORN*, 4:306; ser. 2, 1:160.)

CSS *Norfolk*. Confederate. Screw "Maury" gunboat, 166 tons. Beam 21 feet, depth 8 feet, draft 5 feet. Armed with one 9-inch and one 32-pounder. Constructed in 1862 at the Gosport Navy Yard. Was burned at the Gosport Navy Yard on May 10, 1862, to prevent its capture by Union forces. (*CWC*, 6-277; *WCWN*, 218.)

CSS *Northampton*. Confederate. Side-wheel steamer, 405 tons. Built in 1860 at Baltimore. Was sunk with the CSS *Jamestown* in mid-May 1862, to act as an obstruction below Drewry's Bluff in the James River. A 1982 gradiometer survey by Underwater Archaeological Joint Ventures located few anomalies at the site. Was probably removed after the war. Divers recovered some copper sheathing, cast iron fragments, and brass fasteners. (*ORN*, 10:466; *CWC*, 6-277; Margolin, "Endangered Legacy," Grier and Winter, *Look to the Earth*, 93–95.)

Odd Fellow. Confederate. Schooner. Out of Yeocomico. Was burned by a gig from the USS *Coeur de Lion* on June 11, 1863, on the Coan River. (*ORN*, 5:285.)

Ornament. Confederate. Ship. Was scuttled by Confederates on May 5–10, 1862, at Cooke's Island in the Pamunkey River. (*ORN*, 7:379–80, 382; *CWC*, 6-332.)

O. Whitmond. Confederate. Ship. Was scuttled and burned by Confederates on May 17, 1862, at Newcastle in the Pamunkey River. (*ORN*, 7:379–82; *CWC*, 6-332.)

Oxford. Confederate. Schooner, 85 tons. Draft 7 feet. Was scuttled to act as an obstruction on May 17, 1862, at Bassett's Landing in the Pamunkey River. (*ORN*, 7:378–80, 382; *CWC*, 6-333.)

Palestine. Confederate. Schooner. Was scuttled by Confederates on May 5–10, 1862, at Cooke's Island, in the Pamunkey River. (*ORN*, 7:379–80, 382; *CWC*, 6-332.)

Paragon. Confederate. Sloop. Was scuttled by Confederates to act as an obstruction on May 17, 1862, near Bassett's Landing in the Pamunkey River. (*ORN,* 7:378–80, 382; *CWC,* 6-332.)

CSS *Patrick Henry* (*Patrick*) (*Yorktown*). Confederate. Side-wheel steamer, 1,300 or 1,403 tons. Naval Academy training ship. Length 250 feet, beam 34 feet 6 inches or 34 feet, depth 17 feet or 17 feet 6 inches, draft 13 feet, armor 1-inch iron over the boilers and engines. Complement of 150, with two 10-inch pivot guns and two 8-inch guns (another source—one 10-inch smoothbore, one rifled 64-pounder, six 8-inch guns, and two 32-pounders). Built in 1853 in New York City as the brigantine rigged *Yorktown* by William H. Webb for the New York & Old Dominion Steamship Line. Ran between Richmond and New York City before being seized by the Confederacy. Used as a training ship for 52 Confederate navy midshipmen. Was burned on April 2–3, 1865, at Richmond's Rocketts Navy Yard to prevent its capture. Part of wreck was demolished and removed by Benjamin Maillefert in April 1865. (*OR,* 11:1:636; *ORN,* 12:138; ser. 2, 1:262; Semmes, *Service Afloat,* 812; *WCWN,* 242; *CWC,* 6-280; *LLC,* 327–28.)

Pendulum. Union. Side-wheel steamer, 215 tons. Built in 1851 at Philadelphia. Reportedly foundered on March 8, 1862, at Hampton Roads, but may have been sunk in the USS *Monitor*–CSS *Virginia* engagement. (*MSV,* 170, 289.)

USS *Pennsylvania*. Union. Ship of the line, 3,241 bulk tons, 3,105 tons. Length 247 feet, beam 59 feet 6 inches, depth 54 feet 10 inches. Complement of eleven hundred, with sixteen 8-inch, and one hundred and four 32-pounders in 1850. Started in 1821 and launched in 1837 in the Philadelphia Navy Yard. Used as a receiving ship. Burned to the floorheads the night of April 20–21, 1861, at the Gosport Navy Yard with five guns spiked on one side. (*ORN,* 4:295, 306; ser. 2, 1:174.)

USS *Picket Boat No. 2*. Union. Screw steam torpedo boat. Length 30–40 feet, beam 9 feet 6 inches, depth 4 feet 6 inches. Built at Boston. En route from Baltimore to Hampton Roads to join Lt. William Barker Cushing's expedition against the CSS *Albemarle* when its engine broke down. Anchored in the Great Wicomico Bay near the mouth of Reason Creek. Its commander thought Reason Creek was the Patuxent River, a major tributary of the Potomac River. Was attacked by seventy-five to eighty Confederate guerrillas under Capt. S. Covington on October 8, 1864, and forced to surrender after it ran aground on Potomac River oyster beds. Was almost high and dry at the low tide. The USS *Commodore Read* and USS *Mercury* shelled the USS *Picket Boat No. 2.* The Confederates scuttled it. Union forces salvaged a 12-pounder howitzer and captured a Confederate officer and twelve men on October 19, 1864, at the wreck. (*ORN,* 5:486–88; 10:539–41; Perry, *Infernal Machines,* 156.)

USS *Picket Boat No. 5* (USS *Epsilon*) (*Harry Bumm*) (USS *Tug No. 5*). Union. Screw steam torpedo boat, 51 tons. Length 66 feet, beam 15 feet, depth 7 feet 6 inches, draft 3 feet, speed 8–9 knots. Complement of ten, with one 12-pounder smoothbore. Built in 1864 at Philadelphia. Sank on December 10, 1864, opposite Jamestown in the James River. Was raised and later lost in 1872. (*ORN,* ser. 2, 1:178; Scharf, *History of the Confederate Navy,* 766; *WCWN,* 116.)

Planter. Confederate. Ship. Was sunk by Confederates at Cooke's Island to block the Pamunkey River on May 5–10, 1862. (*ORN,* 7:379–80, 382; *CWC,* 6-332.)

USS *Plymouth* (CSS *Plymouth*). Union. Ship sloop-of-war, 974 or 989 tons. Length 147 feet 6 inches, beam 38 feet 1 inch, draft 18 feet, depth 16 feet 4 inches. Complement of 210, with 20 guns. Laid down and launched in 1843 and completed in 1844 in the Charles Town Navy Yard, Mass. Burned and sank on April 20–21, 1861, at the Gosport Navy Yard while under repair. Was raised by Confederates. Was scuttled by Confederates as the CSS *Plymouth* on May 10, 1862, when they abandoned Norfolk. (*ORN,* 4:306; ser. 2, 1:180; *CWC,* 6-288; *WCWN,* 132.)

CSS *Portsmouth*. Confederate. Steam gunboat, 166 tons. Length 106 feet, beam 21 feet, depth 8 feet, draft 5 feet. Armed with one 9-inch and one 32-pounder. Under construction in the Gosport Navy Yard when destroyed by Confederates on May 10, 1862. (*CWC,* 6-288; *WCWN,* 218.)

Princess. Confederate. Schooner. Was scuttled by Confederates on May 5–10, 1862, at Cooke's Island in the Pamunkey River. (*ORN,* 7:379–80, 382; *CWC,* 6-332.)

USS *Raritan.* Union. Sailing frigate, 1,708 or 1,726 tons. Length 175 feet, beam 45 feet, draft 22 feet 4 inches, depth 14 feet 4 inches. Armed with 44–60 guns. Laid down in 1820 and launched in 1843 at Philadelphia Navy Yard, Pa. Burned and sank on April 20–21, 1861, in the Gosport Navy Yard. The wreck was sold in 1867. (*ORN,* 4:306; ser. 2, 1:189; *WCWN,* 127.)

Reliance. Confederate. Ship. Was burned by Confederates near Indian Town in the Pamunkey River on May 5–10, 1862. (*ORN,* 7:379–80, 382; *CWC,* 6-332.)

USS *Reliance.* Union. Screw steamer, 90 tons. Length 88 feet 2 inches, beam 17 feet, depth 7 feet 5 inches. Complement of forty, with one 30-pounder rifle and one 24-pounder howitzer. Built in 1860 at Keyport, N.J. Was captured on August 23, 1863, at the mouth of the Rappahannock River with the USS *Satellite* by sixty Confederates under Lt. John Taylor Wood in four boats. The Confederates had three wounded, while the Union crew had two killed and seven or eight wounded, including Capt. Henry Walters, who was badly injured. Taken to Port Royal or Port Conway with the captured USS *Satellite.* The USS *Reliance* was destroyed on August 28–31, 1863, to prevent its recapture by Brig. Gen. Judson Kilpatrick's Union cavalry. The engine was removed by the Confederates and sent to Richmond. Raised and became a merchant vessel in 1865. (*OR,* 29:1:96–99; *ORN,* 5:333–46, 358; ser. 2, 1:190; *CWC,* 6-292; Shingleton, *John Taylor Wood,* 82–88.)

CSS *Richmond.* Confederate. Ironclad steam ram, 1,200 tons. Length 150 feet, 172 feet 6 inches, or 180 feet; beam 34 feet; depth 14 feet; draft 12 or 16 feet; speed 5–6 knots. Complement of 150, with four 7-inch Brooke rifled guns, two smoothbore shellguns, and a spar torpedo. Launched on May 6, 1862, at the Gosport Navy Yard with money and scrap iron collected by Virginia citizens. Finished in July 1862 at Richmond. Was scuttled on April 3, 1865, at Chaffin's Bluff in the James River. Part of the wreck was removed in April 1865 by Benjamin Maillefert to clear the channel. A gradiometer survey located a 200 by 80 foot anomaly and divers located some material. (*ORN,* 12:101, 138; ser. 2, 1:265; *CWC,* 6-185; *WCWN,* 205; Margolin, "Endangered Legacy," Grier and Winter, *Look to the Earth,* 95; Still, *Iron Afloat,* 109.)

CSS *Roanoke* (CSS *Raleigh*). Confederate. Wooden steamer, 65 tons. Armed with two 6-pounder howitzers. Escaped the Confederate disaster at the Battle of Elizabeth City on February 10, 1862, by navigating up the Dismal Swamp Canal. Later served as a tender to the CSS *Virginia.* Was blown up in the James River at Drewry's Bluff on April 2–3, 1865. (*ORN,* 12:138; ser. 2, 1:265; *CWC,* 6-290; *WCWN,* 241.)

Robert Wilbur. Confederate. Along with a schooner, sloop, canoe. Was captured and burned by a launch with thirteen men from the USS *Jacob Bell* on November 4, 1862, in a small bay about 5 miles up Nomini Creek. (*ORN,* 5:148–49.)

R. P. Waller. Confederate. Schooner. Was scuttled by Confederates on May 5–10, 1862, at Cooke's Island in the Pamunkey River. (*ORN,* 7:379–80, 382; *CWC,* 6-332.)

***St. Nicholas* (CSS *Rappahannock*).** Confederate. Side-wheel steamer, 413 or 1,200 tons. Armed with one gun. Built in 1845 at Brooklyn, N.Y. A passenger ship running between Baltimore and Georgetown, D.C., Was captured on the Potomac River on June 28, 1861, near Point Lookout, Md., by Confederates posing as passengers. Sailed into the Chesapeake Bay. Was burned at Fredericktown by Confederates on April 19, 1862. (*ORN,* ser. 2, 1:264; *CWC,* 6-290; *WCWN,* 243; *MSV,* 192.)

Sarah Ann. Confederate. Schooner. Was scuttled by Confederates on May 5–10, 1862, at Cooke's Island in the Pamunkey River. (*ORN,* 7:379–80, 382; *CWC,* 6-332.)

Sarah Margaret. Confederate. Schooner. Out of Yeocomico. Was burned by a gig from the USS *Coeur de Lion* on June 11, 1863, on the Coan River. (*ORN,* 5:285, 581.)

Sarah Washington. Confederate. Schooner. Was scuttled by Confederates on May 17, 1862, near Bassett's Landing in the Pamunkey River. (*ORN,* 7:379–80; *CWC,* 6-333.)

USS *Satellite.* Union. Wooden side-wheel gunboat, 217 bulk tons. Length 120 feet 7 inches, beam 22 feet 6 inches, depth 8 feet 6 inches. Complement of forty to forty-three, with one 8-inch smoothbore and one 30-pounder Parrott (another source—one 32-pounder smoothbore and a 12-pounder howitzer). Built in 1854 at New York City.

Was captured the night of August 23–24, 1863, along with the USS *Reliance* at the Rappahannock River's mouth by a Confederate small boat expedition of forty men in two boats under Lt. John Taylor Wood. Union acting ensign Rudolph Sommers and four men were wounded and one or two of the crew were killed in the fight. Went to Port Royal or Port Conway with the captured USS *Reliance*. Was stripped and scuttled by Confederates on August 28–31, 1863, when Brig. Gen. Judson Kilpatrick's cavalry advanced and shelled the boats. On May 31, 1864, the USS *Commodore Read* exploded fifty pounds of gunpowder in a captured Confederate torpedo in the boiler to prevent the vessel's use by the Confederates. (*ORN*, 5:332–46, 439; ser. 2, 1:202; *CWC*, 6-298; *WCWN*, 97–98; Shingleton, *John Taylor Wood*, 82–88.)

Seaboard. Confederate. Wooden side-wheel steam tug, 59 tons. Built in 1859 at Philadelphia. Was captured by Union troops and the USS *Lilac* at Upper Tree Hill Bridge on the James River, below Richmond on April 4, 1865. Hit a snag at Drewry's Bluff and was run aground. Raised and involved in an interservice fight between the Union army and navy over whose prize it was. (*ORN*, 12:167–68; *CWC*, 6-300; *WCWN*, 243.)

Sea Witch. Confederate. Ship. Was scuttled by Confederates on May 17, 1862, near Bassett's Landing in the Pamunkey River. (*ORN*, 7:378–82; *CWC*, 6-333.)

USS Shawsheen (Young America) (Young Racer). Union. Side-wheel steam gunboat, 126 bulk tons, 180 tons. Length 118 feet, beam 22 feet 6 inches, depth 7 feet 3 inches. Complement of thirty-five to forty, with one 30-pounder Parrott, one 20-pounder Parrott, and one 12-pounder Dahlgren howitzer. Built in 1854 at Greenpoint, N.Y. Grounded in 5 feet of water while dragging for torpedoes near Turkey Bend and Turkey Island Plantation in the James River at a bend off Pickett's Farm. A Confederate battery of six cannons from Stark's Battalion of Va. Artillery shelled the vessel, hitting the steam drum on May 7, 1864. The Confederates captured the USS *Shawsheen* along with twenty-five to twenty-seven members of its crew, in the ten-minute fight. Set afire by Confederates upon the approach of two Union ironclads. (*OR*, 36:2:265, 268, 524; *ORN*, 10:30; ser. 2, 1:207; *WCWN*, 98; *MSV*, 235.)

Shrapnel. Union army. Steamer. Was sunk in a canal on November 24, 1864, on its way to Norfolk to be repaired. Was probably raised. (*ORN*, ser. 2, 1:267; *WCWN*, 243.)

CSS Shrapnel. Confederate. Steam tender or picket boat. Was burned at Richmond on the James River on April 3, 1864, by Confederates to prevent its capture. (*OR*, 42:3:716.)

Smith Briggs. Union army. Side-wheel steamer, 237 tons. Built in 1863 at Albany, N.Y. While on its way to attack a Confederate camp at Pagen Creek to flank Confederate scouts at Chuckatuck, the *Smith Briggs* and a Union detachment with one 12-pounder howitzer were captured by Confederates on January 31, 1864. Was burned and blown up on February 1, 1864, near Smithfield. The navy's 12-pounder was later found by the 23rd Mass. Regiment at Day's Point. (*OR*, 33:103–6; 51:2:850; *ORN*, 9:425–31; 10:218; *MSV*, 200.)

Stag. Confederate. Steamer. Was sunk with two schooners near Franklin Depot in the Blackwater River, about a quarter-mile from a railroad bridge. The wreck was found by the USS *Hunchback* on May 29, 1862. (*ORN*, 7:375, 711.)

Star. Confederate. Ship. Was destroyed by Confederates at Garlick's Landing in the Pamunkey River on May 5–10, 1862. (*ORN*, 7:379–82; *CWC*, 6-332.)

Starlight. Confederate. Ship. Was sunk by Confederates at White House on May 5–10, 1862, in the Pamunkey River. (*ORN*, 7:379–80, 382; *CWC*, 6-332.)

Titan. Union army. Steam tug, 113 tons. Armed with one 24-pounder. Built in 1863 at Philadelphia. Was captured while laying cable on March 5, 1864, with the steamer *Aeolus* by Capt. John Taylor Wood, two Confederate navy officers, and thirteen soldiers of Company F, 5th Va. Cavalry Regiment, at Cherrystone Point. On March 7, 1864, the Confederates took the *Titan* upriver and were chased by the USS *Tulip*. The Confederates burned the *Titan* to the waterline at Freeport at the head of the Piankatank River when the USS *Commodore Read*, USS *Jacob Bell*, USS *Fuchsia*, USS *Thomas Freeborn*, and USS *Currituck* arrived. The Union fleet recovered a metallic lifeboat from the *Titan* and broke up the tug's boiler and machinery. (*OR*, 33:231–32; *ORN*, 5:398–402; 9:527–28.)

CSS *Torpedo*. Confederate. Steam screw tug, 150 tons. Length 90 or 70 feet, beam 16 feet, depth 6 feet 6 inches. Armed with two 20-pounder Parrott guns. Used as a torpedo boat tender. Was stripped, partially burned, and scuttled on April 2–3, 1865, at Drewry's Bluff in the James River. Raised and sent to Norfolk Navy Yard in May 1865. (*ORN*, ser. 2, 1:269; *CWC*, 6-317; *WCWN*, 242.)

***Towns* (*W. W. Townes*).** Confederate. Side-wheel steamer, 89 tons. Built in 1855 at Philadelphia. Was scuttled to block the Warwick River in September 1861. (*ORN*, 6:724; *MSV*, 224; *WCWN*, 243.)

***Two Brothers*.** Union. Schooner, 47 tons. Cargo of anchors and anchor chains. En route to Philadelphia. Was captured the night of August 24–25, 1863, by Confederate guerrillas under Lt. John Taylor Wood in the captured USS *Satellite*. Was stripped and burned at Port Royal on August 31, 1863. (*ORN*, 5:344–45; *Naval Records Group 45, M101, Subject File of the Confederate States Navy*.)

***T. W. Riley*.** Union. Sloop. Was scuttled near the sloop *Jane Wright* on the morning of August 20, 1861, by the USS *Yankee* and USS *Restless* at Wades Bay, Potomac River, to prevent its use by Confederates following invasion rumors. (*ORN*, 4:615–17; *WCWN*, 88; Shomette, *Shipwrecks on the Chesapeake*, 141, 253.)

***Umpire*.** Union. Brig. Cargo of sugar and molasses. En route from Cardenas, Cuba, to Boston. Was captured and destroyed on June 15, 1863, by the CSS *Tacony* off Virginia near latitude 37° 40' north, longitude 70° 31' west. (*ORN*, 2:656.)

***Union*.** Confederate. Ship. Was scuttled by Confederates near Bassett's Landing in the Pamunkey River on May 17, 1862. (*ORN*, 7:378–82; *CWC*, 6-333.)

USS *United States* (CSS *Confederate States*). Union. Frigate, 1,526 or 1,607 tons. Length 175 feet 10 inches or 175 feet, beam 44 feet 2 or 8 inches, depth 21 feet 2 inches or 23 feet 6 inches. Complement of 467, with 44 guns. Launched on May 10, 1790, at Southwark, Pa. Commissioned on July 11, 1798, as one of the first three ships built for the U.S. Navy. Abandoned by the Union at Gosport Navy Yard as obsolete. Taken by the Confederates and used as a receiving ship with nineteen 32-pounders and 9-inch Columbiads.

In April 1862 the CSS *Confederate States* was sunk by the Confederates in the Elizabeth River to obstruct the channel to the Gosport Navy Yard. Was raised by Union forces and broken up in 1862. (*ORN*, ser. 2, 1:229, 270; *CWC*, 6-318–19; *WCWN*, 125.)

***Victory*.** U.S. Clipper ship, 670 tons. Built in 1851. Wrecked on February 9, 1861, near Cape Henry. (*EAS*, 145.)

***Virginia*.** Confederate. Ship. Was scuttled to act as an obstruction by Confederates at Newcastle in the Pamunkey River on May 17, 1862. (*ORN*, 7:379–82; *CWC*, 6-332.)

***Virginia*.** Confederate. Side-wheel steamer, 548 tons. Built in 1853 at Washington, D.C. Was burned along with forty private schooners at Fredericksburg by Confederates before April 19, 1862, to prevent their capture by Union forces. (*ORN*, 5:37; *MSV*, 222, 304.)

CSS *Virginia* (USS *Merrimack*). Confederate. Screw steam ironclad, 3,200 tons. Length 275 or 263 feet, beam 38 feet 6 inches or 51 feet 4 inches or 57 feet, draft 22 feet, armor 2-inch iron, armor backing 24-inch wood. Complement of 300–320, with one 6-inch rifled gun, eight 9-inch Dahlgrens, and two rifled 7-inch Dahlgren (another source—two 7-inch rifled guns, two 6-inch rifled guns, six 9-inch rifled guns, and two 12-pounder howitzers). The wreck of the USS *Merrimack* (see **USS *Merrimack***) was raised and rebuilt under Lt. J. M. Brooke. The first Confederate ironclad. Sank the USS *Congress* and USS *Cumberland* at Hampton Roads on March 8, 1862. Had a draw battle with the USS *Monitor* on March 9, 1862, in the first naval engagement between ironclads. On May 11, 1862, the CSS *Virginia* grounded near the south tip of Craney Island while attempting to escape Norfolk before Union troops took control. Blown up that morning by Confederates to prevent its capture. In 1867 salvage operations by a Norfolk wrecker removed 13,000 pounds of iron, armor, and the stern. In 1868 more machinery was salvaged and gunpowder was exploded under the wreck to demolish it. From 1874 to 1876 additional salvage was done with two guns removed. Some salvaged wood was made into canes and iron armor made into paperweights sold as Civil War mementos. Its anchor and other artifacts are in the Museum of the Confederacy at Richmond. (*ORN*, 7:335–38,

791–98; ser. 2, 1:271; Jones, "Aftermath of an Ironclad," *Civil War Times Illustrated*, 21–25; *CWC*, 6-320–23.)

CSS *Virginia II*. Confederate. Ironclad steam sloop, 2,000 tons. Length 197 feet overall or 180 feet between the fore-side of stern and aft side of rudder post, beam 47 feet 6 inches, draft 9 feet 6 inches or 14 feet, speed 10 knots, forward armor 6-inch iron, armor elsewhere 5-inch iron. Complement of 150, with two 8-inch guns and two 6-inch Brooke rifled guns (another source—one 11-inch, one 8-inch, and twelve 6.4-inch rifled guns). Laid down in 1863 and launched in 1864 at Richmond, Va. Flagship of the Confederate James River Squadron. Set afire on April 2–3, 1865, by Adm. Raphael Semmes's men at Drewry's Bluff above the obstructions to block the James River. Its maga-zines were full of shells when it was blown up. In April 1865 part of the wreck was removed by Benjamin Maillefert to clear the channel for vessels. In 1871–72 Maillefert cleared the rest of the wreck out of the river. Novelist Clive Cus-sler's NUMA and Underwater Archaeological Joint Ven-tures performed a gravimetric survey in 1982 at the site. (*OR*, 46:3:574; *ORN*, 12:101, 138; ser. 2, 1:271; *Annual Report of the Secretary of War 1871*, 73; *Chief of Engineers Report 1872*, 690; Semmes, *Service Afloat*, 812; Miller, *Photographic History*, 6:89; *CWC*, 6-321; Margolin, "Endangered Legacy," Grier and Winter, *Look to the Earth*, 92–95; *WCWN*, 209.)

Walton. Confederate. Ship. Was scuttled to act as an ob-struction by Confederates on May 17, 1862, at Newcastle in the Pamunkey River. (*ORN*, 7:379–82; *CWC*, 6-271.)

CSS *Wasp*. Confederate. Torpedo launch. Length 46 feet, beam 6 feet 3 inches, depth 3 feet 9 inches, one 18-foot spar torpedo. Built in 1861 at Richmond, Va. Was sunk by Union artillery fire from Fort McPherson after grounding in January 1865. (*CWC*, 6-322–23; *WCWN*, 219.)

Watchman. Confederate. Was scuttled by Confederates on May 17, 1862, at Newcastle in the Pamunkey River. (*ORN*, 7:379–82; *CWC*, 6-332.)

Wave. Confederate. Was scuttled by Confederates on May 17, 1862, at Newcastle. (*ORN*, 7:379–82; *CWC*, 6-332.)

Way. Confederate. Schooner. Was scuttled by Confeder-ates on May 5–10, 1862, at Cumberland. (*ORN*, 7:379–81, 382; *CWC*, 6-332.)

West Point (*Nellie Pentz*) (*Niagra*). Union. Side-wheel steamer, 409 tons. Built in 1860 at Keyport, N.J. Collided with the *George Peabody* on August 12–13, 1862, at Ragged Point, Potomac River with 76 killed. Was probably raised and renamed *Nellie Pentz*. Foundered on November 25, 1865, at Lynnhaven Bay. (*MSV*, 228, 306; *EAS*, 97; Shom-ette, *Shipwrecks on the Chesapeake*, 255.)

White. Union. Tug. Was destroyed with a dredge owned by the Albemarle & Chesapeake Canal Co. and other vessels at Pungo Landing by Confederates on October 16, 1863. (*OR*, 29:1:483–84.)

USS *Whitehall*. Union. Wooden side-wheel steamer, 326 tons. Length 126 feet, beam 28 feet 2 inches, depth 10 feet, draft 8 feet. Armed with two 30-pounder Parrotts and two 32-pounder smoothbores. A converted ferryboat built in 1850 at Brooklyn, N.Y. Was accidentally destroyed by fire off Fort Monroe's landing at Old Point Comfort on March 10, 1862, at 2:06 a.m. by a fire started in the fireroom, which killed four crewmen. The wreck was moved to Mill Creek and torn up. (*ORN*, 7, 10:82; ser. 2, 1:239; *MSV*, 229.)

Wild Pigeon. Confederate. Was scuttled by Confederates on May 17, 1862, near Bassett's Landing in the Pamunkey River. (*ORN*, 7:378–82; *CWC*, 6-333.)

William Allison. Confederate. Side-wheel steamer, 304 tons. A flag of truce boat. Built in 1854 at Baltimore. Had delivered 983 Union prisoners, and was carrying 212 pack-ages of blankets for Union prisoners still held by Confed-erates on its return trip when it was accidentally sunk by Confederate torpedoes off Cox's Ferry in the James River on the night of February 19, 1865. Was probably raised. (*OR*, 46:2:585; *ORN*, 12:41, 184; *MSV*, 230.)

William and Wesley. Nationality unknown. Was scuttled by Confederates on May 17, 1862, near Bassett's Landing in the Pamunkey River. (*ORN*, 7:378–82; *CWC*, 6-333.)

William Edward. Confederate. Was scuttled by Confeder-ates on May 5–10, 1862, at Cooke's Island in the Pamunkey River. (*ORN*, 7:379–80, 382; *CWC*, 6-332.)

William Francis. Confederate. Was scuttled by Confeder-ates on May 17, 1862, near Bassett's Landing in the Pamun-key River. (*ORN*, 7:378–82; *CWC*, 6-333.)

William Seldon. Confederate. Side-wheel steamer, 378 tons. Built in 1861 at Washington, D.C. Was burned on May 10–11, 1862, at Norfolk when Confederates abandoned the port. Its engines and boilers were probably salvaged by the schooner *Typhoon* for its Union owners in October 1862. (*ORN*, 8:35, 38–39; *MSV*, 232, 307.)

William Shamberg. Nationality unknown. Schooner. Was scuttled by Confederates on May 17, 1862, at Newcastle in the Pamunkey River. (*ORN*, 7:379–82; *CWC*, 6-332.)

William S. Ryland. Nationality unknown. Ship. Was burned by Confederates on May 17, 1862, at Newcastle in the Pamunkey River. (*ORN*, 7:379–82; *CWC*, 6-332.)

Wythe. Nationality unknown. Schooner. Sank in the James River. Removed in 1871 by Benjamin Maillefert under a U.S. Army Corps of Engineers contract. (*Annual Report of the Secretary of War 1871*, 73.)

▶ VESSELS WITHOUT NAMES

barge. Union. Cargo of 250,000 shells and 100,000 bullets. Blown up by a bomb disguised as a lump of coal by Confederate Secret Service agents John Maxwell and R. K. Dillard on August 9, 1864, at Lt. Gen. Ulysses Grant's ordnance depot at City Point (now Hopewell). More than $2 million in property was destroyed, including about 600 feet of warehouses and 180 feet of wharf, with at least 80 killed and 125 wounded. Grant and his headquarters' staff were showered with splinters and shells. (*OR*, 42:1:17, 954–56; 46:3:1250; Stern, *Confederate Navy Pictorial History*, 230–35; Perry, *Infernal Machines*, 130–35.)

boat. Confederate. A large boat was destroyed by the Union vessel *Brinker* about December 1864 in the James River area. (*ORN*, 11:194.)

boats. Confederate. Eighteen to twenty boats. Destroyed by a Union expedition on November 17, 1863, on the Piankatank River in Mathews County, Va. (*OR*, 29:1:653.)

boats. Confederate. Four boats were captured and burned by the Union tug USS *Resolute* on August 31, 1861, at Ferry Landing. (*ORN*, 4:647; *SCH*, 326–27.)

boats. Confederate. Two large boats were scuttled by Confederates in the Elizabeth River about April 17, 1861, near Craney Island to prevent Union vessels at Gosport Navy Yard from escaping to the North. (*ORN*, 4:279.)

canal boats. Confederate. Were sunk by Confederates to act as obstructions at the mouth of the Warwick River at Warwick Bar and in the James River, in the Swash Channel between Mulberry Point and Harden's Bluff from August to September 1861. (*ORA*, pl. 43, no. 1.)

canal boats—James River. Twelve canal boats, *Buena Vista, Commodore Stockton, Fort* (112 tons), *John McHale* (122 tons), *John Mitchell* (114 tons), *Margaret and Rebecca* (125 tons), *Mary Ann, Mary Linda* (116 tons), *Musadora* (123 tons), *Pilgrim* (126 tons), *Richard Vaux* (120 tons), *Rolling Wave* (112 tons), and two unnamed canal boats. Union. Purchased to be sunk in the James River at Trent's Reach. Each was loaded with 60 tons of stone. Three sank while under tow from Baltimore to Hampton Roads after July 13, 1864. Two canal boats were sunk at Hampton Roads, five were sunk on July 20, 1864, and two others were sunk later in Trent's Reach, James River. The sunken canal boats in the James River were probably removed after the Civil War by the U.S. Army Corps of Engineers. Where each named canal boat was sunk does not seem to have been noted. (*ORN*, 10:464; 12:138; *DANFS*, 5:438; Shomette, *Shipwrecks on the Chesapeake*, 256.)

flatboats. Confederate. Two flatboats were captured and destroyed by the USS *Coeur de Lion* on the Rappahannock on December 21, 1861. (*ORN*, 5:581.)

flat-bottomed boat. Confederate. Was destroyed by the USS *Dan Smith* at the head of Floods Creek on November 30, 1862. (*ORN*, 5:199.)

gunboat. Confederate. The gunboat was in the stocks and burned along with two schooners in the North River by a Union expedition from the USS *Mahaska* and *General Putman* on November 25, 1862. (*ORN*, 8:227–28.)

light ship. Confederate. Sank in front of Fort Lowry on the Rappahannock River before April 1862. (*ORN*, 5:34–36.)

light vessel. Nationality unknown. Wrecked and floated onto a beach at Cape Henry in good condition in May 1862. (*ORN*, 7:382.)

schooner. Confederate. Cargo of salt. The cargo was unloaded and sent to Richmond. Was set afire on December 20, 1862, to prevent its capture in the Piankatank River when the USS *Currituck*, USS *Ella*, and USS *Anacostia* approached. (*ORN*, 5:207–8.)

schooner. Confederate. May have been a captured Union large schooner with goods from New York City. Ran ashore at Milford Haven or Old Haven on September 23, 1863. The cargo was being unloaded by a number of men with thirty or more boats when the USS *Anacostia*, USS *Tulip*, and USS *Thomas Freeborn* arrived. Was set on fire. (*ORN*, 5:353, 358.)

schooner. Confederate. Was being refitted as a privateer when grounded. Destroyed on October 5, 1861, by two boats with twenty-three men from the USS *Louisiana* at Chincoteague Inlet at Cockrell Creek. Three hundred Confederates were driven off, with Confederate losses estimated at eight killed and wounded. Union losses were four wounded. (*ORN*, 6:288.)

schooner. Confederate. Was burned by the USS *Currituck* on September 28, 1863, in Old Haven Creek. (*SCH*, 416–17.)

schooner. Confederate. Was captured and burned by howitzer boats from the USS *Mahaska* and *General Putnam* on December 5, 1862, in the Severn River. (*ORN*, 8:262.)

schooner. Confederate. Was captured and destroyed on May 28, 1861, in the Potomac River probably by the USS *Resolute*. (*SCH*, 320–21; *WCWN*, 120.)

schooner. Confederate. Was captured in Quantico Creek and destroyed by two launches from the USS *Rescue*, USS *Resolute*, and USS *Union* on October 11, 1861. (*ORN*, 4:709–10.)

schooner. Confederate. Was sunk by Confederates near the wrecks of the CSS *George Page* and *Fairfax* in early March 1862 in Quantico Creek near Quantico. (Scharf, *History of the Confederate Navy*, 106.)

schooner. Confederate. Was destroyed with the *Jemima* by a Union expedition of thirty-six in small boats from the USS *Crusader* at Milford Haven in the York River on March 14, 1863. (*ORN*, 8:611.)

schooner. Union. Cargo of coal. Was sunk off Urbana in August 1863 by Confederate guerrillas. (*ORN*, 9:179.)

schooner. Union. Cargo of sutler's goods. Was captured and burned by Confederates off Pagan Creek, between 11:00 p.m. and midnight on December 5, 1864, near Smithville. (*OR*, 42:1:961; 42:3:840–41.)

schooner. Union. Transport. Was set afire next to the USS *Minnesota* at Hampton Roads on March 9, 1862, during the USS *Monitor*–CSS *Virginia* battle. (*OR*, 9:9.)

schooner. Union. Was captured and sunk on March 5, 1864, by Capt. John Taylor Wood, two Confederate navy sailors, and thirteen men of Capt. Thad Fitzhugh's Company F, 5th Va. Cavalry Regiment, at Cherrystone during a raid. The tug *Titan* and steamer *Aeolus* were also captured. (*OR*, 33:231–32.)

schooners. Confederate. Three schooners were sunk by Confederates 2–3 miles from the mouth of the Blackwater River. The USS *Hunchback* moved one of the wrecked schooners on May 23, 1862, in order to enter the Blackwater River. (*ORN*, 7:440.)

schooners. Confederate. Two schooners were ashore full of water at Milford Haven when set fire by an expedition from the USS *Crusader* and USS *Western World* on May 1, 1863. (*ORN*, 8:835.)

schooners. Confederate. Two schooners were burned in the North River along with a gunboat in the stocks by a Union expedition from the USS *Mahaska* and *General Putman* on November 25, 1862. (*ORN*, 8:227–28.)

schooners. Confederate. Two schooners were sunk with the *Stag* by Confederates a quarter-mile above a railroad bridge, near Franklin Depot. The USS *Hunchback* discovered the wrecks on May 29, 1862. (*ORN*, 7:711.)

schooners. Confederate. Was burned at Fredericksburg, along with the steamer *Virginia*, by Confederates before April 19, 1862, to prevent the schooners' capture by Union forces. (*ORN*, 5:37; *MSV*, 222, 304.)

sloop. Confederate. Cargo of salt. Driven ashore in the Potomac River on August 11, 1862. (*SCH*, 360–61.)

sloop. Confederate. Was burned at Fredericksburg by the USS *Anacostia* on August 31, 1862. (*ORN*, 5:78.)

sloop. Confederate. Was burned on August 3, 1862, by a cutter from the USS *Delaware* at Smithfield Creek. (Shomette, *Shipwrecks on the Chesapeake*, 255.)

sloop. Confederate. Was captured and destroyed by a detachment from the Union army gunboat *Reno* and 9th N.J. Regiment on April 14, 1864, on the Nansemond River. (*OR*, 33:271–72.)

sloop. Confederate. Was destroyed by the USS *Commodore Morris* on July 3, 1863, at Cumberland. (*SCH*, 342–43.)

sloop. Confederate. Wrecked up King's Creek in January 1863. (*ORN*, 11:717.)

vessel. Confederate. Was burned by Confederates near Fish Haul on the Pamunkey River on May 5–10, 1862. (*ORN*, 7:379–92.)

vessel. Confederate. Was scuttled in June 1861 in the Warwick River. (Shomette, *Shipwrecks on the Chesapeake*, 253.)

vessel. Confederate. Was sunk on January 25, 1862, near Norfolk. (Shomette, *Shipwrecks on the Chesapeake*, 253.)

vessels. Confederate. Along with a schooner, sloop, canoe, and the *Robert Wilbur*. Were captured and burned by a launch with thirteen men from the USS *Jacob Bell* on November 4, 1862, in a small bay about 5 miles up Nomini Creek. (*ORN*, 5:148–49.)

vessels. Confederate. Ferryboat, two sloops, a large scow, two barges, and four pontoon boats along with the small steamer *Little Magruder*. Were destroyed at White House on January 7, 1863, by a Union expedition consisting of the USS *Mahaska*, USS *Commodore Perry*, and army tug *May Queen* with three hundred soldiers of the 5th Pa. Cavalry Regiment, 6th N.Y. Cavalry Regiment, and 115th N.Y. Infantry Regiment. (*OR*, 18:124; *ORN*, 8:409–11.)

vessels. Confederate. Nine or ten sloops and schooners. Confederate. Were burned by a Union expedition of three hundred soldiers in the Union vessel *Fanny* and sailors in five launches with seven cannons from the USS *Minnesota* and USS *Resolute* on July 24, 1861, in the Back River,

midway between Old Point Comfort and the York River. (*ORN*, 6:34–35; *New York Times*, July 27, 1861.)

vessels. Confederate. One hundred and fifty boats and schooners. Destroyed on October 4–9, 1863, by a Union expedition in Matthews County. (*OR*, 29:1:205–8.)

vessels. Confederate. Seven small boats, one large fishing boat, and a scow were destroyed at the mouth of Aquia Creek on August 31, 1861. (*ORN*, 4:768.)

vessels. Confederate. Seventeen boats were destroyed opposite Charles County, Md., by a Union flotilla on the Potomac River on September 27, 1864. (*ORN*, 5:485.)

vessels. Confederate. Skiff and a large flat-bottomed boat were destroyed by USS *Daylight* on December 13, 1864, in the James River area. (*ORN*, 11:194.)

vessels. Confederate. Sloop and nine boats. Were burned and fifteen other boats captured at the head of Queen's Creek by the *General Putnam* and a howitzer boat from the USS *Mahaska* on December 19, 1862. (*ORN*, 8:309–10.)

vessels. Confederate. Sloop, scow, and eight boats. Sloop was 30 tons. Was captured and destroyed by USS *Mahaska* on December 20, 1862, in Fillbates Creek. (*ORN*, 8:310.)

vessels. Confederate. Thirty-one boats and two scows were burned by a Union boat expedition from the USS *Coeur de Lion* and USS *Mercury* on December 15, 1864, on the Coan River. (*ORN*, 5:495; *SCH*, 450–51; Shomette, *Civil War Shipwrecks*, 397.)

vessels. Confederate. Three schooners and four small boats were destroyed by a Union expedition consisting of the USS *Don*, USS *Stepping Stones*, and USS *Heliotrope*. The expedition ascended the Rappahannock River to Mattox Creek near Montrose, and up the right fork of Mattox Creek, where four boats were destroyed on March 16, 1865. Up the left fork three schooners were destroyed. (*ORN*, 5:534–37.)

vessels. Confederate. Three schooners, scows, and boats were captured and burned by three hundred men of the 52nd Pa. Infantry Regiment and the USS *Mahaska*, *General Putnam*, and *May Queen* on November 23, 1863, in the East River, Mobjack Bay. (Shomette, *Civil War Shipwrecks*, 398.)

vessels. Confederate. Twelve boats, one sloop. Were destroyed by a Union expedition on November 18, 1863, at Gwynn's Island. (*OR*, 29:1:653–64.)

vessels. Confederate. Two sloops, a schooner, and several fine boats were captured and burned by howitzer boats from the USS *Mahaska* and *General Putnam* on December 5, 1862, in the Severn River. (*ORN*, 8:262.)

vessels. Confederate. Were burned in the Pamunkey River on January 7, 1862, near West Point and White House. At low tide the wrecks of barges are reported to be visible. (Frassanito, *Grant and Lee*, 168; Shomette, *Shipwrecks on the Chesapeake*, 253.)

vessels. Confederate. Were sunk in March 1862 to obstruct the Nottaway River. (*ORN*, 7:711.)

vessels. Union. Dredge and other vessels. The dredge was owned by the Albemarle & Chesapeake Canal Co. Were destroyed by Confederates at Pungo Landing on October 15, 1863. (*OR*, 29:1:483–84.)

Washington

Washington had a number of wrecks during the Civil War period. All were lost as a result of accidents and storms.

Cadboro. Nationality unknown. Ship. Was lost in October 1862 near Port Angeles. (Gibbs, *Shipwrecks Pacific Ocean*, 274.)

Coquimbo. Nationality unknown. Ship. Was lost on January 22, 1862, east of Dungeness Spit. Salvaged. (Gibbs, *Shipwrecks Pacific Ocean*, 274.)

Decatur. Nationality unknown. Ship. Was lost in 1865 off Grays Harbor. (Gibbs, *Shipwrecks Pacific Ocean*, 275.)

Enterprise. Nationality unknown. Ship. Was lost in 1864 at Point Chehalis. (Gibbs, *Shipwrecks Pacific Ocean*, 274.)

Fanny. Union. Sloop. Lost its masts and became waterlogged. Wrecked off Shoalwater Bay or Willapa Bay in 1864 with the crew escaping in boats. Capsized and later sank after the *Pacific* rammed the hulk. (Gibbs, *Pacific Graveyard*, 251; Gibbs, *Shipwrecks Pacific Ocean*, 274; Marshall, *Oregon Shipwrecks*, 73.)

Frigate Bird. Nationality unknown. Ship. Was lost in 1863 at Applegate Cove. Salvaged. (Gibbs, *Shipwrecks Pacific Ocean*, 274.)

Iwanowa. Nationality unknown. Ship. Was lost on November 24, 1864, off Cape Flattery. (Gibbs, *Shipwrecks Pacific Ocean*, 275.)

Jennie Ford (Jenny Ford). Union. Bark. In ballast. En route from San Francisco to Puget Sound. Hit an underwater rock off the North Head on January 29, 1864. One passenger was lost, but the rest escaped. (Gibbs, *Pacific Graveyard*, 261; Gibbs, *Shipwrecks Pacific Ocean*, 274; Marshall, *Oregon Shipwrecks*, 133.)

Jenny Jones. Union. Schooner. Stranded on May 14, 1864, on Peacock Spit while going upriver. (Gibbs, *Pacific Graveyard*, 261; Marshall, *Oregon Shipwrecks*, 133.)

Kossuth. Nationality unknown. Ship. Was lost in 1862 off Dungeness Spit. (Gibbs, *Shipwrecks Pacific Ocean*, 274.)

Marmon. Nationality unknown. Ship. Was lost off Cape Flattery in 1861. (Gibbs, *Shipwrecks Pacific Ocean*, 274.)

Mary Woodruff. Nationality unknown. Ship. Was lost on July 31, 1862, at Camano Island. Salvaged. (Gibbs, *Shipwrecks Pacific Ocean*, 274.)

Ocean Bird. Union. Bark. Built in 1847 at Augusta, Maine. Ran between Milwaukie, Ore., and San Francisco. Was lost on March 19, 1864, southwest of Cape Flattery, Wash., or disappeared on April 3, 1864. (Gibbs, *Shipwrecks Pacific Ocean*, 274; Marshall, *Oregon Shipwrecks*, 185.)

Persevere. Nationality unknown. Ship. Was lost in September 1861 40 miles off Cape Flattery. (Gibbs, *Shipwrecks Pacific Ocean*, 275.)

Susan Abigal. Nationality unknown. Ship. Was lost in July 1865 off Cape Flattery. (Gibbs, *Shipwrecks Pacific Ocean,* 275.)

Tolo. Nationality unknown. Ship. Was lost in February 1862 at San Juan Island. (Gibbs, *Shipwrecks Pacific Ocean,* 274.)

Willamette. U.S. Schooner, 180 tons. En route from San Francisco to Shoalwater Bay or Willapa Bay. Wrecked in 1861 at the mouth of Shoalwater Bay, with two lost. Capt. John Vail later homesteaded in the area of present Richmond. (Gibbs, *Pacific Graveyard,* 285; Gibbs, *Shipwrecks Pacific Ocean,* 275.)

West Virginia

West Virginia was part of Virginia until it entered the Union as a state on June 18, 1863. Several steamers were lost on its waters during the Civil War.

B. C. Levi (Cuba No. 2) (General Crook). Union. Stern-wheel steamer, 110 tons. Cargo of military stores. Built in 1862 at Belle Vernon, Pa. Was captured by Maj. James H. Nounnan and twenty men of the 16th Va. Cavalry on the Kanawha River at Red House on February 3, 1864. Brig. Gen. Eliakim P. Scammon, one lieutenant and one captain were captured along with the boat's crew and twenty-five other Union soldiers, but the passengers were released. Burned at the mouth of Big Hurricane at Vintorux's Landing with more than $100,000 worth of medicine and one artillery piece with its ammunition. Was probably raised and sold after the war and renamed *Cuba No. 2.* (*OR,* 33:109–12; *WPD,* 35.)

Belle Creole. Union. Side-wheel steamer. Built in 1862 at New Albany, Ind. Sank near West Columbia, W. Va., the winter of 1863–64. Its machinery was removed and taken to Cincinnati. (*WPD,* 42.)

Julia Moffett. Union. Stern-wheel steamer, 56 tons. Built in 1860 at Cincinnati. Burned on August 1, 1861, at Tyler. (*MSV,* 118, 273.)

Kanawha Valley. Union. Stern-wheel steamer, 126 tons. Built in 1857 at Wheeling, Va. (W. Va.). Carried the 22nd Regiment. Was burned on August 1, 1861, at Cannelton on the order of Gen. Henry A. Wise. One aboard was killed by gunfire from shore. Was probably burned to prevent its capture. (*OR,* 2:1011; *MSV,* 119, 273; *WPD,* 35.)

Liberty. Union. Stern-wheel steamer, 261 tons. Built in 1857 at Wheeling, Va. (W. Va.). Was snagged on December 27, 1862, at Twelve Pole Creek below Huntington, W. Va. (*MSV,* 127, 276; *WPD,* 285.)

Wisconsin

Berlin City. Union. Side-wheel steamer, 74 tons. Built in 1856. Stranded on July 8, 1861, at Oshkosh. (*EAS,* 236; *MSV,* 21.)

Shipwrecks of Unknown Location

A number of American vessels were lost or sunk as part of the Union Stone Fleet in the Civil War at locations that the author has been unable to identify.

A. Holly. Union. Schooner. Purchased at Baltimore in August 1861. Was to be sunk as part of the Union Stone Fleet in the Confederacy to block Confederate harbors. (*ORN,* 2: 1:29.)

Alida. Union. Side-wheel steamer, 35 tons. Built in 1856 at East Saginaw, Mich. Burned in 1865. (*MSV,* 7, 240.)

Alvarado. Union. Ship. Purchased at Baltimore in August 1861. Was to be sunk as part of the Union Stone Fleet in the Confederacy to block Confederate harbors. May have been sunk in Hatteras Inlet, N.C. (*ORN,* 2, 1:33.)

Ashland. U.S. Stern-wheel steamer, 274 tons. Built in 1859 at Paducah, Ky. Burned on February 15, 1861. (*MSV,* 14, 243; *WPD,* 31.)

Aunt Letty. U.S. Double stern-wheel steamer, 303 tons. Length 187 feet, beam 36 feet, depth 5 feet. Built in 1855 at Elizabeth, Pa. Snagged on February 11, 1861, at Beram Island. (*MSV,* 16, 243; *WPD,* 33.)

Bob Mills. U.S. Screw steamer, 34 tons. Built in 1864 at Buffalo, N.Y. Exploded on June 12, 1865. Was probably lost in Lake Erie. (*MSV,* 23, 246.)

Brazil. U.S. Stern-wheel steamer, 211 tons. Length 150 feet, beam 31 feet, depth 4 feet, 3 boilers. Built in 1854 at McKeesport, Pa. Collided with the bark *Plymouth* on November 11, 1865, with the loss of two lives. (*MSV,* 24, 246; *WPD,* 60.)

Corea. Union. Ship, 356 tons. Purchased in 1861 at New Haven, Conn. Was to be sunk as part of the Union Stone Fleet in the Confederacy to block Confederate harbors. Was possibly sunk near Savannah. (*ORN,* 2, 1:35.)

Courier. Union. Stern-wheel steamer, 165 tons. Built in 1852 at Parkersburg, Va. (W. Va.). Was lost in 1863. (*MSV,* 47, 253.)

David Cavanagh. Union. Screw steamer, 169 tons. Built in 1864 at East Boston, Mass. Vanished in early 1865 at sea, probably in the Atlantic Ocean. (*MSV,* 51, 254.)

D. E. Crary. Union. Screw steamer, 109 tons. Built in 1863 at Brooklyn, N.Y. Stranded on September 9, 1863. (*MSV,* 49, 254.)

Delaware Farmer. Union. Ship. Purchased in 1861 at Baltimore. Was to be sunk as part of the Union Stone Fleet in the Confederacy to block Confederate harbors. (*ORN,* 2:1:73.)

E. D. Thompson. Union. Schooner. Purchased in 1861 at Baltimore. Was to be sunk as part of the Union Stone Fleet in the Confederacy to block Confederate harbors. (*ORN,* 2:1:76.)

Edward. Union. Bark, 340 tons. Purchased in 1861 at New Bedford, Mass. Was to be sunk as part of the Union Stone Fleet in the Confederacy to block Confederate harbors. (*ORN,* 2, 1:77.)

Ellen Goldsboro. Union. Schooner. Purchased in 1861 at Baltimore. Was to be sunk as part of the Union Stone Fleet in the Confederacy to block Confederate harbors. (*ORN,* 2, 1:78.)

Frederick Greff. Union. Army-chartered side-wheel steamer, 46 tons. Built in 1849 at Philadelphia. Reported as sunk by ice in 1862, possibly in Aquia Creek, Va. Exploded on March 4, 1863. Used in the Peninsula Campaign in Virginia. (*OR,* 21, 884; *MSV,* 77, 262; Gibson and Gibson, *Army's Navy,* 120.)

Friendship. Union. Schooner. Purchased in 1861 at Baltimore. Was to be sunk as part of the Union Stone Fleet in the Confederacy to block Confederate harbors. (*ORN,* ser. 2, 1:88.)

George P. Upshur. Union. Schooner. Purchased in 1861 at Baltimore. Was to be sunk as part of the Union Stone Fleet in the Confederacy to block Confederate harbors. (*ORN,* ser. 2, 1:94.)

George S. Wright. Union. Screw steamer, 199 tons. Built in 1863 at Cornwall, N.Y. Was lost on March 16, 1865. (*MSV,* 84, 263.)

Grampus. Union. Army-chartered stern-wheel steamer, 221 tons. Built in 1850 at Freedom, Pa. Stranded in 1865. (*MSV,* 88, 265.)

Harvest. Union. Bark, 314 tons. Purchased in 1861 at New Bedford, Mass. Was to be sunk as part of the Union Stone Fleet in the Confederacy to block Confederate harbors. (*ORN,* ser. 2, 1:99.)

Hero. Union. Schooner. Purchased in 1861 at Baltimore. Was to be sunk as part of the Union Stone Fleet in the Confederacy to block Confederate harbors. (*ORN,* ser. 2, 1:102.)

John Alexander. Union. Schooner. Purchased in 1861 at Baltimore. Was to be sunk as part of the Union Stone Fleet in the Confederacy to block Confederate harbors. (*ORN,* ser. 2, 1:114.)

Kate Sarchet. U.S. Stern-wheel steamer, 184 tons. Built in 1856 at New Albany, Ind. Stranded on February 18, 1861. (*MSV,* 120, 274; *WPD,* 267.)

Ladonia. U.S. Screw towboat steamer, 75 tons. Built in 1863 at Portsmouth, Ohio. Was lost on August 22, 1865. (*MSV,* 123, 275.)

Leviathan. Union. Steamer, 67 tons. Built in 1857 at Cleveland, Ohio. Was lost in 1865, probably in one of the Great Lakes. (*MSV,* 276.)

Louisville. Union. Stern-wheel steamer, 155 tons. Length 153 feet, beam 30 feet, depth 4 feet. Built in 1854 at Brownsville, Pa. Was lost in 1861, possibly on the Illinois River. (*MSV,* 131, 277; *WPD,* 296.)

Mary Frances. Union. Ship. Purchased in 1861 at Baltimore. Was to be sunk as part of the Union Stone Fleet in the Confederacy to block Confederate harbors. (*ORN,* ser. 2, 1:137.)

Montezuma. Union. Ship, 424 tons. Purchased in 1861 at New London, Conn. Was to be sunk as part of the Union Stone Fleet in the Confederacy to block Confederate harbors. (*ORN,* ser. 2, 1:150.)

North (Cronstadt). Union. Side-wheel steamer, 232 registered tons, 381 tons. Length 149 feet 5 inches, beam 21 feet 7 inches. Built in 1859 at Hull (Kingston-on-the-Hull), England. Was lost in late 1863. Formerly the British vessel *Cronstadt,* which was captured by the USS *Rhode Island* on August 16, 1863. Documented as the *North* on November 11, 1863. (*MSV,* 158, 285; *LLC,* 295.)

Patriot. Union. Schooner. Purchased in 1861 at Baltimore. Was to be sunk as part of the Union Stone Fleet in the Confederacy to block Confederate harbors. (*ORN,* ser. 2, 1:171.)

Saline. Union. Stern-wheel steamer, 176 tons. Built in 1858 at Louisville. Stranded in January 1865 on Clark's Bar. (*MSV,* 192, 295.)

Samuel B. Young (Sam Young). U.S. Stern-wheel steamer, 154 tons. Built in 1855 at Shouseville, Pa. Was lost on July 22, 1865. (*MSV,* 193, 296.)

Sarah M. Kemp. Union. Schooner. Purchased in 1861 at Baltimore. Was to be sunk as part of the Union Stone Fleet in the Confederacy to block Confederate harbors. (*ORN,* ser. 2, 1:201.)

Sea Foam. Nationality unknown. Screw steamer, 135 tons. Built in 1855 at Camden, N.J. Stranded on August 10, 1861. (*MSV,* 192, 297.)

Somerfield. Union. Schooner. Purchased in 1861 at Baltimore. Was to be sunk as part of the Union Stone Fleet in the Confederacy to block Confederate harbors. (*ORN,* ser. 2, 1:210.)

Southerner. Union. Schooner. Purchased in 1861 at Baltimore. Was to be sunk as part of the Union Stone Fleet in the Confederacy to block Confederate harbors. (*ORN,* ser. 2, 1:211.)

South Wind. Union. Schooner. Purchased in 1861 at Baltimore. Was to be sunk as part of the Union Stone Fleet in the Confederacy to block Confederate harbors. (*ORN,* ser. 2, 1:212.)

Vermont. Nationality unknown. Steamer, 255 tons. Built in 1851 at Cleveland, Ohio. Was lost in 1863, probably in the Great Lakes. (*MSV,* 220, 303.)

William L. Jones. Union. Schooner. Purchased in 1861 at Baltimore. Was to be sunk as part of the Union Stone Fleet in the Confederacy to block Confederate harbors. (*ORN*, ser. 2, 1:241.)

W. L. Bartlett. Union. Schooner. Purchased in 1861 at Baltimore. Was to be sunk as part of the Union Stone Fleet in the Confederacy to block Confederate harbors. (*ORN*, ser. 2, 1:234.)

W. W. Burns. Union. Schooner. Purchased in 1861 at Baltimore. Was to be sunk as part of the Union Stone Fleet in the Confederacy to block Confederate harbors. (*ORN*, ser. 2, 1:234.)

Bibliography

GOVERNMENT DOCUMENTS

"Abandoned Shipwreck Act, Final Guidelines, Notice." *Federal Register* 55, no. 233, December 4, 1990, 50, 115–45.

Annual Report of the Chief of Engineers to the Secretary of War for the Year 1870. Washington, D.C.: Government Printing Office, 1870.

Annual Report of the Chief of Engineers to the Secretary of War for the Year 1874. Washington, D.C.: Government Printing Office, 1874.

Annual Report of the Chief of Engineers to the Secretary of War for the Year 1875. Washington, D.C.: Government Printing Office, 1875.

Annual Report of the Chief of Engineers to the Secretary of War for the Year 1876. Washington, D.C.: Government Printing Office, 1876.

Annual Report of the Chief of Engineers to the Secretary of War for the Year 1879. Washington, D.C.: Government Printing Office, 1879.

Annual Report of the Chief of Engineers, United States Army, to the Secretary of War for the Year 1880. Washington, D.C.: Government Printing Office, 1880.

Annual Report of the Chief of Engineers, United States Army, to the Secretary of War for the Year 1881. Washington, D.C.: Government Printing Office, 1881.

Annual Report of the Chief of Engineers, United States Army, to the Secretary of War for the Year 1883. Washington, D.C.: Government Printing Office, 1883.

Annual Report of the Chief of Engineers, United States Army, to the Secretary of War for the Year 1887. Washington, D.C.: Government Printing Office, 1887.

Annual Report of the Chief of Engineers, United States Army, to the Secretary of War for the Year 1888. Washington, D.C.: Government Printing Office, 1888.

Annual Report of the Chief of Engineers, United States Army, to the Secretary of War for the Year 1891. Washington, D.C.: Government Printing Office, 1891.

Annual Report of the Chief of Engineers, United States Army, to the Secretary War for the Year 1893. Washington, D.C.: Government Printing Office, 1893.

Annual Reports of the War Department for the Fiscal Year Ended June 30, 1897, Report of the Chief of Engineers, pt. 6. Washington, D.C.: Government Printing Office, 1897.

Annual Reports of the War Department for the Fiscal Year Ended June 30, 1898, Report of the Chief of Engineers, pt. 2. Washington, D.C.: Government Printing Office, 1898.

Annual Reports of the War Department for the Fiscal Year Ended June 30, 1901, Report of the Chief of Engineers. Washington, D.C.: Government Printing Office, 1901.

Annual Report of the Secretary of War Being Part of the Message and Documents Communicated to the Two Houses of Congress at the Beginning of the Second Session of the Forty-second Congress, 1871. Washington, D.C.: Government Printing Office, 1871.

Annual Report of the Secretary of War on the Operations for the Department for the Fiscal Year Ended June 30, 1872. Washington, D.C.: Government Printing Office, 1872.

Executive Documents of the House of Representatives of the Thirty-eighth Congress, 1st sess., Report No. 123, June 21, 1864. Washington, D.C.: Government Printing Office, 1864.

Executive Documents of the House of Representatives of the First Session of the Forty-eighth Congress, 1883–1884. Washington, D.C.: Government Printing Office, 1884.

Executive Documents of the House of Representatives for the Third Session of the Forty-fifth Congress 1878–1879. Washington, D.C.: Government Printing Office, 1880.

Executive Documents of the House of Representatives of the United States, Second Session of the Fortieth Congress, 1867. Washington, D.C.: Government Printing Office, 1873.

Executive Documents of the House of Representatives of the United States for the Second Session of the Forty-third Congress, 1874–1875. Washington, D.C.: Government Printing Office, 1875.

Goodwin, R. Christopher, Jack Irion, Susan Barrett Smith, David Beard, and Paul Heinrich. *Underwater Cultural Resources Survey for Contraction Dikes at Red Eye Crossing, Mississippi River, Baton Rouge to the Gulf of Mexico, Louisiana.* New Orleans: R. Christopher Goodwin & Associates, Inc., for the U.S. Army Corps of Engineers, 1993.

Granger, M. L. *History of the Savannah District: 1829–1968.* Savannah: U.S. Army Corps of Engineers, 1968.

Irion, Jack B. *Underwater Archaeological Investigations, Mobile Bay Ship Channel, Mobile Harbor, Alabama.* Espey, Huston & Associates, for the U.S. Army Corps of Engineers: 1986.

Irion, Jack B., and Cell L. Bond. *Identification and Excavation of Submerged Anomalies, Mobile Harbor, Alabama,* Espey, Huston & Associates for the U.S. Army Corps of Engineers: October 1984.

Marine Magnetometer Survey . . . Pinellas County, Florida. for the U.S. Army Corps of Engineers, 1988.

Mills, Gary B. *Of Men and Rivers: The Story of the Vicksburg District.* Vicksburg, Miss.: U.S. Army Corps of Engineers, 1978.

Mistovich, Tim S., Vernon James Knight Jr., Carlos Solis, George M. Lamb, and Eugene Wilson. *Cultural Resources Reconnaissance of*

Pascagoula, Mississippi. Mobile, Ala.: U.S. Army Corps of Engineers, 1983.

Moore, Jamie W. *The Lowcountry Engineers: Military Missions and Economic Development in the Charleston District.* Charleston, S.C.: U.S. Army Corps of Engineers, 1981.

Naval Records Collection of the Office of Naval Records and Library Record Group 45, M101, Subject File of the Confederate States Navy, 1861–1865. Washington, D.C.: National Archives Trust Fund Board, National Archives and Records Service, 1983.

Official Records of the Union and Confederate Navies in the War of the Rebellion. 30 vols. Washington, D.C.: Government Printing Office, 1894–1922.

Patrick, David M., Maureen K. Corcoran, Paul E. Albertson, and Lawson M. Smith. *Legacy Resource Management Program.* U.S. Army Corps of Engineers Report GL-94-9, Vicksburg, Miss., March 1994.

Pearson, Charles E., George J. Castillo, Donald Davis, Thomas E. Redard, and Allen R. Saltus. *A History of Waterborne Commerce and Transportation within the U.S. Army Corps of Engineers New Orleans District and an Inventory of Known Underwater Cultural Resource.* New Orleans: Prepared for New Orleans District, U.S. Army Corps of Engineers, December 1989.

Petsche, Jerome E. *The Steamboat Bertrand: History, Excavation, and Architecture.* Publications in Archaeology II. Washington, D.C.: National Park Service, 1974.

Report of the Chief of Engineers Accompanying Report of the Secretary of War, 1867. Washington, D.C.: Government Printing Office, 1867.

Report of the Chief of Engineers to the Secretary of War for the Year 1868. Washington, D.C.: Government Printing Office, 1869.

Report of the Secretary of War, Being Part of the Message and Documents Communicated to the Two Houses of Congress at the Beginning of the First Session of the Forty-second Congress Report of the Chief of Engineers. Washington, D.C.: Government Printing Office, 1873.

U.S. Army Corps of Engineers. *General Design Memorandum, Mobile Harbor Deepening, Alabama, Design Memorandum No. 1, Appendix G, Cultural Resources.* Mobile, Ala., June 1984.

U.S. Department of the Interior, Fish and Wildlife Service. *Bertrand.* Washington, D.C.: Government Printing Office, 1982.

U.S. Department of the Navy. *Civil War Chronology, 1861–1865.* Washington, D.C.: Government Printing Office, 1971.

———. *Dictionary of American Naval Fighting Ships.* 8 vols., Washington, D.C.: Government Printing Office, 1959–81.

War Department Collection of Confederate Records, Record Group 109. Washington, D.C.: National Archives and Records, General Services Administration, 1973.

The War of the Rebellion: A Compilation of the Official Records of the Union and Confederate Armies. 128 vols. Washington, D.C.: Government Printing Office, 1880–1901.

Weinman, Lois J., and E. Gary Stickel. *Los Angeles Beach Harbor Areas, Cultural Resources Survey.* Prepared for U.S. Army Engineer District, Los Angeles, April 1978.

Yoseloff, Thomas, ed. *The Official Atlas of the Civil War.* New York: Harper and Row, 1967.

NEWSPAPERS

Charleston (S.C.) Mercury, 1862.

Daily Dramatic Chronicle (San Francisco, Calif.), 1865.

Daily Examiner (San Francisco, Calif.), 1865.

Daily Illinois State Journal (Springfield), 1863.

Harper's Weekly (New York City), 1863.

New York Times, 1861–1865.

Sacramento (Calif.) Bee, 1999.

Sacramento (Calif.) Union, 1865.

BOOKS

Arnold, J. Barto, III, ed. *Beneath the Waters of Time: The Proceedings of the Ninth Conference on Underwater Archaeology.* Austin: Texas Antiquities Committee, 1978.

———. *Marine Magnetometer Survey of Archeological Materials Found near Galveston, Texas.* Publication No. 10. Austin: Texas Antiquities Committee, 1987.

Bass, George F., ed. *Ships and Shipwrecks of the Americas: A History Based on Underwater Archaeology.* New York: Thomas and Hudson, 1988.

Bearss, Edwin C. *Hardluck Ironclad: The Sinking and Salvage of the Cairo.* Baton Rouge: Louisiana State University Press, 1966.

Berman, Bruce D. *Encyclopedia of American Shipwrecks.* Boston: Mariners Press, 1972.

Bernath, Stuart L. *Squall across the Atlantic.* Berkeley: University of California Press, 1970.

Bright, Leslie S. *The Blockade Runner Modern Greece and Her Cargo.* Raleigh: North Carolina Division of Archives and History, 1977.

Burgess, Robert E. *Sinkings, Salvages, and Shipwrecks.* New York: American Heritage Press, 1970.

California State Lands Commission. *A Map and Record Investigation of Historical Sites and Shipwrecks along the Sacramento River between Sacramento City and Sherman Island.* Sacramento: California State Lands Commission, 1988.

Carnahan, J. W. *4000 Civil War Battles.* Fort Davis, Tex.: Frontier Book Co., 1967.

Carse, Robert. *Blockade: The Civil War at Sea.* New York: Rinehart, 1958.

The Century War Book: The Famous History of the Civil War by the People Who Actually Fought It. New York: Arno Press, 1978.

Chaitin, Peter M., and editors of Time-Life Books. *The Coastal War: Chesapeake Bay to Rio Grande.* Alexandria, Va.: Time-Life Books, 1984.

Chance, Franklin N., Paul C. Chance, and David L. Topper. *Tangled Machinery and Charred Relics: The Historical and Archaeological Investigation of the C.S.S. Nashville.* Orangeburg, S.C.: Sun Printing, 1985.

Cochran, Hamilton. *Blockade Runners of the Confederacy.* New York: Bobbs-Merrill, 1958.

Courtemanche, Regis A. *No Need of Glory: The British Navy in American Waters.* Annapolis, Md.: Naval Institute Press, 1977.

Cussler, Clive, and Craig Dirgo. *The Sea Hunters: True Adventures with Famous Shipwrecks.* New York: Simon and Schuster, 1996.

———. *The Sea Hunters II: More True Adventures with Famous Shipwrecks.* New York: G. P. Putnam's Sons, 2002.

Daly, Robert W., ed. *Aboard the USS Florida, 1863–1865: The Letters of Paymaster William Frederick Keeler, U.S. Navy, to His Wife, Anna.* Annapolis, Md.: Naval Institute Press, 1968.

Dimitry, John. *Confederate Military History: A Library of Confederate States History in Thirteen Volumes, Written by Distinguished Men of the South.* Ed. Clement A. Evans. Vol. 10: *Louisiana.* Secaucus, N.J.: Blue and Gray Press, n.d.

Drago, Harry Sinclair. *The Steamboaters: From the Early Side-Wheelers to Big Packets.* New York: Bramhall House, 1967.

Elliott, Robert G. *Ironclad of the Roanoke: Gilbert Elliott's Albemarle.* Shippensburg, Pa.: White Mane Publishing Co., 1994.

Forrest, Nathan Bedford. *Gunboats and Cavalry.* Memphis: Nathan Bedford Forrest Trail Committee, 1965.

Frassanito, William A. *Grant and Lee: The Virginia Campaign, 1864–1865.* New York: Charles Scribner's Sons, 1983.

Geier, Clarence R., Jr., and Susan E. Winter, eds. *Look to the Earth: Historical Archaeology and the American Civil War.* Nashville: University of Tennessee Press, 1994.

Gibbs, James Atwood. *Pacific Graveyard.* Portland: Binford and Mort, 1964.

———. *Shipwrecks of the Pacific Coast.* Portland: Binford and Mort, 1957.

———. *West Coast Windjammers in Story and Pictures.* Seattle: Superior Publishing Co., 1968.

Gibson, Charles Dana, and E. Kay Gibson. *The Army's Navy Series: Dictionary of Transports and Combatant Vessels, Steam and Sail Employed by the Union Army, 1861–1868.* Camden, Maine: Ensign Press, 1995.

Gould, Richard A., ed. *Shipwreck Anthropology.* Albuquerque: University of New Mexico Press, 1983.

Hearn, Chester G., III. *Gray Raiders of the Sea: How Eight Confederate Warships Destroyed the Union's High Seas Commerce.* Camden, Maine: International Marine Publishing, 1992.

Hewitt, Lawrence Lee. *Port Hudson, Confederate Bastion on the Mississippi.* Baton Rouge: Louisiana State University Press, 1987.

Hicks, Brian, and Schuyler Kropf. *Raising the* Hunley: *The Remarkable History and Recovery of the Lost Confederate Submarine.* New York: Ballantine Books, 2002.

Higginson, Thomas Wentworth. *Army Life in a Black Regiment.* 1864. Reprint. New York: W. W. Norton, 1984.

Hill, D. H. *Confederate Military History: A Library of Confederate States History in Thirteen Volumes, Written by Distinguished Men of the South.* Ed. Clement A. Evans. Vol. 4: *North Carolina.* Secaucus, N.J.: Blue and Gray Press, n.d.

Hoehling, A. A. *Thunder at Hampton Roads.* Englewood Cliffs, N.J.: Prentice-Hall, 1976.

Holden, William M. *Sacramento: Excursions into Its History and Natural World.* Fair Oaks, Calif.: Two Rivers Publishing Co., 1987.

Holmquist, June Drenning, and Ardis Hillman Wheeler, eds. *Diving into the Past: Theories, Techniques, and Applications of Underwater Archaeology.* Proceedings of the First Conference on Underwater Archaeology, April 26–27, 1963. St. Paul: Minnesota Historical Society, 1963.

Hoole, W. Stanley. *The Logs of the CSS Alabama and the CSS Tuscaloosa, 1861–1863: Kept by Lieutenant (Later Captain) John Law.* University, Ala.: Confederate Publishing Co., 1972.

Horan, James D. *Confederate Agent: A Discovery in History,* New York: Fairfax Press, 1954.

———, ed. *C.S.S. Shenandoah: The Memoirs of Lieutenant Commanding James I. Waddell.* New York: Crown Publishers, 1960.

Horner, Dave. *The Blockade-Runners: True Tales of Running the Yankee Blockade of the Confederate Coast.* New York: Dodd, Mead, 1968.

———. *Shipwrecks, Skin Divers, and Sunken Gold.* New York: Dodd, Mead, 1965.

Jackson, Walter A. *The Doghole Schooners.* Volcano: California Traveler, 1969.

Johnson, Robert Underwood, and Clarence Clough Buel, eds. *Battles and Leaders of the Civil War.* New York: Castle Books, 1956.

Johnston, Paul Forsythe, ed. *Proceedings of the Sixteenth Conference on Underwater Archaeology.* Special Publications Series No. 4. Glassboro, N.J.: Society for Historical Archaeology, 1985.

Keats, Henry C., and George C. Farr. *Dive into History.* Vol. 2: *U.S. Submarines.* Houston: Pisces Books, 1991.

Keel, James R. *Florida's Trails to History's Treasures.* Fort Lauderdale, Fla.: Seajay Enterprises, 1981.

Lane, Carl D. *American Paddle Steamboats*. New York: Coward-McCann, 1943.

Lingenfelter, Richard E. *Steamboats of the Colorado River: 1852–1916*. Tucson: University of Arizona Press, 1978.

Longacre, Edward G. *Mounted Raids of the Civil War*. New York: A. S. Barnes and Co., 1975.

Lonsdale, Adrian, and H. R. Kaplan. *A Guide to Sunken Ships in American Waters*. Arlington, Va.: Compass Publications, 1964.

Lytle, William M., and Forrest R. Holdcamper. *Merchant Steam Vessels of the United States: 1790–1868, "The Lytle Holdcamper List."* Ed. C. Bradford Mitchell. Staten Island, N.Y.: Steamship Historical Society of America, 1975.

Marshall, Don B. *California Shipwrecks: Footsteps in the Sea*. Seattle: Superior Publishing Co., 1978.

———. *Oregon Shipwrecks*. Portland, Ore.: Binford and Mort, 1984.

Marx, Robert F., and Jennifer Marx. *The Search for Sunken Treasure: Exploring the World's Great Shipwrecks*. Toronto: Key Porter Books, 1996.

Miller, Edward Stokes. *Civil War Sea Battles: Seafights and Shipwrecks in the War between the States*. Conshohocken, Pa.: Combined Books, 1995.

Miller, Francis Trevelyan. *Photographic History of the Civil War*. 10 vols. 1911–12. Reprint. New York: Castle Books, 1957.

Milligan, John D., ed. *From the Fresh-Water Navy, 1861–64: The Letters of Acting Master's Mate Henry R. Browne and Acting Ensign Symmes E. Brown*. Annapolis, Md.: U.S. Naval Institute, 1970.

Mills, Randall V. *Stern-Wheelers Up Columbia: A Century of Steamboating in the Oregon Country*. Palo Alto, Calif.: Pacific Books, 1947.

Morgan, Murray. *Dixie Raider: The Saga of the C.S.S. Shenandoah*. New York: E. P. Dutton, 1948.

Morris, Paul C., and William P. Quinn. *Shipwrecks in New York Waters: A Chronology of Ship Disasters from Montauk Point to Barnegat Inlet, from the 1880s to the 1930s*. Orleans, Mass.: Parnassus Imprints, 1989.

Nesmith, Robert I., and John S. Potter Jr. *Treasure: How and Where to Find It*. New York: Arco, 1968.

Nesser, Robert Wilden. *Statistical and Chronological History of the U.S. Navy, 1775–1907*. New York: Burt Franklin, 1970.

Owsley, Frank Lawrence, Jr. *The C.S.S. Florida: Her Building and Operations*. Tuscaloosa: University of Alabama Press, 1987.

Perry, Milton F. *Infernal Machines: The Story of Confederate Submarine and Mine Warfare*. Baton Rouge: Louisiana State University Press, 1965.

Pleasants, James A. *North Carolina Wreck List*. MS, 1976.

Porter, David D. *The Naval History of the Civil War*. Secaucus, N.J.: Castle Books, 1984.

Potter, John S. *The Treasure Diver's Guide*. Garden City, N.Y.: Doubleday, 1960.

Pratt, Fletcher. *Civil War on Western Waters*. New York: Holt, 1956.

Quinn, William P. *Shipwrecks along the Atlantic Coast: A Chronology of Maritime Accidents and Disasters from Maine to Florida*. Orleans, Mass.: Parnassus Imprints, 1988.

Reinstedt, Randall. *Shipwrecks, Tall Tales, and Sea Monsters of California's Central Coast*. Carmel, Calif.: Ghost Town Publications, 1975.

Rieseberg, Lt. Harry E. *Fell's Complete Guide to Buried Treasure, Land and Sea*. New York: Frederick Fell, 1970.

Robinson, William Morrison, Jr. *The Confederate Privateers*. New Haven, Conn.: Yale University Press, 1928.

Scharf, J. Thomas. *History of the Confederate Navy*. 1877. Reprint. Wilkes-Barre, Pa.: Fairfax Press, 1977.

Semmes, Adm. Raphael. *Service Afloat; or, The Remarkable Career of the Confederate Cruisers* Sumter *and* Alabama. 1887. Reprint. New York: P. J. Kennedy, 1903.

Shingleton, Royce Gordon. *John Taylor Wood: Sea Ghost of the Confederacy*. Athens: University of Georgia Press, 1982.

Shomette, Donald G. *Shipwrecks of the Civil War: The Encyclopedia of Union and Confederate Naval Losses*. Washington, D.C.: Donie, 1973.

———. *Shipwrecks on the Chesapeake: Maritime Disasters on Chesapeake Bay and Its Tributaries: 1608–1978*. Centreville, Md.: Tidewater Publishers, 1982.

Silverstone, Paul H. *Warships of the Civil War Navies*. Annapolis, Md.: Naval Institute Press, 1989.

Spence, E. Lee. *Shipwrecks of South Carolina and Georgia*. Sullivan Island, S.C.: Sun Research Society, 1984.

Stern, Philip Van Dorn. *The Confederate Navy: A Pictorial History*. Garden City, N.Y.: Doubleday, 1962.

———, ed. *Secret Missions of the Civil War*. New York: Bonanza Books, 1959.

Stick, David. *Graveyard of the Atlantic*. Chapel Hill: University of North Carolina Press, 1952.

Still, William N., Jr. *Iron Afloat: The Story of the Confederate Armorclads*. Columbia: University of South Carolina Press, 1988.

Summersell, Charles G., ed. *The Journal of George Townley Fullam: Boarding Officer of the Confederate Sea Raider Alabama*. Tuscaloosa: University of Alabama Press, 1973.

Turner, Maxine. *Navy Gray: A Story of the Confederate Navy in the Chattahoochee and Apalachicola Rivers*. Tuscaloosa: University of Alabama Press, 1988.

Underwater Archaeology: The Proceedings of the Eleventh Conference on Underwater Archaeology. Ed. Calvin R. Cummings. Fathom Eight Special Edition No. 4. San Marino, Calif.: Fathom Eight, 1982.

Vandiver, Frank E., ed. *Confederate Blockade Running through Bermuda, 1861–1865: Letters and Cargo Manifests*. 1947. Reprint. New York: Kraus Reprinting Co., 1970.

Way, Frederick, Jr. *Way's Packet Directory, 1848–1983*. Athens: Ohio University Press, 1983.

Way, Frederick, Jr., and Joseph W. Rutter. *Way's Steam Towboat Directory*. Athens: Ohio University Press, 1990.

West, Richard S. *Mr. Lincoln's Navy*. New York: Longmans, Green, 1957.

Wiltse, Ernest A. *Gold Rush Steamers of the Pacific*. Lawrence, Mass.: Quarterman Publications, 1976.

Wise, Stephen R. *Lifeline of the Confederacy: Blockade Running in the Civil War*. Columbia: University of South Carolina Press, 1988.

ARTICLES

Ammen, Daniel. "The Navy in the Civil War." *Confederate Military History*. Reprint. Secaucus, N.J.: Blue and Grey Press, n.d.

"Ancient Steamboat Sleeps in Swamp." *Treasure* 9, no. 4 (April 1978): 40.

Anuskiewicz, Richard J. "Marine Archaeology: A Problematic Approach to Resolution of Unidentified Magnetic Anomalies: Session Overview." *Proceedings: Seventh Annual Gulf of Mexico Transfer Meeting* (1986): 233–35.

Anuskiewicz, Richard J., and Ervan G. Garrison. "Underwater Archaeology by Braille: Survey Methodology and Site Characterization Modeling in a Blackwater Environment—A Study of a Scuttled Confederate Ironclad, C.S.S. *Georgia*." *Diving for Science . . . 1992: Proceedings of the American Academy of Underwater Sciences Twelfth Annual Scientific Diving Symposium*. Wilmington, N.C.: American Academy of Underwater Sciences, 1992.

Arnold, J. Barto, III. "Underwater Cultural Resource Management: The Computerized Shipwreck Reference File." *Underwater Archaeology: The Proceedings of the Eleventh Conference on Underwater Archaeology*. Special Edition, no. 4. San Marino, Calif.: Fathom Eight, 1982.

Arnold, J. Barto, III, and Richard J. Anuskiewicz, "USS *Hatteras*: Site Monitoring and Mapping." *Underwater Archaeology Proceedings from the Society for Historical Archaeology Conference* (Washington, D.C.). (January 1995): 82–87.

Babits, Lawrence E. "Exploring a Civil War Sidewheeler." *Archaeology* 47, no. 5 (September–October 1994): 48–50.

Barr, Alwyn. "Texas Coastal Defense, 1861–1865." *Southwestern Historical Quarterly* 45 (July 1961): 1–31.

Bearss, Edwin. "Underwater Archaeology and the Cairo." In *Diving into the Past: Theories, Techniques, and Applications of Underwater Archaeology*. Ed. June Drenning Holmquist and Ardis Hillman Wheeler. Proceedings of the First Conference on Underwater Archaeology, April 26–27, 1963. St. Paul: Minnesota Historical Society, 1963.

Boozer, Jack D. "Chattahoochee's Sunken Guns." *True Treasure* 4, no. 8 (July–August 1970): 28, 30.

Boyd, Ellsworth. "Diving Down to Dixie." *Gold!* no. 13 (Winter 1975): 42–47.

———. "The Enigma of This Civil War Gunboat Has Ironic Twists." *Skin Diver* 36, no. 12 (October 1987): 132–38.

———. "Raise the Monitor." *Skin Diver* 30, no. 8 (August 1981): 18–21.

———. "Top Ten Wrecks of the East Coast." *Skin Diver* 29, no. 9 (September 1980): 20–23, 78–79.

———. "Wreck Facts." *Skin Diver* 37, no. 10 (October 1988): 43–44.

Bright, Leslie S. "Wrecked Blockade Runners of the Lower Cape Fear: Site Environment and Physical Condition." In *Proceedings of the Sixteenth Conference on Underwater Archaeology*, Special Publications Series No. 4. Ed. Paul Forsythe Johnston. Glassboro, N.J.: Society for Historical Archaeology, 1985.

Broussara, Larry W. "The *Judah*: Sunken Civil War Schooner Harbored in Shifting Sands for 125 Years." *Skin Diver* 37, no. 7 (June 1988): 164–68.

Burgess, Robert. "First Dive to the Monitor: Exploring America's First Submarine Sanctuary." *Oceans* 12, no. 5 (September–October 1979): 6–7.

Calhoun, Jessamine A. "A Question of Wood and Time." *Naval History* 10, no. 4 (July–August 1996): 49–50.

Chase, Christopher. "In Search of the CSS *Hunley*: A Twenty-Three Year Mission Ends in Success." *Blue & Gray Magazine* 13, no. 5 (July 1996): 24–26, 28.

Childress, Lt. Cdr. Floyd. "The National Marine Sanctuaries Program as a Cultural Resource Management Tool for the U.S.S. *Monitor*." In *Beneath the Waters of Time: The Proceedings of the Ninth Conference on Underwater Archaeology*. Ed. Barto Arnold III. Austin: Texas Antiquities Committee, 1978.

Christley, James. "The Alligator, the North's Underwater Threat." *Civil War Times Illustrated* 19, no. 10 (February 1981): 26–31.

"Civil War Relic." *Treasure Search* 11, no. 5 (October 1983): 29.

Czura, Kenneth P. "Raider of the Arctic Seas." *America's Civil War* 4, no. 1 (May 1991): 46–52.

Czura, Pete. "The Confederate Navy Rises Again." *Argosy* (October 1968): 28.

Delaney, Norman C. "At Semmes' Hand." *Civil War Times Illustrated* 18, no. 3 (June 1979): 22–27.

———. "Raising the 'Hatteras,'" *Civil War Times Illustrated* 18, no. 8 (December 1979): 28–29.

Dickson, James. "Voyage of Fear and Profit, Part I: The Leavetaking." *Civil War Times Illustrated* 18, no. 7 (November 1979): 14–19.

———. "Voyage of Fear and Profit, Part II: Running the Blockade." *Civil War Times Illustrated* 18, no. 8 (December 1979): 30–36.

Dixon, Lt. William F. "Aboard the *Sultana*." *Civil War Times Illustrated* 12, no. 10 (February 1974): 38–39.

Garrison, Ervan G., J. Alan May, and William H. Marquardt. "Search for the U.S.S. *Queen City*: Instrument Survey 1977." In *Beneath the Waters of Time: The Proceedings of the Ninth Con-*

ference on Underwater Archaeology. Ed. J. Barto Arnold III. Austin: Texas Antiquities Committee, 1978.

Guerout, Max. "Wreck of the C.S.S. *Alabama.*" *National Geographic* 186, no. 6 (December 1994): 66–83.

Hand, Charles C., III. "Confederate Ironclads: Gunboats of the South to Rise Again." *Skin Diver* 38, no. 2 (February 1989): 140–41.

Haydon, Glen E. "Sunken Treasure Every Five Miles." *Saga* 36, no. 6 (September 1968): 20–21, 58–61.

Hollister, Fred[erick F.]. "Revealed: The Phantom Treasure of the Brother Jonathan." *Treasure* 7, no. 12 (December 1976): 58–61.

———. "Sunken Treasure of the Great Lakes." *Western Treasures* 4, no. 3 (March 1969): 22–25.

Hubinger, Bert. "Can We Ever Raise the Monitor." *Civil War Times Illustrated* 36, no. 3 (June 1997): 38–48.

Irion, Jack B. "The Confederate Brick Fleet of Mobile." In *Proceedings of the Sixteenth Conference on Underwater Archaeology.* Ed. Paul Forsythe Johnston. Special Publications Series No. 4. Glassboro, N.J.: Society for Historical Archaeology, 1985.

Jones, Robert A. "Aftermath of an Ironclad." *Civil War Times Illustrated* 11, no. 6 (October 1972): 21–25.

Lambert, C. S. "CSS *Alabama*—Lost and Found." *American History Illustrated* 23, no. 6 (October 1966): 32–37.

Levstick, Frank R. "The Sultana Disaster." *Civil War Times Illustrated* 12, no. 9 (January 1974): 18–25.

Longmire, David. "Vicksburg Discovers Civil War Treasure." *Engineer Update* (U.S. Army Corps of Engineers) 14, no. 10 (October 1990): 4.

Lowry, Mike. "Treasures of the Big Muddy." *True Treasure* 4, no. 1 (January–February 1970): 49–50.

Magruder, Karen. "Divers Explore Underwater Antiques." *Engineer Update* (U.S. Army Corps of Engineers) 9, no. 10 (October 1995): 5.

Margolin, Samuel G. "Civil War Legacy beneath the James." *Archaeology* 40, no. 5 (September–October 1987): 50–56, 84.

———. "Endangered Legacy: Virginia's Civil War Naval Heritage." In *Look to the Earth: Historical Archaeology and the American Civil War.* Ed. Clarence R. Geier Jr. and Susan E. Winter Knoxville: University of Tennessee Press, 1994.

Martin, Cdr. Tyrone G. "North Carolina's Ironclad." *Naval History* 10, no. 4 (July–August 1996): 45–50.

Marx, Robert E. "In Search of the Perfect Wreck." *Sea Frontier* (September–October 1990): 47–51.

McGrath, H. Thomas, Jr. "The Preservation of the U.S.S. *Cairo.*" In *Underwater Archaeology: The Proceedings of the Eleventh Conference on Underwater Archaeology.* Ed. Calvin R. Cummings. Fathom Eight Special Publication No. 4. San Marino, Calif.: Fathom Eight, 1982.

Melton, Maurice. "From Vicksburg to Port Hudson: Porter's River Campaign." *Civil War Times Illustrated* 12, no. 10 (February 1974): 26–37.

Morr, Terry. "Been Blown to Atoms." *Naval History* 10, no. 3 (May–June 1996): 34–36.

Murphy, Geri. "Tropical Shipwrecks." *Skin Diver* 40, no. 10 (October 1991): 29.

Newton, John G. "How We Found the Monitor." *National Geographic* 147, no. 1 (January 1975): 48–61.

Potter, Jerry. "The Sultana Disaster: Conspiracy of Greed." *Blue & Gray Magazine* 7, no. 6 (August 1990): 18–24, 54–59.

Remick, Teddy. "Lake Huron Treasure Ship." *Treasure World* 6, no. 3 (February–March 1971): 26, 28.

———. "Treasure Ships of Lake Huron." *True Treasure* 4, no. 1 (January–February 1970): 37–39.

Riley, Joan. "Brother Jonathan Search Continues." *Treasure Diver* 1, no. 1 (September 1989): 8–12.

Robinson, Lorraine, and Laurence Gould. "Bermuda's Storybook Wreck." *Skin Diver* 30, no. 11 (November 1981): 64–65.

Rooney, Kevin. "Wreck of the Georgiana." *Skin Diver* 29, no. 3 (March 1980): 80–87.

Shugg, Wallace. "Prophet of the Deep: The *H. L. Hunley.*" *Civil War Times Illustrated* 11, no. 10 (February 1973): 4–10, 44–47.

Soley, James Russell. "The Blockade and the Cruisers." *Confederate Military History.* Secaucus, N.J.: Blue and Grey Press, n.d.

Spence, Edward Lee. "Iron Treasure Chest." *Treasure* 2, no. 1 (June 1971): 61–63.

———. "Civil War Shipwrecks." *Argosy Treasure Hunting Annual* (1977): 34–38, 90.

———. "South Carolina's Fabulous Underwater Treasures." *Treasure* 13, no. 7 (July 1982): 75–77.

Stephenson, Richard A. "Physical Processes at the CSS *Chattahoochee* Wreck Site." In *Proceedings of the Sixteenth Conference on Underwater Archaeology.* Ed. Paul Forsythe Johnston. Special Publications Series No. 4. Glassboro, N.J.: Society for Historical Archaeology, 1985.

Still, William N. "Confederate Behemoth: The CSS *Louisiana.*" *Civil War Times Illustrated* 16, no. 7 (November 1977): 20–25.

Thompson, Bruce F. "Legacy of a Fourth-Rate Steam Screw." *Naval History* 10, no. 3 (May–June 1996): 36–39.

Toner, Mike. "Divers Study Long-Sunken Civil War Ship." *Atlanta Journal-Constitution,* July 31, 2003.

Towart, James W. "The *Maple Leaf* in Historical Perspective." Maple Leaf *Shipwreck: An Extraordinary American Civil War Shipwreck.* www.mapleleafshipwreck.com/Book/introduction/intro1.htm.

Tower, Howard B., Jr. "The Dai Ching." *Skin Diver* 38, no. 7 (July 1989): 54–57, 68–69.

——. "Relics Abound on Excavated Civil War Vessel." *Lost Treasure* 8, no. 12 (December 1983): 26–29.

——. "Salvaging the Boston." *Skin Diver* 33, no. 4 (April 1984): 98–99, 102–9.

——. "U.S.S. *Columbine,* Civil War Wreck Story with a Twist." *Skin Diver* 34, no. 1 (January 1985): 54–56, 109.

Townsend, Samuel P. "North Carolina Report." In *Diving into the Past: Theories, Techniques, and Applications of Underwater Archaeology.* Ed. June Drenning Holmquist and Ardis Hillman Wheeler. Proceedings of the First Conference *on Underwater Archaeology,* April 26-27, 1963. St. Paul: Minnesota Historical Society, 1963.

Tzimoulis, Paul. "Best of the Bahamas." *Skin Diver* 30, no. 9 (September 1981): 61–91.

Vesilind, Priit J. "Lost Gold Bounty from a Civil War Ship." Photographs by Jonathan Blair. *National Geographic Magazine* 206, no. 3 (September 2004): 108–27.

Watts, Gordon P. "Bermuda and the American Civil War: A Reconnaissance Investigation of Archival and Submerged Cultural Resources." *International Journal of Nautical Archaeology and Underwater Exploration* 17, no. 2 (1988): 159–71.

——. "The Civil War at Sea: Dawn of an Age of Iron and Engineering." In *Ships and Shipwrecks of the Americas: A History Based on Underwater Archaeology.* Ed. George F. Bass. London: Thames and Hudson, 1996.

——. "Runners of the Union Blockade." *Archaeology* 42, no. 5 (October 1989): 32–39.

Watts, Gordon P., and Leslie S. Bright. "Progress in Underwater Archaeology in North Carolina: 1962–72." *International Journal of Nautical Archaeology and Underwater Exploration* 2, no. 1 (1973): 131–36.

Wegner, Dana M. "The Weehawken's 'Fearful Accident,'" *Civil War Times Illustrated* 11, no. 8 (December 1972): 4–9, 46–47.

Wilkinson, Dave. "Peripatetic Coffin: Civil War Submarine." *Ocean* 11, no. 4 (July–August 1978): 13–17.

Wrigley, Ronald S. "Treasure Ships of the Great Lakes." *Treasure Search* 1, no. 1 (Summer 1973): 75–79, 88.

WEB SITES

American Civil War Homepage. Ships of the Texas Marine Department. http://sunsite.utk.edu/civil-war/warweb.html.

California State Lands Commission. www.slc.ca.gov.

Charleston Illustrated: A Historic District Architectural Map. CSS *H. L. Hunley.* www.charlestonillustrated.com/hunley/index.html.

"Chicord Creek Vessel Update." *Stem to Stern* (Newsletter of Maritime Studies Program, East Carolina University) 12 (Winter 1997). www.ecu.edu/maritime/Publications/s2s97.pdf.

Civil War @ Charleston. www.awod.com/cwchas/main.html.

Civil War Naval Museum at Port Columbus. www.portcolumbus.org.

"Civil War Shipwrecks (1861–1865)." Minerals Management Service. Gulf of Mexico Region. U.S. Department of the Interior. Press releases and reports. www.gomr.mms.gov/homepg/regulate/environ/archaeological/civil_war_shipwrecks.html.

"CSS *Georgia.*" U.S. Army Corps of Engineers, Savannah District, and Georgia Ports Authority. www.sas.usace.army.mil/CSS/index.htm.

"The *Denbigh* Project: Archaeology of a Confederate Blockade Runner." Institute of Nautical Archaeology. Texas A&M University. www.nautarch.tamu.edu/projects/denbigh.

"Exploration of the *Phoenix* Wreck via FSU." Florida State University, Maritime Archaeology. www.anthro.fsu.edu/research/uw/research/ships/phoenix.html.

"CSS *Alabama.*" U.S. Department of the Navy. Naval Historical Center. Press release, July 31, 1995. "Field Work on CSS *Alabama* Site, Summer 1995." www.history.navy.mil/branches/org12-1b.htm.

Florida Division of Historical Resources. www.flheritage.com.

Fort McAllister Historic Park. www.gastateparks.org/net/go/parks.aspx?LocationID=24&s=0.0.1.5.

Friends of the *Hunley,* www.hunley.org.

Georgia Historical Preservation Division. Georgia Department of Natural Resources. http://hpd.dnr.state.ga.us.

"*H. L. Hunley,* Confederate Submarine." U.S. Department of the Navy. Naval Historical Center. www.history.navy.mil/branches/org12-3.htm.

Maple Leaf Shipwreck: An Extraordinary American Civil War Shipwreck. http://mapleleafshipwreck.com.

Monitor National Marine Sanctuary. National Oceanic and Atmospheric Administration. monitor.noaa.gov.

National Park Service, Projects, Submerged Resources Center. http://home.nps.gov/applications/submerged/.

National Underwater and Marine Agency (NUMA). Founded by novelist Clive Cussler. www.numa.net.

Civil War Naval Museum at Port Columbus. www.portcolumbus.org.

"Remote Sensing Investigations of the Civil War Blockade Runner *Ivanhoe.*" Florida State University, Maritime Archaeology. www.anthro.fsu.edu/research/uw/research/ships/ivanhoe.html.

Sea Research Society. www.shipwrecks.com.

South Carolina Institute of Archaeology and Anthropology. University of South Carolina. www.cas.sc.edu/sciaa.

"The Steamboat *Twilight.*" Press release, July 12, 2001. www.lostreasure.com/pressrelease/Sage%Marketing-12-Jul-01.cfm.

Index of Shipwrecks

Shipwrecks of unnamed vessels or vessels whose names are unknown are not included in this index. Readers looking for unnamed vessels or vessels not located by specific name should review the "Vessels without Names" sections at the ends of the geographic sections of this encyclopedia.

CSS *Drewry*	Virginia
Drover	Louisiana
Duchess (see USS *Petrel*)	
Dudley	Florida
Duke	Tennessee
Duke W. Goodman	Alabama
CSS *Dunbar*	Alabama
Dundalk (see *Georgiana C. McCaw*)	
Dunkirk	Canada
Dunleith	Mississippi River
Eager	Texas
Eagle	California
CSS *Eagle*	South Carolina
Eagle Coal Co.	Tennessee
Eagle's Wing	Rhode Island
USS *Eastport*	Louisiana
Ebenezer (see USS *Tawah*)	
Ebenezer Dodge	Atlantic Ocean
Echo	Tennessee
Echo (see *Jefferson Davis*)	
Echo No. 2	Ohio River
Eclipse	Alabama
Eclipse	Tennessee
Eclipse (see *Petrel*)	
Economy	Ohio River
Ed Air	Kentucky
Ed Howard (see CSS *General Polk*)	
Edisto	South Carolina
Edith (see CSS *Chickamauga*)	
Editor	Louisiana
Ed R. Hart (see CSS *Hart*)	
E. D. Thompson	Unknown
Edward	Atlantic Ocean
Edward	Unknown
Edward Carey	Pacific Area
Edward F. Dix	Louisiana / Mississippi River
CSS *Edward J. Gray*	Mississippi
Edwards (see CSS *Forrest*)	
Edwin	South Carolina
Efina Kuyne	California
E. F. Lewis	Atlantic Ocean
E. H. Herbert	North Carolina
E. J. Hart (see CSS *Hart*)	
Electric Spark	Maryland
USS *Elfin*	Tennessee
Elisha Dunbar	Azores
Eliza	California
Eliza	Louisiana
Elizabeth	Florida
Elizabeth	North Carolina
Elizabeth	South Carolina
Elizabeth Ann	Atlantic Ocean
Elizabeth Buckley	California
Eliza G	Arkansas
Eliza Simmons (see CSS *Pontchartrain*)	
Ella (see USS *Philippi*)	
Ella	Arkansas
Ella	North Carolina
Ella Warley (see *Isabel*—New Jersey)	
Ellen	North Carolina
Ellen Forrest	Rhode Island
Ellen Goldsboro	Unknown
USS *Ellis* (CSS *Ellis*)	North Carolina
Ellwood	Arkansas
Ellwood	Tennessee
Elma	Virginia
CSS *Elmea* (*Elmea*)	Texas
El Paraguay (see CSS *Ivy*)	
Elvira	Mississippi River
Emerald	Georgia
Emilie No. 2	Missouri River
Emily (see *Emily of London*)	
Emily	North Carolina
Emily	Texas
Emily of London	North Carolina
Emma (see USS *Bloomer*)	
Emma	Florida
Emma	Georgia
Emma	Louisiana
Emma	Louisiana
Emma Bett	Mississippi
Emma Boyd	Alabama
Emma Jane	Indian Ocean
Emma L. Hall	New York
Emma Tuttle	North Carolina
Emma Valeria (see *Annie*—Georgia)	
Empire	South Carolina
Empire (see CSS *Appomattox*)	
Empire (see *Jennie Hubbs*)	
Empire Parish	Louisiana
Empress	Mississippi River
Empress Theresa	Atlantic Ocean